THE *Making* OF

MODERN *Europe*

BOOK ONE:
THE MIDDLE AGES TO WATERLOO

Edited by

HERMAN AUSUBEL
Columbia University

The Dryden Press · New York

FORMAT

The text has been set in Granjon type, with Nicholas Cochin for the chapter and article titles. The title line on the cover and on the title page is hand lettered.

TO

Anne and Kenneth

Preface

THE PROBLEM of what to do about supplementary readings has disturbed every teacher of European history. He knows that textbooks have become so big and heavy that additional reading assignments would seem to impose too great a burden on students. At the same time, however, he knows that the content of history is so rich and complex that even the most learned textbook writers cannot have a mastery of every topic with which they deal. And he regrets that students should acquire almost all their knowledge of the past from such writers—and not from the experts who have devoted long years of research to the mastery of particular historical subjects.

The result often is that the teacher decides to require several book reviews from his students. Soon, however, he discovers that although reviews are admirable for some purposes, they fail to prepare any large number of students to engage effectively in any large number of class discussions. If he proceeds, therefore, to require scattered weekly readings in specialized secondary works, he soon finds himself in difficulties with the administration. For these days American college libraries are hard pressed. They suffer not only from a lack of money but from a lack of space. As Carl Becker expressed it, "If, some bright afternoon, all the students in philosophy, literature, and the social sciences should take it into their heads to invade the library in order to do what they are conventionally expected to do, there would scarcely be standing room for them, to say nothing about tables to work at. . . ." In short, the teacher continues to be disturbed by the problem of what to do about collateral readings.

The present volume aims to help solve that problem. Designed to accompany any of the standard textbooks in modern European history, it consists mainly of articles that appeared originally in American and British scholarly journals. Written by some of the most gifted of recent specialists in European political, economic, religious, and intellectual history, these articles deserve to be more readily available. First, they are generally interpretative in character; frequently, in fact, they embody relatively new approaches to their subjects. Secondly, they lend themselves readily to classroom discussion; often, indeed, they are provocative enough to give rise to the hope that many a student will descend willingly on the library—despite all the difficulties involved—in order to find out more about particular topics.

For the convenience and guidance of the reader, each article has an introduction and, in almost all cases, a glossary. The introduction is designed to place the selection in its setting and to indicate why the student has been invited to read it. The glossary identifies those names and defines those terms which seem to deserve or require special definition or identification. Except in a few instances—and these are clearly indicated—the articles have been reproduced in their entirety. In order to save space, however, the footnotes which originally appeared with many of the articles have often been omitted. Such omissions have again been clearly indicated.

In conclusion, I should like to express the hope that the reader will find this sampling of the literature of modern European history as stimulating to read as it was to prepare.

H. A.

Columbia University
October 1950

A Note on Sources

The articles in *The Making of Modern Europe* have been selected from both books and periodicals. The periodicals are listed below.

Agricultural History

American Academy of Political and Social Science: Annals

American Economic Review

American Friends of Lafayette: Publications

American Historical Review

American Philosophical Society: Proceedings

American Political Science Review

American Scholar

Association of History Teachers of the Middle States and Maryland: Proceedings

Cambridge Journal

Canadian Historical Review

Catholic Historical Review

Church History

Church Quarterly Review

Columbia University Quarterly

Commentary

Contemporary Review

Current History

Economic History Review

Foreign Affairs

German Life and Letters

Hibbert Journal

History

Huntington Library Quarterly

Isis

Journal of Central European Affairs

Journal of Economic History

Journal of Modern History

Journal of Political Economy

Journal of the History of Ideas

Listener

Lutheran Church Quarterly

Political Science Quarterly

Psychological Review

Public Opinion Quarterly

Queen's Quarterly

Review of Politics

Royal Historical Society: Transactions

Russian Review

Scientific Monthly

Slavonic Review

Social Education

South Atlantic Quarterly

Speculum

Studies

Virginia Quarterly Review

Yale Review

Contents

III · The So-called Renaissance

IV · The Protestant Revolutions and the Catholic Reformation

V · The Expansion of Europe

VI · The Habsburgs in Early Modern Times

VII · France in Early Modern Times

VIII · Late Tudor
and Early Stuart England

IX · The Glorious Revolution
and Its Aftermath

X · The Emergence of Prussia and Russia

XI · Science in Early Modern Times

XII · The Age of Reason

XIII · The French Revolution and Napoleon

I

The Nature of History

⫸⫸⫸⫸⫸⫸⫸⫸⫸⫸⫸⫸⫷⫷⫷⫷⫷⫷⫷⫷⫷⫷⫷⫷

Can History Educate?
ROBERT LIVINGSTON SCHUYLER

Truth in History
WILLIAM A. DUNNING

⫸⫸⫸⫸⫸⫸⫸⫸⫸⫸⫷⫷⫷⫷⫷⫷⫷⫷⫷⫷⫷⫷

➤➤

Can History Educate?

ROBERT LIVINGSTON SCHUYLER

➤➤➤➤➤➤➤➤➤➤➤➤➤➤➤➤➤➤ *Published in 1935* ◄◄◄◄◄◄◄◄◄◄◄◄◄◄◄◄◄◄

Twentieth-century historians, living in a world beset by complicated social, economic, political, religious, and moral problems, have often found themselves in a difficult position. So many of their academic colleagues—chemists, physicists, psychologists, economists, and sociologists—have been able to derive immediately useful results from their respective subjects that many historians have developed an unmistakable sense of guilt. Determined not to be viewed as mere antiquarians, as escapists to an ivory tower, they have frequently come to insist that the study of the past is worth while above all because it can throw light on the difficulties of the contemporary world. So widespread has this pragmatic point of view become among American historians that it is refreshing to come upon a scholar who dares to justify the study of history even when it fails to make easier the reading of the morning newspaper. Such a scholar is Robert Livingston Schuyler, professor of history at Columbia University and the author of numerous books and articles on modern British history. Schuyler's defense of past-mindedness in historical study and his exposure of the dangers growing out of present-mindedness deserve the close attention of everyone who has ever thought about the usefulness of history.

The educational values of historical study and the educational aims which it ought to pursue have long been subjects of discussion and controversy, and the discussion and controversy are at present going forward briskly, not to say clamorously. If we run over in our minds some of the claims that have been made for the educational utility of history, a significant conclusion will, I think, present itself.

Reprinted by special permission from *Columbia University Quarterly*, XXVII (1935), 93-103.

The conception of history as preacher has had a long career. According to Tacitus, the principal function of history was to prevent meritorious actions from being forgotten and to deter men from evil by fear of the reprobation of posterity. This point of view has naturally appealed strongly to moral reformers. Luther, for example, said that from history "we learn what things those who were pious and wise pursued, what they shunned and how they lived, and how it fared with them, or how they were rewarded, and again how they lived who were wicked and obstinate in their ignorance and what punishments overtook them." Lord Bolingbroke—a deist and not exactly a moral reformer—wrote in this tradition. In his *Letters on the Study and Use of History* he says: "Nature gave us curiosity to excite the industry of our minds; but she never intended it should be made the principal, much less the sole object of their application. The true and proper object of this application is a constant improvement in private and public virtue." And the study of history he regarded as "of all others, the most proper to train us up to private and public virtue." To him, as to Dionysius of Halicarnassus, history was "philosophy teaching by examples." If history repeats itself, as was believed by Thucydides and is believed nowadays by the man in the street and by some educators, then it is the great reservoir of wisdom, a veritable helmsman of life for those who can read it aright. According to this view, history is a branch of homiletics, exhorting to virtue and deterring from vice. Its primary function is to preach.

If history does repeat itself, then it gives us the basis for prediction. History becomes prophet. Many historical philosophers have played with this alluring idea. Its most famous contemporary exponent is Oswald Spengler, with his theory of recurring cultural cycles—a theory elaborated with much philosophical embroidery and poetic fervor and presented with unbounded self-confidence and dogmatism. "Every culture," Spengler announces, "every adolescence and maturing and decay of a culture, every one of its intrinsically necessary stages and periods, has a definite duration, always the same, always recurring with the emphasis of a symbol." Before the publication of *Der Untergang des Abendlandes* everybody was free, so he tells us, to hope what he pleased about the future, but now it is everybody's business to inform himself of what *can* happen "and therefore of what, with the unalterable necessity of destiny and irrespective of personal ideals, hopes or desires, *will* happen." If we know what befell Babylon and

Pataliputra, we know what destiny has in store for London and New York. As conceived by Spengler, history offers the possibility of "predetermining the spiritual form, duration, rhythm, meaning and product of the *still* unaccomplished stages of our Western history." If this, or anything approaching this, were true, the educational utility of historical study would need no further justification.

The use of history as teacher of patriotism is thoroughly familiar to us all. It appears to be about as old as patriotism. Professor Henry Johnson in his informing and charming little book, *An Introduction to the History of the Social Sciences in Schools* (a book, by the way, that ought to be read by all teachers of history and especially by all educational administrators and curriculum experts who tell the teachers how to teach) refers to a history textbook published in Germany in 1505. Its purpose, in Johnson's words, was "to make young Germans proud of their German past and to stimulate them to enlarge the fame of Germans." Its author flourished rather early in the history of patriotism, but highly developed patriotic historians of later times have not been able to improve substantially upon his method, for "he wrote," says Johnson, "of anything that promoted his purpose, and anything which did not seem to promote his purpose he simply excluded." He actually accomplished the extraordinary patriotic feat of excluding Canossa. His spiritual descendants are flourishing throughout the world today, and the young of all nations are being made duly proud of their national past by means of history in school. Nobody who has given any attention to the subject would deny that history has in all countries been education's most powerful instrument for the promotion of patriotism.

BOLINGBROKE: English Tory politician and writer of the early eighteenth century. Although his own behavior left much to be desired by the standards of his time, he insisted, in his *Letters on History* (1735), that historical study should serve to inculcate moral principles.

CANOSSA: Village in northern Italy where, in the eleventh century, the Holy Roman Emperor Henry IV sought the forgiveness of Pope Gregory VII. A symbol, therefore, of the humiliation of a secular power by the papacy.

NEW HISTORY: A book of essays (1912) by James Harvey Robinson. Critical of the "old history," it emphasized a broad view of the content of history; it insisted on the need for cooperation between historians and

At present the most "progressive" educational opinion regarding history is that its only value is to explain the present. History is educationally useful, according to this view, only for "background" purposes, only as giving the setting of current events; very recent, or, as it is called, "contemporary" history is necessarily the most important part of history; and to concern oneself with anything in the past that does not help palpably to account for the present is to waste one's time and to be guilty of "mere antiquarianism." The educational claims of "contemporary" history are by no means novel; they have been set forth from time to time during the last two or three hundred years. But the-past-as-explaining-the-present doctrine no doubt owes much of its current vogue to the comparatively recent spread of evolutionary habits of thought. As to the predominance of this doctrine in the teaching of history in our schools there seems to be no question. Speaking from the fullness of his knowledge, Professor Johnson tells us that history in the school curriculum "now revolves around current problems in about the way that history in the eighteenth century revolved around examples of conduct." In both cases, he adds, the principle is "to take out of the past only what is directly useful in the present."

Now the significant thing, it seems to me, about all these theories of the utility of history is this, that the attempt to derive from the study of the past the educational values that are sought for results in a treatment of the past that is repugnant to that spirit of free inquiry which is the essence of the scientific attitude, whether in the study of history or of anything else. Nothing could be more unscientific than to select historical materials, interpret events and organize a

---

other social scientists; and it stressed the idea that historical studies should throw light on the news in the morning paper.

OSWALD SPENGLER: Twentieth-century German writer whose erudite work *The Decline of the West* caused a great stir in intellectual circles almost everywhere in the western world. It became especially popular in Germany, where it fitted in with the disillusionment that followed defeat in World War I. To many a patriotic German it was consoling that the whole western world, not merely Germany, was on the decline.

TACITUS: Roman publicist, moralist, and historian of the first and second centuries. His hostile treatment of such emperors as Tiberius, Claudius, and Nero was based on the notion that the historian should make "the reprobation of posterity a terror to evil words and acts."

narrative in the light of some assumption, and then to claim that "history teaches" the truth of that assumption. It is easy to give the impression that one's country has always been right by judicious omissions and misinterpretations. It is easy to give the impression that the wicked have always been punished for their wickedness by simply saying nothing about the rascals of history who seem, on the whole, to have had a pretty good time of it. It is easy to give the impression that the past explains the present by selecting from past events only those that appear to do so. Such buccaneering historical raids do not acquire scientific respectability even if the objectives which the buccaneers have in view happen to be ethically or socially desirable. It would be a work of supererogation to demonstrate that the attitude of those who look upon history as a means of inculcating morality or patriotism is far removed from the spirit of science. But what about the attitude of those who believe that it is the prime business of history to explain the present? This doctrine has captivated Progressive Education; it is a cherished article of faith of the New History. It surely deserves the thoughtful and critical consideration of all teachers and mature students of history.

The past, of course, leads to the present. But it is the past *as it was* that leads to the present *as it is*. If we were historically omniscient, if we knew the whole past as it was, we should understand the whole present as it is—understand it, I mean, in the sense of knowing all its antecedents. But the worst way to gain insight into the past as it was is to study the past with one eye fixed on the present. Present-mindedness is and always has been the great distorter of the past, the great source of anachronism, the great enemy of historical-mindedness. All propagandist history is present-minded in the sense that it aims at objectives in the present, but what is in question here is something subtler, something more difficult to detect and make allowance for, something of which the writer or teacher of history may himself be quite unconscious. Far from being "new," present-mindedness is extremely old, in fact primitive. It is indeed the natural way of looking at the past, the way in which, we need have little doubt, primitive man looked at *his* past. What is comparatively new, and I believe genuinely progressive, is historical-mindedness, a fair and rare flower of culture, a product of the scientific spirit applied to the study of the past. Using the present as a basis of reference in historical study causes us to see the past through the medium of our own standards and presuppositions, to select for mention and emphasis among past events what seems significant to us rather than what seemed significant to contemporaries, to omit embarrassing Canossas. It leads to an over-simplification of historical processes, and to an exaggeration of the resemblances and an obscuring of the unlikenesses between past and present. Even in our own memories, personal experiences are colored by subsequent events. A description of, say, a state of mind at a critical juncture of life, written from personal recollection fifty years afterwards in an autobiography, would not be identical with a description of it written in a diary at the time. And diaries are notoriously more reliable as historical sources than autobiographies. Mr. H. G. Wells wisely gives up the attempt to reconstruct from memory his schoolboy outlook upon the world. "I find it impossible," he writes in his *Experiment in Autobiography*, "to disentangle the things I saw and read before I was thirteen from the things that came afterwards. The old ideas and impressions were made over in accordance with new material, they were used up to make the new equipment. This reconstruction went on from day to day, and so, in order and detail, they are lost beyond recovery."

Compare the views and interpretations of some past epoch presented by an historical specialist who has saturated himself in the sources for his period with those of the same epoch conveyed by writers of general history textbooks. The latter are not only expressed more briefly; they are simpler and usually much more present-minded. What we get in the textbook is not a living past, multifarious, complex, instinct with individual ambitions and loves and hates, but an artificially simplified and unified stage in historical evolution. It is a leading thesis, and I think a sound thesis, of Mr. Herbert Butterfield's suggestive essay, *The Whig Interpretation of History*, that the very act of summarizing and abridging history makes for present-mindedness. The textbook writer, needing some yardstick for measuring the importance of past events, is impelled almost irresistibly to adopt the fallacious principle that what seems important from the viewpoint of his own day was actually important when it happened. The investigator who has gone deeply into a segment of the past is impressed by the complexity of historical processes, but a treatment of the past that is guided by present-mindedness turns complexity into simplicity. If history is to be likened to a stream, it should be to a stream with many pools and eddies and cross-currents. "I am tired," exclaims

Mr. Henry Seidel Canby, "of seeing the history of these United States interpreted in terms of what the pioneers or soldiers of the Civil War did for the Chicago of 1933 or for John Smith who runs a filling station on the Northern Boulevard. There is a fallacy in this teleological view of history, which would make Lake Ontario important only because it flows into the Gulf of St. Lawrence." Present-mindedness, in making the complex simple and the crooked straight, leads to facile generalizations about historical tendencies—even historical "laws"—it nourishes the fallacy of "fundamental" causes and "inevitable" results, it encourages uncritical belief in a necessary "progress" in human affairs and glib talk about the "verdicts" of history and the "logic" of history. It is the soil in which imposing deliverances concerning the *Zeitgeist* flower most luxuriantly.

Historical-mindedness I have called the scientific spirit applied to the study of the past. A great deal of ink has been spilt in arguing the question of whether history is a science or not. We need not lose our footing in that bog. History is certainly not an "exact" science, but even "exact" sciences are not as exact as was formerly supposed. The most exact of them, physics, has substituted probability for certainty. Whether history is or can be genuinely scientific must obviously depend upon how science is defined, and that much used and much abused term has never been defined to the satisfaction of all persons who regard themselves as scientists. To me the scientific spirit applied to the study of the past means, to put it shortly, disinterested curiosity about the past—some part or aspect of the past—in and for itself, and the satisfaction of that curiosity by the best available means of ascertaining the truth about the subject under investigation. It seeks knowledge of the past as an end in itself, not as a means to some end. It is not perturbed by the utilitarian's contemptuous question, "What's the use of such knowledge?" It is merely sorry for the questioner, because it looks upon knowledge as good in itself, as needing no ulterior justification, as its own reward. If it cared to do so, it could meet the utilitarian on his own ground, for it is almost surely true, as Bertrand Russell says, that "a race of men without a disinterested love of knowledge would never have achieved our present scientific technique." To be inspired by this spirit, it should be understood, does not imply acceptance of any particular tenets associated with the nineteenth-century scientific school of historiography, for example, the belief in the discoverability of laws of history. What it does imply is rejection of the doctrine now preached in high places and widely accepted as a dispensation of advanced thought, that disinterestedness, objectivity and impartiality, as historical ideals, are outmoded shibboleths that ought to be discarded and renounced in favor of historical interpretation based upon social philosophies of the present.

In certain circles it is regarded as evidence of personal illumination and realistic psychological insight to deny the possibility of disinterested motivation and to look upon those who deny this denial as simple-minded and intellectually unsophisticated folk. Let us hear what one of these naïve persons has to say about this. Max Planck, author of the Quantum Theory and admittedly a preëminent master of physical science, writes in a book intended for the laity:

> Every individual science sets about its task by the explicit renunciation of the egocentric and anthropocentric standpoint. In the earlier stages of human thought . . . primitive man made himself and his own interests the center of his system of reasoning. Confronted with the powers of nature around him, he thought that they were animated beings like himself and he divided them into two classes, the one friendly and the other inimical. He divided the plant world into the categories of poisonous and non-poisonous. He divided the animal world into the categories of dangerous and harmless. As long as he remained bound within the limits of this method of treating his environment, it was impossible for him to make any approach towards real scientific knowledge. His first advance in this knowledge was accomplished only after he had taken leave of his own immediate interests and banished them from his thought. At a later stage he succeeded in abandoning the idea that the planet whereon he lives is the central point of the universe. Then he took up the more modest position of keeping as far as possible in the background, so as not to intrude his own idiosyncrasies and personal ideas between himself and his observations of natural phenomena. It was only at this stage that the outer world of nature began to unveil its mystery to him, and at the same time to furnish him with means which he was able to press into his own service and which he could never have discovered if he had continued looking for them with the candlelight of his own egocentric interests. The progress of science is an excellent illustration of the truth of the paradox that man must lose his soul before he can find it. The forces of nature, such as electricity for instance, were not discovered by men who started out with the set purpose of adapting them for utilitarian purposes. Scientific discovery and scientific knowledge have

been achieved only by those who have gone in pursuit of it without any practical purpose whatsoever in view.

Are there, we may now ask, any educational values in historical study which aims simply at learning the truth, so far as is possible, about some aspect of the past, disclaiming as alien to its nature and purpose the object of making us righteous or patriotic, or of giving us the background of the morning's news, though it might, indirectly and incidentally, have any or all of these effects? I believe that the answer to this question is emphatically in the affirmative.

Such study, in the first place, is bound to widen one's temporal horizon, to mitigate at least, if not to cure, that temporal provincialism (if it may be so called) with which our age is sorely afflicted. The historically-minded study of the past has an educative effect comparable to that of foreign travel, in that it gives insight into cultures different from ours and an appreciation of the fact that they were once as vital and vivid as ours is now. It makes for toleration, for it teaches us, indirectly, to see our own age as one among many and not as the norm by which all others are to be judged. It is natural to think of our present ways of life, habits of thought and institutions as normal, and to think of all others as more or less abnormal—as natural as it was to think of the earth as the center of the physical universe. Historical-mindedness in the study of the past puts us where we need to be put—in our proper place. It substitutes a Copernican for our naturally Ptolemaic attitude toward the past. The historian is an explorer in time, and the present-minded, Ptolemaic historian, who searches in the past only for "roots" and "germs" of present-day institutions, is likely to misrepresent a past age as badly as Vasco da Gama misrepresented the Hindu temple which he mistook for a Christian church. He is to be likened not to the enlightened traveller who seeks insight into a different civilization or an alien culture by living in it sympathetically and absorbing something of its spirit, but to the globe-trotter from Main Street who, from his point of vantage on the deck of a Dollar liner, applies to the passing scene the judgments of Gopher Prairie. The student of history who has never felt the need of freeing his mind from bondage to opinions and distinctions and classifications that are matter of course and commonplace in contemporary thought has missed one of history's precious educational gifts.

But educationally speaking, historical method is probably more important than historical information. *How* the historically-minded student learns about the past is of greater educational value than *what* he learns about it. I am thinking primarily of what we call historical research, but even in the elementary study of history some knowledge of historical method can be gained if the teacher is capable of imparting it. By critical use of the textbook and by judiciously chosen exercises in elementary historical criticism the historically trained teacher can give his pupils some appreciation of the comparative reliability of different kinds of sources, can make them aware of the superiority of first-hand to second-hand information, can make them alert to distinguish between statements of carefully ascertained fact and statements of opinion, and so can do something to cure that credulity to which all flesh is heir. If the time spent in our would-be and self-proclaimed "progressive" schools in amateurish attempts to make history explain the morning newspaper were devoted to inculcating in pupils something of that critical sense which scientific historical study is so eminently calculated to develop, school history would be in a far healthier state, educationally, than it is.

So far as the more advanced study of history is concerned, it would be hard to imagine a better discipline in thoroughness and alertness in following up clues than the careful and prolonged search for materials which precedes and accompanies all historical investigation that deserves to be called scientific. There is developed in every real historical scholar something of the detective. He must have a scent for sources, just as the successful newspaper reporter must have a nose for news. Conclusions arrived at by the most approved methods of historical criticism, brilliant historical interpretations, are liable to collapse in deep humiliation if essential sources have not been used. It goes without saying that the writer of history needs something more than industry. Like the natural scientist he needs constructive imagination. But this is very different from the fancy that builds castles in the air. It does not operate without previous research; it does not give rise to fertile hypotheses in uninformed minds. It works under discipline and restraint. Over-indulgence in untested historical hypotheses is a sure indication of an unhistorical mind.

Historical study, it has just been suggested, can do something— it can do much—to cure, or at least to mitigate, natural human credulity. It is here, I am inclined to think, that it can render its crowning educational service. We are innately credulous. We become critical only through education, whether acquired formally or otherwise. The uneducated and the educated differ in nothing more than in this, that the former believe whatever they hear or read, while the latter weigh evidence. Under the pressure of powerful propaganda and the stress of great emotion even the educated may lapse into credulity. In 1914, for example, there was something like a moratorium on the critical faculty, as regards the causes and issues of the war, in all the belligerent countries, and the part then played by historians is not one to which the profession looks back with pride. But the uneducated are always credulous. As a means of ascertaining facts, the historical method is inferior to the method of direct observation. But it is the only method of ascertaining *past* facts. Its very inferiority gives it its chief educational value. Because we cannot observe historical events directly, because we can learn of them only from records of some kind, the obligation is imposed upon us to deal critically with our records, to estimate their comparative trustworthiness, to weigh evidence. It is to facilitate and make more accurate the weighing of evidence that the techniques of historical criticism have been elaborated.

The greatest educational values of historical investigation may come from its methods rather than from its findings. But methods are means, not ends. If the discovery of truth is our end, and we seek for it by the critical methods of scientific history, many good things, educationally speaking, will be added unto us.

Truth in History

WILLIAM A. DUNNING

►►►-►►►-►►►-►►►-►►►-►►►-►►►-►►► *Published in 1914* ◄◄◄-◄◄◄-◄◄◄-◄◄◄-◄◄◄-◄◄◄-◄◄◄-◄◄◄

Few modern historians have had so much influence on methods of writing history as Leopold von Ranke (1795-1886). Distinctly conservative in his outlook, Ranke was disturbed by the propagandistic uses to which many of his eighteenth-century predecessors had subjected historical study. As reformers, many of them had written their accounts of the past for the purpose of encouraging political, social, and religious change in their own time. Ranke, however, insisted that the function of the historian was to find out "what really happened"; and to do this the historian should keep his eyes fixed on the past, not on the present. Though Ranke's own works contained numerous interpretative analyses, he viewed himself primarily as an objective, or factual, historian. And as his conception of the historian's role won adherents in one country after another, more and more emphasis came to be placed on digging up facts from the original sources. The result of this accumulation of vast stores of data was that many previously held notions were disproved; many historical "truths" were converted into falsehoods. In at least one respect, however, this rewriting of history in keeping with the facts that were revealed in original sources proved to be dangerous. It encouraged historians to forget that, from the historical point of view, what people *think* is true—however false it may be—is often far more important than the real truth. This point William A. Dunning, the historian of European political ideas and of Reconstruction in the United States, emphasized in the presidential address which he delivered shortly before World War I to the American Historical Association. One of the most penetrating essays ever written on the nature of historical study, it deserves to be read and reread both for the brilliance of its content and the beauty of its style.

"**P**ilate saith unto Him, What is Truth?" Thus ends the report of one of the most famous conversations ever recorded. That the colloquy should have terminated without an answer to the question of the Roman procurator, must always raise regret in the mind of the reader and the writer of history. For we are told often and conclusively that history has truth for its subject-matter and the discovery of truth for its end. An authoritative definition of truth, therefore, would have been a priceless boon. It has indeed been often asserted that the question of Pilate was interrogative in form only, and that his real thought was to affirm the hopelessness of ever reaching a definition. If such was the case, one might reasonably conjecture that the Roman had lately been engaged in historical research; for in no other occupation is there more powerful stimulus to the despair that his remark expresses. The optimist who has assured us that truth will out, even in an affidavit, was a lawyer; the devotee of history would never commit himself to so cheerful a dogma.

It is a commonplace, however, that the pursuit of an end is as useful, at least, as the attainment. The boy who seeks the pot of gold at the foot of the rainbow acquires valuable information in the quest. No limit can be imagined to the curiosity of man, once having become self-conscious, as to the past. History is the name we give to the result of his efforts to satisfy this curiosity. The earliest beginnings of these efforts bring perplexity. The phenomena of the past are no less complex than those of the present and the truth about them is no less elusive. History, therefore, as an aggregate of facts for investigation, requires subdivision and analysis. Not all truth, but certain aspects or classes of truth, are the subject-matter of the science, if science it be. I know of no serious contention by anybody that all past phenomena, without discrimination, are properly the field of the historian. I likewise am

Reprinted by special permission from *The American Historical Review,* XIX (1914), 217-229. The footnotes which originally appeared with this essay have been omitted.

LIVY: Roman moralist, stylist, and historian (d. A.D. 17). Much of his work was lost, but the parts of his *History of Rome* that did survive were influential for many centuries. Medieval views of ancient Roman history were in large measure derived from his writings. Dante, for example, referred to him as "Livy, who does not err."

aware that no problem will call forth more violent debate than the bounding of the field—the determination of what is within and what is without it.

For my present purpose I am going to assume that the province of history is to ascertain and present in their causal sequence such phenomena of the past as exerted an unmistakable influence on the development of men in social and political life. Such an assumption will occasion, I suppose, certain liftings of the eyebrows and shruggings of the shoulders among colleagues in this association for whom I have the profoundest respect; but I must bear with such fortitude as is vouchsafed to me the consequences of my rashness.

How did the primitive Aryans fatten their swine for slaughtering (if there ever were Aryans, and if they ever were primitive, and if they ate pork); what was the favorite cosmetic of Alcibiades; what was the bacteriological species of the maggots that St. Simeon Stylites piously replaced when they lost their hold on his sores; what was the color of the horse that bore Washington at the battle of Monmouth: all these questions concern truth as to the past, but shall we call the answers to them history?

It would indeed be scientific heresy to deny that any of the phenomena referred to could possibly have been influential in human development. In these days no science is sure of its footing until it has proclaimed its special interpretation of history. The economic, the sociological, the metallurgical, the pathologic, the meteorological, the astronomical, the geological, and for aught I know, the geometrical interpretations are in heated rivalry. It is therefore unsafe to say that the most obscure and least suspected fact of the past will not appear to-morrow as the hinge on which man's whole career has turned. But pending the newest revelation of this sort we are privileged to approach the study of the past under guidance of a series of presumptions, among which is this, that such phenomena as have been mentioned are not of the first importance.

In dealing with matters that *are* presumed to be of high importance

---

NIEBUHR: German historian of the early nineteenth century who was a major figure in the rewriting of ancient Roman history. Highly critical of Livy, he denied the truth of much that had been passing for historical knowledge. Like Livy, however, he dealt with Roman history very much in the manner of a moralist.

the student of history is confronted with the problems concerning truth in all their diversity. He must ascertain the objective actualities —the occurrences that impressed the senses of men; he must ascertain the chronological order of these occurrences; he must strive, at least, to ascertain the causal nexus between them.

The last of these tasks is by no means the least. As we have lately been warned by the dean of the historical gild in America, Dr. Jameson, with his wonted force and precision, "the stream of history is a stream of causation." To resolve the forces and detect the relations that underlie the movement of this current, demands an exceptional endowment and an unstinted application of intellectual strength. For about a century now this particular field of activity has been less diligently cultivated by the scientific historian, and it has been his special aim to achieve exactness in the first of the above-mentioned aspects of truth. He must know precisely what happened and he must know it from the original contemporary evidence. A secondary or derived account of an event must be presumed false. The longer such an account has been accepted as true, the more likely it is false. If the account runs back into immemorial antiquity, the event never happened, and the matter does not concern history at all, but belongs in the outer darkness of anthropology or sociology.

The effects of this trend of thinking on the study and writing of history during the last two generations have been remarkable. A cyclone of criticism has swept through the populous realm of pseudo-historical traditions and the region is thickly strewn with the *disjecta membra* of their proud and often most beautiful forms. The search for original material has occupied the first place in the attention of historical students and has proved beneficent in two ways at least: it has enormously increased the mass of such material for the use of the man competent to make a synthesis from it, and it has furnished an all-engrossing occupation for many who might otherwise have tried their hands, and the patience of their readers, in the hopeless task of synthesizing. The high ratio of monographic collections of material to organized and literary narrative is one of the most familiar characteristics of recent publications in history.

The absorbing and relentless pursuit of the objective fact—of the thing that actually happened in exactly the form and manner of its happening, is, I take it, thus, the typical function of the modern devotee of history. Certain corollaries and consequences of this conception are obvious. In the first place it tends greatly to limit the scope of history. Again, it tends to stress the material as compared with the spiritual or psychic forces and influences in human life. Further, it reduces to the minimum the consideration of causal nexus, and tends to limit history to the *post hoc,* regardless of the *propter hoc.* Finally, it tends unduly to limit regard for the influence of what men believed to be true, as compared with what was true.

Every serious student of history knows the thrill that comes with the discovery of an unknown or a forgotten fact of the past. In comparison, the joy of the gold or diamond hunter over a "find" is indeed moderate. Especially keen and spicy is the satisfaction of historical discovery when it implies the erroneousness of long-standing beliefs and enables the discoverer to proclaim the most eminent and authoritative chroniclers of the past the victims of ignorance and illusion. The "reconstruction of history" is always in the mind of the investigator, whether consciously or unconsciously, and in the intoxication of an actual discovery of new truth he is very prone to foresee a reconstruction vastly greater than what actually takes place. The current of humanity's past obstinately continues to move before his eyes in the same old channel with but a trifling little jog, though the new revelation seems to require a great displacement all along the course.

Why is this so? Why do the achievements of historical research, in bringing to light the truth about the individual events of the past, change so slightly the broad picture? This is the question to which I wish to devote some particular attention in this place. The answer to it cannot be a simple one, and I do not aspire to make mine complete. I would merely suggest, as in some measure, at least, influential, this fact, that the course of human history is determined no more by what is true than by what men believe to be true; and therefore that he who brings to light a past occurrence of which he is the first to have knowledge is likely to be dealing with what is no real part of history. The phenomena of social life, so far as they are determined at all by the will of man, are due in origin and sequence to conditions as they appear to contemporaries, not to conditions as revealed in their reality to the historian centuries later. Or if the lesson of the past is sought as a guide to any policy, the lesson that is learned and acted upon is derived from the error that passes as history at the time, not from the truth that becomes known long after.

Many a fact of history is like the grain of sand that intrudes within the shell of the pearl oyster. Tiny and insignificant, it is quickly lost to sight and knowledge; but about it are deposited the ensphering layers of myth and legend till a glimmering treasure is produced that excites the mightiest passions of men. Under the charm of its beauty, art, religion, civilization, is developed; through the lust to possess it a dynasty is overthrown, an empire falls into ruin. The historian may crush the pearl and bring to light the grain of sand; but he cannot persuade us that the sand made all the intervening history.

Consider some of the salient incidents in the history of history that throw light on this doctrine. Take the history of Rome, for example. Nothing is more familiar or more amazing than the influence of this history on certain phases of civilized life in Europe down to the nineteenth century of our era. So far as the moral, legal, and political development of West-European nations were determined by the conscious purpose of men, that purpose was shaped by the lessons of recorded Roman experience. All the great leaders of thought and action were steeped in the tradition of the Tiberine city—its rise, its greatness, and its decay. Theologians, jurists, and statesmen of both the secular and the ecclesiastical class sought in the institutions of the Roman people solutions for the problems of medieval and modern times. And the solutions were in no rare instances forthcoming. But what was the character of the history on which depended thus the course of civilized life? It was for the most part the history that we find in Livy and Vergil—a congeries of myths, legends, traditions, and patriotic fancies, animated throughout by a purpose to glorify a not too glorious people. The superhuman valor and virtue of the early Roman heroes— Cincinnatus, Camillus, and the rest; the godlike sagacity of the lawmakers who devised and the statesmen who applied the constitution of the republic; the resplendent genius of the military leaders and the perfection of the military system in the days of the great conquests: all these have been reduced to the proper level by the critical historians of the nineteenth century. But this was after the fabulous elements so ruthlessly extirpated from Roman history had served effectively for ages in shaping the thoughts and deeds and aspirations of men. It was after the genius of Dante had fixed the trend of the medieval mind by assigning to Pagan Rome a high place in the favor of God and an indispensable part in the scheme of Christian redemption. It was after the cynical Machiavelli had projected a powerful influence into the affairs of the sixteenth and seventeenth centuries by deriving from the tales of Romulus and Numa and Virginius and Fabius and Scipio his astute but unmoral maxims of both princely and popular polity. And it was after the erudite Montesquieu had found in the annals of Rome's greatness and decay the most impressive illustrations of those principles which he so effectively taught to succeeding generations through his famous *Spirit of the Laws*.

Early in the nineteenth century Niebuhr began the process of proving that Dante and Machiavelli and Montesquieu, however ingenious and impressive in their conclusions, were sadly astray in their assumptions of fact. At the present day what is accepted as the history of Rome, especially in its earliest ages, would scarcely be recognized by either of those thinkers as concerned with any state of which they had ever heard. Romulus and Numa and Servius Tullius and a whole series of personages whose careers furnished delectable lessons have receded into the realm of myth; the curies, centuries, dictators, tribunes, and other stock properties of the drama of Rome have been so transformed as to contradict the deductions that were once drawn from them. The nineteenth-century conception of Roman history is far indeed from the conception that was influential during the centuries when Rome was a name to conjure with.

It may of course be denied that any ideas about Rome, whether true or false, ever had any actual influence on the course of history in later ages. We all have heard that the things which really and truly determine the sequence of human affairs are those of economic significance; that social and political systems take form, flourish, and decline according to the source and volume of the food or metal supply, the vagaries of commerce, and other such matters as are assumed to be independent of the will of men; and that appeals to the conscious human experience of the past are but the futile cries of deluded creatures who will not be reconciled to the idea of their own insignificance. If this is the truth of the matter, if the sufficient explanation of all social and political phenomena is to be found exclusively in the workings of the law of diminishing returns, the fluctuations in the value of gold, and other such impersonal causes, then is it vain indeed to compare the influence of true with that of false history, and this essay must stand as but one more futile cry of a deluded creature.

Let us turn, however, to another familiar illustration of the tendency that we are trying, with interest even if in error, to trace. The most hardened devotee of the economic interpretation of history would hesitate to deny that during the last thousand years, if for no longer, the history of the Jewish nation, as recorded in the Old Testament, has occupied a very large place among the cultural influences of Christendom. To the strongest minds of thirty generations it had the character of a divinely revealed record of the precise facts, given by God to men for the express purpose of infallibly guiding them in their earthly affairs. It was comprehensive in scope, narrating the origin of the human race and pointing by remorseless prophecy to its end. It was detailed in treatment, showing in minute revealings the course of social, legal, and political development among God's chosen people. There was no question of public policy or of private conduct that could not be and was not answered by appeal to this history. Through a thousand years of West-European development emperors, popes, kings, bishops, and all minor authorities sustained themselves on the precedents of the Children of Israel. The succession of phenomena during that thousand years may have been determined in fact by fluctuations in the value of gold or by the law of diminishing returns; but Hildebrand and Innocent III. and Boniface VIII. and Charles V. and Martin Luther all thought, and all said, that the mainspring of the part that they took in trying, at least, to influence affairs, was the will and purpose of God as revealed in the Bible.

In the history of the Israelites the precedents were found for every species of social and political activity that was manifested in Christendom. Kings discovered there divine sanction for absolute monarchy; republicans for popular sovereignty; moderate men, for the mixed form. If a tyrant was to be got rid of the way was pointed out by the achievements of Ehud and of Jehu and of Samuel, when he hewed Agag in pieces before the Lord. If a people was to be destroyed, the fate of the Amalekites and the recalcitrant tribes of Canaan furnished a divinely sanctioned model of efficiency. The Albigenses at Toulouse, the papists at Drogheda, and the Pequots in Connecticut were slaughtered with pious joy, based on the same historical evidence that the will of God was being executed. How thoroughly the social, economic, and political development of our own country in its early life was permeated with ideas derived from the Old-Testament history, it is unnecessary here to set forth. Suffice it to note that one authority at least has gravely ascribed our whole political system to the influence of the ancient Israelitish polity as described in the Scriptures.

What, now, is the present status of this body of historical narrative
that was for so many ages a powerful factor in the conscious activities
of Christendom? How has the critical spirit of the nineteenth century
dealt with the ancient records and traditions of the Jews? The answer
is so familiar as scarcely to need mention. Adam has gone into the
same category of historical significance with Romulus. The trials and
triumphs of the Israelites have taken their place as an epic version
of an actual experience that was paralleled by many a nomad tribe
of the Orient. Their heroes, lawgivers, and deliverers have been reduced, like those of the Romans, to the level of ordinary humanity.
Their social and political institutions are known to have been, not an
exceptional type set for the guidance of the nations, but in substance
not different from what every primitive people in similar circumstances
has evolved. The compilers of their records and the writers of their
annals are proved to have worked under no more unerring inspiration
than that which guided the historians of most other nations.

Will the history of the Israelites as thus transformed ever again influence the motives of men as it did in, say, the sixteenth and seventeenth centuries, while it still retained its ancient character? Will the
Biblical Moses continue to inspire national patriots when it is known
that our record of his career took shape a thousand years after his
death in a literature of moral and religious propaganda, and is about
as trustworthy as would be a life of Alfred the Great written to-day to
promote Anglo-Saxon unity? Will constitution-makers ever again seek
so anxiously for light from the system of the old Jewish government
as they did before that system was known to have been described
more in the light of hope for the future than of knowledge of the
actual workings in a far-distant past? But one answer to these questions
is possible. Of Jewish history as of Roman history it must be said:
The deeds of men have been affected more by the beliefs in what was
false than by the knowledge of what was true.

Here again, however, we must pause and qualify. We shall be
told that we are hopelessly out of date to suppose that the deeds of
medieval men were affected in any significant degree by belief in
Jewish history whether true or false. The interpreter economic will
assure us that the conflict between Papacy and Empire was but a
struggle for land between two grasping monopolies. The interpreter
meteorological will show us, from measurements of Sequoia stumps
in California, that a decline of the rainfall in central Asia determined

the Crusades without any reference to the historical beliefs of Peter the Hermit or of St. Bernard. And a host of miscellaneous interpreters will be sure that the Lutheran revolt was produced by a medley of racial, financial, and artistic incompatibilities amid which the convictions of the leaders in respect to Biblical history became a wholly negligible factor. If all these interpreters are right, the comparisons that have been suggested between the true and the erroneous ideas of Jewish history must be dropped as futile.

What I have sought to illustrate by the broad aspects of Roman and Jewish history may be as readily studied in familiar episodes in other fields. Take, for example, the origin of that mighty sanctuary of liberty and justice, trial by jury. Through six centuries of English history it was devoutly believed that this institution had either its source or its effective guarantee or both in Magna Carta. There in the famous article XXXIX. stood the familiar words: "No free man shall be taken or imprisoned or dispossessed, or outlawed, or banished, or in any way destroyed, nor will we go upon him, nor send upon him, except by the legal judgment of his peers or by the law of the land."

Floods of ink and myriads of goose-quills were consumed by Fortescue and Coke and Hale and Blackstone and all the lesser lights of English constitutional history in the effort adequately to eulogize the foresight and wisdom of the barons of Runnymede in providing for later generations this singularly beneficent safeguard of human rights. It is hard to understand at times, when reading the declamation of the anti-prerogative men and Whigs, that Magna Carta was framed with any other conscious purpose than to furnish a firm basis for trial by jury. This was in large measure the idea that was transmitted to America, so that we find in Tucker and Story and the rest of the juristic Fathers Magna Carta and the jury system inseparably united as the foundation of our free institutions.

That the association of trial by jury with Magna Carta contributed much through the centuries to the realization and maintenance of constitutional government, is beyond all doubt. Nineteenth-century criticism has proved, however, that the association was, as an historical fact, utterly without foundation. The "judgment of his peers" referred to in the thirty-ninth article was a wholly different thing from the verdict of a jury; and no such institution as trial by jury of a person charged with crime was known to the law of the land when Magna Carta was formulated. The great charter of English liberties neither created nor sanctioned nor guaranteed trial by jury. Such is the actual fact of the matter. How great and important has been the part played in English history by the contrary idea, every one even moderately familiar with that history may easily estimate. It is another case where an effective (and apparently a beneficent) influence on the sequence of human affairs has been exercised, not by what really happened, but by what men erroneously believed to have happened.

Thus far I have sought to illustrate my theme by such misconceptions of fact as have been ancient and inveterate, and untraceable to any definite source in human volition. It would be hardly worth our while to detail the thronging examples where history has been deliberately falsified from motives of political or personal advantage. Conscious and willful misrepresentation of the actual facts has always been a feature of politics and diplomacy and has furnished historians with many of their most interesting problems. It is but a little over forty years now since a spectacular instance of such misrepresentation convulsed Europe. In 1870 the present German Empire came into being, and the impulse to its birth was given by a lie. We know this on the fully documented testimony of the liar. Bismarck, in deep despair at the apparent failure of a diplomatic enterprise intended to force a war with France, received a despatch from the Prussian king containing an account of the last interview of the king with the French ambassador. The meeting had been entirely amicable. Bismarck immediately made public a version of the king's despatch so distorted as to produce in Germany the impression that the ambassador had insulted the king, and in France the impression that the king had insulted the ambassador. The result was an outburst of passion in both countries that at once precipitated the momentous war, with the fall of the French and the establishment of the German Empire.

American history teems with instances hardly less flagrant and malicious, though in none, so far as I know, has there been anything so cynically frank as Bismarck's avowal of his part in the fraud. We might refer, for example, to the perversion of the record in the Dred Scott case so as to represent the Chief Justice as declaring that negroes had no rights that a white man was bound to respect—a view of the opinion that appears in more or less pretentious publications even down to the present day. But without multiplying examples, let us consider now some conclusions that may be drawn from the whole matter.

That the critical spirit in the study of history during the nineteenth century has produced some astonishing results, is beyond all controversy. Its reconstructions of human life in the past have been no less significant than the amazing changes wrought by the physical sciences in our ideas of the material universe. No wonder that the mantle of skepticism has enveloped the whole historical gild, so that only the hardiest of the fraternity dares venture a commonplace without the original source as a foot-note to sustain him. No wonder that the restless quest for new facts has overshadowed every other activity of the historical student. And no wonder that, in the search for new facts of the objective sort, familiar old facts of the other sort are neglected and crowded out of their due consideration. We are overwhelmed with the glory of our achievements in discovery and intoxicated with our superiority over the luckless generations that preceded us. A newly detected brick pile in Mesopotamia or a freshly opened tomb along the Nile reveals to us unsuspected information about Tiglath Pileser and the sixteenth dynasty; at once we feel a sense of pity for the Periclean Greeks, that, with all their culture, they lacked these facts. Excavations in Argos and Crete give us knowledge of Homer's heroes that the most learned men of Augustan Rome never dreamed of; we pity the Romans so much the more than we pitied the Greeks, and we feel renewed confidence in the ancient judgment that the civilization of Rome was after all but a thin veneer. The higher criticism shows us that David, king of the Jews, lacked somewhat of both the might and the tunefulness ascribed to him by the Old Testament; away goes all our respect for the Middle Ages, to whose thinkers David was an inspired model in all the larger and finer things of life. Our contempt for the centuries is cumulative and reaches its climax in the eighteenth, when Gibbon, the paragon, historiographically, of his time, described with affecting details the "fall" of the Roman Empire in the West, though every school-boy of our blessed age has learned from one of our brilliant associates that it never "fell" at all.

No long reflection is needed to detect the dangers that flow from exaggerating the importance of new truth in history. If we impute it for unrighteousness to an age or a people that they lacked the knowledge of the past that has become our possession, the age or people in question is affected with a taint that operates to obscure its own history. We enlightened observers scorn to busy ourselves with the doings of those who supposed that Moses and Romulus and Numa were actually what they were long represented to be, and who believed that trial by jury was guaranteed by Magna Carta. We subconsciously feel that so ignorant a people could have had little in its own affairs to warrant the attention of respectable scholarship. Logically this is of course a shocking *non-sequitur,* but its existence and its influence at the present day are unmistakable, and it probably has some share in the rather enthusiastic movement of the younger generation of historical students, especially here in America, away from the field of medieval history. I have in mind three men under forty, each of whom made his doctorate by a noteworthy study of the Middle Age. To-day all three are professors, and in their serious work one of them goes, with much reluctance, as far back as the peace of Westphalia; another centres his effort in the first half of the nineteenth century; and the third declares roundly that he has no real interest in anything that happened prior to 1870.

The corrective for whatever evils may be involved in the tendencies referred to lies ready to our hand. We must recognize frankly that whatever a given age or people believes to be true *is* true for that age and that people. The actual facts as to Adam and Moses and trial by jury and Romulus had no causal relation to the affairs of Europe in the sixteenth century. Erroneous ideas on those topics had very close causal relations to those affairs. For the history of the sixteenth century, therefore, it is the error and not the fact that is important. The business of the historian who studies that century is to ascertain the scope and content of the ideas that constituted the culture of that period. Whether these ideas were true or were false, according to the standards of any other period, has nothing to do with the matter. That they were the ideas which underlay the activities of the men of this time, is all that concerns the work of the historian.

These axioms of the study of history are familiar and undisputed. Living up to them, however, is another matter. Especially in view of the cyclonic sweep of criticism and discovery during the nineteenth century, it has become desperately difficult to maintain an attitude of decent respect for the historical beliefs of less favored ages. Our pride in the attainments of our own day distorts all our judgments of the past. In vain the master-mind of a distant generation rears with matchless ingenuity a system of institutions based on the teachings of Moses or of Numa. We follow out languidly the story of his system, no matter how precisely it fitted the demands of the time. At only one point will our interest revive, where the master-mind, by some chance, hit upon a notion that has acceptance and vogue in our own day. Here we centre our attention and appreciation, and in our history of the affair make the central feature, not the ingenious adaptation of the system to contemporaneous needs and environment, but the accidental fact that there was in the situation something that anticipated the thought or achievement of the wonderful twentieth century.

The crying need in the study of history to-day is humility. The realities of the past will never be scientifically apprehended so long as the student of history stands contemplating in a stupor of admiration the reversals of ancient beliefs effected in our own age. Contempt for those who lacked our light is the worst of equipments for under-standing their deeds. With all their misconceptions about Adam and Romulus and trial by jury, the people of earlier centuries often thought and acted very much as do we, their regenerate posterity. Keen his-torical vision will detect in them at times qualities closely akin to what used to be called human nature. That they acted in many cases under the impulse of ignorance and error, should make their history more rather than less interesting. At least they lived—they acted—they "did things."

Lowes Dickinson, with his usual acuteness, penetrated to the heart of the matter when he wrote:

> To take the philosophy or the religion of the past and put it into your laboratory and test it for truth, and throw it away if it doesn't answer the test, is to misconceive the whole value and meaning of it. The real question is, what extraordinary, fascinating, tragic or comic life went to produce this precious specimen? What new revelation does it give of the possibilities of the world? That's how you look at it, if you have the sense of life.

The study of history is justified by some as furnishing examples for present instruction, by others as merely enlightening us about present conditions by tracing them in their becoming. On either basis the student is under obligation to repress in all humility his scorn for the error that he finds in the beliefs of those with whom he is dealing. For his business is to present past occurrences in their causal sequence. Not this, that, or the other event by itself, but this as the cause of that, and the other as the effect of that. But unless he is ready to adopt in the extreme form the economic and sundryological interpretations and discard the human influence entirely, he must find in the beliefs of men a most powerful factor in the chain of causation. Nor does it matter at all whether a belief is true or false. Montesquieu remarks in his *Esprit des Lois*: "In a free nation it is very often a matter of indifference whether individuals reason right or reason wrong; it is enough that they reason: for from that springs liberty." Much the same is the case in respect to the beliefs of a people about history, whether of their own past or of the past of others: the beliefs are important whether true or false; for out of them is formed the subject-matter of history.

Thus we come again to the sum of the whole matter. It is impossible to exaggerate the significance in many respects of the transformations effected in historical knowledge during the nineteenth century. Least possible of all is it to overestimate the change in the general attitude toward history that has resulted from these transformations. Yet in one respect there is need of the utmost caution in handling the new situation. It behooves the historian to be modest in his rejoicings over the discoveries that have reversed so many long-cherished beliefs. He must keep in mind that the reversal cannot be made retroactive, so as to affect the thoughts and deeds of the generations who knew not the reality. He must remember, in short, that for very, very much history there is more importance in the ancient error than in the new-found truth.

II

Some Glimpses of the Medieval Scene

※※—※※—※※—※※—※※—※※—※※—※※—※※—※≪—≪≪—≪≪—≪≪—≪≪—≪≪—≪≪—≪≪—≪≪—≪≪

What Is Medieval History?

JOSEPH R. STRAYER

Magna Carta

SIDNEY PAINTER

Technology and Invention in the Middle Ages

LYNN WHITE, JR.

※※—※※—※※—※※—※※—※※—※※—※※—※※—※≪—≪≪—≪≪—≪≪—≪≪—≪≪—≪≪—≪≪—≪≪—≪≪

What Is Medieval History?

JOSEPH R. STRAYER

➤➤➤➤➤➤➤➤➤➤ *Published in 1945* ◀◀◀◀◀◀◀◀◀◀

The study of the Middle Ages has suffered serious reverses in American schools and colleges in recent years. Except in Roman Catholic institutions, the tendency has been to cut down on the amount of time and space given to the centuries that passed between the decline of Roman civilization and the age of Columbus. It is understandable, therefore, that specialists in medieval history have come to be regarded as luxuries that few colleges can afford. This situation deserves to be deplored, as Joseph R. Strayer, professor of medieval history at Princeton and one of the most highly respected of present-day American medievalists, insists in the present selection. Strayer emphasizes that medieval history is enormously rich and meaningful in its content. It is significant, however, that he bases his defense of medieval history on grounds quite different from those employed by Schuyler to defend the study of any kind of history. Strayer does not justify the investigation of his subject as an end in itself. Reflecting the insecure position of medievalists in general, he argues that the Middle Ages can throw valuable light on the problems of the contemporary world.

Medieval history has long since disappeared from the curricula of most secondary schools and it is now being squeezed out of the colleges. The reasons for this trend are easy enough to understand. There is so much to learn and so little time in which to learn it; the Middle Ages seem a remote, confused period which contributes little to an understanding of our own age. Why should we waste our time on medieval studies when we have all the problems of recent history to consider?

It must be admitted that medieval history, as it is often taught,

Reprinted by special permission from *Social Education*, IX (1945), 295-298.

justifies this attitude. Courses are too long, too heavily loaded with detail, too antiquarian in their approach. They give no clear picture, either of the essential elements of medieval civilization, or of the importance of that civilization in the development of occidental society. These weaknesses are not inherent in the subject. There is a pattern in the development of medieval society which can be seen with the aid of a relatively small number of examples; there is a medieval achievement which can be understood without memorizing the names of emperors of the Salian dynasty. If we stress these two approaches we can teach a great deal about the Middle Ages in a relatively short time, and we can create enough interest in the subject to encourage students to do further reading. This article is an attempt to discover the basic pattern of medieval history and to point out the essentials of the medieval achievement in order to show the value of medieval studies.

What were the Middle Ages? The conventional answer is that they were the centuries between the fall of the Roman Empire and the beginnings of modern European civilization. Scholars have argued, and will argue endlessly, as to the exact dates of these two terminal points, but we do not have to wait for them to reach an agreement. Most historians would admit that the Roman Empire was well on its way to decline by the fifth century and that many of the characteristic elements of modern civilization were apparent by 1500. We do not have to be more precise than this—we can say that the Middle Ages run, roughly, from the fifth to the fifteenth century. There will be exceptions to this rule-of-thumb definition—aspects of Roman civilization survive in some parts of Europe long after 400 A.D. and elements of modern civilization appear in Italy well before 1500—but no student of medieval history can say that these transitional forms are completely outside his field of interest.

The Middle Ages extend from the fifth to the fifteenth century. This is a long period, so long that many writers will argue that it has no real unity, that there are many middle ages instead of one. There is force in this argument. We have only to think what our ancestors were like a thousand, or even five hundred, years ago to wonder whether one of Clovis's German warriors had much in common with a crusader of the twelfth century or an English baron of the Wars of the Roses. Is there any real unity in the Middle Ages, or have we simply developed a convenient catch-basket phrase in which to dump a number of centuries that do not greatly interest us?

To answer this question let us pick a century which everyone will admit was medieval, say the twelfth. How do the ways of living, the basic ideas and ideals of this century differ from those of the Roman Empire and those of the modern world?

In the first place, it is clear that we are dealing with a civilization which, in its complete form, covers only Western Europe. It has little influence on Eastern Europe and even less on Western Asia and Northern Africa. Graeco-Roman civilization had been Mediterranean, not European; it attained its fullest development in Italy, Greece, Asia Minor, Syria, and North Africa. Modern occidental civilization is oceanic, not European; it is as typical of America, Australia, and parts of Asia and Africa as it is of Western Europe. In the Roman period most of Europe was a backward, colonial region, receiving its institutions and ideas from more advanced communities to the south and east. In the modern period Europe has been first the center and then a segment of a world civilization. But in the twelfth century European civilization stood by itself, neither greatly influencing nor greatly influenced by the civilizations of other continents.

In political and constitutional developments twelfth-century Europe occupies the same middle position. The Roman Empire was not a national state, it was a union of all the peoples who shared the common Mediterranean civilization under a single powerful ruler. The modern world, though it recognizes the fact of a common civilization, is divided into sovereign national states. The twelfth century knew neither the single powerful political unit nor the modern state. Nationalism and sovereignty did not exist, and while the concept of a Commonwealth of Christendom did exist, it found effective expression only in the Church, not in any secular political organization. Every man was

---

ABSOLUTISM: Political doctrine that no power—whether church, feudal aristocrat, or law of nature—limits a ruler in the exercise of his authority. A basic concept in the political history of seventeenth- and eighteenth-century Europe.

SCHOLASTICISM: Medieval philosophy that subordinated philosophy to Christian theology and sought to justify faith by reason. Characterized by an

subject to many overlapping authorities, to the local feudal lord or self-governing town in all ordinary affairs, to the more remote overlord (king, duke, or count) in special cases, to the Church in matters which concerned the welfare of Christendom and the Christian faith. This division of authority made absolutism impossible; neither the unlimited power of the Roman emperor nor the equally unlimited power of the modern sovereign state could exist under such circumstances. On the other hand, the weakness or the absence of large political units increased the cohesiveness of smaller groups. No individual could stand alone; he had to be part of a community, and the community of a village or of a town influenced and controlled the lives of its members to a far greater extent than it does today.

This peculiar political organization was adapted to an equally unusual religious organization. In the Roman Empire the state had controlled religion; the pagan cults were mere agencies of the government, and even the Catholic Church had had to conform to laws and administrative regulations issued by the emperor. In the modern period the churches are usually considered voluntary private associations, completely dissociated from the state, completely dependent on their own moral authority to enforce their rules. In the twelfth century the Church was an independent public authority. It claimed complete freedom of action; no secular ruler could interfere with its officials, its courts, or its laws. But at the same time the twelfth-century Church insisted that lay authority must support its efforts to preserve the unity of the faith and the rules of Christian morality. The Church determined the values and the goals of European society; it held that lay governments were inferior, though independent, agencies whose chief duty was to deal with the sordid details of crime and punishment. The idea of a Commonwealth of Christendom found its expression in the Church, and loyalty to the Church was stronger than loyalty to any lay organization.

Aristotelian stress on systematization, it is associated chiefly with the name of St. Thomas Aquinas (d. 1274).

TROUBADOURS: Medieval poet-musicians who flourished in Southern France. Directing their sentimental love songs mainly at aristocratic women, they did much to shape medieval notions of chivalry, gallantry, courtesy, and romantic love.

It is a little more difficult to appreciate the significance of the twelfth century in economic history. At first glance it would seem that there had been little change since the Late Roman Empire. Both in the fourth and in the twelfth centuries the great majority of the population of Europe was engaged in agriculture, and most of these agricultural laborers were unfree. The great difference between the two periods is that the fourth century was a period of declining economic activity while the twelfth century was a period of economic expansion. The Romans of the Late Empire would have been satisfied if they could have kept production and commerce at their old level; the men of the twelfth century were making a great effort to increase production and commerce. They were clearing forests, draining swamps, building new towns, establishing new trading stations in the East, concentrating certain industries in the towns, and even experimenting with new sources of power, such as the windmill.

This rapid expansion makes the twelfth century, in some of its aspects, resemble our own boom periods. For example, emigration agents in the Rhineland told German peasants the familiar story of fertile land on the eastern frontier which could be had for a song. But the controlling ideas of the twelfth century were so different from ours that the resemblances between the two economic systems are less striking than the differences. Strong community feeling and influence of the Church made group enterprise more important than individual effort. Settlers on the frontier grouped themselves in villages for mutual protection and assistance; they did not set up individual homesteads. The small business men of the town formed strong associations, not only to guard their political rights but also to suppress economic competition. Even the most individualistic enterprisers of the period, the great merchants who traded across the length and breadth of Europe, found that they had to be backed up by associations of their fellow merchants to enjoy any security.

At the same time the Church was very suspicious of profit-seeking individuals. It feared, quite rightly, that such men would become too interested in this world to remember the next. So the Church urged that business be carried on for the good of the community rather than the individual, and encouraged organizations and regulations which subordinated individual profit to the general welfare. This is not to say that the profit motive was completely suppressed in the twelfth century, but no one at that time thought that it was or should be the main-spring of human activity. As a result, neither individual capitalists nor the middle class as a whole had the same importance in the twelfth century that they have had in the modern world.

In art and literature, philosophy and science, formal and informal education, the twelfth century diverged sharply from the Roman tradition. It saw the beginnings of a new type of architecture in the early Gothic churches and a new type of literature in the poems of the troubadours and jongleurs. It witnessed the revival of science, long neglected by the Romans, and the first works of scholastic philosophy. The gradual development of the Universities of Bologna and Paris laid the foundations for a new system of education, characterized by formal lecture courses, examinations, and degrees. At the same time the ideal of the cultured gentleman slowly began to take shape in the active social life of the courts of southern France.

We have inherited all these traditions, but it is hardly necessary to point out that they have been greatly modified by the passage of time. The Renaissance, in reviving the classical tradition, caused a sharp break in the development of medieval forms of expression, and when these forms were revived in their turn in the nineteenth century they had to be fitted into a new intellectual and material environment. Sir Walter Scott could not write medieval ballads, however much he soaked himself in Middle English poetry, and a Gothic church built around a steel skeleton is not the same kind of church as Notre Dame de Chartres. Even where there was no sharp break with the past, as in the field of science, gradual change led to almost complete transformation of values and objectives. We can see how modern physics developed from the Aristotelian works brought back to the West in the twelfth century, but we cannot think the thoughts of a twelfth-century scholar. The intellectual and artistic tradition of the twelfth century has its roots in the past and bears much of its fruit in the future, but it is clearly an independent tradition; it is neither decadent classicism nor primitive modernism.

If we try to summarize the results attained by this brief discussion we might say that the civilization of the twelfth century had characteristics which clearly separated it from the civilizations of Rome and of the modern world. It was a Western European civilization rather than a Mediterranean or an oceanic civilization. Political power was divided among a hierarchy of interdependent governments rather than concentrated in a world empire or a group of sovereign national states. The Church was independent of secular authority, but it was more than a private association with limited functions; it set the standards and defined the goals for all human activities. In economics there was neither state regulation nor *laissez faire*; instead local groups controlled farmers, artisans, and merchants in the interest of the whole community. In Gothic art, chivalric poetry, scholastic philosophy, and the university system of education the twelfth century created forms which were neither classical nor modern. These characteristics of twelfth-century civilization were not only distinct, they were also interdependent; they fused into an organic whole. The economic institutions could not have existed without the political and religious institutions; the art and literature were profoundly affected by the religious and political beliefs of the age. The civilization of the twelfth century was remarkably self-sufficient and self-consistent; it had a flavor, a texture, almost a personality of its own.

Obviously these elements of twelfth-century civilization are not duplicated exactly in any other period of the Middle Ages. But they illustrate the basic assumptions, the social habits, the aspirations of the other medieval centuries. Conscious choice and the force of external circumstances were leading Europeans toward the pattern of twelfth-century civilization long before that pattern could be fully worked out. Conscious choice and force of habit made Europeans cling to the basic pattern of twelfth-century civilization for generations, even though new activities and ideas forced modifications of some of its details. There are important differences between the early and late Middle Ages, but these differences represent different stages in the development of a single civilization. From the fifth to the eighth century the wreckage of an older civilization was slowly cleared away. Europe gradually separated itself from the Mediterranean world and worked out its own independent culture, based on Christianity, survivals of Roman institutions and ideas, and Germanic customs. The ninth, tenth, and eleventh centuries were a period of adjustment and experimentation, in which Europeans slowly and painfully discovered the most effective institutional and ideological expressions of their basic beliefs and aspirations. The twelfth and thirteenth centuries were a period of fruition, of full development of all the potentialities of medieval civilization. In the fourteenth and fifteenth centuries medieval civilization slowly decayed under the impact of the new forces which it had created by its own success. From this point of view there is real unity in the story of the Middle Ages; it is the story of the rise, development, and fall of a great civilization.

It is because the history of the Middle Ages is the history of a civilization that the subject is worth studying. The record of the rise and fall of any civilization deserves careful examination, for the basic problems of all civilizations are similar. When we fully understand how peoples of the past slowly became capable of organizing and integrating their efforts, how they accomplished their great and characteristic work, how they eventually lost their ability to do constructive work and slipped into stagnant or retrogressive patterns of behavior, then we shall better understand the state of our own civilization.

The medieval experience is especially important first, because we have more information about it than any comparable cycle, and second, because it has contributed directly to our own way of life. Too many people still think that the Middle Ages are merely a stagnant pit which lies between the heights of classical and Renaissance civilization, and that all our legacy from the past was carried over the bridges which Renaissance thinkers threw across the medieval pit to the firm ground of Graeco-Roman learning. This is true even of people who deposit money in a bank, who elect representatives to a national assembly, who rely on the precedents of the English common law, who receive degrees from universities and believe that science is an important part of education, who worship in Gothic churches and who read books written in modern European languages. They would find their lives rather limited and unsatisfactory if they could do none of these things and yet the basic idea of every one of these activities was worked out in the Middle Ages and not in ancient Greece or Rome.

Our civilization has roots in the Middle Ages as well as in the classical period, and the medieval roots often contribute more nourishment than the classical ones. The story of medieval civilization is worth knowing and its neglect will impoverish our understanding of the modern world and our own age.

Magna Carta

SIDNEY PAINTER

➤➤➤-➤➤➤-➤➤➤-➤➤➤-➤➤➤-➤➤➤-➤➤➤-➤➤➤-➤➤➤ *Published in 1947* ⬅⬅⬅-⬅⬅⬅-⬅⬅⬅-⬅⬅⬅-⬅⬅⬅-⬅⬅⬅-⬅⬅⬅-⬅⬅⬅

One of the principal themes in the history of the last medieval centuries was the struggle on the part of kings to undermine the institution of feudalism and destroy the decentralization of political authority that was the essence of feudalism. Some kings succeeded in their attempt to increase their power and to deprive their vassals of traditional feudal rights and privileges; others failed. Certainly the most dramatic failure was King John of England, who was so striking a failure that no other English ruler has ventured to be known as John II. The document that embodied his defeat was Magna Carta, the feudal contract by the terms of which he was compelled to recognize the rights and privileges of his vassals as well as the limitations on their obligations to him. Through the centuries, of course, Magna Carta has had thousands of commentators. Few of these commentators, however, have known thirteenth-century England so well as Sidney Painter, of the Johns Hopkins University. Author of a valuable monograph on *The Reign of King John* (1949), Painter is especially qualified to evaluate the significance of the most famous document in European political history.

Magna Carta occupies a unique place in Anglo-American political tradition. What is more it fully deserves this eminence. It contains certain basic ideas and assumptions that have dominated the development of English and American political thought. It has been studied and commented on more often and more ably than any other historical document of European civilization with the possible exception of the New Testament. Certainly every student of medieval

Reprinted by special permission from *The American Historical Review*, LIII (1947), 42-49. The footnotes which originally appeared with this essay have been omitted.

England, and they have been both numerous and distinguished, has contributed his mite to the magnificent total of commentaries on Magna Carta. In this brief paper I am following this long-established tradition by adding my own contribution—or as much of it as is consistent with brevity.

The long and distinguished career of Magna Carta as a political document is one of the most striking ironies of history. Its beginning was certainly far from auspicious. It was an agreement between an able but completely unscrupulous and opportunistic king and a small group of his barons. While this group of barons contained some men of maturity and integrity, two of its leaders, Robert fitz Walter and Saher de Quency, were clearly disreputable and a number of others were reckless young men who had just come into their inheritances. Both sides considered the agreement as a mere truce to give them time to prepare for war. The northern barons did not even wait for the completion of the agreement before rushing off to put their castles in order. John promptly called for Poitevin and Gascon troops and dispatched messengers to Rome to persuade the pope to declare the charter invalid. Moreover, the detailed provisions of Magna Carta were for the most part obsolete when they were written. They dealt with a political system that was rapidly dying and they served to hasten its end.

In order to understand this puzzle as to how a truly great political document sprang from a personal and political mire we must glance at the ideas and motives of those who created it. Let us first consider King John. As his actions led to the demand for the charter, he was as much its author as those who actually framed its clauses. John was not a pleasant person, but he was an active and able monarch. His political difficulties were for the most part caused by factors that were entirely beyond his control. He was faced with the problem of ruling England by a political system that had lost all touch with economic reality. The feudal system was based on the assumption that the all-important political unit was the fully armed knight. A king's or a baron's importance depended on the number of knights who would follow his banner. By the time John came to the throne this assumption was no longer sound. Mercenary crossbowmen were fully as effective as knights, and knights could be hired and equipped for money. Money had become the source of power. Unfortunately, John found himself at a serious disadvantage under a money economy. The prices of agricultural products were rising rapidly and with them the income of those who could tap directly the profits derived from agriculture. But John's predecessors had reduced the royal demesne to a few scattered remnants. Hence the king's direct share in the rising income from the land was very small. His revenue had to come from his feudal rights or from new devices. John did his best to increase the revenue from scutages, aids, and reliefs, but he met with fierce resistance and the results were pitifully small. These dues were based on the knights' fee, and the knights' fee had no reality as an economic unit. A scutage rate that would yield a reasonable return from rich estates would crush poor ones. John turned to new devices such as the thirteenth, but they met with even more bitter resistance. As a result John spent his reign in trying various ways to get his share of the country's growing income and these efforts led directly to Magna Carta. The details of Magna Carta are largely a commentary on John's methods of raising money.

The baronial opposition to King John was essentially conservative if not reactionary. The barons wanted to preserve the feudal system as they believed it had existed in the times of their ancestors. They wanted to fix their feudal obligations to the crown at the ancient rates and to put an end to John's novel financial expedients. Their attack on the writ *praecipe* shows that they were anxious to stop the expansion of the jurisdiction of the royal courts. The fact that there was no general attempt to undo the legal work of Henry II was probably the result of baronial ignorance of the past. They had no idea how recent that enormous expansion of royal authority was. The assembly that they provided to give approval to the levying of scutages and special aids was a thoroughly feudal body and hence essentially obsolete. The assembly of tenants-in-chief contemplated in Magna Carta would have included men of insignificant position and excluded some of the chief men of the realm. In fact one of the twenty-five barons chosen to enforce Magna Carta would not have been entitled to a summons as a

---

DEMESNE: That land which a lord reserved for his own use, as distinguished from those pieces of land which he permitted peasants to hold and use.

FEE OR FIEF: A unit of income. Usually an estate or a number of estates granted to a vassal by an overlord in return for certain services.

GRATIAN: Twelfth-century monk and professor at the University of Bologna. His *Decretum* became the standard work for the study of canon law in medieval times.

tenant-in-chief except as a tenant of an honor in the crown's hands. The barons' efforts led to the result that so often attends reactionary movements—they killed the system they were defending. The feudal revenues of the crown were frozen, and future kings were obliged to place all their hope in new, nonfeudal ways of raising money. There is no evidence that the ideal feudal assembly conceived by the barons ever met. The principles on which it rested, tenure and the possession of knights' fees, soon passed into oblivion.

Thus Magna Carta was essentially an expression of feudal custom. But fortunately for the charter's reputation as a political document the feudal system embodied certain basic assumptions that were to outlive it by many centuries. The most important of these was the conception of the *liber homo*, the free, the privileged man. Let me take this occasion to say that when *liber* or any of its derivatives are found in a medieval document the proper form of "privileged" will render the meaning better than will "free." In the original home of English feudal custom, tenth and eleventh century France, the *liber homo* could do anything he pleased or had the power to do as long as he performed his feudal obligations as they were interpreted by his fellow vassals. He was answerable only to the judgment of his peers in his lord's court. In England feudal custom had failed to replace entirely the ancient laws of the land. Hence the English *liber homo* was also subject to that law. Only a baron could claim the right to answer in no court other than one composed of his feudal peers. This idea of the *liber homo* and his privileges finds expression in the thirty-ninth clause of Magna Carta—"No free man shall be taken, or imprisoned, or disseised, or outlawed, or exiled, or in any way destroyed, nor will we go against him or send against him, except by lawful judgment of his peers or by the law of the land."

By this clause the *liber homo* was guaranteed protection of his per-

---

Peter Lombard: Twelfth-century theologian whose *Sentences* became the leading theological textbook in medieval universities.

Frederick Maurice Powicke: One of the leading twentieth-century English medievalists. Author of such volumes as *Stephen Langton* (1928), *Medieval England* (1931), and *King Henry III and the Lord Edward* (1947).

Scutage: A money payment in lieu of the military service that was usually the major obligation of a vassal (he who received and held a fief) to his overlord (he who granted a fief).

son and property from arbitrary action. When it was written it was not as airtight as it seemed, for the king's judges were rapidly expanding the law of the land at the expense of the privileges of the *liber homo*. But the privileged men of England soon grasped this fact and within a half century the law could be changed only by statute. As time went on, the rights of privileged men were extended to more and more of the people of England. New rights were added as changing conditions made them needful. Thus this basic feudal idea has remained one of the fundamental political principles of Anglo-American peoples. It is, however, important to notice that this concept is not essentially democratic and had no slightest democratic element in the time of Magna Carta. The *liberi homini* were the feudal class, the privileged few. Whenever provisions of the charter seem to benefit the ordinary man, a close examination will show that it is his lord's pocketbook that is the real cause of concern. Finally, it is interesting to notice that while this clause is tucked away obscurely in the middle of the charter, it is the first item in the list of Magna Carta clauses found in a contemporary document in the French archives. Someone at the time evidently saw its great importance.

The second basic assumption of the feudal system grew inevitably out of the first. The *liber homo* was free to go where he willed and to serve any man or no man. When he swore fidelity and did homage to a lord, the relationship was essentially contractual. It was assumed that lord and vassals would co-operate for their mutual benefit. The feudal custom governing the relations between a lord and his vassals was worked out by the vassals in their lord's feudal court. The lord could not change these relations of his own accord. Moreover the lord was expected to take no step that was of importance for the welfare of the fief without consulting his vassals. He was expected to seek the counsel of his vassals before choosing a wife for himself or for his eldest son, before embarking on a war, or before going on a long journey. Now this obligation on the part of the lord to seek counsel cannot be found expressed in documents, but the evidence that it was the usual practice is overwhelming. In fact the idea of the necessity of taking counsel was a central feature of medieval government. While it is expressed most clearly in the great monastic rules, it was fully as important in the secular world. In Magna Carta this right of the vassal to be consulted finds expression in the clauses forbidding the levying of scutages or special aids without consulting the assembly described in the charter.

It has been argued that the fact that an assembly of vassals must be consulted does not necessarily imply that its assent must be obtained. I cannot prove from the wording of Magna Carta that its authors intended that the king had to gain the consent of the assembly for these financial exactions. But it seems clear that it was so interpreted by contemporaries. During the regency of William Marshal, Bishop Peter des Roches went so far as to refuse to pay a scutage on the ground that he himself had not consented to it. While the acceptance of his contention probably demonstrates the bishop's power rather than any general belief in the justness of his cause, it certainly seems to indicate the belief that the vassals had to give their consent to unusual feudal exactions. Under Henry III and Edward I this principle became firmly established and was the basis for the power of Parliament. But there is no reason to believe that the barons who dictated Magna Carta had any general ideas such as we express by the slogans "No taxation without consent" and "Government by the will of the governed." They insisted on the right of the king's vassals to participate in the government. It was the king not the barons who brought burghers into Parliament and gave them a voice in such matters. But the basic principle that the king must seek the assent of some council before levying taxes was a vital one to the development of the English constitution.

The third basic assumption of the feudal system was the result of the contractual nature of the relations between a lord and his vassals. A lord could never be an arbitrary, absolute ruler—he was bound by the contract, by the customs forged in his court. He had no power over a vassal other than that given him by this custom. The terms "feudal law" and "feudal contract" when applied to the feudal states of western Europe as a whole are vague generalizations that have little meaning and less utility, but when applied to a single fief they are extremely concrete. Magna Carta was an official expression of important phases of the feudal custom of England. By issuing it John admitted that he was bound by that custom. This point was fully understood by the barons and their successors. During the thirteenth and fourteenth centuries the kings of England were forced to reissue the charter some thirty times. Most of its specific causes were obsolete and forgotten, but it stood as the symbol of the king's subservience to the law.

This raises a most interesting question—did King John have absolutist ideas? I can find no evidence that is very convincing. Master Alexander Cementarius, one of King John's many intimate clerks, seems to have spoken of the royal power in terms that would have pleased James I, but this is feeble proof of John's views. In his own letters to the pope and to his barons he relied as much on the ancient custom of the realm as did his opponents. I suspect that the seeds of absolutist theory existed among the clergy. Caesar of Heisterback's story of the debate among the clerks at the University of Paris as to whether Thomas Becket had owed his chief duty to his king or to the church seems to support this view. But John was brought up in a thoroughly feudal atmosphere and it seems doubtful that such ideas found a place in his mind.

One other feature of feudalism that was embodied in Magna Carta deserves our notice. The feudal system assumed the willingness of the feudal class to resort to war. If a vassal defied the decision of his lord's court, his fellow vassals took up arms to subdue him. If the lord violated custom, his vassals rose against him. But the line between irresponsible revolt and justified rebellion against violations of feudal custom was hard to draw. A small group that opposed a strong king was likely to suffer as traitors no matter how good their cause might be in theory. The barons wanted machinery set up that could legalize revolt against violations of Magna Carta. The result was the creation of the group of twenty-five who were to watch over the execution of the charter and call for war against John if he violated it. This arrangement was thoroughly feudal in spirit and has strong echoes in later Anglo-American political thought. Both Englishmen and Americans have always had a weakness for the right of rebellion against oppression—when practiced by them instead of against them.

These feudal elements of Magna Carta sprang from Anglo-Norman tradition and the conservatism of the rebel barons. I believe, but I cannot prove, that the clauses expressing them were forged by the most powerful of all English barons, William Marshal, earl of Pembroke. William was a member of the king's party and served as one of the negotiators between him and the barons. He carried the baronial demands to John and urged him to acept them. I am convinced that in the process he shaped the charter. I have two reasons for this belief. If one lays aside the helter-skelter order in which the clauses are arranged, the charter is very ably drawn. Compared to such later documents as the Provisions of Oxford it is incredibly clear and precise.

Moreover, it shows an intimate and accurate knowledge of the working of the English royal government. Professor Powicke argues that any baron would have this knowledge. I must take the liberty of doubting this. I can find no one in the rebel camp who seems to me to have had sufficient experience as a royal official. William Marshal had this experience; he went back and forth to the rebel camp while the charter was being drafted, and the husbands of his two eldest daughters were baronial leaders. Then Magna Carta shows remarkably few signs of the bitter personal animosity that had placed most of the rebel barons in opposition to John. It seems to me that only a wise neutral could have brought so statesmanlike a document out of the rebel camp.

In his capacity as negotiator between John and the barons William Marshal had a colleague, Stephen Langton, archbishop of Canterbury. Through him Professor Powicke has given Magna Carta a place in the main current of political thought of the twelfth and thirteenth centuries. This is largely speculation, but I think well-founded speculation. Langton had been a professor of theology at the University of Paris and a cardinal in the curia of the great pope, Innocent III. As a professor he had devoted his energies to interpreting the work of the two great organizers of Christian thought, Gratian and Peter Lombard. Gratian had taken the confused and often contradictory mass of real and forged papal and conciliar decrees and the works of the fathers and had woven the whole into a consistent system of canon law. Peter Lombard had performed the same service for theology. The ambition of the great popes of the twelfth and thirteenth centuries was to apply these two systems so that the universal church would have one law and one theology. As cardinal, Langton had aided the greatest of these popes in this work. The canon law as drawn up by Gratian and interpreted by his successors governed the internal organization of the church and its relations with the lay world. It governed popes and bishops, kings and nobles. Almost inevitably Langton would believe in the desirability of a similar system of law for purely secular affairs.

Langton arrived in England after his reluctant acceptance by the king to find the barons chafing under John's rule. They had many personal grievances and felt sure that John was continuously violating the ancient customs of the realm, but they had no idea what could be done about it. Langton met with them at St. Albans in the autumn of 1214. He showed them a document which he had probably found in the archepiscopal archives at Lambeth—the Charter of Liberties of

Henry I. It must have been a great boon to the conservative-minded barons. Here was some precise information about what had been considered the custom of the realm in their grandfather's time. More important, here was a program and precedent for it. To this extent Langton was clearly the father of Magna Carta. The belief that he saw it as an attempt to establish an orderly system of law in secular politics is, as I have said, speculation, but I agree with Powicke that he probably did.

It is impossible to label any of the details of Magna Carta as Langton's work with any confidence. Powicke suggests that the first clause providing for a privileged church with all its ancient rights was his attempt to connect secular and canon law. But this clause could just as well have been copied from Henry I's charter. One can advance an argument that Langton was responsible for the clause that stated the rights of the *liber homo*, but it is too speculative to carry much weight. That clause appeared first on a list of items from Magna Carta found in the French archives. One might speculate that these were Langton's notes for the charter which he left with his friend Philip Augustus when he passed through France in 1216. Unfortunately the only support for this theory is that there is no evidence against it. Not even a medievalist can go far with that.

If Langton's purpose was to establish the reign of law in the political affairs of his native land, he was eminently successful. The charter he fathered became the first of many expressions of the slowly developing English constitution. It became besides the symbol of the Anglo-American conception of government. Through it the fundamental features of the feudal system passed into our political tradition. I am inclined to believe that my liberal friends may say—"That is what we have been suspecting all along. Your *liber homo* is at last as obsolete as the system that created him." But he has lasted a long, long time—far longer than the *cives Romanus*—and I am not yet ready to abandon him.

Technology and Invention in the
Middle Ages

LYNN WHITE, Jr.

≫≫-≫≫-≫≫-≫≫-≫≫-≫≫-≫≫-≫≫ *Published in 1940* ≪-≪≪-≪≪-≪≪-≪≪-≪≪-≪≪-≪≪

In popular usage today, the word *medieval* continues to serve as a synonym for backward, ignorant, and barbaric. For many decades, however, medievalists have been struggling to overcome this word association. Pointing proudly to the political and economic achievements of medieval men, they have gloried in the growth of parliaments and of capitalist institutions and practices. Among the cultural and intellectual achievements of medieval men, they have pointed no less proudly to the development of Gothic art, vernacular languages and literatures, university education, scholastic philosophy, and natural science. One of the most recent attempts to rehabilitate the middle ages, undertaken by Lynn White, Jr., now president of Mills College, deals with a subject that has too often suffered from neglect: medieval inventions and technological developments.

Τ he history of technology and invention, especially that of the earlier periods, has been left strangely uncultivated. Our vast technical institutes continue at an ever-accelerating pace to revolutionize the world we live in; yet small effort is being made to place our present technology in the time-sequence, or to give to our technicians that sense of their social responsibility which can only come from an exact understanding of their historical function—one might almost say, of their apostolic succession. By permitting those who work in shops and laboratories to forget the past, we have impoverished the present and

Reprinted by special permission from *Speculum*, XV (1940), 141-156. The extensive documentation which originally appeared with this essay has been omitted.

endangered the future. In the United States this neglect is the less excusable because we Americans boast of being the most technically progressive people of an inventive age. But when the historian of American technology tries to probe the mediaeval and renaissance roots of his subject he runs into difficulties: the materials available to him are scanty and often questionable; for professional mediaevalists have left unmined this vein in the centuries on which they have staked their claim.

Broadly speaking, technology is the way people do things. (In a certain sense there is even a technology of prayer.) Yet it is startling to reflect that we have, as a rule, only the vaguest notion of how the men of the Middle Ages actually did things, and how, from time to time, they learned to do them better. In our museums we cherish mediaeval textiles; we recognize the crucial importance of the cloth industry in the growth of early capitalism. But what do we know of spinning and weaving, of fulling and dyeing, and of the improvements in quality and production which affected both the art and the economics of the time? We all know that St. Louis of France went on crusades. But did he sail towards Orient in the same sort of ship which Godfrey of Bouillon might have used, had not this latter chosen, probably with good reason, to journey by land? How had shipbuilding changed in the intervening century and a half; under what influences had it changed; and what could a ship of 1249 do which one of 1095 could not? And more particularly, what could a ship of 1492 accomplish in addition? Every textbook on American history should begin with a discussion of those mediaeval improvements in shipbuilding and navigation without which the exploration and settlement of the New World would have been technically impossible. That chapter is lacking chiefly because mediaevalists themselves have not studied these matters adequately. To offer a final example: how is it that the impor-

BAYEUX TAPESTRY: Masterpiece of eleventh-century art and an enormously valuable historical source. Twenty inches wide and more than two hundred thirty feet long, it depicts in colored thread a large number of scenes from the Norman Conquest of England in 1066. It throws much light on the conditions of feudal life.

MARC BLOCH: Outstanding French medievalist who was put to death by the Nazis during World War II. Almost all of his important writings on

tance of the late thirteenth-century Italian invention of spectacles has not been more generally appreciated? Anyone familiar with the crescendo of intellectual life in the later Middle Ages would challenge that enthusiast who has ascribed the Renaissance to the discovery of eye-glasses; but surely no one in the bespectacled academic world will be sufficiently discourteous to doubt that this technical development does much to account for the improved standard of education and the almost feverish tempo of thought characteristic of the fourteenth and fifteenth centuries. People were able to read more, and to read in their maturer years.

If, then, we are to understand any one of the many 'Middle Ages' (blessed be the pluralist bias of our tongue!) and their gradual metamorphosis into modern times, we must not neglect technology. Yet at present the laborers in this field are as few as the harvest is plenteous.

Perhaps the chief reason why scholars have been hesitant to explore the subject is the difficulty of delimiting its boundaries: technology knows neither chronological nor geographic frontiers.

The student of the history of invention soon discovers that he must smash the conventional barriers between Greek and barbarian, Roman and German, oriental and occidental. For mediaeval technology is found to consist not simply of the technical equipment inherited from the Roman-Hellenistic world modified by the inventive ingenuity of the western peoples, but also of elements derived from three outside sources: the northern barbarians, the Byzantine and Moslem Near East, and the Far East.

The importance of the first of these, the barbarian influence, has been far too little understood even by those who have dabbled in the history of technology. Students of the fine arts have only recently led the way towards an appreciation of the essential unity and originality of that vast northern world of so-called 'barbarians' which, in ancient

---

medieval history are still untranslated, but any reader who understands French will find his writings rewarding.

PLINY THE ELDER: Roman writer of the first century. His *Natural History* is for all practical purposes a history of civilization. It is filled with useful information concerning ancient manners, customs, inventions, and scientific beliefs.

times, had its focal point on the plains of Russia and of Western Siberia, but which extended from the Altai Mountains to Ireland: we are beginning to learn how profoundly it affected the aesthetic expressions of the Middle Ages. But even before the Germanic migrations, these barbarians had begun to influence Roman technology, and in later centuries they contributed many distinctive ingredients to mediaeval life: trousers and the habit of wearing furs, the easily-heated compact house as contrasted with the Mediterranean patio-house, cloisonné jewelry, feltmaking, the ski, the use of soap for cleansing and of butter in place of olive oil, the making of barrels and tubs, the cultivation of rye, oats, spelt, and hops, perhaps the sport of falconry and certain elements of the number-system. Above all, the great plains invented the stirrup, which made the horse etymologically responsible for chivalry, and, perhaps even more important, the heavy plow which, as we shall see, is the technological basis of the typical mediaeval manor.

Naturally the problem of diffusion to and from the Greek and Saracenic Orient constantly troubles the student of technology. Despite the laborious research which has been lavished on the Levant, each new wise man from the East compels us to revise prevalent notions. First Lawrence of Arabia challenges the long-accepted belief that the rapid development of western military architecture in the twelfth century was based on the crusaders' observation of Moslem and Byzantine models; and now Arthur Upham Pope is bent on proving that the basic principles of gothic construction were derived from Iran.

The various portions of this Oriental legacy can scarcely be enumerated, if only because so few items of it have been satisfactorily established: even the distillation of alcohol, so long thought to be an art borrowed from Islam, is now believed to be a western-European invention. Much work remains to be done—and done over! Let one illustration suffice: the fore-and-aft rig. Until such a rig was developed, mariners were unable to tack effectively against the wind, and oarsmen remained the only dependable nautical motive power. Clearly the development of the fore-and-aft rig would mark an epoch in the history of labor by eliminating the galley, it would cheapen sea transport by increasing the average speed of ships, and, by reducing the size of crews, it would vastly extend the range of ocean voyaging. The earliest form of the fore-and-aft rig was the lateen sail. What is probably the most ancient picture of a lateen is found in a grafito on a ruined church at El-Auja in southern Palestine. The church is pre-Moslem, but unfortunately the scratching cannot be dated. Lateen sails suddenly appear in Greek miniatures of the ninth century; in the twelfth century they are found in objects of art produced at Venice, Amalfi, Benevento, and other Italian centers of Byzantine influence. Thence they spread to all the coasts of Europe and played a great part in speeding up commerce, in displacing rowers and in stimulating exploration.

But it is increasingly evident that Roman Catholic Europe drew technical novelties during the Middle Ages not only from Byzantium and Islam but perhaps in even greater measure from China. Nor were these borrowings always mediated by Greeks and Moslems, as paper was: on the contrary, Europe got some things directly, by way of the caravan routes of Central Asia. Gunpowder, the compass and printing with cast movable type were probably not derived from the Far East: the latest opinion credits them to Europe, whence they spread eastward into Islam. But what of church-bells, practically unknown in the Near East, but appearing at the two extremes of the Old World? Or the crossbow, perhaps known in some form to the Romans, subsequently forgotten save in China, then introduced to Constantinople by the crusaders? Or the fiddle-bow, which revolutionized western music; or the wheelbarrow, which cut in half the number of laborers needed to haul small loads by substituting a wheel for the front man of the hand-barrow (we have been replacing men by wheels ever since!); or the spinning-wheel, which speeded up the cloth industry; or the functional button which, about 1300, started the greatest of revolutions in the history of costume? Above all, was that fundamental invention, the casting of iron, which appears in Europe during the fourteenth century, an importation from the Far East where it was certainly practiced much earlier? Indeed, when even the *Enciclopedia italiana* (*s.v. pasta*) confesses that chow-mein may well be the ancestral form of spaghetti, the whole of the Middle Ages seems to shrivel into a mere appendix to China!

But possibly more careful scrutiny will prove that some of these were gifts of Europe to China rather than the reverse. For the expansive vitality of the late-mediaeval technology of the West spread its influence round half the world, from Gardar to Cambaluc: at the very time when Norse settlers in Greenland were teaching the Eskimos to make coopered tubs, saws, and screws, European engineers were delighting the Great Khan with new siege-engines of western design; while shortly thereafter China received from Europe such diverse inventions as firearms and eye-glasses, and perhaps distilled liquors. We may be sure that the merchants and missionaries who flocked to Cathay under the Yüan dynasty went not devoid of technical skills. Perhaps when Far Eastern studies are more advanced, and particularly when the Harvard-Yenching Institute's historical dictionary of the Chinese language is completed, we may be able to deal with facts rather than with guesses.

The student of European technics, then, is compelled to follow his subject far beyond the usual geographical limits of mediaeval research. Similarly he finds that for his purposes the customary tripartite division of history into ancient, mediaeval and modern is completely arbitrary. In particular he finds no evidence of a break in the continuity of technological development following the decline of the Western Roman Empire.

The Dark Ages doubtless deserve their name: political disintegration, economic depression, the debasement of religion and the collapse of literature surely made the barbarian kingdoms in some ways unimaginably dismal. Yet because many aspects of civilization were in decay we should not assume too quickly that everything was back-sliding. Even an apparent coarsening may indicate merely a shift of interest: in modern painting we recognize that Van Gogh's technical methods were not those of David; so, when we contrast a Hellenistic carved gem with a Merovingian enamel, our judgment should be cautious. Few will dispute that the Irish illumination and the Scandinavian jewelry of the seventh and eighth centuries stand among the supreme arts of all time; yet they are far from classical canons of taste, being rooted in an ancient, and quite separate, tradition of Northern art. So in the history of technology we must be discriminating. Changing tastes and conditions may lead to the degeneration of one technique while the technology of the age as a whole is advancing. The technology of torture, for example, which achieved such hair-raising perfection during the Renaissance, is now happily in eclipse: viewed historically, our modern American 'third degree' is barbaric only in its simplicity.

Indeed, a dark age may stimulate rather than hinder technology. Economic catastrophe in the United States during the past decade has done nothing to halt invention—quite the contrary; and it is a commonplace that war encourages technological advance. Confusion and depression, which bring havoc in so many areas of life, may have just the opposite effect on technics. And the chances of this are particularly good in a period of general migration, when peoples of diverse backgrounds and inheritances are mixing.

There is, in fact, no proof that any important skills of the Graeco-Roman world were lost during the Dark Ages even in the unenlightened West, much less in the flourishing Byzantine and Saracenic Orient. To be sure, the diminished wealth and power of the Germanic kings made engineering on the old Roman scale infrequent; yet the full technology of antiquity was available when required: the 276-ton monolith which crowns the tomb of Theodoric the Ostrogoth was brought to Ravenna from Istria; while more than two centuries later Charlemagne transported not only sizable columns but even a great equestrian statue of Zeno from Ravenna across the Alps to Aachen. Incidentally, we should do well to remember that the northern peoples from remote times were capable of managing great weights, as witness Stonehenge and the dolmens.

In military machines especially we might expect the barbarians to fall below the ancient standard; but at the siege of Paris in 886 we discover the Vikings, who presumably would be as untouched by Roman methods as any western people, using elaborate and powerful artillery; while the city itself was defended with catapults. However, the Dark Ages do not seem to have improved on ancient artillery: the Roman level was not surpassed until the twelfth century when the trebuchet, worked by counterweights, began to drive the less efficient tension and torsion engines from the field.

If the political and economic decay of the Dark Ages affected any technique adversely, it was that of road-building. Yet even here the case is not clear. For northern climates at least, the technical excellence of Roman roads has been exaggerated. They had massive foundations, which sometimes survive to the present day; but the surface, consisting of slabs of masonry cemented together, made no provision for contraction or expansion. Heat made the slabs buckle and crack; water seeped under them and froze, separating them from the foundation. Repairs were difficult and expensive: no modern road-builder would consider imitating Roman methods. It was the Middle Ages which developed the cheaper and more efficient method of laying cubes of stone in a loose bed of earth or sand which permitted expansion and made repairs easy: a type of paving still common.

Indeed, the technical skill of classical times was not simply maintained: it was considerably improved. Our view of history has been too top-lofty. We have been dazzled by aspects of civilization which are in every age the property of an élite, and in which the common man, with rare exceptions, has had little part. The so-called 'higher' realms of culture might decay, government might fall into anarchy, and trade be reduced to a trickle, but through it all, in the face of turmoil and hard times, the peasant and artisan carried on, and even improved their lot. In technology, at least, the Dark Ages mark a steady and uninterrupted advance over the Roman Empire. Evidence is accumulating to show that a serf in the turbulent and insecure tenth century enjoyed a standard of living considerably higher than that of a proletarian in the reign of Augustus.

The basic occupation was, of course, agriculture. We have passed through at least two agricultural revolutions: that which began with 'Turnip' Townshend and Jethro Tull in the early eighteenth century, and another, equally important, in the Dark Ages.

The problem of the development and diffusion of the northern wheeled plow, equipped with colter, horizontal share and moldboard, is too thorny to be discussed here. Experts seem generally agreed: (1) that the new plow greatly increased production by making possible the tillage of rich, heavy, badly-drained river-bottom soils; (2) that it saved labor by making cross-plowing superfluous, and thus produced the typical northern strip-system of land division, as distinct from the older block-system dictated by the cross-plowing necessary with the lighter Mediterranean plow; (3) most important of all, that the heavy plow needed such power that peasants pooled their oxen and plowed together, thus laying the basis for the mediaeval coöperative agricultural community, the manor. But whatever may be the date and origin of the fully developed heavy plow, its effects were supplemented and greatly enhanced in the later eighth century by the invention of the three-field system, an improved rotation of crops and fallow which greatly increased the efficiency of agricultural labor. For example, by switching 600 acres from the two-field to the three-field system, a community of peasants could plant 100 acres more in crops each year with 100 acres less of plowing. Since fallow land was plowed twice to keep down the weeds, the old plan required three acres of plowing for every acre in crops, whereas the new plan required only two acres of plowing for every productive acre.

In a society overwhelmingly agrarian, the result of such an innovation could be nothing less than revolutionary. Pirenne is only the most recent of many historians to speculate as to why the reign of Charlemagne witnessed the shift of the center of European civilization, the change of the focus of history, from the Mediterranean to the plains of Northern Europe. The findings of agricultural history, it seems, have never been applied to this central problem in the study of the growth of the northern races. Since the spring sowing, which was the chief novelty of the three-field system, was unprofitable in the south because of the scarcity of summer rains, the three-field system did not spread below the Alps and the Loire. For obvious reasons of climate the agricultural revolution of the eighth century was confined to Northern Europe. It would appear, therefore, that it was this more efficient and productive use of land and labor which gave to the northern plains an economic advantage over the Mediterranean shores, and which, from Charlemagne's time onward, enabled the Northern Europeans in short order to surpass both in prosperity and in culture the peoples of an older inheritance.

In ways less immediately significant the Dark Ages likewise made ingenious improvements. One of the most important of these was a contribution to practical mechanics. There are two basic forms of motion: reciprocal and rotary. The normal device for connecting these—a device without which our machine civilization is inconceivable—is the crank. The crank is an invention second in importance only to the wheel itself; yet the crank was unknown to the Greeks and the Romans. It appears, even in rudimentary form, only after the Invasions: first, perhaps, in hand-querns, then on rotary grindstones. The later Middle Ages developed its application to all sorts of machinery.

Clearly there are nuggets in this stream for anyone to find. Perhaps the most successful amateur student of early mediaeval technology was the Commandant Lefebvre des Noëttes, who after his retirement from active service in the French cavalry, devoted himself to his hobby, the history of horses. He died in 1936, having made discoveries which must greatly modify our judgment of the Carolingian period. From his investigations Lefebvre des Noëttes concluded that the use of animal power in antiquity was unbelievably inefficient. The ancients did not use nailed shoes on their animals, and broken hooves often rendered beasts useless. Besides, they knew only the yoke-system of harness. While this was adequate for oxen, it was most unsatisfactory for the more rapid horse. The yoke rested on the withers of a team. From each end of the yoke ran two flexible straps: one a girth behind the forelegs, the other circling the horse's neck. As soon as the horse began to pull, the flexible front strap pressed on his windpipe, and the harder he pulled the closer he came to strangulation. Moreover the ancient harness was mechanically defective: the yoke was too high to permit the horse to exert his full force in pulling by flinging his body-weight into the task. Finally, the ancients were unable to harness one animal in front of another. Thus all great weights had to be drawn by gangs of slaves, since animal power was not technically available in sufficient quantities.

According to Lefebvre des Noëttes this condition remained unchanged until the later ninth or early tenth century when, almost simultaneously, three major inventions appear: the modern horse-collar, the tandem harness, and the horseshoe. The modern harness, consisting of a rigid horse-collar resting on the shoulders of the beast, permitted him to breathe freely. This was connected to the load by lateral traces which enabled the horse to throw his whole body into pulling. It has been shown experimentally that this new apparatus so greatly increased the effective animal power that a team which can pull only about one thousand pounds with the antique yoke can pull three or four times that weight when equipped with the new harness. Equally important was the extension of the traces so that tandem harnessing was possible, thus providing an indefinite amount of animal power for the transport of great weights. Finally, the introduction of the nailed horseshoe improved traction and greatly increased the endurance of the newly available animal power. Taken together these three inventions suddenly gave Europe a new supply of non-human power, at no increase of expense or labor. They did for the eleventh and twelfth centuries what the steam-engine did for the nineteenth. Lefebvre des Noëttes has therefore offered an unexpected and plausible solution for the most puzzling problem of the Middle Ages: the sudden upswing of European vitality after the year 1000.

However, Lefebvre des Noëttes failed to point out the relation between this access of energy and the contemporary agricultural revolution. He noted that the new harness made the horse available for agricultural labor: the first picture of a horse so engaged is found in the Bayeux Tapestry. But while the horse is a rapid and efficient power-engine, it burns an expensive fuel—grain—as compared with the slower, but cheaper, hay-burning ox. Under the two-field system the peasant's margin of production was insufficient to support a workhorse; under the three-field system the horse gradually displaced the ox as the normal plow and draft animal of the northern plains. By the later Middle Ages there is a clear correlation on the one hand between the horse and the three-field system and on the other between the ox and the two-field system. The contrast is essentially one between the standards of living and of labor-productivity of the northern and the southern peasantry: the ox saves food; the horse saves man-hours. The new agriculture, therefore, enabled the north to exploit the new power more effectively than the Mediterranean regions could, and thereby the northerners increased their prosperity still further.

Naturally Lefebvre des Noëttes made mistakes: only when his work receives the recognition it deserves will these be rectified. His use of the monuments is not impeccable; his almost exclusive concern with pictures led him to neglect the texts, particularly Pliny's assertion that at times Italian peasants (presumably in the Po valley) plowed with several yokes of oxen; and he overlooks the complex question of the eight-ox plow-team as a basis for land division in pre-Carolingian times. Moreover an etymologist has recently shown that the word for 'horse-collar' in the Teutonic and Slavic tongues (English: hames) is derived from Central-Asiatic sources, implying a diffusion of the modern harness westward from the nomadic steppe-culture. Doubtless criticism will eventually show that Lefebvre des Noëttes' three inventions developed rather more slowly than he thought. But that they grew and spread during the Dark Ages, and that they profoundly affected European society, seems already proved.

These discoveries regarding the utilization of animal power illustrate the novel results which may be expected from the study of mediaeval technology. No less profitable is Marc Bloch's brilliant and thoroughly documented investigation of the origin and spread of the water-driven mill. His conclusion that, while it was invented in the first century before Christ, it did not become common until after the collapse of the Empire, confirms Lefebvre des Noëttes' contention that the technological position of the Dark Ages has been misunderstood.

The development of the windmill has not been so carefully sought out. Windmills are found in tenth-century Persia, but rotating on a vertical rather than on a horizontal axis. The first authenticated windmill in Europe turns up in Normandy ca 1180. Twelve years later Jocelin of Brakelond mentions one near St. Edmundsbury and gives no indication that he considers it unusual. Within a generation this power-engine had become a typical part of the landscape on the plains of northwestern Europe. In such a region it was a great boon; for the fall of rivers was so gradual that expensive dams and mill-ponds often had to be constructed to run water-driven mills; likewise these mill-ponds must often have flooded good agricultural land which the wind-mill freed for production. The spread of the windmill into the more mountainous southern regions, which were better equipped with rapid streams, was slow. The first Italian reference to a windmill seems to be Dante's description (*ante* 1321) of Satan threshing his arms like 'un molin che il vento gira' ['a mill that the wind is turning'] (*Inferno*, xxxiv, 6). This southward and eastward diffusion, together with the horizontal axis of the western mill, probably indicates that the windmill was not an importation from Islam.

The cumulative effect of the newly available animal, water, and wind power upon the culture of Europe has not been carefully studied. But from the twelfth and even from the eleventh, century there was a rapid replacement of human by non-human energy wherever great quantities of power were needed or where the required motion was so simple and monotonous that a man could be replaced by a mechanism. The chief glory of the later Middle Ages was not its cathedrals or its epics or its scholasticism: it was the building for the first time in history of a complex civilization which rested not on the backs of sweating slaves or coolies but primarily on non-human power.

The study of mediaeval technology is therefore far more than an aspect of economic history: it reveals a chapter in the conquest of freedom. More than that, it is a part of the history of religion. The humanitarian technology which our modern world has inherited from the Middle Ages was not rooted in economic necessity; for this 'necessity' is inherent in every society, yet has found inventive expression only in the Occident, nurtured in the activist or voluntarist tradition of Western theology. It is ideas which make necessity conscious. The labor-saving power-machines of the later Middle Ages were produced by the implicit theological assumption of the infinite worth of even the most degraded human personality, by an instinctive repugnance towards subjecting any man to a monotonous drudgery which seems less than human in that it requires the exercise neither of intelligence nor of choice. It has often been remarked that the Latin Middle Ages first discovered the dignity and spiritual value of labor—that to labor is to pray. But the Middle Ages went further: they gradually and very slowly began to explore the practical implications of an essentially Christian paradox: that just as the Heavenly Jerusalem contains no temple, so the goal of labor is to end labor.

III

The So-called Renaissance

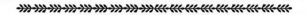

Renaissance or Prenaissance?

LYNN THORNDIKE

Published in 1943

The concept of the Renaissance that continues to dominate many history textbooks and practically all popular publications—*Life* magazine, for example—derives mainly from the writings of Jakob Burckhardt, the nineteenth-century Swiss scholar. The outstanding cultural historian of his time, Burckhardt was the author of *The Civilization of the Renaissance in Italy*, a phenomenal work of historical scholarship that surely deserves to be widely read and discussed. Since Burckhardt's time, however, hundreds of scholars have uncovered a vast amount of material about which he knew little or nothing; and some of these scholars have challenged his approach, insisting that it was based on inadequate knowledge and that it embodied a host of distortions and oversimplifications. One of the most learned of these scholars is the Columbia University medievalist Lynn Thorndike, whose tremendous store of information has enabled him to blast many a neat historical generalization. A vigorous critic of Burckhardt, he has often protested against his concept of the Renaissance. In the following essay he presents his case against the Swiss scholar and gives the reasons for his aversion to one of the best-known terms in history.

Professor Dana B. Durand has accused me of harboring a personal antipathy to the Renaissance. Whether my motive is personal or rational, objective or subjective, conscious or sub-conscious, it must be confessed that my aversion to the term in question is even more sweeping than Durand perhaps thinks and extends to such catchwords as the Carolingian Renaissance and the twelfth-century renaissance, as well as to the more often mentioned Italian Renaissance of the

Reprinted by special permission from *Journal of the History of Ideas*, IV (1943), 65-74.

fifteenth century or somewhere thereabouts. Religion may have its resurrections and revivals, but I have even less faith than Nicodemus in rebirths or restorations of whole periods of human history. I take my stand with the blind writer of Christian hymns, Fanny Crosby, who sang,

> But the bird with the broken pinion never soared so high again;

with William Muldoon who said of former heavy-weight champions,

> They never come back;

with Omar Khayyam who mused,

> The moving finger writes and having writ
> Moves on; nor all your piety nor wit
> May lure it back to cancel half a line
> Nor all your tears wipe out one word of it;

and with a verse from the light opera, Tom Jones,

> Time is not a necromancer;
> Time's a thief and nothing more.

Legacies from the past? Yes. Inheritances from previous periods? Yes. Survivals? Yes. Resemblances to our forebears? Yes. Reformations? Perhaps. Reactions? Unfortunately. But no rebirths and no restorations!

Books and works of art are about all that remains to us of the past. The latter are all too soon sadly altered, and their restoration, whether by some German professor or by a Thorwaldsen or Viollet-le-Duc, only makes them less like what they originally were. Books remain less changed by the lapse of time, but even their text may become corrupt, or the meaning of the very words they use alter in the interim. The humanists of the so-called Italian Renaissance had only a bookish knowledge of antiquity; they failed almost as dismally as have Mussolini and his Fascists to make the reality of ancient Rome live again. If, even in our own day, all the resources of the art of history aided by archeology can give us only a faint and imperfect idea of the past, how can we expect actual renaissances of it or recognize them as such, if they were to occur? At the age of sixty I am perhaps more like myself at the age of twenty than I am like anyone else. But I couldn't possibly put myself back into the frame of mind that I had then. I have a dim recollection of it; my present state of mind is an outgrowth of it; that is all. A girl of eighteen, dressed up in the clothes which her grandmother wore when a girl of eighteen, may look more like her grandmother as she was then than her grandmother herself does now. But she will not feel or act as her grandmother felt and acted half a century or more ago. Much more tenuous is the connection between distant historical periods, and much less likely is it that historians can successfully venture upon glittering generalities about them. Who can evoke from the past more than a wraith, a phantasy, a specter, which murmurs, like the ghost in *Hamlet,* "Historian, remember me!"

It is true that history offers examples of human customs which somewhat resemble the conception of a renaissance. For instance, at Tonalamatl in ancient Mexico the recurrence of the year date 2. acatl every 52 years was considered a critical occasion, it being feared that the sun might fail to rise next day and that the evil spirits might destroy the world and mankind. Accordingly, a festival of ceremonial firemaking was held. All the old fires were carefully extinguished and at midnight on the mountain top the high-priest by rubbing sticks together kindled a new fire on the breast of a prisoner who was forthwith sacrificed. The new fire was then distributed to the temples of the surrounding cities and thence to the adjacent peoples. Old garments were thrown away and household dishes and utensils were broken or freshly painted over in token of the new lease of life given to mankind.[1] But this rekindling and renewal was immediate, continuous, and perfunctory. Only a part of one night intervened between the two periods, not centuries of dark ages. There was no intellectual or spiritual rebirth.

We might also adduce the influence upon our notions of revolutions and periods in history of the astrological theory of conjunctions and revolutions of the planets.

[1] Joyce, *Mexican Archaeology* (1914), 74.

ALBERTUS MAGNUS: Thirteenth-century theologian. Often considered the outstanding natural scientist of the Latin Middle Ages, he drew extensively on Aristotle but also emphasized the use of experimental methods.

CARMINA BURANA: A collection of medieval student poems found in a Bavarian monastery. Critical of the clergy, and filled with enthusiasm for wine and women, these poems demonstrate the extent to which individualism and secularism flourished in the so-called Age of Faith.

JULES MICHELET: Ninteenth-century historian who believed that historical

But let us turn to the development of the concept of an Italian Renaissance and begin with the translation into Latin of Ptolemy's *Geography* in the first decade of the fifteenth century. Durand is inclined to censure the previous medieval translators for neglecting this work. If they did—for a previous translation may have escaped our notice—it is to be remembered that after all the text in question consists largely of lists of ancient place-names, many of which cannot be identified and located with any assurance and are of purely historical and linguistic interest. Moreover, Ptolemy had made the Mediterranean Sea too short by one-third, whereas one of the medieval *portolani* is more accurate than any other map of the Mediterranean until the eighteenth century. Concerning the Far East, too, and islands in the Atlantic the thirteenth and fourteenth centuries were much better informed than Ptolemy. The translation and subsequent vogue of his *Geography* were therefore in some ways regrettable. Be that as it may, in the dedication of his translation to pope Alexander V, Jacobus Angelus, who was a booster of his native town of Florence, says:

> This very age of ours, especially in our city of Florence, has sparkled with how many wits, who to their great glory have resuscitated liberal studies which had grown almost torpid.

In the fifth volume of *A History of Magic and Experimental Science* I have given various examples of this notion of a resuscitation of liberal studies becoming stereotyped and being extended to most inappropriate fields, such as astronomy by Moravus and Santritter, chiromancy and physiognomy by Cocles, anatomy by Vesalius, and magic in the case of Antiochus Tibertus. Abstemius depicted Pope Paul III as restoring astrology after it had lain in darkness, disrepute, barbarism and sordid squalor for many centuries past; Pena praised Charles, cardinal of

---

writing should approach the level of pure literature. His view of the Renaissance as the period which discovered man as well as the world has been extremely influential in subsequent historical writing.

PORTOLANI: Name applied to the maps made by medieval sailors. Some of them are so remarkable for their accurate charting of the Mediterranean coasts that many scholars regard them as the first real maps in the modern sense.

QUATTROCENTO: The 1400's, or the fifteenth century.

Lorraine, for having resuscitated the prostrate mathematical sciences.[2] Just as the humanists who found manuscripts of the Latin classics in monasteries represented themselves as discovering the work in question and rescuing it from neglect and decay, saying nothing of the fact that the monks had copied it in Carolingian times and preserved it ever since, but leaving their own manuscripts when they died to some monastery as the safest place in which to keep them, so publishers who printed a text for the first time, even if it was a typical product of medieval scholasticism, represented themselves as snatching it from Gothic filth and dust and mildew and cobwebs and bringing it to the light of fairest impressions with the text carefully restored to its pristine purity and freed from barbarisms, when in reality they were very likely using a single inferior manuscript and neglecting a dozen older and superior versions.

When was the word, Renaissance, first used? Nicolaus Prucknerus or Prugner approached such usage when, in the preface to his re-edition of the ancient Roman astrologer, Julius Firmicus Maternus, addressed from Strasbourg on January 28, 1551, to young king Edward VI of England, he spoke of religion reviving in that realm. But evidently he was speaking of the Protestant Reformation. Two years later, however, the French naturalist, Pierre Belon, in the dedicatory epistle of his *Les observations . . . de plusieurs singularitez* to François cardinal Tournon, assured him that, as a result of his patronage of learning and education of promising young scholars, it had followed that the minds of men, which were formerly as it were asleep and sunk in a profound slumber of long-standing ignorance, had begun to awake, to come forth from the shadows where they had so long dwelt, and to develop in all sorts of good disciplines a happy and desirable Renaissance, like plants that, after the rigors of winter, regain their strength with the sun and sweetness of springtime.[3]

Peter Ramus, in an oration delivered in 1546, made the following vivid contrast between his own and the preceding century. Suppose, he said, a master of a century ago should return to life now, what progress he would discover, how astounded he would be! He would be as surprised as one who, risen from depths of earth, should see for the first time sun, moon and stars shining bright. For then he heard no one

---

[2] *A History of Magic and Experimental Science,* V, 334-5, 52-3, 524 and 530, 55, 265, 304.

[3] [Footnote omitted.]

speak except in a barbarous and inept manner, while now he would hear countless persons of every age speaking and writing Latin correctly and ornately. Then no one could read Greek, now men not only read it but understand it thoroughly. He used to hear as grammarians, poets and orators, Alexander of Villa-Dei, Facetus, the *Graecismus*; in philosophy, Scotists and followers of Petrus Hispanus; in medicine, the Arabs; in theology, I know not what upstarts. Now he would hear Terence, Caesar, Virgil, Cicero, Aristotle, Plato, Galen, Hippocrates, Moses and the prophets, the Apostles and other true and genuine messengers of the Gospel, and indeed voices in all languages.[4]

Except for the closing allusions to vernacular translations of the Bible, this passage well expresses the original restricted significance of the Renaissance as a purification of Latin diction and grammar, a revival of Greek, and a return from medieval compilers, commentators and originators to the old classical texts. This was all that the revival of learning meant to the Italian humanists of the quattrocento and to their fellows beyond the Alps, and for them it was enough. The mere thought of it aroused in Ramus a grand and glorious feeling of enthusiasm tempered with complacency. He neither sensed any change in the political and economic set-up nor was aware of any alteration in social and moral values.

As the study and reading of Latin and Greek waned, however— and this was partly because the humanists and classicists had substituted a dead for a living language—fewer and fewer persons could sincerely share in this thrill or impart it to others. Such fervor as the concept of the Renaissance still invoked was largely in the realm of the fine arts, where the term had been applied to the post-Gothic period. It was at this juncture that Michelet called the Renaissance "the discovery of the world and of man," and was followed in this lead by the very influential book of Burckhardt, in which, on what seemed too often to be dogmatic or imaginary grounds without sufficient presentation of facts as evidence, the Renaissance was no longer regarded as primarily a rebirth of classical learning and culture but rather as a pre-birth or precursor of present society and of modern civilization—

---

[4] For the Latin of the passage, which I have rendered freely, see K. Waddington, *Ramus, sa vie, ses écrits* (1858), 304-5. For a very similar attitude by Giovanni Ferrerio, in an academic dissertation published at Paris in 1539, see *Magic and Experimental Science*, V, 295.

"a period," to quote the *Boston Transcript* (February 27, 1926) concerning Elizabethan England, "that witnessed the birth pangs of most
that is worth while in modern civilization and government."

This made a well-calculated appeal to the average reader who is
little interested to be told that Erasmus was a great Greek scholar or
that Leonardo da Vinci copied from Albert of Saxony, but whose
ego is titillated to be told that Leonardo was an individual like himself or that Erasmus's chief claim to fame is that he was the first
modern man—the first one like you and me. All this was quite
soothing and flattering and did much to compensate for one's inability
to read Horace or to quote Euripides. It even had its appeal for professors of modern European history and for teachers of the modern
languages. It appears to be the concept of the Renaissance which
such recent advocates thereof or apologists therefor as Wallace K.
Ferguson and Hans Baron are concerned to defend, retreating to new
standing ground of plausible hypothesis and ingenious conjecture,
when some of Burckhardt's old bulwarks are proved to be untenable
by new masses of facts concerning either or both the middle ages and
the quattrocento. But would it not make things clearer, if they ceased
to employ the old name, since the old concept has been abandoned,
and, instead of talking of the Renaissance, spoke of the period or
movement or whatever it is they have in mind as the Prenaissance?

With regard to the work of Burckhardt I may perhaps be permitted a few further comments. Of its six parts, the third on the
Revival of Antiquity seems to me scholarly and just, recognizing the
defects as well as the merits of the Italian humanists and containing
many bits of illuminating detail. But most of the political, social, moral
and religious phenomena which he pictures as Renaissance seem almost
equally characteristic of Italy at any time from the twelfth to the
eighteenth century inclusive. The fourth part on the discovery of the
world and man uses only popular, not scientific literature, nor may this
be dimissed as merely a sin of omission, since elsewhere in the volume
are such atrocious misstatements as that few works of Aristotle had
been translated into Latin by the fourteenth century. By including
such personalities as Frederick II and such authors and literary compo-
sitions as Dante and the *Carmina burana* within the Renaissance,
Burckhardt freed the movement from the embarrassment of chronological limits and made any differentiation between it and medieval

culture well-nigh impossible. At bottom this was a wholesome tendency, equivalent to recognition that there is no dividing line between "medieval" and "renaissance" culture, just as most historical museums have a single section labeled "Middle Ages and Renaissance." In general, Burckhardt devoted so much of his pages and energy to the attempt to trace intangibles, such as personality, imagination, passion, spirit, the popular mind, the feeling for this and that, such and such a sentiment, that his book hardly touches the domain of intellectual history and seems to possess a will-o'-the-wisp sort of character.

The attraction which this kind of writing has for many has been well expressed by Professor Schevill in reviewing another book:

> If the modern scientific method, a well co-ordinated plan, and the view-point regarding the character of the social process which obtains among present-day scholars are the indispensable requirements of a good history, it would have to be conceded that Mrs. Taylor's book stands self-condemned. But if there is salvation outside the ruling formulas, if a work may still be history, and good history, when, instead of building up a solid edifice of facts, it occupies itself with the spirit behind the facts in the hope of communicating the color and perfume of a segment of human experience, this book can be confidently recommended not only to the notoriously unscientific lovers of the Renaissance but to those grave and reverend signors, the professional historians themselves.[5]

The trouble is that this kind of writing is almost invariably based upon an insufficient acquaintance with the facts and misinterpretation of them. Of the same genus is another bête-noire of mine, those writers who proclaim that this or that person was far in advance of his time, like Roger Bacon or Leonardo da Vinci.[6] But should you ask them to name a few contemporaries of the person in question who were typical of that time, they would hardly be able to do so.

Was the individual freed and personality enhanced by the Renaissance or Prenaissance? Burckhardt affirmed that with it "man became a spiritual individual and recognized himself as such," whereas "in the middle ages both sides of human consciousness—that which was

---

[5] Review of Rachel Annand Taylor, *Aspects of the Italian Renaissance: American Historical Review*, XXIX (October, 1923), 122.

[6] Durand has recognized this antipathy, too, in reviewing my fifth and sixth volumes in *Isis*, XXXIII (June, 1942), 691-712, especially 702-3, 704-6.

turned within as that which was turned without—lay dreaming or half awake beneath a common veil."[7] It might be remarked that individualism may be a mark of decline rather than progress. The self-centered sage of the Stoics and Epicureans rang the knell of the Greek city-state. Basil, on the verge of the barbarian invasions, complained that men "for the greater part prefer individual and private life to the union of common life."[8] Carl Neumann held that "true modern individualism has its roots in the strength of the barbarians, in the realism of the barbarians, and in the Christian middle ages."[9] Cunningham believed that the Roman Empire "left little scope for individual aims and tended to check the energy of capitalists and laborers alike," whereas Christianity taught the supreme dignity of man and encouraged the individual and personal responsibility. Moreover, in the thirteenth century there were "fewer barriers to social intercourse than now."[10] According to Schäfer, "So far as public life in the broadest sense, in church and state, city and country, law and society, is concerned, the middle ages are the time of most distinctive individuality and independent personality in volition and action."[11] We may no longer think of the Gothic architects as anonymous, and de Mely discovered hundreds of signatures of miniaturists hidden in the initials and illuminations of medieval manuscripts.[12] No period in the history of philosophy has discussed individuality and its problems more often or more subtly than did the medieval schoolmen. Vittorino da Feltre and other humanist educators may have suited their teaching to the individual pupil; at the medieval university the individual scholar suited himself. The humanists were imitative in their writing, not original. Vitruvius was the Bible of Renaissance architects who came to follow authority far more than their creative Gothic predecessors. For the middle ages loved variety; the Renaissance, uniformity.

Not only has it been demonstrated that the thirteenth and fourteenth centuries were more active and penetrating in natural science

[7] English translation (1890), 129.

[8] *Hexaemeron*, VIII, 7.

[9] "Byzant. Kultur u. Renais. Kultur," *Historische Zeitschrift*, XCI (1903), 215-32; translated in Munro and Sellery, *Medieval Civilization*, 524-46.

[10] *Western Civilization in Its Economic Aspects*, II (1910), 8 *et seq.*, 2.

[11] "Zur Beurtheilung des Wormser Concordats," *Philos. u. Hist. Abhandl. d. kgl. preuss. Akad. d. Wiss.* (1905), 94.

[12] F. de Mely, *Les primitifs et leurs signatures: les miniaturistes* (1913).

than was the quattrocento,[13] but the notion that "appreciation of natural beauty" was "introduced into modern Europe by the Italian
Renaissance"[14] must also be abandoned. Burckhardt admitted that
medieval literature displayed sympathy with nature, but nevertheless
regarded Petrarch's ascent of Mount Ventoux (which is only 6260 feet
high) in 1336 as epoch-making. Petrarch represented an old herdsman
who had tried in vain to climb it fifty years before as beseeching him
to turn back on the ground that he had received only torn clothes
and broken bones for his pains and that no one had attempted the
ascent since. As a matter of fact, Jean Buridan, the Parisian schoolman,
had visited it between 1316 and 1334, had given details as to its altitude,
and had waxed enthusiastic as to the Cevennes. So that all Petrarch's
account proves is his capacity for story-telling and sentimental ability
to make a mountain out of a molehill. Miss Stockmayer, in a book
on feeling for nature in Germany in the tenth and eleventh centuries,
has noted various ascents and descriptions of mountains from that
period. In the closing years of his life archbishop Anno of Cologne
climbed his beloved mountain oftener than usual.[15]

As for the feeling for nature in medieval art, let me repeat what
I have written elsewhere anent the interest displayed by the students
of Albertus Magnus in particular herbs and trees.[16]

This healthy interest in nature and commendable curiosity concerning real things was not confined to Albert's students nor to "rustic
intelligences." One has only to examine the sculpture of the great
thirteenth-century cathedrals to see that the craftsmen of the towns
were close observers of the world of nature, and that every artist
was a naturalist too. In the foliage that twines about the capitals of
the columns in the French Gothic cathedrals it is easy to recognize,

[13] In addition to the bibliography given by Durand may be noted "Science in
the Renaissance," by George Sarton, in *The Civilization of the Renaissance* (Chicago, 1929), 75-95. As Dr. Sarton remarks, "From the scientific point of view the
Renaissance was *not* a renaissance.

[14] J. E. Spingarn, *A History of Literary Criticism in the Renaissance* (1899),
226.

[15] Gertrud Stockmayer, *Uber Naturgefühl in Deutschland im 10. und 11. Jahr-
hundert* (1910), 38 *et seq.* For further bibliography on feeling for nature in the
middle ages consult Paetow, *Guide to the Study of Medieval History* (revised
edition, 1931), 463, which, however, does not mention B. Q. Morgan, *Nature in
Middle High German Lyrics* (1912).

[16] *Magic and Experimental Science*, II, 536-37.

says M. Mâle, a large number of plants: "the plantain, arum, ranunculus, fern, clover, coladine, hepatica, columbine, cress, parsley, strawberry-plant, ivy, snap-dragon, the flower of the broom and the leaf of the oak, a typically French collection of flowers loved from childhood."[17] *Mutatis mutandis,* the same statement could be made concerning the carved vegetation that runs riot in Lincoln cathedral. "The thirteenth-century sculptors sang their *chant de mai.* All the spring delights of the Middle Ages live again in their work—the exhilaration of Palm Sunday, the garlands of flowers, the bouquets fastened on the doors, the strewing of fresh herbs in the chapels, the magical flowers of the feast of Saint John—all the fleeting charm of those old-time springs and summers. The Middle Ages, so often said to have little love for nature, in point of fact gazed at every blade of grass with reverence."[18]

It is not merely love of nature but scientific interest and accuracy that we see revealed in the sculptures of the cathedrals and in the note-book of the thirteenth-century architect, Villard de Honnecourt,[19] with its sketches of insect as well as animal life, of a lobster, two parroquets on a perch, the spirals of a snail's shell, a fly, a dragonfly, and a grasshopper, as well as a bear and a lion from life, and more familiar animals such as the cat and swan. The sculptors of gargoyles and chimeras were not content to reproduce existing animals but showed their command of animal anatomy by creating strange compound and hybrid monsters—one might almost say, evolving new species—which nevertheless have all the verisimilitude of copies from living forms. It was these breeders in stone, these Burbanks of the pencil, these Darwins with the chisel, who knew nature and had studied botany and zoology in a way superior to the scholar who simply pored over the works of Aristotle and Pliny. No wonder that Albert's students were curious about particular things.

Finally, can we accept the altered concept of a Prenaissance as the vestibule to modern times and seed-bed of the modern spirit? Chronologically, perhaps. But, aside from the circumstance that modern times and spirit seem at present to be swiftly shifting, are not our political, economic, charitable, educational and ecclesiastical institutions

[17] Émile Mâle, *Religious Art in France in the Thirteenth Century,* translated from the third edition by Dora Nussey (1913), 52.

[18] *Ibid.,* 53.

[19] Published in facsimile at London (1859), and Paris (1908).

quite as much an outgrowth from medieval life? Without attempting
here to argue this larger question, I would merely recall that medieval
men coined the word, modern, and regularly spoke of themselves or
the last generations of themselves as such. "Maurus, Matthew, Solomon, Peter, Urso are modern physicians through whom reigns the
medicine of Salerno."[20] About 1050 Berengar of Tours was accused
of "introducing ancient heresies in modern times";[20a] about 1108
Hugh of Fleury wrote his *Historia moderna.* "On all sides they
clamor," wrote John of Salisbury in the twelfth century, "what do we
care for the sayings or deeds of the ancients? . . . The golden sayings
of the ancients pleased their times; now only new ones please our
times."[21] When in the next century Robertus Anglicus composed his
treatise on the quadrant, it was called *Tractatus quadrantis secundum
modernos.* But then improvements were made in the quadrant and
Robert's work became *Tractatus quadrantis veteris.*[22] Even scholastic
philosophy had its *via moderna* as well as *via antiqua.*[23]

The concept of the Italian Renaissance or Prenaissance has in my
opinion done a great deal of harm in the past and may continue to
do harm in the future. It is too suggestive of a sensational, miraculous,
extraordinary, magical, human and intellectual development, like unto
the phoenix rising from its ashes after five hundred years. It is contrary to the fact that human nature tends to remain much the same
in all times. It has led to a chorus of rhapsodists as to freedom,
breadth, soaring ideas, horizons, perspectives, out of fetters and
swaddling clothes, and so on. It long discouraged the study of centuries of human development that preceded it, and blinded the French
philosophes and revolutionists to the value of medieval political and
economic institutions. It has kept men in general from recognizing
that our life and thought is based more nearly and actually on the
middle ages than on distant Greece and Rome, from whom our
heritage is more indirect, bookish and sentimental, less institutional,
social, religious, even less economic and experimental.

[20] Epilogue to a *Regimen Salernitanum* in Sloane MS. 554, f. 155, at the British
Museum; S. de Renzi, *Collectio Salernitana,* V, 139.

[20a] *Soc. Hist. Franc.,* 50 (1884), 75.

[21] Hauréau, *Notices et Extraits,* III, 216, quoting the *Entheticus.*

[22] Duhem, *Le système du monde,* III, 306.

[23] The ancients were the thirteenth-century thinkers before William of Ockham, the moderns his followers. See "modern" in the indices of *Magic and
Experimental Science,* vols. II-IV, for other examples of medieval use of the word.

But what is the use of questioning the Renaissance? No one has ever proved its existence; no one has really tried to. So often as one phase of it or conception of it is disproved, or is shown to be equally characteristic of the preceding period, its defenders take up a new position and are just as happy, just as enthusiastic, just as complacent as ever.

> You may break, you may shatter the vase, if you will,
> But the scent of the roses will hang round it still.

Still lingers the sweet perfume of the Renaissance; still hovers about us the blithe spirit of the Prenaissance.

The Renaissance Reconsidered

G. P. V. AKRIGG

➤➤-➤➤-➤➤-➤➤-➤➤-➤➤-➤➤-➤➤-➤➤ *Published in 1945* ◄◄-◄◄-◄◄-◄◄-◄◄-◄◄-◄◄-◄◄-◄◄

Many scholars, though critical of Burckhardt's conception of the Renaissance, have nevertheless been unwilling to go as far as Lynn Thorndike in his repudiation of it. They concede that Burckhardt often misunderstood and misrepresented the Middle Ages. They grant that he frequently exaggerated the individualism and the secularism of the so-called Renaissance and failed to acknowledge sufficiently its nonindividualistic and nonsecular features. For all that, they see good reason for retaining the word *renaissance* to characterize a period in the history of European civilization. Consider, for example, the case that G. P. V. Akrigg, of the University of British Columbia, makes in the present essay. A gifted stylist with a light touch that does not occur often enough in historical writing, Akrigg makes it clear that he agrees with Thorndike about the need to re-examine the traditional conception of the Renaissance. But the results of his reconsideration are quite different from those of the Columbia professor.

I

In the old days in Alberta, our Grade Seven history came to us in the form of a pamphlet. The work can hardly have been much more than sixty pages in length, but its scope was enormous, extending from the Ancient Egyptians to Sir Robert Borden. All that intervened between these two points was presented to us, in condensed form, in numbered chunks; first came the Ancient Egyptians (one page); then the Ancient Greeks (two-and-a-half pages); third, the Ancient Romans; fourth, The Dark Ages, and so on. Each chunk had its number and label in very black print at its head. One always knew where one was, a highly satisfying state of affairs. At the end of the third chunk we

Reprinted by special permission from *Queen's Quarterly*, LII (1945), 311-319.

knew that we had 'done' the Ancient Romans, and with a sense of
secure achievement awaited our envelopment of the next, The Dark
Ages. Like a pageant, the numbered eras came picturesquely rolling
by. It was fun jumping from stepping-stone to stepping-stone across
the creek of time.

The high point in our studies was the fifth chunk, The Renaissance.
Once that was left behind we all foresaw an anticlimax. The Renaissance fascinated us. We twisted our lips around its magnificent, mouth-
filling names—Leonardo da Vinci, Michelangelo, Galileo. In our
imaginations we heard a silver bell ringing out over the dank morose
Europe of The Dark Ages. Then, with a rush, came the Renaissance.
People pulled off monkish costumes, skipped out of the cloisters and
danced in the meadows or raced down to the harbours and started off,
in all directions, on The Great Voyages of Discovery. Except, of course,
for the Renaissance Scholars, who settled down to read Greek and
Latin. But everybody had a wonderful time. "Bliss was it in that
dawn to be alive." Vicariously we in Grade Seven shared in the fun.

Time in its wake brings disillusions. Learning became more and
more paradoxical as one left behind the noble simplicity of elementary
studies. The Equator faded into an abstraction, no longer a superb
tangible girdle about the world. In Senior High School it suddenly
became permissible to begin a sentence with 'And'. Only the structure
of History remained immutable: (1) The Ancient Egyptians; (2) The
Ancient Greeks; (3) The Ancient Romans; (4) The Dark Ages;
(5) The Renaissance. One amassed much detail, but the structure
remained the same. The Renaissance, if anything, became more
brilliant through covert acquaintance with Cellini and Boccaccio.

The first blast came with entry into college. 'The Dark Ages' were
redefined, limited to an "era extending roughly from 600 A.D. to
800 A.D. for which there is practically no recorded history." What

CASTIGLIONE: Italian aristocrat and writer whose *Book of the Courtier*
embodied a humanist's conception of what made for a well-rounded personality and produced a perfect gentleman.

MONTAIGNE: Sixteenth-century writer and moralist. His introspective *Essays*
are important not only for their literary value but for the light they throw
on the ideas of a thoughtful philosopher who lived at the time of the Religious Wars in France.

one had been accustomed to regard as The Dark Ages turned out to
be The Middle Ages. The assault upon the Renaissance was delayed.
Gradually it began to appear that there was more than one Renaissance.
There was the Celtic Renaissance. There was the Renaissance before
the Renaissance. Dates began to waver curiously. The Renaissance
remained a radiance, but was now something of a will-o'-the-wisp,
burning brightly over the fifteenth and sixteenth centuries, wavering
at their fringes, disappearing and recurring strangely when one tried
to establish a point for its beginning or close.

Complete disenchantment came in the graduate school. Here was
laborious study of the documents of The Renaissance, a dredging up
of the minutiae of history. 'Renaissance' and 'Mediaeval' became two
faces on the same head. They came, at times, to be classifications that
hopelessly overlapped and interpenetrated each other. As one attended
to the ponderables of history or literature he became more and more
suspicious of any generalization. The very title of books on 'The
Renaissance Man' induced misgivings. Historical novels made one
feel queasy. The old landmarks had lost their significance. 'The
Revival of Learning'? One snorted and cited Thorndike on the super-
ficiality of Italian Neo-Platonism, reeled off a list of classical authors
known continuously in Western Europe, and commented on the
Greek studies of the Arabs in Spain. To speak of 'The Renaissance'
seemed almost naïve and sentimental. Our seminar papers dwelt on
the continuum of history. What worth had such insubstantial phrases
as 'The Renaissance' for us, working on the rock-face of History?

II

The dogmas of elementary school, the elaborations of high school,
the discoveries of college, the researches of the graduate school, all
these in time are left behind; one turns and reconsiders. The Renais-

---

POGGIO: Fifteenth-century humanist and historian famous for his expedi-
tions to monasteries in search of classical manuscripts. He has become a
symbol of the Renaissance man, whose craving for knowledge of antiquity
was insatiable.

RAMUS: Sixteenth-century French scholar who criticized Aristotle as well
as the cult of Aristotle and stressed the use of reason rather than authority
in the search for truth.

sance—did it ever *happen*? *Was* there ever the Renaissance? The answer to the two questions is not the same. As an event, a phenomenon with ascertainable beginning and end, clearly the Renaissance never did *happen*. It did not happen when Constantinople fell, when Chalcondyles came to Florence, or when Poggio started manuscript-hunting. It did not happen when Petrarch wrote his *Secret*. It is impossible to put a finger on any point and say, "Here the Renaissance began." Neither can anyone affirm, "Here the Renaissance ended."

The Renaissance did not happen, yet there *was* the Renaissance. Not discretely, as an isolated phenomenon, but imperceptibly it came into being, just as one phase of the moon succeeds another, itself waning to give way to a third. A second simile may express this paradox, that while the Renaissance did not happen, it did exist. When one moves through the woods in autumn, the trees succeed one another with a fair uniformity of growth, colour, and species. Changes occur, but they are so gradual that the eye is nowhere aware of a transition. Sometimes, however, at the end of the trail one reaches an eminence and, looking back, sees distinct belts of colour and shade standing forth. One sees that here alder predominated, here birch, here spruce. It is so with history. Taken in the total scene, each age has its particular colour or shade, this being derived from the traits which were predominant in that age, from the ideas and ideals that then prevailed. These ideas and ideals subsequently may not have perished, but continued in a subordinate rôle. To deny, however, that their successive emergence sets up a series of distinguishable areas in history, is like denying the existence of belts of colour in the woods on the ground that, regardless of proportion, birch is encountered all the way, alder all the way, and spruce all the way along the trail. The scholar who becomes so obsessed with the continuity of history as to deny the broad divisions of the ages is simply in the position of not seeing the forest for the trees.

The 'periods' of history do exist. In the nature of things they must exist. The human spirit is capable of many responses. It may be timorous and uncertain or exultantly self-confident; naïvely credulous or coldly sceptical. An age, being the aggregate of the individuals that comprise it, each of his own temperament and condition of life, each experiencing private successes, joys, disasters and pains, cannot be unanimous in spirit—purely timorous or purely self-confident, completely credulous or completely sceptical. On the other hand, all the

individuals within an age, apart from being private persons, are
denizens of the same world, perceiving the same contemporary trends
and responding collectively to them, now with increasing timidity,
now with greater self-confidence. According as they achieve their
collective goals, their age will become optimistic; as they consciously
fall short of them it will become pessimistic. The student of literature
must be sensitive to the atmosphere of the age in which his studies
fall. A man unversed in archaeology, unaware of the stratification
within which an artefact has been found, is as ill qualified to examine
it as a scholar unaware of the trends of feeling through the centuries
is to understand the individual writings that come before him.

III

Having affirmed that there was a Renaissance, one must try to
say *what* the Renaissance was. It was a renaissance in that there was
a rebirth of the old classical studies and philosophies. Unfortunately
the hyperbole 'renaissance' implies a previous death and so fosters a
false concept of the Middle Ages and lends itself too readily to a
rigid departmentalizing of history. A better term than Renaissance
might be Resurgence, for the age was one when men's energies surged
forward and the human spirit felt a new momentum. In part this
new momentum derived from a revitalized awareness of classic antiquity, yet this awareness need not be regarded as cause so much as
consequence, nourishing a felt need for cultural stimulus—the foundations of the new age being economic and political.

Great terms—tragedy, love, heroism and the like—do not lend
themselves to definition, a process which entails delimitation. It is so
with the word 'Renaissance.' Any definition pretending to complete-
ness must be encyclopaedic in scope. No descriptive epigram can be
much more than a half-truth, a stricture which applies even to
Michelet's pregnant phrase, "man's discovery of the world and of
himself." All that is possible in this brief essay is to set forth what
seem to be the chief marks of the Renaissance, the great themes of
the age.

The first is self-confidence. Self-confidence was both the cause and,
augmented, the product of the refutation of authorities unchallenged
during the Middle Ages. Self-confidence lay behind the anti-Aris-
totelian ultimatum of Ramus, the circumnavigation of the globe by
Magellan, and the atheism of Marlowe. In the social field this self-

confidence showed itself in the emergence of merchants and adventurers as magnates and princes; in the physical field in the great explorations of the navigators and the researches of the astronomers; and in the field of religion both in the scepticism of the Italian academies and in the allied phenomenon of the northern Reformation, with its repudiation of the Papacy and its central theme of the individual making his own way to Heaven. Self-confidence is the great mark of the Renaissance. It was this that gave zest and verve to the age, the wonderful sense of all things being possible. It is this spirit that inspired the Elizabethan love of 'action' and expressed itself in the manly word 'resolution.' The Renaissance wanes with the faltering of men's self-confidence at the close of the sixteenth century, when they became oppressed with a sense of frustration of their earlier sanguine hopes, conscious of the minuteness of their world in the Copernican universe, and saddened by their inability to solve the paradoxes that everywhere confronted them.

The second mark of the Renaissance is awareness—awareness of environment and self. The pictorial art of the age reveals an amazing power of perception and representation of the outward world. It is enough to refer to the portraiture of the age, to the incredible veri-similitude of Dürer's paintings of a wood violet or a tangled mass of sedge. Men opened their eyes more widely than before and saw their world more clearly. Colour, shape, texture, rhythm became extremely powerful stimuli. These things being so, it was only natural that the Renaissance should produce a body of poetry, poetry that reflected this awareness of the sensory world, poetry which, in Milton's phrase, was *sensuous*. Puritanism, of course, damned appreciation of the sensuous, and some part of our own age still regards it as suspect. The Renaissance was not troubled by such inhibitions, however, and sensuousness is a great mark of the era. Spenser is at once sensuous and high-minded; Milton's own poetry, which is very late Renaissance, is sensuous too.

If sensuousness is a mark of the Renaissance, so too is the extreme of sensuousness—sensuality. This element is too important to be ignored in any assessing of the Renaissance, especially the Renaissance in Italy. There is no need here, however, to investigate the sonnets of Aretino or the eccentricities of various of the despots.

Besides heightened awareness of environment, and that enjoyment of the processes of perception and awareness which properly constitutes sensuousness, the Renaissance brought increased self-awareness on the part of the individual. Individualism is the third great mark of the Renaissance. The art of the Middle Ages was anonymous, but that of the Renaissance blazons forth the characters and names of individuals. The change might be expected of an age when men became markedly aware of themselves, infatuated, at times, with a sense of their own uniqueness and self-sufficiency. A spokesman here is Webster's Bosola with his cry:

> I will not imitate things glorious,
> No more than base; I'll be mine own example.

Montaigne, who was fascinated by the homeliest imperfections in his own character, provides another example.

To the men of the Renaissance, with their intense sense of self and their unabashed joy in living, the thought of death was particularly abhorrent. The consolations of religion were not enough. Against the horror of not-being, of total disappearance of self, all that seemed possible to some was the perpetuation of one's name among succeeding generations. Thus arose the cult of Fame, whom the Renaissance allegorists loved to depict in triumph over Death. Allied to Fame was Honour. Fame was the perpetuation of name after death: Honour the advancing of a man's name during his lifetime. (Castiglione's courtier was to seek honour in single combats before the gaze of armies, but to avoid general engagements where, his courage going unheeded, there would be no honour.) The allied cults of Fame and Honour represent a fourth great mark of the Renaissance.

Another mark of the Renaissance has been insufficiently emphasized—its idealism. Along with its cruelty and debauchery, the Renaissance contained a stream of pure idealism. Without tracing this stream to its Platonic, Stoic, and Christian sources, one may note how it recurs in the literature of the age—Castiglione's Bembo, who believed that beauty is always good, "a holy thing"; the lofty passages of Spenser's *Hymns*; and the fine idealism of Sidney. The Renaissance, with its inherited sense of hierarchy, of the Great Chain of Being, never lost sight of what was considered the proper position of Man— set above the animal creation, only a little beneath the angels. From this there sprang an exalted concept of the nature and obligations of man. 'Man' was made a term of nobility. All that was sensual and irrational was held to be 'beastly' in the literal sense of the word. By

a significant false etymology 'abominable' was written abhominable.'
"If we will be men," wrote Sidney, "the reasonable part of our soul
is to have absolute commandment." There was, moreover, a cult of
Virtue—Virtue being that which, like the Latin *virtus*, makes a man:
a property compounded of self-sufficiency and integrity, valiancy of
courage and generosity of spirit.

> Vertue is ever sowing of her seedes;
> In the Trenches for the Souldier; in the wakeful study
> For the Scholler; in the furrows of the sea
> For men of our Profession—of all which
> Arise and spring up Honor.

This was the idealism that tempered the sensuousness, rebuked the
sensuality of the age, and produced the noblest spirits of the time.

IV

What of the Renaissance and the modern world? Recent history,
with its succession of economic depressions and increasingly cataclysmic wars, has induced a current of pessimism in all except the
unthinking. People regard the future with foreboding. The science
of the behaviorists and kindred schools has served to write man down
to the lowest valuation that he has yet set upon himself. The doctrines
of materialism and 'realism' which are now everywhere broadcast
beat down assertions of idealism. The arts still survive, but a little
precariously. Meanwhile the increasing regulation of life by the state,
the uniforming of studies and recreations, leave less and less scope
for individuality. In such an age there is something therapeutic in
participation in the Renaissance spirit with its note of confidence,
its assertion of individuality, and its proclaiming of the nobility of the
human spirit. Resort to Renaissance art and literature is not to be
escapism, ivory tower seclusion from the world, but a vital part of
our education, quickening appreciation of values imperilled in our
own age and inspiring us to preserve and proclaim them.

The Survival of Mediaeval Intellectual Interests into Early Modern Times

LYNN THORNDIKE

Published in 1927

Regardless of what view of the Renaissance the reader accepts, the truth remains that many a medieval idea and approach continued to exercise considerable sway in what historians have come to call early modern times (the sixteenth through eighteenth centuries). At first glance, this must seem so obvious as to require no amplification. But since the tendency among scholars has often been to stress the fact of change rather than the fact of continuity in the intellectual history of these centuries, Lynn Thorndike has performed a service by demonstrating the remarkable extent to which medieval interests and ideas continued to thrive in early modern times. It goes without saying that the reader should not be concerned with the mass of detailed evidence that Thorndike marshals in support of his thesis. What matters is the thesis itself, as well as the way in which it is developed.

Those external conditions of life which we call mediaeval largely persisted into early modern times or even until the French Revolution or the nineteenth century. In most parts of Europe the life of the peasant and the land system were little altered. In most towns the picturesque walls and towers, streets and houses, remained essentially unchanged, except that with the falling-off in population whole quarters might be deserted, or with the decline in taste charming Gothic arches, windows, columns, and ornamentation might be walled up, plastered over, cut through, or otherwise concealed and disfigured. To a large extent, save in royal capitals and new commercial centres,

Reprinted by special permission from *Speculum,* II (1927), 147-159. The documentation which originally appeared with this essay has been omitted.

the old buildings were made to suffice. Thus, if a new school were opened, instead of occupying a new building, it would move into some half-ruined monastery or abandoned hospital. The feudal castles were battered down and dismantled only in the seventeenth century. If knighthood was not still in flower in the sixteenth century, nevertheless a captain of that time could say that a good cavalier on a good horse was as superior a being as there could be in this world. The gild system was essentially the same in the seventeenth century as in the thirteenth, and did not disappear on the continent of Europe until the French Revolution and the middle of the nineteenth century. Quaint old custom and procedure, popular festivals and liberties, had been reduced; artisans worked longer and were paid less; in the gilds there was less charity and unity. Nor had the lot of the teacher and writer improved. But all this was in the nature of subtraction rather than alteration and innovation.

The point I wish to make is this: if the external conditions were still so largely mediaeval, why should thought change? If man is largely dependent for his ideas upon his environment, such new thought as there was in the early modern period will be found to be based upon, or connected with, new or newly discovered things: manuscripts of Greek tragedies and comedies, and of the essays of Plutarch and Lucian, new continents across the Atlantic, new scientific instruments like the telescope and microscope which opened up vast realms of nature to discovery. Otherwise the old thought and methods of thought might be expected to go on as before.

Much has been written, it is true, concerning the new spirit of the Renaissance and of the Reformation. But gradually it is becoming recognized that both the humanists and the reformers were singularly lacking in originality. As the seventeenth century opened, Hugo Grotius was the precocious pet of the humanistic circles in which moved Scaliger, Casaubon, and Heinsius. The first text he edited

JEAN BODIN: Sixteenth-century French writer whose works on economics, political theory, and the nature of history have become classics in the study of the development of European thought.

CARDAN: Italian mathematician and philosopher of the sixteenth century whose indebtedness to medieval writers on mathematics was considerable.

was that most early-mediaeval of all early-mediaeval works, the *De nuptiis philologiae et mercurii* of Martianus Capella; his first original poem was on a theme which had been repeatedly treated in the mediaeval religious drama. Nevertheless it may be admitted that in the early modern centuries there was a certain turning away from mediaeval tradition. The humanist, philologer, or antiquarian became enamoured instead of the classical tradition; the reformer turned away in disdain from the traditions of the mediaeval church. Perhaps with most zest of all, absolute monarchs like Francis I cast aside the ancient laws of the realm and the solemn promises of their predecessors, riding roughshod over past privileges, franchises, and institutions, whether Estates, Parlement, or University. This break with the immediate past was undoubtedly important. But, except that it also seriously affected the fine arts, it was in the main limited to such fields as have already been mentioned.

In other fields the course of development already initiated in the mediaeval centuries went on uninterrupted. There was no sufficient occasion, for instance, for a physician or a lawyer or a mathematician or a chemist or an optician or a clock-maker or a cartographer or a munition-manufacturer to reject the mediaeval foundations that had been laid for him. "It was a continuation of a mediaeval tradition," says Rashdall, "that made Montpellier and Padua the centres of European medicine in the sixteenth and seventeenth centuries." And "there were surgical writers at Bologna as early as the second half of the thirteenth century whose works continued in sufficient circulation to be included among the earliest productions of the Venetian press and to be often reprinted up to the middle of the seventeenth century." "In political theory," Dr. Figgis states, "many of the mediaeval arguments and methods subsisted until the eighteenth century."

The divisions of the field of knowledge, the classification of the different subjects studied, the main interests of the human mind, re-

PIERRE DUHEM: French scholar whose writings on the history of science represent one of the major pioneering efforts in twentieth-century historiography.

HUGO GROTIUS: Seventeenth-century Dutch humanist and diplomat whose *On the Law of War and Peace* is a basic work in the growth of the idea of international law.

mained almost the same in early modern times as they had been in the thirteenth century. The humanism of the intervening centuries had added classical philology and antiquities, a more direct and ampler acquaintance with Greek; the new temper of the times and warring sects had added controversies—that was about all. The courses offered in universities, the titles of academic chairs, the subject headings employed in catalogues of libraries—all these remained but little altered. Lives of the saints and commentaries on the Sentences, liturgical works and ascetic treatises were generally abandoned by Protestants, but were still read and written by Catholics. With the secularization of the Reformation period more space in the academic curriculum was given to history and politics, but we must remember that mediaeval historiography had been abundant and that Aristotle's Politics and Economics had even been translated into French in the fourteenth century.

Our main thesis may be excellently illustrated by the case of Descartes, the philosopher who is commonly represented as having made such a sharp break with mediaeval scholasticism. Yet even his celebrated "*Cogito, ergo sum*," merely repeats one of the four states of certitude of Duns Scotus, the schoolman of the early fourteenth century. Descartes was opposed to over-much study and scorned the teachings of the schools. He would begin with a preliminary attitude of sweeping doubt as to all previous traditions and accepted knowledge, and then, by "the easy path" of the natural reason possessed by almost every man, "find in himself, and without borrowing from any, the whole knowledge which is essential to him in the direction of his life, and then by his study succeed in acquiring the most curious forms of knowledge that the human reason is capable of possessing."

Yet we find Descartes concerned with many of the problems, topics, and notions which had occupied the attention of the science and philosophy of previous centuries. He employs such familiar captions of mediaeval physics as Meteorology and Dioptrics. He asks such an old type of question as, Why children and old people weep more easily than others. He repeats the old notion of the formation of animal spirits in the cavities of the brain. Indeed, it was not overthrown until the time of Gall in the nineteenth century. Descartes' doctrine of the pineal gland in the brain as the connecting link between soul and body reminds one of the explanation of thought as the opening and closing of "a particle of the substance of the brain similar to a worm," which we find in the ninth century Arabic treatise of Costa ben Luca, *On the Difference between Soul and Spirit*. Costa ben Luca represented this particle as forming a sort of valve between the anterior and posterior ventricles, and held that when a man was in the act of recalling something to mind, this valve opened and the subtle spirits passed from the anterior to the posterior cavity. Now hear Descartes' explanation: "Thus when the soul desires to recollect something, this desire causes the gland, by inclining successively to different sides, to thrust the spirits towards different parts of the brain until they come across that part where the traces left there by the object which we wish to recollect are found. . . ."

The magnet and the rainbow played about as large a part in Descartes' philosophy as in mediaeval science. To the time-honored problem, Why is the sea not increased by the rivers flowing into it? he gives, not the modern answer, evaporation, but the answer which Ristoro d'Arezzo in the thirteenth century and others since had given, Because the surplus water returns by underground passages to the tops of the mountains. Descartes still had faith in Aristotelian first causes, criticizing Galileo for merely investigating particular phenomena and forces and so building without a foundation. So we might go on to show how Descartes denied the existence of a vacuum, discussed such oft-discussed matters as quicksilver, sulphur, and bitumen, nitre and salts, how stones and minerals are produced by vapors ascending from the interior of the earth, how vermilion or *minium* is made— a stock paragraph in mediaeval chemical treatises and collections of recipes for painters, why the flame of the candle is pointed.

Descartes of course often offered a new explanation, but the fact remains that he was trying to answer the same old set of questions and observing the traditional classification of the arts and sciences. He was still as interested as the thirteenth century had been in the marvelous secrets of nature. Although in one place he states that it will be impossible for him to treat in detail of such matters as the phoenix, he soon expresses a curiosity concerning even "apparitions, illusions, and in a word all the wonderful effects attributed to magic," and promises to gratify it. "Then I shall place before your eyes the works of man upon corporeal objects, and after having struck wonder into you by the sight of machines the most powerful, and automata the most rare, visions the most specious, and tricks the most subtle that artifice can invent, I shall reveal to you secrets which are so simple that you will henceforward wonder at nothing in the works of our hands." These words sound almost like a literal translation of some sentence from the treatise ascribed to Roger Bacon "On the Secret Works of Art and Nature and the Nullity of Magic." Descartes was not without faith in such time-worn marvels and ancient superstitions as the inexhaustible lamps supposed to burn for centuries without addition of new fuel, or the bleeding of the wounds of a corpse at the approach of the murderer. He was confident that his Method could offer satisfactory explanation of the truth of such marvels.

Finally, before taking leave of Descartes, let us recall that even his claim to be the inventor of analytical geometry must be discounted, since Nicholas Oresme had already made use of coördinates in the fourteenth century. Oresme had also employed fractional exponents for powers, an innovation formerly attributed to the sixteenth-century mathematicians, Vieta and Stevin.

These cases illustrate the truth that not only were many intellectual interests of the middle ages perpetuated in the early modern centuries, but that what have been acclaimed as new discoveries resulting from the free spirit of the Renaissance and the Reformation were often mere revivals of, or improvements upon, ideas which had already been broached in the thirteenth or fourteenth century. Duhem has traced the use made by Leonardo da Vinci in his scientific thought of the previous mediaeval literature, and shown that his geological ideas, for example, were largely taken from Albertus Magnus in the thirteenth, and Albert of Saxony in the fourteenth century. Cardan was influenced in his turn by da Vinci, while Palissy plagiarized from Cardan. Torricelli, Galileo's private secretary and demonstrator by his famous experiment of the possibility of a vacuum, in his dynamics often used the reasoning and even the very wording of Jean Buridan, the Parisian schoolman of the fourteenth century. Gesner and Cardan made large use of Albertus Magnus. The thirteenth-century work of Bartholomew of England *On the Properties of Things*, intended by its author only as a handy compilation, was the chief source of scientific information for writers of the Elizabethan age. Mary P. Ramsay has pointed out the mediaeval doctrines in the English poet, Donne, of the seventeenth century. Knight has shown that Grotius' work *On the Law of War and Peace* covered ground already repeatedly trod by the schoolmen. Anatomy and physiology did not begin with Vesalius and Harvey. Guy de Chauliac in the fourteenth century, and the earlier writers whom he cites, possessed anatomical knowledge which has been commonly ascribed to a later period.

Nor did the men of the later centuries always fail to recognize the greatness of their predecessors. Gabriel Naudé in the seventeenth century notes that Scaliger and Cardan in the sixteenth put Richard Suiseth or Swineshead, the "Calculator," of the fourteenth century, in the rank of the ten rarest wits that the world had ever known. Regiomontanus has usually been represented, perhaps especially by German historians, as having resuscitated mathematics from the gloom and neglect of the middle ages. He was better appreciated by Cardan who did not regard him as much of an originator, asserting that he had taken his *Tabulae directionum* in large part from Johannes de Blanchinis of the fourteenth century, his *Epitome* from a still earlier mediaeval writer of Milan, and his treatise on Spherical Triangles from a Hebrew of Spain.

The mediaeval regard for such ancient authorities as Aristotle, Galen, and Ptolemy was not diminished by the classical Renaissance and Protestant Reformation. Sometimes the sixteenth century seems guilty of a blinder adhesion to the letter of such authorities than had previously been the case. Duhem held that the archaic Italian Renaissance brought into honor again doctrines of Aristotle and Averroës which had been abandoned about 1300. John Dryander, in his 1540 edition of the Italian anatomist, Mundinus, of the early fourteenth century, was shocked to find that his author did not always follow Aristotle and Galen (as if they had always been in agreement among themselves!) and he presumed to correct Mundinus by citing Galen. When Francis I in 1544 by royal edict condemned both of the recent works of Ramus against Aristotle and forbade him henceforth to attack Aristotle or other approved authors, his sympathizers held that this was an unprecedented assault upon academic freedom, and that it had hitherto been no crime to oppose Aristotle. Henceforth, however, it was to be, at least in Paris, where as late as 1642 the Sorbonne and Parlement censured certain men for attacking the Aristotelian doctrine of form, matter, and substantial forms. Luther for a time indulged in violent vituperation of Aristotle, but he was much irritated when Carlstadt and Melancthon took his invective literally instead of in a Pickwickian sense. By 1535 Melancthon had seen the light and was convinced that without Aristotle "pure philosophy cannot be retained or indeed any right system of teaching or learning," and that "Aristotle wrote so

eruditely of civil customs that nothing more is needed." For a long
time thereafter the Aristotelian logic, physics, and philosophy remained
as firmly intrenched in most Protestant as in Catholic schools. Even so
critical a spirit as Pierre Bayle, when he became professor of philosophy
at Sedan in 1676, continued to follow Aristotle in logic and morals,
though introducing the Cartesian physics, while his metaphysics remained scholastic with some attention to Cartesianism.

The good old mediaeval teaching of dialectic received severe punishment at the hands of Renaissance critics and satirists, but appears to
have taken it all and come back smiling. When the Collège de Guienne
was instituted in 1533 at Bordeaux, it was regarded as a progressive,
humanistic enterprise, and Tartas, its first principal, was represented
as going south to revive learning, accompanied by twenty-one teachers
of Hebrew, Latin, and Greek. As a matter of fact, only one or two of
them knew any Greek, while Hebrew was never taught at the school.
However, disputations were abandoned, and the emphasis was on the
Latin classics. Nevertheless, dialectic was taught from the start, and although Nicholas de Grouchy at first dictated his lectures in Greek, he
concluded by using the Latin Aristotle of Joachim Périon. The pupils
were dissatisfied with his successor in the chair of dialectic, and we find
efforts being made to secure someone qualified to comment on Aristotle
in Latin. This might sound as if good teachers of logic were becoming
scarce, but at the beginning of the next century, when the study of
Greek had been dropped from the curriculum, we find that the principal of the school was a Scot named Balfour whose most important
work, published in 1616, was a commentary on the *Organon* of
Aristotle.

Similarly in the field of medicine there was at first a marked
tendency in the late fifteenth and first half of the sixteenth century to
revert to the Greek text of Hippocrates and Galen, and to cast aside
the great Arabic medical writers of the intervening period. This movement, however, never went very far, and was soon seen to be an
antiquarian retrogression rather than modern progress. The normal
trend of early modern medicine was rather to continue, with occasional innovations such as those of Paracelsus, the methods and
matter of the numerous mediaeval works and Latin translations. Since
the later mediaeval centuries had seen no little progress in anatomy,
medicine, and surgery, this situation cannot be called one of mediaeval
stagnation, although it perhaps became stagnation in the subsequent

centuries. Be that as it may, we find the candidates for degrees or professorial appointment at Montpellier in 1574 defending theses which can generally be duplicated in the works of the Jewish physician Isaac of the tenth century or of Petrus Hispanus and Pietro d'Abano in the thirteenth. These questions were argued theoretically or scholastically from the usual premises of ancient and mediaeval science and their *Weltanschauung*. This may be further illustrated by quoting the forms followed by candidates for the doctorate at Padua in 1642 and 1665 A.D., as preserved in two manuscripts of the Sloane collection of the British Museum.

> Relying on the inspiration of the divine spirit and your good will, O most wise fathers, I enter on explanation of the points assigned me by lot by the most illustrious presiding officer for today's examination, in expounding which I follow the received order in this dear university and proffer four things. First, I will show the connection of the text with what went before. Second, I'll expose the author's meaning. Third, I'll divide the text into parts. Fourth, I'll explain the various parts and, if any matters are worthy of consideration, I'll note them too. I have to interpret a twofold point, one philosophical, the other medical. The philosophical is from the second book of Aristotle's Physics, and its opening words are: "Quasi natura sit principium . . ." The medical is from the *Ars Parva* of Galen, chapter 43, opening, "Humidius autem et frigidius. . . ."
>
> I come then to the first part of the text, in which Aristotle thus defines nature, that it is the principle and cause of motion and of that rest in which it is first and *per se* and not *secundum accidens*. Moreover, that nature is the principle of motion and rest may be confirmed by this argument: whatever gives the essence to things, gives likewise the operations following the essence. But nature gives things their essence, ergo etc. The major (premise) is clear; for whatever immediately constitutes a cause, the same also immediately constitutes the effect. The minor (premise) is proved by this reasoning. If nature is both the matter of natural things and their form, it also gives them their essence. But the former is true, and hence the latter also. A second argument that I adduce is that whatever is the principle and cause of increase and alteration and progression, the same is the principle of motion and rest. But nature etc., ergo etc. . . .

In another case the candidate is assigned the problem of a youth of hot and dry temperament laboring with intermittent fever complicated by headache. His diagnosis is that the patient has a hot and dry distemper of the heart and entire body, caused by bilious humour putrefying outside the veins in two places. The headache comes from bilious and putrid vapor affecting the brain. Hence the patient requires cold and wet treatment, riddance of the putridity and inhibition of further putrefying by means of attenuating, abstergent, incident, and imminuent remedies, with cordials and liver-pills. Hippocrates is cited to the effect that the disease is not perilous and that a cure may be hoped for. The candidate for the doctorate advises bleeding from the basilic vein of the right arm as much as the patient's constitution will permit.

It should not be thought, however, that the observance of such forms was necessarily incompatible with observation and experiment. The very man who in 1583 had an anatomical theater constructed at Padua, at the same time renewed the practice of disputations which had begun to flag.

In Roman Catholic lands scholastic theology also, which has often been represented as moribund in the fourteenth century, continued to hold its own into the eighteenth. The University of Salamanca was the great centre of Thomism in the sixteenth century. There is a tradition that Duns Scotus was buried alive. Certainly his soul went marching on in many a subsequent disputation and tome. And as his corpse was repeatedly exhumed—in 1476, 1509, 1619, 1642, and 1706—so his philosophy was repeatedly revived. One such occasion was in the seventeenth century when the teaching of two young scholars from southern Italy spread like wildfire through all the Scotist schools. The professors of the University of Rome from 1580 to 1690 were active in publishing works on the philosophy and theology of Aquinas, while Scotism found defenders still in the eighteenth century.

Let us turn very briefly to yet other sides of education. In the schools of Champagne in the second half of the sixteenth century reckoning was still taught by the means of jetons or counters in the mediaeval manner. The old mediaeval textbooks also continued long in use. That meagre epitome of astronomy, the *Sphere* of Sacrobosco, written in 1244, was still taught at the University of Montpellier in 1608. The logic of Paul of Venice, who had a great reputation as an astronomer and philosopher in the early fifteenth century but seems to have done little more than reproduce earlier mediaeval authors, found, according to Momigliano, a last refuge in the schools of the

Jesuits in the sixteenth and seventeenth centuries. Boethius was the text in music at Oxford in the eighteenth century. The brief compendium of the philosophy of Albertus Magnus entitled *Philosophia pauperum* was being used at the University of Cracow in 1777.

Alchemy, astrology, and other occult sciences continued on much the same path as they had followed in the twelfth and thirteenth centuries, and men of note in science and thought still were not above lending a favorable ear or even pen to their claims. The works of Henry Cornelius Agrippa, Porta, and Cardan contain almost no superstition not found in previous works. A Giordano Bruno, an Achillini, a Bodin, a Kepler, a Francis Bacon, a Robert Boyle, all had their little weaknesses in these matters. Such a doctrine as that of Bodin concerning climate, instead of constituting a new modern contribution is little more than a borrowing from mediaeval astrology, whose last sighs have sometimes been mistaken for the first breath of a geographical interpretation of history.

Finally, let us note that, despite the absorption of the humanists in classical history and antiquities, thēre was much historical interest in the mediaeval past manifested from the sixteenth to the eighteenth centuries. Familiar enough to us perhaps is the appeal to history made by Protestants and Catholics and reflected in such rival enterprises as the Magdeburg Centuries and the Annals of Baronius; sufficiently familiar, too, the patriotic national histories and the publication of royal records. But there were also numerous works written upon the past of individual towns and localities, of universities and learned professions. At a time when centralization and unification in a few courts and capitals took away the life and power of the old local centres, it was natural that they should seek solace in a review of their historic past. At a time when absolute monarchy or foreign domination allowed few men the active exercise of citizenship, it was not strange that much intellectual rather than political history was written. And such works almost always convey the impression of intellectual continuity between the mediaeval centuries and their own times.

Machiavelli's *Il Principe*

SIR RICHARD LODGE

Published in 1930

Of all the men of the so-called Renaissance, none has figured more prominently in the history of political thought than Machiavelli (1469-1527).
Within a few generations of his death, his work *The Prince* was well known
in European intellectual circles and his name converted into an adjective synonymous with cunning, ruthless, and unscrupulous. Yet there can
be no doubt that Machiavelli's reputation has suffered because his critics
have often judged him without reference to his historical context. Indeed,
when he is viewed in his setting—as a product and reflection of his times—
he appears in a very different light. As Sir Richard Lodge demonstrated in
his presidential address before the Royal Historical Society, Machiavelli
emerges as a thoughful and well-informed patriot who sought to awaken in
his fellow Italians a feeling of national consciousness—all with a view to
liberating the Italies from the Frenchmen and Spaniards who were plundering it.

Few names are so familiar as that of Machiavelli, who has given
at least an adjective to every European language, and few books
have been subjected to such intense scrutiny and such industrious
commentary as his most impressive work, *The Prince*. It may well be
thought that there is nothing more to be said about either the
author or the book, and that an apology is needed for adding
even an ephemeral address to the enormous mass of literature about
Machiavelli. My apology or explanation is a simple one. The great
majority of the critics and commentators deal with problems which
are of great interest in themselves but do not concern my immediate

Reprinted by special permission from *Transactions of the Royal Historical
Society*, Fourth Series, XIII (1930), 1-16.

object. One of these is the ethical question as to how far the supposed interest of the state—the *raison d'état*—justifies a departure from the ordinary accepted canons of morality or honesty. Another is the place of Machiavelli in the history of what is called Political Science. And a third very fruitful topic is the influence of Machiavelli's teaching upon political action in successive generations after his death. I do not propose to deal with any of these matters, but to concentrate attention upon the narrower problem of the motive and purpose which induced Machiavelli to write one particular book, *Il Principe*. This problem, in comparison with the others to which I have referred, has been largely neglected or obscured because most commentators have treated the book, in connection with the *Discorsi*, as a deliberate statement of Machiavelli's views as to the methods which should be adopted in founding, extending, and maintaining a principality. In this assumption they have been encouraged and confirmed by the author's inveterate habit of stating his propositions in the most general terms.

The book itself has been familiar to me for more than half a century. I first studied it for examination purposes when I was reading for the School of Modern History at Oxford. It was one of the prescribed books for my special subject. For sixteen years after graduation I expounded it to successive generations of undergraduates. In those years I formed a strong opinion as to the motive which induced Machiavelli to write it. The evidence seemed to me so simple and convincing that I expected to find my conclusion generally accepted. It was therefore rather a blow to me when I referred to one authority after another and found that they either evaded the issue or at any rate failed to find or to state what seemed to me a self-evident solution. I remember very vividly going to hear John Morley, as he was then, deliver the Romanes Lecture on Machiavelli, and my disappointment when he abstained from saying what I wanted him to say. And so, when a few weeks ago I cast about in my mind for some suitable subject for a presidential address, I determined to give the eighteenth century a holiday, to go back to a period which at one time was more familiar to me than any other, and to put on record opinions which I had never found reason to alter, though I had never stated them except in oral instruction.

Since I began to write this paper I have at last discovered a historian who is, or rather was, in whole-hearted agreement with me. When

I say that my champion is no less person than Leopold von **Ranke,**
whom I was brought up to regard as perhaps the greatest all-round
historian of the nineteenth century, you will understand how greatly **I**
have been encouraged by the assurance of his posthumous support.
It is true that the essay in which he expressed his views was an
early work, having been published as long ago as 1824, but it was
reprinted with unimportant changes in 1874 and again in 1884, so that
we may conclude that, in spite of hostile criticisms, he found as
little reason to alter his views as I have done. Ranke's main contention is that the commentators have misrepresented Machiavelli by
taking as general maxims for all princes and all time what he wrote
as advice to a particular prince in peculiar and special circumstances
and for his guidance to a definite objective. This is the thesis which
I have always held and which I propose to state and defend this afternoon.

In order to make my position clear it is necessary to offer some
preliminary observations, which I will make as short as possible.
The Prince was written in the later months of 1513, and Machiavelli's
motives were necessarily conditioned by the contemporary state of
affairs (1) in Europe, (2) in Italy generally, and in two Italian
states with which he was peculiarly concerned, (3) the States of
the Church and (4) his own city of Florence.

(1) As to Europe, it is a commonplace to state that the medieval
conception of the Holy Roman Empire was for all practical purposes obsolete at the close of the fifteenth century. Beyond the ever
narrowing bounds of what was still called the Empire, states were
forming themselves under the influence of that novel and undefinable
force which we call nationality. England was politically outside the
Florentine's ken, but two of the newly coherent states, France and

---

BABYLONIAN CAPTIVITY OF THE PAPACY: Expression used to characterize the
years from 1305 to 1378, when the papacy resided at Avignon. Since the
Avignon popes were all Frenchmen, the tendency developed in England and
the Germanies to regard the papacy as a foreign power.

CAESAR BORGIA: Conqueror of most of the Romagna, who came close to
establishing a Borgian dynasty in Central Italy. The death in 1503 of his
father, Pope Alexander VI, effectively ended his scheme.

SAVONAROLA: Dominican friar who sought to achieve a spiritual and reli-

Spain, were vitally concerned with the problems which troubled him. In both these states such unity as had been achieved was associated with a dynasty, with the increased authority of the crown, and with the overthrow of aristocratic privileges and independence. If you wish to realise how strongly this process of unification impressed Machiavelli, you have only to read what he says of the part played by the Parliament of Paris in bringing about the unity of France.

(2) From the prevalent tendency towards a national grouping of states in western Europe, Italy seemed to be comparatively exempt. It is needless to examine into the causes of Italian disunion. A nominal subjection to an alien and distant monarchy in Germany, the quarrels of Empire and Papacy with the resultant factions of Ghibellines and Guelfs, the obstinate traditions of municipal republicanism, all combined with the influence of geography to break up northern and central Italy into a number of minute political units. Such unifying influences as found their way into the peninsula took the form of the substitution of despotisms for democratic or oligarchical institutions, and of the subjection of the lesser states to their more powerful neighbours. By this process of local centralisation Italy came in the fifteenth century to be dominated by five principal states, the duchy of Milan, Venice, Florence, the Papacy, and the Kingdom of Naples. All progress towards more complete unification was checked by temporary coalitions against any state which threatened to overthrow the balance of power between these predominant units. This uneasy and fluctuating balance could at any moment be destroyed by the calling in of a foreign power. For generations southern Italy had been involved in constant wars by the rival claims of the houses of Anjou and Aragon. At the end of the fifteenth century these claims passed to the ruling dynasties of France and Spain, and when Louis

gious regeneration as well as political and economic reform in late-fifteenth-century Florence. For a few years in the 1490's he dominated Florentine life. Having defied the papacy, however, he was excommunicated and finally burned as a heretic.

Francesco Sforza: Military adventurer who suppressed the Republic of Milan and became its Duke in 1450. In order to make his position secure and his rule palatable, he sought to further the economic prosperity of his duchy.

XII added to his Neapolitan claim a pretension to the duchy of Milan, the whole peninsula, north as well as south, was involved in this clash between the two major states of the continent. The German king, by virtue of his claim to imperial suzerainty in Italy, could not hold aloof from the contest, and thus Italy became the cockpit of Europe. In these incessant wars the Italian states themselves could only play an ignoble part, because the mercenary troops which they had employed for generations in their local feuds proved to be no match for the French or the Spaniards or even for the alien mercenaries who were brought in from Switzerland. Thus Italy seemed to lose not only all prospect of unity but almost all hope of independence. Such independence as was left to some of the states was only maintained by playing off one foreign invader against the other, a game which was both difficult and hazardous.

(3) The fifteenth century was a notable epoch in the history of the Papacy. The Latin Church, though more stable and more deeply-rooted than the Holy Roman Empire, appeared to be doomed to share its fate. A mortal blow to its claim to universality was dealt when the Council of Constance was divided into units whose ecclesiastical decisions were largely guided by political interests, thus justifying their academic name of "nations," and when Martin V foiled the schemes of the reforming party by concluding concordats with the separate states. From this it was but a step to the semi-political secessions of the following century. The process of disruption was hastened by the absorption of Martin V and his successors in the task of restoring papal control in the ecclesiastical states, which had been torn to pieces by the great baronial houses during the Babylonish Captivity in Avignon and the Great Schism. After alternating success and failure on the part of intermediate Popes, the suppression of the nobles and princes in Rome and the Romagna was practically completed by Alexander VI and Caesar Borgia, whose policy Machiavelli had occasion to observe closely when he was sent on missions to Caesar's camp. Their aim, as he admits, was to found a secular principality for the house of Borgia, but the fruit of their achievements was reaped by the Papacy under Julius II. Julius was the real founder of the Papal States, and he thrust them into the seething cauldron of Italian politics. After humbling Venice by means of the League of Cambray, he turned against the French, raised the patriotic cry of "down with the foreigner," and organised the Holy League. He suc-

ceeded in his immediate aim, the eviction of the French from Lombardy, but he only did so by an inconsistent alliance with Spain, and thus helped to rivet upon Italy the chains of its first permanent subjection to foreign domination. On his death in 1513 the Papal States, with all the prominence which he had given to them, passed to his successor, Giovanni dei Medici, who took the name of Leo X.

(4) During the fifteenth century Florence had preserved her republican institutions, but the two great Medici, Cosimo, *Pater Patriae*, and his grandson, Lorenzo the Magnificent, had so manipulated them as to establish a personal rule which was none the less absolute because it was disguised. On Lorenzo's death in 1492, a fateful date for Italy and for Europe, this rule was assumed by his incompetent eldest son, Piero. Two years later Charles VIII's famous march through Italy resulted in the expulsion of Piero and his brothers, and Florence became once more a pure Republic. As its revival was due to France, the republican government remained, in spite of some vacillations, loyal to the French alliance during the prolonged wars which followed. It was under this government that Machiavelli was employed and obtained his insight not only into domestic administration but also into the general currents of Italian and European politics. He was Secretary to the Council of Ten and was sent on several legations in Italy and twice to the Court of France. The period of republican revival was not a very triumphant one. Internal disorders, in which the rise and fall of Savonarola were involved, led to the adoption of an extreme remedy, the appointment of a Gonfalonier for life, in imitation of the Venetian Doge. Still more humiliating than domestic strife were the revolt of Pisa, the greatest conquest of the old Republic, and the disasters which accompanied the twelve years' siege that was required before the rebel city was reduced. And in the end the Republic had to pay dearly for its adhesion to France. In 1512, during the war of the Holy League, Spanish and Papal forces, under the guidance of the Cardinal dei Medici, occupied Florence, deposed the Republican Gonfalonier, and restored the constitution as before 1494, which meant the restoration of Medici rule. Machiavelli was deprived of his office and, after a short period of imprisonment for his services to the Republic, retired with his wife and family to his little estate near San Casciano, where he sought consolation for his impotence and poverty in the exercise of his pen. His favourite study was Roman history, and, taking Livy

as his text, he began to write the *Discorsi* in which he commented upon the Roman historian in the light of his own political experience.

This then was the situation in 1513 as Machiavelli surveyed it. Italy was not only more torn and divided than ever but was under the heel of the foreigner: in his own words, "more enslaved than the Hebrews, more servile than the Persians, more dispersed than the Athenians, without a head, without order, beaten, despoiled, ravaged, over-run, and enduring every kind of ruin." It is true that one of the great invaders, France, had been for the moment driven from Italian soil, but it was not likely that its expulsion would be permanent. And in the meantime Spanish rule had been firmly fixed in southern Italy, and the imperial suzerainty, so long purely nominal, had been revived in the north by the return of the Sforzas to Milan. In his own city the Republic which had employed him had been overthrown, and the rule of the Medici had been restored under the protecting patronage of the now powerful Papal State. As long as Leo X was Pope, and he was still a comparatively young man, it was not humanly probable that the power of the ruling house, whether wielded by the Pope's brother, Giuliano, or by his nephew, the youthful Lorenzo, would be overthrown. Gradually there seems to have dawned upon Machiavelli's mind the idea that Italy's salvation might be found in this opportune conjunction of Florence with the Papacy. If only Leo would give to his brother or his nephew the support which Alexander VI had given to Caesar Borgia, and if he would adhere to the anti-foreign programme put forward in his later years by Julius II, there might be built up a central Italian principality strong enough to extend its power to the Alps, and to establish there a barrier against any renewed invasion from France and against any active intervention on the part of Maximilian or his successors in Germany. It is hardly to be supposed that Machiavelli contemplated anything so chimerical as the expulsion of Spain from its southern kingdom. Naples had always been apart from Italy; its whole history was in complete contrast to that of the rest of the peninsula; it had not been included in that Lombard kingdom whose crown had been assumed by the mediaeval Emperors. The Italy which Machiavelli dreamed of as united and free was bounded on the south by the States of the Church.

Having dreamed his dream, Machiavelli was confronted with the problem of its realisation. It was obvious to him that neither pen nor voice could suffice. It would be useless to come out into the open, to denounce Italian degeneracy, to point out its causes, and to prescribe his heroic remedies, which included the formation of a national militia to supersede the fatal mercenaries of the past. He had watched the career of Savonarola, had contrasted it with that of past leaders from Moses downwards, and had come to his famous conclusion that it is only the armed prophets who have prevailed; the unarmed have always been ruined. He would not play the part of the unarmed prophet. Nor could he see any prospect of success in a revival, even if it had been possible, of republican independence. As he looked round Europe, he found that all the great achievements of his time were the work of princes. If the Medici prince, either Giuliano or Lorenzo, would undertake to serve the cause of Italy, it would be a small sacrifice on his own part to abandon any theoretical predilections for a Florentine Republic. Inspired by these conceptions, he turned aside from his *Discorsi* to write with great rapidity his manual of instructions for such member of the ruling family as would be willing to follow them. His first idea seems to have been to send his work to Giuliano, as the more amenable to advice and the more likely to conciliate support both in Florence and outside. But when Giuliano died in 1516, he had no alternative but to dedicate it to Lorenzo, and it is the Letter to Lorenzo which is prefixed to all editions of *The Prince*. There was of course no idea at the time of publication. Nothing could be more fatal to the purpose of the book than publicity. And as a matter of fact it was not printed until 1532, after Machiavelli's death, long after the death of Leo X, at a time when all hope of Italian unity had disappeared.

It is not in the least necessary to assume that Machiavelli believed in the possession by either of the Medici princes of the qualities which he desiderated. But a prince can be guided by a far-seeing and capable minister. As Machiavelli pointed out, it is in the choice of such a minister that the wisdom of the prince is demonstrated. I have never been able to read the brief twenty-second chapter on "the Secretaries of Princes" without a conviction that Machiavelli aspired to play to his prospective patron the part that Antonio da Venafro played to Pandolfo Petrucci of Siena. Nor do I see anything discreditable in the supposition, which I believe to be true, that a minor motive for writing *The Prince* was a desire on the part of the author to pave the way for his own return to political employment.

One last explanatory observation. I have said that Machiavelli turned from writing the *Discorsi* to compose *The Prince*. Any author can understand that he could not altogether free himself from the influence of his previous work. It was largely from this that he took those general assertions that sound so often as if he was laying down the law for all time, and it was wholly from this that he borrowed those classical illustrations and parallels which often seem out of place in a manual for a sixteenth-century ruler, and which rarely add much force to his contentions.

I admit that this reconstruction of Machiavelli's motives is largely conjectural, as indeed most interpretations of past motives must necessarily be. But I claim that it fits in with internal evidence, and it is not, so far as I know, contradicted by any external proof. Of course it may be incomplete: so subtle and complex a mind as that of Machiavelli may well have had other thoughts in reserve. But, so far as it goes, its refutation seems to me difficult and indeed impossible. And it has the supreme merit of removing most of the difficulties which have confronted commentators. It provides a complete answer to those doctrinaire republicans who have denounced Machiavelli as a traitor to his avowed principles because he wrote what appear to be maxims for despots. It explains and justifies the all-important chapter on Ecclesiastical Principalities, with its concluding compliment to Leo X, which appears to be quite irrelevant to the guidance of any normal secular ruler. Above all, it removes what has been a stumbling-block to successive generations of critics, the choice of Caesar Borgia as an exemplar for Machiavelli's Prince. "I do not know," he says, "what better precepts I can give to a new prince than the example of his actions." This is a matter of such vital importance from my point of view that I may be allowed to develop it at some length.

Machiavelli divides new principalities into two categories according to whether they are acquired by *virtu* or by *fortuna*. *Virtu*, which may be regarded as the key-word of the Italian Renaissance, has nothing in common with our own word "virtue." It retains the classical meaning of courage or daring, but has acquired in addition the sense of intellectual ability. Fortune, on the other hand, is opportunity or environment. The man who can suit his conduct to contemporary conditions is called fortunate. If the conditions change and his conduct remains unaltered, he at once becomes unfortunate. If a man is skilful enough to change his conduct to suit changing circumstances—*temporeggiare con gli accidenti*—he will be always fortunate. The man who acquires a principality by *virtu* has all his difficulty in gaining his position, but little trouble in maintaining it; whereas the prince who rises by fortune, leaps suddenly to the summit, but requires all his skill and pains to keep himself there. Admitting Machiavelli's distinction, which of the two categories would be the more likely to fit an imaginary prince? There seems to me to be only one possible answer to the question. A prince who was worth advising might be expected to possess or develop *virtu*, or at least to choose a minister who would supply the desired quality. *Fortuna*, on the other hand, was a matter of luck and could not be had for the bidding. It was to be expected therefore that the preceptor of princes in general would lay stress upon the exercise and the reward of ability, and would pay comparatively little attention to careers which owed their starting-point to the chance of good fortune which was not likely to be repeated. But if we turn to *Il Principe* we find that Machiavelli does the precise opposite. He refers to Francesco Sforza as a prince who owed his elevation to *virtu*, and then dismisses him in a sentence. But to the career of Caesar Borgia, whom he selects as the beneficiary of fortune, he devotes a long and detailed chapter. This was not due, as is generally assumed, to his personal familiarity with the doings of the Borgias, or to any peculiar admiration for Caesar's character or achievements, but solely to the curious similarity of his *fortuna* with that of the restored Medici in Florence. Caesar Borgia was the son of a Pope. It could not be expected that any normal prince in the dim future would find himself so situated. But Giuliano dei Medici was the brother, and Lorenzo was the nephew, of the actually reigning Pope. This fact, and nothing else, made Caesar an apt example, not for all princes, but for the particular ruler to whom *Il Principe* was to be addressed.

This narrows the much-debated problem of political morality. Machiavelli himself leaves no doubt on this matter in his fifteenth chapter. He will say nothing about imaginary princes, but will confine himself to contemporary facts.

"My intention being to write something that may be useful to him who understands, it has seemed to me more fitting to go behind to the actual truth about things rather than to any imaginary condition: and indeed there are many imagined republics and principalities which have never been known to exist in fact; for there is so great a distance between the way men live and the way they ought to live, that he who quits what is actually done for that which ought to be done, will bring about his ruin rather than his safety; because a man who wishes to be virtuous in all his actions must necessarily be ruined among so many who are not virtuous."

The general conclusion of the chapter is that a prince should, if possible, possess all the virtues, but that in a wicked world he must exercise such self-control that, while avoiding all vices which might ruin the state, he should not be too scrupulous about those which are necessary for its salvation. This is no general maxim for all time: it is advice to an Italian prince in the early part of the sixteenth century. The "wicked world" is the world as Machiavelli saw it. And I confess that, startling or even shocking as it may sound to us at the present day, I do not see what other advice he could have given. If Machiavelli's premises are accepted, it is difficult to resist his conclusions. His most voluminous critic does not defend the political morality of Italy, but contends at great length that things were just as bad in England, France, and Spain in the same age. This may be consoling to Italians, but it does not affect the contention that a political writer, like a political actor, must be judged by the prevalent morals of his own time rather than by any absolute code. I once had occasion to read an interesting correspondence on this subject between Lord Acton and Bishop Creighton. The layman was for the moral code, the whole code, and nothing but the code, while the Bishop pleaded for some allowance for the historic wrong-doer. I own that in this controversy I am on the side of the Bishop. And I must reiterate my conviction that Machiavelli was writing not only about his own time but for his own time and for no other.

This last paragraph is a partial digression into one of those topics which I had determined to avoid. But it is difficult, in writing about Machiavelli, to avoid such a digression. I have still my final argument in the famous last chapter in which he urges the recipient of his book to undertake the sublime task of freeing Italy from the barbarians. I have already quoted from it his picture of the forlorn condition of his native country, and I cannot refrain from one last extract, though no translation can do justice to what is perhaps the finest example of Italian prose.

"There is no visible hope for Italy except in your illustrious house, if, with its *virtu* and its *fortuna* [I lay stress upon this last word], favoured by God and the Church, of which it is now the head [I lay stress again on these words], it will take the lead in the country's redemption. . . . No words can express with what joy it will be received in all those provinces which have suffered from these foreign floods, with what thirst for vengeance, with what resolute faith, with what devotion, with what tears. What gates will be closed to the redeemer? What peoples will refuse him obedience? What jealousy will oppose him? What Italian will deny him devotion? In every man's nostrils this barbarous dominion stinks. Let therefore your illustrious house undertake this venture with the courage and the hope with which men embark on just enterprises in order that under its standard this country may be ennobled, and under its auspices this sonnet of Petrarch may be verified:

> 'Virtu contro al furore
> Prendera l'arme, e fia il combatter corto;
> Chè l'antico valore
> Negl' Italici cuor non è ancor morto.' "[1]

I have never been able to understand, much less to sympathise with, the contention advanced in some quarters, that this chapter was mere rhetorical camouflage to conceal and justify the deliberate immorality of the rest of the book. If Machiavelli was not sincere when he wrote this, I should lose all faith in the sincerity of any writer. And a man does not write deliberate camouflage to blind the eyes of posterity when he does not know that what he writes will ever meet those eyes.

I can imagine a destructive critic maintaining that the *Principe*, as I have interpreted it, reveals a scheme so chimerical in itself, and proved to be so chimerical by subsequent events, that it can never have been seriously put forward by a man with such an acute intellect and so much practical experience as Machiavelli possessed. I do not accept the conclusion. Machiavelli very probably underestimated certain difficulties, but, even if he had been less sanguine, he would not be the first advocate of a great cause who believed that it would be more advanced by unsuccessful effort than by passive acquiescence. But I admit that the project was chimerical. Its weakest point was the

---

[1] I have not ventured to translate the lines of Petrarch, but Madame Villari has, quite justifiably, been bolder. Her rendering is:
"When Virtue takes arms against Fury, short will be the fight,
For in Italian hearts still lives the ancient might."

belief that the Papacy would combine with Florence for its promotion. This is probably clearer to us than it was to Machiavelli. For a century before 1513 the Popes had weakened and almost sacrificed their claim to the spiritual headship of a universal Church while they concentrated their efforts on the building up of a temporal lordship. Machiavelli himself had seen Alexander VI lending the papal name and papal support to the unscrupulous schemes of Caesar Borgia. And he had seen Julius II acting as a secular prince, leading troops to the war, and proclaiming a sort of Italian crusade against the French. It was not altogether surprising that he left out of account the spiritual side of the Papacy, and believed that the policy of Leo X would be as frankly secular as that of his recent predecessors. But he reckoned without the Reformation. The Lutheran movement with its threat of schism, the actual secession of England, of the north German princes, and the Scandinavian countries, forced the Popes to revive their old claims, to refurbish their ancient weapons, and in the end to consent to a reform of the old Church. It then became clear that the Papacy was by its very nature pledged to war against the principle of nationality, and especially against nationality in the country in which the Popes lived. One of the first acts of the reformed Papacy was to place the works of Machiavelli upon the Index. When in the nineteenth century Italian unity and independence were at last achieved, the Papacy held obstinately aloof and hostile, and it has been left to our own day to witness the signature of a possibly fragile treaty between the head of the Roman Church and the King of a united Italy. In spite of the treaty, the relations between the Vatican and the Quirinal are likely to be uneasy for some time to come.

While Machiavelli was blind as to the spiritual revival of the Papacy, and its consequent desertion of the cause of Italy, which Julius II had seemed for the moment to have espoused, there was another untoward event which he could not foresee. This was the union under Charles V of the Spanish monarchy with the Austrian inheritance and the Imperial pretensions. The overwhelming power wielded by Charles V was responsible for the establishment of that Spanish domination in Italy, which was transmitted from the Spanish to the Austrian Habsburgs, which was restored in 1815 after the shattering blows of Napoleon, and was not finally overthrown till the middle of last century. And even then it was not overthrown by unaided

Italian effort, but by the classic expedient of playing off one foreign state against another.

Although Machiavelli's dream was unrealised, though no Medici aspired to play the part of Victor Emmanuel, or called upon him to play the part of Cavour, and though Italy was ultimately freed by other methods than those which he had devised, his whole-hearted advocacy of his country's cause has never been forgotten, and ever since the middle of the last century he has stood higher in the estimation of his fellow-countrymen than at any other time since his death.

THE MEDICI.

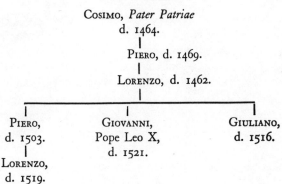

COSIMO, *Pater Patriae*
d. 1464.

PIERO, d. 1469.

LORENZO, d. 1462.

| PIERO, d. 1503. | GIOVANNI, Pope Leo X, d. 1521. | GIULIANO, d. 1516. |

LORENZO, d. 1519.

IV

The Protestant Revolutions and the Catholic Reformation

>>>->>>->>>->>>->>>->>>->>>->>>->>>>>><<<-<<<-<<<-<<<-<<<-<<<-<<<-<<<-<<<

Luther, Luther's Critics, and the Peasant Revolt

HAROLD J. GRIMM

Calvin's "Institutes of the Christian Religion"

WILHELM PAUCK

The Reformation at Home and Abroad

H. MAYNARD SMITH

Survival of the Catholic Faith in the Sixteenth Century

HENRY S. LUCAS

>>>->>>->>>->>>->>>->>>->>>->>>->>>>>><<<-<<<-<<<-<<<-<<<-<<<-<<<-<<<-<<<

Luther, Luther's Critics, and the Peasant Revolt

HAROLD J. GRIMM

Published in 1946

During the years when Luther struggled to bring about the acceptance of his conception of salvation, he was faced with a number of major crises. None of these crises, however, has occasioned such heated discussion as his stand in the Peasant War of 1524-1525. Even today many a loyal Lutheran historian finds himself embarrassed when he remembers the strong words with which Luther exhorted the princes to take action "against the plundering and murdering hordes of the peasantry." Often, of course, the difficulty has been that critics have viewed Luther in the light of their own outlook and times rather than *his*. In the present article, Harold J. Grimm, of Ohio State University, one of the leading American authorities on the German Reformation, calls attention to the dangers of this approach as he attempts to situate Luther in his historical setting.

Although virtually no recognized authority in the field of the Lutheran Reformation accuses Luther of encouraging the German peasants to begin a social revolt and then of repudiating them when their cause appeared doomed, this thesis still persists and perturbs many who are otherwise inclined to recognize the important historical contributions of the German reformer. The reasons for its persistence must be sought chiefly in two powerful intellectual tendencies, the materialist, or positivist, interpretation of history and the revival of Thomistic scholasticism.

Reprinted by special permission from *The Lutheran Church Quarterly*, XIX (1946), 115-132. The extensive documentation which originally appeared with this essay has been omitted.

I

The Marxists, or dialectical materialists, with their emphasis upon the class struggle and the survival of the fittest, cannot understand the strong moral faculties of Martin Luther any more than they can appreciate man's religious and moral struggles in general. As a consequence, they assume that the reformer was motivated by base, selfish, materialist interests and ignore his overwhelming conviction that, since man is justified solely by faith in the Gospel, the preservation of the Gospel is more important than any other consideration—the conviction which alone gives consistency to his whole career. Instead, the late medieval, feudal struggle between the peasants and their lords is interpreted in the light of a modern class struggle and becomes far more significant than the religious movement which only indirectly encouraged the peasants to revolt.

In line with this patent distortion of history, the Marxist historian Karl Kautsky ventures to accuse Luther of riding along "on the tide of popularity, stirring up the expectation of all classes," but, "when it became necessary to decide the question who should appropriate the fruits of church reform, the lower or the higher classes," of coming "to no decision so long as he was not compelled to do so." Instead of helping "the lower classes to derive material benefit from the Reformation," he favored "each step taken by the Princes in this direction." As a consequence, Luther lost the good will of the German people, and Thomas Münzer became "in the eyes of the German working classes . . . the most brilliant embodiment of heretical communism." Not content with accusing Luther of "joining the victorious side after having carried water on both shoulders as long as possible," Kautsky impugns his character as a leader of the German people by stating that "he was not a person who would maintain a position that did not promise success," attributes the direction which the Reformation took to his fear and cowardliness, and explains his role as a reformer by pointing to the unusual "combination of the opportunism and spineless adaptability of the courtier with the natural strength and rudeness of the peasant and with the wild passion of the fanatic."

Georg Adler, in his evaluation of the part which the Peasants' Revolt played in the history of socialism and communism, minimizes the violence of the movement in the areas outside Thuringia and emphasizes the fact that Luther had at first not only seemed to justify revolt as a work pleasing to God, but had provided the masses with such powerful slogans and watchwords as "evangelical freedom," "divine justice," and "universal priesthood."

W. Zimmermann goes much further in laying the responsibility for the uprising on Luther, who, he maintains, "suddenly gave up his position of impartiality" and "turned far to the right," for "his attitude became increasingly despotic, like that of the princes themselves." He ventures to explain this alleged *volte-face* by stating that Luther's vision had become clouded and his emotions aroused; that he was irritated by the fact that his well-meant warning, which he thought would have a miraculous effect, was ignored by the peasants; that "at the head of the popular movement stood Carlstadt, whom he despised because of his position with respect to the Lord's Supper," and "Münzer, of whom he had long been jealous"; and that he had been held responsible by his enemies, particularly by Duke George of Saxony, for the brutalities perpetrated by the peasants at Weinsberg.

Consistently ignoring Luther's basic contention that both peasants and lords were bound by the same moral laws and that neither group had the right to use the Gospel to attain its own ends, Zimmermann charges that

> Without for a moment considering the fact that he had approved most of the Twelve Articles of the peasants, that he had virtually admitted publicly that their cause might be good and just, without realizing that he did not have the complete understanding of a competent, trained jurist, and without considering the fact that the lords at Weinsberg had deserved their punishment for treacherously slaying hundreds of peasants during an armistice, spilling the blood of peasants along the Danube, and making a mockery of all the laws of war and

---

CARLSTADT: German scholar and religious leader. Luther's colleague and defender at Wittenberg, he came to favor a more thoroughgoing break with Roman Catholicism than Luther advocated.

PHILIP MELANCHTHON: A disciple of Luther who drafted the Augsburg Confession (1530), the moderate and conciliatory statement of the position of the Lutherans which was addressed to Charles V. He also played an important part in reorganizing the German school system. After Luther's death, he served as the leader of German Protestantism.

THOMAS MÜNZER: German priest and revolutionist whose religious radical-

of peoples, Luther condemned all the peasants as responsible for the affair at Weinsberg and wrote his bitter pamphlet "Against the Plundering and Murdering Hordes of the Peasantry." Now they were entirely wrong; now they must be attacked, butchered, stabbed, secretly and openly, as one must kill a mad dog.

Luther's subsequent severity in demanding justice instead of mercy for the peasants, Zimmermann avers, was the consequence of the criticism of both friends and foes, for, "as Melanchthon shows, he could stand no opposition," and "as Carlstadt and Münzer said, he hurled himself into the conflict as though he were a second pope."

Finally, Zimmermann states that Luther, because of his fundamental inconsistency in the affair of the peasants, "involved himself in a veritable knot of contradictions and eventually defeated himself and his cause"; that "this dark side of his character, this stormy, reckless, tempestuous tendency, this stiffening of opinion" in the face of opposition, which had made possible "his great work of the Reformation," prevented him from reaching the conclusions suggested in his answer to the Twelve Articles and from discovering the clear implications "of the true point of view." Indulging in wishful thinking with respect to what Luther might have accomplished if he had been a political and social, as well as a religious, reformer, Zimmermann conjures up the following pipe dream:

> If Luther had accepted the consequences of his fundamental principles, if he had remained the leader of the people, . . . if he had exerted a strong influence upon the thousands of undecided people, . . . the Germans would have become a nation, one in faith and with a free constitution; then the religious and political divisions and impotence,

---

ism was matched by his social and economic radicalism. Favoring the extermination of the godless and the dispossession of the landed aristocracy, he played a major role in the Peasant War of 1524-1525. He was executed after the defeat of his supporters.

TWELVE ARTICLES: A statement, drawn up in 1524, of peasant grievances. Although the complaints were mainly social and economic, the tone of the document was distinctly religious. Included were such proposals for reform as the abolition of serfdom, the readjustment of rents, the cessation of enclosure of common lands, the expansion of peasant hunting, fishing, and wood-cutting rights, and the reduction of peasant service obligations.

the want and disgrace of the sixteenth, seventeenth, and eighteenth centuries . . . would have been averted.

The most influential contemporary critics of Luther are Harold Laski and R. H. Tawney, British economic historians who judge Luther's pronouncements upon political, social, and economic matters with an almost total disregard of his primary, religious aims. Laski states that "every concession made by Luther—and he is rarely consistent in his concessions—is a safeguard of the support he needs." Allowing the reader to draw the inference that Luther's sole object was to increase the power of the territorial state, contrary to "the new spirit that was emerging," he argues that "he never hedged about the state with rights which entitled it to deny his religious premises."

Tawney correctly states that Luther and all the early reformers, as well as Catholic leaders, appealed to medieval authorities in questions of social morality and conceived of their society as a church civilization "in which all departments of life, the State and society, education and science, law, commerce and history, were to be regulated in accordance with the law of God." Moreover, he is right in maintaining that "Luther accepted the social hierarchy, with its principles of status and subordination" and was "as fully convinced as any writer that serfdom was the necessary foundation of society." Nevertheless, he wrongly accuses Luther of gross inconsistencies in his attitude toward social problems, stating that his "utterances on social morality are the occasional explosion of a capricious volcano, with only a rare flash of light amid a torrent of smoke and flame, and it is idle to scan them for a coherent and consistent doctrine." Although he recognizes that Luther "drew a sharp antithesis between the external order and the life of the spirit," he proceeds to condemn him for developing "a political theory which exalted the absolutism of secular authorities" without showing that the reason for Luther's support of the princes was consistent with his literal interpretation of biblical, specifically Pauline, references to the authority of rulers in secular matters.

Obviously most historians interested chiefly in political, economic, and social reforms feel that Luther should have opposed the powerful movement toward absolute monarchies in Europe in general, and the growth of the territorial states of the princes in Germany in particular; that this religious reformer, whose training had been con-

fined largely to medieval philosophy and theology, should have understood the complicated legal problems involved in the relations of the
peasants to their lords, should have perceived the economic changes
affecting the society of his day, and should have reflected modern
revolutionary views concerning the proper remedies.

It must be remembered that Luther's attacks upon the evils of
his day and his bold message of evangelical freedom "meant different
things to the several elements of German society," and naturally mean
different things to different elements in our own day. Yet none of his
utterances against prevalent conditions was ever dissociated from the
fundamental purpose of his life and work, that is, to preserve for all
men the Gospel as he had experienced it in his struggle for certainty
concerning salvation. Whether he assailed usury, foreclosure of
mortgages, charging of exorbitant prices, oppression of peasants by
their lords, or extravagance in food and clothing, he was chiefly
motivated by a desire to provide freedom of a purely spiritual kind.
Although he "wished the peasants well," he "seems at times to regard
any direct striving for other things than for the betterment of the
soul as treason to God." That this was his unequivocal position toward
social reform he had already made clear in the year 1520, in his
important tract, *On the Freedom of a Christian*, in which he stated
that "this is the righteous, spiritual, Christian idea of freedom; that
which frees the heart from sins, laws, and edicts; that which overtops
all other kinds of freedom, as heaven does the earth. May God give
us the power to behold and understand it!" To overlook this early
statement concerning Luther's position with respect to "evangelical
freedom," to judge his subsequent actions, specifically his relations
with the peasants, by Marxist standards, and to point to inconsistencies
in matters which were clearly on the periphery of his interests, discloses, on the one hand, a lack of historical objectivity and, on the
other, a desire to utilize history for immediate, materialist ends.

Much of the confusion and misunderstanding concerning Luther's
attitude toward the Peasants' Revolt stems from a misunderstanding of
the nature of the movement itself. The men of the sixteenth century
considered it primarily a political revolution and treated it as such. The
social and economic aspects were considered and emphasized only after
the great mass movements of the American and French revolutions,
after revolutionary thinkers had proclaimed the inalienable rights of
man and the legal equality of all people, regardless of class. And

only after the industrial revolution was well under way did the Marxists point to the peasants of the fifteenth and sixteenth centuries as brethren in a class struggle against their oppressors, while their historians judged Luther almost exclusively according to their own standards of political, economic, and social justice.

The peasants themselves did not evince a strong class consciousness or look upon their movement as a revolt of dispossessed and exploited workers who had "nothing to sell but their labor." On the contrary, as peasants with a late medieval outlook they condemned the infringements upon their feudal rights by the territorial princes who were using every available means, including the introduction of the Roman, as opposed to the customary German, law to increase their political authority, and by the many lesser lords who were imitating the ambitious princes and were in need of increased income in money and services for that purpose. In no substantial respect is the revolt of 1524-1525 to be dissociated from previous peasant uprisings of the Middle Ages, but only in so far as the Lutheran doctrines and slogans were seized upon by the peasants and their leaders to justify their already formulated demands.

For the sake of historical justice, Luther's attitude toward the peasants must be weighed according to the standards of his own day, and not the standards of any modern dialectical system, whereas his specific actions and statements must be judged in the light of his own religious convictions and of Christian ethics. Only when one realizes with what intensity Luther clung to the conviction that the free preaching of the Gospel was the most important consideration, can one understand the reformer; only then can one see the consistency in his attitude toward the peasants.

II

The attack of the Catholic historians upon Luther's role during the Peasants' Revolt rests upon the basic charge that he was a renegade monk and a heretic whose morbidly scrupulous nature was perverted and whose abnormal psychological constitution led him to deny the truth as represented by the dogmas of the Church. Jacques Maritain, the outstanding spokesman of the revival of Thomism, asserts that the basis of Luther's break with the Catholic Church was his "egocentrism: something much deeper, and much more serious, than egoism; a metaphysical egoism," and that the "Reformation unbridled the human self in the spiritual and religious order, as the Renaissance (I mean the hidden spirit of the Renaissance) unbridled the human self in the order of natural and sensible activities."

Luther's doctrine of justification by faith alone and of the certainty of salvation is, according to G. P. Gauss, the outgrowth of his "self-willed positiveness and hypochondriac asceticism," and according to Maritain "but the transference to the human individual and his subjective state of that absolute assurance in the divine promises which was formerly the privilege of the Church and her mission." Maritain further insists that Luther lays the foundation for individualism in religion, as Descartes does in philosophy and Rousseau does in politics, and that individualism is "a blunder; the exaltation of individuality camouflaged as personality, and the corresponding degradation of true personality." Thus Luther "did not free human personality, he led it astray. What he did free was the material individuality . . . , the animal man." The results of this attitude Maritain sees in the reformer's own life for, "as he gets older, his energy becomes less and less a soul's energy, and more and more the energy of a temperament." He is "a man of Will only, characterized by power in action," by "feeling and appetite," by "a profound anti-intellectualism," and according to Hilaire Belloc, "an eloquent man of confused mind but great energy."

One can readily see why Catholic historians accuse Luther of arousing the individualist and materialist interests of all classes, particularly of the peasants, by his vehement attack upon the Church. Many of them admit that the Church was greatly in need of a reformation, that the growing tide of resentment against the hierarchical authority culminating in the papacy was reaching the proportions of a rebellion, and that the "growing rebellion was met by legal method, the use of force, continued and often fearful punishments, but not by that spiritual change which the times demanded." Although not all Catholics follow Janssen in maintaining that the Reformation was directly responsible for the revolt of the peasants, there is a consensus of opinion among them that Luther must carry much of the blame because of his inflammatory utterances, particularly because "he himself summoned his followers to destroy the churches, monasteries, and dioceses of Antichrist. True, he desired this to be done by the authorities, but the peasants felt that they were the authorities." His "doctrines, acting like a leaven on the whole German dough, had raised illusory hopes even among a great part of the peasantry, mercilessly ground under the heels of their lords." They insist that, whereas previous uprisings had occurred in Germany and elsewhere, they had been settled without the destruction and bloodshed of the revolt of 1524-1525, in which the Gospel became a revolutionary program and Luther's utterances became the slogans of the rebellious peasants.

Moreover, Luther is accused of the gravest inconsistencies in his "self-appointed role" of mediator between the peasants and the authorities during the uprising. In the first place, he is upbraided for urging in his *Exhortation to Peace* that the peasants use peaceful means for obtaining some of the ends sought in The Twelve Articles, and for using in the same pamphlet such violent terms against "the oppression and extortion" of the authorities, "on whose neck the sword lies" and whose "presumption will break their necks," that "the desire for revolution could be only strengthened among the masses."

In the second place, Luther is charged with inconsistency in at first showing considerable sympathy with the demands of the peasants and an understanding of their problems, but eventually determining to attach himself to the cause of the princes. Thenceforth he refers to the peasants as "mad dogs" who should be ruthlessly exterminated or at least "compelled to hear the crack of the whip and the whizz of the bullets," for they will not listen to the Word of God.

Janssen maintains, in the third place, that just "as Luther declared his marriage to be a work of the Almighty, so he attributed his pamphlet against the peasants to divine inspiration and stated that God had willed the war so that the peasants "might be brought to see how much too well off they had been and might repent that they had not enjoyed their blessings in peace and contentment."

The Catholic critics of Luther are particularly severe with him for destroying the universal authority of the medieval church and strengthening the hands of the territorial princes. They insist that the entire movement of the Protestant Reformation "was a triumph of the temporal power over the spiritual," for Luther, wishing to escape anarchy, "placed all authority in the hands of the princes." Janssen calls particular attention to the fact that "during the social revolution it was the peasants who had inscribed the word 'Gospel' on their banners and based their claims on the authority of Scripture; now, however, the Gospel was pressed into the service of the governing powers." To substantiate this, he quotes Luther's statement of the year 1526:

Scripture, speaking figuratively, calls rulers drovers, task-masters, and scourges. Like the drivers of donkeys, who must belabour their animals incessantly with rods and whips, or they will not obey, so must the rulers do with the people; they must drive, beat, throttle, hang, burn, behead, and torture, so as to make themselves feared and to keep the people in check. For God is not satisfied with our merely holding up the law before the people; he requires that we should drive them to keep it.

The basic Catholic charge that Luther destroyed the universal authority of the Roman Catholic Church by developing a new theology based upon his personal experience and his doctrine of justification by faith alone cannot be denied. The fundamental difference between Protestant and Catholic is so great that any attempt to unite the two Christian bodies theologically still appears utterly futile. However, the inference that Luther was largely responsible for the political, economic, and social disturbances and bloodshed of the sixteenth century is false, as the Catholic historian Belloc himself recognizes when he states that

the clerical organization, that is, the temporal structure of the Church, was becoming ossified and ceasing to function properly; was raising opposition of every kind; was provoking the anger of those who felt they were not being spiritually fed. . . . In other words, a pile of gunpowder had been accumulating, at any moment a match might be set to the train and an explosion would follow in which the unity of Christendom would be destroyed.

Luther's revolt from Rome would have been inconceivable without the widespread support which he received from people of all classes, including the clergy, not only in Germany, but in Europe as a whole. Moreover, it cannot be denied that the peasants might have revolted without the encouragement of a Lutheran theology, as they had done on previous occasions.

That Luther did not sanction the use of force on the part of the peasants is abundantly clear in his *Exhortation to Peace,* in which he explicitly states that

Since they have mentioned me by name and have asked me to make a frank public statement of my views, I will gladly comply with their wishes so that I shall not be responsible should any grave disturbances follow. . . . Since this is a grave and serious matter which concerns God's kingdom as well as the secular kingdom, both powers will be

destroyed if open revolt spreads. . . . No one has the right to overthrow authority, for Paul says, "let every soul be subject unto the
higher powers."

At the same time Luther shows his fearless attitude toward the princes
when he charges that

> We have no one to thank for all this mischief and revolt than you
> princes and lords, especially you blind bishops and you mad priests and
> monks, who even now with hardened hearts continue to rave and storm
> against the holy Gospel. . . . In secular affairs you consider only your
> splendor and pride until the poor common man can stand it no
> longer. . . . It is not the peasants, my dear lords, who oppose you; it
> is God himself who is punishing you for your madness. . . . The
> government does not exist for the purpose of seeking its own aggrandize-
> ment at the expense of its subjects, but for the purpose of establishing
> the welfare of its subjects.

Moreover, he urges both the princes and the peasants to adjust their
differences amicably, warning them that if they failed to follow his
advice, "all Germany will be utterly destroyed. . . . Although the signs
and wonders of our own day make me solicitous concerning the outcome of these disturbances, I shall still hope for conciliation."

This *Exhortation to Peace* was written toward the end of April,
1525, before the revolt had reached the stage of widespread violence,
while compromises were still being made by various groups of peasants
and their respective lords. As late as April 22nd, Luther published the
Accord of Weingarten, in the introduction of which he recommended
that it be used as a model for future agreements.

By the beginning of May, however, it was apparent to all classes
that compromise was no longer possible. Driven to acts of extreme
violence by fanatical leaders with radical socio-religious programs, the
peasants made increasingly radical demands and supported them by
increasing violence, thereby changing the entire character of the movement and consequently alienating the sympathy of townsmen and
landlords alike. Such a turn of events played into the hands of a number of territorial princes, particularly Philip of Hesse and the members
of the Swabian League, who had from the outset determined to break
the desire of the peasants for greater freedom and thereby to increase
their own power. These factors, and not Luther's alleged inconsistencies,
are responsible for the changed character of the revolt.

When Luther realized that his exhortation was futile, since the revolt had already begun and all the passions of hatred had been aroused,
after he had risked his life in a hopeless attempt to quell the disturbances in Thuringia, and after he had learned that the peasants were
becoming active near Wittenberg, he penned his vehement pamphlet,
Against the Plundering and Murdering Peasant Hordes, urging the
princes to suppress the revolt without mercy. The sins which the peasants had committed against God and man and for which they deserved
severe punishment were, according to Luther, the shameless revolt
against their lords, the wanton plundering of monasteries and castles,
and the use of the Gospel for the purpose of condoning their actions.
Because the revolt was by that time taking a terrific toll of lives and
was causing much destruction, Luther felt called upon to instruct the
princes with respect to their duties:

> Every official who can and wishes to slay and punish these peasants
> without considering the propriety of such a procedure has my sanction,
> provided he will not harm the Gospel. . . . However, the Christian
> government which supports the Gospel must act with discretion, for
> it may be God who has sent the devil to punish us for our sins. . . .
> The prince and lord must realize that he is God's official here on
> earth, that he is the servant of God's wrath, to whom is given the
> sword for punishing such fools. . . . Therefore, dear lords, . . . stab,
> slay, and throttle who can. May God give no good thing to those who
> are not converted. . . . If any one thinks this too severe, let him realize
> what a heinous crime it is to revolt against established authority.

When a number of Luther's own followers, unable to understand
his outburst of wrath and vengeance, protested to him, he answered
them with his *Circular Letter Concerning the Severe Book against the
Peasants,* in which he stated that

> There are two kingdoms, the one God's and the other the world's;
> he who knows how to distinguish between these two will not be angry
> with my pamphlet. God's kingdom is one of grace and mercy, . . . but
> the temporal kingdom, which is nothing else than the servant of God's
> wrath over evil-doers, must not be merciful but stern, severe, and
> wrathful in its office and work.

While he admitted that the lords had gone too far in their vengeance,
he argued that this had nothing to do with his pamphlet, for "if they
misuse their power, that does not indicate that they have learned it

from me." The Gospel, he made clear time and again, "does not concern itself with secular things and pictures this earthly life only as suffering, injustice, the cross, patience, and scorn for temporal goods and life."

Those who charge Luther with using excessively violent language in demanding that the princes suppress the revolt overlook the fact that manners and speech were uniformly coarse and methods of punishment severe in sixteenth-century Europe. The Catholic Ferdinand, brother of Emperor Charles V, commanded the lords to resort to "spearing, flaying, quartering, and every cruel punishment" in suppressing the peasants. Moreover, it must not be overlooked that Münzer, whom Luther feared most as a fanatical communist leader, in exhorting his allies to revolt against established authority in Thuringia, asked them to let their "swords be ever warm with blood." In those cases in which Luther confessed that he had been unusually severe, he explained to his friends that he was not by nature so constituted that he could deal leniently with those whom he considered enemies of the Gospel. As a matter of fact, he believed that all enemies of the Gospel were prompted by the devil in person and could therefore not be overcome by compromise and kind treatment.

With respect to the original demands of the peasants, which were completely ignored during and after the suppression of the revolt, it is clear that Luther was no proponent of Christian or any other kind of socialism. The government, according to him and virtually all his contemporaries, had the right and duty to exterminate revolutionists, while religious dissent was invariably considered a political offense in Europe during the sixteenth century. Luther felt nothing of the urge of the Anabaptists or the Puritans who wished to change political, economic, and social conditions which were not in harmony with their religious views. To him the relation of man's soul was of far more importance than man's relation to the world. If man's soul stood in the proper relation to God, he maintained, his relation to society would right itself. He never considered the kingdom of God as beginning here on earth, as Münzer had taught, but drew a sharp distinction between the here and the hereafter. He would not accept the implications of Augustine's *City of God,* of his conception of a church-state which would rule the people according to the commands of Christ, for this seemed Utopian to him. On the contrary, he consistently limited the application of Christ's Sermon on the Mount to man's private life.

Luther's conception of the state was firmly rooted in the Bible as well as in medieval scholasticism, even though it contained some new features. He accepted the Pauline conception of the state and man's humble position in relation to his political superiors. Mackinnon criticizes Luther for having dethroned an absolute pope and having set up an absolute prince in his place, stating that he "swam with the political current that was bearing the absolute ruler to port in Germany, France, Spain." Yet he himself says that Luther "doubtless acted from a kind of bovine conviction, and not from any desire to gain the favour of the ruling class. . . . He was in principle up to this period opposed to the use of force in behalf of religious or any other reform, and to him religious reform was the thing that mainly mattered."

Luther not only accepted the divine-right theory as supported by the Pauline epistles, but he believed with William of Ockham and other scholastics that the agrarian, feudal division of society into distinct, permanent classes was also of divine origin. The "free Christian," according to him, agreed to submit to an orderly society under the protection of the government. His position in this society was for Luther something divinely ordained, and as a soldier, judge, or hangman the Christian did his duty toward society by punishing crime with severity. This peculiar, conflicting thought process, this careful differentiation between man's duties as a Christian and his duties as a citizen, was characteristically medieval and scholastic.

Always maintaining that there was only one solution to the problem of salvation, Luther proceeded to the conclusion that there was only one truth, only one will of God. Since he was certain that he was appointed by God to preach this will, he insisted that his interpretation was the objective truth. Moreover, his emphasis upon authority at the expense of individual interpretation was also to a large extent influenced by his changing attitude toward the peasants. He lost faith in them when he saw how recklessly they followed leaders like Carlstadt and Münzer and failed to understand and heed his admonitions. They did not make the keen scholastic differentiation between the office and the officeholder, as Luther had done, and they felt that he was inconsistent in not abolishing the secular and ecclesiastical positions filled by scoundrels. The fact that they ignored his suggestions and opposed his methods aroused his fighting spirit, and he saw in them all the hosts of the devils, plotting to destroy the Gospel.

Contemporary historians may regret that Luther was not a "people's leader," that "toward social abuses he was almost completely deaf, dumb, and blind," that "democracy beyond the religious realm remained utterly incomprehensible to him," and that he failed to help the peasants, with whom he had originally sympathized. Nevertheless, if we bear in mind his early bitter struggle for the certainty of salvation and, after he had achieved this certainty, his life-long struggle to preserve the Gospel, we cannot justly accuse him for failing to attach his religious cause to the political and social revolution of the peasants. The fact cannot be denied that he remained consistent in what he considered his divine mission to the end of his life.

Calvin's *Institutes of the Christian Religion*

WILHELM PAUCK

≫≫≫≫≫≫≫≫≫ *Published in 1946* ≪≪≪≪≪≪≪≪≪≪≪

In the rich history of Christian thought, few literary works have exerted so much influence on the religious practices and beliefs of Europeans and Americans as John Calvin's *Institutes of the Christian Religion*. Published first in 1536, it was expanded and modified by Calvin on numerous occasions before his death in 1564. These successive revisions had a simple purpose: they were designed to embody the changes that Calvin's theological ideas—and these were inseparable from his political and social ideas—underwent in the course of his eventful career. Even devout Calvinists, however, are frequently unaware of the significance of the numerous editions of the *Institutes*. It is fortunate, therefore, that the eminent church historian Wilhelm Pauck, now of the Federated Theological Faculty of the University of Chicago, has undertaken to examine the development of Calvin's ideas as mirrored in the successive revisions of the *Institutes*.

O n account of its influence upon many generations of Protestants, Calvin's *Institutes of the Christian Religion* may be regarded as the classical statement of the Protestant Christian faith. It reflects more clearly than any other book produced by the Reformation the thought which inaugurated the whole Protestant movement.

This is all the more remarkable in view of the fact that Calvin was a member of the second generation of the Protestant Reformers. When, in 1536, he appeared on the scene of history as the author of the *Institutes of the Christian Religion,* the Protestant Reformation was firmly

Reprinted by special permission from *Church History*, XV (1946), 17-27; also by permission of the author and publisher from *The Heritage of the Reformation*, copyright 1950 by The Free Press, Glencoe, Illinois. The footnotes which originally appeared with this essay have been omitted.

established not only in Germany and in Switzerland but also in other European countries. In contrast to Luther and others of his contemporaries, Calvin did not have to plow new religious ground. He could rely upon what those who had preceded him had already stated and affirmed. In the light of all this, it is all the more remarkable that, in the course of time, the *Institutes* came to be regarded as *the* theological exposition of Protestantism.

One may say that this book reflects Calvin's total career. It does not represent his entire life work as a writer, for he was the author of numerous volumes of sermons and Biblical commentaries and of essays dealing with theological and ecclesiastical controversy, and particularly of innumerable letters—numbering several thousands—in which he instructed his contemporaries of all European lands in the meaning of the Christian faith as he saw it.

Nevertheless, the *Institutes* reflect Calvin's total work. This is true also in the sense that the book accompanied him throughout his life. It established his fame in 1536; when, in 1559, he produced the last edition, the little book of the beginnings had grown into a volume of large size containing all the theological wisdom that Calvin had gathered in the course of his career.

In order that we may understand this book best, let us consider it in terms of the stages of its growth. The first edition was published in Basle in the early part of 1536. It was conceived as a catechism, i.e., as an introduction to the Christian faith. Yet it was meant to serve also another purpose, namely a political one, for it was dedicated by a letter of introduction and dedication to the King of France, Francis I. The latter, for political reasons, was a staunch defender of Roman Catholicism, resolved to exclude the influence of the Lutheran Reformation from his land. But such prohibition was unsuccessful in view of the fact that during the Reformation age the printing presses had become very quick means of communication all over Europe. Since the beginnings of the Protestant movement, Lutheran influences had thus made themselves felt on French public life.

MARTIN BUCER and WOLFGANG CAPITO: Protestant theologians and religious leaders who were associated with Calvin during the years he spent in Strasbourg, the most important center of Protestantism in Southwest Germany.

One of the first tasks that Calvin, as a spokesman for the Protestant faith, assigned to himself was to justify his religious conviction and to prove to the King and all who were willing to listen that the Protestant faith was not subversive. This is how the *Institutes* came into being.

It is significant that all the editions of the *Institutes* were provided by Calvin himself with the letter of dedication addressed to the French King in 1536:

> I beseech you, Sire,—and surely it is not an unreasonable request,— to take upon yourself the entire cognizance of this cause, which has hitherto been confusedly and carelessly agitated, without any order of law, and with outrageous passion rather than judicial gravity. Think not that I am now meditating my own individual defense, in order to effect a safe return to my native country; for though I feel the affection which every man ought to feel for it, yet, under the existing circumstances, I regret not my removal from it. But I plead the cause of all the Godly, and consequently of Christ himself.
>
> It shall be yours, Sire, not to turn away your ears or thoughts from so just a defense, especially in a cause of such importance as the maintenance of God's glory unimpaired in the world, the preservation of the honor of divine truth, and the continuance of the Kingdom of Christ uninjured among us. This is a cause worthy of your attention, worthy of your cognizance, worthy of your throne. This consideration constitutes true royalty, to acknowledge yourself in the government of your kingdom to be the minister of God. For where the glory of God is not made the end of Government, it is not a legitimate sovereignty but a usurpation.

These statements reflect the true spirit of Calvin. They are especially remarkable in view of the fact that the author of the challenging book that contained them was only twenty-six years old.

The book itself was divided into six chapters. The first three dealt with the "Law," in the form of an explanation of the Decalogue; with "Faith," by way of an interpretation of the Apostles Creed; and with "Prayer," on the basis of an exposition of the Lord's Prayer. Then followed three other chapters, one dealing with the sacraments, namely

---

GUILLAUME FAREL: French Protestant reformer who, in the years before Calvin's arrival in Geneva, played an important part in the movement to convert the French-speaking cantons of Switzerland to Protestantism. Indeed, it was he who convinced Calvin to remain in Geneva.

Baptism and the Lord's Supper, another containing a discussion of the five other Roman Catholic sacraments, the validity of which Calvin denied; and finally there was a chapter on "Christian Liberty," the power of the church and of the political magistrate.

This organization of the earliest edition of the *Institutes* indicates that Calvin was under the influence of the writings of Luther. Indeed, he followed the order of Luther's *Catechism*. The Decalogue, the Apostles Creed, and the Lord's Prayer had been used for centuries as the chief subjects of religious instruction, and depending upon this old tradition, the Reformers, and especially Luther, had used these statements as the means by which to explain the faith which they held.

But it was characteristic of Calvin that going beyond the limits generally set by the writers of catechisms, he dealt extensively also with the church in his interpretation of the Christian faith. What he said about the character of the church and also of the nature of the state he retained unchanged in all the later editions of his book. From the very beginning his mind was so definitely set that he had no need to modify any of the opinions he articulated in his youth.

He showed himself in all respects a true disciple of the early Reformers, especially Luther. The doctrine of justification by faith, according to which no man may trust in his own power to achieve the good but rather must rely upon the mercy of God in order to be enabled to fulfil the moral law, was adopted by Calvin as his major theme. But he added to this interpretation of the Christian faith something very characteristic of his own religious nature: the religious life he taught is one of complete obedience to God. What God's will is is laid down in the law, the law of the Old as well as of the New Testament. That the fulfilment of this law in terms of absolute obedience is the highest good was guaranteed to Calvin by the faith in the merciful God, who in his revelation in Christ shows to anyone who believes that he is not only just but also forgiving.

Throughout his career, Calvin insisted upon this understanding of the nature of the religious faith: unreserved obedience to the law of the divine Lord, who, in Christ, has proved himself trustworthy.

The second edition was issued in 1539, and printed at Strasbourg, where Calvin was then a resident. The first issue of the *Institutes* had established his fame, and when he happened to travel through Geneva in the year 1537, he was recognized as the author of a widely read and representative Protestant book, and his friend and compatriot, Farel, drew him into the service of the Geneva church. This first activity of Calvin in Geneva ended in a fiasco. He did not succeed in persuading the leading citizens of the city of the validity of his conception of Christianity and the principal organization of the church implied therein, and so, in 1539, he resigned his offices and went to settle in Basle, from where he was called to Strasbourg.

He became the minister of a congregation of French Protestant refugees, and, at the same time, a lecturer in the Reformed church of Strasbourg. Of all the German cities, Strasbourg at that time was the most decidedly Protestant. Under the leadership of the two reformers, Bucer and Capito, its whole common life had been transformed according to the principles of the Reformation. The Protestant faith was not only taught in church and school, but it was expressed in organization and discipline.

Calvin, who in Geneva had endeavored to build a city of God in the civil community because he was persuaded that the whole individual and common life of men should be one of obedience to the divine commandments, was profoundly impressed by the accomplishments of the Strasbourgers. He attached himself particularly to Martin Bucer, whom he revered as a father until their friendship was terminated by Bucer's death in 1551.

In the new edition of the *Institutes,* this Strasbourg experience was clearly reflected. The six chapters were extended to seventeen. The parts that were now added were inspired by the studies that Calvin had made in reaction to his own Geneva experience, and in response to the stimuli that he received in Strasbourg.

He had undertaken a new study of Paul's Letters, especially the Epistle to the Romans. Even more definitely than before he had come to the conviction that it was Paul's interpretation of the Christian Gospel which had to be regarded as the central interpretation of Christ to be found in the whole New Testament.

Inspired by this Paulinism, he had turned to a study of the Church fathers, and particularly to Augustine. Thus he had become an accomplished Augustinian, finding in Augustine, however, primarily what agreed with his own Paulinist outlook. From Augustine he directed his attention also to the Greek fathers, especially Chrysostom. Using this knowledge very skillfully, he undertook now to add to the earlier chapters of his *Institutes* certain discussions of what he believed to be the major themes of the Christian faith.

He still talked primarily of the law and of the faith and of prayer and of the sacraments and the church, but the work assumed an entirely new character. These are the chapter headings:

The Knowledge of God; The Knowledge of Man and of Free Will; The Law; Faith; Penitence; Justification by Faith and the Merit of Works; On the Similarity and Difference Between the Old and the New Testaments; On Divine Predestination; On Providence; On Prayer; On the Sacraments; On Baptism; On the Lord's Supper; On Christian Liberty; On the Power of the Church; On the Five False Sacraments; and finally, On the Life of the Christian Man.

Inspired by Paul and by Augustine, Calvin had added to his earlier exposition interpretations of those themes of faith which in the mind of the Reformers were the most decisive and characteristic ones.

He began his exposition with chapters on the knowledge of God and the knowledge of man. This was in accord with the deepest explanations of the religious life as they can be found in the literature of all ages, for religion is always a relation between God and man, a response of man to the action of God made known through a Revealer. The interpretations of this commitment of man to God have always been, generally speaking, of two kinds. One either tried to explain how the soul could rise to God—then the religious life was seen as an interpretation of human existence in so far as it is governed by its own deepest levels. Or one attempted to show that the knowledge of God is the pre-supposition of the best self-knowledge at which man can arrive—then religion was seen as the service of God. The first way of speaking of religion is characteristic especially of the mystics; the second way may be called that of the prophets. The mystics begin with human experience and then cause their mind to be elevated in the search for the vision of God, but the prophetic way of speaking of religion is one in which human existence, and particularly human self-knowledge, is understood in the light of the divine self-disclosure. When religion is thus interpreted, God-knowledge becomes the basis of self-knowledge.

It was highly indicative of Calvin's bent of mind that he chose this second way of interpreting religion. The knowledge of God, he insisted, must be firmly established before one can comprehend the meaning of the divine will for human life. That is why he began this second edition of the *Institutes* with a chapter on the knowledge of God, and for the same reason he ended it with a chapter on the life of the Chris-

tian man. In order to give an impression of the flavor of this second
edition, one can do nothing better than to cite two sections from the
chapter on the Christian life. This chapter, entitled "The Life of a
Christian," has been overlooked by many of the interpreters of Calvin's
ethics. If it were read more often, many of the common misinterpretations of Calvin's ethics would not occur. Calvin wrote:

> Although the divine law contains a most excellent and well arranged
> plan for the regulation of life, yet it has pleased the Heavenly Father
> to conform men by a more accurate doctrine to the rule which he had
> prescribed in the law, and the principle of that doctrine is this: That
> it is the duty of believers to present their bodies a living sacrifice,
> wholly acceptable unto God, and that in this consists the legitimate
> worship of Him. Hence is deduced an argument for exhorting them:
> "be not conformed to this world; but be ye transformed by the renew-
> ing of your mind, that ye may prove what is that will of God."
>
> This is a very important consideration that we are consecrated and
> dedicated to God that we may not hereafter think, speak, meditate, or do
> anything but with a view to his glory, for that which is sacred cannot
> without great injustice toward Him be applied to unholy uses. If we
> are not our own but the Lord's, it is manifest both what error we must
> avoid and to what end all the actions of our lives are to be dedicated.
> We are not our own. Therefore, neither our reason nor our will should
> predominate in our deliberations and actions. We are not our own.
> Therefore, let us not propose it as our end to seek what may be ex-
> pedient for us according to the flesh. We are not our own. Therefore,
> let us as far as possible forget ourselves and all things that are ours.
>
> On the contrary, we are God's. To Him, therefore, let us live and
> die. We are God's. Therefore, let His wisdom and will preside in all
> our actions. We are God's. Toward Him, therefore, as our only
> legitimate end let every part of our lives be directed. Oh, how great a
> proficiency has that man made who having been taught that he is not
> his own, has taken the sovereignty and government of himself from
> his own reason to surrender it to God.

One may say that this passage can serve as a motto for the entire interpretation of the Christian faith that Calvin offers in his *Institutes*.
In the light of these words expressing the theme, "We are not our own,
but we are God's," one can also appreciate why Calvin felt compelled
to attribute so much significance to the two doctrines of predestination
and of providence, doctrines which have been regarded by many as the
central themes of Calvinist Christianity.

Calvin was naturally led to emphasize predestination and providence because he could not but be consistent with himself. He felt it necessary to say that because in all respects man depends upon God, so that he is always God's and never his own, he must let the divine will govern the sovereignty of his reason. He was further driven to say that the divine sovereignty is so absolute that every single aspect of human existence, and also the ultimate end of human life, must be viewed in the light of this divine initiative. In the doctrine of providence Calvin taught, therefore, that a believer must learn to be assured that nothing at all happens in the world without the express will of God. Not being afraid to say too much rather than too little, Calvin chose to be so specific in the explication of this doctrine that he declared that not a single hair falls from the head of a man without the express will of God and that no drop of rain falls from skies without the direct volition of the divine Father. But when he spoke in this way he did not mean to be understood as a determinist, much less as a fatalist. He wished merely to interpret the Christian faith as an absolute confidence in the omnipotent Creator who is the Father. When, therefore, he dealt with the question, to what extent the doctrine of providence is applicable to the daily events of life, he said that one who believes in the all-ordering divine providence does not need to be anxious or filled with dread. He may always be sure that nothing at all can befall him that is not provided for his benefit by the omnipotent will of God who is good.

It is this same spirit that led him to speak so affirmatively concerning predestination.

He warns again and again throughout the *Institutes* and in all its editions of the danger (to which all men are so easily prone) of speculating concerning the divine nature. Just as Luther he was persuaded that religion has nothing whatsoever to do with speculation. It is nothing but an answer to what God has done in his revelation.

In this light, one must see predestination: just as man lives by the gratuitously given grace of God, over which he has no control whatsoever and which he must receive in faith, so he must understand his ultimate destiny as being in all respects dependent upon the will of God. Predestination, therefore, was for Calvin merely an appendix to the doctrine of justification by grace. Calvin, so one may say, was a predestinarian because he believed absolutely in the initiative of the God of mercy. If a man cannot rely upon himself for his salvation but must throw himself upon God's merciful goodness, then he must also be willing to acknowledge that in all respects he is God's and not his own—particularly with regard to his eternal destiny.

Calvin was so consistent in making these explications that he also drew the negative conclusion which makes it appear as if he had been speculative, after all. In other words, as a predestinarian, he spoke as one who believed in rejection as well as in election; yet, when he thus stressed two-fold predestination, he did not mean to yield to the temptation of one who thought speculatively about the divine will, as if he were able to say what was hidden in it. Rather, as a teacher of double predestination he desired to be understood as one who explained what he believed to be actual occurrences. Throughout his career, he had tried to teach men obedience to God. He became most concretely impressed by the fact that some men were utterly incapable, as it seemed, of such obedience. No services of the spokesmen of the divine word could persuade them to yield in their disobedience. So, in the light of the fact that some show a strange propensity for religion while others seem to be excluded from the possibility of opening themselves to it, Calvin believed that it was possible for a theological interpreter of the religious faith to say that some were elected by the saving will of God and others were not.

All these convictions which are characteristic of Calvin's entire work were for the first time most clearly expressed in the second edition of the *Institutes* of 1539.

In 1543, there appeared a third edition. It was again enlarged, although all that the former issues had contained was preserved. In the meantime, Calvin had returned to Geneva. He had arrived there in September, 1541. He had made it the condition of his acceptance of the call of the citizens of Geneva to be their chief minister of the word of God, that they should order the church life of their city according to the "Ecclesiastical Ordinances." Therein Calvin had laid down the principles of that church organization which, throughout the centuries, has proved effective in all Calvinist church groups.

He was interested to establish a church that should be free as far as possible from interference of the state or the political magistrate. He wanted to see the church organized according to what he believed to be the will of God. He knew the will of God, as has already been suggested, through the law. The law was given to him in the Bible, in the Old as well as in the New Testament. The New Testament, according to his conviction, merely clarified all that was enunciated in the Old

Testament, particularly in the passages dealing with the moral law. Therefore, Calvin believed that a church organized according to the will of God had to conform to principles of polity that were derived from Scripture; and he interpreted the ecclesiological chapters of the New Testament, Romans 12 and I Cor. 12, in such a way that he saw therein prescribed four church offices, namely, those of the pastors, the elders, the teachers, and the deacons. No church, he was persuaded, conformed to the law of God unless it was established in these four offices, the purpose of all of which was to be the proclamation and the expression in deeds of the word of God.

According to these principles, he built the church of Geneva, and in this concern he consumed his strength. When, in 1543, it was necessary to bring out a new edition of the *Institutes,* he added to the earlier chapters on the church certain sections in which he made plain his own convictions as to the character of church polity. Furthermore, he took occasion to reject more forcefully than he had done before, the Catholic church order which he believed was contrary to the word of God.

In the form of this third edition the book was issued repeatedly, but more or less unchanged, in 1545, 1550, and 1554.

When the year 1558 came around, Calvin was forty-nine years of age. He believed that the end of his life was near. He suffered with many illnesses. Throughout his career he had been ailing with severe indigestion. In 1558, he suffered not merely of this stomach ailment and of gout, but also of the quartan fever. He was unable to attend to his regular duties and was confined to his house; but, as was characteristic of him, he used this leisure, as he called his sickness, to revise his major book, the *Institutes.* Working on his sick bed, he rearranged the material of all the former editions. He made corrections as he felt the need. He added to what he had written before, particularly that wisdom which had come to him as a Biblical exegete.

The *Institutes* of the first edition of 1536 had been conceived by him as a catechism. In 1539, he had stated that he wished that the book should be used by the students of theology as an elementary text which might help them to understand the major themes of Christian thought. In 1559, when he was able to print the completely revised edition which was to remain the final one of his work, he said that he desired the book to be understood as a statement of Biblical theology. As such he wished it to be used as a basis for the work of interpretation, particularly in exegesis of the Biblical books. The additions he made in this last edition were therefore primarily taken from the Bible.

He believed that as a Protestant thinker he should prove to the world that the only source of his faith was the Bible and nothing else. On this basis he argued against those who fundamentally disagreed with him: turning to the right, he endeavored to refute the Roman Catholics who unjustly, he believed, added to the authority of the Bible that of the tradition; and turning to the left, he criticized just as vehemently the "radicals" of the Reformation, the Anabaptists, who believed it possible to order their lives primarily on the basis of a direct inspiration from God and only secondarily on the basis of the Bible.

The book was now organized in what he called four "books." The first book (in eighteen chapters) dealt with the knowledge of God, the Creator; the second book (in seventeen chapters) treated "the knowledge of God the Redeemer in Christ, which was revealed first to the Fathers under the law and since to us in the Gospel"; the third book (of twenty-five chapters) was entitled "On the Manner of receiving the grace of Christ, the benefits which we receive from it and the effects which follow from it"; and the final book (of twenty chapters) was devoted to a discussion of "the external means or aids by which God calls us into communion with Christ and retains us in it."

All in all, the work now contained eighty-one chapters. In 1536, it consisted of merely six. Now, the fullness of the Calvinistic faith was disclosed. No major theme that was of significance in the Reformation was omitted. One cannot say that the argument of the work was one of continuity. Calvin presents himself as a writer who was able to deal with many diverse subjects. Yet, in spite of the fact that these subjects do not appear to hang together, they are written about by a man who had a clearly delineated intellectual and spiritual character. The interpreters of Calvin's *Institutes* have tried to describe and analyze this character. Some have said that Calvin was primarily oriented to the sovereignty of God; others have attempted to show that the doctrine of predestination was the hinge on which all his arguments turned. Still others believe that providence should be emphasized centrally; and still another group has endeavored to show that Calvin was but a true disciple of the Reformation and that "justification by faith" was his one great theme, articulated in various ways.

I believe that the truest way to describe Calvin's manner of writing and of arguing is to see him as a Biblical theologian. To be sure, he read the Bible in the light of the doctrine of justification by faith and in terms of the absolute lordship of God, but he left room in all he wrote for the great variety of religion that is embodied in the Biblical books, believing that as the revelation of God the Bible was a spiritual unity. Accordingly, one will understand him best as a Biblical theologian.

He did not care to speculate on divine themes or to write as a philosopher. He wished nothing more than to be obedient to what he was persuaded was the voice of God directly made audible in the words of the Bible. Indeed, if one desires to gauge the manner in which the Bible as a whole formed the thought world of a great Christian thinker, one can, I believe, do nothing better than to study Calvin's *Institutes*.

The Reformation at Home and Abroad

H. MAYNARD SMITH

꘏꘏꘏꘏꘏꘏꘏꘏꘏꘏ *Published in 1940* ꘏꘏꘏꘏꘏꘏꘏꘏꘏꘏

It is difficult to find dispassionate discussions of the religious changes that took place in sixteenth-century England. Battles over the religious policies of Henry VIII, Mary, and Elizabeth continue to rage—a fact that emerges clearly from the recent literature of English church history. There are still writers who delight to dwell on the brutality of Henry VIII, the bloodiness of Mary, and the religious opportunism and intolerance of Elizabeth. There are still writers who go out of their way to pass moral judgments on the behavior of the Tudors—judgments that do not take account of the standdards of behavior which people of the sixteenth century accepted. In short, relatively few writers have combined learning and fair-mindedness in their treatment of the religious history of Tudor England. One of the small number who falls into this category is the late H. Maynard Smith, Canon of Gloucester and author of two volumes that are well on the way to becoming standard works: *Pre-Reformation England* (1938) and *Henry VIII and the Reformation* (1948). In the present essay, Dr. Smith attempts to place the religious history of Tudor England in its historical setting. Inevitably, there are points in the essay which Roman Catholics, Lutherans, and Calvinists would dispute. Even some of the author's fellow-Anglicans would question some of his statements. This, however, should not discourage the reader. What matters is that Dr. Smith has generally viewed it as his function to understand the past, not to praise or condemn it.

The Reformation in England followed a different course to the Reformation on the Continent. There it started with a theology but here with a political issue. It began with the King's quarrel with the Pope, in which both were to blame; and the quarrel gave an opportunity for the wicked to despoil, which was exploited to the utmost. Then Reformation doctrines were imported from abroad to justify the spoliation. Some sincerely religious men adopted these doctrines; and they were promoted to episcopal thrones or burnt at the stake as political expediency required. The changes were sudden and violent, but the Church managed to maintain its Catholic creed, its Apostolic Orders and the due administration of the Sacraments.

Luther's teaching about grace had led to loose living; Calvin, with his sense of discipline, had established a Draconian code; England was content with the Ten Commandments, making due allowance for cakes and ale.

Luther had condemned Rome as the Babylon of the Apocalypse; Calvin, having decided that the mediaeval Church was apostate, proceeded to found another, equally autocratic, on a few texts of the New Testament interpreted by himself; Henry VIII was content to decree that the Bishop of Rome hath no authority in this realm of England; and then to seek "in sundry old and authentic histories" for proof that his decree was in accordance with antiquity.

That the proofs he offered are not very convincing does not concern us here; except in so far as they shew that Henry, who was a tradi-

Reprinted by special permission from *The Church Quarterly Review*, CXXX (1940), 278-289.

THOMAS CRANMER: A leading figure in the English Reformation. He championed the royal headship of the church, married Henry VIII to Anne Boleyn, and sponsored the translation of the Bible into English. His most important achievement was the Book of Common Prayer. He suffered martyrdom during the reign of Mary.

ERASTIANISM: Doctrine associated with the name of the sixteenth-century

tionalist, relied on precedents and had no intention of founding a new Church. Proud as he was of being Defender of the Faith, he had no intention of departing from Orthodoxy; and proud as he was of being Supreme Head of the Church, he had every intention that that Church should be worthy of his majesty.

At the beginning of his anti-papal legislation it was declared that:

> "Our said sovereign the King, and all his devout subjects, as well spiritual and temporal, be as obedient, devout, catholic and humble children of God and Holy Church as any people be within any realm christened."

At a later date he declared that there was no intention "to decline and vary from the congregation of Christ's Church in anything concerning the very articles of the Catholic faith of Christendom," and that in the ordinances which he promulgated he was always "ensuing the old ancient customs of the realm." And here, in justice to him, it may be added, that when no selfish interests inspired him, his reforms were often good.

But Henry's creed was very much better than his conduct. When he wanted money and his new aristocracy wanted land, he could not resist the temptation to plunder the Church; when he was afraid of the Emperor and wanted an alliance with the Protestant princes of Germany, he allowed of conferences with Lutheran divines; and when he had freed his clergy from the tyranny of the Pope, he browbeat Convocation and the bishops, so that their last state was worse than their first.

Henry VIII was a dominant personality and made changes from which we benefit and for which we suffer. The Church suffered many things, but she survived him. Other nations of Europe have from time to time been oppressed by kings determined to use the Church for

Swiss theologian Thomas Erastus. In its vulgarized form it came to mean the supremacy of the state in the regulation of ecclesiastical affairs.

RICHARD HOOKER: Elizabethan clergyman, scholar, and controversialist. His *Of the Laws of Ecclesiastical Polity* was the leading scholarly defense of Anglicanism as embodied in the Thirty-nine Articles and the Elizabethan religious settlement in general. He wrote his treatise in order to answer Puritan criticisms of the Elizabethan church and "to satisfy all tender consciences."

their own purposes; but the Church has survived them. Granting that Henry VIII was a bad man, it is equally true that Alexander VI was a bad Pope; but we do not condemn the Roman Church because of Alexander VI, and we should not condemn the Church of England because of Henry VIII.

He broke with Rome because he failed to obtain his divorce, and was tired of the duplicity and shuffling of Clement VII. The divorce was most unpopular in England; but the people, who hated the divorce, were only too glad, for any reason, to repudiate the Pope. They had never heard any good of him; they were not conscious that they had received any good from him; he was a foreigner: and it was believed that he drained the country of gold to spend it on forbidden pleasures.

As soon as Edward VI began to reign, the Church began to move at first slowly but quite definitely in a Protestant direction. This was due to Somerset who was a Protestant but not in a hurry. The pace was quickened through the rapidity with which Cranmer absorbed the very latest doctrines, and through the support which he received from the gangsters, who succeeded Somerset in power and understood the opportunities which a reformation offered for plunder. They were not truly converted to the new opinions. Northumberland, the chief of them, when he was brought to the scaffold, declared that he died in the old religion. The efficient Secretary of State, Sir William Cecil, was an Erastian—his religion was that of his prince; and he served faithfully Somerset, Northumberland, Mary and Elizabeth. During Mary's reign he conformed; but we need not believe Parsons who says that "he laboured a pair of great beads which he continually carried," for if he was adaptable, he was much too clever to overplay his part.

Sir Richard Rich had first become prominent by perjuring himself to ensure the condemnation of Sir Thomas More. Later in an excess of Catholic zeal, when Protestantism was out of favour, he had racked Ann Askew with his own hands. Under Edward VI he saw the Gospel light and became foremost among the lay reformers. Under Mary he founded Felstead School so that boys might be brought up in the Catholic faith, and when Elizabeth succeeded he altered its constitution, and took away the Popish ornaments with which he had endowed it.

During the last two years of Edward VI the Church of England was as Protestant as it could be made by passing Acts and issuing

Ordinances; and these two years have come to be regarded both by Roman and Protestant controversialists as determining the character of the reformed Church of England. This is absurd. During those two years the Church of England was theologically dominated by foreign refugees who had escaped to England after the victory of Charles V at Muhlberg. A Lasko was resident at Lambeth, Bucer was professor at Cambridge with Fagius to assist him. Peter Martyr was professor at Oxford, while Ochino and others were at work here. They were all admonished and directed by Bullinger from Zurich and by Calvin from Geneva. They no doubt made many converts, but their theology had no roots in the English soil. They were welcomed and provided for by the reforming party in England; but that party, though supreme for the moment, did not represent England or her Church. Tunstall and Gardiner, imprisoned in the Tower, were still bishops of the Church of England, and represented a far larger proportion of the population than Cranmer and Ridley.

Reformed doctrines made great progress in the Eastern Counties, and were prevalent in London and other cities, and the irreligious—they are always in the world—were glad of the license that the Reformation afforded them to blaspheme and indulge in ribaldry. But the majority of the people—and the majority lived in villages—were untouched.

The accession of Mary was hailed with relief. The ornaments, when not sufficiently valuable to have been stolen, were replaced in the churches, and the old services were revived. Few except Mary and Pole were anxious on religious grounds to be reconciled with the Pope, though Gardiner and Tunstall had been converted to the belief that for the freedom of the Church it was necessary to have a head outside the realm. Paul IV was most accommodating. He made no demand for the restitution of Church property, and he accepted the deans and chapters who had succeeded the monks in what had been monastic cathedrals. Mary had nothing to fear from men like the Duke of Suffolk, and not much to fear from the scurrilous tracts written by Scory and Knox, which were printed at Emden and sent to England by an organised band of messengers for distribution in the streets of London. The Spanish match cost Mary her popularity, for Englishmen were terribly afraid lest this land should become yet another dominion of the Habsburgs. The persecutions and burnings alienated the country from Rome, for the flames lighted candles which are not yet extinct. The burning of Thomas Cranmer has done as much to ensure the perpetuity of a reformed Church, as the murder of Thomas Becket ensured the supremacy of the Pope and the privileges of the clerical caste.

Elizabeth on succeeding to the throne found herself in a position of great complexity. A Pope had pronounced her a bastard, and as such she had no right to the crown; but, luckily for her, the other claimant was Mary, Queen of Scots, who had just married the Dauphin, and Philip of Spain could not allow England to become an appanage of France. Elizabeth finessed with him on the subject of religion, and was much embarrassed by the exiles returning from Emden, Frankfurt, Geneva and Zurich. She promoted a few of them, but she was steadfastly purposed that she would not substitute a Pope at Geneva for the Pope at Rome. Pole died, happily for her and for himself, so that the See of Canterbury was vacant without any trouble; and she found the right man in Matthew Parker to succeed him. Parker's Protestant sympathies were real, but he was no fanatic. He was, moreover, a keen historian and collected ancient chronicles and statutes to prove the continuity of the English Church, the usurpations of Rome, and the many previous disagreements between England and the Papacy. Jewel followed with his *Apology for the Church of England*, appealing to the Oecumenical councils, the Fathers and the practice of the first six centuries. His contention was that the Church was true to the religion received in 597 from St. Augustine. Both writers had far too static a view of the nature of the Church; but they shared this with their adversaries. The Church of England has never admitted that she is a new body. She has always been ready to vindicate her continuity with the Church of the Middle Ages.

This is not to deny that the Church had passed through a period of confusion and disorder such as it had not experienced since the Danish invasion, and, to go further back, the work of Parker was even harder than that of Theodore in reconciling and disciplining clergy with very different traditions and outlook. There were elderly men who had been ordained before the divorce, there were quondam monks who had been given livings to save their pensions; there were ignorant men who had been thrust into Orders that they might fill vacancies—and how ignorant they were may be learnt from Latimer and Hooper—there were men returned from the Continent full of zeal for Protestant principles; and men who had been ordained in the reign of Mary because they detested them. Few men of university standing had been willing to take Orders when the future was so uncertain; and we read of squires who sent servants, almost illiterate, to the bishops for ordination in order that their parish churches might be served. It says much for the tact of Parker that without much assistance from the Queen he welded the body together. It says much for the administrative ability of Whitgift and Bancroft that the Church was restored to order. It says much for the universities that when Elizabeth died there was a clergy who were more learned and more respectable than any in Europe. It is evident that in this formative period the clergy did not think alike and did not teach alike, but they tended to draw closer together through using the same Prayer Book. Their way had been made easier by the studied ambiguity of some of the new formularies, and because both the Government and the bishops, wherever possible, had very blind eyes.

How were the laity reconciled to the new services and the change in ceremonial? This was the easier because after the rapid and disturbing changes, the most devout people in Europe had become first confused and then indifferent to religion. This indifference is reflected in Elizabethan literature. Continental Protestantism made headway in the towns, because ministers who believed in the supreme importance of preaching liked to have big congregations. In the country, rich squires, Catholic at heart, found it more convenient to attend church than to pay fines, and their children who had never known the old order frequently became stout Churchmen. The children of the poor had no religious instruction, except that they received from their mothers, or in the parish churches which they were bound to attend. The traditions derived from mothers accounts for the many mediaeval survivals found in country districts. The zealous Calvinist who accepted a country living soon found how impossible it was to interest his flock in the truth of supra-lapsarianism, and took to preaching a simpler gospel. The Calvinist who was tempted into accepting a mitre, found that the cap fitted him; it also steadied him—he might remain a Calvinist in theology, but had no longer any patience with Marprelate tracts denouncing prelacy. When Elizabeth died the third generation was growing up and the Anglican settlement was settling down. It was even helped in doing so by the irreconcilable minorities of Papists and Puritans, ready to suffer for the maintenance of their faith, for they helped the Church to think out her position and we have as a consequence Dean Field on *The Church* and Hooker's *Ecclesiastical Polity*.

One sentiment indeed did unite all parties in the Church, and that was a hatred of the Pope. This was due to the excommunication of Elizabeth by Pius V, the assassination plots, the Armada and Gunpowder Treason. It was also due to the Massacre of St. Bartholomew's Day, the assassination of William of Orange and Henri Quatre, and to the stories in circulation about the Spanish Inquisition. I am not here concerned with examining all the facts or the papal responsibility for them. They were assumed by Englishmen as facts at the beginning of the XVII century, and the Pope was hated accordingly. The hatred was inspired by fear. The average Englishman thought of the Pope as always plotting against his life and liberties; he believed that every disaster that occurred abroad was contrived by the Pope, that all disorder at home was fomented by the Pope, and that anyone he particularly disliked was an emissary of the Pope—a Jesuit in disguise. In fact the Pope became a bogey-man of the first magnitude; but the fear and hatred he inspired were due to political facts and fictions, and had no religious origin.

Too conservative to unite with any foreign Protestant body, and too anti-papal to be reunited with Rome, the Church of England became isolated in Christendom, a national Church with an ethos of her own.

It is sometimes maintained that a national Church can have no claim to be called Catholic; but what then is the *Sancta Romana Ecclesia*? For four centuries no one not an Italian has been Pope and the papal curia has been dominated by Italians, while the policy of the Church has been usually dictated by Italian interests. The Roman Church is a national Church, and it is none the less national, because it controls many subject races. It is better to maintain that anyone who professes the Catholic faith has a right to call himself a Catholic, and that any Church which professes that faith is *a* Catholic Church; but that *the* Catholic Church will only be manifest when the scattered flock of the One Shepherd are gathered into one fold.

In many ways by 1600 the spirit of the Church of England was more in harmony with the Catholic Reformers, Colet, Erasmus and More,—than with the Protestant Reformers, Cranmer, Ridley and Hooper, though she owed much to all of them. Many superstitions had been denounced and some abuses had been remedied, and both sets of Reformers would have approved; but the Catholic Reformers would not have approved of the way in which the work had been done. The Church had suffered a rough spring-cleaning, by zealous but rude hands; and it is not surprising that some delicate things had been broken and some beautiful things had been lost. In compensation, the Protestant Reformers had bestowed the inestimable gifts of the English Bible and the English Prayer Book which have done so much to form all that is best in the English character. The Reformers, Catholic and Protestant alike, were responsible for insisting on the need for enquiry and the rights of reverent criticism. They alike thought of the Church as the Body of Christ in which all the baptised were members; and repudiated the idea of Holy Church as a clerical caste dominating a laity whose duty it was to believe what they were told and pay for being told it.

The real distinction between the earlier and later reformers was the attitude that they adopted towards the world. The earlier group believed that the world belonged to God, and that religion should interpenetrate and sanctify the whole of life—its art, science and literature; its business, amusements and its social order. The later group saw a world lying in wickedness which a Christian ought to renounce. They were afraid of life and multiplied inhibitions, touch not, taste not, handle not. The external world was a snare to them, and external ceremonies were a hindrance and not an aid on the way to God. The first group worked for the redemption of the world, the second group to save souls out of the world. There is no doubt that during the last four centuries the Church of England has on the whole followed the more humane tradition; but there has always been within her, as there has been in the Church of Rome, a strong puritan minority. For this we may be grateful, for the Christian humanist, however admirable his ideal, is always in danger of being contented with comfort and respectability. He needs to be reminded that if he sets out to do God's will on earth, he must do it as it is done in heaven. In consequence, if the Church of England owes most to the spirit which inspired the Catholic reformers, it owes also a great debt of gratitude to the reformers who succeeded them; and the Church is really all the more Catholic because it embraces the teaching of both parties. She need not be ashamed of calling herself Catholic and Reformed.

VI

When we consider how complex were the causes that resulted in
the Elizabethan settlement, it is not surprising that foreigners and
outsiders find it hard to understand what the Church really stands
for. Many critics say that anything may be believed or denied in the
Church of England, that it is composed of irreconcilable parties who
are only kept together by the endowments of the Establishment.
Nothing could be more false, for the Anglican Communion has
spread and flourishes in many lands where there are no endowments
and no Establishment. It would be more true to say that she is a body
so confident in her own identity and her continuous existence that
she is not afraid to challenge free enquiry and can welcome criticism;
while she is far too strong to be much disturbed by the eccentricities
of some people who still claim to belong to her.

In the reign of Henry VII Trevisan had reported to the Venetian
Signory on the religion of Englishmen—

> "They do not omit any form incumbent on good Christians; there
> are however many who have various opinions concerning religion."

That is the key to understanding the problem. The Englishman is
in many ways a conservative. He reverences tradition, is careful in
performing his duties, dislikes change, but is resolved to think as he
likes. In the days of the Tudors he acquiesced when traitors were
disembowelled alive, for nothing could be too bad for those who disturbed the order of the realm; but he resented the burning of heretics,
for he believed in the inalienable right of the Englishman to speak
his mind. In later days the Church persecuted Separatists and Nonconformists because they disturbed the order of the realm, but hardly
ever persecuted a man for his opinions. Heresy hunting has never been
a popular amusement in England.

The Church has shown her conservatism by decreeing that the
Apostolic Creeds should be recited in all her churches every day,
that the Dominical sacraments should be duly ministered, that the
ancient feasts and fasts of the Church should be observed, and that
ancient customs and ceremonies, when not superstitious, should be
retained. She defines her position in the XXX canon of 1604:—

> The abuse of a thing doth not take away the lawful use of it, Nay,
> so far was it from the purpose of the Church of England to forsake

and reject the Churches of Italy, France, Spain, Germany, or any such like Churches, in all things that they held and practised, that as the Apology of the Church of England confesseth, it doth with reverence retain those ceremonies, which doth neither endamage the Church of God, nor offend the minds of sober men; and only departed from them in those particular points, wherein they were fallen both from themselves, and from the Apostolical Churches which were their first founders.

On the administrative side there was very little change. The Ecclesiastical Courts continued to sit, and the Canon Law was still valid, not because it had issued from the Pope, but because it was the customary law of England. Chancellors still presided—some of them held their office under Henry VIII, Edward VI, Mary and Elizabeth—issuing the old forms in the old terms and gathering in the accustomed fees. There was still—not counting archdeacons, rural deans, and churchwardens—an army of apparitors and questmen to look after the morals of the people. There were still people put to public penance, and men were still liable to excommunication which had secular consequences; for instance, the will of a man dying excommunicate could not be proved. The Church still concerned itself with the probate of wills; issued marriage licences and heard matrimonial cases. The Archbishops still issued dispensations from fasting.

In the course of four centuries some of these activities have ceased or been transferred to the State; but the Church remains a very conservative body; and, like the State, having no written constitution, it is hard to define. But whatever the change in thoughts and circumstances, few things are more difficult than to alter any canon, article of religion or formulary of the Church of England. She stands in the old ways.

At the same time she inherits the tradition of Colet and Erasmus and has never been afraid of free enquiry and has always claimed to be the Church of sound learning. She has never hampered her scholars or been unduly disturbed at the sometimes unexpected results of their researches. She has favoured free discussion and she has been justified, for the controversies that have taken place within her Communion have ended in the confirmation of orthodoxy. Every educated man to-day knows something of Richard Hooker, but who now reads Cartwright or Travers? Butler's *Analogy* is a classic, but few even know the names of the Deists he confuted.

It is probably true that there is hardly any heresy that has not been advocated by some member of the Church of England, and the most orthodox of her divines have sometimes cherished a private opinion not in accord with her formularies. This is the controversialist's opportunity. He claims to describe the nature of the Church of England by quoting the indiscreet *obiter dicta* of her members. He might as well claim to describe the British Constitution by collecting the silly utterances of some members of Parliament. There are certainly perils in permitting freedom of speech, but heretical opinions are generally very fugitive, they have their day and pass. The Church remains a witness to the Faith—the pillar and ground of the Truth. A Church is strong which can suppress those who deviate from her standards; a Church is still stronger which can afford to tolerate them, confident that in the end Truth will prevail.

Survival of the Catholic Faith in the Sixteenth Century

HENRY S. LUCAS

➤➤➤-➤➤➤-➤➤➤-➤➤➤-➤➤➤-➤➤➤-➤➤➤-➤➤➤-➤➤➤ *Published in 1943* ◀◀◀-◀◀◀-◀◀◀-◀◀◀-◀◀◀-◀◀◀-◀◀◀-◀◀◀-◀◀◀

In the sixteenth century the Roman Catholic Church suffered assaults from one Protestant group after another. It is important, however, not to exaggerate the numerical significance of the defection of Lutherans, Zwinglians, Anglicans, and Calvinists. Indeed, at the end of the sixteenth century, Roman Catholicism had far more adherents in Europe—not to mention the New World—than all the Protestant faiths combined. Historians, in explaining the success of the Catholic, or Counter, Reformation, have usually followed a standardized procedure. They have attributed a vast influence to the activities of St. Ignatius Loyola and the Society of Jesus, to the reform measures of the Council of Trent, and to the operations of the Inquisition and of the Congregation of the Index. Henry S. Lucas, however, one of the most prominent Roman Catholics in the ranks of present-day American historians and the author of a widely used textbook on *The Renaissance and the Reformation,* insists that it is time to give more attention to the role of spiritual forces in accounting for the survival of Roman Catholicism in the age of the Protestant Revolutions. In the present paper, therefore, he analyzes, among other things, the prolific devotional literature of the Catholic Reformation.

That the religious difficulties of the sixteenth century mark a profound crisis in the cultural development of western Europe no one will deny. For then it was that the religious unity which had so mightily assisted in the formation of occidental civilization was shat-

Reprinted by special permission from *The Catholic Historical Review,* XXIX (1943), 25-52. The extensive documentation which originally appeared with this essay has been omitted. The author has made a few minor changes in the present version of his article.

tered apparently beyond repair. At the opening of the century all northern Europe professed the traditional faith. By 1600 large sections had been torn from the Holy See. Competing churches of Lutheran, Zwinglian, Anglican, or Calvinist origin had come into existence—largely on national or political lines.

Nevertheless the traditional Church weathered the worst of the storm. Triumphantly it again proclaimed its teaching, strengthened the allegiance of the wavering to the Holy See, won for the faith vast areas in the newly discovered wilds of the Americas through energetic missionary enterprise, increased its membership, and again took up its ancient role of shaping the religious life of millions—a striking turn in the crisis which began when Martin Luther nailed up his theses in Wittenberg. The questions here to be answered, so far as the brief space of a general article permits, are: How were these things accomplished? What forces enabled the Church to ride out the tempest? What men and women gave their love, strength, and intellect to achieve this end? What institutions were formed which helped them to face the enemies of the faith? What circumstances enabled them to score this significant victory?

To these questions a complete answer is not readily at hand. The Counter-Reformation—a term first applied to this theme, it appears, by Leopold von Ranke, has been variously interpreted and frequently in a most adverse manner. All too often have writers, proceeding from a patent misunderstanding of the movement, brushed it aside without attempting to grasp the spiritual forces which made possible the survival of the ancient faith and its institutions. For this reason the term has acquired a meaning at once inadequate and misleading. Derived

---

CESARE BARONIUS: Roman Catholic church historian whose monumental *Annals* (12 vol., 1588-1607) was designed to bolster the historical claims of Roman Catholicism. He wrote in rebuttal against the Magdeburg Centuriators, who had sought to justify Lutheranism and condemn Roman Catholicism by means of an appeal to history.

CARMELITES: Members of a religious order founded in the twelfth century. Under the influence of St. Teresa of Avila and St. John of the Cross, they underwent a major revival in sixteenth-century Spain.

CARTHUSIANS: Members of a religious order founded in France in the

from the German *Gegenreformation*, it implies that Catholic Reform was mainly a reaction to Protestantism and ignores the substantial spiritual forces still resident in the Church.

Among these forces which helped to bring about reform, we should note first of all a persistent and widely expressed desire for renovation throughout the Church. There can be no question as to such need of reform, for it had been expressed repeatedly during the last two centuries of the Middle Ages, particularly at the Councils of Vienne (1311-1312), Pisa (1409), Constance (1414-1418), and Basel (1431-1449).

Enmeshed in the feudal structure of society and bound to its ancient manorial way of life, the Church in its outward organic existence was hardly free to proceed rapidly and decisively. Even in matters pertaining purely to religion and discipline, it was difficult if not impossible to take effective and speedy action. For priests usually owed their livings in the first instance to secular persons who did not always scrutinize their spiritual fitness. Bishops and archbishops were in effect appointees of princes who bestowed episcopal posts to reward their faithful servants or strengthen themselves in their own political policies. Abbatial posts frequently were in the gift of some prince; and, as monastic inmates were all too often placed in cloisters by influential laymen without asking whether they were fit for the regular life, zeal and discipline declined. Frequently pressure exerted by laymen so interfered with the orderly management and normal religious life of monasteries that chaos, financial as well as disciplinary, resulted. And what was particularly harmful—because it set a bad example and encouraged confusion—was the way secular politics obtruded upon the Curia itself. Finally, the lack of a definite course of professional

---

eleventh century. Hermits, they were influential in encouraging contemplative devotion in medieval times.

LAS CASAS: Sixteenth-century clergyman, missionary, and writer. As "General Protector of all Indians," he sought to combat their exploitation in Spanish America, going so far for a time as to defend the use of African slaves in the hope that this would reduce the death rate among the Indian population.

LUDWIG VON PASTOR: Roman Catholic scholar whose multi-volume *History of the Popes from the Close of the Middle Ages* (1886-1932) embodied his fundamental idea that historical study should serve the interests of the Church.

training for the priesthood made it possible for ambitious persons with little education or spiritual qualification to be promoted to positions with the cure of souls.

Other difficulties, springing from a different source, produced an even more dangerous crisis. The closing Middle Ages witnessed a remarkable concentration of political power in the hands of princes, whether rulers of great national states like England or Spain, or lesser princes like the dukes of Saxony. A new kind of taxation appeared which pushed aside older feudal conceptions of raising revenue; and a new army, a new navy, a new kind of justice, a new military strategy, and, in short, a new type of state emerged whose basic theory tended to be absolutist, based upon divine right. This placed in jeopardy the ancient conception of Church and State as parallel institutions in European society, each possessing authority in its own sphere and respecting the rights naturally belonging to the other. This relationship of co-operating partners could no longer be maintained when ambitious and masterful princes interfered in matters essentially religious.

But this growth of the new state, frequently buoyed by a nascent sentiment of nationalism, was not the sole or even the greatest danger confronting the Church. The temper of civilization itself was changing; the Middle Ages were passing, and a Humanist culture, secular in tendency, was undermining the old asceticism. The growth of commerce and industry, the development of an advanced money economy, the appearance of large towns and a constantly expanding bourgeoisie paralleled this political development. The non-Christian ideals of classical culture now possessed a new appeal, and an esthetic dilettantism began to supplant the rigorous thought of the scholastics. Secularism and materialism, couched in artistic luxury which all too often avoided the hard processes of logic, seemed to sap religious life, thus weakening the ecclesiastical edifice just when its ancient position was being impugned by absolutist princes.

Confronted by such difficulties: external—those induced by the economic, social, and political problems of the time—and internal—such as flowed from the chaos in ecclesiastical management and resulted in confusion and lack of discipline—the Church developed a new and vigorous type of spirituality. It blossomed in a remarkable series of writings, a much neglected type of literature which in its way deserves to be ranked with other aspects of Renaissance literature

such as the sonnet, the drama, history, and the prose essay. Although many little spiritual books like the *Imitation of Christ* and the *Spiritual Exercises* have received the attention of scholars, these phenomena in the religious life of the fifteenth and sixteenth centuries have never been studied sufficiently. What such a study might be like may be illustrated by Henri Brémond's *The Literary History of Religious Thought in France from the Wars of Religion down to Our Own Times*, surely one of the most significant contributions to the history of literature and, we affirm with confidence, indispensable to historians of modern thought. This work traces the development and influence in France of the devout life, beginning with the teaching of Louis Richeôme (1544-1625), a Provençal, a Jesuit, and author of many spiritual treatises, and the noteworthy St. Francis de Sales (d. 1622), about whom we shall have more to say in the proper place.

This new type of devout life was characterized by a great systematization—consistent examination of conscience, methodic prayer, mental prayer, contemplation, and spiritual direction—in which the psychological aspect of religious life is strikingly brought forward. Its roots are to be traced deep into the Middle Ages and even Apostolic times. Its early beginnings may be found in St. Paul's insistence on the ascetic life (spiritual combat) as stated, for example, in his first Epistle to Timothy. Its subsequent development is a complicated theme; Benedictine, Dominican, and Franciscan influences all contributed toward it. But it was the Carthusians, who, because the manner of their life especially favored contemplative devotion, advanced the practice of spiritual exercise more than any other group of religious during the heyday of the Middle Ages.

The *Devotio Moderna* of the Low Countries, which made its first appearance in the fourteenth century, marked great progress in inculcating interior devotion, because its devotees employed practical methods coupled with mysticism, which proved enormously effective in the town life of the Netherlands, Belgium, and neighboring parts. Founded chiefly by Gerrit Groote of Deventer (d. 1384), this *Devotio moderna* became the type of spirituality common among the Brethren of the Common Life as well as their feminine counterpart, the Sisters of the Common Life. Noteworthy especially among Groote's followers in spirituality and as writers of spiritual treatises were Florentius Radewijnszoon (d. 1400), Gerrit Zerbolt of Zutfen (d. 1398), and Thomas à Kempis (d. 1471), each one of whom contributed in some effective way to the devotional life of the time. Out of these circles came that classic of interior devotion, so tremendously popular for five centuries—*The Imitation of Christ*. Likewise the congregation of the Canons Regular of Windesheim, a monastic order which fully embraced the *Devotio moderna* and greatly resembled the Brethren of the Common Life, emphasized interior devotion and helped to spread its influence far and wide. These groups, however, did not possess a fully systematized method of devotion until Wessel Gansfort of Groningen (d. 1489), a pupil of the Common Life and friend of Thomas à Kempis, produced a "ladder of meditation," a work which exercised extensive influence. Henceforth appeared a large number of devotional treatises showing in varying degree remarkable psychological skill in inculcating devotion.

But, contrary to usual representations, the Italian Renaissance also made noteworthy contributions to the psychology and literature of spiritual devotion. Undoubtedly we have all too much stressed the antagonism of the culture of the Quattrocento and Cinquecento to that of the Middle Ages and especially to its asceticism. So far as the achievements of Greek and Roman antiquity are concerned, it is certain that mediaeval theologians owed much to St. Augustine, mediaeval philosophers to Plato and Aristotle, mediaeval medical men to Galen; mediaeval practical men of affairs to Roman Law; and many a mediaeval writer arrayed his thought in the ancient Latin vehicle and sometimes was inspired by classical Latin literary forms as in the case of the scholars of the school of Chartres. Certain it is that the Middle Ages, far from shutting off the Renaissance from the civilization of antiquity, actually provided the medium for the direct transmission of some of the significant achievements of the ancient world to the time of Petrarch and the Platonic Academy.

The Humanist cult of excellence, so marked in the striving of the men of the Renaissance, also had its profound roots in the classical and mediaeval past. Henri Brémond has shown that this cult of excellence, as applied to Christian teaching, definitely had its forerunners in the Middle Ages. He held that the highest artistic and psychological expression of the Renaissance was not limited to secular things, as some historians have thought, but that it also was strikingly united with profound ethical insight and religious inspiration.

Many a Humanist, for example, gave expression to this phenomenon in his religious life and writings. Thus Pietro Paolo Vergerio

(d. 1440) and Vittorino da Feltre (d. 1446) produced a new and fruitful type of education in which Humanist conceptions were wedded to Christian teaching. Ambrogio Traversari (d. 1439), of the Order of Camalduli, combined the new enthusiasm for the ancient classics and particularly for the Church Fathers with Christian thought. Other Humanists followed their example, especially Pico della Mirandola, who tried to harmonize, but none too successfully, the thought of Plato with that of Christ, thus winning a wide audience for the ideas of the Platonic Academy founded by Cosimo de Medici (d. 1464), Gemistos Plethon (d. 1450), Marsiglio Ficino (d. 1499), and others.

From such forces subsequently, in part at least, came the Oratory of Divine Love, a confraternity which received the papal confirmation in 1516 or 1517 and established branches in the larger cities of Italy. Among the best known of the noble spirits that belonged to the Oratory were: Cajetan de Thiene (d. 1547); Giberti (d. 1548), later bishop of Verona; Aloysius Lippomano (d. 1558), Giberti's successor; Giovanni Pietro Caraffa (d. 1559), later Pope Paul IV; and other notables like Pietro Bembo (d. 1547), Sadoleto (d. 1547), Gasparo Contarini (d. 1542), and Giovanni Morone (d. 1580). The Oratory's extensive influence was felt by persons like Michelangelo and Vittoria Colonna. Also outside Italy early in the century some prominent men like Sir Thomas More (d. 1535) and Lefevre Stapulensis (d. 1536) experienced its quickening power.

Although often speculative and flashily critical, appealing to the educated who looked to secular princes for favor, and generally aristocratic in character, the more extreme manifestations of Humanism did not touch vitally the great stream of traditional religious life which still coursed so vitally in Italy. Ludwig von Pastor has demonstrated this fact by giving a long list of notable persons of deep piety and exemplary life, of whom St. Catherine of Genoa (d. 1510) was but one. Even before the close of the Quattrocento there was a growing tendency among many worldly Humanists to adopt a more serious view of life. Devotees of Humanism then turned their attention to the practical religious needs of ordinary men, encouraging interior devotion and personal sanctity. They sought to make the Christian religion a source of spiritual edification as well as a thing of beauty. A serious type of Humanism appeared also beyond the Alps, something which Professor Lindeboom has called "Biblical Humanism."

Henri Brémond, however, named it "Christian Humanism" which, especially after the Council of Trent, became organically bound to Christian thought and practice. After that date the term "Devout Humanism," which Brémond gave it, appears especially appropriate. Thus was the spiritually parched soil nourished and watered. What practical fruits did it produce?

First of all, there appeared a voluminous and widely read literature, composed of small spiritual treatises dealing with methodic prayer. Most influential was the Dominican Giovanni Battista Carioni (d. 1534), or da Crema, who wrote devout treatises based upon his experience as a spiritual director, the most important perhaps being the *Della cognitione et vittoria de si stésso* and the *Via di aperta verità*. A noted priest of San Giovanni in Laterano, Serafino Aceto da Pratis (d. 1534), so admired these works that he too wrote several devotional treatises. Later other gifted priests followed this example, especially Lorenzo Scupoli (d. 1610), a member of the Theatine Order and author of the immensely popular *Combatimento Spirituale*, a work which passed through many editions, being revised and extended by various hands so that its original twenty-eight chapters finally were increased to as many as sixty-six. As a practical spiritual vademecum, this book was decidedly superior to the *Imitation of Christ*, which always remained a popular classic of meditation. The books by Carioni and Scupoli also marked a great advance upon Wessel Gansfort's treatise, for they possessed a surer method and avoided superfluous exercises. Laying out a definite plan of spiritual cultivation—a system of piety—consisting in prayer, frequent communion, and examination of conscience, they were characterized by an entirely new and practical spirit. Such, it should be stressed, were the peculiar characteristics of Italian spirituality more or less under Humanist influence.

But these Italian masters of spirituality, although influenced by Spanish writers, also contributed to the movement in Spain. García de Cisneros' *Ejercitatorio*, dating from the early years of the sixteenth century, undoubtedly owed something to Italian spiritual masters as well as to the writers of the *Devotio moderna*, especially *The Imitation of Christ*. That Cisneros' treatise helped to guide Ignatius Loyola is a well-known fact. But St. Ignatius in his *Spiritual Exercises* was no slavish imitator, for among his contributions was the emphasis upon the efforts of spiritual directors in guiding exercitants. The influence of the *Spiritual Exercises*, first upon members of the Society of

Jesus and next upon the laity with whom the Society came in contact, was truly great.

Spain soon became the classic land of spiritual exercise; in fact, it became part of the Spanish way of religious life. This is clear from the numerous treatises on spirituality of which we shall, however, mention only a few of the greatest. The *Libro de la oración y meditación* and *Guía de pecadores* by the Dominican Luis de Granada (d. 1588) are the work of a capable classicist who joined Humanist refinement with genuine Christian spirituality. His Dominican contemporary, Melchior Cano (d. 1560), a philosopher and most zealous soul in quest of religious knowledge, although entertaining exaggerated suspicions of spiritual exercitants who he feared had too much influence among the distrusted Alumbrados, nevertheless produced the *De la vitoria de si mismo,* reminiscent of one of Carioni's important writings. Among other widely read books of this nature we should note Bartholomew of the Martyrs' *Compendium mysticae doctrinae,* a digest of spiritual doctrine and method, Peter of Alcántara's *Treatise on Prayer and Meditation,* and John of Bonilla's *Pax animae.* But these and other noteworthy Spanish books were not the only great spiritual guides, however, for towards the end of the century there appeared in many lands similar books—to mention but one of numerous examples—Robert Bellarmine's *Ascent of the Mind to God by a Ladder of Things Created,* a book which has never ceased to attract earnest souls.

Far and wide, wherever the influence of the Church reached, these little spiritual classics effectively guided people in devotion. This literature was one of the forces which, according to David Knowles, "combines to give the professional director of consciences a place in the religious life of the times which would have astounded the religious communities of the Middle Ages, and would not a little gall those of today." But we should not assume there was no variety; in fact uniformity in method hardly existed, the chief uniformity being the end constantly kept in view—the stimulation of devout religious life.

Augustine Baker (d. 1641), an Englishman who in spite of the official repression of the ancient faith in England came into the Church as a convert and entered the Benedictine Order, forcibly illustrates this fact. The author of the long popular *Sancta Sophia* and *The Inner Life of Dame Gertrude More* objected to the severe exercises frequently insisted upon by confessors, preferring to lead exercitants to find their own way in spiritual life and not through excessive and what he termed artificial mortifications. He believed the most fruitful mortification was to be found in the trials and tribulations incidental to the experiences of every person who seeks to direct his life according to the counsels of evangelical perfection.

Although Baker worked primarily with men and women in religion, his moderation and particularly his basic conception of ascetic discipline, were peculiarly adapted to the needs of the laity. But it was left to another master, the author of the noteworthy *Treatise on the Love of God*, to produce a book of spiritual counsel for all people. This was the noted Genevan, St. Francis de Sales, who as bishop instructed in spiritual perfection many of his followers, of whom Jeanne de Chantal (d. 1614) was especially noted. His letters are a splendid source of information for all who would study his methods and learn what success crowned his endeavors. In the preface to his *Introduction to the Devout Life* he described his aim and procedure as follows:

> Those who have treated of devotion have almost all had in mind the instruction of persons very much withdrawn from the society of the world, or at all events they have taught a kind of devotion which leads to this complete withdrawal. My intention is to instruct those who live in towns, in households, at the court, and who, by reason of their circumstances, are obliged to lead an ordinary life in outward show; but very often, under color of an alleged impossibility, are not willing even to think of undertaking the devout life, because they are of the opinion that, just as no beast dare taste of the herb called *palma Christi*, so no one ought to aspire to the palm of Christian piety, whilst living in the midst of the press of worldly occupations. And I show them that, as the mother pearls live in the sea without taking one drop of salt water, and as towards the Chelidonian isles there are springs of perfectly fresh water in the midst of the sea, and as the flies called *pirastes* fly in the flames without burning their wings, so a vigorous and constant soul can live in the world without receiving any worldly taint, can find springs of sweet piety in the midst of the briny waters of the world, and fly among the flames of earthly concupiscences without burning the wings of the holy desires of the devout life.

St. Francis de Sales directed many penitents; but none of them responded in so ideal a manner as did Madame de Charmoisy. "I have just found," he said, "in our sacred nets a fish which I had so longed

for these four years. It is a lady all of gold, and magnificently fitted
to serve her Saviour; and if she persevere she will do so with fruit."
In the *Introduction to the Devout Life*, she appears as Philothea; the
book itself is made up of the spiritual counsels directed to her.

Mysticism also flourished during all this period. A concomitant
of the systematic asceticism of the spirituality of the age, it represents
the highest religious life in the Church. But it is quite impossible
to separate the devotional literature of the sixteenth century into two
distinct categories, ascetic and mystic. Manuals of devotion like the
Imitation of Christ and the *Spiritual Exercises* assume the ascetic as
necessary to the latter. The term asceticism as here used, it should be
noted, signifies the pursuit of evangelical perfection guided by love
of God, something very different from the vulgar notion that it refers
simply to extreme austerities. Devout folk arrived at mystical states
only after passing some time in the purgative before gaining the
illuminative and unitive stages. There were many mystics in Renaissance Italy, some of whom lived quietly and unnoticed while others
like St. Catherine of Genoa attracted much attention. Among the
many later proficients in contemplation we may mention the Carmelite
Mary Magdalen dei Pazzi (d. 1607) who also became a considerable
master of theology. The Dominican Catherine de Ricci (d. 1560),
whose biography became a source of spiritual edification to many,
exerted much influence through her letters written to persons of the
noble class. The Poor Clare, Battista Varani (d. 1526), expressed her
tenderest thought, mingled with Platonism, in the typically Franciscan
manner of the Renaissance.

It was in Spain, however, that mysticism found its classic expression. In her numerous monasteries and also among the laity there
literally were thousands of proficients in mystical devotion. Nowhere
in all Christendom did the contemplative life produce so bountiful
a literature. Among feminine mystics we need mention only St.
Teresa of Avila (d. 1582), a masterful woman, able, pious, and reformer of the Carmelites. She had extensive contacts with her contemporaries personally or by letter and exercised great influence. Her
writings—*Letters, Life, Foundations, Way of Perfection*, and *Interior
Castle* rank among the monuments of the Renaissance. Noteworthy
also was another Carmelite, St. John of the Cross (d. 1591) who,
although a follower of St. Teresa, was a genius of the first order. His
Ascent of Mount Carmel, Dilucidario, Spiritual Canticle, The Dark

Night, and *The Living Flame of Love* are perhaps unsurpassed in mystical experience, even by St. Teresa herself.

We have devoted what may appear to some as a disproportionate amount of space to the spirit and literature of spirituality simply because historians as a rule fail to stress it as a decisive element in the life of the time and the reform of the Church. Charity—the love of God and His creation—inculcated by the ascetic and mystical aspects of the new type of devotion, was a dynamic principle certain to find expression in the moral, social, ecclesiastical, intellectual, and artistic activity of the time. To the spiritual rededication outlined above, in which so many people in the bosom of the Church had a part, we must in the first place ascribe the survival of the traditional faith. Certainly the example of Protestantism sorely smote the conscience of earnest folk; it created in them a resolve to straighten out the religious life of the people and even the torpid clergy, who also were very generally submerged by the secular tide. To this extent we may assent to the opinion often advanced that the reform in the ancient Church was due to Protestantism. The emphasis usually placed upon the political influence of the kings of Spain and similarly absolute princes or upon other equally adventitious features of the movement springs in part at least from the failure to appreciate the profundity of the spiritual devotion exhibited in this crisis by many sons and daughters of the Church.

The new spirit of devotion speedily found concrete expression in the creation of new religious orders. It is not to be assumed, however, that the ancient monastic orders had outlived their usefulness. The Benedictine Order had indeed suffered from its contact with feudal and manorial institutions. But there were model Benedictine houses scattered in various countries besides the reformed Benedictine congregations of St. Justina in Italy and Valladolid in Spain. Much as the earlier rigor of the Cistercians may have declined, the order showed considerable vitality during the sixteenth century. The Carthusians were particularly vigorous, and in England produced a number of martyrs. The Franciscans were by no means as corrupt as has so frequently been represented. At least the Franciscan Observants in England were resolute upholders of Franciscan principles and, as a result, frequently suffered martyrdom. Likewise the Dominicans generally remained true to their ancient ideals. So also the Observant part of the Augustinian Order to which Luther belonged. And besides these, there were the Brethren of the Common Life and the Windesheim Congregation of

Canons Regular whose members were staunch upholders of the Church. But none of these ancient institutions which had served the Church so long and so well really could meet the unusual needs of the age. The new orders now created, excepting those founded by women, were as a rule composed of priests bound by the three vows but not subject to the ancient *stabilitas loci*. They were canons regular, but organized to meet some specific need peculiar to the new age. Educated in the newer methods inspired by Humanism, more alert to the great moral crisis before them, they were able to combat rampant evils in public and private life.

Among these new orders we should note first the Theatines, founded in 1524. Recruited from the Oratory of Divine Love, its members felt the rekindling spirit of devotion and addressed themselves to the moral rejuvenation of society by preaching, taking care of the sick in hospitals and private homes, giving catechetical instruction, administering the sacraments, helping the destitute especially when Rome was mercilessly sacked in 1527, and, last but not least, providing for the education of a zealous priesthood. This practical example of noble solicitude for the unfortunate shown by pure-minded and unselfish priests created a profound impression.

The Sommaschi, like the Theatines, were deeply impressed by the misfortunes of the innocent and helpless. The wars of the balance of power between Charles V and Francis I had wrought extensive havoc in the thickly populated Milanese and adjacent parts of Lombardy. The towns and countryside swarmed with orphaned and abandoned children growing up in indolence and vice. The gentle St. Jerome Emiliani (d. 1537), a Venetian nobleman, was so touched by their pathetic condition that he took some of them into his own house and soon founded homes and hospitals for others in Como, Verona, Milan, Venice, and other places. St. Jerome's piety resembled that of the Theatines. His association, confirmed in 1540, affiliated with the Theatines in 1547 and finally, in the seventeenth century, was constituted as a separate order.

A third order, the Barnabites, in 1530 sprang from the same conditions and contributed greatly toward the spiritual rehabilitation of Italian society. Their founder, Antonio Maria Zaccaria, like St. Jerome Emiliani, was tutored in the piety of the Oratory of Divine Love and the Theatines and grieved over the growing laxity in the life of the people, which the Barnabites sought to counteract by moral instruction, preaching, and relief of the poor. "They took pains to stir the feelings of the ruder sort of people by open-air missions and public exercises of penance; they were to be seen, crucifix in hand, preaching in the most crowded thoroughfares; some carried heavy crosses, others confessed their sins aloud," writes Pastor. Possessing great sociological significance, this order grew steadily, founded many houses, and became an important agent in social regeneration.

Springing from the same spiritual needs and out of the devotion which had produced the Theatines, Sommaschi, and Barnabites, was the Congregation of the Oratory. It grew up around the efforts of St. Philip Neri (d. 1594), truly one of the noblest characters of the sixteenth century, who attracted groups of zealous priests seeking spiritual edification through mental prayer, spiritual reading, informal discussions, frequent communion, attendance upon the sick in hospitals, and instruction in the faith. St. Philip's humanity, moderation, unquestioned devotion, and purity of motive won many a soul. The Oratory became powerful in Rome and exercised a mighty influence in the moral uplift of all classes wherever it was most needed.

There were other organizations, each of which in its special way illustrated the contagious example of charity in an environment where rigorous devotion became more and more common. Among these were congregations of secular priests, the Spanish Brothers of Mercy founded in 1540 by St. John of God for the purpose of tending the sick; the Fathers of a Good Death, founded by Camillus de Lellis in 1584, also to care for the sick, spiritually as well as corporeally; the Fathers of Christian Doctrine, established by Caesar de Bus in 1592; the Oblates of St. Charles Borromeo, organized in 1578, who were effective assistants to the great cardinal in his reform of the see of Milan; and the Piarists, who owed their existence (1597) to Joseph Calasanza, a Spaniard interested in the education of boys. Important also were the Capuchins, who in 1528 broke from the Observant Franciscans under the leadership of the Italian Matteo da Bascio. In them appeared an intensified Franciscanism which made the Capuchins a mighty force among the lower classes, especially in towns.

To these striking examples of devotion we should add the Ursulines of St. Angela of Brescia, organized in 1537 for the moral and mental development of young girls, especially waifs and orphans. Significant also as indicating the new trend were the Angelicals or Guastallines, founded by Luigia Torelli, countess of Guastalla. That zealous woman, deeply impressed and directed by Zaccaria, founded a number of houses for women who co-operated with the Barnabites in carrying out their social gospel. Their active work in charity, unfortunately, brought upon them undeserved criticism which caused Pope Paul III to order strict cloister upon them. In France the work of St. Francis of Sales and St. Jeanne de Chantal in 1610 led to the creation of the Nuns of the Visitation. Its members followed the rules laid down by St. Francis de Sales and made it a part of their devotion to visit the sick in their homes and also in the hospitals.

But important as each of these new foundations proved to be—and their significance must not be minimized—even more effective and more widely influential was the Society of Jesus which began in 1534 and received papal confirmation six years later. The story of St. Ignatius Loyola's career is so well known that we need not recount it here. But it is essential to emphasize his remarkable skill as a spiritual drill master in whose hands the *Spiritual Exercises* proved a most successful means to strengthen devotion among his followers, whether in the Society or outside. St. Ignatius had no specific social or religious mission in mind. What he wished to do was well summed up in the Jesuit motto: to labor *Ad Maiorem Dei Gloriam.* As opportunity presented itself, he and his followers successfully put their hands to whatever tasks seemed to demand attention—preaching to the spiritually neglected, helping the poor, teaching the youth, engaging in scholarly study and controversy, bringing the gospel to the heathen, and, finally, taking up the cudgels against heresy. Truly, surveying the history of the time and reflecting upon the spirituality of the century, we can state without hesitation that the Society of Jesus was a vital agency in promoting religious and moral revival and ecclesiastical reform.

Such influences, expressed in so many forceful ways, welled up in the bosom of the traditional Church. That they should express themselves in increased conviction and dogmatic fervor was inevitable. But they also were translated into social action, for the teachings of Christianity are in their aim ascetic as well as dogmatic, moral, and mystical. This is exactly what we should expect if we keep in mind the earlier history of the Church. Each of the great monastic movements had its social and moral significance in the life of the time when it flourished.

Even the smaller orders, limited as to time and place, also exerted a very considerable influence.

How could these forces springing from a newly found strength of conviction be successfully implemented? An ancient institution, embracing a territory more extensive than that of any secular state, enmeshed in the feudal, manorial, town, and national politics of the closing Middle Ages, the Church could not readily act upon the promptings for reform to be heard on every hand. Were not abbots, bishops, archbishops, and popes all too often appointed under pressure of political interests? The election of Adrian VI (1522-1523), a Netherlander who had been under the tuition of the Brethren of the Common Life and besides was deeply stirred by the reforming work of Cardinal Ximenes in Spain, seemed to mark a turning point in papal policy. Unfortunately, his speedy demise frustrated hope for immediate reform. The pontificate of Clement VII (1523-1534) accomplished nothing remarkable and even that of Paul III (1534-1549) at first seemed to promise little.

But Paul III, knowing that changes were long overdue and, in fact, urgently needed if Protestantism were to be checked, finally moved. In 1535 and 1536 he promoted to the cardinalate men of unquestioned piety, some of whom were inspired by the newer type of devotion. Among them were Gasparo Contarini, Caraffa of the Theatines, Sadoleto, and Reginald Pole. On November 13, 1536, the pontiff declared in consistory that reform of the Church in head and members should be the immediate aim of the papal court. Meanwhile the Commission of Nine named by Paul III in May, 1535, had surveyed the need of reform and in 1537 presented a frank report of needed changes and a definite program of action. This memorable document, signed by Contarini, Caraffa, Sadoleto, Pole, Giberti, Cortese—to mention only the most prominent—breathed the spirit of the serious men and women who, in cloister and out, prayed and labored for the renovation of the ecclesiastical organization.

Although Paul III had recognized the urgent need for reform from the beginning of his pontificate, he had found it hard to move consistently. Nevertheless he was responsible for many reform measures. Finally, on May 22, 1542, he issued the bull convoking the great reform council which began its sessions at Trent in 1545 and sat intermittently during the pontificates of Paul III, Julius III, Paul IV, and Pius IV.

The disciplinary decrees of the Council of Trent, which covered most aspects of ecclesiastical life, had been foreshadowed in the report of Paul III's Commission of Nine and in such zealous diocesan administrations as that of Bishop Giberti of the see of Verona. Like them, the decrees and canons concerning religious life sprang from the deepening convictions of the age. This was inevitable, for not only did reforming prelates who had shared in the new devotion attend the Council, but also Jesuit fathers whose piety had been powerfully formed by the *Spiritual Exercises* of St. Ignatius.

Thus auspiciously begun, the reform movement received further stimulus from the energetic—all too energetic, it might be said—Paul IV, as Caraffa was known while occupying the Chair of Peter from 1555 to 1559. This former member of the Oratory of Divine Love and co-founder of the Theatines did not hesitate personally and vigorously to initiate reforms which former pontiffs had shrunk from suggesting even in the most diplomatic manner. The full effect of the labors of the Fathers at Trent, however, became more and more apparent when Pius IV (1559-1565) started to apply the decrees of the Council and began the preparation of the profession of faith based upon them. Under Pius V (1565-1572), surely one of the striking characters of the time, great strides were made in discipline, renovation of abuses, and the stimulation of religious life. The breviary and missal were corrected and the *Roman Catechism* was finished. Gregory XIII (1572-1585) continued this work and founded colleges for training clergy to labor among the Greeks, Maronites, Armenians, Germans, and others. These pontiffs, as well as Sixtus V (1585-1590), also inaugurated many practical reforms.

At once vigorous steps were undertaken to reform the training of the priesthood. Humanist education with its emphasis upon the cultivation of literary style, philology, classical letters, philosophy, and theology was accepted as the indispensable foundation for a successful clerical career. The ancient liberal arts as a propaedeutic now were expanded and the easy-going methods of mediaeval schools abandoned. Further, such educational preparation was coupled with spiritual training in a new institution, the clerical seminary, which combined some of the best ideas of the former schools with the practices of monasteries. The fifth session of Trent laid down the rules for lectureships in biblical literature, the twenty-third prescribed the establishment of seminaries in each diocese.

St. Charles Borromeo, archbishop of Milan, greatly influenced by the practical reforms of Giberti and Lippomano, his successor in the see of Verona, took a lead in establishing a model seminary, an example followed wherever bishops were able to do so, first in Italy and thereafter in other parts of Christendom. By the close of the century the Jesuits, acting upon their unusual success as teachers of youth, produced their *Ratio Studiorum* which henceforth provided a basic pedagogy as well as philosophy of education for the training of laymen as well as candidates for the priesthood. And so it came to pass that many devoted priests brought up in the piety of the *Combatimento spirituale,* the *Spiritual Exercises,* and similar books of devotion presented themselves for the pastoral office.

Soon also appeared eminent scholars who combined the best in Humanism with the new spirituality. To combat the bitter critics of the Church, Cesare Baronius (d. 1607), a member of the Oratory, in 1588 began to publish his *Annales ecclesiasticae,* a truly noteworthy work in which appeared a vast number of documents from papal archives illustrating the history of the papacy. Though defective from a palaeographical standpoint, this monumental work must still be consulted by historians, particularly mediaevalists. As a work of scholarship—considering the general condition of critical historical scholarship at that time—it is distinctly superior to the work of the Magdeburg Centuriators. The Oratory attracted a number of able musicians—among them Giovanni Animuccia (d. 1571), who was *maestro di capello* in St. Peter's, and the renowned Giovanni Pierluigi da Palestrina (d. 1594). These, together with Francisco Soto (d. 1619) and others, brought to full fruition the development of polyphonic music. Soon also appeared the oratorio, a new artistic vehicle for the dissemination of spiritual seriousness, which speedily received universal acclaim.

The deepening devotion of the age could not but leave its mark upon scholarship, particularly in Spain, where the tumults of the century passed more or less unnoticed. There the *philosophia perennis* was cultivated in spite of the emphasis which some Italian Humanists were placing upon a metaphysics based essentially upon naturalism. To give here a list of the large number of distinguished philosophers who did not submit to the tide of misunderstanding criticism, not to mention abuse, of scholastic philosophy is impossible. The Dominican Order produced Francisco Vittorio (d. 1566), Melchior Cano (d. 1560),

Dominico Bánez (d. 1604), and especially John of St. Thomas (d. 1644), the author of a significant commentary on St. Thomas Aquinas' *Summa Theologica*. But extensive as the influence of these distinguished thinkers proved to be, that of the Jesuits proved fully as decisive. Teaching at the universities of Alcalá, Salamanca, Coimbra, Rome, and many schools of less reputation, they guided the development of theology and philosophy in Catholic circles. Among them were Francisco Toledo (d. 1596), Pedro de Fonseca (d. 1597), Luis de Molina (d. 1601), and Francisco Suárez (d. 1617).

The scholarship thus inspired ranks very high in the intellectual history of the century. The *Complutensian Polyglot* produced at Alcalá under the influence of Cardinal Ximenes (d. 1518), uncle of García de Cisneros, certainly was the most significant scholarly work expended upon biblical textual criticism at that time. As a biblical commentator, the Jesuit Maldonatus (d. 1583) had few if any equals. Robert Bellarmine (d. 1621) from Tuscany, also a Jesuit and the author of a number of spiritual treatises, as we have learned, was one of the greatest among the scholars of the age. His works on theology, law, and government attracted general attention. And, besides, in the Jesuit schools, physics, mathematics, astronomy, music, geography, and literature generally received serious attention.

Strengthened by the zeal of a revived faith, the sons of the Church with singular devotion went forth to win new peoples to the faith. St. Francis Xavier traveled to India, Malaya, and Japan; and only death, which came to him at Sancian in 1552, prevented him from entering China, at that time forbidden to foreigners. Abyssinia, the Congo, Mexico, South America, and Central America attracted Jesuits, Franciscans, and Dominicans. And in the wilds of North America Jesuit missioners moved among the Indian tribes, sometimes finding martyrdom and always seeking to advance Christ's kingdom. But nowhere were these missioners so successful as in Mexico, Central America, and South America. New Spain became a cultural offshoot of old Spain. Merging the culture of the old world with that of the American aborigine was a stupendous task; and the story of European exploitation of the native red man is not very pleasant reading. We may, however, oppose to it the labors of Bartolomé de Las Casas (d. 1566), even though he sometimes failed to realize the full implications of the ideals he cherished, a fact which we who are better instructed in a sounder science of cultural anthropology, can, in view of the insurmountable difficulties confronting him in a novel situation, understand and perhaps readily pardon.

In literary expression also we note the effects of the resurgence of a vital and militant faith. This theme, altogether too complex and too significant for the future to be discussed here, must be disposed of in a few words. The new spirit soon began to make itself felt in the realm of literature. Questionable books like Lorenzo Valla's *De voluptate* were banned. Others like Erasmus' *Colloquia familiaria* which emphasized the shortcomings of priests and indulged in exaggerations and half-truths were no longer permitted in the schools. Much regret has been expressed over the rigid removal of these and other Humanist literary productions from active circulation among the devout and loyal. But that it is doubtful whether such stern policy really suppressed literary effort is shown by the attitude of Pietro Bembo (d. 1547), a man whose early career was anything but edifying, but whose later years revealed positive amendment under the influence of reviving seriousness among many of the Humanist elite. A master of elegant diction, Bembo wedded his Latin of Ciceronian purity to the practical uses that the Church had for it. Many a writer expressed his serious convictions in Latin and also in the vernacular.

But merely to list the noteworthy writers of each country would be a tiresome task. In Italy there was Torquato Tasso (d. 1595); in Spain, St. John of the Cross and St. Teresa, to mention only two writers; in the hostile Netherlands, Joost Vanden Vondel (d. 1679)—a writer altogether too much neglected by current scholarship; and in England, a country where one would scarcely expect to find writers championing Catholic piety, there was the poet Richard Crashaw (d. 1649). In France a significant school of writers appeared, all inspired by the "Devout Humanism" which, according to Henri Brémond, now triumphed. We have already noted St. Francis de Sales, but we should add here such names as Pierre de Bérulle (d. 1629), Charles de Condren (d. 1641), Blaise Pascal (d. 1662), Jacques Bossuet (d. 1704), and François de Fénelon (d. 1715).

This new spirit of devotion, the subject of much misunderstanding comment, has been all too much neglected. Issuing in the Baroque Age, it has received less appreciative study than the cultural phenomena of the Quattrocento and Cinquecento, centuries whose thought, art, and letters were given an interpretation fitting the prepossessions of the Enlightenment of the eighteenth century and the Positivists of the nineteenth. But sound historical study no longer is satisfied with these intellectual prejudices. It is wearisome to read the same old conventional and jejune estimates of the work of the great men and women of the Baroque Age, especially at its beginnings.

This spirit of devotion also found expression in painting, sculpture, and engraving. The plastic perfection of the High Renaissance had indeed culminated in the mannerism of the imitators of Michelangelo; but the newer schools nevertheless were able to give serious meaning to their splendid creations. The three Carracci (Augustine, d. 1602; Annibale, d. 1609; and Lodovico, d. 1619) who created the eclectic school of Bologna laid the foundations of their great influence, which was to be felt for several decades. Guido Reni (d. 1642), one of their pupils, painted a large number of splendid pictures combining the radiant anatomy of youth with grief, distress, and ecstasy. The weeping Magdalen, the repenting Peter, the mistreated Savior were favorite topics in his *bottega*. Lorenzo Bernini (d. 1680) translated this same spirit into sculpture and architecture.

But the great influence of the Italian masters of the early Baroque should not blind us to the greater excellences of Spanish masters like El Greco (d. 1615), Gregorio Fernández (d. 1636), José de Ribera (d. 1658), Francesco Zurbarán (d. 1664), Murillo (d. 1682), Diego Velásquez (d. 1660)—at least in his religious pictures—and Luis de Morales (d. 1716). Spanish artistic culture undoubtedly owed much to established political peace, a condition well realized by Philip II. But it owed at least as much to the intense spirit of piety cultivated in the Spain of that century. The piety of the time also found artistic as well as literary expression in the Southern Netherlands in spite of the Eighty Years' War and the rise of Protestantism. As shown by the activity of Peter Paul Rubens (d. 1640), artistic expression approaching even the greatness of Spanish plastic work was attained.

In these paragraphs we have endeavored to make clear just one important aspect of the Catholic Reform of the sixteenth century—the immensely significant influence of the many men and women in cloister or as lay-folk, in aristocratic circles as well as humble, among the clergy as also the laity, who lived devout lives, tried by spiritual exercise to attain to their highest spiritual development, and wrote spiritual manuals for the rejuvenation of the faith and the reform of the Church. Much more might be said upon this subject, but our aim will be realized if we here succeed in calling attention to the importance of an all too much neglected branch of Renaissance literature.

V

The Expansion of Europe

❯❯❯-❯❯❯-❯❯❯-❯❯❯-❯❯❯-❯❯❯-❯❯❯-❯❯❯-❯❯❯❮❮❮-❮❮❮-❮❮❮-❮❮❮-❮❮❮-❮❮❮-❮❮❮-❮❮❮-❮❮❮

The Role of Monopoly in the Overseas Expansion and Colonial Trade of Europe Before 1800

EARL J. HAMILTON

❯❯❯-❯❯❯-❯❯❯-❯❯❯-❯❯❯-❯❯❯-❯❯❯-❯❯❯-❯❯❯❮❮❮-❮❮❮-❮❮❮-❮❮❮-❮❮❮-❮❮❮-❮❮❮-❮❮❮-❮❮❮

The Role of Monopoly in the Overseas Expansion and Colonial Trade of Europe Before 1800

EARL J. HAMILTON

≫≫-≫≫-≫≫-≫≫-≫≫-≫≫-≫≫-≫≫-≫≫ *Published in 1948* ≪-≪≪-≪≪-≪≪-≪≪-≪≪-≪≪-≪≪-≪≪

Just as in the religious history of early modern Europe the basic influence was the growth of Protestantism, so in the economic history of early modern Europe the basic influence was overseas expansion. Not that this expansion affected only the economic life of Europe; it also had unmistakable repercussions on European political, social, intellectual, and religious life. To people who lived in the early modern centuries, however, the economic results of overseas expansion were especially impressive: the Mediterranean became relatively less important than it had been before; the Atlantic ports became increasingly powerful economically; basic changes took place in the volume and nature of European trade; a revolution occurred in the European price structure; and capitalism and mercantilism grew in importance. Among the American scholars who have explored the impact of overseas expansion on European economic life, Earl J. Hamilton, now of the University of Chicago, has made substantial contributions. Indeed, if it is difficult nowadays to take a course in the history of early modern Europe and not hear something about the price revolution, the responsibility rests in no small measure with him. Author of *American Treasure and the Price Revolution in Spain, 1501-1650* (1934), Hamilton has had the rare experience of seeing his research findings embodied in textbook after textbook. Here has been one notable instance where texts have not lagged far behind advanced scholarship. For his part, Hamilton has continued to publish important articles in the field of European economic history. In the present paper, he examines monopoly as a factor in the overseas expansion of Europe in early modern times.

I. *Introduction*

The great European empires of classical antiquity included a fringe in Asia and the Mediterranean littoral of Africa, and the crusading nations and trading states of the late Middle Ages acquired tenuous footholds in Asia Minor and on small islands in the eastern Atlantic. But Europe controlled little territory beyond its own boundaries either in ancient or in medieval times. It remained for the enlightened captains and bold sailors of Prince Henry the Navigator to inaugurate, early in the fifteenth century, the great age of discovery, from which both imperialism and the modern world have emerged. From that time until the Napoleonic Wars suspended expansion by absorbing European energies at home, the leading powers of Europe effectively occupied more than a third of the earth's surface and established claims to more than half of it.

Near the end of this period, Adam Smith concluded, after two decades of reflection and a full year in the British Museum reading on colonial questions, that "the utility which has resulted from . . . the establishment of the European colonies in America and the West Indies . . . is not clear and evident. It was not understood at their first establishment, and was not the motive either of that establishment or of the discoveries which gave occasion to it; and the nature, extent, and limits of that utility are not, perhaps, well understood at this day." Smith was contrasting what the motives should have been with what the uneducated public believed them to be. What they really were he thought he understood well enough; namely, to acquire precious metals and to obtain high profits through monopolistic exploitation of colonial markets. One of Smith's main objectives in writing the *Wealth of Nations* was to refute mercantilism by demonstrating the theoretical folly and practical impossibility of an indefinite accumulation of the precious metals. Nevertheless, monopoly overshadows not only treasure but everything else in his learned and illuminating analysis of colonial policies. Although Smith repeatedly pilloried businessmen and the craft guilds for monopolistic practices in England,

Reprinted by special permission from *Papers and Proceedings of the American Economic Association*, XXXVIII (1948), 33-53. The extensive documentation which originally appeared with this essay has been omitted. The author has made a few minor changes in the present version of his article.

he did not argue, as has been fashionable in recent decades, that limitation by monopolies of domestic opportunities for investment and employment drove capital and labor into imperialistic ventures.

Focusing our attention upon the foundation and the trade of the five leading colonial empires before 1800—the Portuguese, Spanish, Dutch, French, and English—we shall endeavor to determine the extent to which a desire for monopoly motivated the overseas expansion of Europe. We shall also see to what extent and in what respects the colonial trade, governed by the vague principles of mercantilism throughout the three centuries under review, was monopolistic or competitive.

II. *Portugal*

Most writers on mercantilism have neglected Portugal, and its colonial policy has attracted surprisingly little attention. The destruction of a large mass of colonial papers in the Torre do Tombo Archives by the earthquake and ensuing fire on November 1, 1755, and the silence of the early chroniclers on such prosaic matters as trade and navigation have deterred many scholars interested in the Portuguese colonial system and seriously handicapped those who have persevered. Consequently, inadequate knowledge may explain the tendency to dismiss the Portuguese empire with the derogatory conclusions that it consisted only of a chain of forts and trading stations, developed no new institutions, set no important precedents, and made no significant contributions to colonial theory. Although precise information and many details are lacking, we know that Portugal discovered the all-water route to the East Indies, established the first contacts with the natives, forged a colossal empire, exclusively controlled the East India

---

JOHN LAW: Scottish mercantilist, financier, and notorious speculator of the early eighteenth century. He won the support of the French government for an ill-fated scheme to redeem the public debt through the organization of a public bank which was to engage in colonial trade.

METHUEN TREATY: Commercial treaty of 1703 between England and Portugal. By its terms the Portuguese gave special preference to English woolen goods and the English admitted Portuguese wines at one third less duty than French wines. It was this treaty that laid the basis for the popularity of port wine in eighteenth-century England.

trade for almost a century, solved a host of problems before any rival appeared on the scene, and smoothed the paths of Holland, England, and France to trade and empire in the East. Not the least service, or disservice, of Portugal was to furnish other powers a classic example of absolute monopoly in colonial trade.

A key figure in the early overseas expansion of Europe was Prince Henry the Navigator. The conquest of Céuta in 1415 and the expedition he led three years later to repel a Moorish counterattack against this stronghold permanently fixed the attention of Prince Henry upon Africa. The tragic failure of Portuguese arms against Tangier in 1437 convinced him that Portugal's future lay in the utilization of sea power along the western coast of Africa and in the islands of the eastern Atlantic. As an adjunct to his systematic voyages of exploration, Henry began about 1420 to construct the astronomical observatory, naval arsenal, and institute for nautical research on Cape Sagres at what later became known as the *Villa do Infante*. Whether Henry established a formal school of geography remains a disputed issue. But he assembled Christian, Moorish, and Jewish scientists; provided them with excellent facilities; and gave them favorable working conditions. Research in geography, mathematics, and astronomy was pursued intermittently, if not continuously; and the results were applied to nautical instruments, naval architecture, and navigation. Henry's captains went to sea in good vessels and equipped with the best geographic data then known, and their reports at the end of the voyages provided valuable source material for the scientists on shore. Henry pushed his practical and scientific work forward for four decades, and the Portuguese kings continued it after his death. Great advances in the art and instruments of navigation, marine architecture, and geography resulted. The good ships and skilled mariners in Portugal and southwestern Spain, where Portuguese skills infiltrated, were important factors in

POMBAL: Eighteenth-century Portuguese minister who, as a mercantilist, favored government intervention in economic life in order to further the wealth, power, and unity of the state.

PHYSIOCRACY: School of economic thought in eighteenth-century France which stressed the importance of agriculture, the desirability of a minimum of state intervention in economic life, and the unwisdom of colonial monopolies.

the discovery of America and of the all-water route to the East Indies.

The early Portuguese chroniclers pictured Prince Henry as a recluse, who renounced the pleasures of the Court, to live, at least the last two decades of his life, immersed in study, on the sterile promontory of Sagres, motivated only by intellectual curiosity and a zealous desire to turn the flanks of Islam by skirting the western coast of Africa and effecting a union with a fabled Christian potentate somewhere in eastern Africa. His resources were supposedly drawn from the enormous revenues derived from his grand mastership of the Order of Christ, and trade was of strictly secondary importance. The chroniclers regarded Henry's exploits as a prolongation of the crusades. What his ultimate goals were one cannot say. But in his proximate aims and his methods he bore more resemblance to Commodore Vanderbilt than to Saint Francis of Assisi. Recent research has demonstrated that Henry was not a religious zealot devoid of worldly concerns and pecuniary aims but a company promoter, slave trader, and monopolistic exploiter. Through political influence this "ascetic" Prince obtained a monopoly on woad-dyeing in all Portugal, and he controlled the cloth industry in the provinces of Beira and Minho. He had the exclusive right to manufacture and sell white and dark soap in the entire kingdom. In 1440 Henry secured the exclusive privilege of sardine and tuna fishing off the Algarve coast for the Pescaria do Infante, a company ostensibly organized to end the unbearable tolls levied upon fishermen by the owners of vessels and equipment. Yet he claimed one-fifth of the profits for himself. Prince Henry formed a company in 1441 to enjoy a monopoly on trade with the Canary Islands not belonging to Spain. He loaned the company funds of the Order of Christ at 6 per cent and exacted a fifth of the profits for his services as a promoter. Derived from the capture of slaves and the cheap acquisition of produce, the returns amounted to 80 per cent in some years; and apparently Henry levied his toll until his death twenty years later. In 1450 Henry induced the Crown to force the company floated by foreigners the previous decade, to exploit a monopoly on the coral industry, to allow Portuguese subjects, including Henry, of course, to participate in the enterprise.

What interested Prince Henry in Africa, in the beginning, was the gold brought across the Sahara by caravans; after about 1441, the gold dust and the rich slave-raiding territory found on the west African coast; and, finally, the hope of reaching the East Indies by water, thus giving Portugal complete control over the spice trade of all Europe. In view of Henry's acquisitiveness, his unwillingness to permit either foreigners or compatriots to trade or sail along the coast of Africa is not surprising. Until the gold dust and slaves began to pour into Portugal in significant quantities in the early 1440's, trade and exploration were confined to the one or two vessels a year Henry was ordinarily able to send out. Since the new opportunities exceeded Henry's resources, he organized the First Lagos Company in 1444 and the Second Lagos Company in 1447 for trade and exploration—to promote more trade. In 1449 he set up an affiliate of the Pescaria do Infante to monopolize the fisheries off the African coast. After Henry's death the Second Lagos Company was dissolved, but the trade was not thrown open. For the remainder of the fifteenth century it was farmed out by the Crown as an exclusive privilege to Portuguese companies and subjects. Not until after the papal bulls of Alexander VI and the Treaty of Tordesillas of 1494 had divided the "world" between the two Iberian powers did Portugal concede to Spain the right to fish in west African waters.

When the acquisition of gold and slaves progressed, and the prospects of finding an all-water route to the Indies brightened, as the intrepid explorers pushed down the African coast, Portugal obtained one papal bull after another forbidding all other powers to trade in the new territory and to navigate in the new seas. The reluctance of Protestant countries for almost a century to violate the claims of Portugal and Spain suggests that the bulls were not mere scraps of paper, but the formidable sea power of the Iberian states was doubtless the primary factor in the initial success of exclusion. The valuable prizes in hand, and believed to be in the offing, were strong incentives for Portugal's precedent of rigidly excluding other nations from overseas dominions—a precedent followed, with few and generally brief exceptions, by every other colonial power until the nineteenth century. If the rewards of Portuguese discovery and exploration had appeared less valuable, the subsequent pattern of colonial trade might have been more liberal and international relations somewhat less turbulent.

Vasco da Gama returned from his discovery of the Cape of Good Hope route to the East Indies with spices and other oriental products that yielded approximately 6,000 per cent on the entire cost; and Cabral's voyage four years later, which accidentally established the Portuguese claim to Brazil, paid a handsome profit. With such fabulous returns, the Crown was bound to establish the monopolistic system prevailing in the African trade. In the first three quarters of the sixteenth century vessels went to the East Indies only at the expense and at the risk of the king. The king sold licenses to private traders and companies to send goods to the Indies and to import oriental products; but he soon began to take the spice trade into his own hands, and by 1520 his monopoly was complete. Portugal endeavored not only to supply Europe with all her spices but to take over the commerce and the carrying trade of India and the East Indies with China, Japan, Africa, and the Near East. How ruthlessly Portugal pursued this aim is shown by a proclamation of 1524 providing that "the penalty to a native captain found in Indian waters without a Portuguese license was death and seizure of his ship and property. The officials took care, before granting the permit, to secure a lion's share in the profits of the voyage." The Portuguese soon realized they could not attain their objectives without seizing political control over key positions. In the first half of the sixteenth century intrigue and the sword gave Portugal such strategic points as Hormuz, Diu, Goa, Malacca, and Macao; and either directly or through alliances she controlled most of their hinterlands. By establishing or maintaining friendly dynasties or parties in power, the Portuguese dictated many treaties that excluded all alien traders and either exempted the Portuguese from customs duties or granted them lower rates than native merchants paid. Furthermore, the rulers of Calicut, Malabar, Ceylon, and the Moluccas were forced by treaty to sell all the pepper, ginger, cinnamon, cloves, and nutmeg in their kingdoms exclusively to the Portuguese government. Whenever the quantity of any spice was excessive, that is, was greater than would yield the maximum net revenue to the intruding monopolist, the surplus was destroyed on the spot.

For a few years after Magellan's voyage around the world Spain planned to trade with the spice islands via Cape Horn, but Portugal's purchase of the Spanish claim to the Moluccas in 1529 ended this threat. A few French and English interlopers reached the East Indies; but their activities were sporadic and, for the most part, on a small scale.

The only serious violation of the royal monopoly on direct trade with the East Indies was by Portuguese officials. The high prices resulting from the suppression of competition in Portugal and the Indies made smuggling attractive. Since the captains of Portuguese war vessels received less than Dutch sergeants, and other officials were paid accordingly, the temptation to smuggle proved irresistible. Partially to combat this evil, in 1575 the Crown farmed the exclusive right to trade on a twenty-five mile stretch of coast in Cochin-China. Two years later the king began to contract with a company to import spices and deliver them to him at Lisbon at stipulated prices. To another company he farmed the privilege of selling in Lisbon the spices he did not want to market through his factor in the Low Countries. When Philip II succeeded to the Portuguese throne in 1580, he continued to farm the right to import and sell spices and to permit only favorite merchants, willing to pay dearly for royal licenses, to trade with the East Indies. Under the new system spice prices obviously were administered, not competitive; but the corporate monopolists must have been less grasping than their royal predecessor. For in the midst of the Price Revolution, spice prices in Spain dropped precipitately and did not recover the loss for almost half a century. At no time before Portugal lost her supremacy in the East Indies, early in the seventeenth century, did competition govern the purchase or sale of goods either at home or in the colonies.

Portugal attempted to exclude foreigners from the trade with Brazil, but it appears to have been much more open to natives until 1755 than was the East India trade. In 1502 the exclusive privilege of importing Brazil wood was farmed to a company; but the monopoly ended about 1530, when imports from Spanish America rendered it unattractive. From early in the sixteenth century until the middle of the eighteenth century trade with Brazil was confined to fleets that sailed from Lisbon, touched at Oporto, and stopped at four leading Brazilian ports. Apparently all Portuguese subjects were free to participate, but we do not know the extent to which formal associations or informal agreements among businessmen or other trading bodies limited competition. By 1750 concentration of the trade in the hands of the Jesuits was so great that the Marquis of Pombal preferred an absolute legal monopoly. Consequently, he divided the trade between the Maranhao Company, chartered in 1755, and the Pernambuco Company, established in 1759. The companies maintained their monopolies on trade with Brazil until their dissolution in 1778 and 1780 respectively. After experimenting with a concession of the diamond mines discovered in 1730, under a strict limitation on the number of workers who might be employed, the Portuguese government adopted drastic measures to curtail smuggling, limit production, maintain prices, and maximize revenues. No building might be erected, and no unauthorized person might reside, within a hundred leagues of the mine. Apparently the supply of diamonds was restricted, but the resultant increase in their value may not even have equalled the lost output of the agriculture and industry extinguished in the blighted area. Like other colonial powers in America, Portugal restricted or prohibited certain types of industry to protect vested interests at home. To prevent competition with Portuguese wines, olives, and olive oil, no grape vines or olive trees might be planted. The production of raw sugar was encouraged in every possible way, but refineries were banned. Although the Portuguese textile industry languished after the Treaty of Methuen in 1703, only coarse linen and cotton goods to clothe the slaves and poor whites might be produced in Brazil. Early in the nineteenth century skilled spinners who had set up spindles were banished from the colony.

III. *Spain*

The high rewards demanded by Columbus in negotiating the contract for his first voyage show that, whatever other incentives he may have had, his economic motivation was strong; and the delay of the Catholic Kings in accepting his terms, after they had accepted his plans, indicates that they shared his concern for the commercial opportunities. The thorough search by Columbus for the precious metals and valuable objects of commerce and the keen interest of Ferdinand and Isabella in what he found point in the same direction. How far it was from the intention of the Spanish monarchs to share the discovery with any other power is shown by their haste in obtaining a papal bull confirming their claims and by the fact that from the beginning no Spaniards except Castilians were allowed to trade with the New World. Monopolistic chartered companies developed late and never controlled a major portion of the trade. The only important examples were the exclusive privilege of trading with Venezuela granted the Caracas Company in 1728, and exercised for half a century, and the monopoly on trade with the Philippines given the Philippine Company in 1785. But, as in the case of Portugal, royal regulation, semistate shipping, and the funneling of commerce through staple ports facilitated private monopolies.

The early discovery of gold in the Antilles and the fabulous amounts of silver secured after regular mining by Spaniards began in Mexico and Peru, in an age when treasure was supposed to provide the key to wealth and power, naturally induced one of the most rigid systems of state regulation of colonial trade ever adopted by any country. With infrequent and unimportant exceptions, licenses had to be obtained from, or through, the House of Trade (Casa de la Contratación), established at Seville in 1503 and transferred to Cádiz in 1717, for all vessels, merchants, and emigrants bound for America. All ships had to return to the House of Trade to pass a severe inspection, unload their cargoes, and deliver their gold and silver. In a vain effort to obstruct the leakage of Peruvian treasure into foreign hands, Castile imposed destructive restrictions—limitation of tonnage, absolute prohibitions, and prohibitive duties—upon trade between Buenos Aires and Spain on the one hand and Peru on the other. The economic development of the rich River Plate region was retarded for generations. To prevent bullion from being smuggled into, or captured by, other nations, almost all trade with the New World was confined to two convoyed fleets after the middle of the sixteenth century. The fleets sailed from and returned to the House of Trade once a year when commerce was flourishing and once every three or four years when it was stagnant. The irregular and infrequent sailings from Spain, inevitable under the fleet system, facilitated the inroads of Dutch, French, and English interlopers upon Spanish exclusionism. Arbitrary searches of foreign vessels in Caribbean waters and other vigorous measures of Spain to suppress the contraband trade were a factor in several wars and were the principal cause of the long conflict with England in 1739-50.

Despite the pressure of special interests in Spain, the policy toward the commerce and industry of the American colonies was relatively liberal. Intercolonial trade not considered injurious to Castilian interests, nor likely to facilitate the smuggling of specie out of the realm, was subjected to low duties and suffered few restrictions. No systematic attempts were made to prevent manufactures for domestic consumption, and so long as an industry did not compete with Castile in an external market it remained undisturbed. For example, woolen and silk manufactures, objects of great concern to the mercantilist statesmen and rulers in Spain, were permitted. But in the seventeenth century exports to other colonies were impeded; and the requirement in 1628 of a license from the Council of the Indies to make cloth in America, ostensibly to protect the Indians from exploitation, was designed to protect Castilian industry. Yet Spain was the only country to allow legal operation of refineries in the sugar colonies. At various times the government outlawed the cultivation of saffron, hemp, flax, tobacco, and olives; but at other times the production of hemp and flax was heavily subsidized. The early prohibitions against vineyards in Peru

were not enforced; and no attention was paid to the order received by
the Mexican Viceroy early in the nineteenth century to have all the
vineyards in northern Mexico destroyed, because the Cádiz Guild
Merchant had complained that they were disastrously reducing wine
imports from Spain.

Until 1785 goods shipped between Spain and the Philippines had
to pass over the bad roads and high mountains between the Mexican
ports of Veracruz and Acapulco; and the tonnage, value of cargoes,
and amounts of specie that might move between New Spain and the
Philippines were severely restricted. The members of the Guild
Merchant at Mexico City doubtless utilized their opportunity to levy
a monopolistic toll. For more than two centuries all lawful European
imports into Mexico were carried to Veracruz by the New Spain
Fleet and those of the entire western coast of South America to
Lima via Panama by the Galleons. The restriction of the Mexican
and Peruvian commerce to one metropolitan and two colonial ports
enabled small groups of traders in the Merchant Guilds at Seville,
Cádiz, Mexico City, and Lima to control the volume and dictate the
prices of imports and exports in Spain and America. The habilitation
of other ports in Spain and America by the so-called "Free Trade
Acts" (Libre Comercio) of Charles III and his progressive ministers
beginning in 1765 induced some competition. But even in the last
years of peace before the outbreak of the wars of the French Revolution, in 1793, ended peacetime trade between Spain and her colonies
four-fifths of the American commerce passed through Cádiz. It is
highly significant that five of the nine indictments against Spanish
rule circulated throughout Hispanic America by the revolutionaries
in 1808 concerned monopolistic abuses; and the Cádiz Guild Merchant
was bitterly attacked. One of the chief inducements to fight held out
by the intellectual leaders in Latin America during the long War of
Independence was the promise of fair prices for produce and for
imports through the suppression of the Cádiz monopoly.

IV. *Holland*

As Spain declined during the seventeenth century, Holland became
the foremost nation in the colonial trade, and its United East India
Company the leading economic enterprise in Europe. The company
was the instrument through which the Dutch empire in the East was

obtained. But there was much less innovation in the Dutch policies than in those of Portugal and rather less than in those of Spain. Furthermore, the original policies remained surprisingly static until the East India Company expired in 1795. Holland was never a major colonial power in the West.

In the Dutch East Indies the flag not only followed the private trader but was firmly planted there by him. In 1594, when Philip II, closed the Lisbon harbor to the Dutch vessels that had been distributing Portuguese spices in northern Europe, in an effort to bring the Dutch rebellion against Spanish rule to an end, the enterprising traders began to sail directly to the East Indies. Commercial success and the disclosure of unsuspected Portuguese weakness in the East induced voyages in rapid succession. In the last five years of the sixteenth century sixty-odd Dutch vessels sailed to the East Indies. The early traders protested that they had to deal with semibarbarous rulers who did not share European conceptions of law and order or of the sanctity of contracts. The Dutch also complained of cutthroat competition with their compatriots in selling European wares and in buying native products. They did lack knowledge of political conditions and of local markets; and owing to the long period of waiting for the returns, the heavy outlay for transportation, and the great and unpredictable risks involved, their capital was pathetically inadequate. To raise funds and end "abuses," in 1602 the traders and other Dutch businessmen formed the United East India Company. Its charter gave it a monopoly on trade and navigation with the East for twenty-one years and authorized it to acquire territory, establish fortresses, and make war and peace within its sphere of operations.

Historians of colonial policy and of the United East India Company agree that almost the only purpose of the Dutch in the East Indies before 1795 was to earn high profits by acquiring and holding a monopoly on spices. I have found no evidence that they ever pretended to Christianize or to lift up the natives. In fighting the Portuguese and the native rulers for control over spices, the Dutch adopted the Portuguese tactics of supporting a dynasty or faction and exacting monopolistic privileges after placing it in power. They also copied the Portuguese preference for the spice islands rather than for the mainlands and of trying to attain their commercial objectives by holding a chain of island fortresses. Like the Portuguese, the Dutch early began the practice of destroying surplus spices; that is,

the portion of the supply that might depress prices below the point
that would maximize their return. But they pushed this nefarious
policy much farther. They limited production to certain selected areas,
carefully regulated the output, regularly dispatched inspectors to see
that the prohibition of production was obeyed, and not only chopped
down spice trees but lopped off heads, to leave no producers, when
this seemed the only way to enforce compliance.

The ridiculous rigidity in the policies of the East India Company,
into which it may have been lulled by monopoly and conspicuous success in its first hundred years, was a major factor in its decline. Even
in the most peaceful years of the eighteenth century vessels returning
from the Indies had to sail around the Orkneys instead of through
the English Channel, as prudence had dictated during the long
conflicts with England in the second half of the preceding century.
Even after light, fast, and strong English vessels began to compete
most effectively in the carrying trade in the East, the Dutch vessels
had to incur the heavy and needless expense of passing by Batavia
for inspection on each voyage. The monopoly of the East India Company injured not only the natives but the Dutch as well. For example,
when the Cromwellian and Stuart Navigation Acts deprived Dutch
vessels of their normal cargoes, the Eastern carrying trade might have
afforded some relief had it not been closed by the East India Company's monopoly. As in the case of the Portuguese, the chief infringement of the monopoly was by the underpaid officials of the East
India Company. But the natives benefited very little from this breach,
for the officials arbitrarily set up monopolies of their own and exploited them mercilessly. The murder of English subjects at Amboina
in 1623, in defense of the monopoly, embittered relations with England
for generations; and more than once Holland went to war to defend
the territory or the trade of the East India Company.

Even though rich booty from privateering against Spain, high
profits from trading with the Spanish colonies, and a monopoly on
trade from Newfoundland to Tierra del Fuego were held out as
inducements, private Dutch investors were not attracted by the stock
of the Dutch West India Company, organized in 1621. The government had to subscribe for half the shares and to exert the utmost
pressure upon financiers to take the balance. Apparently the clever
Dutch businessman saw no opportunity to profit by war even against
a power at once as weak and as rich in land as was the Spain of

Philip IV. The West India Company has been praised by economists for throwing open the trade with Surinam and taxing it lightly instead of exercising its monopoly, as well as for attempting to develop its possessions in the New World. But apparently these policies did not pay. In 1674 the West India Company was dissolved, after having dissipated most of its capital. "Nevertheless, upon the ruins of the defunct institution another was to rise. The States-General, in 1674, licensed the new organization with a capital of 6,000,000 florins. . . . Although active until 1790 it never flourished, and its possessions were few."

V. *France*

Of the great colonial powers before 1800, France was the last to enter the field, the least original in its policies, and the least successful in the use of monopolies to open up and maintain colonial commerce. Hence, for my purpose, French experience merits only brief attention.

Since nothing had come from the Company of Sumatra, Java, and Moluccas, chartered in 1600, Henry IV established the first French East India Company in 1604, with exclusive rights to trade, navigate, and colonize in India and the East Indies. Except for 1769-84, trade and navigation with the East under the *ancien régime* remained in the hands of a monopoly. After the vigorous efforts of both Richelieu and Mazarin had utterly failed to vitalize the East India trade, Colbert gave his East India Company, chartered in 1664, the exclusive privilege for fifty years of trading and navigating from the Cape of Good Hope east to the Straits of Magellan, a heavy bounty on imports and exports, a royal guarantee against losses in the first six years, and naval escorts for its vessels at public expense whenever needed. In view of the uncritical acceptance by many liberals and even conservatives of the communist theory of imperialism, repeated with increasing asperity by writers and statesmen from Rosa Luxemburg and Rudolf Hilferding to Lenin and Molotov, one might expect that French capitalists in the age of Louis XIV, the war lord of Europe, were the instigators and eager beneficiaries of these opportunities. But neither financiers, nor overseas traders, nor any other capitalists cared to invest. When venture capital was not forthcoming, Colbert and Louis XIV appealed to the public to buy the East India shares for the glory of God, country, and king—in much the same fashion that the Russian Court was to appeal for funds for the exploitation of the financially unattractive timber concessions along the Yalu River on the eve of the Russo-Japanese war. The royal treasury actually had to put up more than half the money for the French East India Company; and most of the remainder came from public officials, less able than businessmen to resist the formidable pressure to invest, exerted not only by Colbert but by Louis XIV himself. The company lost more than two-thirds of its capital in its first twenty years, and it languished until the brief interval when the organizational skill and inflationary policies of John Law injected life into the East India trade. For about three decades after the collapse of the Mississippi Bubble the monopolistic privileges could not keep the East India Company going, without liberal subsidies from the royal treasury. The Seven Years' War stripped the company of most of the territorial gains achieved during the blaze of glory under Dupleix in the middle of the eighteenth century; and in 1769 physiocratic theories, marshalled by Morellet, succeeded in suppressing the monopoly on trade with the East. The flourishing commerce in the brief interval of freedom seemed to vindicate the physiocrats, but in 1785 the monopoly was restored on the ground that cutthroat competition among French traders was ruinously depressing the prices they received and raising those they paid in the East.

Haiti, by far the most important of all the French colonies under the *ancien régime,* was founded by buccaneers and smugglers without the encouragement or even the knowledge of the government. But most of the leading French colonies in the New World were established under patents granting privileges in which a monopoly on trade, in return for the settlement of a certain number of colonists within a limited period, figured prominently. When the colonial entrepreneurs lost money and their privileges lapsed, a new company was usually formed to exploit them. In the century between Mazarin and John Law the trade of most of the French colonies in America was theoretically controlled by a monopoly most of the time. But Colbert forced the West India Company to allow any French vessel to trade in the sugar colonies upon the payment of duties to the company; and the proximity of Canada to the active traders and accomplished smugglers of New England, together with the great need of the Caribbean islands for Anglo-American provisions and timber, meant that a great many vessels came from other countries as well. One can hardly imagine the descendants of freebooters and free traders or the progenitors of Toussaint l'Ouverture's soldiers in Haiti having much respect for monopolistic privileges at any time. Between 1721 and 1731 the trade of the American colonies was thrown open to all Frenchmen, and apparently it remained open during the remainder of the century. In 1784 the vessels of the United States were permitted to trade with the French possessions in the Caribbean. In the freedom of their trade with all subjects of the motherland, the French colonies probably ranked next to those of England, and in *de facto* trade with the outside world the French colonies probably ranked first. The French colonies also suffered from the fewest restrictions to protect vested interests in the mother country. The only obstructions that seem to have hampered the colonies very much were the prohibition on the erection of new sugar refineries in 1684 and the law of 1698 suppressing the ones already in operation. As a. compensation the colonies enjoyed a monopoly on the metropolitan sugar market. The relative economic freedom was doubtless a vital factor in the prosperous agriculture and commerce of Saint Christopher, Martinique, Guadeloupe, and Haiti.

VI. *England*

On the whole, England was the leading colonial power in the East and the West before 1800, as well as after. Through monopoly she established her trade and empire in the East, and through promises of monopoly she motivated her early voyages and first successful and unsuccessful colonial ventures in the West. Except for the first half century, when the colonies were few and feeble, England excluded other countries from direct trade and navigation with her American plantations. Since leading historians and economists interested in the history of economic thought have lavished study upon English colonial experience, the policies are too familiar to economic historians to require detailed examination. Hence, it seems safe to assume that the general features are known and to limit our consideration to the salient characteristics and results.

The English East India Company, chartered in 1600, was given a monopoly on trade and navigation in the area between the Cape of Good Hope and the Straits of Magellan not occupied by a friendly power. It was the company, formed and administered by merchants, not the government, that built up the empire in the East—to protect and promote trade. The monopoly of navigation lasted until 1813, but from late in the seventeenth century merchants willing to pay the exorbitant freight rates on the company's vessels had the right to send a limited tonnage of goods to the East. The energy and ingenuity of traders and the freedom and vigor of thought in England combined to make interloping much commoner than in any other country, and on several occasions the impecunious Crown granted exemptions from the monopoly for particular voyages in return for substantial fees. Opposition to the monopoly by interloping merchants and liberal economists generally enabled the government to exact increasing rewards, ordinarily in the form of loans at less than the going rate of interest, whenever the privileges were renewed. But in 1793 the company secured an extension of its monopoly by demonstrating the enormous profits of recent years and asking whether the objections of mere theorists should delude Parliament into tampering with such a successful enterprise. The "theorists" happened to be interloping merchants as innocent of, and unsympathetic toward, economics as is a typical member of the National Association of Manufacturers. Despite the relatively high and steadily increasing remuneration of the company's employees, it had almost as much difficulty in preventing the abuse of the company and the natives by the petty private monopolies of its servants in the East as did Portugal or Holland. Even as late as the 1760's, the company's Eastern employees dictated the prices they paid for native products and the prices they charged for such imported necessities as salt, tobacco, and betel nuts. Furthermore, they attempted to limit the output of the produce they purchased and to require the natives to buy minimum amounts of what they sold—after the fashion of the seventeenth-century tax farmers in France and Spain who forced the poor to pay for a certain amount of salt whether they used it or not. How prevalent private trading by the company's officers must have been is shown by a minute from Lord Clive on September 19, 1766. He informed the Select Committee that "'a Governor ought not to be embarrassed with private business. He ought to be free from every occupation in which his judgment can possibly be biased by his interest.' He, therefore, proposed, that the Governor should receive a commission of one and one-eighth per cent upon the revenues; and in return should take a solemn and public oath, and bind himself in a penalty of £150,000 to derive no emolument or advantage from his situation as Governor of Bengal, beyond this commission, with the usual salary and perquisites: and a covenant to this effect was formally executed by him." Nevertheless, to combat private trading, in 1784, servants of the company returning to England were required to give under oath an inventory of their property and rendered liable to imprisonment and the forfeiture of all their wealth for a false statement.

From Henry VII to James I, English patents for voyages of discovery and for colonization generally provided a monopoly of trade as one of the incentives. The companies that established the initial settlements in Virginia and Massachusetts, the first and most important two of the Thirteen Colonies, had either exclusive privileges or the right to tax commerce conducted by others. But these privileges soon lapsed and were not revived. After the first quarter of the seventeenth century no commercial company monopolized trade with the American colonies south of the Hudson Bay region. The Dutch, whose capital is said to have aided in the foundation of the first English sugar colonies, soon supplied the shipping and took over a considerable percentage of the trade of the Anglo-American plantations. In 1625 England forbade imports of tobacco in foreign vessels, but frequent repetition of the prohibition suggests that it was not enforced. Amendments to the Navigation Acts beginning about 1663 shifted the colonial trade to English vessels, allowed imports only from England, and required that exports of enumerated articles—for the most part industrial raw materials in short supply—be shipped to England. In compensation for these restrictions the colonies were given a virtual monopoly on the metropolitan market for enumerated articles through prohibitions and prohibitive duties. Particularly after 1699, the manufacture and intercolonial shipment of various manufactures were banned in order to protect English industries. Adam Smith probably underestimated the efficacy of these restrictions when he dismissed them as "only impertinent badges of slavery," that neither "cramped" nor "restrained" our industry; but the plethora of advertisements of proscribed manufactures in colonial newspapers indicates that we were "restrained" very little.

In his study of the Navigation Acts, Professor L. A. Harper, who has thoroughly combed the manuscript sources in England and America, concluded that the Acts gave England and the colonies virtual control over the colonial export trade. Through facts and logic he shows that most of the imports came into the Thirteen Colonies in English vessels through legal channels. In his exhaustive study of the records of Thomas and John Hancock, both of whom were notorious smugglers, W. T. Baxter found no evidence that a single foreign vessel participated in trade with the American colonies in the half century prior to the Revolution, when the temptation to smuggle reached its zenith. As Professor Harper has maintained, the Navigation Acts ousted the Dutch from the American trade and gave England the lion's share for several decades. Whether either the colonies or England gained by this diversion is another matter. But there is reason to wonder whether England would not have retained at least as great a proportion of the trade if she had repealed the Navigation Acts at the end of the Seven Years' War. The overwhelming industrial superiority of England over every rival in 1763-75 and the fact that the percentage of American trade obtained by England rose phenomenally in the first quarter-century after the Revolution—in spite of bitter war memories, the loss of commercial connections by English exporters with American importers, and the irritation in this country over our exclusion from legal trade with England's sugar colonies—suggests that a timely repeal of the Navigation Acts and the other restrictions on our economic life might have retained our trade, gained our good will, and possibly averted or delayed the Revolution. But even if the Navigation Acts, not the efficiency of English industry and commerce, did confine the trade of America largely to England, the deleterious effects of the restriction were reduced by the fact that the commerce was not in the hands of a monopolistic company, carried by convoyed fleets at irregular and infrequent intervals, or channeled through a few ports. Adam Smith, who was a keen observer of the American trade in the thriving port of Glasgow and who was disposed to see a monopolist wherever he looked, felt that "the number and dispersed situation of the different traders [exporting to America] renders it impossible for them to enter into any general combination" in restraint of trade.

VII. *Conclusions*

The leading motive for the discovery of America and the Good-Hope route to the East Indies, which marked the dawn of modern times, was the hope of material gain from the spice trade. It is inconceivable that any country would have willingly shared access to such fabulous riches as the spices of the Eastern seas or the gold and silver of the Mexican and Peruvian mines. Following the example of the Iberian kings, every other European monarch refused to permit any other power to trade with his colonies before the end of the eighteenth century. Furthermore, staple ports, convoyed fleets, prescribed routes, and special privileges—designed to extend and protect commerce and empire—closed most of the colonies to most of the subjects of most of the colonial powers most of the time.

The Portuguese concessions of monopolies on trade and navigation to companies and court favorites in the days of Prince Henry the Navigator required exploration at a specified rate, and the kings of England and France promised exclusive trading privileges in their early patents for discovery and colonization. Hence, a monopoly on colonial trade was contractually connected with European expansion into the West. The monopoly on trade granted the Dutch, English, and French East India Companies afforded the incentive to commerce and empire in the East. The issuing governments were convinced that without a joint-stock company enjoying an exclusive privilege of trade and navigation enough capital could not be raised to tide over the long period of waiting for returns, bear the enormous risks, defray the cost of providing and equipping vessels, and "protect" cargoes, merchants, and ships against semibarbarous natives and rulers. Even such an ardent "laissez-fairist" as Jean-Baptiste Say justified monopoly to induce the establishment of trade in "a distant or barbarous area," just as a patent is granted to reward invention; and Adam Smith had taken a similar position. But both authors insisted that, like a patent, the monopoly should be tolerated for a limited time only. The East India Companies not only held their privileges much longer than was warranted on economic grounds but abused their authority, and petty monopolies by officers and servants on internal trade in the colonies often paralleled the hold of the companies on external commerce.

The monopolistic trading companies depressed the prices of exports and raised those of imports in Europe and the Eastern colonies. In the short run producers suffered, and consumers were permanently oppressed. The high prices paid for imports in colonial and metropolitan markets went to monopolistic middlemen instead of to producers in the exporting countries, who, under perfect competition, could have been expected to increase their output. Factors of production were diverted from their most fruitful use and were underemployed during the transition. In reality the cost of occupying and exploiting backward areas was defrayed by a sort of tax, paid not to the government presumably for the benefit of the body politic, but to a favored group of courtiers and monopolistic traders. The tax was not rational in its amount or incidence; and the poor in the colonies, upon whom a large share of the burden fell, were taxed without representation or even consultation. The monopolistic toll bore no relation to the cost of the "service," but was based on what the traffic would bear.

Without monopoly, there probably would have been no European empire in the East before 1800. Hence, in the final analysis, one's appraisal of the role of monopoly in the expansion to the East depends upon his view as to how well the white man bore his burden. To economic liberals it is gratifying that the American colonies of England and France, where industry and trade enjoyed the greatest freedom, were the ones that achieved the greatest material progress.

VI

The Habsburgs in Early Modern Times

❯❯❯❯❯❯❯❯❯❯❯❯❯❯❮❮❮❮❮❮❮❮❮❮❮❮❮❮

Tendencies and Individuals. Charles V and Philip II

SIR CHARLES OMAN

The Thirty Years' War: A New Interpretation

S. H. STEINBERG

The Decline of Spain

EARL J. HAMILTON

❯❯❯❯❯❯❯❯❯❯❯❯❯❯❮❮❮❮❮❮❮❮❮❮❮❮❮❮

Tendencies and Individuals. Charles V and Philip II

SIR CHARLES OMAN

➤➤➤➤➤➤➤➤➤ *Published in 1937* ◀◀◀◀◀◀◀◀◀◀◀

Since Spain was the dominant power in sixteenth-century Europe, the political life and international relations of the time can be studied most accurately by an analysis of the policies of the Habsburg rulers of Spain— Charles I (1516-56; Charles V as Holy Roman Emperor) and Philip II (1556-98). These Habsburg rulers have attracted the attention of scores of historians. As a matter of fact, in the eighteenth and nineteenth centuries the two rulers figured in a number of works that rapidly became historical classics: William Robertson's *Charles V*, William H. Prescott's *Philip II*, and John Lothrop Motley's *Rise of the Dutch Republic*. In more recent years Charles and Philip have rarely been treated by a scholar with so much insight as Sir Charles Oman, the talented military historian. Strongly sympathetic to Charles but distinctly hostile to Philip, Sir Charles compares and contrasts their problems and policies in this chapter from his valuable book of essays *The Sixteenth Century* (1937).

There was one personage whose activities cover all the most important years of the century, and whose position was so abnormal and unprecedented that at the first glance it might seem that he ought to have become the dictator of Europe, and to have set his impress on the whole of Christendom. Yet he failed to do so. Napoleon, whose knowledge of history was somewhat sketchy, once expressed his surprise that Charles V did not succeed in mastering the world.

Certainly his opportunities appeared to be great, and his personal character was high: though not a genius, he was a most level-headed,
intelligent and hard-working monarch, not plagued with vices like his
contemporaries Francis I and Henry VIII, and entirely destitute of
the megalomania or 'kaiserwahnsin' which ruined many princes of
less ability in all ages. On the whole he was a moderate, well-meaning,
religious man, with a strong sense of duty and an infinite capacity
for hard work.

The election of Charles as Emperor in 1519, in succession to his
grandfather Maximilian, gave him a position which no sovereign
since Charlemagne had enjoyed, since he was not only the sole owner
of the heritages of Hapsburg, Burgundy, Castile and Aragon, and the
possessor of the southern half of Italy, but also the titular head of the
Holy Roman Empire. The imperial title had come to mean little when
it was in the hands of princes with a moderate territorial endowment,
like Charles' great-grandfather Frederic III, or the Schwartzburg,
Palatine, Nassau, and Dutch emperors of earlier centuries. But the
immense possessions of Charles outside Germany gave him a chance
of making the imperial power a reality, after centuries of impotence.
For no emperor before him had ever possessed such resources, territorial, financial, and military. Nothing looked more likely in 1519
than the establishment of a Hapsburg domination over all central
and southern Europe. For the new Emperor inherited a share of the
diplomatic ability of his Spanish grandfather Ferdinand, and no small
portion of the magnanimous and adventurous temperament of his
Austrian grandfather Maximilian.

This being so, it may appear extraordinary that Charles did not
attain to what appeared to be his obvious destiny, and after many
wars and many victories, retired in his old age to a monastery, as a
broken old man who had failed to achieve his purpose.

The reasons for the frustration of his career were three—one
psychological, and two military. The first was, of course, the outbreak
of the Protestant Reformation—a religious movement far more complicated and serious than any preceding phenomena of a more or less
similar character, such as the waves of indignation that followed on
the great schism of 1378, or the national unrest that resulted in certain regions from the teaching of John Wyclif in England or John
Huss in Bohemia. The disruption of Germany that started with the

Lutheran protest was undoubtedly one of the main causes of the failure of Charles in his life-work.

But the two military causes must be considered. The first was the irruption of the Ottoman Turks into Central Europe. They had been checked on the Danube for a hundred years, and no one foresaw the sudden collapse of the Hungarian monarchy at the battle of Mohacs (1526), or the further advance when the Turk thundered at the gates of Vienna in 1528. These catastrophes gave the Emperor a suddenly developed eastern war-front, which distracted his attention, and drew away his arms from France and Italy. Nor was it only on the Danube that the new peril became obvious. A few years after the disaster of Mohacs Turkish pirate chiefs, who had conquered Algiers and Tunis in 1516-17, offered their allegiance to Sultan Soliman, and placed their fleets at his disposal. The western Mediterranean ceased to be the 'mare nostrum' of the Italians, where for 500 years no non-Christian flag had been seen. A new and serious naval peril grew up for Sicily, Sardinia and Southern Spain—all in the Emperor's charge —and forced Charles during his short intervals of peace in Europe to direct his efforts against the pirate-scourge. His two great African campaigns against Tunis (1535) and Algiers (1542) were the one a transient success, the other a dreadful disaster, which destroyed an army that would have been invaluable in Italy a year later. It was the misfortune of Charles V that he had to deal with the most capable and ambitious of all the sultans who ever reigned at Constantinople, a monarch as steadfast and as obstinate as himself, and even more physically vigorous, for Soliman died in his tent, still campaigning, at seventy-three, while Charles had retired, worn out, to his monastery at the age of fifty-six.

If he had been engaged with the Turk alone the great Emperor

AUTO-DA-FÉ: Act of faith. The ceremony for the public confession of repentant heretics and for the condemnation and punishment of those who did not repent.

CONCILIAR MOVEMENT: The unsuccessful series of attempts in the fifteenth century to reform the Roman Catholic Church by reducing the authority of the papacy and by increasing the power of the general councils of the Church.

might possibly have restored the boundary of Christendom on the Danube, and swept the Mediterranean free of the Barbary pirates. But the Turk was only his secondary enemy, against whom he marched or sailed at moments of special crisis or opportunity. His real foes were the Kings of France, still set beyond all reason on continuing the vain venture which had been started by Charles VIII, the conquest of Italy, though it had already led to a dozen lost campaigns, and drained the best blood of France in many disastrous battles. This persistent attempt to establish a French domination beyond the Alps was pursued with obstinacy, not only by Francis I, whose military career had started with that brilliant success at Marignano which obsessed his mind for many years, but by his son Henry II, who never had any such intoxicating glimpse of personal glory. It was not only the kings who were besotted, but the whole nation—an appeal to the charms of adventure and easily-got gain never failed in its effect on the French noblesse. Though regularly beaten off, the invasion of Italy was resumed again and again, whenever Charles V was distracted by some urgent problem in Germany or Hungary, or on the High Seas that face Africa.

The most immoral and the most effective policy of the French kings was alliance with the Turk, the common enemy of Christendom, which both Francis I and Henry II took up without shame. There was some protest against it among Frenchmen of the better and more religious type, as has been mentioned before, but no effective opposition, even when a combined Franco-Turkish fleet was ravaging the coasts of Corsica or Nice, and sending thousands of Christian captives to be sold in the slave-market of Constantinople.

As it turned out, the systematic stab in the back which the French kings used to deliver when Charles was deeply engaged with the

---

COMUNEROS: Castilians who participated in the uprising of 1520-1521 against Charles I. Led at the outset by aristocrats as well as bourgeois, they sought to restrict the growth of royal power and reassert the traditional rights and privileges of the towns and feudal aristocracy. They were crushed by 1521.

SEA BEGGARS: Naval contingents from the Netherlands, not much different from pirates, who, in the years when Dutch-Spanish relations were deteriorating, plundered Spanish vessels as well as vessels of their own countrymen.

Turk in Africa or Hungary, or worried by rebellions of Protestant princes in Germany, just sufficed to keep the Emperor from making a success of his reign. He had to have armies everywhere—on the Pyrenees, in Italy, in Flanders, on the Meuse and Rhine, and in his precarious African garrisons. And money to pay them was not always forthcoming—for the treasures of Mexico and Peru, on which his son could depend, were only just beginning to drift across the Atlantic to his treasury. He was often in a semi-bankrupt condition. When his mercenary troops were unpaid, they indulged in mutinies, or fell upon the civil population, or simply deserted. The princes of the empire grudged the money and contingents which they ought to have provided under the rules of the *Matricula*. Some of them, like Charles of Guelders and Robert of Bouillon, openly took sides with the French in the earlier years of the strife. Later on the Protestants of the Schmalkaldic League were far more dangerous in 1547, when a new king, quite as perverse in his ambitions as his father Francis, had just come to the throne, and eagerly linked his fortunes with those of the German heretics.

Victorious for a moment at Mühlberg over the rebel princes, and vainly in hopes that he had settled the religious troubles of Germany by the *Interim,* Charles was destined after a short pause to face the last and most unhappy of all his wars. He was attacked by Henry II, by Sultan Soliman, and by the German rebellion that flared up again under the leadership of the unscrupulous Maurice of Saxony. After some years of indecisive and sometimes disastrous campaigning the French had taken Metz, and had once more got a foothold in central Italy at Siena—the Turk was threatening Naples. Charles failed to get his son Philip elected as Emperor in his stead—the favourite scheme of his old age—and then feeling himself no better than a gout-ridden invalid, whose life's work had been a failure, abdicated, and retired to spend the short remainder of his life in the very remote Estremaduran Monastery of Juste. The legend that he spent his last months in the vain endeavour to make several clocks keep exactly the same time is probably an allegory, hinting that he had so many problems under his hand at one time that the happy moment when all should be solved simultaneously never arrived.

The life of Charles was not all failure—he had won the domination of Italy for the House of Hapsburg, and he had fought the Turks to a standstill. The French danger had been staved off, and before the old emperor had been long dead, France fell into the interminable wars of Catholic and Huguenot, and ceased for a long generation to be an aggressive power. The Ottoman empire, a few years later, passed from the hands of the great Soliman into those of a sot, who was followed on the divan by a miser. But Charles did not live to see the passing away of the perils which he had spent his life in confronting.

Nevertheless his career was a disappointment in its main lines. He had failed to make the Emperor once more a dictatorial ruler in Germany, and he had failed equally in the attempt to reunite Christendom under a reformed Roman Church. By the end of his life he had come to regard Protestantism as no less a danger than the Turk, but his method of dealing with it by reviving the great Conciliar Movement for the consideration of all religious questions, was foiled at Trent, by the triumph of the intransigent elements and the diplomacy of the popes and the Jesuits. For the future neither councils nor lay sovereigns could meddle with the Papacy or with doctrine.

There had, of course, been many conjunctures when Charles might, if he had chosen, have put himself at the head of a national German demand for Church reform and revision of doctrine, a move which would have crushed the Papacy—for the popes were still behaving as intriguing Italian princes of no spiritual insight. But his personal character rendered this course impossible. He was a respectable and sincere Conformist, quite uninterested in such questions as Justification by Faith, or Free Will, or the meaning of the Sacrament of the Eucharist. And he had been profoundly shocked by some of the freakish developments of Protestantism, such as the antinomian outbursts of the Anabaptists, and the iconoclasm which devastated churches. The conduct of his own army in the sack of Rome in 1527 had made him feel ashamed—no Good Christian should have had any responsibility for the wrecking of St. Peter's, or the ransoming of cardinals, however tiresome and provocative the conduct of Clement VII might have been. He was all for reforming the administration of the Church, but not by violence, or by the breaking up of all time-honoured institutions. And, looking at matters from the point of view of an emperor, he naturally resented the conduct of his vassals—German princes and free cities—who introduced sweeping changes in Church government without consulting him or getting his permission. If he accepted the extraordinary decision of the Diet of Speier in 1526, running to the conclusion *'cujus regio ejus religio'* (15 August), it was because the

Pope and the King of France had formed the League of Cognac against him on 22 May, and he had no attention to spare for German quarrels at the moment. His real religious policy was embodied in the *Interim* of 1547, published after his victory at Mühlberg, and this imposed a creed on Germany founded on his good pleasure alone. His defeat was marked by the treaty of Passau (1552), which conceded local liberty of conscience, and his failure was formally proclaimed at the Diet of Augsburg (September, 1555), where it was enacted 'that no emperor or prince should offer any violence to any state on account of its religion or faith, but leave them quietly alone,' while religious differences should be adjusted by 'peaceful Christian methods.' In the same autumn (25 October) Charles announced his approaching retirement, and in January 1556 transferred the administration of his Spanish possessions to his son. In the following autumn he carried out the ceremony of resigning the Imperial Crown to his brother Ferdinand, and retired to Spain.

By assenting to the conclusions of Passau and Augsburg he had acknowledged that his whole policy had failed, so far as religious matters went. He handed over to his son not only the charge of the last act of the French war, which was soon brought to a successful close at Cateau Cambrésis, but a recommendation that peace with France should be accompanied by a joint action of both powers against heresy. A firm adherent of the old religion, he had permitted the persecution of heretics in his own hereditary states, though he had been forced to watch their multiplication in Germany ever since the Diet of Speier in 1526. But he was neither fanatical nor personally cruel, and his efforts to suppress Protestantism by the stake and sword were not very vigorous. It was reserved for his dull and ruthless son to make the Netherlands smoke from end to end with *autos-da-fé*, and to root out heresy completely from his Spanish and Italian dominions.

Putting aside the matter of religious persecution, a custom to which all princes in that age were equally addicted—there is little to criticize in the character of this laborious and not ungenerous emperor. He was courteous and even genial to his subjects—an extraordinary contrast to his awkward and arrogant heir. He was not revengeful or wilfully cruel—most victors would have beheaded the prisoners of the campaign of Mühlberg instead of merely imprisoning them. He was liberal when he had the wherewithal for liberality, which was not at all times. He was an enlightened patron of art—and was well repaid by Titian's magnificent picture of him in his old age. Though he won battles by the sword of his great captains, not by his personal guidance, he took the field in several years, and showed himself deficient neither in courage nor in endurance, though he was accused of lacking initiative, and showing over-caution in his last campaign on the northern frontiers of France. The indictment that he played false to Henry of England both in the campaign of 1523 and that of 1544, when his armies on each occasion failed to join hands with the English expeditionary force, may be parried by the allegation that Henry on his side failed to carry out his part of the co-operation—Suffolk's army on the one occasion, the King's own army on the other, never struck deep into France according to the original plan of campaign. Nevertheless a certain shadow of broken pledges hangs over the peace of Crépy, which left the English army stranded alone around Boulogne and Montreuil: though Charles perhaps knew that his ally also was intriguing for a separate peace with France.

Charles was a competent man, on the whole a man of laudable aspirations, he bestrode all Europe for nearly forty years, yet he left no permanent impression behind him. This was due partly to his own limitations, but much more to the extraordinary complication of hindrances which fell to his lot—the simultaneous attacks by the Kings of France and the Sultan coming precisely at the moment when the outbreak of the Reformation in Germany produced an unforeseen religious cataclysm with which no ordinary sovereign, however capable, could cope.

Oddly enough the great Emperor's detestable son left more of a trace on the history of the century than his brilliant father. The one had been a prince of the Renaissance, the other was a most perfect example of a prince of the Counter-Reformation. Considering the opportunities for evil that lay before 'el rey prudente,' we can only express a feeling of relief that his procrastination and indecision, his distrust of his best friends and his nearest kin, his leaden hand and his faithless pen, his secret treacheries and his open persecutions, saved Europe from falling under the black tyranny of a hypochondriac.

His armies fought many a good fight, his generals were the best in their generation. Fortunately the inspiration at the centre was missing. Philip himself was neither a general nor an organizer, and the strength which he wielded was due to his father's work, and to the line of great leaders bred in the old Italian wars. He himself, shut up in the Escurial, an ascetic Tiberius in a very bleak Capreae, contributed nothing to his wars but orders difficult and sometimes impossible to execute, always received with dismay by the reluctant commanders of his formidable hosts.

When we say that Philip left a permanent impression on his age we mean that he accomplished the remarkable feat of ruining the great empire which his father had left him, of leaving Spain drained of vitality and condemned to spiritual lethargy. A series of unsuccessful wars, combined with the deadening influence of systematic persecution and espionage worked by the Inquisition, broke the spirit of the Spanish race. Not all the gold of Peru and Mexico would compensate for the loss of initiative and energy caused by Philip's minute and detailed tyranny. For the misfortune of Spain his reign extended over more than forty years—destined to be almost exactly parallel with those of his shifty and unscrupulous rival Elizabeth of England —he started three years before her (1555 as against 1558); she outlived him by five years (they died in 1598 and 1603 respectively). By the time of his death he had crushed the spirits of a whole generation of his subjects, and left ruin behind him.

Philip, therefore, may be reckoned as one of the dominating figures of his age, though his domination was entirely of the negative sort— he saw to it that the inspiration alike of the Renaissance and the Reformation was killed in southern Europe—having the effective but not always willingly given co-operation of the Counter-Reformation popes and the Order of the Jesuits. They would not have accomplished all they did without the help of his sword, nor he have carried out his policy without the aid of their propaganda. But being a single figure with forty years of activity before him, he stands out more prominently as an individual than Paul IV or Pius IV or Pius V, all of whom were short-lived rulers, working for the same general end, no doubt, but in ways determined by their personal idiosyncrasies. Between them, Philip, the popes and the Jesuits kept half Europe in the Roman obedience, though the other half slipped free after a final struggle.

It should be noted that Philip was, in the early years of his reign, after the Peace of Cateau Cambrésis (1559), in a much more favourable position for exercising general influence in Europe than his father had ever been. The two great hindrances which had stood in the way of

Charles V had been removed. France, after the death of Henry II (1560), had plunged into a long series of civil wars, and was 'out of the picture.' Turkey, after the death of Soliman the Magnificent, had fallen into the hands of incompetent and eccentric sultans. The German problem had been taken out of Philip's hands by the fact that his uncle Ferdinand and his cousin Maximilian successively wore the imperial crown, and had to deal with the situation created by the Augsburg compromise, with which they worked on an opportunist policy, anxious to keep the peace at all costs. They were not of much use to the fanatical Philip, and could not prevent their Protestant vassals from sending intermittent help to his revolted subjects. But on the other hand they took off from his shoulders the weight of the German burden, which had broken down his father's strength. If they gave him little help, they at least guarded his rear, and saved him from any serious interference on a large scale on the part of the German Protestant princes. It may be added that they took over the land-front of Christendom for defence against the Turk, though the Turk was growing very much less formidable than he had been in the days of Charles V.

Absolutely dominant in Italy by virtue of his possession of Milan, Naples, and Sicily, and his predominance over the minor states— the Dukes of Savoy and Parma served as generals of his armies, while the popes had reluctantly dropped their ambitions as secular princes —Philip had no danger to fear in the lands which his ancestors had won by so much hard fighting. Spain was already tamed by his father —the days of the *Comuneros* and the rebellious feudal nobility were long past. In the middle of his reign Portugal fell into his hands by inheritance—unwillingly, but with hardly a blow struck to preserve its independence, and with Portugal went all its empire in the eastern seas, 'the wealth of Ormuz and of Ind,' which Pope Alexander VI, with such splendid disregard of other people's rights, had granted to Manuel the Fortunate eighty years back. But the Portuguese colonial empire, great as it was, was far less important than the American empire which the *Conquistadors* had won for Charles V, while he was engrossed in his Italian wars. The gold and silver of America had begun to pour into the Spanish treasury in the later years of Philip's father, but not in such regularity as was to be the case when exploitation had replaced military conquest. The Emperor had profited from the hoarded wealth of Montezuma or Atahualpa, captured once in bulk and irreplaceable: his son got the regular produce of mines worked systematically by slave labour, a vast annual income. He could depend upon it as a normal item of his revenue, till in the second half of his reign the buccaneering English began to interfere in the Atlantic with the precious ever-welcome *flota*. The American gold, long the monopoly of Spain, upset all the scale of prices in Europe, when it began to be dispersed around, mainly in war expenses. Already in the time of Charles V it had caused financial troubles in many lands, the gold-owning sovereign having an immense advantage over his political rivals. But Philip was a much greater gold-monopolist than his father: he found ways to get rid of his primary advantage by means of unsuccessful wars and lavish subsidies to allies, till all that was left to him was the fact that prices were higher in Spain than in any other country of Europe, and that national industries flagged, because they could not compete with those of countries where the costs of production were not so abnormally high.

With such resources it might have been supposed that Philip might have controlled all Europe, or at least all southern and western Europe. That he failed to do so was entirely his own fault. He was governed by a curious mixture of obstinacy and procrastination; when he had made up his mind he was hard to move from his resolve, even when circumstances continued to prove that his decision had been unwise. But it took a very long time for him to arrive at any decision, because he profoundly distrusted all advice given him by his ministers or generals. He was always suspecting interested personal motives in any course suggested to him by his subordinates: and their reports, preserved in the Spanish archives, show countless marginal notes arguing criticism and distrust in his own hand. For he read everything, important or unimportant, that came into his chancery, and wasted endless hours in commenting on things trivial as well as on things of real moment.

If Philip had been merely an honest fanatic, ready to wade through any amount of blood, and to kindle any amount of fires for heretics, he would have been much less hateful than was actually the case. But he was also a systematic liar and hypocrite, who thought no means too base to secure his two great ideals—autocratic power for himself, triumph for the Roman Church. He made no scruple of violating the most solemn written engagements—other princes did that in his time—but his habit of subsidizing hired assassins even contemporary opinion thought unworthy of a man of ostentatious piety. He lured suspected persons into his clutches, and put them secretly to death without a trial: suspicion was as fatal as proved treason. But the word treason might be made to cover almost any action that savoured of criticism or disobedience. His chosen tool, the Duke of Alva, once wrote a letter to him which expresses the whole mental attitude of master and man: 'Lawyers are only accustomed to pass sentence on a crime being *proved*: that will never do here.' One of his most odious habits was to utilize the Inquisition for his own political interests, where religion was not in the least in question. Indeed, it may perhaps be said that he was a tyrant first, and a fanatic only in the second place. It will be remembered that he dealt most drastically with Paul IV when the old Neapolitan pope ventured to assail him by force of arms and with French aid. But it was seldom that the interest of the autocrat clashed with that of the orthodox Catholic. And his faith was as sincere as his belief in his own essential infallibility—the two inspirations generally worked together with perfect ease when some particularly treacherous scheme was afoot.

A certain additional distaste has—perhaps a little unfairly—attached itself to the unamiable figure of the despot from his unsocial and secretive habit of life—a curious contrast to that of his blatant and boisterous father-in-law Henry VIII of England. Henry loved to show himself off, to advertise his wit, his learning, his taste in costly apparel and in tournaments and pageants, to appear surrounded by a splendid court, and to show ostentatious liberality. Philip disliked all public ceremonials save *autos-da-fé,* at which he was a regular attendant: it was hard to interest him even in the obligatory official shows which attended his third and fourth marriages. He was awkward in company—as had been very much remarked in his father's day, when he was in Germany and Flanders. He had no gracious small-talk such as some kings successfully cultivate, and disguised his unreadiness of speech by a rebarbative affectation of haughty silence. In his mature years he shut himself up for months in the Escurial, where the gloomy bed-chamber in which he died looks out on the high altar of the chapel. The habit of mind which induced him to rear this great palace-monastery in a rocky corner of the most uninviting mountain-range in central Spain is obvious. He disliked human society, and preferred to seclude himself with a few secretaries in apartments that are more like cells than ordinary rooms. Here he carried out his interminable desk-work in bleak surroundings. Louis XI of France, a spider of the same sort, had at least the lovely country-side of Touraine around him at Pleissis-les-Tours. Philip looked out on nothing but barren rocks—sun-blasted in summer, wrapped in rain-fogs in winter. Here he could in his more hypochondriacal moments practise self-maceration with the celebrated scourge, which he bequeathed on his death-bed to his insignificant son Philip III.

Philip's character explains his failure to be a world power, even in days when France was become a battle-field of civil wars, and Elizabeth of England was practising all her shifty diplomacy to put off her inevitable fight with Spain for as long as possible. If Philip had been wise he would have declared war on her in her earlier years, while she was still hardly safe upon her throne, and had not accumulated the navy which was to foil the great effort of Spain in 1588. He imagined himself a diplomatist of great finesse—but the English Queen was almost as unscrupulous and quite as cunning as himself. A study of their insincerities is amusing, but leads to the conclusion that her procrastination was politic, and his temperamental and misplaced. He would have been wise to declare war on her in 1568 over the matter of his seized treasure ships, just before the 'Rising in the North'; she had given him quite sufficient provocation.

Despite the distractions of his Algerine wars (1559-65) and Morisco rebellion, Philip's main interest was in the furthering of autocracy and the suppression of heresy in the Netherlands. Here both his ambitions were concerned: he was determined to govern the curious amalgam of old Low-Country duchies and counties, not by their ancient customs as his father had done, but by his arbitrary will. And he was also determined to root out the growing Protestantism which had survived the old Emperor's comparatively mild persecutions. He first imposed on the Netherlands as regent his bastard sister Margaret, the wife of Ottavio Farnese Duke of Parma, with Cardinal Granvelle, a stranger from the Franche Comté, as her minister (1560-64). It was wrongly supposed that the change in the spirit of government, and the terrible increase of executions for heresy, were due to Margaret and Granvelle. This was entirely an error: everything done by the regent was under strict orders from Madrid. Protests proved futile, and only led Philip to send to the Netherlands his ruthless general Alva, with 10,000 veteran troops from Italy (1567). Alva practically relieved Margaret of all power, and set to work to govern by the sword, the axe, and the stake. His decisive act, which made revolt inevitable, was the seizure under circumstances of gross treachery of the nobles who had headed the protest to the King against mis-government in 1565—the Counts of Egmont and Horn. The former was the victor of the battle of Gravelines, the last defeat of the French in the great war; the latter High Admiral. They were both Catholics of unimpeachable orthodoxy, perfectly loyal to the Crown, and idolized by all the nobility of the Netherlands. For the idiotic cruelty of their execution, under a ridiculous charge of treason, Alva was responsible; but he took the precaution of getting the King's leave. Philip signified his complete approval—the counts were kept for several months in prison till the royal mandate arrived (May, 1568). Alva's 'Council of Blood' put to death many hundred Netherland nobles and citizens, by no means confining its attention to Protestants: all constitutional protests had become treason. Hence in its earlier stages the Revolt of the Netherlands was not in fact an entirely Protestant movement—some Catholics joined in the rising as directed for the repression of tyranny, not for the protection of heresy. Philip's two foibles co-operated to make the discontent general: many of the old faith disliked tyranny, though they had no love for Lutherans.

It is surprising that Alva's reckless governance by the sword and stake, accompanied by crushing financial exactions, went on for several years before any general explosion. Partial risings backed by German help he succeeded in crushing: the real war only began with the seizure of Brill by the 'Sea Beggars' on 1 April 1572, after which it never ceased for the rest of King Philip's life, despite an abortive pacification on terms of compromise made by Don John of Austria, the most moderate of Alva's successors, in 1577. The terms would never have suited Philip; he disavowed the acts of his able and ambitious bastard brother, who was aiming at building up a kingdom of his own in the Low Countries. The war that went on against the unaided Netherlands from 1572 to 1585, and against the Netherlands backed by the parsimonious aid of Queen Elizabeth from 1585 down to the end of the century, was the 'running sore' that sapped all Philip's resources, drained his treasury, and finally broke his heart. The only small measure of success that came from all his efforts and intrigues was that the seven southern provinces of the Netherlands were recon-quered, and remained in his hands—half ruined by the expulsion of all their Protestant inhabitants. Pressed in between France and the new Dutch republic, they were more of a charge than a profit to Spain. Aware of this, in his last moments, Philip separated them from the Hapsburg monarchy, and bequeathed them at his death to his daughter Isabella. If she had left heirs a kingdom of Belgium would have come into existence two centuries before its time!

Though hampered for the last thirty years of his life with the interminable Dutch War, Philip found energy enough to interfere with the internal affairs of France on the side of the Catholic Leaguers —some of whom promised him the French crown—and to plan a number of attacks on the dominions of Elizabeth of England. His great Armada of 1588 was only the largest and the most unlucky of several naval ventures. At sea he was always unfortunate, and the most humiliating episode of his old age was to see Cadiz, his most important harbour-city, taken and sacked by an English expedition (1596). His pose during his last years was that of the blameless man afflicted by inscrutable decrees of Providence—like Job of old. But he never realized that his own character was the cause of all his misfortunes.

If we designate Philip II as one of the figures dominating the sixteenth century, it is firstly because he might, if his character had been different, have turned the fate of Europe into ways very different from those which his father had tried; but secondly (and this is most important), because he accomplished a definite feat—he left Spain ruined in reputation, finance, and spirit, though when he took over her rule she was by far the most powerful state in Christendom, and had not only Europe but 'the Two Worlds' at her feet. I have failed to find in him any redeeming traits save his quite genuine affection for his daughters, and his dislike for the paintings of El Greco.

The Thirty Years' War: A New Interpretation

S. H. STEINBERG

➤➤➤➤➤➤➤➤➤ *Published in 1947* ◄◄◄◄◄◄◄◄◄◄◄

Clichés dominate most accounts of the Thirty Years' War. It is presented usually as the last of the great religious struggles ushered in by the Protestant Revolutions. And its repercussions on German history are generally described in terms of disaster. A tremendous decrease in the size of the German population, a vast impoverishment of the German economy, a serious deterioration of cultural life, of science, art, and letters, a marked growth of immorality—all these alleged developments and many more have been ascribed to the impact of the Thirty Years' War. Indeed, few wars in history have been blamed for so much as this struggle that determined the fate of both the Austrian and the Spanish Habsburgs. There are, nevertheless, good reasons for challenging the validity of many of the traditional assertions concerning the Thirty Years' War. It is with some of these reasons that S. H. Steinberg, author of a useful *Short History of Germany* (1945), deals in the present article.

The author of the most recent book on the "Thirty Years' War" sums up its causes and results as follows.[1] "The larger issue was that between the dynasties of Hapsburg and Bourbon. . . . But . . . the geography and politics of Germany alone give the key to the problem. The signal for war was given . . . in May, 1618, by revolt in Bohemia. There was no compulsion towards a conflict. . . . The war solved no problem. Its effects, both immediate and indirect, were either

Reprinted by special permission from *History*, XXXII (1947), 89-102.
[1] C. V. Wedgwood, *The Thirty Years' War* (1938), pp. 31, 65, 526.

negative or disastrous. Morally subversive, economically destructive, socially degrading, confused in its causes, devious in its course, futile in its result, it is the outstanding example in European history of meaningless conflict."

Apart from the first dozen words quoted here almost every word of this statement is debatable. However, Miss Wedgwood only voices what may be called the *consensus gentium*; and it will take time and patience to uproot the prejudices and misconceptions of historians which have been strongly backed by playwrights, novelists and poets.[2] To Miss Wedgwood's version the following may be opposed. The various European wars fought between 1609 and 1660 decided the issue between the dynasties of Hapsburg and Bourbon. France's need to break her encirclement gives the key to the problem. Open warfare ensued over the Hapsburg effort to strengthen their grip on France to the north and north-east (truce with the Netherlands and attempted seizure of Jülich-Cleve, April, 1609). The only alternative to armed conflict was tame submission to Hapsburg domination. The series of wars ending with the peace of the Pyrenees (1659) solved the outstanding problem of Europe: the final overthrow of the Hapsburg hegemony established the principle of the balance of power, which henceforth would militate against every attempt to set up a single-state rule over Europe. The immediate effects of most of the wars were negligible; cumulatively and indirectly, they were momentous. Morally, the age of rationalism affirmed the equality of the Christian denominations and, implicitly, the freedom of worship and thought; economically, the age of mercantilism rid Europe from the curse of the American gold which had wrecked the economics of the sixteenth

[2] There can be no doubt that Schiller's *Geschichte des Dreissigjährigen Krieges*, first published in 1792, and his dramatic trilogy *Wallenstein* (1799) have crystallized and popularized the main features of the traditional concept.

JOHN AMOS COMENIUS: Seventeenth-century Bohemian theologian and writer on educational reform. Filled with optimism and faith in human nature, he saw in scientific research and the spread of education the key to the elimination of religious and international disputes.

EDICT OF RESTITUTION: Issued in 1629 by Ferdinand II, the Holy Roman Emperor, it authorized Catholic territorial princes to exile their Protestant subjects except those who adhered to the Augsburg Confession. In addition,

century; socially, the age of absolutism dissolved the feudal structure of society. It is the outstanding example in European history of an intrinsically successful settlement.

The traditional concept of the Thirty Years' War is based on two main groups of sources: deliberate official propaganda and unwittingly one-sided private records. The first reflect the opinions of the victorious powers—France, Sweden, the Netherlands, Brandenburg; the second, those of the educated middle class which was hit hardest by the economic upheaval of the time. That these distortions should have gained credence may perhaps be ascribed to two failings of the nineteenth-century schools of German historians: they consciously or unconsciously made the political interests of the Prussian monarchy the criterion by which they judged the course of German history; and they preferred narrative sources and dispositive documents to administrative and business records.

Now of the two German powers which gained most by the peace of Westphalia—Brandenburg and Bavaria—the latter lapsed into a state of indolence and complacency after the death of Maximilian I (1651), whereas in the former, Frederick William I, the Great Elector, pursued a vigorous policy of aggrandizement. He was a master of political propaganda, the first to put over the identification of Hohenzollern and German interests; and he laid the foundations of the Prussian monarchy in the ideological sphere as well as in that of power politics. In Samuel von Pufendorf (1632-94) he secured as court historiographer a scholar and pamphleteer of European reputation who had already served the Dutch, Swedish and Palatine governments. Pufendorf's interpretation of the Thirty Years' War was taken up by Frederick the Great in his *Mémoires pour servir à l'histoire de la maison de Brandebourg,* and has become part and parcel of the national-liberal historiography of the nineteenth century.

The original "atrocity" propaganda emanating from Berlin had a

---

church property that had been confiscated since 1552 was to be restored. The Edict was viewed by Protestants as a threat to their rights and as a prelude to the establishment of a strong, centralized Holy Roman Empire.

SAMUEL VON PUFENDORF: Seventeenth-century political theorist, writer on international law, and court historian at Berlin. It was he who popularized the misleading label "Thirty Years' War."

double aim: for home consumption it was meant to accentuate the magnitude of the political, economic and cultural successes, real or alleged, of the Great Elector by painting the background as black as possible; while at the same time the darker aspects of his policy—the abandonment of the peasantry to the tender mercies of the Junkers, the oppressive taxation of the poorer classes in general and of the townspeople in particular, the tax exemption of the Junkers, and the inordinate expenses for the standing army—could, to the more gullible, be justified as unavoidable consequences of the war. As an instrument of foreign policy, the Brandenburg version of the Thirty Years' War —Brandenburg as the defender of the protestant religion and of the "German liberties" against Hapsburg interference and foreign aggression in general—was meant to serve the shifts and vagaries of the Great Elector's policy: one aspect or another of this picture could always be turned against his *pro tempore* enemy—the emperor, Sweden, Poland, France, Denmark—and incidentally win for him the moral support of the German and Dutch Protestants or of the anti-Hapsburg German Catholic princes, or the latent German patriotism of the liberal professions.

This picture of the Thirty Years' War, born of the needs of the Brandenburg propaganda of 1650-90, more or less coincided with the historical preconceptions of nineteenth-century national liberalism. The current version of the Thirty Years' War therefore largely reflects the Prusso-German attitude of Bismarck's fight against the German middle states, Austria and France, the *Kulturkampf* against the Roman Church, and the cultural and economic expansionism of the Hohenzollern Empire.

While the official records reflect the light in which the victorious party wished the nexus and causality of events to be seen, the private sources—chronicles, annals, diaries, letters—chiefly show the results of the war as experienced by those who lost most. These documents have been used to fill in the lurid details of famine and starvation, epidemics and cannibalism, ruin of town and country, decline of civilization, extinction of large sections of the population and complete pauperization of the remainder. It is not the purpose of the present paper to glorify the Thirty Years' War; and much misery, brutality, cruelty and suffering no doubt added to the terror and slaughter of purely military actions. But nothing is gained by putting the Thirty Years' War in a class by itself: its destructive aspects are common to

every war—and were in any case smaller than those of "total war" in
the twentieth century—and an impartial assessment of the facts will
lead to the conclusion that some of the features most commonly
attributed to it are unconnected with the war itself, while others have
been generalized and exaggerated. The generalization of isolated
events, the exaggeration of facts and, above all, figures, the special
pleading for a particular cause, lay the contemporary chroniclers and
diarists less open to criticism than modern historians who have failed
to recognise the distorted perspective from which these accounts have
been written: for the compilers of town chronicles, parish registers,
family albums and personal diaries, all belonged to the same class of
educated, professional men—clerks, priests, officials, lawyers—who were
hit by every vicissitude of the times, and always hit hardest. Whenever
circumstances forced upon the treasury a cut in expenditure, it was
the educational and cultural departments which were the first victims.[3]

The very term "Thirty Years' War" is fraught with misunderstanding. Seventeenth-century authors speak of the military events of the
first half of the century as "wars," "*bella*" in the plural and clearly
distinguish between the *"bellum Bohemicum," "bellum Suecicum"*
and so forth. The figure "thirty" and the singular "war" seem to occur
for the first time in Pufendorf's *De statu imperii Germanici* (1667).
One of the liveliest and still most readable pamphlets of seventeenth-
century political science, its success was immediate and far-reaching:
German, French, English and Dutch translations, popular adaptations
and polemical treatises secured the rapid spread of its arguments
throughout Europe. Here we have already all the well-known theses
of later historians: the Bohemian revolt of 1618 as the beginning, the
peace of Westphalia as the end of the war; its character as a religious
conflict; its extension over the whole of Germany; the omission of
its European setting; the economic ruin and exhaustion; and the in-
sinuation that Austria is a foreign power like France and Turkey.

From the political point of view the Thirty Years' War offers two
aspects: the general European, and the particular German one. Both
issues can be traced to the foreign and home policies of the emperors
Maximilian I and Charles V. In the European field, Maximilian started

---

[3] To give an illustration: as a result of a general change in financial policy,
the imperial city   Goslar, from 1625 to 1630, reduced its expenditure from
221,744 guilders to 54,342 guilders; expenditure on defence dropped from 590
to 460 guilders, on schools from 102 to 4 guilders.

the antagonism between the houses of Hapsburg and Valois by claiming the inheritance of Charles the Bold of Burgundy, and made it
permanent by marrying his only son to the daughter and heiress of
the Spanish world-monarchy. He thereby welded a ring of Hapsburg possessions round France which every French statesman was
bound to try his utmost to break.

In Germany, Maximilian deliberately wrecked the last prospect of
equitable settlement of the constitutional dispute between centralism
and federalism. As at the same time the imperial crown became hereditary in the house of Hapsburg, in all but legal prescription, he made
this dynasty the permanent champion of that centralism which had
become unattainable and was therefore by force of circumstances reactionary; so that any combination of forces, which for different
reasons might be opposed to the Hapsburgs or the empire or centralisation, might appear as fighting for progress.

Charles V, Maximilian's grandson, intensified this development.
He completed the total encirclement of France by acquiring the duchy
of Milan, subduing the papacy, and drawing Portugal, England, Denmark and Poland into the Hapsburg orbit. The very greatness of his
successes made a reaction inevitable. The exploits of Elizabethan England, the secession of the Spanish Netherlands, the alliance between
France and the German Protestants (1552), the pacification of France
by the edict of Nantes (1598)—are all signs of the growing restive-
ness against Hapsburg universalism. In fact, during the fifty years
following the death of Charles V (1556) all European powers were
jockeying for position.

France was obviously the rallying point of every opponent of
Hapsburg domination throughout the whole of western Europe and
the New World. The aggressive and expansionist policies of Louis XIV
and Napoleon I have obliterated the fact that up to the death of
Mazarin (1661) it was France which was the protagonist of the
European balance of power against the domination of the continent
by a single power.

The political struggle was accompanied by an ideological struggle.
The antagonism between the old and the new faith made itself felt
in the early stages of the conflict, and religious catchwords and
propaganda were meant as sincerely or insincerely as were in more
recent times the slogans of democracy and totalitarianism. The Hapsburgs, it is true, represented all the life-forces and the spirit of the

reformed church of Rome; and the defeat of the Hapsburgs undoubtedly benefited the Protestant powers of Sweden, the Netherlands, England and Brandenburg. But the victory was chiefly a victory
of Catholic France, which during the war was successively led by
two cardinals of the Roman church; and the papacy itself had from
1523 to 1644 consistently opposed the Hapsburgs and even lent its
support to the Protestant hero, Gustavus Adolphus of Sweden.

France could become the ideological leader of Europe as well as
its political protagonist as she herself had solved the fight between
Protestantism and Catholicism in a *tertium quid* which transcended
both these sixteenth-century points of argument. Because the French
leaders—the Protestants Henry IV and Sully and the Catholics Richelieu and Mazarin alike—recognised that the absolute claims inherent in
every religious system were irreconcilable, they replaced religious
standards by the criterion of the *raison d'état*. This enabled France to
destroy Protestantism within her own frontiers and to save Protestantism
in Germany, Sweden and the Low Countries, to secure religious unity
at home, and to perpetuate the split of western Christendom abroad.
Catholic apologists tried in vain to counter this onslaught of secularism
by elaborating a *ragione della chiesa* [apologia for the church]; it has
never been a serious challenge to the *raison d'état*.

Seen against this European background, German affairs are of
minor importance. Germany, as such, i.e. the "German section of the
Holy Roman Empire," was not at all involved in any of the European
wars of the period. The individual German states entered and left
one war or another as partisans of the European antagonists; only
the emperor was engaged in every conflict, not, however, as German
king, but as the head of the Austrian branch of the house of Hapsburg. The German wars started in 1609 with the war of the Jülich-
Cleve succession and ended in 1648 with the treaties of Münster and
Osnabrück. They decided the political future of the empire, in that
the last attempt to set up a centralistic government was defeated in
favour of a loose confederation of virtually independent states. The
concerted action by which the electors forced the emperor to dismiss
his generalissimo Wallenstein in 1630 was their last achievement as
a corporate body. They, too, who for centuries had represented the
federal principle of the German constitution, henceforth showed an
ever diminishing concern with the affairs of the empire and were
content to look after their own interests. However, the constitution

agreed upon in 1648 proved its soundness in that it lasted for more than 200 years, until 1866, with the short interval of the Napoleonic settlement. The wars also decided the dynastic rivalries within the leading German houses—curiously, every time in favour of the younger branch: the Palatine Wittelsbachs, the Thuringian Wettiners and the Wolfenbüttel Guelphs had to give way to their cousins of Bavaria, Saxony and Hanover, who henceforth formed the leading group of German powers. The most far-reaching result, however, was the rise of the electorate of Brandenburg, before 1609 the least important of the bigger principalities; it came to equal Bavaria and Saxony and was to outstrip them in the following century.

The conception of the Thirty Years' War as a "war of religion" has been abandoned to a large extent since it has been recognized that religious divisions coincided largely with political, constitutional and economic ones. It will always remain a matter of dispute which of these motives was decisive at a given moment. It does, however, seem that rational considerations of political and economic gains determined the policies of the cabinets to the same extent to which religious emotions held a strong sway over the masses, sufficient to whip up their passions in battle and to make them endure with fortitude their plight in adversity. The Swedes, under Gustavus, fought for the pure gospel, caring little for the *"dominium maris Baltici"* ["dominion of the Baltic Sea"] and knowing nothing of the French subsidies on which they subsisted; while Tilly's men were fired by an equal zeal for the Holy Virgin, with no stake in the power politics of the Wittelsbachs and ignorant of the pope's support of the heretic Swede.

Political and dynastic, religious and personal motives are inextricably mixed in the actions of the champions of the Protestant and Catholic causes. Both Gustavus Adolphus of Sweden and Maximilian of Bavaria were fervent devotees of their creeds. At the same time, the Lutheran establishment was also Gustavus's strongest bulwark against the claims to the Swedish throne, made by his Catholic cousin, Sigismund of Poland; and as the Palatine Wittelsbachs had assumed the leadership of the Protestant estates of the empire, the head of the Bavarian branch found safety and prospect of gain in rallying the Catholic princes under his standard. The struggle for the *"dominium maris Baltici"* set Gustavus in opposition to Protestant Denmark, Catholic Poland and Orthodox Russia. The occupation of the Hartz mines by the imperial forces (1624) endangered the Swedish copper market; Wallenstein's appointment as "General of the Atlantic and Baltic Seas" (1628) threatened Sweden's maritime position: her vital interests demanded armed intervention against the Catholic Hapsburgs and alliance with Catholic France, and the edict of restitution (1629) only added religious zeal to the dictates of power politics. Likewise, political considerations brought Maximilian into conflict with the Lutheran imperial cities of Swabia and Fran- conia, Catholic Austria and Spain, and the Calvinistic Netherlands and Palatinate; but after he had overawed the cities and, in alliance with Austria and Spain, crushed the elector Palatine, his interests as a prince of the empire and member of the college of electors made him turn against the Hapsburgs as his chief opponents. The reduction of the dominant position of the emperor and the removal of the Spaniards from the empire were from 1627 onward his over-riding aims which, in co-operation with the pope, Catholic France and Lutheran Saxony, were brought to a successful consummation.

The ruinous effect of the war years on German economic and cultural life has been very much exaggerated. War is by its very nature destructive, and the wars of the seventeenth century are no exceptions. But all the campaigns of the period 1609-1648 were of short duration and the armies themselves of a very small size.[4] It was only the districts of primary strategic importance which had to bear the brunt of successive invasions in the seventeenth century, as they have been the focal points of every fight in central Europe, from Caesar's to Eisenhower's campaigns: the Rhine crossings of Breisach and Wesel, the Leipzig plain, the passes across the Black Forest and the roads to Regensburg and the Danube Valley. Other tracts of Germany were hardly affected at all, some only for a few weeks; the majority of towns never saw an enemy inside their walls.

From the middle of the thirteenth century the towns were the

[4] The Catholic League had an effective strength of about 15,000 men; Gustavus Adolphus landed in Germany with 15,000 men; the imperial army under Wallenstein may have exceeded 20,000 men; Bernhard of Weimar received French subsidies for 18,000 men—Richelieu had originally only bargained for 14,000; Condé's army in 1645, the strongest French contingent to be employed in Germany, numbered 12,000 men. The numbers of "regiments," "squadrons," "standards" etc. are meaningless in themselves: for instance, in the battle of Breitenfeld, the 15,000 troops of the League were organized in 10 regiments, the 15,000 imperialists in 28 regiments.

undisputed masters of German economics. Even agriculture, if not brought under direct control of city financiers, was at least completely dependent upon the town markets for home consumption as well as exportation (with the notable exception of the Teutonic Order in Prussia, whose totalitarian economy comprised production as well as commerce and excluded the citizen middlemen). This whole system of German economics was breaking down in a series of disastrous events from the middle of the sixteenth century: the south German cities were ruined by the repeated bankruptcies of the Spanish crown (1557, 1575, 1596, 1607), in which they lost every financial gain accumulated in the preceding century. The Hanse towns of North Germany were equally hit by the sack of Antwerp (1585) and the closing of the London Steelyard (1598) which deprived them of the two western pillars of their trading system; and even more by the separation of the Netherlands from Spain. The new republic vigorously asserted its independence in the economic sphere, intruding into the Baltic trade, hitherto the jealously-guarded monopoly of the Hanse.

About 1620 the German towns still presented an outward picture of opulence and solidity—very much emphasized to the casual observer by the splendour of their architectural achievements, as shown in Mathias Merian's topographical engravings published from 1640. Yet the foundations of their prosperity had gone, and the big inflation of the years 1619-23 only set the seal upon the utter ruin of German economics which had started some fifty years earlier.

In reality, the crisis of the inflation was the fever which preceded the patient's recovery. The contemporaries of the "clippers and counterfeiters of coins" (*Kipper und Wipper*) were altogether non-plussed by the upheaval of all standards of financial honesty and security, especially as the devaluation of currency was worst in the countries whose prolific output of silver had made them appear the very pillars of affluence and stability: the petty principality of Brunswick-Wolfenbüttel had thirty-two mints operating in 1622, and the emperor Ferdinand II lent his active support to a combine of racketeers who exploited Austria, Bohemia and Moravia for three or four years. When by 1624 the currency was stabilized again, a violent and thorough-going transfer of property had occurred; hardly any of the old firms of international repute survived, and successful speculators, army contractors and black marketeers took their place, many of them Jews and newly converted Roman Catholics, of whom Wallenstein was to become the most conspicuous. All through the following decades, this change-over of family and business fortunes continued: the proscription of Wallenstein and his lieutenants in 1634 threw the biggest and best estates of Bohemia and Silesia upon the market; the new principles of the "mercantilist" system of economics gave openings to fresh and quick brains, and the losses sustained by the one were counter-balanced by the gains of the other. On the whole, the national income, productive power and standard of living were higher about 1650 than they had been fifty years earlier.[5]

The part of the economic structure which was hit hardest by the immediate effects of the war was agriculture, especially for medium-sized and small farmers. To big land-owners, on the other hand, the war itself, the maintenance of troops over wide distances and the new methods of logistics and commissariat as introduced by Wallenstein and Gustavus Adolphus, offered fresh possibilities of enrichment. In fact, the seventeenth century is the period of the growth of the big *latifundia* [landed estates] of the Junkers at the smallholders' expense. The eviction of peasants, and the sequestration of peasant land by the lord of the manor had started at the end of the sixteenth century, caused by the steady rise of corn prices which made large-scale farming and bulk selling more profitable. The depopulation of the countryside and the disappearance of whole villages were in full swing before the first shot of the "Thirty Years' War" was fired, and went on long after the conclusion of the peace of Westphalia.

On the other hand, the improved organization of the commissariat resulted in increasing the apparent burdens of occupied countries. Indiscriminate pillaging by a band of marauders may have done greater damage, but it appeared as a natural phenomenon, whereas the methodical requisitioning by quarter-masters was felt the more irksome as it was planned and therefore rigid, thorough and therefore inescapable, fixed in writing and therefore long remembered and resented.

[5] Sumptuary laws show this very clearly if one disregards the moralizing introductions and looks at the factual clauses. A comparison of the sumptuary laws issued by the town council of Brunswick in 1579 and 1650 indicates the greater affluence of all classes in the latter year. New clauses, not found in 1579, render punishable the wearing of more than four golden rings in addition to the wedding ring, and of coral and amber by servant girls: despite the "difficult times" and the "rod of God's wrath with which he has chastised our beloved fatherland."

Ignorance of scientific demography and inability to visualize large figures account for the legend of the enormous loss of population, which is variously given as ranging from a third to half or more of the total. All these figures are purely imaginary. Such statistical surveys as were occasionally made were always designed to support some special pleading: to obtain a grant in aid, a reduction of payments, or an alleviation of services.[6] The main sources, however, are contemporary reports and, rarely, records of deaths, to the virtual exclusion of registers of births. In view of the huge birthrate this neglect amounts to thirty to fifty per cent.;[7] in other words, exactly that third or half by which the population is said to have been reduced. It is, of course, indisputable that the irregular movements of troops, especially of ill-disciplined mercenaries, and the migration of refugees greatly contributed to the spreading of epidemics, such as the various kinds of typhoid (the greatest terror of the seventeenth century) or, to a lesser degree, of the plague and syphilis. On the other hand, the mortality of the urban population shows a surprising likeness in a place which was far remote from the European battlefields, and one which was right in their midst: it has been computed at seventy *per mille* for London in 1620-43, and at sixty-eight *per mille* for Frankfurt in 1600-50.

What actually happened was an extensive inner migration chiefly from the agrarian countryside into the industrial town, and from the economically retrograde town to the prosperous one. As with the ownership of movable and immovable property, so with regard to the population it is more appropriate to speak of redistribution than of destruction.[8]

The net result is that of an all-round, though very limited increase. This almost imperceptible rise, and over long periods, virtual stagna-

[6] For example, the district of Militsch in Silesia in 1619 furnished the government in Breslau with a list of 976 men available for military service; whereas at the actual census, 1,527 men had been recorded in this category.

[7] These percentages are based on eighteenth-century statistics (when the birthrate was already beginning to decline) for Prussia and Saxony where the surplus of births over deaths was 30 per cent. and 50 per cent. respectively.

[8] Between 1594 and 1637 more than a hundred of the richest merchants of Cologne, whose trade and industry were declining, settled in Frankfurt. There was a considerable emigration from the Altmark to Hamburg, Holstein, Saxony and Poland in 1640-50, and at the same time a remarkable immigration from Bremen, Holstein and East Frisia. In three Thuringian counties the population decreased between 1631 and 1659 by 66 per cent., 73 per cent. and 87 per cent., while in three others it increased by 78 per cent., 89 per cent. and 125 per cent.

tion, is characteristic of every community of a predominantly agricultural type. Keeping in mind the vagueness of the term "Germany," it seems safe to assume a population of fifteen to seventeen million in 1600. A loss of five to eight million by 1650 could not possibly have been made good by 1700, for which year a population of seventeen to twenty million is fairly well documented.

The legend of cultural exhaustion and desolation as a concomitant and result of the "Thirty Years' War" is perhaps easiest to refute. It is solely due to the aesthetic standards of nineteenth-century criticism in literature, art, architecture and music. The culture of the seventeenth century is essentially baroque; and "baroque" was anathema to the critics of the nineteenth century, as "gothic" had been to those of the eighteenth. The revaluation which has taken place within the last thirty years or so makes unnecessary a defence of the writers, architects and musicians of the period of the "Thirty Years' War." The war itself had little and certainly no detrimental influence upon the cultural life of Germany.

The lowest ebb of intellectual and artistic activities was the last third of the sixteenth century. A fresh tide set in at the turn of the century. Kepler's *De proportione coelestium orbium* (1596) and Scultetus's *Medulla Theologiae Patrum* (1598) herald the reawakening of science and learning; Althusius's *Politica Methodice Digesta* (1603) and Johann Arnd's *Vom wahren Christentum* (1605) break the sterility of political science and sectarian dogmatics; Jacob Boehme's *Aurora* (1612) and Heinrich Schütz's appointment as court composer at Dresden (1614) are milestones in German philosophy and music. The foundation of the "Fruchtbringende Gesellschaft" in Weimar (1617) and of the "Naturwissenschaftliche Gesellschaft" in Rostock (1622) gave fresh impetus to the advancement of literature and science. Lyrical poetry reached new heights with Georg Rudolf Weckherlin (better known to English historians as an English under-secretary of state), Simon Dach, Paulus Gerhardt, Friedrich von Spee, and Friedrich von Logau. Martin Opitz's *Buch von der teutschen Poeterey* (1624), Schottel's *Deutsche Sprachkunst* (1641) standardized New High German poetics and grammar, which the many learned societies and poetical associations were assiduously cultivating. The plays of Andreas Gryphius,[9] the novels of Philipp von Zesen and Philipp

---

[9] His *Carolus Stuardus,* written and produced in the year of the king's execution (1649), is remarkable as one of the first European plays dealing with a topical political subject.

Moscherosch, the educational treatises of Amos Comenius, the translations from the Italian, Spanish, French—all show a flourishing
literary life, eager to keep abreast of the general trend of European
letters and thought.

The situation as regards painting, sculpture and architecture is
different only in degree and quality. As German painting since the
death of Dürer (1528) and German sculpture since the death of
Riemenschneider (1531) have been of no account in European art,
the "Thirty Years' War" neither improved nor impaired the position.
In architecture the period after *c.* 1620 is of no great aesthetic importance; but the reason is to be found in the mania for building
during the preceding period: the sixteenth-century palaces and patrician
houses, town halls and churches needed no replacement and little
enlarging. It is only newcomers in church and state who were not
yet provided for, and they certainly did not leave architects unemployed: Wallenstein erected his spacious palaces in Jičin, Sagan,
Prague and elsewhere; Maximilian of Bavaria built Schleissheim
Palace and rebuilt the Munich *Residenz;* Prince Eggenberg, the
emperor's favourite, laid out his magnificent castle near Graz; and
all the new religious orders of the counter-Reformation were busy
everywhere to outrival the older foundations in every Roman Catholic
part of Germany. Protestant churches in Emden, Rudolstadt, Regensburg, Hanau, Hamburg, and elsewhere, though less numerous, show
that Lutherans and Calvinists, too, had the will and money to build
when necessary, regardless of political circumstances.

As regards private buildings, their comparative insignificance
from the artistic standpoint has prevented them from being given
prominence in the handbooks of architecture; and large numbers of
them have, of course, been destroyed by fire or pulled down to make
room for later buildings. Yet that there was no lack of enterprise
during and after the war years, is best shown by the large number
of textbooks for the instruction of builders and masons: Rüdiger
Kossmann of Cologne brought out a textbook of architecture in 1630,
of which revised editions appeared in 1644 and 1653. Josef Furtenbach,
of Ulm, published an *Architectura Civilis* in 1628, followed by an
Architectura Recreationis (1640) and *Architectura Privata* (1641).
G. A. Böckler's writings, from 1648, dominated the post-war reconstruction period, culminating in his first German edition of Palladio.

The Thirty Years' War, put in its proper perspective, was therefore not such a catastrophe as popular historians have made out. Perhaps the one irreparable damage Germany sustained in the first half of the seventeenth century was that German civilization and German politics parted company. This separation may be the greatest misfortune of German history.

The Decline of Spain

EARL J. HAMILTON

➢➢➢-➢➢➢-➢➢➢-➢➢➢-➢➢➢-➢➢➢-➢➢➢-➢➢➢-➢➢➢ *Published in 1938* ⫷⫷-⫷⫷⫷-⫷⫷⫷-⫷⫷⫷-⫷⫷⫷-⫷⫷⫷-⫷⫷⫷-⫷⫷⫷

If the sixteenth was the Spanish century, the seventeenth became increasingly the French century. To those who lived at the time of Charles V and of Philip II, it would have seemed unbelievable that the power and the glory of the Spain of the 1500's would turn into the impotence and the ignominy of the Spain of the late 1600's. Contemporaries, of course, often sought to determine the causes of the Spanish descent from power; and historians have been attempting to do so ever since. One of the most recent attempts—and one of the most thoughtful—has been made by Earl J. Hamilton, to whose work on the economic history of early modern Spain reference has already been made (see p. 170). It seems hardly necessary to add that Hamilton's analysis deserves to be carefully considered. As long as people turn to the study of the past, it is likely that they will be especially drawn to discussions of the decline of civilizations.

T he union of Castile and Aragon, the overthrow of the Moslem kingdom of Granada, the discovery of America, the conquest of Naples, and the annexation of Navarre under the Catholic Kings; the acquisition of Burgundy, Flanders, the Low Countries, Franche-Comté, and Milan under Charles V; and the addition of Portugal, with its vast oriental possessions, under Philip II gave Spain the political hegemony of Europe and an empire far greater than any other nation had ever controlled. Even the boldest proponents of an economic interpretation of history would probably hesitate to explain

Reprinted by special permission from *The Economic History Review*, VIII (1938), 168-179. The extensive documentation which originally appeared with this essay has been omitted. The author has made a few minor changes in the present version of his article.

the rise of the Spanish empire in materialistic terms; but, despite un-satisfactory knowledge of almost every phase of Spanish economic history, it seems safe to say that agriculture, industry, and commerce moved forward throughout most of the sixteenth century, and that the economic support of the empire under Charles V and Philip II was not drawn solely from Flanders, Italy, and America.

The Navigation Acts of Ferdinand and Isabella, subsidies for the construction and operation of ships meeting royal specifications by the Catholic Kings and Charles V, and the maritime problems entailed by world dominions gave Spain at least the second largest merchant marine in Europe during the reign of Philip II. In fact, with the Portuguese fleets included, in 1585 the Spanish merchant marine rivalled, if it did not outrank, the Dutch, doubled the German, and trebled the English and French.

Inasmuch as the lag of wages behind prices, the chief cause of industrial progress in all countries during the Price Revolution pre-cipitated by the influx of Mexican and Peruvian silver, was consider-ably less than in England and France, Spanish manufactures advanced less rapidly than the English and French in the sixteenth century; but the phenomenal growth of all industrial cities, with the virtual doubling of the population of such centres as Burgos, Segovia, and Toledo between the censuses of 1530 and 1594, attests the industrial progress of the kingdom in the *siglo de oro* [Golden Century]. It is true that Spain remained, as always, primarily a producer of raw materials, exporting wine, olive oil, and wool in return for foreign wares; but, although satisfactory data on the development of manu-factures are not available, it seems that the silk, wool, glove, leather, and cutlery industries not only supplied a large part of the domestic market but furnished considerable exports to the Indies. The increase of population in peninsular Spain, exclusive of Portugal, by approx-imately 15 per cent. (in spite of emigration to the New World, the garrisoning of fortresses in Italy, Flanders, and Africa, and heavy losses in continuous wars) reflected substantial economic progress in the sixteenth century.

Obviously it is impossible to date with precision the beginning of economic decline. Some of the causes extended back into the Middle Ages, and there is evidence that decadence was incipient late in the reign of Philip II; but catastrophic changes did not occur before 1598. In broad terms one can say that it took Spain only a century (from the union of Castile and Aragon, in 1479, to the annexation of Portugal, in 1580) to attain political pre-eminence and only a century (from the death of Philip II, in 1598, to that of Charles II, in 1700) to fall into the rank of a second-rate power. Economics and politics were clearly interrelated, but a loss of economic strength appears to have been more largely a cause than a result of the political decline.

Strong biases, pulling in the same direction, have infused into economico-historical literature an exaggeration of Spanish economic decadence in the seventeenth century. The Germans have tended to magnify the extent of the collapse in order to glorify the Emperor Charles V through contrast; the French in order to exalt the economic policy of the first Bourbons; and the liberals of all countries in order to place absolutism, the Inquisition, the persecution of minorities, and the Moorish expulsion in a more unfavourable light. But no reasonable allowance for overestimation by economic historians can invalidate the abundant evidence that agriculture, industry, and commerce declined sharply in the seventeenth century. Contemporary economic literature and the proceedings of the Cortes complain of economic retrogression, and the inductive evidence available corroborates the jeremiads of authors and statesmen.

From the last quarter of the sixteenth century to the last quarter of the seventeenth the tonnage of the ships plying between Spain and the Indies fell by approximately 75 per cent., and in the latter period the trade had virtually passed into the hands of foreigners who supplied "five-sixths of the cargoes of the outbound fleets." It has been said that by the middle of the seventeenth century not enough fishermen could be found to equip a fleet. Despite the attempts of Philip IV and Charles II to stimulate maritime revival, shipbuilding

---

CHRONOLOGY:

Philip II (d. 1598)

Philip III (1598-1621), contemporary of Elizabeth and James I and of Henry IV and Louis XIII.

Philip IV (1621-1665), contemporary of James I, Charles I, Cromwell, and Charles II, and of Richelieu, Mazarin, and Louis XIV.

Charles II (1665-1702), the last of the Spanish Habsburgs, contemporary of Charles II, James II, and William and Mary, and of Louis XIV.

in Spain virtually ceased; and, with the naval losses in Europe and America, the Spanish flag almost disappeared from the seas.

Dr. Julius Klein has shown that the number of sheep in the flocks of the Mesta, or guild of migratory herders, diminished after 1560 and fell precipitately in the seventeenth century; but it seems that gains in sedentary grazing partially compensated for this loss. In 1619 it was reported that the livestock in the bishopric of Salamanca had declined by 60 per cent. since 1600, and in the same year the Council of Castile complained that villages were falling into ruins and fields becoming deserts. The lag of agricultural behind non-agricultural prices in the second quarter of the seventeenth century indicates that in this period agricultural decadence was less severe than industrial, but the complaints of rural depopulation and agricultural distress continued throughout the century. In fact, at the end of the century agriculture remained rudimentary; and the country was on the verge of famine.

The increasing dependence on foreign markets for masts, tar, hemp, sailcloth, and other naval supplies after 1600 reflected industrial decadence. By 1619 industrial stagnation had proceeded far enough to evoke a *consulta* from the Council of Castile, and the following year Philip III formed a *junta* to consider remedies for languishing industry. Complaints of impoverishment from such important manufacturing cities as Toledo, Cordova, Seville, Granada, and Valencia received the attention of the Crown in 1655. In the same year Francisco Martínez Mata noted the disappearance of numerous craft guilds, including workers in iron, steel, copper, tin, sulphur, and alum; and the once flourishing glove industry was almost dead. According to contemporary complaints, Burgos was in ruins, and Segovia was a desert. The num-

---

ENTAILED ESTATES: Lands that have been given as an inalienable possession to an individual and his heirs.

MORTMAIN: Dead hand. The possession of lands by a corporation that cannot dispose of them. In medieval and early modern times it referred usually to the Roman Catholic Church, whose lands, by the teachings of medieval canon law, were inalienable.

COUNT OF OLIVARES: Minister of Philip IV. His efforts to augment royal authority and further the cause of centralization encouraged the outbreak in 1640 of the successful Portuguese war of independence from Spanish rule.

ber of woollen manufactures in Toledo declined about three-fourths in the first two-thirds of the seventeenth century; and the manufacture of arms, the one industry that should have flourished under the stimulus of perpetual wars, reached such a low ebb that the Cortes petitioned the Crown to import artisans to revive it. In 1674 the Aragonese established a *junta* to formulate remedies for industrial ruin. Almost all manufacturing cities suffered a catastrophic decline in population between the censuses of 1594 and 1694; Valladolid, Toledo, and Segovia, for example, lost more than half of their inhabitants. The decrease of the Spanish population by approximately 25 per cent. in the seventeenth century leaves little doubt that, unlike the Italian city states in the sixteenth century, Spain suffered an absolute as well as a relative economic decline.

With almost complete unanimity, previous writers since the seventeenth century have regarded the Moorish expulsion of 1609-14 as the overshadowing cause of Spanish economic decadence. There has been common agreement that the Moors were the most industrious, intelligent, persevering, and thrifty inhabitants of Spain, "the flower of her artisans," the cream of her agriculturalists, and almost the only subjects who did not disdain manual labour, routine operations, and prosaic toil. We are told that the expulsion of the Moriscos utterly ruined the rice fields of Valencia, the sugar industry of Granada, and the vineyards of Spain; that irrigation channels immediately fell into hopeless disrepair; and that artisans were lacking and unskilled labourers scarce.

Facts are not in accord with the accepted thesis concerning the economic consequences of the Moorish expulsion. It is difficult to see how a race largely denied educational opportunities, social privileges, civil liberties, and equality before the law could have been the most enlightened portion of the Spanish nation. If the Moors were strikingly superior and if great numbers were expelled, why did they not develop the geographically similar Barbary States into which most of them passed?

The price stability of most of the commodities formerly produced by the Moriscos in the decade following their expulsion affords strong evidence that this despicable act of religious intolerance was not a major cause of economic decadence. The Moors were outstanding producers of wine, and the Koran deterred them from consuming alcoholic beverages; yet the movement of wine prices in 1610-20 fails to reflect a notable decrease in supply with little, or no, countervailing drop in demand. The downward trend of rice quotations (against the current of general prices) in the decade following the expulsion indicates that the loss of Morisco labour from the Valencian fields, which largely supplied Spain, had no significant effect upon production. The continuation of sugar purchases from Granada by the Hospital dels Inocents at Valencia on the usual scale after 1609 (despite increasing competition with low-cost producers in America) and the approval by the Cortes in 1617 of an excise tax on sugar produced in Granada, as one means of relieving a bankrupt treasury, demonstrate that the Moorish expulsion did not wreck this industry. "Although a considerable part of the Moriscos were peddlers, traders, and mendicants, by far the greater number were peasant agriculturalists." Agricultural prices actually dropped in the two years following the great expulsion of 1609, when most of the deportation took place; failed to rise faster than non-agricultural in 1612-25; and lagged far behind the non-agricultural series in the second quarter of the seventeenth century. The expulsion obviously did not ruin agriculture.

The complete failure of the Moorish expulsion to raise either wages in general or the remuneration of any particular class of workers affords the strongest evidence available that the exodus of the Moriscos was not the chief cause of the decadence of Spain. That wage movements were not too sluggish to reflect the loss of a large percentage of the workers is shown by the rise of wages by nearly 30 per cent. throughout the country in the three years following the severe pestilence of 1599-1600 and by an even higher percentage in Andalusia after the great plague of 1648-50.

The Inquisition certainly would have prevented strong condemnation of the Moorish expulsion by the economists who witnessed it, but the Church could hardly have compelled the unqualified approval which pervades the economic literature of the first half of the seventeenth century. In the famous *consulta* of 1619 the Council of Castile did not list the Moorish expulsion among the numerous causes of economic distress; and the debates in the Cortes in the following four decades, which were by no means devoid of opposition to the Church, failed to register denunciations of this act of intolerance. The literary and artistic talents of Velásquez, Cervantes, and Lope de Vega eulogised the expulsion; and, in fact, "all Spain regarded the expulsion of the Moors as the most glorious event in the reign of Philip III."

The failure of wages and prices to reflect the expulsion strongly suggests that few Moors were expelled. The figure of 101,694, exclusive of nursing infants, compiled by the royal commissioners in charge of deportation was apparently much more complete than economic historians have believed. On July 13th, 1626, a deputy from Granada complained in the Cortes that there was a great number of Moors in Andalusia, "none of whom are willing to work in the fields or to take care of cattle, for which there is a notable lack of hands." The strong traces of Moorish blood in Andalusia and Valencia at present suggest that many Moors remained in Spain. Perhaps the resistance of the nobility and large landowners, which the Crown envisaged and attempted to placate by promising them the immobile property of deported tenants, took the form of shielding the Moors (more docile and easily exploited than Christians) against expulsion.

There has been general agreement among scholars that one of the salient causes of Spanish economic decadence was the progressive decline in the character of the rulers from Philip II until the advent of the Bourbons. Through their absolutism and tireless energy Charles V and Philip II greatly extended the centralisation of authority in the Crown begun by the Catholic Kings. Owing to their devotion to duty and amazing capacity for work, Charles V and Philip II were able to govern the empire almost single-handed. But the mediocrity of Philip III and the dissolute character of Philip IV led them to abandon the affairs of state to court favourites. During the reign of Philip III economic progress was stifled by the unscrupulousness and insatiable avarice of the Duke of Lerma. Under the guidance of his imperialistic favourite, the Count of Olivares, Philip IV played a pitiable and ridiculous role while trying to emulate Philip II. Unmindful of the nation's weakness, he pitted Spain against France in 1635 and England in 1655. On several occasions a tottering Spain attempted to stand alone against the combined might of Europe. The Thirty Years' War was for Spain a thirty-nine years' war; and while it was in progress internal weakness permitted a revolt of the Catalans, which lasted twelve years and exhausted the economic life of that region to such a point that a hundred years was required for recovery. There were also serious uprisings in Andalusia, Biscaya, Sicily, and Naples; and, frightened by the prospect of complete absorption under the imperialistic Olivares, Portugal waged a successful war for independence.

Although dependent upon favourites, Philip III and Philip IV were able to provide political stability by keeping their prime ministers in power for long periods. Diseased in mind and body from infancy, and constantly preoccupied with his health and eternal salvation, Charles II was incapable not only of governing personally but of either selecting his ministers or maintaining them in power. From the assumption of the regency by the Queen Mother, Mary Anne of Austria (too young, too ignorant of politics, and too addicted to the pleasures of the court to govern wisely), to the death of Charles II not one of the many individuals who rose to power displayed genuine ability. For years the King was expected to die at any moment, and his impotence early became evident. Consequently the whole reign of this imbecilic creature, aptly characterised as "royal anarchy," was a protracted plot for the succession. Spain was spared the internal revolts of the previous reign; but, taking advantage of her weakness, Louis XIV dismembered the European empire. In more than half of the thirty-five years' reign of Charles II Spain was at war against the powerful forces of the Sun King.

Great military conflicts (precipitated by imperialism, religious fanaticism, and lavish expenditures) had increased the state debt and the burden of taxation under Charles V and Philip II; but when the rulers were able and the Spanish infantry was the terror of Europe, the results of these policies were less disastrous than under the weak kings of the seventeenth century, when Spanish arms were no longer invincible.

All economists recognise the evil effects of misgovernment even under *laissez-faire*; but, with the state intervention and paternalism prevailing in Spain, the economic consequences of progressively inferior administration were catastrophic.

It was the crushing burden of taxation resulting from costly wars, the extravagance of the royal household, the inefficiency of tax farmers and collectors, and the avidity of court favourites rather than the expulsion of the Moriscos that ruined the sugar industry of Granada. As taxes rose, the number of taxpayers fell with the decline in population and the increase in the ranks of the clergy and the nobility. The unbearable burden of taxation at the end of the sixteenth century and throughout the seventeenth was an important factor in the decline of Spain.

During the century of decline the Church seems to have been the only institution that grew. Long before the close of the Middle Ages the extension of mortmain and the increase in the number of convents were condemned in the Cortes and in the writings of moral philosophers; but throughout the sixteenth century the Church gained ground, and in the seventeenth it marched forward at a phenomenal pace. In 1619 the Council of Castile reported that the excessive number of ecclesiastics and ecclesiastical institutions was ruining Spain, and the Spanish economists of the seventeenth century almost unanimously concurred in this judgment. There is reason to believe that the combined number of priests, monks, and nuns approximately doubled in the seventeenth century and constituted at the end of the period almost 180,000 out of a total population of less than 6,000,000. The celibacy of the ecclesiastics contributed to depopulation, and the indiscriminate distribution of alms aggravated the grave problem of vagrancy and vagabondage. Although the incompetence of the Church as a landowner has generally been exaggerated, the increase in mortmain accompanying ecclesiastical expansion was probably a factor in the decline of agriculture. In every European country during the seventeenth century religious censorship of the press and speech undoubtedly stifled the intellectual progress upon which economic advancement has always largely depended; but, owing to the heavy hand of the Inquisition, the interference of the Church with learning was at its worst in Spain.

Dr. Julius Klein has shown that the migratory sheep herds of the Mesta contributed in various ways to deforestation and deterred the development of arable agriculture. During the semi-annual migrations the shepherds enjoyed the privilege of cutting enough branches from trees to make corrals, fences, cabins, tanbark, fuel, and dairy implements. Furthermore, they were entitled to trim or even to fell trees in time of drought, during the winter, and whenever for any other reason pasturage was scarce. Far more serious was the practice (by migratory and sedentary herders alike) of burning the trees in autumn to provide better spring pasturage. Erosion was increased by the damage done to tender shoots and moisture-retaining turf by the sheep themselves. The right to pasture on waste lands, crown lands, and even on town commons was conferred by the *Fuero Juzgo,* or Visigothic Code. Profiting by the growing power of the Crown, its ally, in the sixteenth century, the Mesta prevented the enclosure of commons for arable. Throughout the two centuries of Hapsburg rule continuous legislation provided for the return to pasture of land converted into arable; but under the weak rulers of the seventeenth century the laws were not enforced. The suppression of competitive bidding for pastures by the Mesta organisation lowered the incomes of the owners, and during the sixteenth century the judicial authority vested in Mesta officials prevented adequate indemnities for the depredations of the migratory herds. But, with the decline of royal authority in the seventeenth century, the Mesta itself suffered through arbitrary levies by the local officials. The Mesta began to lose ground early in the reign of Philip II and became but a shadow of its former self in the seventeenth century, when, according to writers prior to Dr. Klein, its flocks crowded out other forms of agriculture. By the end of the reign of Charles II wool growing was absorbing the attention of nearly every Castilian peasant. Arable agriculture had given way to sheep raising in a large part of Spain, but it was to the sedentary pastoral industry in no way connected with the Mesta.

The growing of *latifundia* through primogeniture, entailed estates, and mortmain apparently gave grazing an advantage over arable agriculture. In the last quarter of the sixteenth century and the first half of the seventeenth grain prices in Andalusia and New Castile forged considerably ahead of the general price level, while the prices of animal products were moving harmoniously with those of general commodities. The growth of large estates, the crushing burden of taxes, and the decline in consumer demand following the decimation of the population by the great plagues of 1599-1600 and 1648-50 were the major causes of agricultural decadence. The sharp rise in the prices of forest products in the first half of the seventeenth century suggests sufficiently rapid deforestation to aggravate the dearth of rainfall. That legal maximum grain prices were not a factor in the decline of agriculture, as has been alleged, is evident from their complete lack of control over market quotations.

Though by no means generally effective, to some extent the mercantilist obstructions to the outflow of specie impounded in Spain a part of the great influx of Mexican and Peruvian silver. Before the end of the century this process had raised prices and costs above the level in other European countries and thus handicapped export industries, naval construction, and navigation. The illusion of prosperity created by American gold and silver in the age of mercantilism was partially responsible for the aggressive foreign policy, contempt for manual arts, vagrancy, vagabondage, luxury, and extravagance, which led to the economic decadence of the seventeenth century. After 1600 the imports of American treasure fell precipitately, and by 1660 shrank to a small fraction of their volume in the reign of Philip II. Since Spanish industry and commerce were geared to this steady and increasing stream of treasure, the sharp drop in the returns from the American mines was a severe shock to the economic life of the nation.

The industrial and commercial progress stimulated by the lag of wages behind prices during the first eight decades of the sixteenth century, while technology was advancing, was checked by the parallel movement at the close of the century. In the first half of the seventeenth century the index numbers of wages on a 1571-80 base were considerably above those of prices in all except five years. Without technological progress to reduce costs correspondingly, business profits were eliminated; and under capitalism a ruinous decline of industry and commerce inevitably resulted.

The golden age in literature and the fine arts and the silver age in money (during the sixteenth century) were succeeded by a bronze age in the seventeenth century. While universally envied because of her monopoly of the American gold and silver mines, Spain saw the precious metals driven completely out of circulation by a cumbersome medium of exchange. Like almost all monetary derangement from medieval debasement of the coinage to the inflation of currency and central bank credit of modern times, the unbridled alteration of the coinage in Spain, which began near the end of the reign of Philip II and gained momentum as the seventeenth century progressed, was largely due to a chronically unbalanced budget. At frequent intervals in the last three-quarters of the seventeenth century the evils of inflation called forth corrective deflation, with sharp declines in the commodity price level and severe commercial crises as inevitable consequences. The deflationary decree of 1628 brought prices downward by 9 per cent. From March 1641 to August 1642 wholesale prices at Seville rose by 93 per cent.; and in a few days following the deflation of September 15th, 1642, they dropped about 87 per cent. In 1680-82 commodity prices fell by 45·43 per cent. as a result of deflation in 1680. From September 1929 to February 1933 wholesale commodity prices in the United States fell only 37·86 per cent., and the drop in the annual index from 1929 to 1933 was but 30·9 per cent.

While many beneficial effects flowed from the constant, and therefore dependable and predictable, rise in prices in the sixteenth century, it was not so with the sudden inflation and deflation in the seventeenth. The numerous and sharp fluctuations in prices upset calculations, stifled initiative, impeded the vigorous conduct of business enterprise, and wreaked havoc upon the economic life of Spain.

In a grave national emergency economists were right, for once, in their diagnoses and prescriptions. With prophetic vision, the Spanish economists of the seventeenth century (Sancho de Moncada, Pedro Fernández Navarrete, Gerónimo de Cevallos, José Pellicer de Ossau, Diego Saavedra Fajardo, Francisco Martínez Mata, Miguel Alvarez Osorio y Redín, and many others) denounced most of the evils leading Spain to ruin—such as primogeniture, mortmain, vagabondage, deforestation, redundance of ecclesiastics, contempt for manual labour and arts, indiscriminate alms, monetary chaos, and oppressive taxation. Their reform programme comprised technological education, immigration of artisans, monetary stability, extension of irrigation, and improvement of internal waterways. History records few instances of either such able diagnosis of fatal social ills by any group of moral philosophers or of such utter disregard by statesmen of sound advice.

VII

France in Early Modern Times

The Characteristic Features of French Economic History from the Middle of the Sixteenth to the Middle of the Eighteenth Century

HENRI HAUSER

The Huguenot Policy of Louis XIV and Pope Innocent XI

LOUIS O'BRIEN

>>>->>>->>>->>>->>>->>>->>>->>>->>>->%-<<<-<<<-<<<-<<<-<<<-<<<-<<<-<<<-<<<-<<<

The Characteristic Features of French Economic History from the Middle of the Sixteenth to the Middle of the Eighteenth Century

HENRI HAUSER

>>>->>>->>>->>>->>>->>>->>>->>> *Published in 1933* <<<-<<<-<<<-<<<-<<<-<<<-<<<-<<<

Textbook treatments of French history in the early modern (the sixteenth through eighteenth) centuries have usually centered on the more dramatic features of the life of the time: on the frequent wars of Francis I, the Huguenot Civil Wars, and the careers and domestic and foreign policies of Henry IV, Sully, Richelieu, Mazarin, and Louis XIV. It is a welcome change, therefore, to come upon an essay that focuses on French economic development rather than on politics and war—important though they were in the life of the times. Nor have there been many scholars more competent than the late Henri Hauser to undertake such a treatment. One of the most important historians in twentieth-century France, Hauser did much to stimulate the investigation of the economic development of early modern times; and in the present essay he shows some of the gifts that placed him in the front ranks of recent economic historians.

I t is my intention, without entering into details or multiplying figures, to trace the evolution of French economic life between the financial crisis which shook the country, together with others, towards 1557-59 and the great crisis which proved the ruin of the *ancien régime*. In this summary I shall endeavour to disengage the charactcristic fca-tures which gave France her particular economic physiognomy.

Reprinted by special permission from *The Economic History Review*, IV (1933), 257-272.

I

In the middle of the sixteenth century France possessed, in the "exchange" at Lyons, one of the great international centres for monetary and commercial transactions. The business of exchange, or in other words the transference from place to place of sums which were to be paid at their destination in money different from that which had been paid by the original debtor, was carried on at Antwerp, particularly for business between the German bank and Spain, at Genoa which served as a centre for the inter-imperial transactions of the Spanish crown or for dealings between it and the Hapsburgs, and at Lyons for business with all the countries with which France had dealings. The Lyons commodity fair, where Spanish wool, Breton linen, Italian silks, lace and gloves, were exchanged for the books which were the pride of the Lyons press, the wines of the Rhône and Saône, the cloth of the Midi and spices brought from the Levant, had quite naturally developed into a financial market, as a consequence of the fact that each of the four great annual fairs was followed by a period of eight or fifteen days, called "settling days," when buyers and sellers who had been content during the fair to enter their debts and credits in their books, were occupied in balancing those books and paying their differences either in specie, or more often in new bills of exchange for a specific period, to fall due at the next fair. At the end of three months these bills might be renewed, from fair to fair, at an additional commission of about 4 per cent. for each period. To ensure the working of this system, which really deserves the name of clearing house, the bankers of Lyons made use of a standard money of account, imitated from the imaginary "banco" money which had early been adopted at Venice and Florence.

It was thus, through the absolute security which it offered to capital, that the city had become the centre which regulated the exchanges. London merchants needed bills on Lyons to pay, not only for the wine which they bought at Bordeaux, but for the Indian goods which they procured in Spain. In this way the Lyons exchange fixed the terms to be observed not only at Rome, where the Curia received the ecclesiastical taxes through this channel, but in a part of Germany and even in Scandinavia and the Baltic countries.

This money power concentrated in a small number of hands was not slow to exercise its influence on European policy. It was the *fuorusciti,* the representatives of the Italian banks who had been the victims of the revolutions there, who financed the wars of the French kings in Italy, and ceaselessly urged them to cross to the southern side of the Alps. In opposition to the bankers of Protestant Germany who tried to attract Henri II across the Rhine, it was the Florentine exiles, who had been vanquished by the Medici-Spanish policy, who drove him into a second Italian adventure.

Thus, in their dealings with the French Government, the Lyons bankers were constantly inflating credit. It was a terribly dangerous temptation for a State, which was perpetually short of money, to have this enormous and easy reservoir of capital at hand. A local agent of the Crown, the Cardinal de Tournon, devised a grandiose plan involving a combination of public and private credit in a direct appeal to the public to invest its savings in return for a promise of fixed interest, and the utilization of the funds thus obtained for a vast scheme for amortizing the public debt. Such, at least, is the conception of this *grand parti* to be derived from the present state of the evidence, a gigantic project of paper credit which needed a French victory as a condition of its success. The defeat of St. Quentin entailed the downfall of the paper issued by the Crown, a crisis which coincided with the bankruptcy of Spain and had repercussions even in Germany.

This crisis descended upon a nation which was generally considered to be passing through an era of prosperity. The France of that period had certainly the densest population in Europe. From the end of the English and feudal wars of the fifteenth century the work of clearing

BANALITÉS: Such utilities as the lord's flour mill, oven, and wine press, which the peasant in pre-Revolutionary France was generally obliged to use and pay for. The banalités represented a source of income for the lord, but they were frequently viewed as burdensome by the peasant.

BARTHÉLEMY DE LAFFEMAS: Influential controller-general of commerce during the reign of Henry IV and a leading champion of economic reforms in the mercantilist direction. In particular, he advocated French industrial expansion. His ideas, set forth in a large number of tracts, did much to shape the approach of Colbert.

RENTIERS: Receivers of a fixed income from investments; people whose economic position, therefore, depends on price movements. In sixteenth-century

the ground for cultivation had been carried on with such vigour that the seigneurs were experiencing a great need of labour, with the result of a rise in the peasants' standard of life. Serfdom had almost completely disappeared. From the thirteenth century the dominant tendency among the seigneurs themselves, when they were in need of money, had been to replace payments in kind by fixed money dues. The constant depreciation of the monetary unit (the *livre tournois* divided into *sols* and *deniers*), and then the fall in the value of money, doubly lightened the charge on the tenant; and he was also getting a better price for his products. France remained a nation of peasants, with rural property divided between a very large number of labourers who enjoyed almost complete property rights, and a numerous *petite noblesse* of country gentlemen who cultivated part of their domains themselves and received for the remainder a rent which was nominally fixed but really decreasing in value. The methods of both seigneurs and tenants were very rudimentary, the three-year course (with a fallow every third year) in the north and a two-year course in the south, on ground parcelled out since time immemorial into a multitude of little separate plots, generally long and narrow, which were mainly devoted to the culture of cereals—wheat on the good land, rye on the rest—and to a primitive species of cattle rearing. The latter provided farm manure, the only improvement known. The whole sufficed, however, for the needs of a population whose demands were not large and, apart from biological or meteorological disturbances and political or military crises, even left a certain margin for

France they suffered considerable hardships as a result of the price revolution.

BATTLE OF ST. QUENTIN: French defeat by the Spaniards and the English in 1557 (during the reign of Henry II).

TREATY OF COMMERCE OF 1786: Eden Treaty between England and France. By its terms customs duties were reduced appreciably for so protectionist-minded a century as the eighteenth. A step in the direction of freer trade, it represented a victory for the ideas of Adam Smith and the physiocrats. Strongly opposed by most French manufacturers, the treaty came to an end in the early years of the French Revolution.

export. On hills with the right exposure the vine was a source of wealth which enjoyed a great reputation abroad, dating from the time when Bordeaux had been an English town and Dijon the capital of a state which included Flanders.

In spite of this essentially peasant character of the French nation the towns had become increasingly important, especially from the end of the fifteenth century. They were to preserve for many years, sometimes even to our own day, their semi-rural character as markets for agricultural produce and dormitories for those who worked in the fields by day. The Paris of France I and Henri II was generally supposed to be the most populous town in Christian Europe, even more populous than Lisbon, or the Italian or Flemish towns. It was believed to contain 300,000 or sometimes 500,000 inhabitants—no doubt an exaggeration explainable by the effect produced on visitors by the swarming and cosmopolitan crowd of students at its University, the number of its legal and financial officials who gravitated round the Court, the crowded state of its narrow shop-lined streets, the scene of activity on its river and the influx of foreigners.

But Paris was not alone. Rouen is generally mentioned as the second city in the kingdom: the point where the smaller craft from Paris exchanged goods with the sea-going ships for England and the Netherlands, and also the principal centre of the cloth industry. Her claim to the second place is disputed by Lyons, the ancient Gallo-Roman metropolis at the junction of the Rhône and the Saône: the historical point where the road leading from the Mediterranean provinces and upper Italy to the northern seas crosses that which makes its way into Central Europe. Lyons was at that time a frontier town and full of foreigners—Italians, Germans, Swiss, even Dutch, besides French from the centre, east and south; the Italians especially were so numerous that they earned for it the name of a French Tuscany. We have already spoken of its commercial and financial importance. To these must be added Marseilles, which began its career as a port for the eastern Mediterranean trade as soon as the relations between the Valois kings and the Porte opened to France an unrivalled position in the Levant and the States of Barbary. In the west Bordeaux has already been mentioned, but there must be added the Basque fishing ports, such as Bayonne, ports of whalers and cod-fishers, the merchant republic of La Rochelle, Nantes at the mouth of a river which was then navigable, and, finally, those cities on the Loire between which a constantly itinerant royal family was always moving its court, indeed, one may say, its capital—namely, Amboise, Tours, Blois and Orléans. France had the reputation of being a country in that happy condition in which she could dispense with her neighbours while they could not do without her. If the word *autarchy* had existed it might have been applied to the France of the sixteenth century. Scarcely anything was believed to be lacking to her, unless it were one or two commodities such as the precious metals, and minerals, such as alum, which were useful for industry.

From the time when internal peace was established by a monarchy which tended towards absolutism and centralization, and from the time of the improvement of the means of communication (an improvement which was relative only, but noticeable to contemporaries), France had greatly increased her commerce and had seen the avenues of the ocean open before her. Although she had arrived too late to compete seriously for the routes of Cathay with the inhabitants of the Iberian peninsula, and although the attempts of Coligny in Florida and Brazil had ended in checks, she had done her best, like the Dutch and English, to deprive the Hanse towns of the empire of the Baltic. She had found a way of acquiring her share of the treasure of the New World by selling the needy Spaniards what they lacked both for themselves and for their overseas territories—corn, cloth, and men. Groups which in real truth deserve the name of "French colonies," attracted by the difference in the value of money on the two sides of the Pyrenees, went marching off to Spain as carters, gardeners, carpenters, and so on, and brought back with them the balance of their high wages. It was to enrich the French, ran the saying, that the Spaniards worked the mines of El Dorado.

II

The crisis of 1559 would probably have been settled, like every crisis which shakes out unsound concerns and brings the country back to a healthy state, by a few financial failures, had it not been for two events: on the one hand the breaking out of the civil wars which followed the death of Henri II and lasted for more than thirty years; on the other, the fact that the wave of high prices which had broken over Spain now began to reach France—which, we must not forget, was bordered by Spain not only in the Pyrenees but on the Saône and the sources of the Oise. The phenomenon of the rapid rise in prices disconcerted contemporaries who saw not only the money of account, the *livre tournois,* but also metal money losing its value. In 1577 a desperate effort was made to re-establish the *livre* by making it one-third of the *écu d'or,* but in contrast with English experience this effort failed.

What were the results of this monetary revolution? As in all periods of inflation, the rise of prices ended in a species of expropriation of the classes living on fixed incomes in favour of their debtors. The *petite noblesse* who lived on their rents saw them entirely disappear. The only ones to survive were the families who left their manors to go and live in the circle of the court. Land belonging to noble families was often bought at a low price by the town bourgeoisie who had grown rich in business or in the public service, and were now in their turn to found families of gentlefolk. The peasants should have been the chief beneficiaries of this revolution; but the Wars of Religion, with their sequence of the systematic pillage of land and the destruction of flocks, often the wiping-out of whole villages by the armies of the two parties, prevented the free play of economic laws —a movement too often checked in France by political catastrophes.

The chief victim was the working class, the members of which lived on their wages. We must not forget the development of industry which had taken place in France since the beginning of the century, if indeed "industry" is the right word for a period when the prominent figure was the artisan. Certain of the traditional industries had already taken on a definitely capitalist aspect, such as the cloth trade with its strict division between the different operations and the relative complication of its machinery. But much more serious was the situation of the new industries introduced at the Renaissance, printing and the silk manufacture, which had escaped the rule of the gilds. The rise in prices was only very slowly followed by a rise in wages, a nominal rise which the journeymen only forced out of the masters by using the weapon of the strike. The formation of a definite working-class proletariat, combined with religious persecution, was the cause of considerable emigration.

Two classes, above all, increased in importance. First, the dealers in money, the bankers and financiers, particularly those who, either alone or grouped in companies or *partis,* advanced to the State the product of the indirect taxes—a product which by nature could not be other than hypothetical. As the Court, and in imitation of it, the towns, were always increasing the sources of their extraordinary

revenue, the number of these *partisans* was always growing. At first
they had been foreigners used to the practice of finance, Italians from
Lyons and elsewhere, or Germans; later the French began to take
part, even down to the servants, who, after enriching themselves by
lending to their masters, began to make their savings bear fruit in
public business. From the time of Henri IV this domination by revenue farmers became one of the prominent features of French economic life. The social ladder soon enabled them or their sons to
climb into the upper strata of society, more particularly because, after
having made their fortunes, they often entered another class which
had benefited by the new regime, the class of public officials. The
offices of justice, finance, administration, even the little posts created by
the poverty of the Treasury, were all to be bought, and were almost,
one might say, put up to auction; thus bringing to the administration, in exchange for a future revenue, a capital which was immediately available. Once paid for, the official posts produced salaries for
those who held them and other advantages with a monetary value.
From the end of the reign of Henri IV they were practically hereditary, or at any rate transferable at the will of the holder. Besides, in a
large number of cases, they conferred noble rank on the possessor,
with privileges among which was that of exemption from direct taxation, especially the land tax. For this reason titles to official posts were
greatly in demand and were sold over and over again.

The establishment of a market in this particular kind of transferable security had incalculable effects upon national economic life.
While in Holland and even in England a merchant, manufacturer,
or financier, having made his fortune, had no other desire but to see
his sons extend the range of his business, in France the dream of every
self-made man was to buy his eldest son an official post; if he was
at the top of the ladder, he would make him a Councillor in one
of the Parliaments or the Chambres des Comptes; if he was a small
shopkeeper, he would make him a clerk. Thus there was a constant
haemorrhage of capital, which removed it from business as soon as it
had been created; and the commercial class was decapitated by the
transformation of its best representatives into professional men. The
younger sons of these families, by entering the Church, also obtained
fixed incomes. This is the explanation of that narrowing down of the
French commercial horizon, that diminution of the spirit of adventure
and enterprise, that triumph of the love of fixed income, which was

to give to France, which had been noted of old for its travellers and conquerors of distant lands, the psychology of a nation of *rentiers*.

The Huguenot element deserves separate mention. Calvin's opinions on the lawfulness of lending at a moderate interest, and his theory about the necessity of saving one's soul in the practice of one's profession, resulted in France, as elsewhere, in a kind of equation between capitalism and puritanism, success in business being a sign that one was walking in the way of the Lord. The honesty of the Huguenot bankers and the strictness of their bookkeeping gained them the confidence of their clientele. It was not by chance that Cardinal Richelieu entrusted to Protestant bankers, not only his personal fortune but in many cases even State business. On the other hand, in spite of the equality of treatment stipulated in the Edict of Nantes, it was only with difficulty that the Protestants entered the public service. From 1661 it was practically, though not yet legally, closed to them. The Protestant families of La Rochelle, Bordeaux, Nîmes, Lyons and Paris had not, therefore, the temptation or the possibility of investing their commercial capital in the purchase of official posts. Even after the revocation of the Edict of Nantes the families of the newly converted preserved these habits and aptitudes. At the time of the great exodus there was a cleavage in a large number of the wealthy and active families, some of the sons emigrating to Protestant countries, the others allowing themselves to be converted to a catholicism more or less sincere in order to avoid the confiscation of the family fortune; but the two branches of the family remained in touch in business. Even Louis XIV, during the great famines of 1694 and 1709, lowered his pride before the bankers of Rouen and elsewhere, who, by means of their relations who had emigrated, were able to procure credits at Amsterdam, London, Hamburg and Danzig.

In the industrial sphere the crisis caused by the rise in prices between 1566 and 1578, which was to last until the end of the seventeenth century, favoured the growth of a theory which was already well known and increasingly upheld by the deputies of the Third Estate (*i.e.,* the craft communities) in the States General—the theory to which later centuries were to give the name of Mercantilism. In the France of the Valois and early Bourbons, as in the England of Lord Burleigh, it was not only a question of attracting gold and silver into the kingdom and of preventing the export of the precious metals, it was also a question of finding work for its subjects, and therefore

of admitting into the kingdom only goods to which as small a part
as possible of foreign labour had contributed: raw materials, which
were indispensable to French products, or partly manufactured goods
in the first stages of their manufacture. The work of restoration to
which Henri IV devoted himself after the devastation of the civil
wars, and the attempts of Richelieu, much earlier than those of Colbert,
had as their object the settlement in France of all the industries whose
products had been bought abroad, both luxury goods as silks, lace,
tapestry, and glass, and those commodities which were of immediate
use for national production such as agricultural implements, or capable
of being largely exported such as the various branches of the cloth
industry. This result was arrived at in two ways: the more or less
complete prohibition of goods which might compete with those which
henceforth it was intended to make in France, and the introduction of
expert workers from foreign countries to instruct the French.

In the time of Henri IV there was an attempt to go further by
promoting the spirit of invention. The Bureau de Commerce summoned by this king acted almost as a Commission on Inventions, and
its minutes seem to herald an early triumph of machinery. But any
attempt at industrial progress failed before an essentially conservative
social organization—the craft corporations. Even in the trades which,
as we have seen, were legally exempt from regulations, even in the
many towns which had no corporations and where one might suppose that labour was free, in reality the masters' oligarchy was sovereign, and its interest was to keep the position and the habits which
it had acquired and to limit competition both in numbers and in
dynamic force. Twice, in 1587 and 1597, the Crown, as much and
more in the interest of revenue as in that of mercantilism, endeavoured
to unify and at the same time to render less mischievous the rules of
the corporations. It failed before the combination of vested interests.
Those who desired the rise of new industries, such as the silk manufacturers of Tours, were opposed by those who were purely merchants,
such as the Lyons importers of Italian silks. The latter found allies
in the many Frenchmen who, in their attachment to the purely rural
traditions of the nation, opposed what they would have called, if they
had had our vocabulary, an excessive industrialism. It is this clash of
theory which gives such a dramatic aspect to the struggle between the
two councillors of Henri IV, Barthélemy de Laffemas and Sully, who
appears as the precursor of the physiocratic theory.

In the upshot, France never had its Statute of Artificers, and the creation of new industries, which was not indeed negligible, was only undertaken under the guise of *manufactures royales*: in other words, the establishment of industries by the State or with privileges from the State.

III

The economic achievement of Colbert has been called State Socialism. On all the evidence this is an anachronism. But it is still possible to say that this great clerk, who was certainly less intelligent than Richelieu, but more tenacious and better served by circumstances, thought of the production and distribution of wealth as a State service. It cannot be denied that, materially, the system produced results in the industrial system. Sheltered by privileges, administered under the control of divisional Intendants under the inspection of the Controller-General, it is incontestable that the *manufactures royales* were brought into being, existed, produced and sold goods. The cloth of Languedoc retained a large market in the Levant for a long period, in spite of Dutch and English competition. The new industries, copied from Venice or the United Provinces, were prosperous. In particular, many industries of artistic value, which contributed to raise the reputation of France still higher, were acclimatized in the country. The workers in the *manufactures royales* became, whether they liked it or not, a kind of industrial army subject to authority, and their attempts to strike were considered as revolts. The spontaneous forms of workers' organization, *compagnonnages* or journeyman's societies for instance, only existed in secret, and the State put all its weight on the side of the employers. In the small trades which, in spite of the growth of manufactures, represented the greater part of the industrial activity of the country, the statutes of the corporations had become the laws of the State. Here, as in the *grande industrie*, regulation reigned supreme, not only regulation of labour but regulation of the goods made, a system hostile to every innovation and every attempt to perfect machinery or to make any alteration in the employment or combination of raw materials. This regime, severe as it was, had at least the advantage of giving French productions the reputation of a standard product with invariable characteristics. It was an assistance to the export trade to have a trade mark which was universally appreciated.

But trade is difficult to regulate. The struggle between the

Controller-General and the town which was the greatest commercial centre of that period, Marseilles, was in the true vein of heroic comedy. The inhabitants of Marseilles, who considered themselves as a sort of merchant republic, were masters of the trade to Barbary and the Levant from Morocco to Constantinople; the *nation française* or French consuls in the Levantine ports were all Marseillais. These people's chief desire was to do business; but the opinions of the minister on the Levant trade were those held by all the men of his time with perhaps two exceptions, Richelieu in France and Thomas Mun in England. It was, it was said, an unfavourable trade, since it caused the export of money from the country in exchange for the import of luxury, and therefore superfluous, commodities. The quarrel was carried on by Colbert's successor, Louvois, on a particular point, that of calico printed and dyed in the Indies. In France, as in England, the prohibition of Indian cottons was to be the great question of the day for a whole century; and when the rigidity of the theory begins to give way under the blows dealt it by the beneficial practice of smuggling, a new stage in economic life will have begun.

For Colbert, as for his predecessors Henri IV and Richelieu, the model for sea-going trade on a large scale was furnished by the Dutch with their companies. It seemed only necessary to imitate them as had been done in England; but it is here that we can best measure the harm done to French economic life by the prejudice against trade which had descended from the nobility to the upper middle-classes, and by the spread of the practice of purchasing official posts. The Dutch companies, which were an economic copy of the political organization of the United Provinces, were a spontaneous growth of capitalist endeavour. Colbert thought he could achieve the same result by royal orders, summonses to take up shares and threats against recalcitrants. There lay the great weakness of the French colonial companies; they were never to strike root in the capitalist classes of the nation. It followed that, in spite of a sumptuous appearance, French colonial enterprise after the seventeenth century was to be feeble and inconsistent. There was little voluntary emigration, since New France had been closed to the only Frenchmen who would gladly have put the Atlantic between them and the authorities which persecuted them—an intolerant and dominating Church, a rigid seigneurial regime, and the unfaltering application of a colonial system which prevented all local enterprise both in the West Indies and Canada. This first French colonial empire was nothing but a façade.

The finance of foreign commerce was no less defective. The square of Lyons had indeed preserved the tradition of its fairs, but they no longer had a European reputation. There were no great banks in France, but only houses which carried on commerce and banking combined. To do business with the Baltic countries, even when a Compagnie du Nord had been formed to compete with Dutch trade there, the French had to procure bills on Amsterdam unless they could get them on Hamburg. Thus, the French rate of exchange was deplorable. The louis was quoted under par in Holland and in England all through the reign of Louis XIV.

It is a simplified view of history which is responsible for the antithesis, "Prosperity in Colbert's time, decadence after his death." This is not the case. In 1661 Colbert made a great effort at financial reform by clarifying the budget and lightening the taxes; but he could not see that the most important thing of all in this rural country was the prosperity of the peasants, and he was not able to increase agricultural production. The policy of regulated industry and of the Companies was expensive. The court was even more expensive, and Colbert could not refuse the king Versailles and its fêtes, nor the luxury of war for the sake of glory. He himself was ruined by that evil counsellor a bitter hatred, the hatred of Holland [sic]. It was he who drove the king into the war with the United Provinces. He began by a tariff war in 1667, and from this economic strife war was bound to come. Thus Colbert's policy ended ruinously in a contradiction.

It was after his day, it is true, that the Revocation of the Edict of Nantes took place, and it was without him, indeed one may say against his will, that the policy of the revocation was begun before his death, driving French employers and workmen and French industry to her competitors. What France lost, directly through the loss of creative energy and indirectly through the creation of rival energies, has been told a thousand times. The war which followed has been well called the Anglo-Dutch war against French trade; and the next, the war of the Spanish Succession, was to have the same character. When, in 1713, Queen Anne celebrated her victory, she told Parliament very truly that it was the victory of British trade. It was for this end that Louis XIV had definitely ruined his finances, already seriously impaired in Colbert's later days. The permanent deficit, the growing indebtedness of the Treasury, the increase of taxes, monetary instability and inflation in all its forms, the misery of the peasants which reached even to under-nourishment and famine, the spectacle of France importing corn and unable to find the credit with which to import it— these were not conditions very favourable to the activity of commerce and industry. What classes remained wealthy? They were the court nobility, who lived on subsidies from the king, the Parliamentary councillors, who had become large landed proprietors, and especially the dealers in money who enriched themselves. It was the reign of the Farmers-General.

IV

It is common knowledge that after the establishment of peace between 1713 and 1715 there was everywhere, but especially in France and England, a fever of speculation. In France it ended in the creation and then in the spectacular fall of Law's "system." We are beginning to understand better the historical value of this experience, which has been too often judged from the point of view of orthodox economic theory. Law was ruined, in fact, by forces created or maintained by the past history of France; the timidity of a nation of peasants and *rentiers*, the privileges of the possessing classes, the traditional hostility of the magistracy and the administrative system to financiers, and the insufficiency of the credit organization. The unpopularity of banking theory had increased, and in consequence the normal evolution of credit was retarded.

It would be, however, a denial of the evidence not to recognize that the "System" gave new life to overseas commerce and to industry. If France was able to withstand the very unfavourable commercial situation created for her by the Treaty of Utrecht, she owed it to this stimulus in 1720; and from then onwards progress continued. All the evidence which we are gradually accumulating points to the years about 1740 as a period of remarkable commercial activity. Certainly there were many failures, but that was because there were many enterprises and company creations. In spite of the commercial domination of England in Spanish-American waters, it is worth notice that the commercial bankers of St. Malo, who drew capital from the whole of France and were in control of the domestic industry of the peasant weavers of Brittany, furnished goods to Spain and, via Cadiz, to the Spanish colonies, not to mention the smuggling trade which they succeeded in carrying on directly with those colonies. Nantes was enriched by the slave trade from the coast of Guinea to the West Indies, in return for which she received sugar for her refineries and rum, besides the provisions, calico, porcelain, and so on, brought from the East by the Compagnie des Indes.

In spite of the war of the Austrian Succession and the Seven Years' War, in spite of the American War and the commercial disappointments which were to follow the peace of 1783, in spite of the competition in the Mediterranean, French commerce continued to increase both in amount and in value. The Treaty of Commerce with England in 1786 appeared as a death-blow in the eyes of the mercantilists, but the same was said in London—a proof that this treaty was, on the whole, advantageous for both nations. In 1789 the total value of French trade for the first time passed the figure of a milliard *livres tournois* (£40,000,000), a figure which, in francs, was not to be reached again until a much later date, in 1806, only to be once more lost. This trade was carried on to a large extent with the French colonial empire which, although it had been grievously curtailed in 1793, still preserved St. Domingo, "the pearl of the Antilles." Bordeaux, the principal refuge of the Portuguese Jews, also played a very considerable part in colonial trade. Marseilles was no less prosperous. Paris had not yet become an industrial town, but she was becoming a great commercial distributing centre and could no longer be called merely a large city of small shopkeepers.

The weakness in this trade was the organization of credit. It was only with Turgot's ministry that a *Caisse d'Escompte* was set up (the name of bank was suspect since Law), in which one may legitimately see the origin of the Bank of France. When the French Government decided, indirectly at first but openly after 1776, to finance the revolt of the American rebels, it had to act by means of the Dutch banks.

This commercial activity made very difficult the maintenance of the system of regulation elaborated by Colbert. In the deliberations of the Council of Commerce, especially after 1750, may be noticed a growing liberalism and a tendency to allow exceptions. In 1759 the permission granted to import Indian cottons was completed by that given to manufacture similar products almost without restriction, and it is well known that the cotton industry is by nature revolutionary and breaks through all the old boundaries. When Turgot suppressed the corporations he only struck at an institution which was already at the point of death. When they were re-established after his resignation they were in reality very different. In imitation of England the spirit of invention became increasingly prevalent. For example, missions were sent from the Academy of Sciences to study the English method of producing steel with coal and coke, rewards were given to inventors, industrial museums or museums of scientific societies were established, there was a system of industrial espionage, designs and machines were sought for and workmen bribed, British firms were established in France, and every means was employed by the Government and by the great nobles who prided themselves on their knowledge of science. About the 1780's, France experienced a first stage of the industrial revolution. Large workshops were set up with a great number of workmen, and it was not chance which gave the word *industrie* its modern meaning about that time. Coal began to be a factor, thanks principally to the mining law of 1744, which was due to the scarcity of vegetable fuel.

It may be asked whether the rate of agricultural evolution kept pace with this development. In the middle of the eighteenth century the character of the French countryside remained almost of the traditional type. The culture of cereals, so indispensable to a nation of bread-eaters, continued to predominate, and the rye, or even buckwheat, grown on the granite lands of the west and centre, had hardly given way at all to wheat or maslin. It was so uncertain a culture that there was always fear of famine in one province while others were enjoying abundance. The Crown, therefore, was always oscillating between two contradictory policies—freedom for the grain trade or prohibition of all internal trade—no one daring to go so far as general freedom of imports and exports. When a famine was very widespread the partisans of *laissez faire* were obliged to give the lie to their beliefs, like Turgot in the Limousin, and to carry on State purchase of grain in the Baltic to prevent the king's subjects from dying of hunger.

The industry of cattle-rearing produced only mediocre beasts, utilized indifferently for hauling or for killing. The use of artificial meadows, which had spread from Flanders to England, had not yet become the custom, and it was difficult to extend its adoption because of the minute division of land and the persistence of old rural usages; the extent of common land, the prevalence of waste where the small-holders had the right of pasturing their half-starved flocks and of gathering wood and litter for their stables, the prohibition of enclosing and the maintenance of what in England was called open field, where pasture was allowed on the fields after harvest; and in consequence the faithful maintenance of a system of rotation with a fallow between the crops.

This backward condition of agriculture was slowly modified from about 1750 onwards. The doctrine of the physiocrats was only the translation into the language of philosophy of the practice followed by various large landowners who knew of the English experiments and who had to provide for the needs of a population which was rapidly growing. Although the part played by the increasing number of agricultural societies must not be exaggerated, they did at least carry on propaganda. France began to have her agricultural experts, who knew that an ox which drew the plough on the plateaux of Central France had nothing but the name in common with a prize Durham steer of an English agricultural show. Many experimented with secondary crops, especially with the famous turnips which Arthur Young, on his travels in France, looked upon as the sign and instrument of agricultural progress. Turnips were in front of potatoes, which, in spite of Parmentier's efforts, were hardly used except as cattle-food, and whose remarkable future no one could foresee. Arthur Young notes the appearance of enclosures, which were traditional in the wooded land of the west and even in a part of the south-west. The Government favoured this change by permitting (by an Edict of 1750) the sale of communal property, and later (1771) its partition among the inhabitants. A fierce struggle developed between the shepherd and the agriculturist, but ancestral customs resisted change up to the Revolution. The edict of 1767 abolished the obligation of permitting the entry of cattle to ploughed fields and allowed the enclosure of such fields, but here again it was necessary to await a law of 1791 to protect both fields and artificial meadows. There was practically no unanimity between the shepherd and the agriculturist except in face of their common enemy the forest, which was already threatened by the development of industry.

To understand the resistance of the peasants to innovations it must be remembered that, although rural property was very much divided, and although before the Revolution there was a great number of small owners, the organization of property was still very feudal—in other words, the land which belonged to the cultivator was burdened with charges, taxes which the privileged classes did not pay, seigneurial dues, ecclesiastical tithe and royal or seigneurial *corvées*, and labour dues which were perhaps more severe and irritating than the charges, such as the *droit de chasse* [hunting rights] and the *banalités*. It has been maintained that manorial rights had even become more oppressive at the end of the eighteenth century; the new nobility of the law and of commerce were more jealous of their rights than the old, and the general absenteeism of all the nobility caused the collection of the dues to be left in the hands of agents from whom no pity was to be expected. The peasants, with their intense desire for land, looked with anger at the immense domains kept by the nobility and clergy, which were often taken out of cultivation for purposes of mere luxury and amusement.

It was not, therefore, an extreme misery which engendered the revolt of the countryside against the privileged classes. If the Revolution of 1789 was essentially a peasant revolution, it was not a revolution of landless men to divide between themselves the land of those in possession, but a revolution of small owners who wanted both to round off their properties and, above all, to shake off the yoke which weighed on them. The principal effect of the Revolution was not to cause any considerable increase in the division of ownership, which was already a characteristic feature of the French countryside, nor to augment the number of properties to enormous proportions, but to liberate peasant property. Agricultural progress, which in Arthur Young's time was limited to the vast estates of certain large owners in the English style, could only gradually become general when this liberation had taken place. The slowness, the love of routine, the individualism, the obstinacy, but also the avidity for work and the passion for acquiring land, the spirit of economy and resistance which remain in the twentieth century the characteristics of the French peasant, are very largely explained by this history.

It is impossible for us to say when and how the agricultural revolution would have taken place if economic life had not been dominated by the financial question. When we remember the commercial prosperity of the France of Louis XVI and compare it with the distress of his Treasury we are describing the position of a State at the last resources of its poverty in the midst of a nation comparatively rich. The chronic deficit had never been made up since the time of Louis XIV, and the State only continued to survive by means of successive bankruptcies. Towards the middle of the Seven Years' War, in 1759, there was an opportunity of paying off the public debt; the Protestant bank, which, as we have seen, continued to exist under a regime which apparently required unity of faith, offered the means to do so in return for the grant of civil rights to members of the reformed religion. The Catholic clergy stigmatized the negotiations as simony and caused them to be broken off. Later, Turgot made a supreme effort to put the finances in order by economizing; his plan, besides being difficult to reconcile with the intervention of France in the American War, failed before the resistance of the privileged classes, from the queen down to the lowest official. The often praiseworthy efforts of his successors could only retard and perhaps aggravate the crisis.

Thus the Revolution of 1789 appears as the last act in an economic drama, the beginning of which was played in 1557-59; and the varying fortunes of this long drama have imprinted on the economic physiognomy of the French nation features which have not disappeared to the present day.

The Huguenot Policy of Louis XIV
and Pope Innocent XI

LOUIS O'BRIEN

>>>->>>->>>->>>->>>->>>->>>->>>->>> *Published in 1931* <<<-<<<-<<<-<<<-<<<-<<<-<<<-<<<-<<<

Few events in the long reign of Louis XIV have received so much attention as the revocation in 1685 of the 87-year-old Edict of Nantes. Louis'
reasons for depriving French Protestants of the limited degree of religious
toleration that they had enjoyed since the time of Henry IV continue to be
disputed. Some historians attribute Louis' action mainly to the influence of
his mistress, Madame de Maintenon, a devout Roman Catholic, who viewed
Protestants as heretics, as slayers of souls. Other historians ascribe much more
importance to political considerations—to Louis' search for unity at home
at a time when he was anticipating foreign war. Whatever the explanation
of the revocation of the Edict of Nantes, the fact is that Protestants who
remained in France suffered numerous atrocities. And these atrocities played
an important role in mobilizing anti-French sentiment in Protestant countries, as anyone who has read Macaulay will remember. The Pope himself
disapproved of the methods used in the France of Louis XIV to win Protestants back to Roman Catholicism. Louis O'Brien, author of a valuable
monograph on *Innocent XI and the Revocation of the Edict of Nantes*
(1930), makes this point, among others, in the following essay on religious
intolerance in seventeenth-century France.

Popular conceptions of the relationship of Pope Innocent XI to the
Huguenot policy of Louis XIV have shown an extraordinary variance. While some historians have maintained that the pontiff wholeheartedly approved of the royal program, others have considered him
actually to have been unsympathetic.

Reprinted by special permission from *The Catholic Historical Review*, XVII
(1931), 29-42. The footnotes which originally appeared with this essay have been
omitted.

Such a wide range of concepts cannot be accounted for by any justifiable difference of opinion. Rather would I suggest that the advocates of the opposing interpretations have failed to weigh the facts of the case at their proper relative values. Almost unanimously they have assumed that Louis' policy was an entity to be taken or rejected as a whole. In this light they have aimed to create one or another consistent attitude for the pope. Such a procedure has obliged the exponents of each point of view either to ignore the evidence which was out of harmony with their interpretation or to discard it as irrelevant.

If the practice be abandoned of considering in its entirety something which can be reduced to its elements, what appears to be an historical problem will be greatly simplified. The Huguenot policy of the Grand Monarch resolves itself into an end and a means to its fulfillment. Religious uniformity in France was the royal ambition; its attainment was to be sought in various ways. To appreciate the relation in which the pontiff stood to the whole subject we must examine his attitude toward the king's aims and also his opinion of the methods employed.

While Innocent XI had no part in the formulation of Louis' Huguenot policy nor was in any way directly responsible for it, the assumption must not be drawn that he lacked sympathy with its purpose. Such was most certainly not the case. It is not surprising that the Supreme Pontiff was interested in the efforts of the Eldest Son of the Church to gain converts. He was constantly informed of the success which attended Louis' proselyting zeal, and he did not hesitate to make his sentiments known to the king through the French ambassador at Rome and the nuncio at Paris. Both of them testified frequently to the satisfaction of the Holy Father with His Majesty's "indefatigable application to the conversion of heretics."

Furthermore Louis XIV received three papal briefs in which the

---

PIERRE BAYLE: French scholar, publicist, and opponent of dogmatism. He not only criticized the forcible conversions that were taking place in the France of Louis XIV but advocated the toleration even of atheists—a policy that such major figures in the history of tolerance as John Milton and Locke did not favor.

CHRISTINA: Daughter of Gustavus Adolphus, and scholarly Queen of

pope expressed gratification at the royal zeal for the propagation of the faith. The first of these followed the revocation of the Edict of Nantes. It was superlative in its approbation. On this occasion Innocent said in part:

> We have deemed it to be our duty to commend lavishly your glorious religious spirit by this distinguished and enduring evidence, our letter, and to congratulate you exceedingly on the crown of immortal praises which, through a signal deed of this kind, you have added to your hitherto nobly performed achievements.

Again some six months later Innocent wrote:

> Moreover, assigning abundant and deserved praises to the extraordinary zeal with which you strive each day further to advance piety and the Catholic religion in that flourishing realm of yours, we pray God, from Whom all blessings flow, for Your Majesty's continuously unbroken happiness and prosperity.

The third brief which touches upon the king's Huguenot policy was dated January 15, 1689. In it the pontiff approves

> that extraordinary zeal (never sufficiently commended by any praises) with which you have set as your illustrious goal to extend the Catholic religion and to guard it vigorously against heretics.

Likewise in the first consistory to be held after news of the edict of revocation had reached Rome, Innocent praised Louis' zeal in similarly glowing terms. The pope at this time also authorized the representatives of His Most Christian Majesty in Rome to conduct a three day celebration in honor of their master's achievement for religion. There is no indication that Innocent XI at any time showed displeasure with the king's aim. Indeed, it would have been exceedingly strange had he done so. Let us see if the same can be said with regard to the means by which that end was sought.

Sweden. She abandoned Protestantism and returned to Roman Catholicism after her abdication in 1654. She died in Rome in 1689.

DRAGONNADES: Troops who were quartered in the homes of Protestants during the reign of Louis XIV in order to "encourage" them to return to Roman Catholicism. It is sometimes believed that the practice originated with the royal official Marillac, who reported that he had remarkable results in bringing about conversions to Roman Catholicism by lodging troops in Protestant dwellings.

By a gradual withdrawal of their political rights and freedom of worship Louis hoped to induce his Huguenot subjects to forsake their religion. In pursuance of this policy he set about, by royal ordinance, to restrict the activities of the dissenters. Before 1680 the royal program developed slowly but thereafter it was pursued with vigor.

Monsignore Ranuzzi, the nuncio, informed the Holy See of each of the crown's encroachments upon the privileges of the Protestants. Invariably the pope signified his satisfaction with the royal regulations. An examination of the correspondence which passed between the Vatican and the Paris nunciature makes it clear that Innocent was pleased with the crusade against heresy in France, at least insofar as the political and religious restrictions on the Huguenots were concerned.

The papal attitude is entirely intelligible. Seventeenth-century Europe still professed belief in the Christian state. Naturally the pontiff subscribed to that opinion. According to it the secular authority was responsible to God for the faith of its subjects. Thus the duty devolved upon the state of protecting orthodoxy and preventing heresy. The least the state could do in fulfilling its obligation was to deny political rights and freedom of worship to those refusing to conform to its established religion.

To a certain extent France had ceased to do this after 1598. The Holy See, like the Gallican church, viewed the Edict of Nantes as an abandonment on the part of France of her obligation as a Christian state. In other words, official recognition of the Huguenots as French subjects having equal rights with their Catholic compatriots and permitted to worship publicly in their own way was interpreted as encouraging Protestantism. Consequently all the ecclesiastical influence which could be summoned opposed the religious settlement of Henry IV from the beginning and continually thereafter. Thus it was that Innocent XI was also ranged against religious toleration in France. For this reason he was gratified to learn of the royal policy which aimed at its withdrawal. But the fact that the pontiff approved of the abrogation of the Huguenots' political rights and freedom of worship does not establish his acceptance of Louis' whole program for the propagation of the faith.

The first indication of papal dissatisfaction with the royal proselyting campaign manifested itself when attempts were made to modify the customary method of admitting converts to the Church. The established practice required that an abjuration of heresy be followed by a declaration of faith prescribed by the Council of Trent. On June 20, 1685, the nuncio informed the Vatican that His Most Christian Majesty desired a new formula to replace that of Trent. It was to be designed, he said, "to close the mouths of heretics who perverted the minds of untutored persons by misrepresenting Catholic doctrine."

Two months later the proposed declaration, drawn up by the Assembly of the Clergy, made its appearance. So vague were its terms that it was even unacceptable to the court, consequently the Archbishop of Paris forbade its use. Louis considered the matter closed, but the pope did not. The Paris formulary was submitted to the Holy Office for inspection and several months afterwards was solemnly condemned by that body.

To facilitate conversions and in default of a more palatable means of submission to the church than the declaration of the Council of Trent, some bishops now permitted Huguenot converts to abjure heresy in general terms without specifically declaring the articles of faith to which they subscribed as Catholics. Ranuzzi reported this practice to the Holy See and received the prompt reply:

> The Huguenots who abjure in general terms without professing the articles expressed in the formulary of Pius IV, as prescribed by the Council of Trent, cannot be good Catholics; and the bishops who have approved such abjurations will not be able to justify their conduct.

Louis was exceedingly annoyed at the pope's refusal to overlook the methods used to gain converts in France. He expressed this annoyance in a letter to Cardinal d'Estrées, the brother of the French ambassador at Rome. The king said that it would be better for the Church if the Vatican bothered itself less about the means employed by the French prelates in their work, "for nothing is more capable," he concluded, "of strengthening the stubbornness of heretics than Rome's continual censures of everything which does not conform with her doctrines"!

Innocent XI, then, condemned a practice which permitted the Huguenots to be received into the Church without explicitly forswearing their former beliefs. He was unwilling to tolerate the dilution of Catholic doctrine, as promulgated by the Council of Trent, for the purpose of making conversions among the French Protestants. His Most Christian Majesty was thus made to realize that he could not depend upon unqualified support from the Holy See in his proselyting plans.

But if Innocent was disturbed by such practices as that just mentioned, how much more alarmed must he have been to learn of the actual use of force in the king's Huguenot program! There is reason to believe that the pope was uninformed of the French persecution until sometime after the revocation of the Edict of Nantes. It is to be recalled that the abrogation of the famous ordinance of Henry IV did not *ipso facto* abolish freedom of conscience. The last article of the edict of revocation explicitly stated that the Protestants remaining in the realm would not be "troubled or hindered on the pretext of their religion." Innocent did not know that this clause was to remain a dead letter.

Shortly after the revocation the pope expressed the belief that no force had been employed in gaining conversions. On November 13, 1685, Innocent received the French ambassador in audience. The latter reported the Holy Father's remark that a cardinal had accused the French king of gaining converts by compulsion. Innocent assured the ambassador that he had denied the allegation and made known to the prelate in question that His Most Christian Majesty had purged his kingdom of heretics by kindness and by the expenditure of great sums of money. Three weeks earlier the pope had similarly defended Louis' policy in an audience granted the representatives of Austria and Spain. On this occasion, other than religious motives had been imputed to Louis in his attack on Calvinism. "The Most Christian king," replied the pope, "is not inspired by political considerations, but by piety, service to God, and zeal for religion."

Moreover, the pontiff had very definite opinions as to the efficacy of persecution as a means of suppressing heresy, opinions which he had expressed in a conversation with Queen Christina of Sweden in October, 1685. Innocent said on this occasion: "Heresy is of such a nature that if it be not extinguished, persecution augments rather than diminishes it." Surely anyone thus convinced would not condone the religious persecution to which the French resorted.

Since it is to be assumed that the pope was unaware of the impious travesty which in France was termed "conversion" at the time he made the foregoing remarks, it is well to examine how he could have been deluded.

The two principal channels through which the pope received information regarding France were the French embassy at Rome and the apostolic nunciature at Paris. If the d'Estrées brothers themselves knew of the persecution in France their knowledge was obtained through some unofficial channel. None of the despatches addressed to them from Paris gave any hint that conversions were insincere, much less mentioned the use of force. Even were duke and cardinal informed of the true state of affairs, to have imparted their knowledge to the pope would have prejudiced their cause needlessly. They were making the most of Louis' zeal for religion in an effort to induce the Holy Father to grant certain concessions to the Eldest Son of the Church. When they addressed His Holiness on their master's Huguenot policy they undoubtedly presented it in its most favorable aspects. There was no possibility that Innocent should learn the truth from them.

The Paris nunciature presented an entirely different situation. Ranuzzi and his assistants sent voluminous reports to the Vatican and apparently related all they knew. Prior to September, 1685, there was nothing in any of their despatches to justify the apprehension of Rome concerning the conversions on the grounds of intimidation. But during and after that month references to compulsion appear in the correspondence. On September 17, for example, the nuncio spoke of the abjuration of 60,000 converts in a few months in the generality of Bordeaux and added that the troops hitherto lodged there had been removed in accordance with a privilege which the king had granted the new Catholics. A week later he again alluded to the dragonnades, this time still more openly. He reported that it was believed the king intended to send troops into Dauphiny to frighten the Huguenots and to compel them to become Catholics "as is done elsewhere." On October 15, a despatch from the nunciature contained the following statement:

> As the means practiced heretofore in different parts of the realm have been efficacious in gaining converts, they will be pushed more vigorously in the future . . . namely, the quartering of dragoons and guardsmen in the homes of Huguenots to live and act as they please until their hosts become Catholics.

A month later this was followed by a report from the secretary of the nunciature in which there is an allusion to the use of force, with the statement that although there were many abjurations there were few conversions. Henceforth the nuncio's despatches contained frequent references to the Huguenot persecution, which was gradually assuming alarming proportions.

If the pope was unaware of conditions in France it was certainly not the fault of the Paris nunciature. It seems significant, however, that the Vatican's replies to the foregoing despatches made no reference whatever to the persecution although it was usual for the cardinal secretary to express his opinion or to repeat that of the Holy Father on any important matter.

All the correspondence of the nuncios was addressed to the papal secretary of state. Obviously the pope saw very few, if any, of these reports. He was dependent for his information upon the cardinal secretary, in this case Cybo. There is reason to believe that Cardinal Cybo was a pensioner of the French Crown. That he was on exceedingly good terms with the brothers d'Estrées is attested by their reports in which appear frequent references to the cardinal's attachment to the interests of France. Moreover, Cybo had personal reasons for fostering Franco-Roman amity. Most of his income was derived from Avignon, and Louis' unfriendliness toward the pope constituted a serious threat against the continued possession of that territory by the Holy See.

Naturally Cardinal Cybo, knowing Innocent's temperament, realized that the pope could not be expected to condone the forceful measures undertaken to coerce the Huguenots into rendering a lip-service to the church and pretending to be converted. That a condemnation of these proceedings by the pope would be exceedingly distasteful to the Grand Monarch was also apparent to the astute secretary of state. There was only one way in which Cybo could be certain that the pontiff would remain silent on the matter and that was to withhold the information which he alone had.

No evidence has been found which proves that the cardinal deliberately suppressed reports from the Paris nunciature. However it is a plausible assumption that for a time the pope was kept in ignorance of actual conditions in France. The cardinal admitted his devotion to Louis XIV and his solicitude for "diverting difficulties." And the fact that no comment was made by the secretary of state in reply to Ranuzzi's information relating to the use of force strengthens the case against him.

However it may have happened, Innocent seems to have been unaware of the French situation at least until the time of the consistory of March, 1686, in which he publicly commended the Grand Monarch's zeal. Fate played into the hands of those who were anxious to keep him in the dark, for early in December, 1685, he fell ill, and for four months was unable to grant audiences save to a few of his ministers.

After the consistory and the Roman celebrations in honor of the destruction of heresy in France, Innocent was more or less publicly committed to the French program.

When or how the pope first learned of the forceful methods by which the faith was being propagated in France is unknown. Cardinal Cybo would have had less reason to withhold his information after the Holy See's commitment to Louis' policy. Possibly the French persecution was brought to Innocent's attention by the retaliatory measures of the Dutch government against the Catholics of the Netherlands. The pope earnestly sought to mitigate their sufferings and he was informed of its cause in no uncertain terms by his representatives at Cologne, London and Brussels. Again, the truth may have reached Innocent through Queen Christina who so violently condemned the French policy. The Spanish and Austrian ambassadors likewise had no reason to shield the actions of the Grand Monarch's government. In any case the pontiff eventually came to be informed of the French situation, and, while he on no occasion officially took cognizance of the use of force in the conversion of the Huguenots, from time to time he gave evidence of his feelings in one way or another.

In an audience granted to a Dutch priest in 1688, the latter reported the Holy Father, in speaking of conditions in France, to have said: "We do not approve in any sense these forced conversions which as a rule are not sincere." Moreover at about the same time, in a letter to Emperor Leopold, Innocent referred to the French persecution in these words:

> He [Louis XIV] prides himself on having contributed with all his power to conserving the rights of the Holy See, and to increasing the number of Catholics, in that he has brought several million to reenter the bosom of the church. To be sure this number would be considerable if the conversions had been made by the holy and pious exhortations of his clergy rather than by violence and by the fury of his soldiers. For what likelihood is there that conversions obtained by torture are real conversions? We have wept, we have bemoaned them instead of rejoicing in them. The horrible thought of so many sacrileges which have been committed will cause me to shudder for the rest of my days. . . . Would it not have been a thousand times better for the glory of the name of Jesus and for the salvation of so many souls to whom God will not grant grace since they are impious and sin against the Holy Ghost, would it not have been better to have left them in their former com-

plete liberty than to have made them fall into this callousness from which they will never be able to extricate themselves?

Furthermore Queen Christina seized the opportunity several times to make known Innocent's attitude. On one occasion a letter which she wrote criticising conditions in France was published by Pierre Bayle in his *Nouvelles de la république des Lettres*. It had not been intended for publication but in a second letter stating she did not regret the publicity given the first, she added: "To the credit of Rome it must be said that all here of good sense and worth, who are animated by true zeal, are not duped by France any more than I."

Christina would hardly have made such a generalization had she not intended to include the Holy Father. This point is substantiated by a third letter in which the queen said that Innocent rendered her opinion its just due although he was overcareful not to offend the Grand Monarch and was unable to speak for reasons of policy.

Two other contemporaries of Innocent XI have left us evidence that they correctly judged his opinion in the matter. Neither of them could have had his knowledge directly from the pope but both occupied positions from which it may be assumed that they were reliably informed, particularly since their statements are correct. The individuals in question are Girolamo Venier, the Venetian ambassador at Versailles, and Abbé Le Gendre, the secretary of the Archbishop of Paris. In neither case are we told of the sources of their information.

Venier, in the *relazione* which he submitted to the Venetian Senate at the expiration of his mission to France, spoke of the papal attitude regarding the methods used against the Huguenots in the following manner:

> Although meritorious the Court of Rome abstained from praising the measures taken against the Huguenots, proclaiming the impropriety of using armed apostles as missionaries, and showing this new method not to be best since Christ had not adopted it to convert the world.

So also the Abbé Le Gendre complained in his *Mémoires* that scarcely anyone at Rome rejoiced over the suppression of heresy in France; "Innocent XI less than any other," he added, "excusing himself by saying that he could approve neither the motive nor the methods of these conversions by thousands where none were voluntary."

In forming our conclusions with regard to Innocent's attitude toward the use of force in the French conversions we are not entirely dependent upon the pope's private statements nor on the careful judgments of certain of his contemporaries. The pontiff's treatment of Etienne Le Camus, Bishop of Grenoble, is also highly illuminating.

Le Camus was the one prelate in France who, more than any other, stood out against the Huguenot persecution. Not that he believed in religious toleration as a principle. To expect such a thing from a seventeenth-century cleric of almost any denomination would be an anachronism. The Bishop of Grenoble was as enthusiastic as any of his confrères in accepting the abrogation of the ordinances permitting the Huguenots publicly to practice their religion; but this was as far as he cared to go in the matter. The use of force in gaining adherents to Catholicism was entirely repugnant to him. Le Camus bitterly opposed the dragonnades and was instrumental in securing the withdrawal from his diocese of troops sent there to intimidate the Protestants.

In September, 1686, Le Camus was elevated to the sacred college. This was a shock to Louis XIV. Not only did the prelate lack the royal nomination; the crown had not even been consulted in the matter. To make the situation still worse Louis' candidate, the Bishop of Beauvais, was ignored. It would be ridiculous to claim that the promotion of Le Camus was primarily a recognition of his opposition to the Huguenot persecution. The Bishop of Grenoble merited his new dignity by his fine qualities of mind and character. But it must be remembered that his stand on the subject of conversion was generally known and that his elevation had been made entirely on the initiative of the Holy See. Furthermore in April, 1687, the cardinal issued a pastoral letter to his clergy dealing with the so-called "newly converted." In it the *curés* were charged to abstain from any form of coercion in their treatment of the former Huguenots. The tenor of the letter may be fairly judged by this excerpt from it: "God wished the service rendered Him to be voluntary."

The effect of Le Camus' pastoral may be easily imagined. At once a protest was raised by the court prelates. When the cardinal saw the storm of disapproval which greeted his letter he sent it to Rome together with his other writings. The pontiff at once replied with a brief of commendation stating that he had taken no notice of the protests and even going so far as to characterize them as "the vain calumnies of a group of ignoramuses." Several months later Innocent addressed the cardinal another brief full of the most laudatory terms.

These letters from the pontiff can signify but one thing: Innocent shared Le Camus' point of view with regard to the Huguenots. A deduction which would have been possible since the red hat had been conferred upon the prelate becomes imperative in consequence of the papal approbation of the cardinal's instructions to his clergy.

Since it seems clear that Innocent disapproved of the use of force in Louis' campaign to convert the Huguenots the question at once suggests itself: "Why did not the pope formally reprove these actions as publicly as he had endorsed Louis' zeal for the propagation of the faith?" Although Innocent himself does not give us an answer, it is not difficult to find one.

The relations between the Holy See and the Eldest Son of the Church, never cordial during the pontificate of Innocent XI, were increasingly strained in its latter years. It was impossible for the pontiff to foresee the lengths to which the king might go if he considered himself sufficiently provoked. An outspoken denunciation of the forced conversions would probably have been misunderstood at the French Court and interpreted as an attack on the Huguenot policy so dear to the Grand Monarch. It might have precipitated a crisis in Franco-Roman relations. It is even conceivable that the Gallican Church would have declared the pope a heretic; his orthodoxy had been challenged not only by the Parisian pamphleteers but by the advocate general of the *Parlement* of Paris, who was known to speak the mind of the court. Such an action would have led to an open rupture and possibly to the creation of an independent church of France.

What the attitude of Innocent XI was, then, to the king's Huguenot policy may be readily understood. He was wholeheartedly in sympathy with its aim—the propagation of the faith in France. True to his seventeenth-century environment, the Holy Father approved of Louis' determination to abolish freedom of worship and to deprive the Huguenots of their political rights. Innocent, however, was unwilling to sanction the use of questionable means to gain converts. He repudiated the dilution of Catholic doctrine for the purpose of facilitating submission to the church and he, at least privately, condemned the use of force as a proselyting agency.

When we see the papal position in all its aspects it becomes clear to us why historians have persisted in misrepresenting it. Conscious of the fact that Innocent approved or condemned some phase of Louis' policy, and imbued with the idea that that policy was an entity to be taken or rejected as a whole, they have placed the pope squarely for or against the king when in fact, with limitations, he was both.

VIII

Late Tudor and Early Stuart England

➤➤

The Elizabethan House of Commons
J. E. NEALE

English Political Sermons, 1603-1640
GODFREY DAVIES

A Democratic Tercentenary
WILHELM SCHENK

Man in Armor
WILBUR CORTEZ ABBOTT

➤➤➤

The Elizabethan House of Commons

J. E. NEALE

Published in 1950

England was not the only European country that had a parliament in the sixteenth century. But whereas most European parliaments underwent a decline during the course of that century, the English parliament—of which the Crown was the key element—grew in power. The reason for this is that the Tudor monarchs used their parliaments in order to carry out many of the changes they wished to make. It is wise, however, not to think of a Tudor parliament in twentieth-century terms, for on the basis of modern standards it was a remarkably weak institution. Although parliamentary history has long been a favorite field of research for Englishmen, many scholars would agree that the most valuable of recent contributions to English parliamentary history was made by J. E. Neale. Indeed, his *Elizabethan House of Commons*, published in 1949, has already become standard in the field. Although based on a prodigious amount of research, it is not a work designed merely for scholars, candidates for the doctorate, and students who have to prepare a book review. Neale, who is also the author of a penetrating biography of Elizabeth, believes that it is part of the historian's task to make the people of the past live again. In the present selection, which originated as a radio program of the British Broadcasting Corporation, Neale indicates his enthusiasm for the humanization even of parliamentary history.

Every schoolboy has heard about 'Tudor despotism.' It has been part of the accepted canon of historical truth so long that it will be an age dying. After a wonderful display of independence at the beginning of the fifteenth century—known in our history books as 'the Lancastrian experiment'—parliament, we used to be told, touched the

Reprinted by special permission from *The Listener*, January 26, 1950.

lowest depths of subservience under the Tudors. Reduced to the simple form of the mathematician's graph, this theory made the line of political liberty drop suddenly in the sixteenth century and then shoot up again under James I, to reach unprecedented heights under Charles I.

The theory was not so silly as I may have made it sound. It appeared to stand on good foundations. That masterful figure, Henry VIII: how well the idea of despotism suited him! Then there was Queen Elizabeth, who apparently treated her parliaments with the greatest disrespect. At the close of one parliament she was said to have vetoed forty-seven bills; and when Mr. Asquith, in the debate on the Parliament Bill of 1911, drew a parallel between the need in the past to diminish the power of the Crown and the need in the present to restrain that of the House of Lords, he cited this famous incident. It was the culmination of royal despotism. Then again, Queen Elizabeth was supposed to have told the House of Commons that its vital privilege of freedom of speech was limited to saying Aye or No. And when parliament petitioned for the execution of Mary Queen of Scots in 1586, she answered—or so it was thought: 'If I should say unto you that I mean to grant your petition, I should then tell you more than is fit for you to know.'

We need not be surprised at the legend of Tudor despotism. But it is a legend. In our generation, historians have got the Lancastrian experiment into better perspective; Henry VIII—of all people!—has been called 'the architect of parliament'; Queen Elizabeth's veto of forty-seven bills has been proved a myth—a mistake in arithmetic by a seventeenth-century scribe; and better texts have been found of her rude speeches, completely reversing the impression they once made. In fact, it is now clear beyond any peradventure that if it had not been for the apprenticeship of the sixteenth century, and particularly the latter part of it, parliament could never have opposed one Stuart sovereign with such skill and confidence, nor have relieved another of his head.

When we speak of parliament in Elizabeth's reign, it is really the House of Commons that must be in our thoughts; and an interesting point, not unconnected with the leading role then played by the Lower House, is that in this reign, for the first time in its long history, we can bring our famous assembly to life and build a detailed picture of its working. Part of this picture I am to describe here.

First, about the composition of the House. All the English counties, with the exception of Durham, elected two members of parliament, while the Welsh counties, which had been brought into the parliamentary system by Henry VIII, each elected one. In all there were ninety of these county members. In addition, there was a large number of parliamentary boroughs, most of which also elected two members. It is here that a very remarkable change took place in the sixteenth century. There was no obvious reason, except that of custom, why one borough should be sending representatives, and not a score of others. And, in fact, the Tudor monarchs began to create new parliamentary boroughs. From 1547 the pace quickened until the House of Commons, from being an assembly of 296 members at the beginning of the century, became an assembly of 462 in the latter part of Elizabeth's reign. Behind this striking growth in the size of the House there was nothing that we today would recognise as a principle of representation. To a certain extent this is not surprising, because sixteenth-century Englishmen, like their medieval ancestors, did not think, as we do, of proportioning representation to population. They thought of communities: the county, the borough. But, even making allowance for this difference of outlook, there remains the fact that the pettiest of places were enfranchised—'rotten' boroughs from the beginning to the end of their story. To the modern mind, dominated by nineteenth-century ideas, this appears so scandalous that only one explanation can account for it. The Tudors packed their parliaments. Tudor despotism once more.

But once more the truth is the reverse. We shall be better able to appreciate the fallacy in the old view if we first consider what sort of people sat in the parliaments of Elizabeth's reign. The law had something to say on this subject. According to the law, county members were to be country gentlemen and borough members burgesses. That is to say, the House of Commons in late Elizabethan times ought to have consisted of 90 country gentlemen and 372 burgesses and

---

ADDLED PARLIAMENT: Name used to describe the second parliament of James I. The two months it met in 1614 were largely consumed in a quarrel with the King. It received its name because by the time it was dissolved it had failed to make a single enactment.

LANCASTRIAN EXPERIMENT: A term referring to the growth of parliamentary influence and strength during the reigns of the rulers of the House of

townsmen. If the membership had really been like this, one result would have been certain. The Commons, lacking in self-reliance and social courage, could not have stood up to the Lords, much less to the Crown; and Charles I would not have lost his head in 1649. But the law was deliberately, flagrantly broken. The proportion of gentlemen and townsmen was reversed. In Queen Elizabeth's House of Commons there were at least four gentlemen to every townsman. They got there by invading the borough seats.

In the Middle Ages M.P.s had been paid wages: 4s. per day for county members and 2s. for borough members, paid by the constituencies. These payments were still legally enforceable in the sixteenth century. But about the middle of the century increasing competition prompted county members to forgo their wages; and the gentlemen who invaded the borough seats also wooed their constituencies by waiving their right. Thus, small boroughs no longer had any reason to fear being enfranchised: on the contrary, the right to send members to parliament provided them with favours to bestow on the gentry and their powerful patrons, in return for which they expected aristocratic protection and support. As for larger boroughs, these found themselves confronted with pressing letters from noble lords and other great men, whose good will meant much to them, asking for seats to bestow on their friends and followers among the gentry. Often, boroughs just sent blank election returns, leaving these powerful men to fill in the members' names. Shocking! you will say: but it was not shocking to the sixteenth century. From the Reformation on, this urge of the gentry to get into parliament grew. It was a snowball process. The keener the competition, the higher the quality of the House and the fascination of a seat there. No other explanation is needed for the remarkable increase in the size of the House of Commons. Tudor sovereigns were simply responding to the clamour of the gentry for more seats.

Lancaster (1399-1461). Owing to the flimsiness of their claim to the throne and to the pressing financial burdens growing out of the war with France, the Lancastrian kings came to raise taxes by the "advice and assent of the lords spiritual and temporal and of the commons, and by the authority of parliament." Even so, parliamentary power in the fifteenth century should not be exaggerated, for parliaments were short in duration and met infrequently.

A Meeting of the Elite

In these circumstances it is not surprising that there was increasing continuity and cohesion in the membership of the House. Over two-thirds of the members sat in more than one parliament. Some made a life-hobby of it; and there was a core of old parliament-hands in all Elizabeth's parliaments. One distinguished gentleman, who made his first entry in 1534, had probably been a member of fourteen parliaments when in 1593 at the age of seventy-nine he sat for the last time; and he then had as fellow-member a young man who was to sit in the Long Parliament in 1640—spanning between them over a hundred years. What revolutionary changes such men had seen; what experience enriched their minds! The elite of the country went to parliament in Elizabethan days: almost every gentleman with a claim to fame was there. By the end of the reign well over half of the House had been educated at the University or the Inns of Court, or both. These were not men to cower before the monarch. In the very first parliament they forced the Queen to change her policy; in the next they fought a battle which would have ended in an addled parliament in James I's reign. And so it went on. They worshipped the Queen, but they fought against her policies. She, for her part, cursed them in private, trounced them in public, yet wooed them with such art that, as a contemporary said, she converted her reign into a kind of romance. She was brilliantly successful, but to her less skilful successors she left a desperate problem.

Parliament in those days was not a continuous assembly. It would be better to speak in the plural of parliaments, rather than in the singular of parliament. They met at what must seem to us very long intervals. There were ten parliaments but only thirteen sessions in a reign of over forty-four years. And the sessions were brief. The average duration was less than ten weeks. The fact is that parliament was not an ordinary but an extraordinary part of the constitution. Its two chief functions—to pass legislation and to grant taxes—required no more frequent and no longer sessions. It was not part of its business to exercise supervision over the government of the country. The age was still one of personal monarchy, not parliamentary government.

The day began early for Elizabethans; and the Commons met for business at 8 a.m. Even at Court, with its late nights, the Queen might grant audience to an ambassador at that hour. As with the Law Courts, sittings were supposed to end at 11 a.m., though it was often nearer twelve before the House rose. When that hour approached, members were eager to get away to their dinner; and, as the House grew more troublesome and loquacious, the government tried to time the reading of controversial bills near to eleven o'clock. On one occasion, in order to force through a distasteful bill before the end of the session, privy councillors had the doors shut and kept them at it until after 3 p.m. When on another occasion we find the House sitting and talking about its liberties until 2 p.m., those last two hours, on empty stomachs, speak eloquently to us of the temper of members.

Normally the House did not sit in the afternoon, nor, of course, in the evening, though towards the end of the session there might be afternoon sittings to deal with the private bills in which members and their constituencies were interested. They can be likened to our all-night sittings, except that they were not imposed by government business. Members were averse to returning to Westminster after the midday meal, eaten, one supposes, at ordinaries or eating houses in the City; and though committees met in the afternoon, these were usually held at some Inn of Court or similar convenient place. The fact is that the House possessed no other accommodation than St. Stephen's Chapel and its porch or lobby. It was a member's duty to sit in this Chamber all the morning, every day of the week except Sunday. While many were slack in their attendance, risking disciplinary measures such as fines or contributions to the poor-box, and while the lawyers among them—then as now a substantial body—were always slipping out, down the steps and into the adjacent Westminster Hall to plead before the law-courts there, one member at least was compelled to bear the full drudgery of the routine. He was the Speaker. He had no deputy.

It was during Elizabeth's reign that the main lines of modern parliamentary procedure were established. Indeed, it was only in this reign that the House of Commons, noticing that its clerk had recently begun to keep a private diary or *aide-memoire*, adopted this diary as an official Journal. From now on, procedure could be made to rest, not on the memory of an intermittent and changing assembly, but on official entries in the Journal. And it is a sign of the times that Elizabethan members themselves occasionally kept private parliamentary diaries, in some of which the interest is so largely procedural as to show that we are in a new age. With the aid of these written records and the memory and committee-sense of old parliament-hands, the House was constantly defining procedure, refining its details, substituting formalism for flexibility. It may sound humdrum. But those who appreciate the significance of procedure will probably agree that the secret of our parliament today is to be found in Erskine May's *Parliamentary Practice* rather than Hansard's *Debates*.

We are all familiar with our modern procedure in legislation; the almost mystical three readings of a bill, the very odd convention by which the first reading is purely formal and the first debate takes place on the second reading, followed by the committee-stage. The Elizabethan period makes the historical reason for all this quite clear; and indeed, it was in this reign that our practice finally crystallised. In those days bills were written, not printed, and the House was informed of their contents by the clerk reading them aloud. Usually, the first reading gave members their first knowledge of a bill, and they were therefore not ready to discuss it profitably. There tended to be no debate. What Elizabeth's reign did was to eliminate debate at this stage. Between the first and second readings those who were specially interested could buy copies of the bill or read it for themselves in the clerk's presence. Briefed in this way, and by listening to the second reading, members were now ready for debate, if debate proved necessary. And out of the debate came indication whether the bill needed alteration. If it did, it was committed; and this gave us our committee-stage after the second reading. Any alterations made in committee were reported back to the House and in turn read twice. Then the amended bill was sent to be written out anew, on parchment; and before being passed, this final text was read in the House—our third reading. Thus we see that our modern procedure on bills arose from the fact that in olden days they were written, not printed, and that the House was apprised of their contents by hearing them read aloud.

The Committee System

At the beginning of Elizabeth's reign bills were only committed if the debate showed that they required alteration. Many were not committed. Indeed, it looks as if in earlier reigns the serious scrutiny of most bills had been left to the House of Lords, where there were judges and other legal dignitaries to give expert assistance. But as Elizabeth's reign progressed, the mounting quality and experience of members of the House of Commons led to a sustained, critical spirit and an increasing propensity to talk. Time became more and more precious. Also, there were outside bodies and persons with bills to promote or oppose. Their activities, which we know as lobbying, took on a sudden spurt. We might almost say that in a single reign lobbying became modern. London had long had the Speaker and the Clerk in fee: they reluctantly added a tip to the Sergeant-at-Arms. They now organised their promotion of bills, concentrating the attack on the House of Commons. Other corporate bodies and individuals paid counsel, paid members to speak for them, and tipped the officials. If their money did not always buy success it bought time. What with more debating and more lobbying, gone were the old leisurely days. The Queen, in her masterful way, continued to insist on short parliaments; and therefore, the House was driven to invent more time by diverting as much of the debate as possible to the committee-chamber. By the end of the reign all bills were being committed. The committee had become a definite stage in legislation, though as yet theory did not admit the change.

This development in procedure, of which I have given only a glimpse, was the surest sign that parliament had come of age. The members of the House of Commons in those days were richly representative of that section of the nation which was politically articulate —the independent-minded country gentry. They had a will of their own. And once that will and the will of the Crown came into collision, nothing could stop the unfolding of modern parliamentary government. It was in Elizabeth's reign that the collision occurred, principally over religious questions; but so skilful was the Queen in averting any dramatic consequences that her very success has deceived us. We have failed to realise that this was one of the crucial periods in English parliamentary history.

English Political Sermons, 1603-1640

GODFREY DAVIES

Published in 1939

One of the most important themes in the history of early Stuart England was the growth of opposition to the religious, political, economic, and diplomatic policies of James I (1603-1625) and of Charles I (1625-1649). To counteract the objections that numerous elements in the population were raising to these policies, the early Stuart kings did what all contemporary rulers in Europe did: they enforced existing restrictions on freedom of expression and imposed further restrictions. At the same time, because they were well aware of the importance of pulpit utterances in the shaping of an obedient public opinion, they encouraged the ministers of the realm to preach sermons that would fit in with royal policy. Although most of the sermons of their reigns have not survived, enough are extant to warrant some conclusions. In the present essay, Godfrey Davies, of the Huntington Library, the foremost American authority on early-seventeenth-century England, draws attention to the role of sermons in the life of the times and to the attempts of James I and Charles I to control preaching.

How many sermons were preached throughout the length and breadth of England and Wales during the first forty years of the seventeenth century is utterly unknown, and any estimate must be pure guesswork. Even at the meager allowance of one sermon per parish per year, the total would be 360,000 sermons delivered. The number printed and surviving is extremely small in comparison with the number preached. Edith L. Klotz, who made a subject analysis of English imprints for every tenth year from 1480 to 1640,

Reprinted by permission of the Trustees of the Huntington Library from *The Huntington Library Quarterly*, III (1939), 1-22. The footnotes which originally appeared with this essay have been omitted.

tells me that clearly identifiable sermons in the *Short-Title Catalogue*, for the years 1600, 1610, 1620, 1630, and 1640, number 7, 29, 46, 43, and 34, respectively. Supposing that the average is forty, the total, 1600-1640, would be 1,600; therefore, the scholar who had read all the sermons extant for those years would necessarily have to generalize on very imperfect data. The present writer freely acknowledges that he has not been able to peruse all, or nearly all, the printed sermons. He has merely sampled here and there, and regards as only tentative such conclusions as he has ventured to indicate. Indeed, his main purpose has not been to reach conclusions but to call attention to a very neglected aspect of early-Stuart history—the important part then played by sermons in the formation of public opinion, and the highly significant attempt by the crown to control pulpit utterances.

Hitherto, such studies of seventeenth-century sermons as have appeared have been concerned rather with form than substance. Surely the time has come for historians to turn their attention to the pulpits, which, as Macaulay said long ago, were "to a large portion of the population what the periodical press now is." Writing of the Exclusion Bill contest the great historian said, "At every important conjuncture, invectives against the Whigs and exhortations to obey the Lord's anointed resounded at once from many thousands of pulpits; and the effect was formidable indeed." What Macaulay wrote is, *mutatis mutandis*, as applicable to the early as to the later Stuarts.

Before examining the use of the pulpit for political purposes, a brief résumé of the other organs of public opinion is given.

All sorts and conditions of men remarked, in the seventeenth century, that the English people were politically minded. Early in his reign James I found cause to complain of the unsatiable curiosity, "an itching in the tongues and pens," of most of his subjects, so that they searched to the bottom, both in talking and writing, "the deepest mysteries that belong to the persons or state of kings and princes." Fifty years later an Italian observer, in the suite of the Grand Duke of Tuscany, noted "the insolence and capricious disposition of the people" who, as they smoked their pipes in their leisure hours, did not scruple to censure the King's actions, "talking with unbecoming liberty of public affairs." People in much humbler walks of life also testified to the general interest in politics. Tom Tell-Troath, apparently writing about 1621, claimed to be "one of the greatest company-keepers" in London, and assured the King that, whenever a group assembled, they talked of the wars of Christendom and the honor of their native land, drawing invidious comparisons between James's government and Queen Elizabeth's, mocking the King's fondness for the phrase "Great Brittaine" and offering to prove that it was much less than "little England was wont to be." The perusal of private diaries, such as those of John Rous or Sir Simonds D'Ewes, affords the same evidence of a widespread interest in public affairs.

Englishmen had various means for satisfying, or trying to satisfy, their curiosity about questions of the day. In London much news doubtless passed by word of mouth, though in the first half of the seventeenth century there were no coffeehouses or chocolate houses to act as centers of gossip. The various measures taken against tippling in alehouses were probably partly inspired by the wish to prevent political discussions. People living in the country may occasionally have received news from returned travelers, carriers, casual passers-by, or peddlers.

The growing habit of the nobles and country gentry of visiting, or even staying for weeks or months, in London, may have originated partly in the desire to be near the center of things and to learn what was going on in governmental circles. Indeed, one reason for the various proclamations against this new habit may have been royal resentment at all attempts to explore the arcana of politics. The carrier was a recognized purveyor of news. He is likened by Earle, the well-known character writer, to a whispering gallery, "for he takes the sound out of your mouth at York, and makes it be heard as far as London." The peddler was naturally a gossip and doubtless

ARMINIANS: Strictly speaking, followers of the Dutch Protestant theologian James Arminius, who challenged Calvin's conception of predestination. Because of the supposed resemblances between Arminius' views and those of Archbishop Laud, the name Arminian came to be applied to the High Church group in England, which stressed the Roman Catholic rather than the Protestant background of Anglicanism.

BENEVOLENCES: Supposedly loans granted willingly to the crown. In fact, however, they were often forced loans to which English kings had recourse in times of financial distress.

COVENANTERS: The Presbyterian Scots who, in 1638, signed the national

spread many a rumor over the countryside. Maybe his propensity for talking politics was one reason for the proclamation of July 6, 1618, suppressing all peddlers not licensed after receiving testimonials from two justices of the peace.

Printed sources of news were very few. Proclamations and declarations were sometimes issued by king and council as propaganda to inform subjects of this or that event, and, especially, to interpret it. *The First Newspapers of England* contains reprints of news books published in Holland in 1620-21 for the benefit of English soldiers then serving abroad, but neither they, nor their successors printed in England, include any domestic news—only foreign intelligence—until the meeting of the Long Parliament temporarily freed the press. Pamphlets sometimes contain news as well as comments on policy. The increasing strictness of the censorship from 1623 onward made difficult the publication in England of news or criticism unpalatable to the crown, and recourse was had to secret, or to foreign, presses. The amount of political news disseminated in this way was small, but pamphleteers were more successful in molding opinion or creating prejudices. Ballads sometimes dealt with contemporary events and supply guidance to the quantity and kind of knowledge of their own times that was possessed by the meaner sort. Newsletters were sources of information available to the rich, but not to the poor. Sometimes friends wrote weekly letters full of public news. Sometimes professional intelligencers drew up newsletters and made as many copies of them as they had clients. Both kinds of letters contained good, bad, and indifferent news, depending on such varied factors as access to the Secretary of State's office or to the court, acquaintance with the

---

covenant and proclaimed their opposition to the attempts of Charles I to Anglicanize their church.

SIR SIMONDS D'EWES: Meticulous antiquarian and keeper of a private record of proceedings during the early years of the Long Parliament. Although much of his journal remains in manuscript, the parts that have been published more than justify the words of praise that scholars have heaped on it.

THOMAS FULLER: Seventeenth-century scholar and Anglican divine. His *Church History of Britain* still deserves to be read; and his *History of the Worthies of England* is still worth the attention of anyone who wishes to examine an early attempt to compile a dictionary of national biography.

great or their servants, and attendance at, or absence from, public events. Unfortunately, no one has ever attempted a census of existing sets of newsletters written during 1603-1640, so speculation about their numbers is rash, but probably most magnates and some squires were kept more or less informed of the course of politics.

There is good evidence that the Englishman's interest in politics was much intensified after the outbreak, in 1618, of the Thirty Years' War in Germany, and after James made it clear to his subjects that he was pursuing a pro-Spanish policy. Immediately, complaints were made against the Spanish match, in an increasing number of tracts generally written by ministers, particularly by the prolific Thomas Scott, a Norwich rector, whose *Vox Populi* is the best-known. The printing of these tracts was responsible for the appearance of a drastic proclamation (December 24, 1620) against lavish and licentious speech about matters of state. Englishmen were warned that, because there was more bold censure in matters of state than "hath been heretofore, or is fit to be suffered," all of them, from the highest to the lowest, must take heed not to intermeddle by pen or speech with secrets of empire, either at home or abroad. D'Ewes comments on this proclamation, that all men conceived it to have been procured by Gondomar, the Spanish ambassador, because the pamphlet, *Vox Populi*, had become "the subject of many men's discourses." The proclamation appeared the more unseasonable and harsh because the disasters to the Protestant cause in Germany had given the Reformation the greatest blow it had ever received. When the very existence of continental Protestantism seemed at stake, James found that pamphleteers were as determined as the House of Commons to discuss his unpopular foreign policy. Apparently, even pictures or rudimentary caricatures were used to enlighten the illiterate or to amuse the literate. A news writer says that Mr. Ward, a minister at Ipswich, had been imprisoned upon Gondomar's complaint that he had put forth a picture of the Gunpowder Plot, depicting the Pope sitting in a council with a cardinal on one hand and the devil on the other. The houses of Parliament are shown, and Fawkes therein with his lantern. Over them is the eye of Divine Providence, darting its beams down into the cellar where Fawkes is. Another scene apparently showed the Armada in full flight, with the English ships in pursuit. As a result, no doubt, of this and other manifestations of popular disapproval of his pro-Spanish policy, James reissued, on July 26,

1621, the proclamation that had first appeared the previous December.

Unlicensed printing was as obnoxious to the early Stuarts as licentious speech. The campaign against "disorderly printing" started a little later than that against free speech. On September 25, 1623, a proclamation was published against the printing and selling of books contrary to the laws of the land and the regulations of the Company of Stationers—both of which had been evaded by printing books beyond the seas. The next year, on August 15, another proclamation, complaining of the swarm of popish and seditious Puritan books, prohibited the printing or importing of any work on religion, church government, or state, unless it had been approved by the Archbishop of Canterbury or of York, the Bishop of London, and the Vice-Chancellors of Oxford or Cambridge, or their deputies. In 1637 a decree of the Star Chamber, by restricting the number of printers in London to twenty, made unlicensed printing still more difficult.

Meanwhile Charles I, by dissolving his third Parliament and by his determination never to call another, hoped that he had silenced permanently the voice of parliamentary criticism. He himself carried on an active propaganda to justify the dissolution—a subject worthy of further study—but permitted no counter propaganda.

The efforts of the crown to suppress freedom of speech and freedom of the press were the natural and logical consequences of the conception of monarchy then prevalent at court. Both James I and Charles I were convinced that their subjects ought not to busy themselves with state affairs. They expected Englishmen in general to remain ignorant of the course of events and devoid of ambition to influence it. They hoped that their paternalistic government would be accepted without question. In the speech Charles intended to deliver against the jurisdiction of the High Court of Justice, he quoted, with full approval, "Where the word of a king is, there is power, and who may say unto him 'what doest thou?'" On the scaffold he said plainly that he did not believe subjects should have any share in governing. Holding such views, Charles, like his father before him, tried to suppress all criticism, regarding it as a sign of disloyalty. He might have met with greater success had the chief differences of opinion between crown and people remained the same as when they were first openly manifested—over foreign policy. Englishmen's interest in continental affairs is liable to be intermittent, and there was a notable diminution of the concern with which they followed the wars in Germany in the 1630's as compared with the 1620's. In any case, after the victories of Gustavus Adolphus, the Thirty Years' War was prolonged rather to decide the victors' spoils than to save Protestantism. But, as Englishmen became less anxious about the fate of Protestantism abroad, they grew more apprehensive about its preservation at home. The spread of Arminianism, especially rapid after Laud had gained the royal ear, and the influence that Henrietta Maria exercised on behalf of Roman Catholicism, seemed to be undermining Protestantism and very definitely postponing to the Greek calends the further reformation the Puritans desired.

Charles, therefore, might expect opposition from Puritans who hated Laudism, from constitutionalists who felt that their liberty was at stake, from patriots who deplored the inglorious foreign policy pursued, and from groups with any kind of grievance. Whether he or his opponents would prevail depended largely upon whether he could enlist on his side the mass of Englishmen. The press could be controlled and political meetings were almost unknown. There remained the most influential of all the organs of public opinion— the pulpit, with whose control was largely bound up the future of the English constitution.

The attempt to control the pulpit, under the early Stuarts, involved both the prescription of certain topics and the prohibition of others. To prevent criticism was the more urgent task, and precedes the attempt to dictate pulpit utterances. On the whole, what might almost be called the censorship of sermons runs parallel to the censorship of the press, the former becoming more stringent at the same time as the latter. In other words, identical factors were operative in both cases.

The definite attempts made from time to time to dictate the contents of sermons belong to Charles's rather than to James's reign. There are instances, throughout James I's reign, of royal indignation at indiscreet pulpit utterances, but they are much more frequent during the last few years. We are told, for example, by the Venetian Ambassador, of James's anger that preachers dared to inveigh against the peace made with Spain in 1604. An early victim of indiscretion was John Burges, who was imprisoned in 1604 for preaching an offensive sermon before the King. In 1612 the author of a sermon was called before the Council for saying that some of the members hear Mass in the morning, then attend Anglican service, sit in Council all the afternoon, and at night tell their wives all that has passed; the latter, being papists, would relate all again to their confessors, who would send it abroad. The discovery of notes for a seditious sermon, in the house of Edmund Peacham, a Somerset rector, caused his condemnation to death, though he died a natural death in prison. An Oxonian cited Proverbs to prove that kings as well as meaner men might steal, both by borrowing without paying and by laying unreasonable impositions upon their subjects. His discourse was at Paul's Cross (near St. Paul's cathedral), and attracted the more attention because sermons there were often in the nature of inspired declarations, being, in Carlyle's happy phrase, a kind of *Times* leader. In 1617, in one of the famous Spital sermons before the Lord Mayor and aldermen of London, a preacher inveighed against the Spanish match. These sermons in London were of special importance, and were often made the occasion for an announcement, or a pronouncement, of policy. One preacher at Paul's Cross began his discourse: "Being called to this high place, in this great assembly, where is accustomed to be a concourse, not onely from all the parts of the City, but almost of every nation under heaven."

In 1618 occurred a striking example of the not uncommon practice of using the pulpit for reading royal messages. In that year every minister was directed to read from the pulpit the so-called *Book of Sports*—an order which was repeated in 1633, when the *Book of Sports* was reissued. The permission thus given to engage in certain lawful recreations after attendance at divine service was of course extremely offensive to Puritans.

The outbreak of the Thirty Years' War and the acceptance of the throne of Bohemia by Frederick V of the Palatinate, James's son-in-law, excited great popular interest in England. The early years of the war, which opened badly for Protestantism, were occupied in England with the negotiations James was carrying on to arrange the Spanish match for his eldest son Charles. Englishmen were bitterly opposed to this projected marriage between the heir to the throne and a daughter of the most Catholic king, and a number of pamphleteers and preachers braved the King's anger by vehemently protesting against such a policy. Perhaps their protests constitute the first definite example of an attempt to marshal public opinion in opposition to the foreign policy of a government in England. It is not surprising, therefore, that punishment of preachers criticizing the King's foreign policy became much more frequent and closely followed the proclamations of 1620 and 1621 against meddling, with speech or pen, in secrets of state. The Venetian Ambassador thought worthy of report to his government James's order to the bishops and clergy to exhort the people not to refer to the affairs of princes. A newsletter writer noted the King's command to the Bishop of London to warn his clergy, in their sermons, not to discuss the Spanish match, "but they do not obey." A few weeks later a Dr. Price, of Oxford, was sent to prison for making too many political applications when preaching about Isaiah's foretelling the Babylonian captivity. John Everard was one of the most pertinacious of James's critics. In an address to the reader, prefixed to his *The Gospel Treasury Opened*, he is acclaimed as "the only noted man that opposed."

> Preached against and held it out to the utmost, against the late king's matching with the Infanta of Spain, when others durst but whisper their consciences and thoughts: he chose texts on purpose to shew the unlawfulness of great sin of matching with idolators, being often committed to prison for it, when he was preacher at Martins in the Fields; and then by the next Sabbath day one lord or other would beg his liberty of the King, and presently no sooner out but he would go on and mannage the same more fully, not withstanding all the power of the bishops, being committed again and again: being as I heard him say six or seven times in prison, insomuch they coming so oft to King James about him he began to take more notice of him, asking What is this Dr. Everout you come so oft about? His name hence forth on my soul (saith he) shall be Dr. Neverout and not Dr. Everout.

His eulogist claimed rather too much, for Everard acknowledged, in a petition, that he had been long and justly imprisoned for some rash words, against the Spanish match, uttered in St. Martin-in-the-Fields.

When in 1622 a clergyman preaching at Whitehall ventured to compare the Palatinate to the soul and its Spanish invader, Spinola, to the devil, he was temporarily confined in the Tower. About the same time the Privy Council took cognizance of the frank views expressed from the pulpit. The Vice-Chancellor, the heads of colleges, and others of the University of Oxford, were informed that a wicked sermon had been preached in the University, the last Lent, by one Knight, "an unadvised young man, tending to noe lesse then sedicion, treason, and rebellion against princes and, being called in question for the same, hee did shelter himself upon doctrine taught by Pareus in his comentaries upon the 13th of the Romanes." Because the doctrine there delivered was seditious, scandalous, and contrary to the Scriptures, the authorities at Oxford were to search diligently all libraries and studies, both private and public, in the University, as also bookshops, and publicly burn every copy of the works of David Pareus they could find. Wood quotes a decree of Convocation (June 25, 1622) which censured "certain propositions of Pareus and declared that according to the canon of Holy Scripture it was not lawfull for the subject to resist his soveraigne by force of arms, or to make warre against him, either offensive or defensive, whether it were for the cause of religion, or upon any other pretence whatsoever." In London, too, the offending volumes were committed to the flames, after a sermon in which the Bishop had denounced Pareus' opinions concerning the people's authority over tyrannical princes. He also urged a generous response to the royal demand for a benevolence, arguing that "what we have is not our own, and that giving to the King is only restoration."

At court, according to Thomas Fuller, it was thought high time "to apply some cure to the pulpits, as sick of a sermon-surfeit, and other exhorbitances." Preachers meddled with state affairs, and generally, "by an improper transposition, the people's duty was preached to the king at court; the king's to the people in the country." Shallow preachers lost themselves when dealing with profound theological questions, while others merely satirized papists and nonconformists. Accordingly, at the royal order the Archbishop of Canterbury sent to the bishops directions, concerning preachers, which they were to enforce in their several dioceses. For the future preachers were to adhere rigidly to their texts and confine their afternoon sermons to some part of the catechism or to a text from the Creed, the Ten Commandments, or the Lord's Prayer, and not to preach about predestination and such other doctrinal differences as separated the Arminians and Calvinists. Moreover, all preachers were forbidden to advocate restrictions on "the power, prerogative, jurisdiction, authority, or duty of sovereign princes or otherwise meddle" with affairs of state. Fuller, the nearly contemporary historian of the Church of England, states that Puritans deplored the loss of half the preaching in England by the restriction placed on the afternoon sermons. Tom Tell-Troath's comment is that, "though there be orders given to preach nothing but courte divinitie, yet a man may easily perceive, by the very choyce of their texts, and the very teares in their eyes, that if they durst, they would speak their consciences." Consternation seems to have been so general that John Donne was called upon to relieve it. On September 15 he preached at Paul's Cross the sermon subsequently printed with the following title: "A sermon upon the xv verse of the xx chapter of the booke of Judges, wherein occasion was justly taken for the publication of some reasons, which his sacred maiestie had beene pleased to give, of those directions for preachers, which he had formerly sent forth." In it Donne explained that, although the King might well have expected his subjects to receive his directions "upon implicite obedience," yet he vouchsafed to explain the reasons that moved him. Donne's main argument was that, by "that primitive way of preaching"—that is, by catechizing—Englishmen might be armed against all kinds of adversaries in fundamental truths. Although some had made sinister constructions of the King's sincere intentions, he never meant his directions to restrain the exercise of preaching or abate the number of sermons. The King was an open adversary to papists and Anabaptists. Preaching against either of these groups he commended, "if it bee done without rude and undecent reviling."

Nevertheless, there were preachers who found opportunities to denounce the proposed marriage of Prince Charles with a daughter of Spain, and opinions that the Venetian Ambassador thought "seditious and most dangerous" were expressed. Among the offenders may have been two preachers mentioned in a newsletter. The one preached on the text, "If any man worship the beast and his image . . . the same shall drink of the wine of the wrath of God" (Revelation 14:9-10). The second spoke of the great murrain that was supposed to have afflicted sheep in Edward VI's reign and to have been caused by the importation of scabbed sheep from Spain. But others were more cautious. One divine, after a discourse of the damnable condition of those who should forsake their faith, concluded that the congregation might expect some present application but he was not ambitious of lying in prison, and so ended.

The visit of Prince Charles and the Duke of Buckingham to Madrid, during the first half of 1623, called forth a fresh crop of sermons that at court were adjudged seditious. The London clergy at least were warned only to pray for the Prince's prosperous journey and safe return, but some did not forbear to add, "now that he was going into the house of Rimmon." One preacher, hearing that he was to pray for the Prince's safe journey and return, "and no more," offered up the prayer—whether through inadvertence or design is uncertain—that "God would return our noble prince home again unto us, and no more."

The tremendous rejoicings that greeted Charles's return without a Spanish bride may perhaps be in part attributed to the effect sermons against the match had had upon their hearers. Certainly, a temporary lull in sermons offensive to the court seems to have occurred after the breach with Spain had quieted fears that Roman Catholicism in England would be encouraged by the Spanish alliance, and for the years 1624 and 1625 there is a marked diminution in the number of contemporary references to sermons that incurred the royal resentment.

Unfortunately for Charles I, who succeeded his father on March 27, 1625, the early years of his reign afforded ample ground for complaint. His foreign policy was disastrous and his evident encouragement of Arminianism seemed to many Protestants only slightly less dangerous than favor to popery. Controversialists were again busy on the differences between Calvinism and Arminianism. This seemed the more serious inasmuch as Charles, in his anger, had just dissolved his second Parliament, to prevent the presentation of a spirited remonstrance.

Heylyn, the biographer of Archbishop Laud, tells us that Charles now determined to take a leaf out of the book of Queen Elizabeth, who, when she wished to rally her people, "used to tune the pulpits, as her saying was," by having ministers in and about London, and elsewhere, to preach up her desires in their public sermons and in their private conferences. Her example was now to be followed to prepare the people for "a dutifull compliance" with the King's wishes.

Charles, therefore, issued one proclamation to suppress copies of the above-mentioned remonstrance, which had been distributed, and another against preaching any opinions concerning religion that were not clearly warranted by the doctrine and discipline of the Church of England. Clerics and laymen alike were warned that stern punishment would fall upon those who dared to disturb the peace, either in church or state.

In Heylyn's opinion the proclamation against disturbers of the peace of church or state was very imperfectly obeyed, and Puritan ministers in the country took little notice of it. Therefore Bishop Laud persuaded the King to have the Book of Articles reprinted and a declaration prefixed. In it the King declared that the articles contained the true Anglican doctrine agreeable to God's word, and that henceforth no man must, either in print or in the pulpit, put his own sense or comment upon any article but take it in the literal and grammatical sense.

Apparently about the same time, the Privy Council drew up a letter to be sent to the Archbishops of Canterbury and York. The letter is worth very careful study, inasmuch as it is an admirable statement of the Stuart conception of the relations of church and state. It begins with the assertion that the church and the state are so closely united that, though they may seem two bodies, yet in some respects they might be regarded as one, inasmuch as both were made up of the same men, "differenced onely in relacions to spirituall or civill ends." This nearness makes the church call upon the state for help whenever she was oppressed beyond her strength and, in similar circumstances, the state calls for the help of the church, "both to teach that duety which her members knowe not and to exhort them to and encourage them in that duety which they knowe." Recently the state served the church and by a timely proclamation settled its peace. Now "the state lookes for the lyke assistance from the church, that shee and all her ministers may serve God and us by preaching peace and unity at home." Therefore instructions setting forth the dangers of the time were to be sent to the archbishops, to be distributed by them to the bishops, who in their turn would inform all the ministers throughout the several dioceses. According to these directions the ministers were to "instruct and exhort the people and labour by their prayers to divert the dangers," both external and internal, hanging over England. On the Continent the house of Austria was nearly master of Germany, and its complete triumph would permit Spain to do what she pleased in the western parts of Christendom. In that event "you are to weigh how it will advantage" the Spaniard "by sea and make him strong against us . . . which is of easie apprehension to all men." To prevent this outcome, men and supplies must be sent to England's ally, the King of Denmark, to enable him to keep the field, because his defeat was likely to involve "the exterpacion of true religion and the replanting of Romish supersticion in all the neighbouring parts of Christendome." Ministers were to warn those committed to their charge that the war with Spain was begun by the counsel of both houses of Parliament, and the King could not be left to carry it on without supplies "but with the sinne and shame of all men." Aid and supply for the "defense of the kingdome and the like affaires of state, especially such as are advised and assumed by parliamentarie counsell, are due to the King from his people by all lawe both of God and men." The internal danger was the breach of unity "which is growne too great and common amongst men of all sorts." The King had endeavored by all means to promote unity and the clergy were to preach it. They were to explain the miseries that differences had wrought upon this and many other kingdoms and to urge union against the powerful and growing enemy. First, last, and at all times to be insisted upon was prayer for the safety of the King of Denmark and his army. The three heavy and usual judgments which God "darts downe upon disobedient and unthankfull people, are pestilence, famine and the sworde. The pestilence did never rage more in this kingdome then of late . . . and the ceasing of the judgement was little lesse then a miracle. The famine threatned us this present yeare," but again the judgment was stayed and a blessed season and a most plentiful harvest ensued. The sword is a thing that might now be expected unless averted by the prayers of some and the arms of others.

The effect of this letter was the delivery of a large number of loyal discourses, some of which seem to have particularly recommended their auditors to contribute liberally to a free gift to the King. The best-known of these sermons was preached by Robert Sibthorpe, the vicar of Brackley, on the text, "Render therefore to all their dues." (Romans 13:7.) The contents of the sermon are well explained on its title-page: *Apostolic Obedience. Shewing the Duty of Subjects to pay Tribute and Taxes to their Princes, according to the Word of God, in the Law and the Gospell, and the Rules of Religion, and Cases of Conscience; Determined by the Ancient Fathers, and the best Moderne Divines.* In the dedication Sibthorpe states that he first conceived the sermon upon reading the King's instructions to the bishops, brought it forth when the Lord President of the Council and others asked him, with other divines, to deliver his opinion, "in case of conscience and religion, whether it were lawfull to lend to the King or not," and spoke it at the assizes at Northampton.

During 1626 and 1627 many preachers imitated Sibthorpe and urged upon their congregations the duty of contributing to the forced loan, and of passive obedience. According to one minister, religion should "be the life of spotlesse allegiance, and the quickning soule of all civill obedience." Isaac Bargrave, whose *Sermon Preached before King*

Charles, March 27, 1627, was published by his Majesty's special command, had as its text, "Rebellion is as the sinne of witch-craft, and stubbornesse as the wickednesse of idolatry." According to this cleric, obedience was the chiefest of the moral virtues. In a word, active obedience was the father, and passive obedience the mother, of all virtue. He goes on to wish that there were none to say that to obey the King was to betray the country, none to brand the clergy because they preached obedience. Few voices were raised in protest against such views. Burton says that, on November 5, 1627, he preached on the "forerunning signes of the ruine of a state"—for which he was summoned before the Court of High Commission but not examined.

The pendulum swung the other way, or seemed to be doing so, when Parliament was summoned. Laud uttered a vigorous exhortation to Parliament, when it met, March 17, 1628, on the text, "Endeavoring to keep the unity of the spirit in the bond of peace." In his opening speech the King made a direct allusion to this sermon, but the Commons were not impressed. They did not hesitate to censure the active share the clergy had taken in urging subscriptions to the forced loan. In 1628 the Commons impeached Mainwaring. The accusations against him were: (1) that, in two sermons lately preached before his Majesty and since published, he had urged that the King was not bound to keep and observe the good laws and customs of the realm, and that the subjects could not refuse to pay unparliamentary loans and taxes demanded by the royal will, without peril of eternal damnation; (2) that those subjects who refused to make the loan above mentioned offended against the law of God and the King's supreme authority and so became guilty of impiety, disloyalty, rebellion, and disobedience; and (3) that the authority of Parliament is not necessary for the raising of aids and subsidies, and that its slow proceedings were unfitted to supply the urgent necessities of the state and apt to induce sundry impediments to the just designs of princes.

The debates in 1629 supply highly significant evidence of the new realization of the importance of political sermons, especially when similar references are conspicuous, in the seven volumes of the *Commons Debates, 1621,* by their absence. During the session of 1629 there were many voices raised against the political discourses of the clergy. One member complained of the Bishop of Durham's chaplain, who preached that all who refused the loan were damned. Oliver Cromwell made his first recorded speech in Parliament, in order to denounce

Neale, who, as Bishop of Winchester, had forbidden Cromwell's old schoolmaster, Dr. Beard, to refute, in a sermon at the Spital, a previous utterance, there, full of "tenets of popery." Another member asserted that a bishop had told one of his divines that he had often heard him preach against popery, which had pleased King James well, but that he must desist now. The abrupt termination of Parliament in 1629 silenced it for eleven years. Unimpeded by parliamentary criticisms, Charles could carry on his plan of using the clergy to educate his subjects in the ways he wished them to follow.

Full advantage was now taken of the opportunities afforded, by anniversary or other services likely to be largely attended, for delivering loyal sermons. On March 27, 1631, Laud preached at Paul's Cross *A Commemoration of King Charles his Inauguration.* Choosing his text from the Psalms—"Give the King Thy judgments, O God, and Thy righteousness unto the King's Son"—Laud soon proceeded to tell his hearers that the age was so bad as not to endure a good king to be commended, but he hoped none would be offended if he prayed for the King. After saying that the King daily prayed for his people, he recalled how Shimei, for cursing and reviling David, was punished for blasphemous iniquity. The people should bless God for their great happiness in living under Charles, who distributed justice equally among his people. Take heed, Laud warned his hearers, that "no sin, of unthankfulness, no base, detracting, murmuring sin, possess your souls, or whet your tongues." Let them accept as a double blessing that there are no subjects in any state who "live in that plenty, at that ease, with those liberties and immunities that you do. There is no nation under heaven so happy, if it did but know and understand its own happiness." The people, therefore, should "show their loving obedience to the King."

For some years after the dissolution of Parliament in 1629, very few sermons seem to have been preached against the royal policy in church and state. At Oxford one Thomas Hall was bold enough to denounce Arminianism, as "popish darts whet afresh on a Dutch grinston have pierced deep, and without speedy succour will prove mortal." He acknowledged his error, on his knees, in convocation, July 16, 1631. After that, according to Wood (who, in his turn, is relying on Prynne), the Arminians grew bold and "vented their errors" in pulpits and the schools without check, but when their opponents answered them they got into trouble and involved the proctors, who were expelled from the University. Wood also mentions "the college or society of wormes," that appointed lecturers to deride the Puritans. "They imitated them in their whining tones, with the lifting up of eyes, in their antick actions and left nothing undone, whereby they might make them ridiculous." They were not interfered with until one published a ludicrous prayer and attributed it to a noted Puritan.

On the whole, Charles seemed to be gaining ground in his attempt to establish absolutism during 1629-35. At least, this is the opinion of a notable Protestant champion, Henry Burton. He tells us how he saw the supporters of absolutism and tyrannical government gain ground, every day, in the hearts of simple and credulous people. He felt they were laboring to undermine the true Protestant religion and the just liberties of the subjects. He therefore determined to do his duty, to God, his church, and his country, as he saw it. Accordingly, on November 5, 1636, the anniversary of the deliverance of King and Parliament from the Gunpowder treason, he preached two sermons on the text, "My son, fear thou the Lord and the King: and meddle not with them that are given to change: for their calamity shall rise suddenly; and who knoweth the ruin of them both." The sermons were printed with the title, *For God and the King.* Clearly Burton delivered a severe—perhaps it would be fair to say a savage—attack on the bishops, although he was careful to try to draw a distinction between their iniquities and the King's innocence. In other words, Burton anticipated the Long Parliament in attributing the misgovernment of the King to evil ministers. The boldness of the stand Burton made may be gathered from the bitter diatribes Heylyn wrote against him, in his *Brief and Moderate Answer to the Seditious and Scandalous Challenges of Henry Burton.* Heylyn quoted Burton as saying that Christ "hath called me forth to be a publicke witnesse of this great cause," and declared that the preacher had made the pulpit a sanctuary whence to rail against the times, to cry down all the orders of the church, and to distract the people with needless controversy. Burton is also charged with purposely exciting his hearers against their superiors and startling them with dreadful fears, as if both tyranny and popery were likely to be thrust upon them shortly. He had made himself the general superintendent of all the churches, the forlorn hope, the "sentinel perdu," of the whole brotherhood.

When Henry Burton came up for punishment before the Star Chamber, William Prynne, a lawyer, and John Bastwick, a physician, shared his sentence. Their crime was that they had dared to criticize—

the one in the pulpit, all three in the press—the ecclesiastical system of Archbishop Laud. Any reader of their sermons or pamphlets will agree with Laud's description of them as men "whose mouths are spears and arrows, and their tongues a sharp sword" (Psalms 57:4). Yet they were the champions—self-appointed, if you will—of a great cause, and their importance is that they stood forth at a time when the royal policy seemed to be triumphant, when Charles I seemed to have tuned the pulpits and gagged the press. The elaborate refutation of their charges, which Laud delivered when they were sentenced and which he promptly published at Charles's command, suggests that the Archbishop realized the immense damage Burton and his associates had done to the cause of absolutism. The same conclusion might be drawn from the cruel sentences pronounced and the intense chagrin Laud expressed when he heard that sympathetic crowds had attended the prisoners, and that their speeches were taken down and distributed. It seems as if the royal advisers had felt snap a link of the fetters they had placed upon the powerful organs of public opinion—the pulpit and the press.

The beginning of the Scottish troubles, shortly after the condemnation of Burton, Bastwick, and Prynne, makes it difficult to estimate exactly their contribution to the cause of liberty in England, but probably the complacent attitude many Englishmen assumed when the Covenanters were successful may be attributed in part to the stand made by the dauntless three, and by John Hampden in the famous ship-money case. Evidence is absent, but the temptation is strong to place among the crowds that watched the mutilations of the prisoners, or cheered them on their several ways to their distant jails, some who resolved that they, too, would venture all for their religion and liberty, when the call came. Maybe some present that day were to stand fast at Edgehill and with pike and musket to wrest a drawn battle out of a seemingly disastrous rout. At least it is probable that others were to serve with the trained bands of London that repulsed the royalist cavalry at Newbury and extorted the reluctant admiration of their enemies.

Even in the face of plain evidence of widespread sympathy with the Scots during the Bishops' Wars, Charles and his advisers continued their policy of trying to direct public opinion from the pulpit. A correspondent of Coke, Secretary of State, notes that the Archbishop of Canterbury "made an excellent sermon for these times on Sunday last," on the text, "I counsel thee to keep the King's commandment, and that in regard of the oath of God." The letter continues: "To-morrow he hath promised us the application of his doctrine; my pur-pose is to move that his Lordship shall print it, in regard he was not sparing towards" the Scotch. Unfortunately, no information is available about the sermons Laud preached on this occasion.

The importance of the struggle James I and Charles I had made to direct public opinion by controlling the pulpits could be illustrated in a variety of ways, after the attempt had failed. Within a week of the meeting of the Long Parliament, members were denouncing the royal advisers, both ecclesiastical and lay, because they "have a minde to quell preaching and to drawe the religion to olde ceremonies." In John Pym's great speech on November 7 he denounced, as a terrible grievance, "preaching for absolute monarchy that the King may doe what hee list." The famous London petition against episcopacy, pre-sented to Parliament on December 11, 1641, enumerates among the manifold grievances caused by the prelates and their dependents:

> The faint-heartedness of ministers to preach the truth of God, lest they should displease the prelates; as namely, the doctrine of predestination, of free-grace, of perseverance, of original sin remaining after baptisme, of the Sabbath, the doctrine against universal grace, election for faith foreseen, free-will, against Antichrist, non-residents, humane inventions in God's worship; all which are generally with-held from the peoples knowledge, because not relishing to the bishops.

Further illustrations of the importance the parliamentary leaders attached to the pulpit could easily be drawn from their employment of ministers as propagandists and as chaplains to the army. In the latter capacity their sermons figure prominently in all crises—the most striking being the diatribes of Hugh Peter (on a text from Psalm 149, which included, "Bind their kings with chains and their nobles in fetters of iron") against Charles I, just before his execution.

To the end, the King remained convinced that he must retain control of the pulpits, above all else. Writing, when in captivity, to his wife, he tells her that, although "the absolute grant of the militia to the Parliament dethrone the King," yet keeping it is not so important as was thought, "without the concurrence of other things . . . certainly if the pulpits teach not obedience (which will never be if presbyterian government be absolutely established), the King will have but small comfort in the militia."

A Democratic Tercentenary

WILHELM SCHENK

➤➤➤-➤➤➤-➤➤➤-➤➤➤-➤➤➤-➤➤➤-➤➤➤-➤➤➤-➤➤➤ *Published in 1947* ◄◄◄-◄◄◄-◄◄◄-◄◄◄-◄◄◄-◄◄◄-◄◄◄-◄◄◄-◄◄◄

The age of the Puritan Revolutions witnessed a luxuriant growth of radical ideas—political, social, and economic. Expressed in pamphlet after pamphlet in the 1640's and 1650's, these ideas have frequently been examined and re-examined by twentieth-century scholars. Some of these scholars, impressed with the obvious relevance to the contemporary world of many of the radical doctrines of the Puritan Revolutions, have tended, unfortunately, to take them out of their historical context. The result has often been, for example, a toning down of the importance of religion as a force in the shaping of the political, social, and economic radicalism of seventeenth-century England. It is against this tendency that Wilhelm Schenk, author of a suggestive monograph on *The Concern for Social Justice in the Puritan Revolution* (1949), protests in the present essay. Dr. Schenk, who died recently at a very early age, was one of the most past-minded and promising scholars in English historical circles. His contention that seventeenth-century radicalism be viewed in its religious context deserves the careful consideration of anyone who seeks to understand the age of Charles I and Cromwell.

Three-hundred years ago, from October 28 to November 1, 1647, the Parish Church of Putney was the scene of highly interesting debates. The participants were members of the Council of the victorious Parliamentary Army. This Council was unusual enough in itself to deserve special notice: it included, in addition to the Army leaders and appointed representatives of the other officers, two soldiers from each regiment elected by the rank and file. These so-called "Agitators" had been spontaneously created by the soldiers in April and May of that year, and the Army leaders had met this pressure from below

Reprinted by special permission from *The Hibbert Journal*, XLVI (1947), 69-74.

by inviting them to the General Council of the Army. Tommy Atkins (or "Buff-Coat," as he was called on this occasion by a rushed stenographer) was, for once, admitted to the august presence of the Generals and Colonels.

The Army was at that time engaged in a serious quarrel with the House of Commons, which, naturally enough, was eager to disband it as quickly as possible. The Army, however, insisted on adequate provisions for its considerable arrears of pay and on other safeguards, and when these were not forthcoming, it seized the King, who was in the hands of Parliament, entered London and forced some of its strongest opponents among the M.P.'s to leave the country. But soon it became evident that the Army itself was divided. The Agitators joined hands with a group of radicals round John Lilburne (himself an ex-member of the Army) and produced a set of proposals for the political settlement of the country, known as the "Agreement of the People." The "Agreement" envisaged the dissolution of the Long Parliament before September 1648, demanded a more equal distribution of seats, and provided for biennial Parliaments with full sovereignty apart from the safeguarding of certain fundamental rights. It contained the phrases: "The people do of course choose themselves a Parliament" and "These things we declare to be our native rights." The manifesto of the Agitators ("The Case of the Army truly stated") added that "all the freeborn at the age of 21 years and upwards" should be entitled to take part in parliamentary elections.

These documents were discussed at Putney, and the phrases just quoted provided the focal point of the debates. One of the spokesmen of the "Levellers" (as they came to be called just then), Colonel Rainborough (their only adherent among the senior officers), demanded

HUNDRED: A subdivision of the shire (county) that dates from Anglo-Saxon times. It came to be used by the crown for administrative, fiscal, and judicial purposes. The Levellers, who hated all things Norman, idealized the hundred as a symbol of local self-government and of the decentralization of political authority.

JOHN LILBURNE: Leading radical in the England of the late 1640's and early 1650's. During the Civil War he fought on the side of parliament, but by 1645 his fears of parliamentary oppression became as pronounced as his fears of royal oppression. Hostile to the religious and political views of both Presbyterians and Cromwellians, he expressed his opposition in pamphlets

universal franchise as the natural birthright of every Englishman; "every man," he said, "that is to live under a government ought first by his own consent to put himself under that government." The main attack on this view came from Commissary-General Ireton, Cromwell's son-in-law, a brilliant debater. Ireton argued that, when it came to the question of natural rights, all men had equal rights to everything:

> "By that same right of nature (whatever it be) that you pretend, by which you can say, one man hath an equal right with another to the choosing of him that shall govern him—by the same right of nature, he hath the same equal right in any goods he sees—meat, drink, clothes— to take and use them for his sustenance."

Ireton tried to show that democracy as advocated by Rainborough logically leads to communism and might easily do so in fact by a majority vote abolishing all private property. This, above all, he wished to prevent; "all the main thing that I speak for," he said, "is because I would have an eye to property." He therefore suggested that only those should have a vote who had "a permanent fixed interest in this kingdom, . . . that is, the persons in whom all land lies, and those in corporations in whom all trading lies." For Ireton, the political term "the people of England" continued to mean what, on the whole, it had meant before: the land-owners, and the merchants of the towns. This conservatism drew angry protests from the Levellers. Sexby, one of the Agitators, claimed to speak for the common soldiers:

> "We have engaged in this kingdom and ventured our lives, and it was all for this: to recover our birthrights and privileges as Englishmen;

---

with such forthright titles as *England's Birth-right Justified Against All Arbitrary Usurpation, Whether Regall or Parliamentary, or under What Vizor Soever* (1645), *England's New Chains Discovered* (1648-1649), and *An Impeachment of High Treason Against Oliver Cromwell and Henry Ireton* (1649).

PIERS PLOWMAN: Fourteenth-century poem written by a contemporary of Chaucer and traditionally ascribed to William Langland. One of the masterpieces in the literature of social protest, it is distinctly religious in tone. Indeed, its social criticism is directed mainly at the failure of Christians to live and act like Christians.

and by the arguments urged there is none. . . . It seems now, except a man hath a fixed estate in this kingdom, he hath no right in this kingdom. I wonder we were so much deceived. If we had not a right to the kingdom, we were mercenary soldiers."

And Rainborough added bitterly:

"I would fain know what the soldier hath fought for all this while. He hath fought to enslave himself, to give power to men of riches, men of estates, to make him a perpetual slave."

Now nobody could miss the modern ring of all these statements. Ireton was echoed by Locke and all those who insisted on a property qualification for political citizenship, and the ghosts of the Agitators haunted many a barrack-room during the late war. It is therefore understandable that recent historians have expressed the view that the Levellers were among the heralds of modern democracy; the statement of two distinguished American scholars, W. Haller and G. Davies, that "Lilburne had his feet on the main track to the democratic future" is fairly typical. Nor can it be doubted that, in a sense, this view is correct. The Levellers were indeed the first to demand manhood suffrage, and they are therefore entitled to a share in the praise or blame we may feel inclined to bestow on this mainstay of modern democracy. But there is much more to it than that. One sometimes cannot help feeling that some modern democrats like to be linked with people of the seventeenth century rather like nouveaux-riches who try to acquire an ancient pedigree. In the latter case one's possessions seem more assured, in the former one's intellectual position. But closer scrutiny reveals such wide differences between the Levellers and their modern successors as to make the pedigree, in an important sense, appear to be spurious.

To discuss all these differences would require much more than an article. Here we shall have to limit ourselves to two of them. But for this purpose we must go beyond the range of the Putney debates and consult the extensive pamphlet literature of the time, which affords us an extremely interesting insight into the mind of the seventeenth-century "man-in-the-street." The Puritan Revolution was, of course, an Age of Faith and the democratic thought of that time had a firm religious basis. It so happens that the chief Leveller spokesmen at Putney, Rainborough and Wildman, supported their views mainly by secular arguments; Wildman, indeed, seems to have been a purely secular thinker. But the two most important Leveller leaders were not present at the Putney debates: John Lilburne for the perfectly good reason that he was in prison, and William Walwyn for reasons unknown to us. A study of Lilburne's and Walwyn's writings reveals that both of them were intensely concerned with religious questions and that their views on all matters were, in varying degrees, influenced by their religious convictions. We arrive at a similar conclusion when we investigate the thought of the rank-and-file Levellers. There was, indeed, an extremely close connection between the Levellers and some of the Independent sects, particularly the Baptists (Lilburne himself was a Baptist, and Walwyn, without joining any of the sects, persistently defended them against their adversaries).

The fundamental conception of the Leveller philosophy was not, as is often thought, liberty, but equality. One of Rainborough's sayings at Putney has become famous: "Really I think that the poorest he that is in England hath a life to live as the greatest he." This is a memorable way of putting it, but it is not very articulate. Nobody would have doubted its literal meaning. But, of course, something more was implied: the conviction that the poorest person is yet a person and as such worthy of respect, and that the greatest person is no more than a person and not entitled to any additional respect on account of his power or riches. Here are more explicit statements on this point from Leveller writings.

> "God, the absolute Sovereign Lord and King" [wrote Lilburne], "created all men equal and alike in power, dignity, authority and majesty, none of them having (by nature) any authority, dominion or magisterial power one over or above another."

The Buckinghamshire Levellers echoed this idea when they expressed their belief that it was "the end of the redemption by Jesus, to restore all things"—and that restoration, they thought, implied equality, because before the Fall God had allowed man to rule only over "inferior creatures, but not over his own kind." Walwyn inveighed against "the unworthiness of our times, in making riches and estates and the things of this world the great badge of distinction between man and man"; this was evidently opposed to the practice of Christ, for "were not the poor and unlearned Fishermen and Tent-makers . . . made choice of for Christ's Disciples and Apostles"?

These quotations, which could be easily multiplied, clearly connect

the Leveller movement with the ancient tradition of Christian radicalism stressing the absence of gentlemen at the time of Adam and
Eve and the equality of all men in Christ.

> "For all we are Christ's creatures and of his coffers rich,
> And brethren as of one blood as well beggars and earls,
> For on Calvary of Christ's blood Christendom gave spring,
> And blood brethren we became there of one body won."
>
> (PIERS PLOWMAN.)

To men like Lilburne and Walwyn the event on Calvary was of
central importance, and so they could share in this tradition which
has its firm roots in the Gospel itself. There, equality is inseparably
bound up with brotherly love: all men are children of the same Father
and therefore brothers of His Son. William Walwyn, in particular,
never ceased to extol Christian love.

> "We should love" [he wrote], "as Christ has loved, Who gave him-
> self an Offering and a Sacrifice for us: so that if we would try each other's
> faith, we are to consider each other's love; so much faith, so much love;
> so much love, so much pure and undefiled religion."

This insistence on an intimate family-feeling in social matters is
closely linked with the second important difference between the
Levellers and the democrats of our time.

Almost all contemporary democrats, whether they are aware of
it or not, think in terms of the modern state, but the Levellers' mental
picture of society was different. They looked back to what they
believed was the society of pre-Norman England: a loose federation
of small communities of neighbours, fairly equal in ownership and
status, ruling themselves without the interference of professional
magistrates or lawyers according to simple and well-known laws. It
was particularly the centralised legal system of their day that the
Levellers denounced as "Norman bondage." They praised the Saxon
legal practices and compared them angrily with the costly, incon-
venient and dilatory proceedings of the "Norman law," made into an
instrument of oppression by the "subtlety of the lawyers." Every man,
was a typical demand, should "have Justice administered at his own
door, as in the days of King Edward and King Alfred." In an appendix
to the second version of the Agreement of the People, published in
1648, Lilburne suggested that the next Parliament should be asked

"to erect a court of justice in every hundred in the nation, for the ending
of all differences arising in that hundred, by twelve men of the same
hundred annually chosen by freemen of that hundred, with express and
plain rules in English . . . to guide their judgment by."

If after this there was any need for further public officials they should
all be elected annually from among the members of the local communities. Except for a general supervision exercised by Parliament
these proposals would have brought to an end all central jurisdiction
and all activities of professional lawyers. It is also significant that all
the versions of the Agreement of the People contain a list of matters
which were to be exempt from legislation. To the Levellers the centre
of gravity obviously lay in the small social unit whose members knew
each other personally and could therefore be expected to regard themselves as belonging, in a sense, to the same family. This attitude can,
indeed, be interpreted as a protest against the growing tendency
towards centralisation in the sixteenth and seventeenth centuries. The
Levellers cannot be held to have been builders of the modern Leviathan.

Having clearly distinguished the Levellers from their modern
counterparts we can now consider another aspect of the question. It
is true that Lilburne's doctrine of the law of nature and the Agitators'
insistence on their birthright has a certain affinity with later democratic theory. It is particularly interesting to observe this growth of
secular thought in a thoroughly Protestant atmosphere. Professor
Woodhouse has suggested that the Protestant separation of Nature
and Grace had an unintentional secularising effect, especially among
some of the extreme sectarians. According to them, the Holy Community of believers was under the exclusive rule of Grace, which
was utterly different from the rule imposed on those who remained
outside. A church had to legislate for the just and the unjust; a sect
could not and would not. Thus, by shutting the gates of Grace on
the many who were not chosen, these sectarians made room for
purely secular influences outside the realm of Grace. This line of
thought, in Woodhouse's words, "which issues in a purely spiritual
view of the church issues just as certainly in a purely secular view
of the State." Now we have seen that the thought of the Levellers
was neither purely secular nor primarily concerned with the State.
But in so far as they did imply a secular view of the State (and it
is this that links them with our own time) they can be regarded as

having done so not in spite, but because of their Protestant sectarianism.

Another consideration leads to the same conclusion. The Levellers, like all the other radicals of the Puritan Revolution, were violent opponents of Church and University. Walwyn rarely failed to compare clergymen to those silversmiths of Ephesus who cried "Great is Diana of the Ephesians" lest they should lose their trade. University men generally he accused of using their learning "as an Art to deceive and abuse the understandings of men." The Leveller news-sheet spoke of clergymen as called "by Oxford and Cambridge, but whether by Christ is questionable," and another Leveller writer maintained that clergymen were no more "priests than the common people, who were reasonable creatures, in possession of God's Word and therefore not in need of any clerical help." Now it must be admitted that then, as always, a case could be made out against the failings of the clergy and of all educated men. But this was more than legitimate criticism, it amounted to a break with the traditional culture of England and therefore to a squandering of a rich heritage, however imperfectly preserved, of contemplation and wisdom. In this way the Levellers helped to destroy the precarious balance of their civilisation and laid it open to the onslaught of a narrowly scientific and utilitarian conception of life. Their indiscriminate attack could easily combine with the contempt spread by the "New Philosophy" for the learning of the "Schools," and with all its consequences. All this gives added support to the view that Protestantism directly and indirectly paved the way for a predominantly secular society.

It is with such thoughts in our mind that we should remember the tercentenary of the Putney debates. This anniversary, unlike many others of its kind, should not be an occasion for self-congratulation or uncritical praise. If there were any public celebration, the speakers should choose as their text the following remark by Lord Lindsay: "The fundamental ideas of democracy, if divorced from the religious context in which they belong, become cheap and shallow and easy of reputation." The Levellers did not divorce these ideas from their religious context, and this should be regarded as their chief claim to fame. Man, as seen by them, was not a creature without any metaphysical bonds; they were therefore able to realise that the brotherhood of Man depends on the Fatherhood of God. Dr. Toynbee, in discussing this fundamental truth, goes on to say:

"If the divine father of the human family is left out of the reckoning, there is no possibility of forging any alternative bond of purely human texture which will avail by itself to hold mankind together."

There is nothing in the history of modern democracy to refute this. On the contrary, this history provides ample reasons for the conviction that mankind without God cannot retain its human level and must fall into inhumanity. In this sense there may be a special message for us in what the Levellers had to say 300 years ago. But it must be added that the intellectual and spiritual equipment of the Levellers was not quite free from those influences which have brought about the all but complete secularisation of our age. Meanwhile, in remembering the Buff-Coats of Putney Church and their friends, we shall think of their courage and honesty in grappling with problems which must continue to engage our most serious attention.

‑‑

Man in Armor

WILBUR CORTEZ ABBOTT

‑‑‑‑‑‑‑‑‑‑‑‑‑‑‑‑‑‑‑‑ *Published in 1935* ‑‑‑‑‑‑‑‑‑‑‑‑‑‑‑‑‑‑

Through the centuries Oliver Cromwell has had scores of biographers—among them such prominent names as Thomas Carlyle and Theodore Roosevelt. Yet it was in the 1930's that for an obvious reason interest in him and his policies seemed to reach a new high. With dictators triumphant in several of the leading countries of Europe, a number of writers proceeded to re-examine Cromwell's career, working on the assumption that such a re-examination would cast light on the contemporary scene. The most popular and the most widely reviewed biography of Cromwell that appeared in the 'thirties was written by the Canadian statesman, historian, and novelist John Buchan (Lord Tweedsmuir); and among its reviewers none was better informed than Wilbur Cortez Abbott, of Harvard University. A man who had devoted his scholarly life to the study of Cromwell, Abbott was engaged at the time in preparing what has proved to be one of the monuments of twentieth-century historical scholarship, his four-volume *Writings and Speeches of Oliver Cromwell* (1937-1947). In view of his qualifications, Abbott's review of Buchan's biography is well worth reading—the more so because it contains his own evaluation of Cromwell's place in English history.

He who would write of worthy deeds worthily," wrote John Milton nearly three hundred years ago, "must write with mental endowments and experience of affairs not less than were the doers of the same, so as to be able with equal mind to comprehend and measure even the greatest of them, and when he has comprehended them, to relate distinctly and gravely in pure and chosen speech."

In such fashion did he condemn, by anticipation, a great mass of modern biography, for reasons which are all too obvious. For biography, in the hands of the subjective biographer, has fallen on evil days. Much of it is too much like the frank confession of the French writer who observed that when he wrote of Shakespeare, he really wrote of himself as affected by Shakespeare. With equal frankness, Mr. Belloc has written such a book on Cromwell, remarking that there were already too many lives of Cromwell now.

Mr. Buchan has chosen rather to follow the admonition of Milton, and, thirty-second in the list of his works which fills the first page of this volume, he has written a Life of Oliver Cromwell, in defiance of Mr. Belloc's judgment. It is a real Life of Cromwell; and though even real Lives of real persons must, perforce, have in them something of the element which the Frenchman described, though they must have a subjective as well as an objective quality if they are to be alive, he has kept that quality in due subjection to the facts of his story, and the result is a good Life of the Protector. No! it is not quite that; no one has as yet quite written that; and even Mr. Buchan has devoted scarcely more than an eighth of his volume to Cromwell in power. He has written chiefly the Life of the man who became Protector, before he reached that eminence.

That is what nearly everyone has done. It was long ago observed that the most interesting part of a man's life was his ascent to power, not what he did with it once it was achieved. It is an old debating question, whether pursuit or attainment is more satisfying, but biographers have leaned generally to pursuit. Here Mr. Buchan is excellent; and nowhere more than in his account of the clash of arms. His battle-scenes are clearly drawn and not overcolored and, with the aid of Gardiner and of Firth, he has been able to pick his way through a mass of details to a satisfactory conclusion in general politics.

His book is not, and, in the nature of the case, could hardly be, a contribution to what is called "pure scholarship." It is derived from sources which he sets out before us with the utmost frankness. It is a piece of writing and a most attractive one, somewhere between the style of Trevelyan and that of Firth, clear, picturesque, sometimes philosophical, sympathetic, understanding, and what is called "interesting." It leans perhaps to the side of eulogy, as is natural. It stresses the "human" qualities, as is right. It tends to minimize the sterner qualities of a man who, with all his tenderness to his family and his devotion to his friends, took such fierce delight in battle, pursuit and slaughter of his enemies, as is revealed in his despatches from the field. He smelt the battle from afar, the smoke of it was in his nostrils, and, like the war horse of the Scriptures, he said "Ha, Ha!" For Oliver Cromwell was a man of the Old Testament rather than of the New; and one may question whether it is not better to paint him as he was, "wart and all," in the old hackneyed phrase.

To his enemies he was a man of wrath, a son of thunder, else he would never have played the part he did in history. If he was a tender husband and father and friend, he was a fierce and bitter foe, as those whom "God made stubble to our swords," those of "whom we had the execution for some miles," and those women and priests knocked on the head at Drogheda might bear witness. He was feared rather than loved in his own day even, for the most part, by his own followers, as any man in such a position must be feared to be successful. He was essentially a fighting man, never happier than in the thick of conflict, as Mr. Buchan himself points out.

He was, in short the Protestant, Puritan champion; he owed his eminence and the success of his cause not to his meekness and humility

---

DROGHEDA: Leading royalist stronghold in Ireland. Its siege in 1649 was the outstanding event in Cromwell's subjugation of Ireland. It is estimated that some four thousand people, combatants as well as noncombatants, were slaughtered by Cromwell's army. The memory of Drogheda has been important in perpetuating Irish hostility to England.

SAMUEL R. GARDINER: Nineteenth-century English scholar who wrote the standard account of English political history from the accession of James I to the Age of Cromwell. His historical writing has often been criticized for

and loving-kindness and humanity, but to his military skill. He has been too often portrayed in too soft colors. Had he been what so many of his biographers have painted him, he would never have been painted at all; and it is notable that of his contemporary portraits there is not one which does not depict him in armor. His triumphs were rather in the field than in the council; and it is fitting that in his biography Mr. Buchan has, consciously or unconsciously, but with true artistic recognition of that fact, stressed this side of him.

So far as his administrative and statesmanlike qualities and activities are concerned, Cromwell's own estimate of his services is the true one. He was a constable set over the parish of England to keep order, and, in the words of an unconscious humorist—who also touched the truth—he "belaboured effectually to keep the peace." Even in power, his triumphs were those of a war leader, of victories over Holland and Spain, his reputation was that of one who made England great abroad through fear. His visions of Protestant alliances were such materials as dreams are made of; his administration was financed largely by confiscation; it was, in effect, a military despotism of an armed minority; it had no widespread popular support and a single general parliamentary election, free from government interference, would at any moment have overthrown it. In effect Cromwell was the government. He was a great leader of men, whether in the field or in his own party, through his military skill. He was, perhaps, the greatest of Englishmen in that respect. But it is no tribute to his greatness to paint him other than he was, and it is to the credit of Mr. Buchan that he has, in general, avoided on the one side denunciation and on the other eulogy.

---

its dullness and colorlessness, but these criticisms are basically unfair. For Gardiner, a descendant of Cromwell, made a noble effort to deal impartially with the most controversial period in all English history.

CHARLES H. FIRTH: Twentieth-century English historian and editor. He continued in the tradition of Gardiner and completed his predecessor's multi-volume account of the Cromwellian period. His masterpiece was a study of *Cromwell's Army* (1902), a vivid account of the life of the enlisted man in mid-seventeenth-century England.

IX

The Glorious Revolution and Its Aftermath

※>>>

Introductory, "The English Revolution,
1688-1689

G. M. TREVELYAN

The Farming Writers of Eighteenth-
Century England

G. E. FUSSELL

"The Industrial Revolution"

HERBERT HEATON

Mercantilism and the American Revolution

LAWRENCE A. HARPER

※>>>

Introductory, *The English Revolution* 1688-1689

G. M. TREVELYAN

➤➤➤➤➤➤➤➤➤ *Published in 1938* ◄◄◄◄◄◄◄◄◄◄

Like the early Stuart kings, the later ones (Charles II, 1660-1685; James II, 1685-1688) had as their objective the establishment of an absolutist regime. In addition, however—and unlike their predecessors—the later Stuart kings sought to restore Roman Catholicism in their realm. The fears aroused by their policies led many Englishmen to conclude that their country was to become more and more like the France of Louis XIV; and the birth of a son to James II made likely an indefinite succession of Roman Catholic rulers. The upshot was that in 1688 the so-called Glorious Revolution took place. It is with the origin and significance of this revolution that the great George Macaulay Trevelyan deals in the present selection. Indeed, if contemporary British and American historians conducted an election to determine the most talented twentieth-century historians, Trevelyan would be among the certain winners. A descendant of Thomas Babington Macaulay, he has carried on in the literary tradition that his ancestor did much to further; and his conviction that history is an art as well as a scientific discipline dominates all his writings, among them such important volumes as *England in the Age of Wycliffe* (1899), *England under the Stuarts* (1904), *England under Queen Anne* (3 vol., 1930-1934) and *The English Revolution, 1688-1689* (1938). It is from the introduction to the last-named volume that the following selection is taken.

Why do historians regard the Revolution of 1688 as important? And did it deserve the title of "glorious" which was long its distinctive epithet? "The Sensible Revolution" would perhaps have been a more appropriate title and certainly would have distinguished it more clearly as among other revolutions.

But in so far as it was indeed "glorious," in what does its "glory" consist? It is not the Napoleonic brand of glory. It is not to be sought in the glamour of its events, the drama of its scenes, and the heroism of its actors, though these also rouse the imagination and stir the blood. The Seven Bishops passing to the Tower through the kneeling throngs; William's fleet floating into Torbay before the Protestant wind; the flight of James II, following his wife and infant son to France, none of them ever to return—doubtless these are romantic scenes, that live in memory. Such also are the events that followed more bloodily in Scotland and in Ireland—the roaring pass of Killiecrankie, the haggard watch on Londonderry walls, and Boyne water bristling with musket and pike. Yet all these are not, like the fall of the Bastille or Napoleon's Empire, a new birth of time, a new shape of terror. They are spirited variations on themes invented forty years before by a more heroic, creative and imprudent generation.

The Seven Bishops whom James II prosecuted were milder and more conservative men than the Five Members whom Charles I attempted to arrest, yet the second story reads much like a repetition of the first: in both cases the King rashly attacks popular leaders who are protected by the law, and by the mass opinion of the capital. In both cases the King's downfall shortly follows. Much else indeed is very different: there is no English Civil War on the second occasion, for in 1688 even the Cavaliers (renamed Tories) were against the King. But the men of the Revolution, James and William, Danby, Halifax, Sancroft, Dundee, are manipulating forces, parties and ideas which had first been evoked in the days of Laud, Strafford, Pym, Hampden, Hyde, Cromwell, Rupert, Milton and Montrose. In the later Revolution there are no new ideas, for even Toleration had been eagerly discussed round Cromwell's camp-fires. But in 1688 there is a very different grouping of the old parties, and a new and happier turn is given to the old issues, in England though not in Ireland, by compromise, agreement and toleration. An heroic age raises questions, but it takes a sensible age to solve them. Roundheads and Cavaliers, high in hope, had broken up the soil, but the Whigs and Tories soberly garnered the harvest.

A certain amount of disillusionment helps to make men wise, and by 1688 men had been doubly disillusioned, first by the rule of the Saints under Cromwell, and then by the rule of the Lord's Anointed under James. Above all, taught by experience, men shrank from another civil war. The burnt child fears the fire. The merit of this Revolution lay not in the shouting and the tumult, but in the still, small voice of prudence and wisdom that prevailed through all the din.

The true "glory" of the Revolution lies not in the minimum of violence which was necessary for its success, but in the way of escape from violence which the Revolution Settlement found for future generations of Englishmen. There is nothing specially glorious in the victory which our ancestors managed to win, with the aid of foreign arms, over an ill-advised king who forced an issue with nine-tenths of his English subjects on the fundamentals of law, politics and religion. To have been beaten at such odds would have been national ignominy indeed. The "glory" of that brief and bloodless campaign lies with William, who laid deep and complicated plans and took great risks in coming over at all, rather than with the English who had only to throw up their caps for him with sufficient unanimity when once he and his troops had landed. But it is England's true glory that the cataclysm of James's overthrow was not accompanied by the shedding of English blood either on the field or on the scaffold. The political instincts of our people appeared in the avoidance of a second Civil War, for which all the elements were present. Our enemy Louis XIV of France had confidently expected that another long period of confusion and strife would ensue in our factious island if William should land there; if he had thought otherwise, he could have threatened the frontiers of Holland, and so prevented his rival from setting sail at all.

But the Convention Parliament of February 1689, by uniting England, baffled the policy of France. By wise compromise it stanched for ever the blood feud of Roundhead and Cavalier, of Anglican and Puritan, which had broken out first at Edgehill and Naseby, and bled

---

LORD ELDON: Lord chancellor famous for his slowness in the dispatch of cases. An unrelenting Tory, who hated innovations, he was a major figure in the struggle against constitutional and legal reform in the early decades of the nineteenth century.

LATITUDINARIAN: An Anglican who believes that conflicting conceptions of church government and of religious doctrine and worship should be allowed within the church.

SEDGEMOOR: Battle of 1685. The decisive engagement in the crushing of the

afresh only four years back at Sedgemoor. Whig and Tory, having risen together in rebellion against James, seized the fleeting moment of their union to fix a new-old form of Government, known in history as the Revolution Settlement. Under it, England has lived at peace within herself ever since. The Revolution Settlement in Church and State proved to have the quality of permanence. It stood almost unaltered until the era of the Reform Bill of 1832. And throughout the successive stages of rapid change that have followed, its fundamentals have remained to bear the weight of the vast democratic superstructure which the nineteenth and twentieth centuries have raised upon its sure foundation. Here, seen at long range, is "glory," burning steadily for 250 years: it is not the fierce, short, destructive blaze of *la gloire*.

The expulsion of James was a revolutionary act, but otherwise the spirit of this strange Revolution was the opposite of revolutionary. It came not to overthrow the law but to confirm it against a law-breaking king. It came not to coerce people into one pattern of opinion in politics or religion, but to give them freedom under and by the law. It was at once liberal and conservative; most revolutions are neither one nor the other, but overthrow the laws, and then tolerate no way of thinking save one. But in our Revolution the two great parties in Church and State united to save the laws of the land from destruction by James; having done so, and having thereby become jointly and severally masters of the situation in February 1689, neither the Whig nor the Tory party would suffer its clients to be any longer subject to persecution, either by the Royal power or by the opposite party in the State. Under these circumstances the keynote of the Revolution Settlement was personal freedom under the law, both in religion and in politics. The most conservative of all revolutions in history was also the most liberal. If James had been

---

rebellion led by the illegitimate son of Charles II, the Duke of Monmouth, who had proclaimed himself king. It was to crush the rebels that the notorious Judge Jeffreys was sent on the judicial circuit that resulted in the "Bloody Assizes."

THE CASE OF THE SEVEN BISHOPS: Archbishop of Canterbury Sancroft and six other Anglican bishops were sent to the Tower for having aroused the displeasure of James II. Tried for seditious libel, they were acquitted in June 1688—a fact of tremendous significance in the mobilization of the opposition to James II.

overthrown either by the Whigs alone or by the Tories alone, the settlement that followed his downfall would not have been so liberal, or so permanent.[1]

In the realm of thought and religion, individual liberty was secured by the abandonment of the cherished idea that all subjects of the State must also be members of the State Church. The Toleration Act of 1689 granted the right of religious worship, though not complete political equality, to Protestant Dissenters; and so strong was the latitudinarian and tolerant spirit of the age ushered in by the Revolution, that these privileges were soon extended in practice though not in law to the Roman Catholics, against whom the Revolution had in one aspect been specially directed.

The political freedom of the individual was secured in a like spirit, by the abolition of the Censorship (1695), by the milder and less partial administration of political justice, and by the balance of power between the Whig and Tory parties, under whose rival banners almost everyone in some sort found shelter. In these ways the distinctively English idea of the freedom of opinion and the rights of the individual were immensely enhanced by the peculiar character of this Revolution.

James had tried to put the King above Parliament and above the Law. The Revolution, while leaving the King the source of executive authority, subjected him to the Law, which was henceforth to be interpreted by independent and irremovable Judges, and could only be altered by Act of Parliament. At the same time, by the annual Mutiny Act that made the army dependent of Parliament, and by the refusal to grant to William for life the supplies that had been granted for the lives of Charles and James II, the House of Commons obtained a power of bargaining with Government that rendered it even more important than the House of Lords; indeed, from the Revolution onwards the Commons gradually gained a control even over the executive power of the King, through the Cabinet system which grew up step by step under William, Anne and the first two Georges. All this was not foreseen by the men of 1689, whose intention was only to subject the

---

[1] The remarks in this introduction refer to England alone. In Scotland, where the Revolution in the winter of 1688 was made by the Presbyterian or Whig party with little aid from the Episcopalians, the settlement of 1689 was one-sidedly Presbyterian. And the result was that civil war remained endemic in Scotland until 1746. In Ireland, the Revolution Settlement was a racial and religious reconquest of the most brutal kind.

kingly power to the bounds of law as defined by the parliamentary lawyers. But the Hanoverian Constitution of Walpole and the Pitts grew straight out of the Revolution Settlement by the logic of experience.

The Revolution has been branded as aristocratic. It was effected by the whole nation, by a union of all classes; but in a society still mainly agricultural, where the economic and social structure rendered the landlords the natural and accepted leaders of the countryside, noblemen and squires like the Tories Danby and Seymour, the Whigs Devonshire and Shrewsbury took the lead when resistance to government had to be improvised. The nation indeed recognized no other chiefs through whom it could act in such an emergency. A similar aristocratic and squirearchical leadership of the country had organized both the Roundhead and Cavalier armies at the beginning of the Civil War; it had, indeed, been partially eclipsed during the rule of Cromwell's military saints, but had been fully re-established at the Restoration of 1660. It continued after 1689 as before, and would in any case have continued until the Industrial Revolution gradually raised up a new social order. Even Despotism, if James had succeeded in setting it up, must in that age have governed through nobles and squires. James attempted to use the lords and country gentlemen who were the Lieutenants and J.P.'s of their counties as the instruments of his Catholicizing policy, but they, like everyone else, turned against him. Having no other bureaucracy through which to work, he fell.

So far, the Revolution was indeed a demonstration of the power of the landlord classes, Whig and Tory alike. They were politically powerful because in the then formation of English Society they were indispensable. Any form of English government must in those days have worked through them.

The Revolution did quite as much for the legal, mercantile and popular elements in our national life as for the aristocratic or squirearchical. The worst permanent result of the Revolution was not the alleged increase in the power of the aristocracy but the undue conservatism that continued throughout the whole eighteenth century. The result of the reaction against James II's innovations was to put too great a stress, for many years to come, on the perpetuation of institutions in their existing form. James, in the interest of Roman Catholicism and Despotism, had remodeled the Town Corporations, invaded the liberties of the Universities and of the Church, and attempted to pack the

House of Commons. In the rebound, the Ministries and Parliaments of the eighteenth century feared to reform the corporations, Universities, Church benefices and Parliamentary Constituencies, even in the interest of purer and more efficient government. James had treated charters as waste paper, so the men of the eighteenth century regarded sheepskin with superstitious reverence. They held that whatever is is right—if it can show a charter. The hundred and fifty years that followed the Revolution are the most conservative in our annals though by no means the least free, happy or prosperous.

The Whig Governments before Burke, and the Tory Governments after him, all had too much reverence for the letter of the Revolution Settlement. It became a flag of ultra conservatism, first Whig then Tory. To Walpole, Blackstone, Burke, Eldon and the anti-Jacobin Tories of the early nineteenth century, the year 1689 seemed the last year of creation, when God looked upon England and saw that it was good.

But when this ultra-conservative mood at length passed away, the bases of the Revolution Settlement still remained as the foundations of the new era of rapid Reform, in which we are still living after more than a hundred years. The relation of the Crown to Parliament and to the Law; the independence of Judges; the annual meeting of Parliament; the financial supremacy of the Commons; the position of the Church of England; the Toleration of religious Dissent; freedom of political speech and writing subject to no control but the opinion of a jury; in short, a Constitutional Monarchy for a free people, these are the bases of our polity and they were well and truly laid by the Whigs and Tories, the nobles, squires, lawyers, merchants and populace who rose up against James II.

But unless strength upholds the free, freedom cannot live. And the Revolution Settlement gave us strength as well as freedom. The Marlborough wars soon demonstrated that; and England was never so safe and so powerful as in the eighteenth century, especially after the Parliamentary Union with Scotland, made in 1707, had united the whole island of Britain "on a Revolution basis."

Between the death of Elizabeth and the Revolution of 1688, the constant struggle between Parliament and King had rendered England weak in the face of the world, except during the few years when Cromwell had given her strength at a heavy price. Our civil broils had occupied our energies and attention; sometimes both the King and the statesmen of the Opposition were pensioners of France; always Parliament had been chary of supply to governments whose policy they could not continuously control. In the reigns of the Jameses and Charleses, foreign countries had regarded our Parliament as a source of weakness, hampering the executive power: the Constitution of England was contemptuously compared to that of Poland.

But after the Revolution the world began to see that our parliamentary government, when fully established, was capable of becoming a source of national strength. Supplies that had been refused to Kings whom the Commons could not trust, were lavished on Ministries that had the confidence of the House. The money must be voted afresh annually, not granted for the King's life; and the Commons must see to its appropriation. On these strict conditions, the governments of William, Anne and the Georges had the run of the national purse such as their predecessors had not enjoyed. Moreover, the "Revolution Governments" had the confidence of the City as well as of Parliament. The system of loans based on taxes gave England the key to power. It was "Revolution finance" and Revolution policy that enabled Marlborough to defeat the Grand Monarch, when free government and religious toleration triumphed over the revoker of the Edict of Nantes. As a result of that victory, the European philosophers of the eighteenth century turned against political despotism and religious intolerance as causes of national weakness, and proclaimed to the world the peculiar merits of England's "happy constitution in Church and State."

Speaking of the wars of William and Anne, and more generally of the eighteenth century, Professor G. N. Clark writes:

"In France and Prussia and almost everywhere militarism and autocracy went hand in hand, but what enabled Britain to deploy its strength was the Revolution Settlement. The main lines of policy were laid down by a small gathering of Ministers who had at their disposal full departmental information about foreign affairs, finance, military and naval preparations and trade. By means of Parliament the Ministers brought into the service of that policy the wealth and man-power of the nation. . . . Parliament was a meeting-place where divergent economic interests were reconciled and combined so as to provide an adequate body of support for the government of the day."[1]

[1] "The Later Stuarts," by Professor G. N. Clark, in the *Oxford History of England,* 1934.

In this way Britain obtained, not only political and religious liberty, but national power, greater than that of the unlimited monarchy of France. Such are the reasons why modern historians regard the Revolution a turning-point in the history of our country and of the world.

The Farming Writers of Eighteenth-Century England

G. E. FUSSELL

>>>->>>->>>->>>->>>->>>->>>->>> *Published in 1947* <<<-<<<-<<<-<<<-<<<-<<<-<<<-<<<

To describe the transformations that took place in farming practices in eighteenth-century England as an "agricultural revolution" leaves much to be desired. The expression is too sensational in its implications, and it overdramatizes and exaggerates the rate and the extent of the changes in the agricultural life of the time. It is true, nonetheless, that in the eighteenth century segments of the English agricultural economy did undergo important alterations, many of which were inspired by the example of the Dutch. The obvious question arises: How did those English farmers who were not afraid to break with traditional methods find out about the relatively novel techniques that the Dutch were using? Part of the answer is not far to seek. G. E. Fussell, of the British Ministry of Agriculture and Fisheries, who probably knows more about the history of modern English agriculture than any other man alive today, makes it clear that a prolific farming literature developed in the eighteenth century. Writer after writer attempted to capitalize on the interest in a more efficient and more profitable agriculture. Undaunted by the widespread illiteracy of many of those whose attention they sought to attract, these writers turned out books designed to keep English farmers informed on the latest developments in husbandry.

E verybody in eighteenth-century England was interested in farming. Even the distinctly urban minority was acquainted with farms, fields, and trees, and since farming became more profitable as the century progressed, interest in it grew greater. When so large a proportion of the population is interested in a subject, all sorts and conditions of

Reprinted by special permission from *Agricultural History,* XXI (1947), 1-8. The footnotes which originally appeared with this essay have been omitted.

men write about it. Not only was there money to be made out of the land, but there was money and reputation as well to be made by writing advice for the farmer.

Most of those who wrote farming textbooks professed to have had practical experience and to be recording that experience, but they were a motley crew and almost every one of them cast doubt upon the abilities and knowledge of all the rest. Four of the most voluminous writers were Richard Bradley, William Ellis, William Marshall, and Arthur Young. Bradley was professor of botany at Cambridge, but the last three certainly were farmers, and I am inclined to think that they, like some moderns, made more money out of their books than they did out of their farms. Amongst the other writers were clergymen, schoolmasters, self-styled gentlemen, and self-styled farmers. Some also were probably barristers or at least members of the inns as so many small and large landowners of the day were. They were undoubtedly men of enterprise and were all too eager to accept novelties without very much consideration simply because they were novelties. This makes it all the more difficult to decide whether what they say reflects current practice or merely the trend of advanced thought in farming theory.

To decide that point it is really necessary to know something about the writers themselves, where they lived, and how they got or failed to get a living. Only a few of them are to be found in *The Dictionary of National Biography*, and those who are were usually included because they did something besides writing a book or so on farming. All that is known of many of the others is to be found in their own works. They do not give anything away, and what can be learned is sufficiently meager although never very modest.

The little that is known of the four most voluminous writers is not altogether reassuring. Richard Bradley, the earliest of them, was a fellow of the Royal Society, but I am very much afraid that such a fellowship meant very little in those days. By the aid of this fellowship and his

JETHRO TULL: Early-eighteenth-century agricultural reformer remembered for his invention of a drill and of a horse hoe. It should be pointed out, however, that he opposed the rotation of crops and the use of manure, viewing them as harmful practices.

ARTHUR YOUNG: English writer on farming, and propagandist for the adop-

natural abilities Bradley became professor of botany at Cambridge in 1720. When applying for the post, Bradley pretended that he had a verbal recommendation from Dr. William Sherard to Dr. William Bentley. This he supported with the offer to found a public botanic garden at the university. Any balance of the expense that he could not raise from interested and philanthropic persons of his acquaintance he promised to provide out of his own pocket. This he did not do although he got the job. He held it for twelve years and died timely to avoid his expulsion for scandalous behavior.

Not only did Bradley fail to carry out his undertaking to found a botanic garden, but he had no knowledge of classical languages and he failed to deliver the required lectures. This part of his work had to be done by Dr. John Martyn, who later succeeded him. By and large Richard Bradley, F.R.S., was a curious character to hold a university appointment. His farming books were numerous. Ninety years ago only two were to be found in the British Museum, today there are nearly thirty, and I fear that more may be discovered.

I imagine that Bradley was more interested in his farming books than in his job, and they probably brought him in a good deal of money. He was an advanced farmer and did not only concern himself with writing. He was interested in the suggestion for a seed drill that had been made in the previous century, and he tried to build a machine along the lines suggested by John Worlidge, who included a drawing of it in his book. When Bradley made it, it would not work. Whether that was the fault of Worlidge's instructions and drawing or of Bradley's failure to construe them I cannot say.

Ernle, writing in the Ministry of Agriculture *Journal* in 1922 on "The Wisdom and Folly of Ancient Book-Farmers," commented unfavorably on the want of books dealing with animal breeding before the nineteenth century. Bradley, however, wrote a book on cattle, the first that had been devoted to that subject since Leonard Mascal wrote *The Government of Cattell* in the sixteenth century. It is characteristic

---

tion of advanced agricultural techniques. An almost unbelievably prolific writer, he became well known not only in the British Isles but on the Continent, where many of his works were translated. His *Travels in France* is one of the most important sources for the study of economic conditions in the last years of the *ancien régime*.

of the time that the arrangement of the book should be sheep, pigs, cattle, and horses. One might almost say sheep for the ubiquitous woolen industry, pigs to feed the rural population, cattle for sale to the towns, and horses for both rural and urban draft.

Bradley, of course, wrote at length on almost every subject connected with farming, and he seems to have read most of the earlier writers. A curiosity amongst his publications, since he is said to have been no classical scholar, is *A Survey of the Ancient Husbandry and Gardening* (1725). He also reprinted in a condensed form John Houghton's weekly miscellany devoted to the improvement of husbandry.

Ellis, who wrote the first English book on sheep and many other things, was certainly a farmer and presumably made his farming pay if only because he lived at Little Gaddesden in Hertfordshire all the time he was writing books. He was not so voluminous a scribe as Bradley, but his works take up a fair space in a bookcase. They are rambling and informative on all sorts of subjects. Ellis was aware of the life around him, and he filled out his books with a farrago of incidental matters. Gypsies particularly were an anathema to him. They were cunning thieves and hard to catch. Once indeed he suspected a party camped on the waste at the edge of some open fields of stealing a sheep. He went to accuse them and demanded to inspect their camp, but they put him off with the pretext that one of their women was in labor and it would be indecent to advance farther. He was furious and unbelieving but what could he do. Many other anecdotes of the sort enliven his pages, and his works can be used as sources for the conditions of contemporary rural life. He was a man who trained servants, tried to sell "improved" implements, and indulged in a variety of business activities in addition to his farming and his writing. Subject to some reserve he can be accepted as presenting a good contemporary description of farming in Hertfordshire, and his record of what was done in other counties may also be trusted.

Marshall and Young, bitter rivals at the end of the century, were both even more prolific than Bradley at the beginning and Ellis in the middle of the period, but no one could rival Young's output, not even Marshall with his Rural Economy series and his massive Reviews of the reports to the old Board of Agriculture. Today it is the fashion to believe that Marshall's writings are likely to be more accurate than Young's and with a show of reason. Marshall lived in most of the districts he described; Young only visited them. Young's method of gathering information was doubtless cursory observations combined with quasi-detective conversations with all and sundry. This is no bad method of gathering information, although the suggestion I once made to a tyro research worker that he should visit the village pub and drink beer with the locals was received with some reserve.

The important thing about these two men is not their personal idiosyncrasies but their method which was new. They did not sit at home and write about farming. They went about the country and found out how it was done. They were determined to find out the facts, and they recorded what they learned in exact terms. The result is that their published works—Young's massive treatise on The Elements of Agriculture has yet to see the light of print—with the county reports of the old Board of Agriculture form a mass of exact evidence on the state of agriculture during the last thirty years of the eighteenth century that is almost impossible for one man to assimilate.

The less well-known writers were more prone to declare that they were men of practical experience. Neither Marshall nor Young needed to have any qualms on this point, but both were sensitive when attacked and like most other farming authors of the day capable of venomous invective in reply to their adversaries.

The age was one of hearty living and the habits of the time made men full-blooded: as the contemporary incidence of diseases shows. Young was himself an embodiment of the age and did not hesitate to condemn the valueless writings of his contemporaries. In one of his earliest books he made a fierce attack on all general treatises, systems, and dictionaries and complained of the large number published. He declared that they were useless, "consisting of the most heterogeneous parts, purloined out of former books on the same subjects, without a common knowledge to discover the good from the bad."

Young was thoroughly acquainted with the literature of his subject and in more than one of his books commented upon the writers who had preceded him, usually with the harshest criticism. John Mills, for instance, who was a translator and compiler in the middle of the century, he credited as a good man, but his writings often advised "The vilest heap of absurdity that ever disgraced common sense!" Such words leave no one in any doubt. One of the worst results of this sort of thing was that experiments suggested by the writers failed owing to their ignorance and caused practical farmers to regard all books on farming with derision.

A few years later in *A Course of Experimental Agriculture* (1770), Young returned to this subject and pointed the moral. "The first point an inquisitive reader attends to," he wrote, "is the reality of the experiments; an enquiry not a little necessary in an age so fertile in book-making, which produces so many experimental husbandmen, whose fields yield such great crops without soil, and whose cattle are fattened so nobly without food—farmers without farms. But geniuses, in whom invention supplies the defect of land, seed, cattle, implements, and every requisite save pens and paper, while such continue to write, it is very necessary, in works of this nature, for the author to set his name to his labours, with that of the place where his experiments were made. . . ." *A Course of Experimental Agriculture* contains a very large number of experiments, all accurately described and with figures attached to them. One wonders whether all these experiments could really have been carried out in the field by so young a man as Young then was. Were they real experiments or were they Young's estimates of probable results?

On another occasion when he had been attacked, Young protested that because he had been addressed in the language of Billingsgate was no reason for replying in the words of a fishwife, but it would be difficult to distinguish this difference in the virulence of his reply. His opinion of the book farmers, like so many of his other views, changed, and fifteen years later he expressed himself as satisfied that the disadvantages of the textbooks had vanished. "The art of writing books on Agriculture in a London lodging," he wrote in 1785, "and dictating the management of farms, without the occupation of a field, died probably with Dr. [John] Hill; this age has too much good sense to be imposed upon." Lucky and incredible age!

When so great a man as Young indulged in such courtesies of debate, lesser men might be expected to profit by his example. Many of them did, although that is not quite fair. It was a fashion of the day that all men followed. Many of the minor writers, not content with condemning the works of their fellows, condemned the farmers as well. The farmers did not profit by the books. They did not read them or so the authors suggested. The majority of them probably could not had they wished. They were, as many modern writers have so ably and so often said, full of reverence for traditional methods which amounted to stupidity. Indeed it is a strange thing in the light of such well founded opinion that farming has ever made any progress at all. Curiously enough Henry Home accused his fellows of the same acceptance of tradition. "Writers on agriculture," he said, "very few excepted, deliver their precepts from a study lined with books, without even pretending to experience. Principles and propositions are assumed on the authority of former writers: opinions pass current from generation to generation; and no person inquires whether they wear the livery of truth."

A few years later the Rev. Dr. John Trusler, whose imagination and pen were almost as versatile as those of Daniel Defoe (who produced *A Descriptive Account of the Islands Lately Discovered in the South Sea* without having been further afield than Leyden), complained that the average book on farming was too full of theory. It led gentlemen to try experiments instead of farming for profit like an ordinary farmer. His own book was, of course, quite free from that fault and prescribed the common practice for the advantage of gentlemen who lived in the country and kept some land in hand. Trusler himself was a commercial adventurer although he was a clergyman. He wrote all sorts of things and finally undertook to publish and issue them himself. He tried to sell his book of holograph sermons by mail order, circularizing the whole of the parish clergy of the country for the purpose. He is indeed a type of the ingenious men who wrote farming books and adopted all sorts of schemes to sell them.

One of them, a schoolmaster, John Randall, adopted, or so I suspect, the disguise of Mr. Ladnar of Kroy as the author of one book mainly to give himself an opportunity of praising his own other works. Actually Randall had a school at Heath near Wakefield, but that is no reason why he should not adopt the simple ruse of spelling York and his own name backwards. Ladnar dedicated his book ironically to the Monthly Reviewers, a body which seems to have been unduly severe upon farming books and which had attacked Randall's *Semi-Virgilian Husbandry* (1764). This work he had presented to the *London Chronicle* possibly because he thought it would advertise a seed drill he wanted to sell or perhaps out of pure philanthropy. Since Ladnar offered what seems to have been the same Universal Seed Plough, I think there is little doubt that Randall and Ladnar were one and the same. Such a method is almost worthy of a modern advertising agency.

Another man, whose name I have not been able to trace, but who signed himself "A Real Farmer," supported his claim to that title by an autobiographical preface. He had a most adventurous life. His history is as romantic as the contemporary picaresque novel, and curiously enough the details are very similar to the established routine of the fiction writers of the time. It may be, of course, that the fiction described a type of life that was common in the eighteenth century, or possibly "A Real Farmer" was cooking the evidence. It would be too much to give the story here, but it began in his childhood. He ran away from home because he was ill-treated by his stepmother and got a job on a farm. When he gave that up he set out for America but only got to London, narrowly escaping the press gang. This was enough for him, and he took horse for home. On the way he got a job on another farm; so clearly he had farming experience.

When such tricks were adopted to sell books and to convince the public that the writers were really authorities on their subject, every writer's jealousy of all others is easily understood. A storm of controversy arose about particular books and their authors. I do not mean the kind of controversy that raged about the drill husbandry that owed its inception to Jethro Tull and did not terminate until over a hundred years after his book appeared. It has already been exhaustively dealt with elsewhere.

The kind of controversy I have in mind was much more personal. It concerned the qualifications of a writer and the value of his work. It was not concerned with particular proposals—indeed the more fantastic the proposals the more readily they were accepted—but with the presumed uselessness of a book and incompetence of its author.

An example is the storm aroused by George Winter's *New and Compendious System of Husbandry* (1787). Winter was one of the numerous persons who invented seed drills, and of course he wanted to sell his, so he wrote a book about farming to advertise it. This was not an original idea, but he really was a farmer and lived in Gloucestershire. There is some want of frankness about his own statement of his object. He said that he wrote the book primarily to place his twenty years of farming experience at the disposal of the public, but that is only to be expected of an advertiser. The book is quite a useful textbook and certainly did not deserve the harsh treatment it received at the hands of the *Monthly Review*. Probably Thomas Comber, a contemporary farming author, wrote the review and that may explain its severity. He shed crocodile tears because his integrity of judgment forced him to condemn the book, painful as it was for him to wound the writer in that most sensitive part, his self-love. Winter was, he wrote, a well-meaning person, who by thinking and talking with ignorant neighbors, persuaded himself in good earnest that his book would be of great general service. If recording the experience and practice of working farmers is of service, the book did its job, but the reviewer thought it trivial and superficial most likely because it lacked wonders and was written from a not particularly advanced district.

Almost immediately an old experienced farmer who called himself Benjamin Bramble came to the rescue. He issued a reprint of Winter's book with a preface by himself entitled *The Farmer Convinced, or the Reviewers of the Monthly Review Anatomized*. He condemned the review in fine resounding terms. Its statements were vague, futile, and fallacious. For himself he was only a country ignoramus, but sometimes he entered into company with what the world called sensible men. Far from this a reviewer is commonly supposed to be some mercenary needy wretch who writes for hire and is equally ready to praise or condemn, as his employers direct. Both sides proclaimed their natural politeness, but it is difficult for a modern eye to discern it.

The *Monthly Review* was never anything less than severe, and no less a person than Young complained of its treatment. In the preface to his Eastern Tour he reasonably claimed that a writer of husbandry should be tried by a jury of real farmers instead of falling into the hands of such a motley crew. Clearly none of the writers trusted each other although they did not scruple to copy from each other even while condemning the work from which they were appropriating ideas; and many of the appropriated ideas were very odd.

The problem of reclaiming the uncultivated land in the country was one that occupied a good deal of attention, and an idea that occurs here and there in the literature was outlined fairly concisely by Matthew Peters in the 1770s. At that time the total area of the country was not precisely known, but some estimates came very near the truth. Peters accepted 39 million acres as a proper computation of the area of England and Wales, and of this area, he thought 9 million acres were waste of some sort or another. With the optimism of his age he thought that the whole of this area could be added to the arable land. In addition there were 6 million acres of forest, chase, and common heath and 2 million acres of downs and plains, all available for cultivation. This makes a total of 17 million acres of reclaimable land, a largish proportion even for those days. His idea, or perhaps I should rather say, the idea adumbrated by the various people who took it up, was that the forest and chase should be divided into 500-acre farms and let at £125 per annum. These farms were to be made one-third pasture, and of the balance 80 acres was to be under wheat, so presumably Peters had the four-course system in mind for this land. He anticipated with the same optimism that the yield of wheat would average 32 bushels an acre although the national average at that date can have been no more than 20 as he himself admitted. The heaths were also to be cut up into farms of the same size but to be let at £62.10.0d. on 25-year leases in order to allow the tenant to get the benefit of his reclamation work. This was a grandiose scheme and not likely to be successful, although what was done in Lincolnshire and north Northumberland slightly later on lends color to the assumption that it was possible. The curious thing to my mind is that the writers who dealt in this project chose 500 acres as the optimum size of farm. Neither then nor at any other time, so far as I am aware, has the major number of farms in England been of this size and nothing would lead one to suppose that it is in fact the most economic size of holding.

If it had been carried out this scheme would obviously have been of the very greatest value to the community, as well as bringing a profit to the man who did the work—a not unimportant consideration. These writers, however, did not intend that the reclamation of the uncultivated land should be carried out gradually as it was but that it should all be done at a stroke. This is clearly impossible, but it is no less impossible than the rewards offered for adopting other plans.

The new crops, turnips, clover, lucerne, sainfoin, timothy, and ryegrass are all discussed at length in the general works, and some of them are honored in specific treatises. I have no doubt that the highly improbable rewards to be gained from their cultivation which many books offered played some part in the slow rate at which they were brought into the normal routine of everyday farming. It is indeed refreshing to turn from some of the more speculative writings to the casual notes made by a farming squire who recorded what he and his neighbors actually did. Such a man was Edward Lisle of Crux Easton, Hampshire.

Lisle was a landowner who had either estates or relations in Hampshire, Dorset, Wiltshire, the Isle of Wight, and Leicester. His book is a series of notes on what he actually did on his farms and what he learned in conversation and correspondence about what other farmers were doing. Such evidence is invaluable for the districts touched upon, and I could wish that more landowners had made similar notes. We must be duly thankful that a descendant had the book printed in 1756. Few such records of farming practice, scrappy as these notes are, have come down to us, and indeed it was not till Young began his tours that anything of comparable worth was written. Of course I use the word worth in the sense of value to the historian.

At about the same date John Mortimer issued his *Whole Art of Husbandry* (1707). This book is a compilation although Mortimer had some practical experience. He had come into an estate in Essex in 1693. The book supplies some details about the farming of Essex, and these are perhaps derived from personal experience or conversation. It also contains references to farming practice in other counties, and since most of these references are identified in place they may be accepted with one reservation. Mortimer used books by other writers, and these sources and their dates must be identified before the time when these practices were usual can be ascertained. These two writers, different as their methods were, do supply something more than mere speculation and the provocative theorizing that brought the "book farmers" into disrepute with each other as well as the audience they intended to reach.

Another man who wished to obtain information about the actual practice of farming in different parts of the country was John Houghton, F.R.S. He founded the earliest farming periodical. His weekly, *A Collection for Improvement of Husbandry and Trade,* was an ambitious project designed to be quite encyclopedic. It followed his earlier attempt at the same sort of thing that had been issued at irregular intervals. Houghton secured contributions from some of the most famous men of the day and from less well-known farmers and so on, but not so many as he may have wished. Here again can be found information descriptive of systems or parts of systems actually practiced. That is the important thing about these three men! They described things that were done instead of proposing things to be done that must have seemed extraordinarily fantastic to the common man.

Young himself set the seal of approval on Houghton's enterprise, but Houghton had no imitators for fifty years, if Bradley's reprint of a condensed version of the Collections is excepted. In 1764 the *Museum Rusticum* began publication, and this also purported to be written by practical men who described things they were personally acquainted with, but it fell into some disrepute because at first the articles were unsigned. It ran to six annual volumes, in Young's words, "as long a duration as it merited." Some of the papers it contains are of the usual theoretic character, but others are valuable, and Young was, I feel, unnecessarily severe upon a publication to which he himself contributed. There were a few other short-lived periodicals before Young commenced the *Annals of Agriculture,* but none of them is important. Such a work as *The Farmer's Magazine* for instance was almost entirely a scissors and paste production, from which I judge its proprietors were economical.

I have already mentioned Young's dislike of dictionaries, encyclopedias, and so on. Only seven were published during the century, and some of these must have been useful to farmers if they saw them. The information they provide is mainly second-hand, but that is more or less natural because all such compilations rely on the authority of earlier works. Of course some of the material they reprinted is no less odd because it is reprinted, but there is a good deal of sound advice to be discovered amongst the rubbish. Though they may have been practically useful, however, they must be used with caution as historical sources. Their own sources must in turn be traced and dated. When that has been done they may be used, but only then. Again some of them contain details of experiments with costings, many of which I have no doubt were carried out only in the imaginations of the writers, but they have a value. They must have been able to pass muster, and to do that the costs must have been of an order that would not be ridiculous in the eyes of the reader. Probably then some idea of the normal expenses of ordinary farm operations can be obtained from them. As much or as little may be said for the costings applied to experiments described in individual writings.

Compared with such works as the dictionaries the treatises on farriery and other subjects are comparatively insignificant in bulk. Farriery was a term for what we might now call veterinary science and treated largely of the cure of animal diseases. I am not competent to offer any opinion of these works, but some of the cures are quaint, and one of them has stuck in my mind. At that time antimony was used as a medicine, and one bright spirit invented what he was pleased to call an everlasting pill compounded of antimony and other things. This was about the size of a round bullet of the kind used in the muzzle loaders of the day and was forced down a cow's throat. When it had performed its function, it was sought in the pasture where the cow grazed and if recovered used again and again. Time cannot have been so precious then as it is reputed to be now, and patience much less easily exhausted.

This can hardly be paralleled, but some of the secret manures suggested were nearly as good. One invented by a Mr. Liveing whose name is all that remains to us is discussed with approbation by Samuel Trowell in 1739. It was a secret preparation composed of "foul salt fermented with other ingredients to be had in great plenty in all parts of Great Britain." It was omnipotent. It increased seed and strengthened the plant; it destroyed rushes, grubs, moss, and worms; it preserved turnips from fly and killed snails, slugs, and all other insects; and it could be carried to the field on horses' backs, thus saving cost and the damage done by heavy wagons. What more could heart desire? Only the formula is lacking.

But it is not in such frivolities as these that the true value of the agricultural literature of the day is to be found. Towards the end of the century real science was emerging. The theory of soils, of plant growth, of the mechanics of the plow, and so on were all being discussed in separate works. I cannot pretend to estimate the value of the more scientific works, but Russell M. Garnier in a book that is now almost forgotten has provided an excellent summary. Many modern scientific works also have prefaces that give outlines of the history of their particular subject.

I have pointed out with perhaps too much emphasis that the different writers almost invariably cast slurs upon each other. Quite a large proportion of this mutual condemnation is well-deserved, but I think the books must have served a good purpose. They probably were effective in rousing popular interest and in engaging the attention of landowners, quasi-scientific bodies, and the local agricultural societies formed towards the end of the century. The farmer himself probably learned a good deal more from example than he did from precept if only because he was usually quite illiterate. In the rural mind here as in Missouri there was a distinct feeling that "you've got to show me."

Our modern interest in these books is, of course, quite different. We value them because they tell us something of how farming developed, but the fact that they distrusted each other's pretensions so largely makes it necessary to bring a highly critical faculty to bear upon them when using them as historical sources. Such men as Houghton, Mortimer, Lisle, Ellis, Young and Marshall are all too few. They dealt in facts; many of the others dealt in highly imaginative theory. The most extravagant rewards were promised for such contradictory things as increasing rabbit warrens and destroying warrens to increase the arable area, for breaking up grass and laying land down to grass—these are, of course, not necessarily incompatible —and for using a light two-horse plow in land for which it was quite unsuited. But something can usually be abstracted from the worst of them. Almost all hint or state boldly that such and such a method was common in a particular place. The danger of making such statements is at once apparent; and they may, therefore, be accepted. They must be examined, however, because they may have been copied from earlier works, and it is only when their origin is traced that their literary—not necessarily the same thing as physical— date can be determined. Used with due caution the farming textbooks written in the eighteenth century afford a background to the history of the development of the industry in that century, but they must be supplemented by other sources of information. For the last thirty years the tours and surveys made by Young, the Board of Agriculture, and Marshall provide almost too much, but for the first seventy there is nothing but the comments of travelers, contemporary novels, essays, and descriptive writings generally. Neverthless a fairly complete story can be made out.

I am afraid that I have dealt with the more frivolous aspects of eighteenth-century agricultural authors here, but those aspects are important because they provide a standard of criticism, perhaps a little severe, which can be applied by the modern research worker in weighing the evidence these writers provide.

"The Industrial Revolution"

HERBERT HEATON

Published in 1938

Few subjects are more solidly embedded in American textbooks of modern European history than the English Industrial Revolution. Yet the approach to the subject that continues to dominate many of these textbooks has been under fire for several decades. The more specialists in economic history have dug into the sources, the more suspicious have they become of the dramatic and sensational features of the traditional approach to the Industrial Revolution. They insist that this approach is based on a fundamental misunderstanding of the industrial evolution of late medieval and early modern times. No less important, they maintain that it is based on an exaggeration of the rate of industrial change in the late eighteenth and early nineteenth centuries. In recent years, these specialists have written much to dispel some of the misconceptions that have surrounded the history of English industrial development. It would be difficult, however, to find a statement of the newer approach to the growth of English industry that can rival the present essay by Herbert Heaton, of the University of Minnesota. Indeed, readers would not complain so often about the dullness of much of the secondary literature on economic history if more economic historians had Heaton's insight, critical power, sense of humor, and style.

The Editor's letter asked for an article on the industrial revolution, "with the view to bringing teachers up to date on newer scholarship and interpretations." So I spent the morning of Thanksgiving Day examining several recent high school or university history or social science texts to see how they handled economic developments. I soon found I had a new reason for being thankful. One *History of Europe* gives 102 pages out of 845 to economic conditions and trends, and an-

Reprinted by special permission from *Social Education*, II (1938), 159-165.

other gives 136 pages out of 1024. This is a mighty advance since the 'eighties, when Fyffe wrote over a thousand pages and never mentioned a machine or a railroad. It is even better than conditions were thirty years ago, when the *Cambridge Modern History* included only three economic chapters in its fourteen volumes. The "Manor," the "Commercial Revolution," "Mercantilism," and the "Industrial Revolution" have definitely been admitted to the texts. My daughter tells me she has heard the manor described in five different lecture courses, and I notice that in her prescribed books the famous plan of a "typical manor" has been improved: a stork stands forlornly in the swamp, and the landlord is hunting a deer and a boar—simultaneously—in the Woodland.

This flush of gratitude for the many crumbs that are now falling from the general historian's table is, however, tempered a little by the staleness of some of the crumbs. Even the best of the university texts have provoked me to make several query marks in the margin; and some of the high school books ought to have whole paragraphs or even pages torn out. A teacher who said that the Roman Empire fell in 476, that the renaissance began when a Greek scholar migrated from Constantinople to Florence in 1397, that the American Constitution was a popular document, or that Germany was solely responsible for the World War would be accused of being old fashioned. Yet that is what often happens when general surveyors or writers of historical introductions to social science deal with economic history. This is inevitable, for the subject is being overhauled by higher criticism of the contents and the ideas of the founding fathers. Those men began their serious study only about sixty years ago and did a grand job with the limited data at their disposal. The second generation, working with a vastly enlarged mass of material, has revised or scrapped some of the

JOHN U. NEF: Professor of economic history at the University of Chicago, he is the author of numerous articles and books dealing with the economic development of early modern Europe. His two-volume study of *The Rise of the British Coal Industry* (1932) and his *Industry and Government in France and England, 1540-1640* (1940) are basic works for anyone interested in economic history.

DAVID RICARDO: English economist of the early nineteenth century who built on Adam Smith's *Wealth of Nations* and on Thomas Robert Malthus' *Essay on Population*. One of the chief formulators of "classical economics," he was frequently misinterpreted by his contemporaries and his followers,

pioneers' conclusions, and the third generation is now knocking at the door, or rather knocking some doors down. Almost every issue of the special periodicals forces us to change an opinion or an emphasis; the subject is as living, as exciting, as contemporary physics. But the task of keeping up with the bright young people on the research front line is hard on the heart and lungs of those of us who are over forty. It is even more strenuous for those who wish to be well informed academic general practitioners.

Such higher criticism has been devastating in two fields well known to history teachers. These are the "Manor" and the "Industrial Revolution." Of the "Manor" there is room here only to say that anyone who thinks he has done justice to the medieval countryside when he has described the manorial system is almost as wrong as he would be if he passed off a picture of a slave plantation as an adequate account of the American countryside. Of the "Industrial Revolution," the sharp lines and strong colors—chiefly rose and black—of the old picture have become so blurred that some of us now put the title in quotation marks or avoid using it.

That old picture, painted about 1880 by Arnold Toynbee, is a triptych, or a melodrama in three acts. First there is "The Eve," still, placid, quiet, at the end of a long day that reaches back to the Normans, Nero, or even Noah. The methods of agriculture, industry, and transportation have changed little in a thousand years. Production is carried on by small manufacturers or farmers. The former, like the latter, live in the country, combine industry and agriculture, and supplement the family labor supply by training an apprentice and perhaps employing a journeyman or two. The wage earner usually works, aided by his family, in his own home on materials put out to

and his ideas came often to be used as weapons in the struggle against government intervention in economic life. Although in general he defended *laissez faire*, he himself favored government intervention in instance after instance.

ARNOLD TOYNBEE: English historian and social reformer after whom the social settlement house Toynbee Hall, located in the East End of London, is named. His posthumously published *Lectures on the Industrial Revolution of the Eighteenth Century in England* (1884) did much to popularize one of the most famous labels in historical literature. He was the uncle of the present Arnold Toynbee, of *A Study of History* fame.

him by his employer; but he may work under his master's roof. Between master and man is a "warm attachment"; they call each other by their Christian nicknames. The class of capitalist employers is still "in its infancy"; some merchant-employers put out material to be processed in the homes of their employees or of small masters, and a few factories or central workshops exist. But in general the family firm and the family farm prevail. Division of class and of labor is slight. The worker can express his personality in his work, though what happens if it is crooked is not clear. Production is for local markets or for the producer's larder and wardrobe, since defective means of transportation and mercantilistic policies shut off distant consumers. No one earns great rewards, but the domestic system insures on the whole a sound and healthy life under conditions favorable to the development of mind, body, and personal dignity. Contentment spins at the cottage door; there is plenty of honeysuckle, ivy, and good ale in this "quiet world" of "scarcely perceptible movement." A comprehensive code of state regulation of production and trade combines with technical inertia to prevent anything from changing.

Then, with a rapidity known in the tropics, "The Night" falls, a night full of noise and action. Seven men—four Lancashire men (Kay, Hargreaves, Arkwright, and Crompton), two Scots (Adam Smith and James Watt), and one Episcopalian parson (Cartwright)—invent some textile machines, improve the steam engine, or write *The Wealth of Nations*. Meanwhile other men revolutionize agriculture and redraw the village map, while others improve roads and rivers or cut canals. But it is the seven men who get their names on the record, for their actions or thoughts "destroyed the old world and built a new one." And what they did was crowded into a brief night that lasted from about 1760 to 1780.

Act Three is "The Murky Dawn," in which the effects become visible. It is a period of "economic revolution and anarchy," as machinery and steam overrun industry, and Smith's plea for laissez faire sweeps the statute book clear of the mercantilistic devil. Population is "torn up by the roots" and dragged "from cottages in distant valleys into factories and cities"; independent farmers, expelled from their lands and impoverished by the extension of sheep raising and the inclosure movement, join the small manufacturing master or journeymen in this rural exodus. In the towns a landless propertyless proletariat is the victim of the seven deadly sins of unrestrained inhuman industrial capitalists. The sins are the factory system, long hours, child labor, the exploitation of women, low wages, periodical or chronic unemployment, and slums. If the victims dislike the contrast between their deplorable lot and the fortunes made by fat factory owners; if they object, riot, join labor unions, or become chartists or socialists, they are shot down, put in jail, or sent to Botany Bay. Their economic masters become their political lords by displacing the landowners in the seats of government, and then legislate—or refuse to do so—with one eye on the cashbox and the other on some page of Smith, Ricardo, or Malthus. A dreary, tragic, selfish, sort of dawn! But by lunch time the weather is improving. The exploited grow class-conscious and organized, some employers grow softhearted, laws are passed to permit unions, to regulate child labor, or to provide a better water supply. Mass production makes goods cheaper, the corn laws are repealed, Victoria becomes queen, Albert the Good builds the Crystal Palace, and by the time it is opened in 1851 the grim tragedy is promising to turn into whatever the urban counterpart of a pastoral should be called.

This story has got into the general books, and the title for it has become so widely accepted that some wit has said all college courses now begin with the amoeba, Aristotle, or the industrial revolution. That is—all courses except those given by the economic historian, for he is getting more and more suspicious of the name and of the crisp dramatic conception. In the great university schools of economic history, Manchester admits that the name was useful when first adopted but thinks it has now served its turn and can scarcely be applied aptly to a movement which was in preparation for two centuries and then occupied at least one more. Oxford finds there is "no hiatus in economic development, but always a constant tide of progress and change, in which the old is blended almost imperceptibly with the new." Edinburgh chimes in with the remark that "sudden catastrophic change is inconsistent with the slow gradual process of human evolution." Harvard insists that the technological changes of the eighteenth century were "only the completion of tendencies which had been significantly evident since Leonardo da Vinci." Birmingham reinforces this by asserting that the developments between 1760 and 1830 "did but carry further, though on a far greater scale and with far greater rapidity, changes which had been proceeding long before." Cambridge finds the period presents a study in slow motion, and in London they tell the pass students there was an industrial revolution, but tell the honors students there never was any such thing.

These quotations give a composite picture of the revised view of the industrial revolution. Let me put it in three generalizations. (1) Steam and the textile machines did not break in on an almost unchanging world of smallscale slightly capitalistic enterprise. (2) The rate of technical change was *lento* rather than *allegro* for a long time; it took decades or even generations to transform old industries and build up new ones. (3) The social and economic "evils" were not new; they were not as black or as widespread as is usually asserted; their causes were often due to special or non-economic factors; and they were in no small measure offset by a substantial improvement in the real wages and living standards of a large part of the wage-earning population. Sentimental unhistorical hysteria is not a good approach to a problem, whether present or past, but it dominated much of the discussion a hundred years ago and the description of a hundred years ago.

Let me elaborate these three contentions. In Toynbee's day little was known of sixteenth-century economic life, and little of any eighteenth-century industry except textiles. Now we know that during this period there were important changes in methods of production, and a quickening spirit of scientific inquiry and of inventive curiosity. New methods of extracting and refining metals were discovered; the preparation of silk yarn, the knitting of hose, the weaving of ribbons, the making of clocks, the finishing of cloth, all obtained new or improved equipment, as did shipbuilding, brewing, mining, sugar refining, and the manufacture of chemicals. The harnessing of wind, water, and animal power was made more efficient, and coal was used in increasing quantities by industries which needed heat. Professor Nef has shown that England had an industrial revolution between 1540 and 1640, and that the rate of technical change was possibly as striking during the age of Shakespeare as during that of Wordsworth or Byron. Holland, Sweden, France, and England alike contributed to technical progress, and by 1700 scientists, especially physicists, had learned enough to be able to answer some questions asked by industrialists. True, some industries or processes stood still, and spinning and weaving did not change much; but many were on the march.

At the same time the organization of production was changing.

Small craftsmen did not have the capital necessary for some of the new equipment, or for bridging the long gap between buying raw material and getting paid for the finished article by a dilatory or distant customer. Hence where materials were costly or came from afar, where equipment was expensive, where the market was large or distant, the initiative had to be taken by merchants or large producers. Some of them bought the raw materials and put them out to be processed by small masters or by wage earners. Sometimes they supplied the equipment as well and paid the master only for his labor, just as he in turn might pay wages to his journeymen. Some of them gathered workers in, because the material could not be put out. You could not put out coal mining, smelting, sugar refining, building, cloth finishing, shipbuilding, calico printing, or the making of glass, bricks, paper, leather, or gunpowder. As these industries grew, so did the number of persons working for wages in their employer's plant; and the combined expansion of putting out and gathering in had created a large propertyless proletariat long before 1760. It may be true that in 1640 the great majority of industrial workers "laboured in their homes, in town cellars or garrets, or in village cottages. But that majority was by no means so overwhelming as has been supposed" (Nef) and was declining rapidly before a flying shuttle flew or a spinning jenny was devised, even in Lancashire cotton production. Wherever men worked, many of them were wage earners.

If they were, their wages tended to be low; but so were all returns in an age of low productivity. Their hours were long—twelve or more a day—but so were those of their employers and of independent workers, since the rate of production was so slow. Their children and their wives had to work, for every scrap of labor was needed; but so did all children and wives, except those of the rich. Unemployment was frequent and severe, industrial diseases and accidents were common, living and working conditions were often dank, unhealthy, and malodorous, whether in town or village. Labor unions were formed, class conflicts occurred, and the state usually took the employers' side.

This sketch of the period before 1760 takes much of the melodrama out of the next seventy years. Some of the remainder disappears, when we examine the pace at which the textile machines and the improved steam engines were adopted. The cotton industry, which was the scene of the famous inventions, has been used as a sample case. But it was not typical; various factors, such as the newness of the industry, the suitability of the cotton fiber for mechanical treatment, and the great market existing for cheap cotton cloth, prevent the story of cotton from being typical of the changes in industry at large. The transfer from domestic hand spinning of cotton to factory machine spinning was rapid—a matter of about twenty years. By 1815 "the power loom was entering into effective rivalry with the hand loom in the cotton industry, though another generation was to elapse before the battle was finally decided." But cotton was a lonely hare in an industrial world of tortoises. It loomed far less large in that world than it has done in the textbooks, for even in the 1830's the number of its employees was only two-thirds that of the number of female domestic servants.

When we get our eyes off this exception, we find the pace of change in the rest of industry much more sedate. Wool spinning, on hand jennies instead of on wheels, was still being done in Yorkshire homes in 1850. Power looms had not seriously threatened the woolen hand weaver at that date; the transfer from hand to power weaving came quietly during the next twenty-five years, but even in 1877 I find one manufacturer contending that the old method was as cheap as the new. As for steam power, Watt had only 320 of his engines at work in England in 1800, and in 1830 a quarter of the power used by cotton mills was still drawn from waterwheels. Mining had no great technical change, but a series of little ones. Building remained a manual industry until the concrete mixer came. The pottery industry relied less on machinery than on other factors. Clothes making, glass blowing, and printing were late in getting mechanical equipment, while mechanical engineering only slowly developed the tools it needed for shaping metal parts cheaply and accurately. In 1850 everything was not over except the shouting. Cheap steel, cheap lubricants, industrial chemistry, and cheap electricity were still to come. The railroad had won its battle, but the steamship was still fighting its sailing rival, even on the North Atlantic. Away from Lancashire and the railroad tracks, technical change between 1760 and 1850 had been gradual, slow, and unspectacular.

What then of the social and economic consequences and of the seven deadly sins? In the first place, if we leave out one or two exceptional industries or areas, people were not torn loose from a rural life of pleasant and virtually independent enterprise and plunged almost overnight into the horrible existence of an urban factory slum-dwelling proletariat. Many of them were already proletarian; many of them already lived in industrial towns which now grew large or in villages which grew into towns; and some of them already worked under the employer's roof. For them there was not much shift of habitat or of economic class. There was little mass migration, and little long distance movement, except by the Irish, who swarmed into England before they swarmed into North America, and who made many labor and urban problems much more acute than they would otherwise have been.

In the second place, before we beat our anger to white heat in describing the slums, the foul streets, the smoke-laden atmosphere, the lack of water or sanitation, the ravages of disease, etc., let us remember three controlling considerations. (a) Technical. Cheap bricks, cheap sewer or water pipes, and cheap house fixtures were not available till at least 1840, and knowledge concerning public health was still scanty. Compare conditions in the industrial towns with those of non-industrial communities or with rural housing facilities; then it is evident that the housing and sanitary shortcomings of the manufacturing districts were not wholly due to the new machinery and the factory system. (b) Constitutional. Until 1835 no town government had adequate powers to cope with the new urban problems. (c) Economic. The provision of houses was never, until recent years, regarded as a public duty. It was left to private enterprise and the stimulus of investment or speculation. The potential builder considered whether his capital would yield a better return in houses than in the many other fields that were thirsty for capital; and the amount he put into a dwelling was limited by what the tenant could afford to pay. In one English town 76 per cent of the houses were rented at a dollar a week or less in 1839; the total capital outlay for one house could not be more than six hundred dollars. In view of the western world's housing impasse since 1914, we must speak more kindly of the builder who a century ago put a roof over the head of the poor, without the aid of mass-produced materials, machinery, or government subsidies.

In the third place, few of the factory working conditions were new. Not even the discipline of fixed hours of work was new to industries which had been conducted in central workshops. Night work may have been new, but long and late hours were not. The cruel treatment of some children by foremen was a personal matter; parents had not been free from it in the domestic workshop, and it was part of that streak of cruelty common in prisons, the army and navy, schools, and homes. The thing that was new and revolutionary was not the "evils," but the discovery that they were evils. For that we have to thank those employers who were heartless. We have to thank the factory for making noticeable in the mass what had been ignored in scattered small instances. We can thank onlookers, whether lay or ecclesiastic, and even Tory politicians who saw in factory conditions a new whip with which to flog their Whig industrial opponents. Finally, much credit must go to those employers—and they were many—who treated their workers decently. These men belonged to that growing army of humanitarians who cleaned up slavery, made the penal code less fierce, welcomed the attack on excessive drinking, pushed the cause of education, built hospitals, dispensaries, and charitable institutions, organized the relief of the unemployed in depressed days, established good working conditions, and fought for better factory laws and better town government.

One final comment may help us to understand better the years between 1760 and 1830. Twenty-six of those years (1789-1815) were dominated by the emotions and strain of the French Revolution and the Napoleonic war, and sixteen of them (1815-1830) were filled with the task of readjustment after a generation of war. The first period was torn by the fear of Jacobinism and the stress of war and famine. There could be little tolerance of mutterings of social discontent or of organized protest during those years; and there was little time to think of domestic problems. The second period we understand better because we have lived through a similar one. The legacies of war were high prices which collapsed, high interest rates and taxes which did not, a scarcity of houses, wide agrarian distress, a disarranged currency, a chaotic credit system, economic nationalism, choked trade channels, prohibitive tariffs, demobilized soldiers without jobs, and so forth. Much that has been blamed on the economic transition was not new, and much of the rest has to be put on the shoulders of the war. The remarkable thing is that by 1830 British opinion had got rid of most of its war phobias and was tackling its problems realistically and constructively by a combination of voluntary organization and state action. If anything was rapid and revolutionary in this whole period it was the change in outlook that between 1824 and 1835 removed the ban on labor organization, passed an effective factory act, reformed the poor law, lowered the tariff wall, made a hole in the navigation laws, remodelled urban government, reformed the House of Commons, liberated the slaves, emancipated Roman Catholics, fashioned a good banking system, and sowed the seeds of national education, trade unionism, and the cooperative movement.

Behind all this was the intense energy of manufacturers and merchants who, either with old equipment or new, enterprised and adventured. This energy is denounced by some as "an orgy of soulless cupidity," and praised by others as "a triumph of the spirit of enterprise." In general it was a bit of both. Cupidity, yes, as in all ages and occupations. Enterprise, yes, but not always triumphant, for the field was strewn with the wreckage of men who failed. When the classical economists said profit was the reward of risk and interest the reward of abstinence, they meant it. Not the abstinence that today would lead a man to pick a Buick for his twelfth car instead of a Rolls Royce, but one which meant meager living and the ploughing back of every spare penny into the business. As for risk, some day somebody will study the industrial revolution through the bankruptcy records; but we know enough to realize on what a treacherous sea the entrepreneur launched his tiny bark.

How does all this affect the teacher's presentation of economic aspects of modern Europe? It takes out some of the heroics—and the villainics, if I can coin a word—it cuts down the pace, and leaves the tale that of a trend rather than of a tumult. But there is enough left, and space has been made available for more that is of first class importance. Any survey of the making of modern Europe should have something to say about the gradual industrialization of parts of the continent, including the effect of hydro-electricity, industrial chemistry, and post-Bessemer metallurgical developments; the emergence of intensive agriculture; the effect of good roads, canals, railroads, steamships, and refrigeration; the end of serfdom in other countries than Russia and the evolution of an efficient peasant proprietor economy; the growing need for more capital and better banking; the unprecedented growth of population and the mass migration of 50,000,000 Europeans to other continents in a century; the steady advance of voluntary association and the influence of the social conscience in producing the social service state; the instability of a complex capitalistic system in a world economy; the twentyfold increase in the value of world trade; the impact of the new world on the old; and the ability of Europe to raise greatly the standard of living of an expanding population, thanks to better technique, better organization, and freedom for a hundred years from Armageddon. And if textbooks must have illustrations, I would dispense with pictures of the spinning jenny, Louis Blanc, and even Karl Marx, if thereby I had room for two graphs, one of the movement of general prices and one of the business cycle. These two would explain a lot of social, political, and even diplomatic history.

Mercantilism and the American Revolution

LAWRENCE A. HARPER

»»-»»-»»-»»-»»-»»-»»-»» *Published in 1942* «««-«««-«««-«««-«««-«««-«««-«««

Few eighteenth-century developments were so important in the political, economic, and intellectual history of Europe as the American War of Independence; and few historical subjects have attracted a greater number of American writers. The fact is, however, that there are still many basic differences that keep these writers from reaching any real agreement as to the causes of the war. In recent years economic interpretations have gained widespread currency; but this is not to say that such interpretations did not exist earlier. Indeed, they go back to the eighteenth century. Edmund Burke, who found the major economic cause of the war in parliamentary taxation, and Adam Smith and Josiah Tucker, who found it in British mercantilist regulations and restrictions, were the formulators of the two leading economic interpretations that have held sway through the present time. Historians, nevertheless, are no closer to agreement as to the relative significance of mercantilism and parliamentary taxation than writers were in the days of Burke, Smith, and Tucker. Among recent investigators of mercantilism as a force that prepared the way for the Revolution, no writer has made so scholarly a contribution as Lawrence A. Harper, author of a valuable monograph on *The English Navigation Laws* (1939). In the present article he states some of the conclusions that grew out of the years of study that he devoted to the subject of mercantilism.

The cynic who declared that history is the process whereby a complex truth becomes a simplified falsehood may have had in mind interpretations of the American Revolution. Even before the Revolution occurred, Vergennes prophesied that France's loss of Canada

Reprinted by special permission from *The Canadian Historical Review*, XXIII (1942), 1-15. The extensive documentation which originally appeared with this essay has been omitted.

would eventually bring it about. The very document which made the severance final attributed the blame to George III, a fashion which has been generally followed, and some years ago was ardently expounded by a former mayor of this city, Big Bill Thompson. These points, however, are called to attention merely to remind us of what Professor Root will expound more fully—that there are many interpretations. Our immediate task is to concentrate upon one—the relation of English mercantilism to the American Revolution.

The term "mercantilism" is one of those words which have different meanings for different people. On the one hand, George Louis Beer claimed that English mercantilism was a well-balanced system designed for the benefit of the colonies as well as the mother country, and on the other, Sir William Ashley declared that the regulations of English mercantilism were either pious formulas nullified in the actual world of commerce by fraud and evasion, or merely a codification of commercial habits which would have been followed in any case. For reasons which have been explained more fully elsewhere we shall reject Beer's claim that there was no exploitation and accept the statements of the mercantilists themselves that they planned to exploit the colonies for the benefit of the mother country. We shall deny the Ashley view that there was no actual regulation and conclude from more recent studies of the evidence that the English laws did regulate trade and commerce.

These two conclusions provide us with a working definition of English mercantilism in its colonial aspects. It had as its purpose, exploitation, and as its means, regulation. Both phases of the problem, exploitation *and* regulation, are important. To understand the relationship of mercantilism and the Revolution we must not only analyse the extent to which the colonists were exploited but also consider the skill with which they were regulated.

An analysis of how the colonists were exploited is no easy task, as any one knows who has struggled with the many statutory ambiguities

---

GEORGE LOUIS BEER: American historian of the early twentieth century. Distinctly pro-British in his outlook, he played an important part in encouraging a more sympathetic approach to the Old Empire in American historical circles. His major works were *The Origins of the British Colonial System, 1578-1660* (1908), the unfinished *The Old Colonial System, 1660-1754* (1912), and *British Colonial Policy, 1754-1765* (1907).

involved. The calculations involved in estimating the burdens placed upon the colonial economy are complicated. They call for arithmetical computations involving duties, preferences, or drawbacks of such odd amounts as 1s. 10d. and 15 16/75 of a twentieth of a penny per pound of tobacco. They run afoul of complicated analyses of costs and close decisions about the incidence of taxation. The answer required some thousands of hours of WPA and NYA labour in tabulating the necessary data and hundreds more in analysing and correlating them, the details of which have been compressed in thirty-eight rather dull pages. All that can be attempted here is to state the conclusions and indicate the grounds upon which they are based. We can, however, simplify our analysis of the mercantilist code which exploited the colonies by dividing it into four parts: first, the basic provisions concerning the trans-Atlantic trade; second, the supplementary measures restricting manufactures; third, the subsidiary rules with reference to the American trade; and fourth, the much discussed measures enacted after the French and Indian War.

In examining the first part, we find that the basic provisions concerning the trans-Atlantic trade placed a heavy burden upon the colonies. By means of the Navigation Acts England attempted both to keep foreign vessels out of the colonies and to enable English merchants to share in the more profitable parts of the trans-Atlantic trade. The enumeration of key colonial exports in various Acts from 1660 to 1766 and the Staple Act of 1663 hit at colonial trade both coming and going. The Acts required the colonies to allow English middlemen to distribute such crops as tobacco and rice and stipulated that if the colonies would not buy English manufactures, at least they should purchase their European goods in England. The greatest element in the burden laid upon the colonies was not the taxes assessed. It consisted in the increased costs of shipment, trans-shipment, and middleman's profits arising out of the requirement that England be used as an *entrepôt*.

ARTHUR M. SCHLESINGER: American social historian and professor of history at Harvard. He is the author of one of the few doctoral dissertations that turned out to be a historical classic, *The Colonial Merchants and the American Revolution, 1763-1776* (1918). He should not be confused with his son, the author of *The Age of Jackson*.

The burdens were somewhat lightened by legislation favouring the colonies, but not as much as usually alleged. The suppression of tobacco production in England, for example, was comparatively unimportant to the colonies since the great quantities of colonial tobacco re-exported caused its price to be determined by a world rather than an English market. Moreover, the motive was not goodwill for the colonists but fiscal, since the heavy revenues derived from tobacco could be collected more easily at the waterfront than upon the farm. Likewise, although colonial shipbuilders and shipowners approved the clauses of the Navigation Acts which eliminated Dutch rivals, they did not need such protection. They had managed to carry cargoes and to build ships which could be sold in the world market before the laws were enacted and they continued to do so after the Revolution. The fact is that colonial shipowners suffered, directly, and colonial shipbuilders, indirectly, under the Navigation Acts since other clauses enabled English shipowners (as contrasted with American) to carry eighty per cent of the trade between the British Isles and the Thirteen Colonies whereas they carried only twenty per cent after the Revolution.

Similarly the drawbacks, bounties, and tariff preferences, of which we are so often reminded, did not materially offset the burdens placed upon the trans-Atlantic trade. The drawbacks paid by English customs authorities on foreign products re-exported to the colonies should not be listed as a benefit to the colonies. There would have been no duties to be drawn back except for the requirement that the colonists purchase their European goods in England. The portion of the duties which England retained, while less than it might have been, was obviously greater than nothing at all. Likewise, *bounties paid upon English manufactures* exported to the colonies, were of advantage to the English producer, who received them whether his goods were exported to the colonies or anywhere else, rather than of benefit to the colonial consumer who otherwise would, and often did, buy competitive European goods.

On the other hand, however, the bounties paid upon colonial products were of real advantage to the colonies. They sustained the growth of indigo in South Carolina, did much to foster the development of naval stores in North Carolina, encouraged the lumber industry in New England, and at the end of the colonial period averaged more than £65,000 a year for the Thirteen Colonies alone. Similarly the preferences granted colonial products were beneficial in so far as they operated. Although they had no effect upon such commodities as tobacco and rice and their effect upon other commodities is somewhat uncertain, colonial raw silk, naval stores, and lumber definitely benefited. Yet the total sum represented by such preferences was never great and it is doubtful whether the benefit the Thirteen Colonies thus derived amounted to even one-twentieth of that obtained by the British West Indian planters who in the year 1773 alone, pocketed £446,000, thanks to a preferential rate which enabled their sugar to hold the English market despite a five-shilling-per-hundred-weight differential in price.

The uncertainties underlying many of our calculations do not permit an exact statement, but judging from calculations for the year 1773, it would seem that after all proper allowances have been made for bounties and other preferences, the net burden imposed upon the Thirteen Colonies by the restraints upon the trans-Atlantic trade was between two million and seven million dollars a year. In these days of astronomical budgets such figures do not seem especially impressive, but the annual per capita burden represented by the lower estimate would come close to meeting all the expenses of operating the national government during Washington's administration, and an annual per capita tax based upon the higher estimate would, in addition to paying the current expenses of government, have raised in twelve years (from 1790-1801) a sum sufficient to pay both the domestic and foreign debt incurred by the United States government during the Revolutionary War.

When we turn to the second part of our discussion, the supplementary measures restricting manufacture, we find a difference of opinion concerning the effect of English restrictions upon manufacturing wool, hats, and iron. The earlier tendency was to dismiss the regulations as immaterial, but recently some have swung the pendulum to the other extreme and argue that the restraints were very important. Neither extreme appears to accord with the facts. In the case of hats, proximity to the source of supply of furs and the comparatively simple process of manufacturing had led to the development of an industry which appears to have been injured by the legislation, but the hat industry played only a minor part in the total economy. Woollen manufactures were, of course, much more important, but there is much evidence to indicate that the English prohibitions had little material effect. The colonies found that they were handicapped by an inadequate supply of good wool when they tried to develop home-spun goods at the time of the Revolution—and even as late as 1791 Hamilton found that an adequate supply of labour was one of the chief stumbling blocks to his programme for encouraging industry. It required an embargo, a war, and a protective tariff before large-scale woollen manufacturing began to develop, and it did not pass beyond the household stage until many years after being freed of English mercantilism—which, incidentally, had never forbidden the manufacture of homespun for domestic use or local distribution.

In the case of iron manufactures the British legislation encouraged the development of pig and bar iron and tried to discourage the manu-facture of more advanced forms, but in both respects the influence of the legislation is doubtful. Because of the proximity of iron ore to forests America had a great advantage in producing crude iron, before coke replaced charcoal, and probably did not need legislative encourage-ment. With such an advantage in producing crude iron it was only natural that some more advanced iron articles would be produced in the colonies, whatever thorough-going mercantilists might dream about having the crude iron sent over to England and having it returned in the form of pots, pans, and other manufactures.

The various disallowances of colonial laws which were intended to foster colonial manufacturing further illustrate the English intention of discouraging it but, despite that intent, English mercantilism as a whole probably had a greater tendency to promote than to hinder colonial industry. The colonies' most dangerous industrial competitors were in many respects, not the English, but the Dutch, the Germans, and other Europeans—to say nothing of the natives of India—against whose competition the provisoes of the Staple Act of 1663 provided a very useful tariff barrier. Moreover, the large sums which mercantil-ism withheld from the colonies reduced their available cash, and prob-ably forced many colonists to use homespun or other American products instead of buying British.

The third point of our inquiry into colonial exploitation by Eng-land should not detain us long. Until the Molasses Act of 1733 the inter-American trade had been left virtually alone except for the re-quirement that the English colonies trade in English or colonial ships. Even after 1733, the prohibitive duties on foreign sugar, molasses, and rum were usually evaded. Such evasion required bribery, fraud, or concealment which probably served as a mildly protective tariff in favour of the British sugar islands, but the prices quoted in the Thirteen Colonies for sugar, molasses, and rum do not indicate that the legislation had any radical effect upon the trade.

The fourth part of our inquiry—that relating to the period after 1763—is a different matter. The researches of Schlesinger and others have demonstrated how the British measures of that period aroused the resentment of the merchants who unleashed an avalanche of agitation which soon went beyond their control. The agitation was not directed toward revolution at first, but agitation by its very nature promotes conditions favourable for revolution—and revolution followed as a natural sequence. Yet, conceding all the irritation thus aroused, we must still face the questions: Were the measures unduly exploitive? Did they fundamentally upset the economic equilibrium? Were they fatal ills which would inevitably lead to the death of the Empire, or merely minor upsets from which the Empire might have recovered—granted otherwise favourable conditions and good luck?

In reviewing the period it does not seem fair to blame British mercantilism for prescribing regulations which were demanded by the circumstances of the time. The British currency and land policies seem to fall under this category. The restrictions upon paper money undoubtedly distressed those who lacked funds, but they merely affirmed a truth which Americans had to learn from sad experience— that in the eighteenth century at least, no political alchemy could transmute paper into gold. Similarly the Proclamation of 1763 and the Quebec Act of 1774 essentially concerned imperial problems and American imitation of the policy after independence was not mere flattery but a tribute to its inherent soundness. The measures disappointed those who had hoped to acquire fortunes from land speculation, but what else could the British have done? Neither they nor the United States government after them could allow private individuals to stir up trouble by moving into Indian territory before the way had been prepared for settlement by negotiations which extinguished the Indians' claims to the area. In view of the British debt it was merely good fiscal policy to charge for the land, and the prices and terms of sale proposed by the British mercantilists seem very reasonable when compared with the prices and terms adopted by the federal government after 1787. And what solution did the Thirteen States themselves find for the conflicting claims to the territory west of the Alleghanies except to create a new governmental unit?

To one who frankly does not profess to be an expert on the point, it is difficult to understand how British mercantilism discriminated materially against the colonists. It is true that in the manoeuvering for land grants, British interests sometimes clashed with colonial interests, but we hear fully as much about clashes between different colonial groups. Both the small frontiersmen and the big speculators were charged more for land than they were accustomed to pay, but it was not as much as they were to be charged by the United States government thereafter. In the readjustments which accompanied the establishment of the new policies the fur traders of the Thirteen Colonies suffered somewhat because of the machinations of British opponents but their loss was not great, and in any event by the Revolutionary period trade in furs formed only a negligible fraction of the colonial economy.

The pre-Revolutionary taxation measures, however, are a different matter, and one for which British mercantilism must bear full responsibility. Yet in analysing the figures we find that the average annual revenue raised by the Sugar Acts, the Townshend Acts, and all the other taxes collected in the Thirteen Colonies by the British government amounted to only £31,000. This sum barely exceeded the indirect taxes which were collected on colonial merchandise passing through England. Moreover, both the taxes collected indirectly in England and directly in the colonies failed to equal the bounties which the British government was paying to the colonies—to say nothing of the advantages which they were deriving from preferential duties on their shipments to England. More interesting still, calculated on an annual per capita basis, the taxes collected during the Revolutionary period directly in the colonies and indirectly in England, totalled less than one-seventh of the taxes assessed at the beginning of the century.

Yet even though the amount of taxation was not great, we must consider the possibility that the form of its assessment detrimentally affected colonial interests. The Tea Act, for one, definitely injured the illicit trade in tea by so reducing the price of the legal article that it lessened, if it did not eliminate, the profit from smuggling. However unfair smugglers may have thought such tactics, they can hardly be said to have injured the economy of the country—especially since tea was not a pivotal commodity.

Molasses, the rum which was made from it, and the provision

trade which accompanied it, however, were vital factors in colonial economy, and historians have often called attention to their importance in such books as *Rum, Romance, and Rebellion*. The Sugar Act of 1764 served notice that the British government intended to make its regulations effective when it lowered the duty on foreign sugar and molasses and prohibited the importation of foreign rum entirely. The provisions concerning sugar and rum were comparatively immaterial since no great quantities were imported, but the duty of 3d. per gallon on molasses was another matter, since literally millions of gallons came from the foreign West Indies. Many feared that the trade could not bear a tax of 3d. per gallon, and in response to their pleas the duty was reduced in 1766 to 1d. per gallon and the tax was assessed on both British and foreign molasses. The excitement aroused by these taxes leads one to look for evidence of the havoc which they wrought in trade, but an examination of the wholesale prices of molasses does not disclose any noticeable change attributable to the legislation. And if we carry our investigations further we find that the tax which the federal government placed and kept upon imports of molasses after 1790 almost equaled the 3d. per gallon placed upon foreign molasses in 1764 and materially exceeded the 1d. duty retained after 1766. In brief, whatever the connection between rum and romance, the statistics of colonial trade disclose no correlation between rum and rebellion.

In so far as the statistics can be followed, the correlation between wine and rebellion is much closer. The Sugar Act of 1764 had also placed a duty upon wines which gave those imported by way of Britain a preferential rate of £3 per ton. The preference was not sufficient to enable the English to capture the trade in Madeira wine, but it enabled them to gain a flourishing trade in port which previously had been negligible. Yet such an infringement of colonial taste hardly seems to justify a revolt—especially when we note that the quantity involved was not large, and that by the post-Revolutionary period Americans preferred port and other wines to Madeira.

Thus, an analysis of the economic effects of British mercantilism fails to establish its exploitive aspects as the proximate cause of the Revolution. The only measures which afforded a sufficient economic grievance were the *entrepôt* provisions of the Navigation Acts, which governed the trans-Atlantic trade. They helped to create a fundamental economic unbalance, but cannot be connected directly with the Revolution. The colonists had lived under them for more than a century without desiring independence and even in the Revolutionary period with few exceptions the *entrepôt* provisions were accepted as the mother country's due for the protection which she afforded. In fact, the official representatives of the colonies were willing to guarantee the British commercial system provided that the measures of political taxation were withdrawn. If there were any inexorable economic forces which were inevitably drawing the colonies toward revolution, they are hard to detect and the colonists were unaware of them.

Anyone who maintains that the Revolution resulted from the inevitable clash of competing capitalisms must reckon with several points: That burdens upon the trans-Atlantic trade were proportionately greater at the beginning of the eighteenth century than in 1776; that the restraints of the land and currency policies were basically the same as those prescribed by the federal government; and that after 1766 the taxes laid on molasses by Britain were less than those imposed by the United States after 1790. He should also explain why the surplus colonial capital alleged to be bursting its confines did not venture into the manufacturing enterprises which the law did not prohibit; why the colonists did not finance their own middlemen in England; and, finally, why they did not pay their debts. If by a clash of expanding capitalism is meant that colonists with money were irritated because their freedom of action was restrained by outside regulation, one must immediately concede that the charge is justified; but such colonial resentment seems more properly classified as a political rather than an economic factor. It is merely an old point dressed in new garb and was better expressed by John Adams when he declared that the American Revolution began when the first plantation was settled.

When we turn, however, from the economic effects of mercantilism to its regulatory aspects, we are faced with a different story. We can establish a direct correlation between mercantilism and the Revolution. Although earlier English regulations had been reasonably satisfactory the regulatory technique of the British government under George III was pitifully defective. As a mother country, Britain had much to learn. Any modern parents' magazine could have told George III's ministers that the one mistake not to make is to take a stand and then to yield to howls of anguish. It was a mistake which the British government made repeatedly. It placed a duty of 3d. per gallon on molasses, and when it encountered opposition, reduced it to 1d. It provided for a Stamp Act and withdrew it in the face of temper tantrums. It provided for external taxes to meet the colonial objections and then yielded again by removing all except one. When finally it attempted to enforce discipline it was too late. Under the circumstances, no self-respecting child—or colonist—would be willing to yield.

Moreover, British reforming zeal came at a very bad time. The colonists were in a particularly sensitive state due to the post-war deflation and the economic distress which accompanied it. The British also attempted to exert unusual control at a time when the removal of the French from Canada had minimized the colonists' dependence upon Britain. Most important of all, the reforms followed one another too rapidly.

In social reform, irritation often is to be measured not so much by what a regulation attempts to achieve as by the extent to which it changes established habits. The early history of English mercantilism itself offers a good illustration of the point. Bitter complaints came from Virginia and Barbados when tobacco and sugar were first enumerated because those colonies had become accustomed to conditions of comparatively free trade, whereas few or no complaints were heard from Jamaica which had developed under the restrictive system. The mercantilist system was geared for leisurely operation and before George III's reign succeeded by virtue of that fact. Its early restraints led to Bacon's rebellion in Virginia but fortunately for the mother country the pressure against New England was deferred until the next decade when it, too, led to an explosion in the form of revolt against Andros. These uprisings were separated both geographically and chronologically so that neither attained dangerous proportions, and both were followed by a reasonably satisfactory settlement of at least some of the colonial grievances.

During the Revolutionary era, however, the tempo of reform was not leisurely. Doubtless all the colonists were not irritated by any one British reform, but each individual had his own feeling of grievance which enabled him to agree fervently with the complaints of others against British policy and thus add to the heated tempers of the time. The politician who objected to the political implications in taxation reforms found an audience in the land speculators and frontiersmen who complained that the colonists were being deprived of the reward of their blood and suffering by the Proclamation of 1763 and the

Quebec Act of 1774. Debtors and inflationists chimed in to tell of the iniquities of the Currency Act; lawyers and printers could not forget the threat to their interests in the Stamp Act. On Sundays the preachers thundered against the dangers of popery in Quebec and voiced their fear that Britain planned to establish an Anglican Church in the colonies. The merchant was always ready to explain not merely how harmful British taxes were to colonial economy, but how irksome were the new administrative rules and regulations. Such chronological and geographical barriers as existed were overcome and a community of antagonisms was maintained by the Committees of Correspondence and other agitators, but such revolutionary forces could not have succeeded if the different elements of the colonies had not recently experienced a mutual sense of grievance.

In short, many of the misunderstandings which have arisen in connection with mercantilism and the American Revolution have grown out of the failure to distinguish between the two phases of mercantilism: exploitation and regulation. The fact that the colonists were exploited by English mercantilism does not necessarily mean that mercantilism caused the American Revolution. Economic forces are not magnets which inexorably move men in predetermined patterns. For better or for worse, men try to regulate their economic as well as their political destiny. A large part of governmental activity consists in attempting to mould economic conduct and to minimize the friction which results from clashes or constraints. English mercantilism was such an attempt. It succeeded rather well in minimizing friction until 1764. For the next decade it bungled badly, and the penalty was the loss of the Thirteen Colonies.

X

The Emergence of Prussia and Russia

❯❯❯-❯❯❯-❯❯❯-❯❯❯-❯❯❯-❯❯❯-❯❯❯-❯❯❯-❯❯❮❮❮-❮❮❮-❮❮❮-❮❮❮-❮❮❮-❮❮❮-❮❮❮-❮❮❮

The Prussian Bureaucracy in the Eighteenth Century

WALTER L. DORN

Peter the Great

B. H. SUMNER

Some Forerunners of the Decembrists

D. M. LANG

❯❯❯-❯❯❯-❯❯❯-❯❯❯-❯❯❯-❯❯❯-❯❯❯-❯❯❯-❯❯❮❮❮-❮❮❮-❮❮❮-❮❮❮-❮❮❮-❮❮❮-❮❮❮-❮❮❮

The Prussian Bureaucracy in the Eighteenth Century

WALTER L. DORN

Published in 1931-1932

Most treatments of the history of Brandenburg in the late seventeenth century and of Brandenburg-Prussia in the eighteenth century are based on a "great man" approach to the past. There is, of course, much to be said in favor of such an approach in the case of Brandenburg-Prussia. In view of the very limited natural resources of the area and the limited taxpaying ability of its population, great power status for Prussia could be created only artificially. Much depended, in short, on the attitudes and policies of such rulers as the Great Elector (1640-1688), Frederick William I (1713-1740), and Frederick the Great (1740-1786). It is unfortunate, nevertheless, that the "great man" approach has often obscured the potentialities of an institutional approach to the development of Brandenburg-Prussia. After all, such institutions as the army and the bureaucracy did much to make possible the recognition that Prussia received as a great power in the eighteenth century. Fortunately, Walter Dorn, of Ohio State University—author of *Competition for Empire,* one of the best volumes in "The Rise of Modern Europe" series—has attempted to deal with Prussian history from the institutional standpoint. The selection that follows consists of the first and third of a series of three articles that Professor Dorn published in the *Political Science Quarterly.*

The uniqueness, the extraordinary strength but also the weakness, of modern Prussia lay in the fusion of the economic and military power of its nobility with the order, system and efficiency of its bureaucracy. The combination of these two basic elements of the

Reprinted by special permission from *Political Science Quarterly,* XLVI (1931), 403-423; XLVII (1932), 259-273. The extensive documentation which originally appeared with this essay has been omitted.

Prussian state warded off the rising tide of the strongest currents of nineteenth-century liberal thought and ceased to be a decisive factor in Prussian politics only with the Revolution of 1918. Whatever judgment one may eventually pass on the Prussian army as an instrument of social organization and discipline, no one conversant with the evolution of modern Prussia can fail to see that the Prussian bureaucracy was for many decades the most creative force in Prussian history. Established in the first quarter of the eighteenth century by Frederick William I, under Stein and Hardenberg this bureaucracy not merely reformed itself but adapted the Prussian state to the conditions of modern life, and in the first half of the nineteenth century played a leading rôle in Prussian politics.

At no time, however, in the entire course of its history did it perform services of greater importance for the future of the Prussian monarchy than in the second half of the reign of Frederick the Great. Under the guidance and inspiration of this enlightened autocrat, the Prussian bureaucracy contrived to produce, on the economic resources of what was then the least prosperous section of Germany, a public revenue which was greater than that of Russia on the accession of Catherine II, with a *per capita* burden of taxation no greater than that of Austria and considerably less than that of France. It managed to support the army of a first-rate power on the resources of a third-rate state and at the same time accumulated a large reserve in the public treasury; it opened up the mining industry in Silesia and in the Ruhr district; it carried through a project for extensive internal colonization in urban and rural districts which added upwards of 300,000 inhabitants to the sparsely populated provinces of Prussia, thus making in 1786 every fifth inhabitant a colonist; it did much to introduce the improved British agricultural methods among the backward Prussian peasantry; it liberalized the craft guilds and adapted them to the needs of capitalistic industry while it endeavored to execute, and not altogether without success, a comprehensive plan to industrialize an almost wholly agricultural country. While in Great Britain, Hanover and Saxony the civil service was still controlled by the system of official patronage, Prussia was remarkably free from it; nor was it possible here to purchase or inherit an office as in France. After 1770 and even before, no Prussian official was appointed to office without having undergone a special training and passed several examinations. Prussian civil servants were neither very numerous nor were they handsomely paid, for to *travailler pour le roi de Prusse* [to work for the king of Prussia] had become the byword of Europe.

The intense pressure and severe discipline under which the Prussian bureaucracy labored is comprehensible only as a natural reaction against the intense pressure that arose from the insecure and precarious position of Prussia among the Powers of Europe. Without his army the rôle of the Prussian monarch in the international politics of Europe would have been utterly negligible. To support the growing financial needs of this army was the pivotal function of the Prussian bureaucracy. All improvements in administrative methods and the wider scope and greater intensity of bureaucratic activity were made to serve the supreme end of producing a maximum public revenue. In the process this bureaucracy became a remarkably effective administrative instrument, if one which, with the progress of the century, it became steadily more difficult to manipulate from a common center. The Prussian bureaucracy of the eighteenth century was not without glaring defects, but whatever its shortcomings, it was superior, *mutatis mutandis*, to the German bureaucracy of our own day; indeed, it may be said that, whereas in post-war Germany the larger private business corporations possess a more highly rationalized and economical bureaucratic organization as compared with the German state, in eighteenth-century Prussia the situation was reversed. The civil servant of Frederick II was still capable of instructing the Prussian merchant in more efficient methods of accounting, just as he was more active in searching for markets than the manufacturer himself.

In its architectonic structure the Prussian bureaucracy possessed certain peculiarities not found in the more familiar French system. In the French bureaucracy the modern monocratic official, the ministerial *chef de bureau* in Paris and the *intendant* in the provinces, predominated in all branches of the administration, while in Prussia all administrative activity was gathered in boards or "colleges," as

---

AUFKLÄRUNG: German word for the eighteenth-century Enlightenment, or Age of Reason. Some of its main literary spokesmen were Frederick the Great, Lessing, Moses Mendelssohn, and Wieland.

POTSDAM: Town near Berlin where the Hohenzollerns resided; Prussian equivalent of Versailles. It became the symbol of militarism and repression in contrast to Weimar, the symbol of sweetness, light, and the humane spirit.

they were called, which subjected the individual civil servant to group discipline and collective responsibility. Not only were there no Prussian equivalents for the French ministries in 1740, but the four members of the supreme Prussian administrative body, the General Directory, exercised identical functions in different provinces in such a manner that each was dependent upon the other three for decisions even in his own department. In provincial affairs the French *intendants* had their Prussian counterpart in the seventeen provincial chambers (*Kriegs-und Domänen-Kammern*), where the principle of group solidarity was observed with even greater consistency than in the General Directory. In this Prussian bureaucratic mechanism authority was more effectively centralized than even in France, just as there was a greater uniformity in the application of administrative maxims, partly because of the incessant personal intervention of the Prussian monarch in all branches of the administration, partly because the organization of the Prussian civil service into collective boards made supervision and control from above at once more difficult and more necessary. Not only did these provincial chambers exercise less discretionary authority than the French *intendants*, but they were bound by elaborate written instructions which embraced the entire range of their activities and provided an invariable rule for every administrative act. Doubtless, the French bureaucracy offered freer play for personal capacity and initiative, as can be seen by recalling the careers of such reforming *intendants* as Le Pelletier de Beaupré, Aubert de Tourny, Turgot and Trudaine. In Prussia, however, where feudal forces continued more vital and where consequently it was more necessary to combat the feudal conception of office, administration was systematically calculated to eliminate all personal influence whatever, first by fettering the individual civil servant to a collective board, then by subjecting both to bureaucratic regulations of imperative and canonical authority. The Prussian bureaucracy was dominated

---

RÉGIE: French financial institution introduced into Prussia by Frederick the Great in the period following the economically exhausting Seven Years' War. Its function was to supervise the collection of the excise tax in all the provinces of the Prussian kingdom. Its officials were responsible only to the crown.

less by personalities than by the *règlement*. Of the two bureaucratic systems the French was technically sounder, although the Prussian bureaucracy was not less efficient and perhaps more active.

The greater uniformity of bureaucratic procedure and administrative maxims characteristic of the Prussian system was admirably suited to the undifferentiated feudal and agrarian society of the heart of Prussia, east of the Elbe river. It harmonized but poorly with the free industrial communities of the Rhenish provinces, where Prussian bureaucrats were perpetually at daggers' points with the native population. It was in the region east of the Elbe that this bureaucratic hierarchy with its General Directory, provincial chambers, local commissaries (*Steuerräte*), and municipal magistrates became the veritable *ecclesia militans* of the Prussian monarchy, amalgamating heterogeneous provinces into a compact unit and disciplining the people to the needs of a Spartan military state. In a profounder sense than was true of the army, the Prussian bureaucracy served as the loadstone which attracted and absorbed into the service of the monarchy the most industrious and intelligent section of the population, thus binding their interests closely to those of the state. Like another Society of Jesus, here was an organization in which military discipline, absolute subordination, and centralization were complete. Prussian municipal magistrates could neither adopt a budget nor lodge a complaint without the consent of the local commissary, and he, not equipped with independent competence, reported all matters to the provincial chamber, which body, having made a preliminary decision, finally referred the matter to the General Directory. But this complicated meshwork of boards and individual officials had the supreme function of collecting data, correlating facts, drawing up balances of trade or contracts for leasing the royal domains, preparing budgets and drafting statistical reports, in other words of supplying the autocratic king, the highest civil servant and only real man of action in the realm, with the indispensable information on which to base his decisions.

Never did absolute monarchs take their autocracy more seriously than the Hohenzollerns of the eighteenth century. Mirabeau could truthfully say that the Prussian government had become for the science of despotism what Egypt was to the ancients in search of knowledge. Prussia was and remained the classic country of monarchical autocracy. Any study of the Prussian bureaucracy as an operating concern must begin with the central bureau or "cabinet," as it was curiously called, of the Prussian king.

I

Prussian administration in the eighteenth century was rooted in the fiction that the king knows everything, that he can do everything and does everything that is done. From Frederick William I onward all matters which were decreed by the higher administrative bodies appeared in the form of royal orders issued by the king in person. The artisan to whom the royal guild statue was a solemn guarantee of his economic security; the peasant who received a marriage license; the merchant entrepreneur who was exempted from the payment of duty on importing a specified article, all of them received their privileges from the king. When on Sunday the village pastor read a patent or an ordinance from the pulpit, it was the king who addressed the assembled congregation, even when the document in question had been issued only by a subaltern authority. This fiction was not merely an administrative device which had taken possession of the popular imagination. Frequently it was no fiction at all. For the bitter quarrel with the obstructionist feudal estates of the numerous provinces of the kingdom had forced on the Prussian monarchs the settled conviction that Prussia could thrive only under an autocracy, that only a king who in person attended to diplomacy, military affairs, finance and current administration could effectually concentrate all the resources of his kingdom and apply them at the point where they were most urgently needed. Frederick the Great was convinced that the large independence of the French ministries was wholly unsuited to Prussia, for under a monarch like Louis XV it inevitably resulted in "lack of system, because each minister possessed a system of his own." He was convinced that the Prussian king, to be able to construct and follow a rational system of politics, must be the actual head of all the departments of the government. It was quite in keeping with this principle that in Prussia administrative tasks were allotted to the various departments in such a manner that the king was literally the only person in the kingdom whose purview embraced the entire field of administration, domestic, military and foreign. The system was so conceived that the king alone came into daily and intimate contact with all the branches of administration. The full burden of coördination, therefore, could not possibly fall into any other hands save his own. Even in purely domestic affairs the General Directory, with entire provinces and departments withdrawn from its jurisdiction, could not serve as an adequate modern central coördinating body. No one but the king possessed complete information of the total public revenues of the kingdom. But this was equally true of other branches of the administration. It is obvious that under these circumstances Prussian ministers could not become, as was the case in France, vehicles of opinions and programs, but must content themselves with the more modest functions of royal clerks who attended to such administrative bagatelles as the king chose to surrender to them. Autocracy could not have been carried to a greater extreme.

Unlike the French king, the Prussian monarch did not make his decisions in the council chamber in the presence of his assembled ministers. As a matter of fact the Prussian king rarely saw his ministers. Apart from the annual "review of ministers," usually held in the middle of June, at which the king met his ministers to approve the budgets and to discuss with each one the affairs of his department, the king saw them perhaps once or twice a year. He remained in Potsdam, immured in his royal chambers, while his ministers labored in Berlin, and no official, not even a minister, ventured to appear at the royal palace without a written leave of the monarch. All transactions were negotiated in writing. They sent him their reports, memorials and requests, and the king replied by means of cabinet orders. It would have been difficult to improve on the order and regularity that prevailed in the royal cabinet. Every evening when the courier from Berlin arrived, five secretaries arranged the letters according to the nature of the business and placed each group into a sealed portfolio to be laid before the king early in the morning. One of these secretaries, Mencken, has left us a description of Frederick the Great at work in his cabinet:

> He began his work early in the morning with foreign affairs; he had already read the deciphered dispatches of his ambassadors and now he dictated to his secretary an answer to every dispatch, whether important or not, from the first letter to the last, often several pages. Thereupon he dictated to another secretary answers to all letters on domestic affairs, to reports of the chambers on accounting and finance, and to the reports of the military inspectors on the army. Some of these he had already decreed by marginal notes. While this was being done,

another secretary prepared a brief extract of all less important letters and petitions from private persons. This was then placed before the king who decreed each item in a few words.

This done, the secretaries retired to write out the orders in full. Late in the afternoon these completed cabinet orders were once more brought to the king for examination and signature. They were always brief, pointed, stripped of superfluous verbiage, quite unlike the unctuous verbosity of the documents which officials sent to the king.

The chief merit of this system was its rapidity. All matters were dispatched forthwith, if circumstances did not require a special investigation. Since everything was done by letter and the king's mind worked with extraordinary speed, there was no reason for delay. It should be remembered that the military order and precision of the king's life in Potsdam was conducive to hard work, that he had with him neither wife nor family, that there was neither court nor French court etiquette, that he never observed a religious holiday and never was distracted by undesired interruptions. There was something like puritanical zeal in his unremitting application to work. His secretaries and ministers testify to the tyrannical discipline which he exercised over his mind and body. With punctilious regularity he disposed of everything as soon as it came to him, sometimes issuing as many as thirty or forty cabinet orders on a single day, and rarely did he postpone any matter from one day to another. Nowhere in the entire Prussian bureaucratic system was there such impeccable order as in the cabinet of the king. Just as each hour of the day, each week and month, so the entire year was arranged in such a manner that no business crowded on the heels of another. A calendar on his table indicated not only the duties of each day and week, but informed him when all outstanding reports, replies, and other matters fell due. Even when in May, June and August of every year the monarch regularly embarked on his inspection journeys through the provinces his secretaries and correspondence accompanied him. Any official who addressed himself to the king could expect an immediate answer. He could even calculate, according to his distance from the royal residence and the time required by the post, the very day when he was to receive his answer. If he did not receive his answer then, none would be forthcoming at all.

This extreme concentration of administrative leadership and control required not only a monarch of great capacity for work, but a man of large intellect and good judgment, for the slightest relaxation or error at the center was sufficient to drive legislation and initiative imperceptibly into the bureaucracy. To be sure, Frederick II was one of those rare persons who are always equal in capacity if not in temper. He was the essence of practicality and good sense. He knew his kingdom as an open page. Yet it was impossible for even so industrious a man as Frederick II to read all the lengthy reports and documents which accumulated in his cabinet. He was compelled to order his ministers to send reports of no more than two folio pages, stating briefly the reasons pro and con. At the beginning of every document sent to the royal cabinet there was a succinct summary of the matter dealt with to serve as a means of rapid orientation. The king was forever threatening officials with disgrace and dismissal if their reports were not drawn up with the utmost brevity, an insistence which had the result that the official might daily spend hours of futile labor in the aggregate not on what action he must take—that was probably simple enough—but on what phraseology would pass the barrage of royal criticism. These reports which came to him from all administrative authorities were not always intelligible to him. He frequently found it necessary to order his civil servants never to employ a Latin or German bureaucratic jargon which he did not understand. But these were minor difficulties easily simplified by ingenious devices in which every bureaucracy is fertile. The basic difficulty of the system was of another sort.

The main anxiety of the Prussian monarch must be to maintain his autocracy in the face of enormous difficulties which came from crowding affairs of such variety and complexity into his cabinet, affairs which often required a thorough investigation and an expert technical knowledge of detail. If under the modern democratic system a bureaucracy with its special training, expert knowledge, and continuous professional experience often exercises a decisive influence on legislation, even in matters of finance, in spite of parliaments and legislatures, its influence was no less subtle and strong even under an exceptionally intelligent and active king such as Frederick the Great, not to say a king who had a conscience in the matter of attending in person to the entire range of administrative problems. While the king resolutely insisted that all impulses must proceed from him alone, he incessantly dealt with officials whose specialized functions and mastery of every detail in their circumscribed field gave them much the same advantage over the king which the modern expert has over the dilettante legislator. The king's withdrawal from personal contact with his officials to the secrecy of his royal cabinet, where he was at leisure to make his decisions alone, was no real solution of the problem. The escape from the person of the expert made the monarch all the more dependent on the documents which the latter sent him.

Instinct and reason might have convinced another man that the system required a degree of autocracy which was impossible, yet Frederick II was inflexible on the principle that neither his ministers, nor the General Directory, nor the provincial chambers could be allowed any initiative as independent administrative bodies. He wrote to the provincial chamber of Breslau in 1783, "You have no right of initiative whatever. All matters must be reported to me directly. The General Directory must do so likewise." After the Seven Years' War the volume of public business swelled to such unprecedented proportions that no single person, however industrious, could inspire and control all measures which were necessary, but the king still firmly held to the principle of exclusive royal initiative and control.

Frederick II was shrewd enough to realize that his bureaucracy was not an impersonal machine which could be manipulated by a capricious master, but a body of men with opinions, passions and habits hardened by routine, a body over which he could maintain his ascendency only by the severest military discipline. To retain that ascendency he assumed the studied pose of infallibility. As a matter of principle he never revoked an order and never openly admitted an error. Frederick managed his bureaucracy in the spirit of the general who places obedience above wisdom. If serious mistakes did occur, he was convinced that the continuity of uniform measures would soon remedy the harm caused by such intermittent errors. Without prompt and obedient response to royal orders the king's autocracy must become illusory. When Frederick suspected a minister of dissent, he brusquely declined all the latter's recommendations, even though he might later advance them as his own. To criticize the king's measures openly was to court disaster. The unhappy Ursinus, one of the most brilliant officials in the General Directory, paid heavily for some mildly critical observations on the king's commercial policy by being condemned to push the wheelbarrow in the Spandau prison. It was inevitable that a king so jealous of his authority should sometimes give instructions to his ministers on matters concerning which he should have listened to them. Wöllner, not always the most enlightened critic of Frederick II, is correct in stating that Frederick frequently gave orders on matters of detail on which it was impossible for him to be thoroughly informed. On such occasions the king might suspect the incompleteness of his information, but he was convinced that the ignorance of others was greater. This royal intervention in technical matters not infrequently disturbed the orderly process of administration, for which officials were nevertheless held responsible.

Against such disturbing interference the only effective weapon was to resort to concealment or even to deception, of course always within the prudent limits of safety. Ministers practised it and the General Directory also on occasion had recourse to it. Minister von Schulenburg, who in his memoirs avers that it was useless to attempt to conceal anything from the king because sooner or later he discovered almost everything, was himself a past master in the art of concealing matters which might provoke a confusing cabinet order if the king were informed of them. When this same Schulenburg was appointed president of the provincial chamber of Magdeburg in 1770 he began to report faithfully the precise quantities of grain which were exported from this province each month. He promptly received from the General Directory the advice that henceforth he would do better to choose more adroitly the materials upon which he reported to the king, for the latter was inclined to be too hasty in prohibiting the exportation of grain entirely, much to the harm of the province. But there were instances of systematic deception which could not be justified on the ground of uninformed royal intervention. Officials sometimes resorted to it when they encountered insuperable practical difficulties, to report which would only provoke a storm of royal criticism of their incompetence.

The most notorious offender in this glib and oily art, the man who deceived the king more than any other, was the Silesian minister Hoym, of whom Frederick II once said that he was really the only official who fully understood the Prussian monarch. This nimble-witted minister understood not only how to omit from his reports items which he knew to be unpleasant to the king but did not scruple to falsify facts. He added 20,000 to a Silesian population report because he knew that Frederick liked high population figures. In spite of the king's express orders to settle only foreign colonists in Silesia

Hoym permitted his underlings to use native Prussian inhabitants for this purpose, insisting only that the colonists along the principal road over which the king ordinarily traveled on his inspection journeys must be foreigners. Under Hoym's régime in Silesia an incident occurred which is without parallel in the history of the Prussian bureaucracy in the eighteenth century. It was one of the central features of Frederick's agrarian policy to secure for Silesian peasants hereditary tenures of their holdings. The energetic Schlabrendorff, Hoym's predecessor in Silesia, had caused much bad blood among Silesian nobles in a vain effort to carry out this measure. No sooner had Hoym assumed control of Silesian affairs than all trouble suddenly ceased. He announced that now serfs held secure hereditary tenures and that the matter was permanently settled. But in 1785 a special commission sent to upper Silesia reported to the king that almost nowhere did serfs possess hereditary titles to their holdings. To satisfy the angry king Hoym was compelled to exhibit the strongest indignation, for suddenly it became apparent that the reports of the rural commissioners (*Landräte*) had deceitfully misrepresented the facts for years; that, while the orders of the king had been executed on paper, things in reality remained as before. And this was the province where administration proceeded as smoothly, as Frederick said, as a piece of music. Indeed, Hoym understood the king only too well.

This silent contest between the monarch and his bureaucracy thus took on different aspects. Sometimes it was the result of official inertia and reluctance to deviate from the established bureaucratic routine; sometimes it was prompted by an effort to forestall or render harmless confusing orders which issued from the cabinet of the king; again it might be the result of an official propensity to interpret royal orders generously enough to suit either the circumstances or bureaucratic convenience. Rarely was it the result of actual corruption. This contest never developed into open bureaucratic opposition, and on the single occasion when consistent opposition was secretly attempted, the king discovered and scotched it at once. But the contest was none the less real and involved more or less the entire bureaucratic hierarchy. It was even rumored that in the persons of the king's private secretaries it entered into the royal cabinet itself. Contemporaries had an overwhelming sense of the influence and importance of these men. Living constantly at the center of affairs, they were informed on everything that happened. They frequently had access to information which never reached the king himself. A shrewd secretary who worked with the king day after day for decades and knew all the latter's limitations and behavior patterns, could, on occasion, place the facts before his master in such a manner as to influence his decision; he could, to be sure at some risk, withhold a letter entirely or delay informing the king of it until he could take advantage of a propitious moment; he could in writing out a cabinet order which the king had turned over to him for expedition either moderate its language or give it a deadly edge. We find these secretaries corresponding freely with ministers and other officials, offering them good counsel on drawing up documents and approaching the king with proper caution. Ministers in turn sought their favor with a cautious solicitude and often requested them to suggest to the king matters which they did not venture to propose themselves. It is quite probable that now and then their intervention thwarted the intentions of the king. But to do so consistently without discovery was impossible. In his long reign Frederick the Great punished but a single secretary because of irregularities on the nature of which we are not accurately informed.

To imagine that Frederick was oblivious to these tendencies in his bureaucracy would be both to mistake his suspicious nature and to underrate his active intelligence. He cherished the inveterate belief that his officials were bent on deceiving him, deceiving him often, as he once admitted, with the best intentions. He inherited this distrust from his Hohenzollern ancestors. The Great Elector had already written in his political testament, "The more civil servants, the more thieves." With Frederick II, however, this distrust became an integral part of the bureaucratic system. Unreserved confidence he reposed in none of his ministers. He kept them in a perpetual state of uncertainty as to what he thought of their honesty and capacity, and one could easily duplicate the instance of the minister who received a letter from the king in fear and trembling expecting his immediate dismissal but received instead the Order of the Black Eagle. It was especially subordinate officials whom he regarded with ineradicable distrust. He once wrote to the provincial chamber of West Prussia that among a hundred officials you could always hang ninety-nine with a good conscience, for if a single official was honest it was much. He spent much time and thought on devising adequate guarantees for the accuracy of reports and reliability in the faithful execution of his orders. Some measure of guarantee he found in the annual journeys through his kingdom which he undertook with great regularity from May until August of each year. During these months he proceeded from province to province, examining officials and interviewing private citizens, personally inspecting public enterprises and inquiring into the condition of the peasants, and consulting with burgomasters, merchants and manufacturers. In this way he attempted to make himself in some sense independent of written reports and control in person the execution of his orders. So imbued was he with the necessity of these journeys that he commended them to his successor as an indispensable means of controlling his officials.

Yet all this did not alter the fact that he was chiefly dependent on written reports and that attempts to control the bureaucracy must proceed from the royal cabinet itself. To prevent bureaucratic hoodwinking the king employed a number of safeguards. He frequently struck upon the expedient of committing the task of reporting on any particular piece of business to two or three different officials none of whom was aware that others were engaged in the same mission. When he did not wholly trust an official he charged an underling with secret supervision. To control his ministers, he regularly corresponded with the presidents of the provincial chambers, and to assure himself of the veracity of the latter he often dealt with the individual members of the provincial chambers. By this continuous correspondence with officials and their subordinates, by controlling ministers through their subalterns and subordinates through their equals, the king tapped extraordinary sources of information which, besides the ordinary channels of information to be discussed presently, acquainted him with everything he seriously desired to know. Now and then shady facts might be cloaked by an impenetrable smoke screen of bureaucratic verbosity. Now and then the king might even become the unconscious dupe of his bureaucracy. But the fact remains that sooner or later the king discovered almost everything.

*   *   *   *   *

IV

The ultimate test of any system of administration is its management and control of finance. It is the financial engine that drives the state along and all other particulars of good government profit a state little unless its system of public finance is well designed. The success of the Prussian monarchy in the eighteenth century must finally be explained in terms of its financial history. Edmund Burke was profoundly impressed with the excellence of the Prussian financial system and admonished the British Parliament to emulate the example of Prussia. We are concerned here not so much with Prussian financial policy as with its bureaucratic control of public finance. Unlike France, which before 1789 could maintain no adequate system of budgetary control because the accounts of past years were not closed off, Prussia under Frederick II developed an effective centralized scheme for the control of public budgets and of its central and local treasuries. It was a capital offense for a provincial chamber to exceed its budgetary allowance in making expenditures or fail to collect its full quota of public revenues or present to the king a sloppy account that was not perspicuous at a glance.

The Supreme Chamber of Accounts (*Ober-Rechnungs-Kammer*) which examined the accounts of the entire kingdom was, like all other Prussian administrative organs, a collective body and attached to the General Directory. This body was composed of experienced financial experts who had served for some years in the provincial chambers. They examined all accounts above one *thaler* in the entire kingdom including those of the *Régie* and government monopolies, in short of all the receivers and spenders of public money down to the municipal magistrates. At the same time they played the rôle of modern efficiency experts in that they suggested to the king ways and means to increase revenues and reduce public expenditures. They were well paid, could accept no gifts or perquisites, and were under oath to accept no accounts not properly authorized.

All accounts in the entire kingdom were due in the Supreme Chamber of Accounts one month or, as in the case of the remoter provinces, six weeks after the close of the financial year. The heavy penalty of a fine of five *thalers* was exacted for every account overdue. Even if small sums were still in arrears the account must be closed at the end of the financial year and sent to the Chamber of Accounts on the appointed time. For every error detected in the accounts sent to them the members of this chamber received from four to twelve *groschen* to be paid by the offending official. Whatever might be said of the ethics of augmenting the salaries of one group of officials at the expense of all the rest, it gave a sharp edge to the alertness of the accountants who desire to make their occupation as profitable as possible. These men corresponded with every collecting and spending official until every feature of the account in question had been satisfactorily explained. They proceeded on the modern assumption that everything could and must be accounted for unless it were either a mistake or an instance of corruption. It was their particular duty to ferret out unauthorized expenditures not provided for in the regular budgets of the provincial chambers. To make this financial control doubly effective the Chamber periodically examined local treasuries and sent the king a list of all delinquent officials. Every official could be certain that sooner or later his defective account would be reported to the king, who might content himself with a verbal reprimand or appoint a special investigating commission or, after the third offense, dismiss the guilty official without more ado. As a protection against corruption and embezzlement the Prussian king required a *Kautionsgeld* or security deposit from every treasury official before he was appointed to office. No treasury official was permitted to accumulate in his treasury more fluid funds than the amount of the security deposit he had placed with the state. His superiors were held responsible for seeing that the money in his treasury never exceeded that amount. In this way responsibility for treasury deficiencies could always be traced to some point in the mechanism. Although instances of official dishonesty were not wanting, a prolonged and systematic plunder of public treasuries was impossible.

V

Notwithstanding the formidable paternalism of the Prussian state in which scarcely a phase of public or private life escaped regulation, the number of Prussian officials was surprisingly small. In the entire kingdom there were no more than 14,000 officials of every category. While in the France of the old régime the persistent popular complaint was that there were too many officials, in Prussia it was that there were not enough. The Prussian king could not afford to employ any superfluous officials. Although the number of provisional chambers increased with the territorial expansion of the monarchy, the king kept these bodies to an irreducible minimum.

The energetic early French monarchs had scored their most brilliant triumphs over the independent jurisdiction of the nobility and the church by appointing bourgeois jurists to all important administrative

374 THE EMERGENCE OF PRUSSIA AND RUSSIA

posts. This alliance between the French crown and bourgeois jurists created the bed-rock foundation of French absolutism and administrative centralization. For a space it appeared as though the most far-sighted Prussian rulers would follow in their footsteps. In their long and bitter struggle against the political and juridical feudalism of the Prussian nobility the Great Elector and Frederick William I had drawn heavily, though not exclusively, on the bourgeois class. Frederick William I, the most bourgeois of the whole line of Prussian kings, was intensely suspicious of noble officials because of their tendency to consider themselves as the representatives not so much of the state as of those feudal interests with which the king was engaged in a struggle to the knife. He grimly derided the nobility when he made his court jester Gundling a noble *Freiherr*. Not that nobles were not represented in the bureaucracy of Frederick William I, but they were not the preponderant element. For every two nobles appointed to the provincial chambers the king added two officials of bourgeois origin to hold the balance between the classes.

Under Frederick the Great, however, there was a sharp change in favor of the nobility. The Prussian crown had stripped its nobility of the last remnants of political power in the provinces. Further triumphs would have reduced Prussian nobles to economic ruin and uprooted them from the soil as completely as was the case with the nobility of France. But in a military state such as Prussia, where the nobility was the backbone of the army, this would have been an irreparable calamity. The Prussian nobility was not like the British aristocracy a wealthy class. The Prussian junkers east of the Elbe were essentially a class of farmers whose principal occupation was to manage their estates, to organize and employ as agricultural laborers the peasant subjects who lived on their lands. They were the organs of local government through whom the king dealt with the serfs. The noble landowner was responsible for the trial of peasant criminals, he pledged the collection of taxes, and supplied from among the peasants of his estate the recruits for the army. He was the local official of the king in much the same way as the British justice of the peace. Unlike the nobles of western and southern Germany who lived exclusively from the ground rents which they drew from their serfs, the Prussian nobles possessed a considerable business and governing experience. Yet the estates of large numbers of them were not extensive enough to guarantee them an existence of assured economic independence. In a random list of 1700 nobles of the

Electoral Mark and Pomerania we find 1300 who were forced to eke out their incomes by some form of public employment. Even in Silesia, the wealthiest province of the Prussian monarchy, 2700 out of a total of 8000 nobles found it necessary to seek public employment either because their estates were too small or because, having no estates, public service was their only means of livelihood. Frederick the Great therefore admitted them to the civil service in greater numbers. But there was another reason for Frederick's predilection for the nobility. Himself an aristocrat to the bone, he was convinced of their superior moral fiber and character, their greater capacity to command and obey as compared with the timorous and often pusillanimous Prussian middle classes, who were still small in numbers and poor in spirit. Thus there came into existence that peculiar class of noble bureaucrats who from generation to generation gravitated to similar branches of public service and sent their children to be trained in the same careers.

Not only were all ministerial posts, with but few exceptions, and the leading offices in the provincial chambers reserved for the nobility alone, but nobles began by imperceptible degrees to multiply in the rank and file of the Prussian bureaucracy. It has been estimated that among 108 understudies who entered the Silesian chambers, between 1742 and 1806, some 70 were of noble and 38 of bourgeois extraction. Among these understudies most of the nobles were appointed to permanent positions after an apprenticeship of four or five years while the bourgeois had to ascend the arduous ladder of several subaltern offices before they achieved the same object and then only after a lapse of fifteen or twenty years. Thus the young bourgeois official suddenly awoke to the fact that the stone walls in which he was immured were literally his sarcophagus in which the flesh of numbers of his fellows had actually been devoured for years under the relentless grind of the same monotonous duties without much chance of advancement. But the predominance of the nobility in the other provinces was not so marked as in Silesia. In the important provincial chambers of the Mark Brandenburg, Magdeburg and Pomerania noble and bourgeois elements faced each other in nearly equal proportions. It cannot be said that Frederick II was blindly prejudiced against officials of bourgeois origin. For positions where technical knowledge was more valuable than the dignified carriage of the noble, Frederick did not hesitate to choose a man from the middle classes. Sometimes bourgeois rose to ministerial posts. Some of the ablest presidents of provincial

chambers—Lentz, Colomb, Domhardt, Puttkammer—were *roturiers*.
Yet these men had to atone for this lack of noble extraction by a re-
doubled zeal and abilities of unquestioned superiority. All this did
not alter the fact that noble birth was considered requisite for high
office in the Prussian bureaucracy and that, although nobles and
bourgeois might balance each other numerically in some provincial
chambers, preponderance of influence, authority, and often of numbers
lay with the nobility.

This ascendancy of the nobility in the Prussian bureaucracy had
its effects upon the larger aspects of Prussian administration in the
eighteenth century. The sharply marked anti-feudal tendency of the
administration of Frederick William I came to a sudden halt. All
further progress in recasting the social and political institutions of
Prussia could be effected only at the expense of the economic and social
privileges of the nobility. But the more pronounced the influence of the
nobility in the Prussian bureaucracy became in the course of the century, the more did the provincial chambers abate their zeal for social
and economic reform. With nobles everywhere in possession of leading
positions it was they who set the pace, and bourgeois officials, learned
but wanting social prestige, humbly followed their leading. It might
be argued with some plausibility that in a bureaucratic system which
dealt so largely with purely agrarian problems there was some reason
for appointing as leading officials representatives of the land-owning and
farming Prussian nobility. In this matter the superiority of noble
over bourgeois officials was unchallenged, and it cannot be denied that
they gave a new vitality to Prussian economic feudalism at a time
when feudal institutions in Western Europe had long been superannuated. On the other hand it is equally true that they sometimes
thwarted or even sabotaged Frederick's efforts at enlightened social reform. They opposed his attempt to emancipate Prussian serfs and to
improve their titles to their holdings. They were responsible for the
failure of the enclosure movement which the king pushed with energy
and enthusiasm. They failed to provide peasants, as the king had
desired, with adequate legal guaranties against extortionate and un-
lawful noble exactions. Prussian bureaucrats were an essentially conservative class. Their conservatism, however, was also due to the peculiar
manner in which they were remunerated. Besides receiving their fixed
salaries, they received *tantièmes* and other emoluments which they
could increase by redoubling their labor. By increasing public revenues

they could increase their salaries. Their private interests were involved with the maintenance of the existing social order in a manner not unlike that by which the employees of a modern business concern share in the profits of the enterprise. They would be the first to feel the smart of drastic social reforms. They did not desire to leave the beaten path.

Of scarcely less importance for the future of the Prussian bureaucracy was the progressive invasion of the military element, a movement which rose to its height at the end of the century. The appointment of former army officers to important administrative posts was nothing new. In the opening years of the eighteenth century Chancellor Ludwig of Halle recorded it as one of the significant signs of the times that everywhere in Prussia military generals were sitting at the writing table. The fact is not astonishing if we remember that the reform of the Prussian army had preceded the reorganization of the civil service; indeed, in the first two decades of the eighteenth century the administration of the army was the most modern feature of the entire Prussian state. The reorganization of the Prussian administrative system under Frederick William I was in the first instance designed to meet the growing financial needs of the army and was in part carried out by former army officers with the army as their model. In this Prussian society where feudal classes were so strongly intrenched army officers were the most dependable and unsparing executors of the royal will. The Prussian army officer brought a number of peculiarly Prussian virtues to the civil service: faithfulness to duty, subordination, thrift with none of that acquisitive self-seeking which made the bourgeois official so obnoxious to Frederick the Great. By transferring men from the army to the civil service the Prussian kings inoculated the bureaucracy with a military sense of promptitude and obedience. By imperceptible degrees the Prussian civil service absorbed the spirit and discipline of the army. The Prussian bureaucracy wore a distinctly military aspect, a feature which distinguished it from any other administrative system of Europe.

If Frederick William I employed former army officers by preference, his son, Frederick II, did so from necessity. Wanting the wherewithal to grant pensions to superannuated and invalid army officers, increased to formidable proportions by his many and bloody wars, he was reduced to the necessity, if he wished to provide for them at all, of reserving an ever larger number of subaltern offices for them. From that day down to our own the former army officers predominated in all the subaltern positions of the Prussian civil service. Ex-officers were found in greatest numbers in the postal service, in the lower grades of the excise administration, in the government salt and tobacco monopolies, as foresters and customs officials. They were also employed extensively as municipal magistrates. The Adjutant General of the Prussian army kept a list of all military invalids and as soon as a vacancy occurred anywhere the person at the head of the list received the position.

This penetration of superannuated and invalid army officers into the lower ranks of the service caused a radical transformation in the character of the Prussian bureaucracy. Hitherto Prussian monarchs had utilized subaltern officers as the most suitable means of educating higher officials. Frederick II himself employed in each provincial chamber a number of unpaid understudies, carefully selected from men of education and good family, who served in subaltern posts only to study the complicated bureaucratic routine as a preliminary step to higher appointments. The highest offices in the realm were open to such subaltern officials. But the royal decree of July 30, 1799, reserved all subaltern offices in the entire kingdom for military invalids to the exclusion of all others. The result was a sudden and conspicuous decline in the quality of subaltern officials because military invalids were generally uneducated men who possessed neither the ability nor the ambition to rise to higher positions. This deterioration in the quality of subaltern officials drew in its train a marked increase of bureaucratic formalities, a multiplication of checks and counter-checks, and encouraged that baneful *Vielschreiberei* [mania for keeping written records] of which Frederick the Great was the deadliest enemy. To control this new type of official, business had to be transacted in the most circumstantial way. The people at large soon began to feel the effects of this transformation of the lower ranks of the service into an insurance institution for military invalids. From that day to this they have recognized in the subaltern official the demobilized soldier who was honest and reliable when fully instructed and controlled but who could not be expected by taking thought to add a cubit to his stature. Henceforth there was a sharp division between the educated higher officials and the subalterns, a distinction which was legalized in 1817 when higher careers were closed to subalterns by law.

The overwhelming majority of French civil servants under the old régime were jurists. In Prussia they were practical economists. While attendance at a university was not a necessary requirement for admission to the service, such attendance became customary, especially in the second half of the century. It was one of the principal functions of Prussian universities to train future civil servants in Cameralism, as the study of economics was called, and jurisprudence. At the end of the century most civil servants had studied at one or more of the Prussian universities. After having passed an examination administered by the president of a provincial chamber, the applicant was admitted to the chamber as an *Auskultator* which was a special educational post for aspiring officials. As such he was admitted to the study of the arcana of the bureaucratic routine. This stage of his training usually continued over a period of two or three years. He was permitted to read the documents of the chamber, work in the chancellery, and generally familiarize himself with the duties of the various officials of the chamber. But this was only half of his preparation. It was a universal practice, prescribed by the king, for each understudy, before taking his final examination, to live on a royal farm for one or two years to make a personal acquaintance with the practical details of agriculture and the management of the royal domains. This practical experience in the management of the royal domains was indispensable for every higher official. Here the future official came into personal contact with some of the most important problems of the Prussian state: intelligent agricultural methods, the financial questions involved in drawing up a contract for leasing the royal domains, and the realities of the lord-serf relationship. It was a traditional conviction among Prussian bureaucrats that no theoretical training, however excellent, could replace this practical experience. Indeed as long as the state possessed a fourth of all the land in the kingdom it would be difficult to suggest a more valuable training for future officials. Once in possession of this practical experience, the candidate could apply, on the recommendation of the president of the provincial chamber, for his final examination with the examination commission of the General Directory in Berlin. This examination embraced the whole field of the activities of the future official. It was an examination in economics, jurisprudence and administrative law and practice. If one may generalize from the case of Theodore von Schön, who has left us a record of his examination, it presupposed an uncommonly thorough and extensive knowledge.

Yet the absence of any system for selecting officials for the highest positions was painfully felt. Each time when a ministry or the presidency of a provincial chamber fell vacant the king was in a quandary over finding the most suitable candidate. The device of governing the realm from the royal cabinet now revenged itself upon the king. He possessed only a limited personal acquaintance of his officials, and the manner in which he was compelled to choose his higher civil servants was and remained unsatisfactory. He had perforce to rely upon his ministers for recommendations, and in consequence there crystallized about each minister a group of protégés for whose advancement he became responsible. The king then called the various candidates to Potsdam and, after a single interview, made his decision. Frederick II was no bad judge of men, but his judgment was far from being always reliable. There was something obviously unsatisfactory in making an appointment on the basis of a single interview. Within the limits of a single conversation the king could do no more than apply his customary tests of bureaucratic ability. It is possible to describe with some precision the attributes of the official who made the deepest impression upon him. The official must be thoroughly posted in his branch of the service, work rapidly, be always ready with a quick reply, display a military bearing and be extremely punctilious in observing all bureaucratic proprieties. But being such an official was perfectly compatible with being a petrified and pedantic formalist, and formalists were not rare phenomena in the Prussian civil service. Among Frederick's ministers v. Heinitz was the only man of learning and independent ideas; in his special province of mining he was an authority of truly European stature. Other ministers like v. Schulenburg and v. Hagen did not rise above being able and industrious men of routine. They were not men to pierce the heart of a problem or to propose incisive measures. Von Hagen boasted that he never read a printed line; indeed, he had such a horror of the printed word that when on his birthday a friend presented him with a printed poem he returned it with the request that he might have it in writing. Lesser officials were more intellectually active. Many of them wrote treatises, valuable in their day, on statistics, agriculture and public finance. In Silesia and East Prussia members of the provincial chambers took a lively part in the movement of the *Aufklärung*. In Breslau the members of the chamber even founded a scientific and literary periodical, the *Schlesische Provinzialblätter*, which was edited by one of the secretaries of the chamber.

Socially, civil servants belonged to the leading classes of Prussian society. In a state where there were few bankers and practically no wealthy merchants or manufacturers, where the masses of the urban population were small shopkeepers, artisans and their apprentices, civil servants were to the urban population what the nobility was to the rural districts. They had the best residences in the towns, kept several servants, horses and a chaise, and employed tutors for their children. While their salaries were not munificent, they were paid better than their equals in surrounding countries and usually held their positions for life.

Peter the Great

B. H. SUMNER

≫≫-≫≫-≫≫-≫≫-≫≫-≫≫-≫≫ *Published in 1947* ≪≪-≪≪-≪≪-≪≪-≪≪-≪≪-≪≪-≪≪

Many experts insist that any discussion of modern Russia should begin **no** later than the reign of Ivan the Terrible (1533-1584). But most general European history textbooks begin with Peter the Great (1689-1725) and his much publicized attempts to Europeanize his realm. As a result, he is often given credit for much that was not his historical due. Yet, although it is certainly true that Peter owed much to pre-Petrine Russia, it is no less true that post-Petrine Russia has owed much to Peter. Through the centuries, his policies have continued to provoke lively controversies—controversies in which the truth about Peter has been much less important than what Russians have thought the truth to be. In the present article, B. H. Sumner, one of the leading British experts in the field of modern Russian history, deals with the problem of Peter's historical reputation, discussing its importance not only in the Tsar's own time but in the centuries that have followed.

Peter the Great has returned to his own—"*skoro, skoro, Petr I, skoro, skoro.*" ("Coming, Peter I, Coming"). I remember seeing the Leningrad cinemas streaming with that advertisement in September 1937, just while the film was having its first performance in Moscow. *Petr I*: Peter I: he was not yet again *Pyotr Veliki*, Peter the Great, but I notice now that since last year Soviet writers can use either title. He is now, as it were, reinstated in the national pantheon. (When Viborg was reconquered from Finland in the winter of 1940, his statue there was immediately restored. Viborg had first come to Russia thanks to Peter, who captured it from the Swedes in 1710.) Peter ranks almost with the new medallists—Kutuzov, Suvorov and Alexander Nevsky; and the Soviet Navy is proud to claim him as its founder. The war has

Reprinted by special permission from *History*, XXXII (1947), 39-50.

given a resounding impetus to Soviet patriotism in all forms; a patriotism which combines intense pride in the October Revolution and its fruits, with pride in the great deeds and creative achievements of the Russian past, a mighty fusing of the old and the new, in which Russian history and Russian leaders, whether in war, or government, or the arts and sciences, received their meed, often with strident exaggeration. Indeed there has now begun a reaction among Soviet historians against what may be called war-time nationalist history. Among the leaders of the past, Peter keeps his new place. This potent revival of patriotic interest in and feeling for the past of Russia is not by any means purely a phenomenon due to the War, though that has immeasurably stimulated it. The revival began a dozen years ago or so, and it represented a deliberate reaction, decided upon in the highest quarters, against what had been the prevailing trend in Soviet schools and education ever since the early days of the Revolution. History—except that of the Bolsheviks and the October Revolution—had been reduced to almost nothing in the curriculum, and what there was, was extremely abstract, and more or less akin to sociology. I am speaking broadly and there were of course exceptions. A great deal of the little history that was taught was directly or indirectly infected with the heresy of economic materialism; and I should myself quite agree that that is a heresy, and a very dangerous one. The times of Peter the Great were too often represented in terms of Pokrovsky's theory of the rise and triumph of "trading capitalism." Peter himself, like any other historical personage, more or less disappeared beneath a string of -isms or a page of, not always well-founded, statistics. The battle of Poltava was scarcely mentioned; nor the foundation of the Academy of Sciences. It is true that some learned, specialist work on Peter's reign was being done between 1917 and 1934, but comparatively little was published. Since then, in the last dozen years, there has been a very marked reversal. A number of specialist books and articles have appeared covering various aspects and events of Peter's reign—not only economic, social and military, but in addition dealing, for instance, with administration, diplomacy,[1] education, or the Streltsy. A beginning has been made with the continuation of the indispensable series of his *Letters and Papers (Pisma i Bumagi)*,

---

[1] Notably T. Korylova's series of articles on Russian diplomacy, 1700-1711, in *Istoricheskie Zapiski*, vols. 7, 10 and 19 and *Petr Veliky: sbornik statei*, vol. 1 (Moscow, 1947), pp. 104-166.

which ceased in 1918 after only having reached the year before Poltava, 1708 (vol. 7, part 2; Moscow, 1946).

In various popular editions and in the rewritten textbooks Peter and his reign are now duly prominent, and the film on him and Alexis Tolstoy's remarkable novel have still further served towards his reinstatement. In the historical treatment of Peter's reign the man himself is given his due. His Russian detractors (particularly Milyukov and of course Pokrovsky) are sharply handled. Peter is called great because he was a man of exceptional gifts and force of character who sensed many of the greatest needs of Russia and bent himself to the task of meeting them; because he appreciated certain of the most important forces or tendencies working within Muscovy of the second half of the seventeenth century; because with his tempestuous (and indeed spendthrift) energy, with his immense power of (and indeed at times immersion in) detail, with his steadfastness and courage in overcoming failures (and indeed at times recklessness and obstinacy), he hastened into being that new Russia which was in process of gestation in the womb of the seventeenth century. He was not so much the *"révolutionnaire couronné"* ["royal revolutionary"] of Herzen,[2] or the tsar-carpenter of the masses: he was rather the "tsar-midwife." But in Peter's own words "it is impossible for a smith to work without tongs"[3]; and his tongs were certainly terribly gripping. As Lenin put it—these words are constantly quoted in the Union—Peter in his Europeanising of Russia did not hesitate to use "barbarous means of

[2] Herzen, *Polnoe sobranie sochinenii,* ed. Lemko, vol. vi, p. 222.

[3] *Pisma i Bumagi imperatora Petra Velikogo,* vol. iii, p. 304, referring to his immense efforts at supplying the Smolensk front with munitions and supplies for 50,000 men for the summer campaign of 1705.

M. N. POKROVSKY: Soviet historian and vice-commissar of education until his death in 1932. With the intensification of Soviet nationalism in the 1930's, his approach, as embodied in his *History of Russia,* went out of fashion. He was repudiated, among other reasons, for his failure to "appreciate" the contributions of such rulers as Ivan the Terrible and Peter the Great.

POLTAVA: Battle of 1709 at which the tired troops of Charles XII of Sweden were decisively defeated by the superior artillery of Peter's army. Although the Great Northern War dragged on until 1721, Poltava proved to be the decisive engagement.

struggle against barbarism." As a typical example of the present attitude to Peter among Soviet historians I will quote the close of an article on "The Army Reform of Peter the Great."[4]

"Peter was the founder of the Russian regular, national army. With masterly foresight, Peter knew how to pick out and assimilate what was useful and progressive and how to reject what was useless. By his creation of the regular army Peter the Great raised an indestructible monument to himself in the history of the Russian State. In his grandiose reorganisation of the armed forces of Russia, Peter showed himself a wise and far-sighted statesman. Under the conditions of the exhausting Northern War and of the backwardness of Russia, Peter the Great successfully decided this historical task."

Soviet historians themselves fully allow that much work remains to be done on Peter's times and his reforms, and one notable lack is still that of an up-to-date, complete, large-scale biography and evaluation of his reign as a whole.[5] But there is certainly now no longer any lack of interest in Peter. I have already pointed out one broad reason for this renewed interest in him. There are other, more particular reasons, why the new Soviet state and society, born out of Revolution and fiercely

---

[4] By P. Epifanov in *Voprosy istorii*, 1945, no. 1, p. 58. The same general attitude appears in his later article on Peter's army regulations of 1716 in *Petr Veliky; sbornik statei*, vol. 1 (Moscow, 1947), pp. 167-213.

[5] The late M. M. Bogoslovsky's minutely detailed biography, *Peter I* (Moscow; 3 vols., 1940-6), is the work of the most learned of the Russian historians on Peter and is an indispensable quarry, but it only goes down to 1699. His brief study *Petr Veliky i ego reforma*, which is the best short survey of Peter's work, was published as long ago as 1920, and does not differ substantially from his lecture course given in Moscow in 1911-12, and reproduced in lithographed form with the title *Istoriya Rossii* xviii-go vyeka.

STRELTSY: Members of the Moscow garrison organized by Ivan the Terrible. It was with the aid of part of the garrison that Peter came to power in 1689; but when some of its members revolted in 1698, the uprising was crushed with a severity that conjured up memories of the days of Ivan the Terrible.

ALEXIS TOLSTOY: Soviet novelist who, with the death of Gorky, and until his own death in 1945, was widely viewed as the foremost Soviet writer. He was the author of *The Road to Calvary*, a trilogy dealing with Russia before, during, and after the Revolution, and of *Peter the Great*, a historical novel that idealizes the Tsar as a precursor of Lenin and Stalin.

tempered in the furnace of struggle, privation and war, should appreciate Peter the Great and his times.

Peter was an iconoclast: he broke with many externals, and with the ritualistic, traditional orthodox manner of life that hitherto had been part and parcel of the nationalism and religion of the court and the magnates and landed families, and in some degree of the bulk of the Russian people. He was lay and secular in his interests, aims, and habit of mind and of life; rationalism and utility were uppermost. He had dynamic energy, violent unbreakable determination, and unfailing courage: therewith he triumphed in the long run over all his adversities, defeats and setbacks—except one, and that one curiously enough his defeat at the hands of the Turks, in 1711, on the Pruth. He was a patriot, devoted to Russia, not sparing his subjects, but least of all himself, in unremitting service to her. He worked upon her "like nitric acid on iron."[6] He was untiring in his plans for the development of Russia's economic resources, particularly her industries, and among those especially metallurgy. In this he had much success, and the great iron and copper industries in the Urals owe their origin to Peter. He was the initiator of what may be called modern education in Russia, not confined to one class, though mainly confined to the immediately useful and the technical. He devoted great attention to Asiatic lands and to Siberia, marched in person into Transcaucasia in war against Persia, sought out Central Asian routes to India and initiated the final successful search for a North-East passage, discovered shortly after his death by Behring. He made the Russian navy out of nothing. He remade the Russian army, on the model of the up-to-date European armies of that day, armed for the greater part with flint-locks and bayonets, well-equipped with a varied artillery, munitioned in the end for the most part from Russian resources. With this army and navy he defeated Sweden, ultimately, after twenty-one consecutive years of war; and Sweden ranked among the foremost military powers of the day, and had in her King Charles XII, a military leader who was the compeer of Marlborough and Prince Eugene, however lacking he was as statesman. (Thanks to Creasy, Macaulay's schoolboy used to know of Poltava, for it is numbered among his fifteen decisive battles of the world—the only Russian one to be so: Poltava, "the Russian resurrection," as Peter and his wife Catherine refer to it in their inti-

[6] Frederick the Great's description of Peter: *Oeuvres,* vol. 2 (Berlin, 1846), p. 21.

mate letters.)[7] With this army and navy Peter gained for Russia the Baltic provinces and the mouth of the Neva, where he founded his new capital St. Petersburg, achievements which obviously enough during the last seven years have been brought home again and again to the Russian people.

Such are some of the salient aspects of Peter's character and deeds which link up easily enough with much that is of absorbing interest to the Soviet Union. But I would like at this point to utter a caveat against facile comparisons which are often made between Peter and Stalin or Lenin, or between what was accomplished under Peter and what has happened in the last thirty years in Russia. There is, in my opinion, nothing truly corresponding to the October Revolution in Peter's transformation of Muscovy into Russia—or indeed in any period of Russian history. Peter stood for a new outlook on life, but not for a radically new type of society or of state. He has often been compared to a thunderstorm, with blinding, searing lightning, with drenching but fruitful and irrigating rain, a thunderstorm in spring *from a clear sky*. That is an untrue comparison. The thunderstorm had been slowly working up, growling and flickering on the horizon, long before it burst with Peter. His methods were extreme and violent and shocking to many, perhaps most, of his subjects—so had been Ivan the Terrible's methods a century and more before him—and in that sense he may be called revolutionary; as Herzen styled him: *"un jacobin anticipé et un terroriste révolutionnaire"* ["a premature Jacobin and revolutionary terrorist,"][8] who wrought "grimly and terribly against the will of the people, relying on autocratic authority and personal strength."[9] But he did not seek either to build upon entirely new foundations or to sweep away the essentials of the Muscovite social structure. Especially, he not only did not change the basic fact of serfdom: in various ways he extended serfdom and clamped it down more heavily. His achievements were very great, even though many of them were undone or warped after his death, but they constituted a great era of reforms, rushed through at breakneck speed, rather than a revolution in comparison with so all-embracing and far spreading and profound a Revolution as that begun in 1917.

[7] *Pisma russkikh gosudarei* . . . (Moscow; 1861), pp. 71, 94, 97.
[8] Herzen, op. cit., vol. VI, p. 240.
[9] *ibid., vol.* IX, p. 2.

There is, however, one respect in which Peter and his effects may perhaps be said to constitute a revolution in a sense. For two hundred years he has divided Russia, very broadly speaking, into two groups. Already his contemporaries were ranged against each other, some opposing him in the name of "the old and ancient faith, of holy orthodox Rus," others supporting him in the name of "the new European science and culture, of 'enlightened' Petrine Russia."[10] On the conclusion of the Great Northern War in 1721 Peter was officially acclaimed as "Father of the Fatherland, All-Russian Emperor, Peter the Great."[11] On his death in 1725 his favoured ecclesiastic, Feofan Prokopovich, Archbishop of Novgorod and ruler of Peter's newly created Synod, preached a funeral oration lauding him as "having raised Russia as from the dead," and comparing him to Samson, mighty man of arms, Japhet the creator of a fleet, Moses the law giver, and Solomon the wise.[12] That on the one side. But also on his death there appeared an unsparing cartoon, one of the most popular of the cheap woodcuts that for long circulated underground in Russia, entitled "The mice bury the cat."[13] Many rejoiced that Anti-Christ was no more, that "the bloodsucker," "the cruel beast of prey" had gone to join Beelzebub from whom he had sprung.[14] For many their dearest wish was that St. Petersburg should be abandoned and Moscow should once again be the capital; and so it was for a very brief span. The two cities symbolised the opposed attitudes to Peter and all that he stood for.

Thus from the very time of Peter himself there appears what has been called "the ideological schism"—*ideologichesky raskol*, the word *raskol*, schism, harking back to the great religious schism in

---

[10] B. Syromyatnikov, '*Regulyarnoe*' *gosudarstvo Petra I i ego ideologiya*, pt. 1, (Moscow; 1943), p. 17, apparently quoting from contemporary sources but not stating which.

[11] The text of the request from the Senate for the assumption of these titles and of the official account of their assumption is in N. A. Voskresensky, *Zakonodatelnye Akty Petra I*, vol. 1 (Moscow; 1945), pp. 155-61.

[12] A reprint of the text of the sermon is in I. I. Golikov, *Dyeyaniya Petra Velikogo* . . . , vol. 9 (Moscow; 1789), pp. 238-44. There is an English translation in T. Consett, *The present state and regulations of the Church of Russia* . . . (London, 1729), pp. 279-85.

[13] E. Shmurlo, *Petr Veliky v otsenkye sovremennikov i potomstva* (St. Petersburg; 1912), p. 13.

[14] Syromyatnikov, op. cit., pp. 6, 155.

the 60's of the seventeenth century—"the ideological schism" between the conception of Russia as part of Europe and of Muscovy as a world of her own, neither Europe nor Asia. In eighteenth century literature for obvious reasons public expression could not be given to direct criticism of the personality or role of Peter and hence to direct discussion of the fundamental problem "what is the nature of Russia, what is her future?" (This actual formula was coined much later by the historian Kavelin in writing of Peter in 1866.) But the subsequent publication of the manuscripts of Shcherbatov and Radishchev show that in Catherine the Great's reign there were definitely formulated, highly critical views of the direction given to Russian life and culture by Peter, "the mighty (*vlastny*) autocrat, who destroyed the last signs of rude freedom in his fatherland" (Radishchev).[15] At the beginning of the nineteenth century with Karamzin, in his later period of old-style, nationalist-patriot, there is openly posed, and in the grand manner, the question how Peter and his work should be evaluated in terms of Russia's national life and future. Thenceforward, above all in the great controversies between the Westerners and the Slavophils, this question is regarded as fundamental in the historico-philosophical disquisitions on the relation of Russia to Europe, on the place of Russia in the world, on the meaning of "national culture" or "national spirit," of orthodoxy, the *mir* (the village commune) or of governmental power. It is perhaps true to say that the reign of Peter has been for Russians, and not at all only for Russian historians, what the French Revolution has been for five generations of Frenchmen. The interpretation of Peter and his reforms has been a political declaration of faith; it has tended to be part and parcel of a view of life, whether primarily religious or mystical, rationalist or materialist, conservative or liberal.

This prolonged public debate has as its central theme, as I have said, the problem "what is the nature of Russia and what is her future?." Because it turned so frequently upon Peter the Great another problem of equal importance was raised: can a centralised, dictatorial government *impose* successfully from above, radical changes, or a revolution, especially at extreme speed and by violent means? These, as I see it, are the biggest reasons why Peter the Great has filled so large and so disputed a place in subsequent Russian history,

[15] Shmurlo, op. cit., pp. 84-90; Radishchev, *Polnoe sobranie sochinenii* (Moscow, 1938), vol. 2, pp. 150-1.

and they raise issues of universal import which make the study of Peter and his times almost as absorbingly interesting to us as to his fellow countrymen. In the last eighty years, however, there has come about so great a change in our historical knowledge of seventeenth and eighteenth century Russia, that these issues are now raised in less simple form in relation to Peter.

In the great cultural struggle between what may be loosely described as the adherents of the old, *stariny*, and the adherents of the new, *novizny,* there are two points most of them had in common with each other. They were weak, sometimes absurdly weak, in their historical knowledge, especially of the earlier centuries and pre-Petrine Russia. Secondly, they were agreed in placing the greatest emphasis on Peter himself and on regarding his reign as a catastrophic, dividing watershed. For Lomonosov or Shcherbatov, Karamzin or Chaadayev, Byelinsky or Kireyevsky, Herzen or Aksakov, Dobrolyubov or Khomyakov, Peter was a giant and a genius, a thunder tempest whether deforming with lightning or enriching with rain, a cataclysm, whether the regimenting despot importing narrow foreign bureaucrats and noxious foreign ways, or a *bogatyr*, the enlightened autocrat, who, in the words of Byelinsky, "opened the door for his people to the light of God and little by little dispersed the darkness of ignorance."[16]

Thus Peter was emphatically the Great for both sides, whether for good or for evil, and what he did was something wholly novel, a paroxysm of revolution. Since the 1860's a series of Russian historians, beginning with the monumental Soloviev, have exploded this idea that Peter worked as it were on a *tabula rasa*, that he came as it were out of a clear sky. Some, though not many, of these historians have also belittled his capacities, "written him down" on the whole, and minimised his personal share in the reforms with which his name is linked. It is now generally recognised that Peter, in almost all spheres of his activities, had his precursors; that seventeenth century Muscovy was in travail with something new, that Peter's reforms did not, with certain exceptions, mean a complete break with the past but rather an immense jolt of the past, and the infusion in a strong, sometimes scalding jet of the new that had hitherto been

---

[16] Byelinsky: *Izbrannye filosoficheskie sochineniya* (Moscow; 1941), p. 145: in the second of his articles on Golikov's Peter the Great.

only slowly and tentatively trickling into Muscovy. That is not to
decry Peter or his work, but to make them more comprehensible.

If you take eight essential fields in which Peter wrought profound
changes, you will find that in all of these there were beginnings in
the generation before him, and sometimes much further back than
that. That applies to the greater part of his foreign policy, to his
army reorganisation, to his reorganisation of the central government,
to his reorganisation of taxation and serfdom, to his employment of
foreigners in Russia and education reforms, to his insistence on
compulsory service, to his economic and industrial developments, and
lastly to his break with the prevailing traditional and ritualistic
ordering of life typified in so much of seventeenth century orthodoxy.
I can think of only four changes wrought by Peter (though they
were great and lasting) which had either nothing leading towards
them in the immediate past or so very little that it scarcely counts.
These were the education of Russians abroad, the abolition of the
Patriarchate, the creation of the navy, and the making of a new
capital, St. Petersburg. Further, however much in many ways Peter
was enamoured of the West and borrowed from it, he did not do so
indiscriminately or wholesale, and he remained thoroughly Russian.
It is a striking fact that Milyukov, who was perhaps the strongest
of Peter's critics among recent historians, should sum up on Peter's
reforms thus:—"Their fortuitousness, arbitrariness, individual stamp,
and violence are necessary elements in them. Despite their sharply
anti-national externals, they are entirely rooted in the conditions of
national life. The country received nothing but the reforms for which
she was fitted."[17]

I have mentioned in passing Peter's foreign policy. His imposing
success in this field had, as we all know, one novel and lasting result
of the greatest consequence; Russia at a bound, in thirty years, became
one of the European powers. Contemporaries in Europe were well
aware of this sudden portent, and many, British included, were much
disturbed by it. When Peter came to England in 1698, his capture
of Azov and league against Turkey had inspired no alarms. On the
contrary, a congratulatory poem of welcome coupled William III
with Peter as "Christ's firmest Pillars and the Christians' Prop" on
the West and East, "whose powerful Work Subdues both Mahomet

[17] *Ocherki po istorii russkoi kultury*, vol. III. *Natsionalizm i evropeizm* (Paris; 1930), p. 195.

and the Christian Turk"; and it closed, "May Roman Conquests be out done by Thee And Czar to more than Caesar then extended be."[18] By the close of the Great Northern War this polite hyperbole had turned into an ominously true prophecy in the eyes of many British, and Hanoverian, statesmen. For them the balance of power in northern Germany and the Baltic had been all too rudely upset, and Peter's new creation was in secret denounced as "that fleet which will disturb the world whilst it is steered by ambition and revenge."[19] They were apt in effect to re-echo Burnet's words: "How long he is to be the scourge of that nation or of his neighbours, God only knows."[20] Others who were not concerned with affairs of state judged differently, and one main current of eighteenth-century British opinion on Peter tended to be most impressed with the idea that here was a great example of Reason, forcing men to be both obedient and civilised and progressive. Thanks to Peter, in the words of Voltaire, the Russians "ont fait plus de progrès en cinquante ans qu'aucune nation n'en avait fait par elle-même en cinq cent années" [made more progress in fifty years than any other nation had made by itself in five hundred years"].[21] I have neither the time nor the ability to

[18] Congratulatory poem on Peter's arrival in England on 21st January, 1698 (new style): London 1698: in Bodleian Library, Firth, MSS, b. 21, 44.

[19] Carteret to Admiral Norris, in command of the British Fleet in the Baltic, 30th August (new style), 1719; W. Michael, *England under George I*, vol. II (London; 1939), p. 263, citing British Museum, Add, MSS. 22511.

[20] *History of His Own Time* (1823 ed.), vol. IV, p. 398. This well-known passage in Burnet was written with the vivid impress on his mind of the terrible accounts he had heard of the massacre of the Streltsy: "It was said that he cut off many heads with his own hand, and . . . seemed delighted with it." A year before, when Burnet was seeing Peter in London, and discoursing to him on Church and State, the Filioque and icons, he formed a very different impression of him: "The Czar will either perish by the way or become a great man." Bodleian Library, Add MMS. D. 23, f. 10, letter of Burnet to Dr. Falk of York, 19/29 March, 1698. Leibniz, already deeply interested in Peter and Russia and later to be an adviser of his on scientific and educational matters, was likewise revolted by the massacre of the Streltsy; he feared it would jeopardise Peter's reforms, and Peter for him still remained, "ohne Zweifel ein grosser Fürst." (Letter to Witsen, 12/24 March, 1699, quoted in W. Guerrier, *Leibniz in seinen Beziehungen zu Russland und Peter dem Grossen* (St. Petersburg; 1873), pp. 29-30). The accounts of the massacre in the West all came from the same source, the Austrian embassy in Moscow.

[21] Voltaire, *Histoire de l'Empire de Russie sous Pierre le Grand: Oeuvres Complètes* (1784 ed.), vol. 24, p. 59.

attempt an estimate of the different British attitudes to Peter and
his work, and I must close. I should like to do so by quoting from
a Scottish poet who dwelt in England, James Thomson, who is now
most remembered as the author of "Rule Britannia," but for long
was best known, and is still most highly appreciated, as the author of
"The Seasons." The passage comes towards the end of "Winter."[22]
It is exaggerated and overdrawn, but it is typical of much eighteenth-
century opinion, and it has a core of truth—and also, coming where
it does, a pleasurable snap of the unexpected.

> "What cannot active government perform,
> New-moulding man? Wide-stretching from these shores,
> A people savage from remotest time,
> A huge neglected empire, one vast mind,
> By Heaven inspired, from gothic darkness called.
> Immortal Peter! first of monarchs! he
> His stubborn country tam'd, her rocks, her fens,
> Her floods, her seas, her ill-submitting sons;
> And while the fierce barbarian he subdu'd,
> To more exalted soul he rais'd the man.
> Ye shades of ancient heroes, ye who toil'd
> Through long successive ages to build up
> A labouring plan of state, behold at once
> The wonder done! behold the matchless prince!
> Who left his native throne, where reign'd till then
> A mighty shadow of unreal power;
> Who greatly spurn'd the slothful pomp of courts;
> And roaming every land, in every port
> His sceptre laid aside, with glorious hand
> Unwearied plying the mechanic tool,
> Gather'd the seeds of trade, of useful arts,
> Of civil wisdom and of martial skill.

[22] The first edition of "Winter" was published in 1726, the year after Peter's
death, but these lines did not appear until the greatly altered and enlarged
edition of 1744. I cannot find, even in Leon Morel's *James Thomson, Sa Vie et
ses Oeuvres* (Paris; 1895), any suggestion of the origin of the lines or of
Thomson's interest in Peter, except the suggestion of O. Zippel that they may owe
something to Thomson's friend, the author Aaron Hill, who in 1718 published,
"The Northern Star"; *Entstehungs-und Entwickelungs-geschichte von Thomson's
"Winter."* (Berlin; 1908), p. xl. The third edition of "The Northern Star," which
appeared in 1725 just after Peter's death, had in addition on the title page, "a
poem sacred to the name and memory of the immortal Czar of Russia." It is a
very undistinguished glorification of Peter and his achievements.

Charged with the stores of Europe home he goes!
Then cities rise amid th' illumin'd waste;
O'er joyless deserts smiles the rural reign;
Far-distant flood to flood is social joined;
Th' astonished Euxine hears the Baltic roar;
Proud navies ride on seas that never foam'd
With daring keel before; and armies stretch
Each way their dazzling files, repressing here
The frantic Alexander of the north,
And awing there stern Othman's shrinking sons.
Sloth flies the land, and Ignorance, and Vice,
Of old dishonour proud: it glows around,
Taught by the Royal Hand that rous'd the whole,
One scene of arts, of arms, of rising trade:
For what his wisdom planned, and power enforc'd,
More potent still, his great example show'd."

Some Forerunners of the Decembrists

D. M. LANG

➤➤➤➤➤➤➤➤➤➤ *Published in 1948* ᐊᐊᐊᐊᐊᐊᐊᐊᐊᐊ

Catherine the Great continues to figure prominently, along with Frederick the Great and Joseph II of Austria, as an outstanding example of the enlightened despot of the eighteenth century. Catherine, of course, did much to foster this conception of herself, but it is a conception that can hardly stand critical analysis. Catherine's early flirtation with enlightenment was mainly a reflection of her own insecure position. As a widow of a tsar, she had only a flimsy claim to the throne. In order, therefore, to win aristocratic support, she toyed with reform projects. In the mid-1770's, however, the outbreak of a formidable series of peasant uprisings made clear the dependence of the landed aristocracy on the armed forces of the monarchy, and once Catherine could count on the support of her landed aristocracy she abandoned her interest in enlightenment. The upshot was that her reign saw the growth of a literature of disillusionment and social protest. After the fashion of the French *philosophes,* a number of writers sought to expose abuses and suggest the need for reform. In the following article, D. M. Lang, fellow of St. John's College, Cambridge, presents the basic ideas of some of the more important of these writers who were obsessed with the condition-of-Russia question. Both learned and perceptive, Lang shows great promise as a historian of modern Russia.

The Government is deaf, blind and insensitive . . . If posterity
believes my words, what will it say about our century?
PRINCE M. M. SHCHERBATOV (1733-90)

1

Catherine the Great's version of her own reign as the Golden Age of Russian enlightenment and tolerance continues to be widely accepted. The Empress was, of course, an excellent propagandist. She enjoyed the considerable advantage of being able to correspond in French, the established medium of international contact, with such skilled publicists as Voltaire and Baron Grimm, with the result that her name is constantly linked with theirs and with that of Denis Diderot, who visited her in St. Petersburg. Thus Western Europe came to entertain a most favourable idea of her 'progressive' outlook.

There is nevertheless another side to the picture. The fate of those eighteenth-century Russian writers who presumed to criticise the existing order of 'benevolent despotism' was not a happy one. Nothing, officially speaking, could be published in Russia without the concurrence of the Censorship—that semi-illiterate Censorship which once forbade a conventional poetic reference to Cupid, that artful Deity, on the grounds that Gods must not be mentioned in a disrespectful spirit. Even if the Censorship raised no preliminary objection to his writings, an author was liable after publication to be haled before the chief of the so-called Secret Expedition, Stepan Sheshkovsky, whose usual opening gambit was to strike the victim's jaw with his stick so that the teeth flew out. Catherine's more cautious critics accordingly left their works unpublished, and certain

Reprinted by special permission from *The Cambridge Journal*, I (1948), 623-634. Publishers, Bowes & Bowes, Ltd.

DECEMBRISTS: Aristocratic conspirators who participated in the uprising of December 1825. Social and political reformers, they believed in restricting the authority of the tsar and in abolishing the institution of serfdom. They took advantage of the confusion that followed the death of Alexander I and staged a "revolution" that proved to be a complete fiasco.

LETTRES PERSANES: Earliest work of Montesquieu. Published anonymously in 1721, it contained criticisms of such abuses in eighteenth-century France

of them have only recently come to light. In any case, most Russian political writings of the eighteenth century are in the crabbed and difficult prose of the period and have never gained anything like the international fame of the Empress's own works. By the end of her reign, however, there existed in Russia a number of intelligent and critical writers on social and political themes, who suffered in many cases from those same methods of Governmental suppression which were to become increasingly familiar in later decades.

It would be misleading to suppose that Russian literature had remained closed to Western liberal ideas until Catherine's accession in 1762 opened the floodgates of 'enlightenment.' From this point of view, her reign was to a great extent a continuation of the processes of assimilation begun under Peter the Great. The works of John Locke circulated in manuscript well before 1750, and Prince Kantemir, who died in 1744, was personally acquainted with Montesquieu and translated his trenchant *Lettres Persanes* into Russian. Alexander Sumarokov (1718-77), who completed many of his best tragedies before Catherine's accession, owed a great deal to the 'philosophic' dramas of Voltaire and was not afraid to imitate him in attacking 'Fanaticism' and 'Tyranny.' It would be excessive to claim that these were symptoms of a widespread mental unrest. But one feels that Catherine took undue credit for the spreading of Western ideas in Russia and that too little attention is paid to the pioneer work done under her predecessors.

Catherine's early 'radicalism' has also been somewhat exaggerated by certain of her historians. The convocation of deputies at Moscow in 1767 and the publication of the Empress's celebrated *Nakaz* or Instruction to guide them in framing a new code of laws raised high hopes of a new and more liberal era. But the deputies eventually departed without completing their main task. The *Nakaz* itself was

---

as the privileges of the aristocracy, the intolerance of the clergy, and the incompetence and inefficiency of the financial administration.

PUGACHEV: Don Cossack who declared himself emperor, decreed the abolition of serfdom, and emerged as the leader of the peasant rebellion of 1773-1775. He was executed in 1775. Although a failure, Pugachev's rebellion aroused tremendous fears and served to strengthen the alliance between aristocracy and monarchy in Russia.

later shelved. As Kizevetter, a prominent authority on the period, has remarked when discussing the episode: 'It is simply the attempt to adorn with the flowers of fashionable ideology a régime based on the real conditions of Russian life.' Unfortunately, these ideological blossoms concealed a sharp thorn, as those of her subjects who were over hasty in taking advantage of the apparent liberal-mindedness of the 'Russian Minerva' were shortly to discover.

The years immediately following the publication of the *Nakaz* were marked by the appearance of Novikov's satirical journals: *The Drone* (1769), *The Painter* (1772-3) and *The Purse* (1774). Nikolai Ivanovich Novikov (1744-1818) was one of the most talented and public-spirited men of his age and it is to be regretted that his work has never been widely known outside Russia. At the time of the Commission for the new code of laws, he worked as a secretary in the Assembly and acquired a knowledge of the state of Russia which he put to good use in *The Drone*. While this, like other Russian periodicals of the time, was an imitation of Addison and Steele's celebrated *Spectator*, Novikov soon became involved in topical comment and social criticism which brought him a sharp rap on the knuckles from the editor of a rival St. Petersburg journal, *All Sorts*, who was none other than the Empress Catherine herself.

To give some idea of the tone of Novikov's journalistic writing, the following extract, taken from the *Drone*, of an imaginary squire's orders to his bailiff on the steps to be taken to deal with a poverty and famine stricken village on his estate may serve as an example of his mood of indignation at the abuses of serfdom:

> To our man, Simon Grigoriev.
> You are to proceed to our village of X and on arrival to carry out these measures:
> (1) Your journey from here to our estate and back to be at the expense of our village elder, Andrew Lazarev.
> (2) On arrival, you are to flog the village elder with the utmost severity before all the peasants for supervising the peasants badly and letting the quit-rent fall into arrears; and then to deprive him of the eldership; and furthermore to exact from him a fine of one hundred roubles.
> (3) Discover most exactly how and for what bribes the elder deceived us with his false report? First of all, have him flogged and then begin the investigation of the matter entrusted to you. . . .
> (8) Settle the division of land between the peasants as you think fit; but tell them that there will be no reduction in their quit-rent and that

without any false excuses they must pay up promptly; flog any defaulters pitilessly in the presence of all the peasants. . . .
(16) After carrying out everything prescribed above, you are to return here; and order the elder most strictly to keep a vigilant watch on the collection of the quit-rent money.

The moral of all this was clear enough. There are indications that those at whom it was aimed did not fail to see what Novikov was driving at. *The Drone* had to cease publication after a few months.

In 1772, however, Novikov undeterred launched a new periodical, *The Painter*. This was, if anything, more outspoken than *The Drone*. A series of articles on serfdom and other social problems was followed by a number of letters, supposedly addressed to a young country bumpkin, Faliley, by his family, a collection of clownish provincial squires resembling the Prostakovs and Skotinin (i.e. *Pigsbody*) of Denis Fonvizin's famous comedy *The Minor* (1782). Here is an extract from one of these letters to Faliley, protesting against Novikov's exposure of the wretched state of the peasantry:

> Who is this Painter fellow who has turned up where you are? Some German, I suppose, since no Orthodox Russian would have written all this. He says the landlords torment the peasants and calls them tyrants. . . . He presumes to say the peasants are poor! What a shame! I suppose he wants them to get rich and us, the gentry, to grow poor? Our Lord never ordained that: someone has to be rich, either squire or peasant. Not every monk can be an abbot. And in the Scriptures it is written: Bear one another's burdens and thus you will fulfil the law of Christ. They work for us and we flog them if they start idling, and so we are all square—I know how to deal with the boors! . . . If I was a great lord, I'd send him (i.e. the Painter) off to Siberia.

Apart from the peasant question, Novikov pilloried such social pests as venal judges, fops and extortioners. His satire aroused a good deal of comment and enough opposition to oblige him eventually to abandon this form of satirical journalism altogether. At the same time, *The Painter* was a great success from the publishing point of view and was frequently reprinted until well into the nineteenth century.

The extracts given above are certainly strongly worded by Russian standards, and it is perhaps surprising that they were allowed to appear without direct interference from the Censorship. Of course, Novikov carefully refrained from touching on really fundamental political matters. He did not, for example, advocate the wholesale abolition of serfdom, except by implication, and never suggested any modification of the structure of Russian autocracy. This led the later Radical critic Nicholas Dobrolyubov (1836-61) to reproach him for having attacked merely superficial abuses without taking into account the chronic weaknesses of the Russian administrative system. Novikov had condemned the corruption of the civil service. What is the use, asked Dobrolyubov, in an article in the review *The Contemporary*, of expecting an underpaid functionary to refuse bribes if he cannot otherwise support himself and his family? You might as well reproach a poor man for being ill-lodged and undernourished.

Another weakness of Novikov's satirical technique was, in Dobrolyubov's opinion, that he took good care to represent the type of people whom he attacked as enemies of the state and, in particular, of the reforms introduced by the Empress. The brutal parents of Faliley in *The Painter* are for ever deploring that the present times are not so propitious for bullying their neighbours, flogging their serfs and defrauding the Government as the good old days of Catherine's less efficient predecessors. The satirist in this way could hope to justify his occasional audacity by pleading that he merely meant to imply praise of the progressive measures taken by the Empress. While Novikov's strictures may have failed to touch the roots of Russia's troubles—ignorance, backwardness, feudalism, despotism—the satirical journals of 1769-74 nevertheless did a great service in awakening public opinion and may be recognised as forerunners of such influential organs of Russian nineteenth-century radicalism as Herzen's *Bell* and the *Contemporary* of Dubrolyubov and Chernishevsky.

While the satirical journals were largely compounded of shrewd Russian wit with an element of Addisonian urbanity, there were a number of writers in Russia who went to the French *philosophes* for political guidance, as well as to British authorities like Blackstone and Adam Smith. The Empress herself, by her friendship with Voltaire, Grimm and Diderot and enthusiasm for such works as Blackstone's *Commentaries* and Montesquieu's *De l'Esprit des Lois* helped to encourage this trend. Admittedly there was nothing revolutionary about Blackstone, but when S. I. Desnitsky of Moscow University translated the *Commentaries* into Russian at the Empress's command (1780-2), it was easy for the reading public to compare the rule of law which the English jurist appeared to take as a matter of course with the arbitrariness and unreliability of Russian justice. Desnitsky himself was a graduate of Glasgow University, where he had studied under Adam Smith. On his return to Russia he submitted to the Empress at the time of the convocation of Deputies a memorandum entitled *Idea for the Institution of Legislative, Judiciary and Executive Powers in the Russian Empire*, inspired by Montesquieu's theory of the division of powers. This project failed to arouse any enthusiasm in official quarters.

During the middle period of Catherine's reign, official distrust of the more extreme forms of Western 'enlightenment' increased noticeably. When her own position had been precarious and opposition to her usurped authority strong, the weapons of Voltairean publicism had been useful additions to her political armoury. But when the conclusion of the Turkish War (Treaty of Kutchuk-Kainarji, 1774) and the execution of the Cossack pretender Emelian Pugachev in 1775 had consolidated her power, she began to find the strictures of French writers such as Rousseau and the Abbé Raynal and their Russian disciples against 'despots' and 'tyrants' a positive embarrassment, now that they could not be explained away as attacks on her die-hard opponents. After 1775, most of these opponents had been either liquidated or reconciled to the existing order. Attacks on administrative abuses could no longer be interpreted as being directed against the Empress's enemies and not her government.

In any case, the French *philosophes* were not by any means unanimous in their eulogies of 'philosophy on the throne', as she liked to be called. Raynal's *Histoire Philosophique et Politique des deux Indes* (1770, 3rd. enlarged ed. 1780) contained a violent diatribe against the very foundations of Russian absolutism and particularly the horrors of serfdom, which he painted in the most lurid colours. On hearing of this, she wrote to Grimm: 'As for the apostle Raynal, I spare you the boredom of scanning him, since he is not worth the trouble.' She was later heard to say that of all the 'learned French Gentlemen' whom she had welcomed at St. Petersburg or corresponded with, Voltaire was the only one who had not bored her.

The outbreak of the French Revolution further increased her dislike of what she called the 'half-baked sages (in Russian—*polumudretsy*) of this age.' The Russian Minister in Paris, Simolin, sent alarming accounts of the effect of philosophic free-thinking on the course of events. These reports were confirmed by the French émigrés constantly arriving at St. Petersburg. The Jesuits, who had found asylum in Russia after their expulsion from France in 1762, lost no opportunity of emphasising the dangers of the sinister Jacobinical activities which they alleged, quite unwarrantedly, that the Russian Freemasons and rationalists were carrying on. Catherine's distrust of Western social and political thought turned to positive hostility. As Masson noted in his *Mémoires Secrets sur la Russie*, the Empress, like so many other crowned philosophers, only liked the liberal sciences in so far as they appeared adapted to propagate her own glory. So long as she could set the pace and maintain a sort of personal monopoly in the importation of Western ideas, all was well. But if anyone attempted to draw independent conclusions from them, or, worse still, to advocate putting them into practice, he was certain sooner or later to incur the Imperial displeasure. As the French Revolution continued, displeasure turned to repression. The British Minister at St. Petersburg, Charles Whitworth, summed up the position very well when he reported in September, 1790 to the Duke of Leeds, then Foreign Secretary: 'So accustomed has this Sovereign been to the stile of Servility and Adulation that she can but ill brook the Language of Truth and Sincerity altho' it evidently conduces to Her own Happiness and to that of Her Country.'

One of the principal victims of this reaction was Novikov. Since the satirical journals had ceased publication in 1774, he had devoted himself more and more to practical philanthropy, Freemasonry, the publishing of original Russian books and translations and to educative activities of all kinds. In 1792 he was arrested and after a parody of a trial sentenced on the vaguest and most undemonstrable charges to fifteen years' confinement in the Schlüsselburg Fortress. He was pardoned by Paul I immediately on his accession in 1796, which was only just, considering that Novikov's acquaintanceship with him when Crown Prince had probably been one of the reasons for his arrest. (Catherine's almost pathological dislike of her son and his friends was notorious.) Novikov's health was permanently undermined by the rigours of his confinement and he emerged from captivity a broken man. Although he lingered on until 1818 he was never able to resume his former activities. In this way Catherine revenged herself on one of her most sincere and well-intentioned critics.

As an illustration of the prevailing attitude, it may be recalled that even the eminent Court Poet Gabriel Romanovich Derzhavin (1743-

1816) was not exempt from suspicion. In the early days of the French
Revolution, he submitted to the Empress a selection of his composi-
tions which included a paraphrase of the 82nd Psalm. Soon afterwards he was horrified to hear that the Secret Expedition had been
instructed to interrogate him on his motive in writing this subversive
poem. The passage mainly objected to contained such lines as these:

> O Kings! I imagined you to be powerful Gods; no one is judge over
> you. But you, like me, have passions and are mortal, just as I. And you
> will fall like the withered leaf from the tree and die just as the last
> of your slaves will die! Arise, O God, God of the Just, and hear their
> prayer: Come, O Judge, chastise the evil and be the one and only King
> of the earth!

With some difficulty, Derzhavin succeeded in convincing the
authorities that the offending Psalm, which he had paraphrased in
1787, before Jacobins had even been heard of, was not an original
composition of his, but was by a King David, who was quite reliable
in his political views.

In these circumstances, the acute political satirist and historian,
Prince M. M. Shcherbatov, from one of whose works the epigraph
to this essay is taken, took care that his trenchant writings on the
contemporary state of Russia should never appear in print during his
lifetime. Shcherbatov's position under Catherine was something like
that of the Duc de Saint-Simon under Louis XIV and the Regency.
He entertained an unbounded contempt for the set of upstart
oligarchs and favourites whose rule was marked by the disintegration
of traditional standards of public and private morality. The importation of foreign luxuries and manners had, in his view, brought about
most of the prevailing abuses. In a memorandum written in 1787
and entitled *The Condition of Russia with regard to Bread and
Money*, Shcherbatov vigorously condemned the government's indifference to the widespread famine conditions and its failure to alleviate
the people's plight. Another work, *On the Degradation of Morals in
Russia*, first published in 1858, gives a lurid picture of the depravity
of Catherine's court and the decay of standards of decency and
honesty in her administration. But, like Saint Simon, Shcherbatov was
far from advocating reform on liberal lines and insisted that Russia's
salvation could come only from a return to the benevolent rule of a
patriarchal aristocracy.

A less circumspect critic of Catherine the Great was an obscure but prolific pamphleteer named Theodore Krechetov, who was arrested in 1793 by the agents of Sheshkovsky, the Empress's secret inquisitor. He confessed under interrogation to having been carried away by enthusiasm for the ideas of Blackstone and of Diderot's *Encyclopédie*, and to having advocated the setting up of representative bodies in order to limit the absolute authority of the Russian autocrat. Tactlessly enough, he cited as a precedent the constitutional demands presented to the Empress Anna Ivanovna in 1730. Krechetov had also written an article in which he made some disparaging remarks about the hereditary aristocracy:

> That man should be deemed most honourable who is honourable to the public advantage, and not he who merely vaunts his birth as a means to acquire consideration . . . What advantage does the state derive from one who can reckon his ancestry back five hundred years, never did anything for the common good, and merely retains the privileges which his Grandfather held? Another man may be a hundred times worthier—but then his Grandfather was no aristocrat, and his efforts are in vain.

The investigators reported that Krechetov's writings were 'full of thoughts about liberty' and might 'cause a breach of the peace'. He was therefore incarcerated in the Schlüsselburg Fortress until the accession of Alexander I in 1801.

2

In 1790, at this most unpropitious moment, an official of the St. Petersburg Customs named Alexander Radishchev printed on his private press a work of his own composition entitled *Journey from St. Petersburg to Moscow*. In it, he attacked in emphatic terms the whole system of Russian autocracy, the corruption of the civil and military administration, the selfishness and incompetence of the nobility, the superstitious ignorance of the priesthood and above all, the iniquitous system of serfdom, the 'bestial custom of enslaving one's fellow-men', which he likened to a hundred headed monster devouring Russia. Only about fifty copies of this work were put on sale, but the sensation which it caused soon attracted the personal attention of the Empress Catherine. She read it with indignation and covered the margins of her copy with angry refutations of Radishchev's arguments.

Radishchev was promptly arrested. He pleaded in reply to Shesh-kovsky's threats that he had merely tried to imitate Sterne's *Senti-mental Journey* and had been led astray by enthusiasm for the oratorical attacks on slavery in Raynal's *Histoire des deux Indes.* Comparison of the *Journey from St. Petersburg to Moscow* with these two works shows that Radishchev had in fact borrowed a good deal from both of them, but this excuse did not mollify his accusers. When he further pleaded that his book, which was issued in a very small edition, was written in a literary style unlikely to be intelligible to the common people and was simply intended to convince the author-ities of the pressing need for reform, Catherine noted that he was a 'rebel worse than Pugachev'. There existed no law to cover the publication of what was regarded as a seditious libel against the government. Radishchev was therefore condemned on several com-pletely fictitious charges, based on clauses of the Military and Naval Codes involving such offences as attempts to harm the sovereign's health and mutinously attacking military installations. The Senate and High Criminal Court pronounced the death sentence. Radishchev was reprieved by the Empress, who commuted his punishment to ten years' exile at Ilimsk, a remote settlement in Central Siberia.

Radishchev may be considered as one of the first of the 'repentant aristocrats' who feature so prominently in Russian social thought. He belonged to a family of provincial gentry who owned a large number of serfs, and studied for five years under the personal patronage of the Empress Catherine at Leipzig University, where he read, as he records himself, the works of Helvétius, the French precursor of the Utilitarian school, and Mably, the Utopian Socialist, as well as Rousseau's *Contrat Social.* On his return to Russia, he translated Mably's work on Greek History into Russian (St. Petersburg, 1773), rendering in one place the word *despotisme* as *samoderzhavstvo* or *autocracy*, and adding his own definition of the word:

> Autocracy is the condition most repugnant to human nature. We cannot give anyone unlimited power over ourselves, and even the law, the expression of the general will, has no other right to punish criminals than that of self-preservation. If we live under the authority of the laws, it is not because we are irrevocably bound to do so, but because it is to our advantage. If we resign to the law some part of our rights and natural powers, we do this in order that the part which we renounce may be turned to our own good; in this we conclude a tacit contract

with society. If it is broken, we are released from our obligations. In-justice on the part of the ruler gives to the nation as his judge a right over him which is just as great, and even greater than that which the law gives the ruler over criminals. *The ruler is the first citizen of the national society.*

It is this idea of an implicit social contract which Radishchev uses in the *Journey* to demonstrate the fundamental iniquity of serfdom. The peasants did not enter into society, he argues, in order to suffer exploitation by a clique of ruthless landowners. By their inhumanity, the squirearchy have broken the social contract and thus released their serfs from all duty of obedience:

> If only the slaves, weighed down by their heavy bonds, inflamed by despair, were to break our heads with the iron which hinders their freedom, the heads of their cruel masters, and crimsoned the fields with our blood! What would the state lose by that? Soon from their midst would arise great men to replace the slain generation; but they would think differently of themselves and be without the power of oppression. This is no fancy; my gaze pierces the thick curtain of time which hides the future from our eyes; I see through a whole century.

But Radishchev looked on revolution as only a last desperate resort, a sword of Damocles hanging over the landowners and ready to fall if they failed to respond to his warnings and improve the lot of the peasantry. He proposed in the *Journey from St. Petersburg to Moscow* that a scheme for doing away with serfdom be set on foot immediately, beginning with the abolition of domestic slavery and extending gradually to all categories of serfs. (The Empress wrote in the margin: 'He is trying to persuade the proprietors to free the peasants: no one will listen!') Unless some such measure was adopted, Radishchev predicted the most terrible disasters for Russia:

> The bell tolls . . . We shall see around us sword and poison. Death and flames will be our reward for our cruelty and inhumanity.

The *Journey from St. Petersburg to Moscow* is one of the most remarkable works of Russian literature, but it will be mainly re-membered as the first serious and profound manifestation of the Russian social conscience. 'I looked around me', said Radishchev in the Dedication, 'and my soul was afflicted with the sufferings of mankind . . . I felt that every man may contribute to the welfare of his fellows.' With these words, as Nicholas Berdyaev has justly said, the Russian Intelligentsia was born.

3

Another outstanding figure in Russian liberal thought of this period was Ivan Petrovich Pnin (1773-1805), an illegitimate son of Prince Repnin. He was a personal friend of Radishchev, whom he knew at St. Petersburg after Alexander I had summoned the latter to take part in the work of the Commission for the Drafting of Laws. Radishchev committed suicide in 1802, and Pnin wrote a poem on his death which expressed the sincere affection and respect which he felt for him.

Pnin's first serious literary venture was the editing of a periodical called *The St. Petersburg Journal*, which appeared in 1798 during the darkest days of the reign of the mad Tsar Paul I. In it Pnin published translations of extracts from Montesquieu's *De l'Esprit des Lois*, Baron Holbach's celebrated *Système de la Nature* and *Morale Universelle* and Volney's *Les Ruines*. To reprint extracts from Montesquieu may have been safe enough, but it required a certain audacity to reproduce passages from the work of a professed atheist like Holbach or a Girondin like Volney at a time when the Emperor Paul's xenophobic and anti-revolutionary mania had reached its height. Pnin therefore prudently refrained from stating the sources of his material, and also resorted from time to time to the familiar device of disguising his topical allusions in the guise of oriental parables. 'Do you think', a vizier asks a caliph, 'that *educated* people will obey you better?' 'Yes', answers the liberal-minded caliph, 'because my people will then be better able to appreciate the justice of my laws.' 'But the sages', continued the vizier, 'will want to interfere with the state administration.' 'All the better', said the caliph, 'they ought to say freely whatever they think. If they did not speak freely, then their precepts would be incomplete. Other people will always be ready to refute their errors.' Pnin was an ardent advocate of free speech and improved standards of education. He even suggested in an article in the *St. Petersburg Journal* that women should enjoy the same academic opportunities as men.

Pnin's principal work, the *Essay on Education as applied to Russia* (1804), bears the motto: 'Happy are those monarchs and those lands where the citizen, possessing liberty of thought, may fearlessly communicate truths which involve the good of society.' The *Essay* is largely inspired by Jeremy Bentham's *Traités de Législation Civile et Pénale* (Paris, 1802, in Dumont's French edition) and expounds a form of social Utilitarianism. The aim of government, says Pnin, should be 'the greatest happiness of the greatest number of persons'. The key to political progress is education. There is a great difference between a brutish mob of ignorant slaves, tyrannised over by a despotic autocrat, and an organic body politic governed by a liberal-minded monarch. When each member of society recognises and fulfils his social obligations, and the Government, refraining from overstepping the boundary of its own legitimate power, respects the rights of the individual—then education has attained its aim. From such axioms as these, Pnin passed on to consider the immediate steps to be taken in order to regenerate Russian society. Naturally enough, he immediately concluded that serfdom was incompatible with social justice, as Radishchev had done before him. He pointed out that not only was slavery a crime against the serfs themselves, but that it ruled out any sense of civic responsibility among a vast section of the community and might at any moment plunge the country into chaos and utter ruin. He recommended that the Government should guarantee the inviolability of personal property and security and proceed to the formal abolition of serfdom.

The first edition of the *Essay* appeared with the approval and encouragement of the Emperor Paul's successor, Alexander I, whose accession was greeted with enthusiasm by all those whom Paul's reign had depressed and exasperated. The book sold so rapidly, however, and attracted so much public interest that the Censorship promptly took fright, prohibited a reprint, and seized and destroyed all available copies of the original edition. It contained, said the Censorship, 'an eloquent description of the sufferings of the peasant serfs, combined with a demand for the abolition of serfdom'. Such a work could not be tolerated.

Pnin promptly published what he alleged to be a translation of an ancient Manchurian manuscript entitled *The Author and the Censor*:

> *Author*: I have, Sir, a composition which I wish to publish.
> *Censor*: It must first be examined. What is its title?
> *Author*: Truth, Sir.
> *Censor*: Truth? Oh, we must examine and most carefully examine it.
> *Author*: It seems to me that you are taking a lot of superfluous

trouble. Examine the Truth? What does that mean? I tell you that it does not belong to me and has been in existence for several thousand years . . . Mortals, love one another, do not injure one another, be just one to another . . . that is the content of my composition.

Censor: Do not take anything one from another! Be just one to another! Sir, your composition must definitely be examined. Show it to me at once. . . . Not *every* Truth may be printed. . .

In spite of the light-hearted irony of this dialogue, Pnin was deeply injured by the suppression of his book. It accelerated the course of the consumptive ailment from which he suffered, and in a few weeks he was dead.

Certain of the reforms demanded by Pnin and Radishchev were carried out under Alexander I and his great minister Speransky, but the serfs were not freed until 1861. Meanwhile the Decembrists perished in a gallant but hopeless attempt to precipitate the changes in the Russian political system which they felt to be indispensable and overdue. But the investigation of the problem of social justice, which remained the absorbing preoccupation of Russian thinkers throughout the nineteenth century, had already been begun in the writings of men who believed, more sincerely than Catherine, in the efficacy of the doctrines of the Age of Reason.

XI

Science in Early Modern Times

➤➤

The Myth about Bacon and the Inductive Method

MORRIS R. COHEN

Sir Isaac Newton, 1642-1727

HENRY CREW

L'Encyclopédie and the History of Science

LYNN THORNDIKE

➤➤

The Myth about Bacon and the Inductive Method

MORRIS R. COHEN

>>>->>>->>>->>>->>>->>>->>>->>> *Published in 1926* <<<-<<<-<<<-<<<-<<<-<<<-<<<-<<<

No early modern philosopher of science has been so much written about as Sir Francis Bacon, the early-seventeenth-century essayist and politician, and the bulk of the literature that deals with his conception of science has been highly adulatory. This is due partly, no doubt, to the inability of many commentators to divorce content from style; and since Bacon has been universally admired as a stylist, his ideas on practically all subjects have often been credited with a validity that at times they lacked. Not that Bacon's conception of scientific method has always gone unchallenged. Even in his own time a number of his contemporaries criticized him for his failure to consult with scientists about procedures, to keep abreast of the experiments that were being conducted, and to appreciate the importance of mathematics. In more recent years the gifted American philosopher Morris R. Cohen added his voice to the minority group that challenged Bacon's approach. Not one to accept on faith the reputations even of the very great, Cohen makes a convincing case for his assertion that Bacon had a fundamental misunderstanding of the essential character of scientific method.

T he popular belief that Francis Bacon was the founder of modern science is so flagrantly in contradiction with all the facts of the history of science and so patently belied by the contents of Bacon's "Sylva Sylvarum" or the second book of his "Novum Organum" that it is most instructive to inquire how such an absurd belief ever gained currency among educated people. Unfortunately, however, the history

Reprinted by special permission from *The Scientific Monthly*, XXIII (1926), 504-508. The footnotes which originally appeared with this essay have been omitted.

of science previous to the seventeenth century is practically a closed book to those without both a classical and a scientific training. Even professional historians like Professor Robinson in his "Mind in the Making" seem to confirm the conventional fable that there was no science before the seventeenth century. Some indications, therefore, of the actual situation must be set down at the beginning.

(1) No one can well dispute the fact that the great body of modern science rests on foundations already laid before the appearance of the "Novum Organum" in 1620. One needs only to mention the work of men like Copernicus, Kepler, Galileo, Stevinus and Gilbert in physics, or of Vesalius and Harvey in biology—omitting, for simplicity of argument, the great mathematicians from Archimedes to Tartaglio and Cardanus. As all these men had long lines of predecessors as well as fellow-workers, Bacon's repeated claim that there was altogether no well-established science based on experience before he came on the scene would in any other man be characterized as the claim of a crank or charlatan. Ignorance on Bacon's part is too generous an excuse. For he certainly must have known something of the epoch-making scientific work of Harvey, whom he knew personally. Does this not make it appear that Bacon's exaggerated claim to originality as to scientific method was the courtier's desire to gain prestige in the eyes of King James? Certainly his treatment of Gilbert's unpublished writings which were entrusted to him did not show any disinterested desire for the spread of truth.

(2) But whatever we may think of the fact and the motives for Bacon's ignoring the scientific work of his own and previous time, there is the still more significant fact that he positively opposed the great constructive scientific achievements of his day—the achievements on which subsequent scientific progress has in fact been based.

(a) He opposed, for instance, the Copernican astronomy which had received notable confirmation in his day through the scientific work of Kepler and Galileo. This fact is so glaring that many of Bacon's admirers have resorted to strange arguments to minimize it. They have attempted to do so either by softening the statement of the fact or by trying to find some justification for Bacon's position. Neither of these arguments, however, is in the least tenable.

Despite the beclouding efforts of Whewell and others, Bacon's opposition to the Copernican astronomy was emphatically explicit.

In his "De Augmen. Scient.," he speaks of "the extravagant idea of diurnal motion of the earth, an opinion which we can demonstrate to be most false." This he repeats in the "Novum Organum."

Those who try to save the prestige of Bacon by claiming that in his day the evidence for the Copernican astronomy was inadequate, imply that Bacon's sense of evidence was superior to that of Kepler, Galileo and Gilbert. But this can not for a moment be tolerated by any one familiar with the mathematical work of Kepler, with Galileo's demonstration of the phases of Venus and especially with the very flimsy character of the evidence which Bacon himself adduced for the older view. His boasted proof consisted of nothing else but the naïve repetition of the Aristotelian doctrine that "the eternal motion of revolution appears peculiar to the heavenly bodies, rest to this globe."

(b) Bacon also opposed the growing and fruitful method of explaining physical phenomena as far as possible in terms of mechanics. This method, begun by the ancient Greeks and developed by the Italians in the latter part of the sixteenth century, did not appeal to Bacon, who believed in *species spiritualis* as the explanation of sound and that the "human understanding is perverted by observing the power of mechanical arts." Despite a few grudgingly approving words, Gilbert's genuinely experimental philosophy is rejected in principle. His experiments with magnets are called a waste of time, and his fundamental discoveries in electricity and magnetism which have proved basic are characterized as fables.

(3) Not only did Bacon ignore or oppose what was sound in the science of his day, but he himself, despite all his grandiloquent claims, failed to make a single important contribution to science.

The only two claims in this respect that I have ever seen are that

WILLIAM GILBERT: Late-sixteenth-century scientist remembered mainly for his studies of the magnet and magnetic bodies, his insistence on the use of experimental methods, and his differentiation between electrical and magnetic phenomena. Although he denied that the magnet had many of the medicinal uses ascribed to it in the past, he thought it valuable for the treatment of lax livers, among other ailments.

WILLIAM HARVEY: Seventeenth-century scientist and court physician to both James I and Charles I. His *On the Movement of the Heart and Blood,* dedicated to Charles I, was fundamental to the development of a science of physiology. Like all his contemporaries, he held to many scientific notions

Bacon anticipated Newton's discovery of gravitation and that he discovered heat to be a form of motion. Neither of these claims is true.

The first claim is made by Voltaire in the famous essay which
did more than anything else to establish Bacon's great European
reputation. But the claim that Bacon anticipated Newton's law of
gravitation is absurd on the face of it, since the Newtonian theory
is based on the Copernican astronomy, which Bacon rejected. Moreover, Voltaire, like other admirers of Bacon, does not seem to have
read Bacon with care or noticed his distinct assertion that bodies lose
weight below the surface of the earth. Newton could certainly not
have been influenced by such nonsense. Bacon's knowledge that the
speed of falling bodies increases as they approach the earth—which
Voltaire confuses with the law of gravitation—was an old commonplace in no way discovered by Bacon, whose views went no deeper
than the observation that some bodies are heavy, some light, and some
neither.

The second claim, that Bacon anticipated the modern doctrine of
heat as a form of motion, is likewise untenable. For Bacon rejected
the atomic theory ("Novum Organum," II, 8), and his method of
induction led him to infer that the motion which produces heat
"should take place not in the very minutest particles but rather in
those of some tolerable dimensions."

How far Bacon himself was from making any fruitful contributions to science is amply illustrated by the observations and conclusions
on almost every page of his "Sylva Sylvarum" and other pretended
scientific works. A few examples from the more widely read "Novum
Organum" may be cited: Refusing to grant that fire can ever separate

_____

that have since been exploded as myths. He believed, for example, that the
application of garlic to the soles of the feet aided expectoration.

LINCEAN SOCIETY, OR ACADEMY OF LYNXES: Organization founded in early-
seventeenth-century Rome for the advancement of scientific learning. Just
as the eyes of the lynx were supposed to penetrate even solid walls, so the
brains of its members were to get at the most intimate mysteries of nature.
Galileo became its most famous member, but after his condemnation in 1633
the society was so divided that by 1657 it went out of existence.

JUAN LUIS VIVES: Sixteenth-century scholar who championed the use of
experimental methods of research. What was much rarer for his time, he
insisted that women were as capable of learning as men.

the elements of a compound, he recommends the study of the spirit in every body, "whether that spirit is copious and exuberant, or meager and scarce, fine or coarse, aeriform or igniform, etc." Or consider the queer jumble of unrelated phenomena in his tables of instances on which an induction as to heat is to be based, containing the following gems: Confined air is particularly warm in winter, and "the irritation of surrounding cold increases heat as may be seen in fires during a sharp frost." All shaggy substances are warm, and so are spirits of wine. Boiling water surpasses in heat some flames, etc. I am not unaware that with due diligence somewhat similar absurdities may be culled from the pages of Gilbert, Kepler, Galileo, Boyle and even later writers in the Transactions of the Royal Society. But these men have positive achievement in science to their credit. Bacon has none. Nor could he very well have made any scientific discoveries so long as he believed in explaining things by "spirits" and relying on "axioms" whereby "gold or any metal or stone is generated from the original menstruum."

(4) Others have urged that while Bacon did not himself make any direct contribution to science, he founded the true method of science, the method of induction. There is, however, not a single authenticated record of any one ever making any important discovery in science by following Bacon's method and its mechanical tables and twenty-seven prerogative instances. It would, indeed, be most amazing if the man who ignored or rejected what was soundest in the science of his day, and put down as fact or conclusion so many absurdities as Bacon did, should become the originator or true expounder of scientific method.

It is true that some scientists, e.g., Boyle and other founders of the Royal Society, paid great tribute to Bacon. But none of their really scientific contributions was determined by the Baconian method. It was rather the methods which Bacon rejected, the methods of Kepler, Galileo and Gilbert, that they followed in their successful efforts. Also, the idea of a society for the promotion of natural and experimental knowledge was developed by the Italians (e.g., the Lincean Society, of which Galileo was a member) long before Bacon.

We need not ignore the fact that in the first book of the "Novum Organum" and more especially in his doctrine of the idols, Bacon has given us a most vivid, stirring and still applicable account of the perennial difficulties in the scientific study of nature. But his unusually eloquent appeal for the study of facts as opposed to idle speculation was neither new nor in fact very effective in the actual development of science. In the century before Bacon the Spaniard Vives had made the same criticisms, the same exhortations and almost the same grandiose plans. Indeed, we find the same appeal for the direct study of nature continually urged as far back as the twelfth century by the scholastic Adelard of Bath. But it is all rather futile. Science flourishes not on good intentions produced by pious exhortations, but on the suggestion of definite directions of inquiry and definite workable methods, and these Bacon entirely failed to produce.

Bacon's failure is most instructive because it shows the illusory character of the idea of induction which he and Mill after him made popular. According to this view the scientist begins without any regard for previous thought. Resolved not to anticipate nature, he lets the facts record their own tale. All this is purely Utopian. The facts of nature do not stream in on us with all their relevant characteristics duly marked. The number of possible circumstances that can be noted about any object is indefinitely large. Scientific progress depends upon considering only the circumstances that turn out to be relevant to the point of our inquiry. But what we consider relevant, e.g., in the inquiry as to the cause of cancer, depends upon previous knowledge. Hence scientific discoveries are not made by those who begin with an unbiased mind in the form of a *tabula rasa*, but by those who have derived fruitful ideas from the study of previous science. In the absence of carefully considered methods of observation that depend upon previous knowledge and critical reflection, the observation of nature herself is sterile. Those who think they can start any natural inquiry without "anticipating nature" or making any assumptions at all are just complacently ignorant. In any case, any one who begins, in the Baconian fashion, to observe nature *de novo* is bound to find many "facts" which are not so. Thus Bacon himself observes that cold diminishes after passing a certain altitude, that air is transformed into water, that clear nights are cooler than cloudy ones, that water in wells is warmer in winter than in summer, and that the moon draws forth heat, induces putrefaction, increases moisture and excites the motions of spirits. Of course many of the absurd observations that crowd the pages of Bacon were made for him by some of his assistants, like the Reverend Rawley, or taken from popular manuals of his day. But they are in any case typical of what untrained observers can and do record. No reader of Bacon can question his genius or the fertility of his mind; but a comparison of his ideas on science with the works of previous scientists upon whom he heaped rhetorical scorn shows the utter irrelevance of Bacon's ideas to the actual progress of science. Thus his classification of the types of motion displays great ingenuity. But all such concepts as the "motion of liberty," in which bodies "strive with all their power to rebound and resume their former density," lack the direct relevance which we find in the ideas of the sixteenth-century Italian predecessors of Galileo, like Benedetti. Compare similarly Bacon's vague statements about colors as "solitary" instances or white color as a "migratory" instance with the observations of Kepler's "Dioptrics" or even with the observations on the rainbow in Vitello's Optics published in 1270. The utter futility of the untrained amateur in science is borne in on us when we compare Bacon's ideas on the motion of the pulse, or his explanation of sex organs with the contemporary work of Harvey.

No wonder that a real scientist like Harvey was moved to say that Bacon wrote science like a lord chancellor.

How, then, in the light of the foregoing readily verifiable facts, are we to explain the tremendous extent and persistence of the tradition that looks to Bacon as the founder of modern science?

The first point to note is that Bacon is still eminently readable, while the scientific works of Kepler, Galileo, Gilbert and Harvey, not to mention their predecessors, are inaccessible to the general reader. The change from Latin to the vernacular as the language of the learned, together with the rapid growth of new technical methods since the eighteenth century, has made it difficult for scientists themselves to read the works of their predecessors of the sixteenth or previous centuries. But Bacon can be read by everybody. His pithy sayings are sententious and quotable like Cicero's. The general reader is carried away by the splendid rhetoric with which Bacon denounces as useless all previous work in science; and his errors of fact or irrelevance of ideas are either not recognized as such or else covered by the very broad but unhistorical reflection that they were good enough for Bacon's times.

The main source, however, of the Baconian myth is the great romantic appeal which inheres in the fundamental idea of organizing science on a new basis calling for no special aptitude or technical training. Technical science involves an arduous routine which can not be popular with the uninitiated. The multitude (including scientists away from their special domain) will always delight in any plan for a new deal in science—"a discovery which will lead to the discovery of everything else," or "a synopsis of all the natures that exist in the universe." That which makes utopias spring up perennially is found in Bacon's idea that if his system could be established "the invention of all causes and sciences would be the labor of but a few years." Especially in an age that believes in democracy and mechanical progress it is pleasant to be told that science exists for material enrichment and that everything can be achieved by rules leaving little to superior wits. It requires painful efforts to disabuse ourselves of such pleasant illusion.

Sir Isaac Newton, 1642-1727

HENRY CREW

Published in 1942

The story of the achievements of Isaac Newton in mathematics, physics, and astronomy, if not in theology, politics, and government service, has been told countless times. But it is a story that deserves to be retold. After all, few minds in the history of mankind have had the power and penetration of the English farm boy whose understanding family did not compel him to remain on the farm; and few minds have made so immense and basic a contribution to the advancement of man's knowledge of the world. There is even less need to justify the re-examination of the career of Newton when the examiner happens to be a scientist such as Henry Crew, former president of the History of Science Society and author of a valuable study, *The Rise of Modern Physics*, and of several volumes that have introduced thousands of American students to the intricacies of mechanics and physics.

Some seven miles south of Grantham in Lincolnshire lies the small village of Woolsthorpe. By going a mile or so beyond this tiny town, one may still see the farm which belonged to Newton's parents and may also visit the large stone house—and even the room—in which he was born. The event of his birth, the tercentenary of which is now being celebrated on both sides of the Atlantic, occurred on Christmas Day, 1642. Here in the quiet surroundings of Woolsthorpe the lad spent the first twelve years of his life. At the end of this period, while Oliver Cromwell was still Protector of England and science was just becoming the fashion of the day, the young boy was sent off to the "public" school in Grantham, where he spent the next five years.

Following this experience, came a brief attempt on the part of his mother—the father had died before the son's birth—to make a farmer

Reprinted by special permission from *The Scientific Monthly*, LV (1942), 279-284.

of him. She and her brother, the Reverend W. Ayscough, a Trinity College man, were however wise enough to see that the interests of the young Newton lay along the line of kites, windmills, water wheels, sun dials—in short, that he was devoted to mechanics and mathematics.

On the 5th of June, 1661, in his nineteenth year, he was admitted to Trinity College, Cambridge: and in 1665 was graduated B.A. Unfortunately, little is known about what subjects Newton pursued during these undergraduate years; even his class standing is unknown. Papers in Newton's handwriting show, however, that it was in this year that the first ideas of a differential calculus occurred to him. In the summer of 1665 the students of Trinity College were "forced from Cambridge by the plague." The same thing happened again in the following summer. Consequently, a long period of enforced leisure was enjoyed at his Woolsthorpe home. On the first of October, 1667, Trinity College elected him to a fellowship; and he again returned to Lincolnshire until the spring of the next year, when he received the Master of Arts degree. It was about this time that Dr. Isaac Barrow, distinguished mathematician and churchman, resigned the Lucasian professorship at Cambridge. To this chair, his pupil, Isaac Newton, now twenty-seven years of age, was promptly elected in 1669. The crowning honor for any young man—that of election to fellowship in the Royal Society of London—came on the 11th of January, 1672.

The key to such a rapid rise is doubtless to be found in the fact that, during two years of leisure at Woolsthorpe, this young mind had not only developed his invention of the calculus, but had also pondered over Kepler's laws and had wondered whether the curved orbit of the moon was not to be explained by the same force which makes a cannon ball take a curved path and an apple fall, from rest, in a straight line. The inverse square law had occurred to other minds, as indicated in the "Principia" (Scholium to Prop. IV of Bk. I.); but Newton set about to verify the law by experiment and thus give it validity and acceptance. He knew fairly well the size of the earth; knew also that the distance of the apple from the attracting center was one radius of the earth, while the distance of the moon was sixty times as great. To obtain the ratio of the squares of these distances is a matter of the simplest arithmetic.

To compare the earth's attraction at the distance of the moon with that at the surface of the earth, Newton relied upon the definition of force which, by universal experience and consent, makes it proportional to the acceleration produced. The problem is then reduced to a comparison of the distance which an apple falls from rest in one second with the distance which the moon falls away from the straight line tangent to its orbit in one second. But the ratio of these two accelerations did not agree as closely as he had hoped with the ratio of the inverse squared distances. Two uncertainties lingered in his mind: one as to the size of the earth; the other as to whether a sphere, such as the earth, attracts as if its entire mass were concentrated at its center. The first of these doubts was removed by the measures of Picard (1672): the second by a theorem of his own, proving, by his method of fluxions, that any solid sphere, in which the density is uniform over each concentric shell, attracts as if its mass were all at the center. The result was that the law of inverse squares was rendered highly probable.

A few years later this law was firmly established when Newton showed, again by use of his calculus, that, given two spheres attracting each other according to the inverse square law, the orbit of either body about their common center of gravity must be a conic. The great paper containing this research was presented to the Royal Society on the 28th of April, 1686.

We are still considering the use which Newton made of his leisure at Woolsthorpe during the years of 1665-66. Among his purchases during this period, one finds listed in his note book certain prisms, lenses, drills, putty, "glass bubbles," betraying his early interest in light and in the explanation of color. It is also significant that when, in 1669, he entered upon the duties of the Lucasian chair the subject which he chose for his lectures was optics. A memorable paper containing the outcome of these early optical experiments was presented to the Royal

LEIBNIZ: Mathematician who invented the calculus at about the same time as Newton. His interests and activities were not limited, however, to mathematics. As a statesman, he sought to push plans for the reform of the Holy Roman Empire so that it could protect itself against the expansionist policies of Louis XIV. As a philosopher, he formulated some of the basic doctrines that were to dominate the thought of the Enlightenment. As a religious reformer, he attempted to further a movement for the union of the Christian churches.

CHARLES MONTAGU: Whig politician and financier. Extremely influential in the reorganization of English public finance in the 1690's—when England was engaged in the War of the League of Augsburg—he played an

Society on the 8th of February, 1672, approximately one month after his election. A few sentences from this paper will illustrate the manner in which he disposes of the hitherto diverse and fantastic notions concerning color.

> Colours are not qualifications of light, derived from Refractions or Reflections of natural Bodies (as is generally believed) but *original and connate properties.* . . . To the same degree of Refrangibility ever belongs the same colour, and to the same colour ever belongs the same degree of Refrangibility. . . . The species of colour and degree of Refrangibility proper to any particular sort of Rays is not mutable by Refraction nor by Reflection from natural bodies nor by any other cause that I could yet observe.

Looking back over the four years that intervened between his graduation from Trinity College and his appointment to a professorship, one observes that the three outstanding achievements of his life were fairly initiated during this quadrennium. These were as follows:

1. The invention of the calculus—an honor which Newton shares with the German mathematician and philosopher, G. W. Leibniz (1646-1716). Oddly enough the first printed account of the Method of Fluxions, as it was then called, is to be found in Wallis's "Algebra," pp. 390-396, which appeared in 1693: and then only because some of Newton's friends in Holland had informed him that, on the continent, the "Method of Fluxions" was becoming known as "Leibniz's Calculus."

2. The idea that the moon and the planets are held in their respective orbits by an attractive force varying inversely as the square of the

---

important part in the early history of the Bank of England and in the formal establishment of the institution of the national debt.

THE ROYAL SOCIETY FOR IMPROVING NATURAL KNOWLEDGE: Organization of scientists which began to hold informal meetings about 1645 but whose official history dates from 1662, when Charles II became its patron. Filled with supporters of the King, it was granted numerous rights and privileges, among them, for example, the right to dissect the bodies of criminals. According to its statutes, it was to "question and canvass all opinions, adopting nor adhering to none, till by mature debate and clear arguments, chiefly such as are deduced from legitimate experience, the truth of such experiments be demonstrated invincibly."

distance from the central body. The mathematical proof of this theorem—presented to the Royal Society on 28th April, 1686—became the basis of the "Principia."

3. The simple theory of spectral colors, experimentally established in his youth—together with some later discoveries in interference and diffraction. These first came to light in his "Opticks," published in 1704.

From the preceding, it is clear that this young man at the age of thirty had definitely outlined three monumental contributions to human knowledge, had been elected fellow of Trinity College as well as fellow of the Royal Society and was now filling the leading chair of science at Cambridge University. Among the multitudinous activities of his later life, none exceeds in importance the publication of the "Principia—The Mathematical Principles of Natural Philosophy"—in 1687. Here we owe much to the astronomer, Edmund Halley (1656-1742), who, having come to believe in the inverse square law, went to Cambridge especially to visit Newton in August of 1684. Halley put to Newton this question, "What will be the curve described by a planet round the sun on the assumption that the sun's force diminishes as the square of the distance increases?" To this Newton promptly answered, "an ellipse." When asked for his reason, his reply was, "I have computed it." Halley then secured a promise from Newton to send this demonstration to the Royal Society for record. The promise was fulfilled in February of 1685. The paper carried the title "De Motu." Its four theorems and seven problems proved to be identical with some of the most important parts of the "Principia." We owe still more to Halley; because the Royal Society thrust upon him the responsibility of printing this great work, but gave him no funds to meet the expense. However Halley's brain was not only nimble enough to appreciate the difference between thinking that the moon's motion was consistent with the inverse square law and proving that the orbit of the moon must be a conic, but he was also generous enough to see the "Principia" through the press. The first edition was practically exhausted within four years of its publication; and a second edition did not appear until 1713. First published in Latin, the one language then understood by men of science in all the countries of Europe, the "Principia" became available to many students in England and in America only after 1729, when it was translated into English by Andrew Motte. It is this edition which the late Professor Cajori has revised and enriched with a scholarly fifty-page appendix. The simple elegance of this volume leaves nothing to be desired. On turning its pages one's only regret is that the pioneer who invented the calculus did not have the courage and wisdom to employ it here in his own book.

In the 382 pages of the "Opticks" (third edition, 1721), which first appeared in 1704, Newton thoroughly established the nature of spectral colors, the interference of thin plates, the phenomena of inflexion and the periodicity inherent in every ray of light.

Twice between the appearance of the "Principia" and the "Opticks" Newton represented Cambridge University in Parliament; but it does not appear that he ever took any very active part in the proceedings.

About this same time, early in the reign of William and Mary, Newton received another governmental appointment of considerable importance. The coinage of England had, since the Restoration, fallen into such a bad condition (owing to clipping and other mutilations) that a large percentage of it was refused acceptance in the payment of taxes. So when Charles Montagu was appointed Chancellor of the Exchequer he shortly afterward invited Newton to become Warden of the Mint. In this position the author of the "Principia" ably directed the recoinage of the entire metallic currency of England. In 1697, he was appointed to a still more important post, that of Master of the Mint. During all this while, he retained his Lucasian professorship at Cambridge; and it was only after occupying it for thirty-two years that he resigned it in December of 1701 and at the same time his fellowship in Trinity College.

English citizens generally consider the presidency of the Royal Society to be the highest honor which any British man of science can receive. It was in November of 1703 that Newton was elected to this post and annually reelected until his death in 1727. Knighthood came to him in April of 1705, when Queen Anne held court in Trinity Lodge at Cambridge.

The professional student will seek the acquaintance of Newton through the "Principia": but the layman will find a shorter and happier route through the reading of Bernard Shaw's recent play, "In Good King Charles's Golden Days." Here, in the first act, this accurate Irish scholar brings on to the stage (set for the drawing room in Newton's London house) the following persons in addition to Sir Isaac himself: King Charles II; Godfrey Kneller, the portrait-painter; the Duke of York, later James II; George Fox, the Quaker; Nell Gwynne; Bar-

bara Villiers; Mrs. Basham, Newton's housekeeper, and Sally, the housemaid. Far from being a romance, the play is one in which Shaw, with penetrating knowledge and marvelous skill, makes each reader personally acquainted with the historical characters represented by the *dramatis personae*. Space permits of only a brief sample of the conversation.

> CHARLES. We must not waste any more of Mr. Newton's time, Mistress Gwynne. He is at work on fluxions.
>
> NELLY. On what?
>
> CHARLES. Fluxions I think you said, Mr. Newton.
>
> NELLY. What are fluxions?
>
> CHARLES. Mr. Newton will tell you. I should be glad to know, myself.
>
> NEWTON. Fluxions, Madam, are the rates of change of continuously varying quantities.
>
> NELLY. I must go home and think about that, Mr. Philosopher.
>
> NEWTON. [*very seriously*] I shall be much indebted to you, Madam, if you will communicate to me the result of your reflections. The truth is, I am not quite satisfied that my method—or perhaps I had better say the notation of my method—is the easiest that can be devised. On that account I have never dared to publish it.
>
> NELLY. You really think I could teach you something, Mr. Newton? What a compliment! Did you hear that, Rowley darling?
>
> NEWTON. In these very simple matters one may learn from any one. And you, Madam, must have very remarkable mental powers. You repeat long parts from memory in the theater. I could not do that.
>
> NELLY. Bless me, so I do, Mr. Newton. You are the first man I ever met who did not think an actress must be an ignorant ninny—except schoolboys, who think she is a goddess. I declare you are the wisest man in England, and the kindest.
>
> CHARLES. And the busiest, Nelly. Come. He has given us as much of his time as we have any right to ask for.

Here must be left the story of the man whose laws of physics are employed in the design of every motor car, every airplane, every Diesel locomotive, every safe railway bridge.

L'Encyclopédie and the History of Science

LYNN THORNDIKE

➤➤➤-➤➤➤-➤➤➤-➤➤➤-➤➤➤-➤➤➤-➤➤➤-➤➤➤-➤➤➤ *Published in 1924* ⫷⫷⫷-⫷⫷⫷-⫷⫷⫷-⫷⫷⫷-⫷⫷⫷-⫷⫷⫷-⫷⫷⫷-⫷⫷⫷-⫷⫷⫷

The growth of science in early modern times (the sixteenth, seventeenth, and eighteenth centuries) has usually been written according to a "great man" conception of history. Copernicus, Tycho Brahe, Kepler, Galileo, Newton—these are some of the more important figures around whom the development of science has been made to revolve. It is refreshing, therefore, to read an article such as the present one by Lynn Thorndike, which is based on a quite different approach. Working on the assumption that the encyclopedias of an age throw a great deal of light on the scientific notions of that age, Thorndike has undertaken an examination of one of the most famous and influential reference works of all times, the *Encyclopédie* of Diderot and d'Alembert. And he emerges with several noteworthy conclusions. First, he discloses the dependence of eighteenth-century scientific thought on earlier thought. Secondly, he makes it clear that eighteenth-century scientific thought was closer in many respects to medieval than to contemporary thought. Finally, he points out that many an eighteenth-century scientific truth is now viewed as little more than a superstition—a fact that encourages the suspicion that many a scientific truth to which we hold today will in future times be regarded in the same way.

E ncyclopedias are perhaps the most important monuments of the history of science and of civilization. Not only do they comprise a wealth of detail brought together with the prime purpose of giving information, so that they are at least less intentionally misleading than many other documents. They also aim to cover the entire field

Reprinted by special permission from *Isis*, VI (1924), 361-386. The extensive documentation which originally appeared with this essay has been omitted.

of human interest in their day, so that the argument from silence can be employed in their case with more assurance than in other cases, and some quantitative conclusions may be ventured upon from the way in which their space is apportioned among the different fields of human endeavour, although of course this is to some extent a matter of chance, and the editors of the famous French *Encyclopédie* which is the object of the present study had occasion to complain that their contributors often composed articles of a length disparate to the relative importance of the subject treated. Even a one-man compilation such as the *Natural History* of Pliny the Elder appears to be our most comprehensive source for ancient civilization. A modern encyclopedia, to which various authorities in different departments are supposed to contribute, although a certain amount of unintelligent hack-work and repetition of previous encyclopedias may creep in, should, in its many-sided reflection of various aspects of civilization from different points of view, constitute a far more valuable picture of our civilization.

This possibility was well recognized by the editors of the eighteenth century French *Encyclopédie*. Diderot in the article *"Encyclopédie"* often adverts to the invaluable handy information which posterity may glean from their work concerning the conditions then prevalent. In defending certain historical disquisitions on such themes as cooking and fashions in clothing, which some readers and critics of the previous volumes had regarded with disfavor, he affirmed,—not perhaps without a touch of that playful irony which gives the *Encyclopédie* a spice

---

ALMAGEST: The Great Work. The name given by Arabic writers to the *Syntaxis* of Ptolemy, the influential second-century writer on astronomy and geography.

BUFFON: Eighteenth-century naturalist who had a talent for writing. His massive *Natural History of Animals* is one of the masterpieces in the literature of science. From the historical point of view, it is unfortunate that today he is remembered not so much for those scientific ideas that rooted him in his own time as for the fact that he anticipated the idea of biological evolution.

JANSENISTS: Roman Catholic followers of the early-seventeenth-century Flemish bishop Cornelis Jansen. In general they upheld the Augustinian doctrine of predestination and denied the free will which the Jesuits stressed. The result was a series of bitter controversies between Jansenists and Jesuits in seventeenth- and eighteenth-century France. Pascal's *Provincial Letters*

generally lacking in its more recent imitators, although Pliny its ancient predecessor had likewise indulged in satire and irony,—that "the most succinct of our articles of this sort will perhaps save our descendants years of research and volumes of dissertations," and that "a writing on our modes which is today thought frivolous will be regarded two thousand years from now as a learned and profound work on French costume, a work very instructive for men of letters, painters, and sculptors." Whatever his publisher thought, Diderot did not conceive of l'*Encyclopédie* as a commercial undertaking nor as of the nature of ephemeral or popular literature, but as *"un dictionnaire universel et raisonné"* ["a universal, analytical dictionary"], intended for the general and permanent instruction of mankind. It is as such that we shall accept it and examine it in the following pages. Our survey will be based primarily upon the original folio edition of 1751 and following, and our illustrations will be drawn chiefly from the earlier volumes in which the editors were freer in working out their plan and ideals without interference, and not from the last ten volumes which, after the suspension of the undertaking by the Parlement of Paris and the withdrawal of the scientist d'Alembert from the co-editorship in 1759, were hurriedly and secretly completed by Diderot and then, without Diderot's knowledge, were much mutilated by the timid publisher, Lebreton. Only in a few instances shall we include articles from the supplementary volumes which were issued in 1776.

Our concern will be with the place of l'*Encyclopédie* in the history

---

(1656) and Racine's plays were the outstanding literary products of Jansenism.

JOHN MORLEY: English Liberal politician and writer (d. 1923). A vigorous rationalist, he expressed his hostility to clerical influence in a number of historical studies that were published in the years when the science-religion controversy, growing out of Darwinism, was raging: *Voltaire* (1872), *Rousseau* (1873), and *Diderot and the Encyclopaedists* (1878).

PHLOGISTON THEORY: The fire theory which dominated the history of eighteenth-century chemistry. What escaped when substances were burned was called phlogiston. And since metals increased in weight when burned, the notion was that phlogiston had negative weight. Sometimes phlogiston was believed to be sulfur, sometimes alcohol, sometimes light. Joseph Priestley, Henry Cavendish, and James Watt all accepted the theory. It was Lavoisier who was most instrumental in bringing about its rejection.

of science. This topic appears to have hitherto received little attention, either from the historians of the sciences or from students of the eve and background of the French Revolution. Diderot is noted individually in the history of medicine for his *Letters on the Blind* and as a biologist has been represented as a forerunner of Bichat, Lavoisier, Gall and Darwin. D'Alembert is of course a well known name in the history of mathematical science and celestial mechanics. But when the Encyclopedists are viewed collectively, it is usually as materialistic "philosophers" who attacked the church and Bible and Christian religion, also *"les abus"* generally, and who agitated or paved the way for political and social reform. For John Morley "philosophy" in the French eighteenth century sense of the word and as used in l'*Encyclopédie* was more or less identical with liberalism and the idea of progress. But I cannot interpret its meaning as quite in that sense. Not only does it, like the philosophy of ancient Greece, include all the sciences, natural, mathematical, and social; scientific research is its very essence. In its very title science came first: *Encyclopédie ou dictionnaire raisonné des sciences, des arts et des métiers par la société des gens de lettres.* When d'Alembert in the *Discours préliminaire* states that "the Renaissance of letters . . . that memorable epoch. . . , began with erudition, continued with Belles-Lettres, and ended in philosophy," he has in mind especially the scientific advance of the eighteenth century. Diderot, too, in the article *"Encyclopédie,"* in comparing his own age with the seventeenth century, says, "Those sciences least common in the century past become more common from day to day," and speaks of the "general movement toward natural history, anatomy, chemistry, and experimental physics." He even had confidence that the expressions proper to those sciences would change the face of even popular speech, and that before another century passed a dictionary of the Age of Louis XIV or even of his own would not contain two-thirds of the words then in use. Alas! the technical vocabulary of the various sciences has increased too rapidly for any general assimilation of it into human speech, or, which is even more regrettable, for any adequate absorption of scientific discovery and method into the general current of human thought.

Yet this last, too, was what Diderot and d'Alembert and their collaborators hoped and worked for, although they realized the need of two sets of workers, namely, researchers and winnowers. And it was in this connection that much of the philosophizing, more strictly called, of the two editors themselves came in. "Every science, every art has its metaphysics," says Diderot. "This side is always abstract, lofty, and difficult. Yet it should be the chief concern of a philosophic dictionary," such as l'*Encyclopédie*. Similarly d'Alembert in treating the topic, "*éléments des sciences*," states that what is most needed is a metaphysics of propositions, which should be nothing more than a clear and precise exposition of the general and philosophic truths on which the principles of the science are founded. D'Alembert would perhaps agree with Diderot that the problem of making such an exposition was difficult, but he believed that the result should be easy to assimilate. "The simpler, easier, and, so to speak, more popular this metaphysics is, the more precious it is," for "truth is simple and should be treated as it is." Yet d'Alembert had no patience with mere speculation or theorizing in physical science, and in both his articles on *Physique* and on experimental method strongly advised against "giving reasons for what escapes us" and against "that craze for explaining everything which Descartes introduced into physical science." In both articles he gives the same illustration that, supposing the barometer rose before rain, physicists would explain the action by saying that the air had become heavier through being charged with vapors, and this would seem a reasonable explanation. But it is not satisfactory because the barometer falls instead of rising before rain. Or if it were the case that snow fell in summer and hail in winter, the explanation might be given that this was because in summer the heat of the air kept the particles from congealing completely, while in winter the cold air near the earth hardened them into hail-stones. This explanation would satisfy everyone, says d'Alembert, and pass for demonstrative. Yet the fact which it explains is false. D'Alembert also quotes with approval from Musschenbroeck's *Essai de Physique* the assertion that "when one examines everything exactly, one finds that there are many more particular laws than general laws." So much for some indication that, while somewhat more spirited and readable, not to say better written, than most modern encyclopedia articles and scientific monographs, l'*Encyclopédie* is not dominated by some facile philosophy but is permeated by a truly scientific spirit. And lest I seem unfair to Lord Morley, let me hasten to add that he was aware that Diderot, unlike Voltaire and Rousseau, had the idea of scientific method as well as the "rare faculty of true philosophical meditation," and that the social philosophy of *Encyclopédie* was founded in positive science. But Lord Morley was mainly interested in the social philosophy; we shall interest ourselves in the science.

Since, however, our investigation is an historical one, and since history may be regarded as one of the sciences—just as some of them are still classed as *Histoires* in *l'Encyclopédie*, while d'Alembert closes his article on experimental method with the suggestion that in addition to the chair of experimental physical science recently established by the king at the University of Paris there should be three others in Ethics, Public Law, and History—since this is the case, we may well commence with the attitude of *l'Encyclopédie* toward history and the history of science. "It is not enough for us," observes d'Alembert in the *Discours préliminaire*, "to live with our contemporaries and to lord it over them. Moved by curiosity and self-love, and seeking with natural avidity to embrace at once past, present, and future, we wish at the same time to live with those who will follow us and to have lived with our predecessors. Hence the origin and the study of history." Nor is it a science without high utility. "Philosophy, often powerless to correct abuses, can at least disentangle their origin." Diderot for his part, in listing the qualifications of the ideal author and the ideal editor for an encyclopedia, stated some of the most essential traits in an historian. He should narrate events of his own time, "as if he were a thousand years off, and those of his native place, as if he were two thousand leagues away." He should never be enthusiastic except for truth, virtue, and humanity. A great knowledge of bibliography is necessary or he will "repeatedly compose in mediocre style at much labor, time, and expense what others have done better," and will go to great trouble to discover what is already known. Finally, "the exact citation of sources would be of great utility; one ought to make it a rule."

The value of the history of science is recognized in the *Discours préliminaire*, where it is said that "the historical exposition of the order in which our sciences have followed one another will . . . enlighten us ourselves as to the way in which we should transmit these sciences to our readers." And some of the particular articles, such as "Anatomie" (by Haller, which appeared first in the supplementary volumes of 1776), "Chirurgie" and "Bibliothèque" contain very good or full historical summaries for the time when they were written. From them the historian of science might possibly get some valuable hints even today.

But an unfortunate philosophy of history and interpretation of the course of civilization tends to vitiate the historical outlook of *l'Encyclo-*

pédie as a whole, and has similarly affected the study of the history of science since, although I do not know if this is a direct legacy from the French encyclopedia passed on through its various successors. First there is the notion that the history of science "is naturally bound up with that of a small number of great geniuses," such as Hippocrates in antiquity, Roger Bacon and Albertus Magnus in the middle ages—who, though they lived in times when the profoundest ignorance prevailed, yet possessed a universality of knowledge in all the sciences "so uncommon in our enlightened age that they would pass even today for prodigies"—, Francis Bacon, that great forerunner of the light, though "born in the bosom of blackest night," Descartes, who "changed the face of philosophy," Galileo, and especially Locke and Newton. As a matter of fact, of course, the works attributed to Hippocrates were composed by a number of subsequent writers over a considerable lapse of time, which is perhaps a sufficient indication that great names are apt to have more credited to them than is their due. Second, there is far too emphatic and exaggerated generalization, as we have just incidentally noted, to the effect that the middle ages were "a long interval of ignorance," when for twelve centuries the chief works of the ancients were forgotten, when the church persecuted scientists, and when scholasticism "constituted all the pretended science of centuries of ignorance."

The short article "Architecture" by Blondel is written from the academic Palladian standpoint which idolized the "simplicity, beauty, and proportion of ancient architecture" and insisted upon "propriety and correctness of design." The article "Cathédrale" is even briefer, while full descriptions are given of military matters and industrial processes. It may be noted, however, that Blondel applied the term "Gothic" to the architecture of the early medieval period before Charlemagne, which he regarded as heavy and northern and the opposite extreme from the later medieval building, which went in his opinion to an excess of delicacy and profuse ornament under southern Saracen influence. Blondel evidently had a very imperfect knowledge of the history and dates of medieval architecture, and ascribed great influence on its course to Hugh Capet and his son Robert.

As far as the disparagement of medieval science is concerned, some of the particular articles contain mentions of medieval scientists such as Al-Hazen and Witelo which are scarcely consistent with it. D'Alembert concedes the discovery of the musical scale to Guido d'Arezzo (c.

995-1050 A.D.), and has the grace to recognize that the origin of all our ideas in sensations had been held axiomatic by the scholastic philosophers long before Locke, but had been rejected during the Renaissance along with the rest of scholasticism. But such concessions and mentions of individuals affect not at all the general attitude of l'*Encyclopédie* towards antiquity, middle ages, and "Renaissance." The difficulty is that the names of medieval scientists, when mentioned, have simply been taken from previous histories of the sciences; there is no evidence that their works had been looked into, much less read through, by the writers of the articles in l'*Encyclopédie*. It would have been better had d'Alembert applied to the middle ages as well his *bon mot* concerning the ancients, "to whom we believe ourselves very superior in the sciences because we find it shorter and more agreeable to prefer ourselves to them than to read them." Then he might have realized that it was not the ancients alone who "have not neglected *la physique expérimentale* as we ordinarily suppose," and might have avoided such errors as placing John Campanus of Novara in the eleventh century instead of the last half of the thirteenth, calling Adelard of Bath a monk, making Guido Bonati come from Friuli, dating Peter of Abano in 1320, and asserting that the only medieval version of the *Almagest* was a Jewish translation of an Arabic translation of a Syriac translation. But usually l'*Encyclopédie* makes no such recondite allusions as these to medieval science but contents itself with such legends as that of the condemnation of Bishop Virgilius for believing in the Antipodes or the persecutions suffered by Friar Bacon, whom Jebb's publication of the *Opus Maius* in 1733 had recently recalled to men's minds and whom d'Alembert does characterize as "the monk (*sic*) Bacon, too little known and too little read today." Haller's long account of the history of anatomy totally omits the middle ages and is valuable and very detailed for the period from Vesalius on. And in general it is only for the sixteenth and seventeenth and early eighteenth centuries that l'*Encyclopédie* gives any accurate, interesting information anent scientific men and discoveries, some of whom are possibly now in their turn too forgotten.

We have already implied that l'*Encyclopédie* held the now much shattered and well nigh totally abandoned theory of the Renaissance in the closing fifteenth and sixteenth century, which it regarded as "one of those revolutions" which are necessary to free mankind from barbarism and which change the face of the earth. "The Greek Empire is destroyed, its ruin causes the little learning that still survived to flow back into Europe: the invention of printing, the protection of the Medicis and of Francis I revived the mind of man; and light everywhere had new birth." What an improbable, insufficient, irrelevant, rhetorical set of explanations! D'Alembert would have been ashamed to approach a problem in physics in this manner. Yet such explanations of the "Renaissance" satisfied most writers and readers for over a century longer. But d'Alembert was at least keen enough to see that the humanists had the defects of servile imitation of the ancients and too great self-complacency, and that they too narrowly devoted themselves to literary erudition, to the exclusion of scientific research and political and social reform.

The philosophy of history, then, is a weak point of l'Encyclopédie, not in harmony with the scientific spirit evidenced elsewhere in it, lending justification to the charge of shallow thinking and too great trust in "reason" which has been made against the French "philosophers." Sometimes, however, d'Alembert makes a happy observation, as when he says that "the infancy of the sciences is long, or better, eternal." And the theory of revolutions expressed so frequently in l'Encyclopédie is interesting both as a sort of survival of the astrological doctrine of revolutions, and in view of the approaching French Revolution at which the encyclopedists more than once hint darkly.

Along with this faulty philosophy of history goes an uncritical attitude in historical matters generally Indeed, the fact that at first "all the articles in ancient and modern history," as well as "all the articles concerning poetry, eloquence, and literature in general," were the work of Mallet (1713-1755), a doctor of theology and professor at Paris, who further was responsible for the theological articles, does not augur well for the independent treatment of history in l'Encyclopédie. However, he does not seem to have had much to do either with its philosophy of history or its treatment of the history of science.

At first it amazes the reader that a work supposed to represent a revolt against the Christian church should unquestioningly accept the chronology of the Old Testament as the opening chapter of human history, and begin its historical introduction concerning almost any topic with an account of the belief or practice of the ancient Hebrews in this regard. I fail to detect any satire or mental reservation in such passages; they seem the regular course of procedure and quite matter-of-fact. It must be kept in mind that scientific excavation and archaeology had not yet disclosed the early history of man; that

Africa, Australasia, and most of America were still unknown continents, while countries like Russia and Japan were outside the pale of civilized intercourse; that none of the ancient oriental languages had been deciphered, so that a scholar could seriously argue that the arts of divination had arisen from the ancient Egyptians forgetting the meaning of their hieroglyphic symbols and attaching themselves to the mere letters. Sanskrit, too, was as yet unknown to European scholars, so that the chief accounts of the early history of man were the Old Testament, Homeric poems, and legends of the seven early kings of Rome. The encyclopedists accepted the last of these three as historic fact, and might equally well accept the first. When Newton had gravely discussed the duration of the world on the basis of the chronological implications of *The Book of Genesis* and had come to the conclusion that the Argonautic expedition would have to be dated in 900 rather than 1400 B. C., is it surprising that d'Alembert, though rejecting as ridiculous the story of the Babylonians having made astronomical observations for 470,000 years, should incline to accept Porphyry's assertion that when Alexander the Great took Babylon these observations had been in process for some 1903 years, which would fix the origin of them 115 years after the deluge and fifteen years after the erection of the tower of Babel in a plain where no mountains cut off the view of the stars? Yet on such a topic as the Concordat of 1516 and its relation to the Pragmatic Sanction of Bourges l'*Encyclopédie* offers an admirably clear and precise account.

Indeed in general there is less either of open attack or covert satire against theology and religion than I had expected in l'*Encyclopédie*, and also, perhaps, less than many of its readers were hoping for, as would appear to have been the case from the letters of Voltaire to d'Alembert and the letter of d'Alembert to Voltaire quoted by Lord Morley. D'Alembert himself, rather than Diderot, seems to have been the one most ready to break a lance with orthodoxy or the clergy, and sometimes apparently went outside his proper scientific field to write articles which would give him that opportunity, for instance, those on Geneva, the Jewish Cabbala, *Forme substantielle*, *Formulaire*, and Fornication. In dealing with the last topic, as might have been expected, he was ably aided and abetted by Voltaire. The article "*Formulaire*" administers a stinging rebuke to religious quarrels in general and that connected with the Jansenists in particular.

I have never been able to see that the deluge theory in geology was especially the work of the church. Certainly it was not a product of the middle ages,—when there seems to have been rather less respect for the literal sense of the Bible than there was after the invention of printing and the Protestant Revolt—but, as the article on Fossils in l'*Encyclopédie* states, began to develop in the sixteenth century. Even the letter of the Bible was not here in question, for, as our article further states, *The Book of Genesis* does not say that the fossil fauna and flora buried in the earth or the shells and marine bodies found at great heights above sea level were deposited by Noah's flood. The theory presumably developed because that flood, like King Numa or Romulus, often suggested itself to the minds of the scientists of that supposedly more enlightened age. If any of them actually desisted from another explanation from fear of religious persecution, one suspects that they must have been under a misapprehension or troubled by their own morbid consciences. Certainly the writer in l'*Encyclopédie* makes no bones of rejecting the deluge as an explanation of the present location of fossils.

On the whole, Christian theology and institutions seem to have been minimized by brevity of treatment and reduction of the amount of space devoted to them rather than by devoting unfavorable attention to them. Thus the writer of the article on Faith, l'Abbé Morellet of the Sorbonne, whose contributions Lord Morley noted as "the chief examples . . . of a distinctively and deliberately historic treatment of religion," apologizes for the extreme length of his article. But it is shorter than that on Fountains or *Forges* or Furnaces, while the article on Fundamentals of Faith occupies less than a page. The success of l'*Encyclopédie*, despite its faults, was ascribed by Diderot to the great number of new things in it which could not be found elsewhere. And where l'*Encyclopédie* has perhaps had the most lasting and distant effect upon the Christian religion is that people today refer to an encyclopedia rather than read the Bible.

The new matter which crowded out or reduced the relative importance of theological, scholastic, and classical interests was in large measure the full discussion of the mechanical arts, industrial and agricultural processes, and especially machines. And this was the especial department of Diderot, himself the son of a cutler. Thus the article on the stocking knitting frame and its 2,500 parts was over ten times as long as the article on cathedrals. At that time this frame was "one of the most complicated and important machines that we have." It is indeed remarkable that Diderot should have laid so much stress upon machinery at a time when it was so little developed, and we must regard him as a prophet of the industrial revolution as well as of the French Revolution. The mention of Jethro Tull in the article on agriculture shows l'*Encyclopédie* in touch also with recent progress in that direction. The article *Bateau*, on the other hand, is very brief, and in general the problem of transportation does not seem to have received great attention. The utilitarian argument advanced in the *Discours préliminaire* on behalf of the mechanical as against the liberal arts would hardly seem to cover the generous space accorded to the art of war. And it is with regret that one finds the article *Machine* occupied more with the infernal machine than any other, and that one further finds its introduction into warfare ascribed not to cruel tyrants but to the Dutch against Alexander of Parma and the English against the coast towns of France.

Diderot found difficulty in learning about the arts from artisans, who wished to keep their profitable processes secret or feared governmental interference and taxation and often told him "the most ridiculous falsehoods." He also was interested in the history of the mechanical arts and felt the need of an account of their origin, but feared that little historical material would be available and that it would have to be largely hypothetical. D'Alembert, too, in the *Discours préliminaire* asked why those who had developed the mechanical clock and watches should not be as esteemed as those who had successively perfected algebra. In his account of whale-fishing Diderot goes into its past history, mentioning the contention of some that sailors from Cap Breton near Bayonne, in following the whales far to sea to discover their retreats, discovered Newfoundland and Canada a century before Columbus, while others held that the first voyage to America for whales was made in 1504 by the Basques.

The need of science in the arts was strongly felt by Diderot. A well trained naturalist would "recognize at a glance the substances employed by artisans of which they commonly make so much mystery." Their absurd lies would not impose on a chemist for a moment. A physicist would see the "explanation of no end of phenomena at which the workingmen remain astonished all their lives." So we may credit l'*Encyclopédie* with having done not a little to encourage the development of applied science.

But we now turn to the science more strictly speaking of l'*Encyclopédie* with the particular purpose of examining how far its scientific articles have advanced from the conceptions current in ancient and medieval science to those of recent years, and what their attitude is to the occult science, the magic, and the superstition of which there were so many traces in ancient and medieval science. On the whole it may be said that l'*Encyclopédie* shows us science fairly thoroughly purged of magic, and that its opposition of science against superstition is more frequent and manifest than that of deism against Christianity. But it is further to be observed that neither is much light thrown on the problem how these magical beliefs and practices came to be abandoned, nor are we usually given any more satisfactory or scientific arguments against them than had been adduced in the past. Such superstitious notions are commonly simply dismissed with a stock formula of condemnation to the effect that in this present enlightened century it is unnecessary to demonstrate their chimaerical character. This airy waving aside of past tradition and this confidence in contemporary enlightenment does not, however, entirely satisfy us, especially when we read in l'*Encyclopédie* itself that as recent and distinguished a scientist as Boyle had believed that some amulets were effective, because he had finally succeeded in checking a nosebleed when other remedies failed by the method of applying some of a powdered human skull on the skin, while Van Helmont had cured patients of the plague by troches of pulverized toads worn as amulets. As for philtres, after citing Van Helmont, Hartmann and Langius in their favor, l'*Encyclopédie* concludes that while there may be ones which drive persons mad or cause loss of memory, it is difficult to believe that there are any which inspire love for one particular person rather than for another.

Most of the articles on specific magic arts were written by the aforesaid general utility man, Mallet, perhaps being considered to fall under the caption of Theology, which was one of his departments. They are usually disappointing, displaying little originality or breadth of knowledge and being largely based upon Delrio's *Disquisition on the Magic Arts*. The article on *Magie* itself, however, forms somewhat of an exception, belittling the importance of natural and supernatural (or diabolical) magic, although pronouncing both natural and divine magic unobjectionable. Greek fire is mentioned as an example of the natural magic of the ancients, who are regarded as more advanced in this field than the moderns. But already we find magic regarded as to-day as especially the affair of savage and barbarous peoples. It is briefly defined as "an occult science or art which trains one to do things which seem beyond human power." Another exceptional article is that on divination, written by Diderot himself, but it is less notable for its discussion of its proper subject than for its conclusion urging the writer's contemporaries to stand out fearlessly against error as Cicero did against divination and the early Christian martyrs did against paganism. However, it also enters on speculations as to the origin of divination under the stimulus of Condillac's *Philosophic Conjectures on the Origin and Progress of Divination*, and, besides the usual division of artificial from natural divination, distinguishes from chimaerical divination the experimental variety drawn from natural causes—such as, presumably, weather prediction. The divining rod is handled rather tenderly in the article *Baguette*. Physiognomy, however, is called a pretended art, and the arguments of Buffon against it are cited, which reduce to the contention that the soul has no connection with the lineaments of the face or the figure of the body—a line of argument which would hardly be adopted by a materialistic philosophy such as is sometimes thought to have characterized l'*Encyclopédie*. Similarly the chief argument against judicial astrology is the favorite patristic and theological one of human free will and morality. All the other arguments are stale and stock, nearly as old as the art of astrology itself, and directed chiefly if not exclusively against horoscope-casting. The attack upon astrology in Voltaire's *Philosophical Dictionary* is even less considerable and made up partly of pleasantries.

Mallet holds fast with Boyle to natural astrology or astrometeorology, affirming that humidity, heat and cold, and the like are dependent on the revolutions, movements, and positions of the other planets as well as sun and moon; that each planet has its own light, modifying the reflected rays of the sun so that the rays are endowed with a specific power of the planet's own which varies with that planet's aspects in reference to the sun and distance from the sun, and so exerts an energetic virtue on sublunar beings. Astrology thus seems to have lost nothing as a result of the change from geocentric to heliocentric hypothesis. Likewise the preliminary *Explication du système des connoissances humaines*, besides physical astronomy, recognizes as distinct from "the chimaera of judicial astrology" that science of the influences of the stars known as physical astrology. When therefore d'Alembert, writing the article *Astrologue*, says that, while formerly the greatest men seem to have believed in astrology, now the name of astrologer has become so ridiculous "that even the lower classes put but little faith in the predictions of our almanachs," he perhaps means to censure only the prediction of human fate. However, his articles *Ascendant* and *Configuration* are also unfavorable and in the articles *Fœtus* and *Generation* no reference is made to the influence of the planets on the process of the formation of the child in the womb. Here again, as in the case of religion and the mechanical arts, it is perhaps a case of the attention being diverted to new things, for the space formerly occupied by astrological doctrine is now filled with an account of observations through the microscope. Mallet's article *Arithmancie* warns the reader that the passage in *The Book of Revelation* concerning the number of the beast should not be confused with this divination by means of numbers nor cited to justify it,—possibly a mischievous dig at the Bible.

Diderot's distinction between chimaerical divination and the experimental variety drawn from natural causes reminds one of the close connection between magic and experimental books in the middle ages. In d'Alembert's article on experimental method he makes a distinction between observation or even ordinary human experience and the experimental method. To the last the ancients did not apply themselves to any great extent, contenting themselves with reading the book of nature, but very assiduously and with better eyes than moderns think, but cultivating experiment proper only in the useful arts and not to satisfy, like us, a purely philosophical (or scientific) curiosity. Experimental method seeks to penetrate more deeply into nature's secrets, to create somehow by different combinations of bodies new phenomena to study: in fine, it does not merely listen to nature but questions and heckles her (*la presse*). One might call it occult physics, provided the word "occult" be understood in a more philosophic (scientific) and true sense than by certain modern physicians (or, physicists) and restricted to knowledge of concealed facts, not applied to the romance of supposed facts. Here again the association of the experimental with the occult, but passing from the magical to the scientific realm! And while we have heard d'Alembert advise against "giving reasons for what escapes us," he would only encourage "that spirit of conjecture which, at once timid and enlightened, leads sometimes to discoveries," provided it remains conjectural until real discovery is assured.

D'Alembert's use of the word "occult" suggests the question, how far does the belief in occult virtues survive in l'*Encyclopédie*. We have already touched somewhat on the point in speaking of amulets and philtres. The marvelous properties that had been once attributed to gems are totally discredited and even the medicinal properties are usually omitted in the articles on the stones themselves. As M. de Vandernesse remarks in his article on the agate, "Great virtues are attributed to the agate the same as to other precious stones; but they are all imaginary." Even the bezoard is discussed at some length without mention of the virtues ascribed to it. Chemistry is described in the introductory *Explication du système des connoissances humaines* as artificial research for the interior and occult properties of natural bodies, but here the meaning is evidently of the scientific sort desired by d'Alembert. However, it is also stated that "chemistry has given birth to alchemy and natural magic." And Mamouin, writing on alchemy, complains that "chemistry makes ungrateful use of the advantages she has received from alchemy; alchemy is maltreated in most chemical books"; and he distinguishes between the true alchemist and the charlatan. Venel, in a long article on *Chymie* which has at least this much in common with the writings of the alchemists that it is muddy to the uninitiated, regards Boyle as a mere physicist and longs for chemistry to come into its own and not be tied down by physics or subordinated to physics as the more general science.

L'*Encyclopédie* displays not a little scepticism on the subject of *materia medica*. The article on the cat warns us that while most authors of works of *materia medica* have recommended the use of different parts of the animal for this and that, not one of them has confirmed it by his own experience, and that it doubts *"ces prétentions de livre en livre"* [these claims that have been copied by one book after another]. It adds, however, perhaps for our amusement, that one author enjoins that the sex of the cat employed be the same as the sex of the patient. The article on the dog, however, appears to be more credulous as to its medicinal properties. The oldwife's remedy of opening a little dog and applying it all hot to the head is characterized as "perhaps too neglected today." Dog fat is recommended. The excrement of the dog is said to be used by apothecaries under the name *album graecum*, and in this case we encounter the old familiar suggestion that the dog be fed on bones. The recipe of stewing three new-born puppies in olive oil is given, but the comment is added that the only value of the puppies is their fat; that is, the attendant circumstances are really useless. The writer on the cabbage states that most of the medicinal properties ascribed to it by the ancients are today doubted, and that he is inclined to go still further and rank it only as a food and not as a medicine at all. On the other hand, the article *Cigogne* lists the use of various parts of the stork against poisons and the pest, for eye-troubles and other complaints. The Chevalier de Jaucourt rejects all that Pliny and Paul of Aegina, Van Helmont and Muller have said concerning the virtues of ear-wax as wretched stuff. "Let's tell the truth: that humour of the glands which appears from its consistency and bitterness a compound of wax and oil may have some slight cleansing, abstergent, and detersive quality," but there are many better remedies of that sort. On the subject of poisons the contributor Daubenton, Buffon's "faithful lieutenant and squire at arms," was quite sceptical, doubting, for instance, from his own experience and that of others who had worked with antimony without experiencing bad effects, if its vapors were poisonous, as most chemists and Paracelsus held, and also if spiders at least in France were poisonous except for inflaming the skin. Vandernesse added to this the comment, "The medical man treats the poison and sting of the spider a little more seriously than the naturalist," but he declares that experience does not support the belief that a spider's web is a specific against intermittent fever.

Yet the naturalist affirmed that little spiders grew at the same rapid rate whether they ate or not. According to his account they grow almost as you watch them. If they can catch a fly, they eat it, but they sometimes go for a day or two or even longer without being seen to take nourishment, "yet they enlarge always at the same rate, and their increase is so rapid that each day they more than double in size." We are assured, however, that the chameleon does not live on air. It is a little discouraging to note that l'*Encyclopédie* still finds it necessary to enter into full and explicit denial of the old tale of the beaver's biting off his testicles to save himself from the hunters, when it had already repeatedly been shown false both in antiquity and the middle ages. And we find the article *Chameau* still citing Solinus to the effect that the camel has but one hump, and Aristotle and Pliny to the effect that it has two humps and the dromedary only one. The article on the bat states that most authors have taken it for a bird, but that it is a quadruped. The long article on the carp and its anatomy is Galen-like in regarding the marvelous structure of its parts as evidence of "the hand of the sovereign Artist." Similarly the article *Coquillage* urges the study of such species in many different localities in order to gain "a new idea of nature's resources and of the sovereign Intelligence who is their Author." The article on the brain gives the opinions of different authorities as to what part of the brain the soul resides in, and discusses whether the brain is necessary to life, citing the case of three children who were born without any, and one who was born without a head. Thus the marvels of animals have not entirely disappeared from l'*Encyclopédie*. On the other hand, of course, positive progress was being made and registered. For example, the article on coral refers to the discovery of the coral insects in 1725 by Peysonnel on the Barbary coast and to his subsequent investigation of similar species of so-called marine plants (madrepores, lithophytes, and sponges) at Guadeloupe, whence in 1753 he sent Buffon and Daubenton a work in manuscript which they hoped soon to publish. In the meantime Daubenton quotes from Donati's *Della storia naturale marina dell' Adriatico saggio,* published at Venice in 1750.

The old problem of animal psychology is touched on by d'Alembert in the article *Forme substantielle*. Descartes had held that animals do not suffer pain but only seem to do so. This d'Alembert rejects but cannot explain why other animals who have similar organs and sometimes keener sensations than man should not have attained the power of reflection and abstract ideas. He comes to the somewhat lame conclusion that we must be content to believe that beasts suffer, that our souls are spiritual and immortal, that God is always wise and just, and to remain in ignorance of the rest. The article on physiology by Haller retains the old classification of the actions and functions of the human body as vital or natural or animal, but holds that everything which is purely corporal in man can be fully explained by laws of mechanics and physics, and that "the definition of the circle is no clearer in geometry than the light that often guides a wise (medical) practitioner." "As for the mutual intercourse of soul and body it is not only the most inconceivable thing in the world but even the most useless to the medical man." A cure is a change made in the human body by the action of other bodies, so the physician should attend solely to the body.

We are thus brought back again to the subject of medicine. The encyclopedists were none too well satisfied with the medical learning or practice of their time. In praising the Hippocratic collection in his article upon experimental method d'Alembert said: "In place of those systems, if not murderous, at least ridiculous, to which modern medicine has given birth only to reject them shortly, one finds facts well envisaged and well put together; one sees a system of observations which still serves today and which apparently always will serve as a basis for the healing art." Similarly the Chevalier de Jaucourt affirmed that no one had described cholera better than Caelius Aurelianus and Aretaeus or indicated a better treatment for it; that moderns added nothing, but rather too often deviated from the almost forgotten practice of the ancients in this disease. Galen was perhaps mentally associated too closely with the despised middle ages to receive such unqualified praise. However, the article *Galenisme* admits his personal greatness and sketches some of his life, but holds that he subjected medicine too much to general ideas and made it too easy—which explains why everybody followed him; that he made too much of the four qualities; and that his association of critical days with the stars or moon was erroneous. The article *Complexion* (in the sense of state of health or natural habitude of the body) rather apologizes for rehearsing the ancient fourfold division into temperaments: sanguine, connected with air, and hot and wet; flegmatic, connected with water, and cold and wet; choleric or bilious, connected with fire, and hot and dry; melancholy, connected with earth, and cold and dry. "Not much attention is any longer paid to such divisions; experience has proved an eye-opener on many prejudices and opinions, of which it is nevertheless necessary to give an account, so that each person can accept or disregard them as he judges fit." Yet we find Vandernesse arguing that a sea bath is the best remedy for mania because the qualities of fluidity, humidity, and heaviness are increased by the salt in the water, while the terror of the patient may excite a reaction which will restore his deranged imagination. And several experiences seem to show that a cold ducking is good for frenzy. Bleeding still remained a favorite medical procedure. The article on Phlebotomy enters upon arguments in justification of it that would put a scholastic to blush. When the blood is too viscous and slow-moving, blood-letting will enliven it and make it hotter; but in a plethora resulting from too great a quantity of spirituous aliment— the secretion of spirit goes on in the brain—or a diminution of transpiration, phlebotomy will make the blood circulate more slowly and refresh it. In the former case blood-letting by lessening the resistance in the blood-vessels will increase their contractive power; in the latter case it will have the opposite effect, since the heart and arteries will no longer contract so often and so vigorously as before. Venel's article on climate disputes the medical theory that one ought to drink a great deal of water in hot climates in order to repair the dried-up blood, holding that to drink undiluted water there is very harmful, and that acids, spices, wines and spirituous liquors are much better and are more salutary in hot than in cold countries, although admitting that the *abuse* of strong liquors is more injurious in a hot climate. The article on wine repeats this contention, adducing the habits of the peasants of the *Midi,* and is also inclined to agree with Hippocrates, Dioscorides, Avicenna, and the Stoics that it may be a good thing to get drunk occasionally.

A chief reason for the scepticism shown in l'*Encyclopédie* on the subject of *materia medica* was the advance being made in chemical knowledge. This was especially destructive to the elaborate compound medicines recommended in pharmacopeias, since it could be shown that some at least of their ingredients had properties which would nullify one another. Pharmaceutical chemistry for a considerable period before l'*Encyclopédie* had been reducing the vast number and reforming the constituents of these confections and electuaries, but had not gone far enough to suit Venel. He says that of about thirty in the *Universal Pharmacopeia* of Nicolas Lémery (1697) only three are now in usage in France, which three Venel proceeds to describe and criticize. The *confection d'hyacinthe* as modified by Lémery contained 1 and ½ ounces of prepared hyacinth, although powdered sapphires and emeralds were now omitted; one ounce each of red coral, *terra sigillata,* and "*santal citrin*"; six gross of raspings of deer's horn; three gross each of bone from a deer's heart, root of tormentil, white dittany, dittany of Crete, saffron, myrrh, red roses, sorrel seeds, lemon, purslain; four scruples of crabs' eyes, and of the skins of lemons and sour oranges; ten grains each of ambergris and musk; one ounce of sirup of kermes;

and three pounds—which Venel criticizes as far too much—of sirup of carnation pinks. Another compound comes down, somewhat altered, from Mesuë, and "old theriac" is still in use and not unfavorably regarded by l'*Encyclopédie* itself. Coral was employed as an ingredient in many other troches, pills, powders, opiates, and tablets than the confections above mentioned.

Willy-nilly, then, the encyclopedists still retained many conceptions of past science—and even of the medieval past which they scorned —which have since been abandoned. Their very chart of the departments of human knowledge has a medieval character with its optic, dioptic, and catoptric, its classified prodigies and monstrosities of nature, its science of God and science of spirits, its pneumatology or science of the soul, its mention of falconry under zoology. The conception of four elements was far from having been completely abandoned, as we have seen, and the phlogistic theory of the principle of fire was, of course, still in force. The article, *Froid (Economie animale)*, opens with the statement that the element fire is found more or less in all bodies.

Inasmuch as the phlogiston theory continued through the century, and the nature of heat was not clearly understood until the middle of the nineteenth century, it is interesting to note the discussion of heat and cold in l'*Encyclopédie*. Venel's article, *Froid (Physique)*, after giving and criticizing the views of ancient philosophers, says that most modern natural philosophers (*physiciens*) hold that in general cold is only less heat, and that the thermometer marks equally degrees of heat and cold. The article, *Chaleur,* states that some call heat a quality; others, a substance; others, a mechanical affection. Bacon, Boyle, and Newton are cited as conceiving of heat not as a property originally inherent, but produced mechanically within a body, while Descartes is quoted as saying that heat is the movement of the parts of a body.

But we must bring our account of l'*Encyclopédie* and its attitude toward science and related fields to a close. While it was inevitable in the circumstances of the case that it should sometimes take up an inconsistent position or halfway attitude, on the whole it shows a brave and intelligent and fairly well sustained effort to maintain a critical and scientific attitude, and to free itself from the errors and unwarranted prepossessions of the past. To those who regard its "philosophy" as shallow we may answer in the words that d'Alembert used in defending the old Greek atomist from the charge of madness, words which not inaptly describe the spirit of l'*Encyclopédie* itself: "Democritus a fool! He who, to say it here in passing, had found the most philosophic way of enjoying both nature and mankind, that is, to study the one and to laugh at the other."

XII

The Age of Reason

>>>->>>->>>->>>->>>->>>->>>->>>-<<<-<<<-<<<-<<<-<<<-<<<-<<<-<<<-<<<-

Rationalists and Religion in the Eighteenth Century

SHELBY T. MC CLOY

The Influence of Eighteenth Century Ideas on the French Revolution

HENRI PEYRE

>>>->>>->>>->>>->>>->>>->>>->>>-<<<-<<<-<<<-<<<-<<<-<<<-<<<-<<<-<<<-

Rationalists and Religion in the Eighteenth Century

SHELBY T. McCLOY

⋙-⋙-⋙-⋙-⋙-⋙-⋙-⋙-⋙ *Published in 1947* ⋘-⋘-⋘-⋘-⋘-⋘-⋘-⋘-⋘-⋘

One of the most significant themes in the intellectual history of eighteenth-century Europe was the growth of rationalism—faith in the power of reason. In the interest of accuracy, however, it is important not to exaggerate the extent of this rationalism. It certainly had no appreciable influence on the lives of most of the people who lived in what historians have come to call the Age of Reason. In fact, most eighteenth-century Europeans would have been quite shocked to hear that they lived in an age of reason; they would have insisted, rather, that theirs was an age of religion. The extent of this rationalism even in intellectual circles has probably been overstressed. The fact remains, however, that more than ever before in the Christian era orthodox religion was found wanting when it was subjected by intellectuals to the test of reason. In the present article, Shelby T. McCloy, of the University of Kentucky, who has made several important contributions to the study of eighteenth-century English and French history, deals with the origins of rationalism as well as with the attitude toward orthodox religion of some of the outstanding rationalists of the so-called Age of Reason.

S teadily after the time of the Renaissance rationalism grew in Europe until in the eighteenth century it was a more formidable force than ever before in history. Historians disagree as to the number of rationalists in the 1700's. Perhaps the actual number will never be known. It is possible to check those who left writings to posterity, but it is not so easy to count those who did not leave records. The wide

Reprinted by special permission from *The South Atlantic Quarterly*, XLVI (1947), 467-482.

sale of books by Voltaire and others indicates little. One might as logically believe that the millions of Americans who read *Mein Kampf* were Nazis. People of the eighteenth century, like those of today, were interested in bizarre ideas, in humor, and in clever literary expression. The people who read Voltaire, Gibbon, Paine, and others represented all shades of intellectual opinion; in fact, occasional readers wrote and published replies. That there were multitudinous scoffers at religion, especially in England and France, is altogether clear, but to call them rationalists is to honor them with a title which they do not deserve. Thus, though the number of rationalists in eighteenth-century Europe is not clear, it was a small but very influential segment of the population.

It was influential in that it embraced some of the leading European monarchs of that day, such as Frederick the Great, Catherine the Great, Joseph II, Leopold II, Charles III, and Gustavus III. It included ministers of state like Turgot and Pombal, the French *philosophes,* and men of other countries associated with them in literary and sociological activity, e.g., Adam Smith, Hume, Gibbon, Beccaria, and D'Holbach. It contained certain of the German *littérateurs* of the *Sturm und Drang* period, such as Lessing and Herder, and Wolf and Kant among the philosophers. The brilliance of these names awed Europe then, and even today they are impressive.

There were, of course, different shades of rationalism, e.g., deism, skepticism, and atheism. Also there was Unitarianism, then often called Socinianism. Indeed all the shades of left-wing or radical opinion beyond the limits of orthodoxy, founded not upon sentiment but upon intellectual activity, may appropriately be designated as "rationalism." The various brands of pietism of the seventeenth and eighteenth centuries that sprang up within Protestant and Catholic folds, although certain of these sects held opinions regarded as unorthodox, would obviously not be included.

Four factors are commonly said to explain the steady growth of rationalism in Europe. One was the influence of ancient Greek and Roman rational thinkers. It will be recalled that during the Renaissance the most highly regarded studies were the *litterae humaniores,* or the "human letters" of Greek and Roman literature, history, and philosophy. Latin, of course, was taught in all of the medieval universities, being, in fact, the language in which all the lectures and the disputations were given. Greek was an intruder and was slow in gaining admission, even during the Renaissance. Nevertheless, it was taught in the Italian cities after the late fourteenth century by wandering Greek scholars from the Byzantine Empire. Not a few of the ancient Greek and Latin writers were skeptical or censorious of religion, among them Cicero, Lucretius, Lucian, and Julian. The last two were very critical of early Christianity in the period of the church which most Christians have regarded as its Golden Age. Yet, of all the ancient writers, Cicero exerted the greatest influence toward rationalism on the minds of Europeans during the Renaissance according to Henri Busson (*Les Sources et le développement du rationalisme dans la littérature française de la renaissance, 1533-1601,* Paris, 1922), who reveals that in France as well as Italy skepticism, deism, atheism, and blasphemy were widespread in that era. The same was true in England, nor was Germany different if we are to accept the findings of J. M. Robertson (*A Short History of Free Thought,* London, 1906).

A second cause of the growth of rationalism was the religious intolerance and warfare of the sixteenth and subsequent centuries. The Middle Ages had also a record of intolerance, evident in the extirpation of Arianism, Averroism, and Albigensianism, and in the attempts to extirpate Waldensianism and the Hussite faith. That this intolerance provoked disgust and skepticism, however, is not apparent. But from 1517 to 1650, the Protestant Reformation and the religious wars arrayed Western Europe into warring camps. Bitterness was displayed between Protestants and Catholics and even between the different camps of the Protestants. Lutherans hated Calvinists, and both hated and persecuted Anabaptists and Socinians. At the Conference at Marburg (1529) Zwingli and Luther agreed on fourteen tenets of Christianity and

---

Beccaria: Eighteenth-century Italian criminal-law reformer. His *Essay on Crimes and Punishments* embodied a series of basic criticisms of the penal system of the *ancien régime* everywhere in Europe. The work was highly praised by such eminent figures as Voltaire, Blackstone, and Bentham.

Condorcet: French *philosophe* who believed in progress, the perfectibility of man, woman suffrage, civil marriage, birth control, a national system of free education, coeducation, and adult education.

Socinians: Followers of Lelio and Fausto Sozzini, the radical Protestants of

differed on a single one, namely, the presence of Christ in the Lord's Supper. This single point kept apart at that time the Lutheran and Zwinglian and later the Calvinist sects. The presence of Christ in the Lord's Supper was in fact a point on which all the Christian groups differed. Little or no tolerance was shown. The fierce persecution that ensued terminated in a series of religious wars, running approximately from 1550 to 1650, that deluged Western Europe in blood, caused the death of several hundred thousand people, and brought untold misery to those that remained. Germany lost from one third to one half of her population. Nor was much tolerance shown even in Voltaire's day. France still sent Protestants to the galleys for assembling in religious worship and put their clergymen to death. The English and Scotch treatment of Catholics was not greatly better. Amid such conditions of intolerance, many thoughtful people were naturally disgusted, were led to question the bases of religious belief, and emerged with some form of rationalistic philosophy. Gibbon in his *Autobiography* relates the story of his own religious experience, saying that this was the cause or prelude of his emergence into skepticism. He alleges the same explanation for the rationalism of Chillingworth and Bayle.

A third cause of the growth of rationalism was European exploration and contact with new peoples, new customs, and new religions. The voyages of the Portuguese and Spaniards in the late 1400's and early 1500's encouraged a vogue for exploration in which seamen of England, France, and the Netherlands likewise participated. These travelers came home with their stories, some of which found their way into printed form. According to Preserved Smith (*History of Modern Culture*, I, 404):

---

the sixteenth century. They denied the Trinity and were therefore persecuted by Roman Catholics, Lutherans, Calvinists, and Anglicans.

STURM UND DRANG: Storm and stress. Term used to characterize such tendencies in late-eighteenth-century German literature as the stress on individualism, emotion, intuition, and instincts and the worship of Shakespeare and Rousseau. Goethe's *Werther* and Schiller's *Robbers* are two of its most famous literary monuments.

TARTUFFE: Chief character in one of Molière's best known and most provocative plays. Tartuffe is a religious scoundrel, and already in seventeenth-century France he came to serve as a symbol of hypocrisy.

No works were so popular during the two centuries following the discovery of America, as the tales of travellers describing the marvellous new lands and the strange peoples of the Far East and of the Far West. Some of them told of naked savages living in piety, virtue, and happiness, without priests, Bibles, or creeds. Along with the Noble Savage the Chinese Sage became the great critic of European faith and morals. In India and in China were found, or imagined, cities more populous than European states, empires more powerful than that of ancient Rome, wealth beyond the dreams of occidental avarice, civilizations more polished than that of Greece, and religions more rational than, and as beneficent as, Christianity.

Some writers insisted that higher morals were practised by the Chinese and the natives of the New World than by the Christians of Europe. Among the Asiatics and the American redskins they found stories of miracles and gods rivaling those of Christianity. Even some of the Jesuit missionaries admired the morality of the peoples among whom they went. Under these circumstances it was natural that traveler and reader should be brought to reconsider what they had been taught about so-called heathen religions and indeed about Christianity itself. They were led to ask whether the God of the Christians was not also the god of non-Christian peoples; whether all revelation was confined to the Bible; whether Christians might not be the victims of priest-craft and superstition, even as they regarded other peoples as being; whether religion, after all, did not consist in moral living rather than in correct belief; and, finally, whether Christians could claim to possess and follow a higher system of morality than peoples of other color and religious belief. The study of comparative religions was thus begun, and its effect upon the European mind was destined to be considerable.

The fourth solvent of what may be called the medieval mind was the influence of modern science. With the 1500's natural science began to make some remarkable if slow developments; certain of these drew fire from the theologians. Very notable was the Copernican controversy, which, beginning in the 1540's, continued until 1835, when all the guns were silenced and the works of Copernicus, Kepler, and Galileo removed from the Index of Prohibited Books. The Copernican hypothesis, which brought fierce attacks from the Church of Rome and led to the burning of Giordano Bruno in 1600 and to the trials and recantation of Galileo before the cardinals of the Inquisition in 1616 and 1633, was condemned also by Luther and Calvin and theologians associated with them. Vesalius's book, *De humani corporis fabrica*, which was published in 1543, the same year as the work by Copernicus, and produced the same revolution in anatomical study that Copernicus's work did in astronomy, provoked attacks from theologians because it stated that the number of ribs in men and women was the same, in contrast to the story in Genesis, which stated that God had taken one of man's ribs to form woman. The discovery of the circulation of the blood by Harvey in the 1600's and the practice of inoculation for smallpox in the 1700's drew fire on both theological and medical grounds, and controversy waxed long in each instance.

Through all centuries of the modern age, in fact, there has run a conflict between science and theology, which has had devastating effects for the exponents of conservative theology. Andrew Dickson White, first president of Cornell University, was so incensed at attempts of churchmen in the late nineteenth century to prevent the erection of a great institution in New York state for the furtherance of science that he utilized his brilliant gifts to write his notable *History of the Warfare of Science with Theology in Christendom*. The work is Voltairian as an exposé and polemic. This and later works recording this conflict reveal that the church has constantly had to give ground. In the 1700's science was already entrenched, advancing in many fields, and in general backed by strong popular support. Encyclopedias giving much attention to science were beginning to appear, as evidenced by those of Chambers in England, Diderot and D'Alembert and Panckoucke in France, and Zedler in Germany. Thinking men saw that theology stood in need of revision at many places. Some went so far as to decide that either theology or science had to be discarded and then discarded theology.

Such were the strong solvents at work in the eighteenth century leading to changes in the minds of men. It was not a static age; thinking men everywhere were trying to adjust themselves to new learning and new experiences. At several points Christianity and the church were severely attacked.

Perhaps the chief of these was the field of the miraculous. With one accord, deist, skeptic, and atheist threw out the miracles of the Bible. The Unitarian did pretty much the same. Miracles came to be regarded as absurd tales, employed by priests to abuse and shackle the minds of the ignorant. In their attack on miracles, however, writers were commonly wary about criticizing those of the New Testament for fear of the law. Rather, they turned their guns upon the alleged miracles of post-Apostolic days, upon relics, upon saints, upon miracles of the Old Testament. Pierre Bayle in his notable *Dictionnaire historique et critique* (1697) took a critical attitude toward miracles in general. Observing that Saint Augustine in his day upbraided the heathen for refusal to believe the Christian miracles, although they believed in miracles of their own religion, Bayle criticized the Christian communions, Protestant and Catholic, for refusal to believe in miracles not of their own particular group, saying:

> It is well known how easily the Roman Catholics give their assent to an infinite number of miracles. They proudly believe thousands of stories which are daily published, and look upon the most plausible reasons of those who deny them as mere cavils of obstinate heretics. But if they hear that the Protestants spread abroad any miracles, they assume a quite different spirit. . . . They deny the fact, challenge the witnesses, reproach them with imposture, or a distempered brain. If they cannot deny the fact, they explain it by natural causes, and collect from the relations of travelers a thousand similar cases.

At another place he said of the Protestants:

> How many things are practiced by the Protestants nowadays which would not have been approved a hundred years ago? I am sure that the author of the Pastoral Epistles (Jurieu) has published more false miracles than he should. And yet only a few, and they laymen, have expressed their disapproval.

Bayle was free in his criticism of post-biblical miracles, casting aspersions upon many stories of Old Testament history, though he was careful to criticize those of the New Testament only by indirection. In speaking of the miracles of Jesus, he quoted pagan opinion. "Nothing," he remarked, "is a more sensible proof of the impertinent credulity of the pagans than their saying that Apuleius had wrought many miracles, and that they equalled or even surpassed those of Jesus Christ." In a note he added: "Apuleius has had the fate of many other persons; his miracles were not spoken of till after his death." Bayle also commented on the similarity between Apollonius of Tyana and Jesus. Apollonius, he said, was "one of the most extraordinary persons that ever appeared in the world," and added that the pagans likened his miracles to those of

Jesus. Bayle's *Dictionary* was one of the most widely read works of the eighteenth century, especially in France and Britain; other rationalists like Gibbon and Voltaire were heavily indebted to him.

His cautious stand on Biblical miracles was long followed; an attack on them was prohibited by statute, and public opinion would hardly have permitted such an attack. For example, neither in Conyers Middleton's *Free Inquiry into the Miraculous Powers which are supposed to have subsisted in the Christian Church from the Earliest Ages through Several Successive Centuries* (1749) nor in Edward Gibbon's *History of the Decline and Fall of the Roman Empire* (1776-88) did the author care to lay himself open to fine or imprisonment. The approach was similar to that of Bayle: both authors ridiculed post-Apostolic miracles and by subtle innuendo cast doubt even upon those of the Bible. The publication of these writings scandalized many of their readers, and various replies were made in book and pamphlet and literary review. University degrees were conferred upon certain of those replying.

Some eighteenth-century writers went further, among them Jean Meslier, curé of Etrépigny in Champagne, who died in 1733 at the age of fifty-five, leaving three manuscript copies of a book setting forth his views on religion. For two or three decades Meslier had humbly and faithfully served the parishioners of Etrépigny, and no one had suspected him of unorthodoxy on any point. By his own words, however, he had long since come to disbelieve the dogmas he was teaching. A thousand times, he says, he would have liked to come out boldly and confess his real attitude, but he dared not:

> It was necessary that I should acquit myself as a priest of my ministry, but how often have I not suffered within myself when I was forced to preach to you those pious lies which I despised in my heart. What a disdain I had for my ministry, and particularly for that superstitious Mass, and those ridiculous administrations of sacraments, especially if I was compelled to perform them with the solemnity which awakened all your piety and all your good faith. What remorse I had for exciting your credulity! A thousand times upon the point of bursting forth publicly, I was going to open your eyes, but a fear superior to my strength restrained me and forced me to silence until my death.

One copy of his work was placed, at his direction, in the archives of Sainte-Menehould; another, strangely enough, was permitted to circulate among the public, and it is said that there were about a hundred copies at Paris, bringing ten louis d'or ($50) each. Voltaire got a copy and was so attracted by it that he published an excerpt from it. In the excerpt occurs a statement on miracles:

> Let us come to the pretended miracles of the New Testament. They consist, as is pretended, in this: that Jesus Christ and His apostles cured, through the Deity, all kinds of diseases and infirmities, giving sight to the blind, hearing to the deaf, speech to the dumb, making the lame to walk, curing the paralytics, driving the devils from those who were possessed, and bringing the dead to life.
>
> We find several of these miracles in the Gospels, but we see a good many more of them in the books that our Christ-worshippers have written of the admirable lives of the saints; for in these lives we nearly everywhere read that these pretended blessed ones cured diseases and infirmities, expelled the devils, wherever they encountered them, solely in the name of Jesus or by the sign of the cross; that they controlled the elements; that God favored them so much that He even preserved to them His Divine power after their death, and that this Divine power could be communicated even to the least of their clothing, even to their shadows, and even to the infamous instruments of their death. It is said that the shoe of St. Honorius raised a dead man on the sixth of January; that the staff of St. Peter, that of St. James, and that of St. Bernard performed miracles. . . .
>
> It is certainly not without reason that we consider these things as lies; for it is easy to see that all of these pretended miracles have been invented but by imitating the fables of the Pagan poets. This is sufficiently obvious by the resemblance which they bear one to another.

Thomas Paine in Part I of his *Age of Reason*, written in a cell in 1794 while he was awaiting trial during the Reign of Terror, argues that the world operates under scientific laws and that the odds are "at least millions to one that the reporter of a miracle tells a lie." He says:

> If we are to suppose a miracle to be something so entirely out of the course of what is called nature that she must go out of that course to accomplish it, and we see an account given of such miracle by the person who said he saw it, it raises a question in the mind very easily decided, which is, is it more probable that nature should go out of her course, or that a man should tell a lie? We have never seen, in our time, nature go out of her course; but we have good reason to believe that millions of lies have been told in the same time. It is, therefore, at least millions to one that the reporter of a miracle tells a lie.

Paine ridicules the story of Jonah and the whale, saying that "it would have approached nearer the idea of miracle if Jonah had swallowed the whale." Had Jonah gone to Ninevah with the whale in his stomach and cast him up in the sight of the public, would not the people have believed him to be the devil rather than a prophet? On the other hand, if the whale had gone to Ninevah and cast up Jonah in the same public fashion, would not "the people have believed the whale to have been the devil, and Jonah one of his imps?" Likewise he ridicules the story of the devil taking Jesus to the top of a high mountain and to the highest pinnacle of the temple and promising him "all the kingdoms of the world." He asks, "How happened it that he did not discover America? or, is it only with *kingdoms* that his sooty highness has any interest?" He comments that he has "too much respect for the moral character of Jesus Christ to believe that he told this whale of a miracle himself." Summarizing, he says: "In every point of view in which those things called miracles can be placed and considered, the reality of them is improbable, and their existence unnecessary."

In the second half of the century there were not a few writers, like Paine, who questioned or criticized Biblical miracles. Most of them were French writers of the philosophic group, e.g., Voltaire, D'Holbach, D'Argens, and La Mettrie. Reimarus of Germany and Hume of Britain likewise called in question the possibility of miracles. It is well known that Thomas Jefferson published a New Testament from which he expurgated all accounts of the miraculous.

Expurgation of the miraculous, of course, carried quite a bit with it, for tied up with the miracles of the Bible are the stories of the miraculous birth of Jesus, the sacrificial atonement for sin, the resurrection, the Trinity, the efficacy of prayer, the Divine revelation of the Bible, and the question of man's soul. Criticism of all these tenets of Christian faith can in fact be found in the more outspoken of the eighteenth-century rationalists like Meslier and Paine. Paine makes of Jesus "a virtuous and an amiable man," and says that "the virtue that he preached and practiced was of the most benevolent kind." The story of his resurrection and ascension, however, are not proved. "The story . . . has every mark of fraud." Paine questions the validity of the Atonement, saying that no person can assume responsibility for another's crime, and that the idea of bearing responsibility for another person's debt does not meet the situation. The Biblical account here is mythical. Even as a child, he says, he was shocked at the idea of God's killing his own son. The Bible story makes God in the likeness of a passionate man. A man doing such a thing would be hanged. As for Jesus's death, he asks, why could not he have paid the debt of man's sin by merely dying of a fever or smallpox or old age, rather than by suffering on the cross? Since he did not regard Jesus as being a divine person, he naturally did not believe in the Christian Trinity. Such a doctrine is but an atavistic relic of polytheism. So too is belief in the power of the Virgin Mary and the saints. "It is curious," says Paine,

> to observe how the theory of what is called the Christian Church spring[s] out of the tail of heathen mythology. A direct incorporation took place in the first instance, by making the reputed founder to be celestially begotten. The trinity of gods that then followed was no more than a reduction of the former plurality, which was about twenty or thirty thousand; the statue of Mary succeeded the statue of Diana of Ephesus; the deification of heroes change[d] into the canonization of saints; the mythologists had gods for everything; the Christian Mythologists had saints for everything; the church became as crowded with the one as the pantheon had been with the other; and Rome was the place of both. The Christian theory is little else than the idolatry of the Mythologists, accommodated to the purposes of power and revenue. . . .

In common with all or nearly all of the Deists, Paine repudiated the claim of Divine revelation for the Bible. The Bible and its stories are but the concoctions of priests, who have written them for their own power and avarice. More than half of the Bible, he charges, is devoted to stories of debauchery, obscenity, and cruelty that make it rather the work of a demon than of God. It is a history of wickedness, and it serves rather to brutalize and corrupt mankind than to improve it. So he wrote in the first part of his *Age of Reason*. In the preface to Part II of the book, written in October, 1795, he says that since writing the former part he has obtained a copy of the Bible and has found it to be worse than he had conceived. "If I have erred in anything in the former part of 'The Age of Reason,'" he adds, "it has been by speaking better of some parts of those books [i.e., the Old and New Testaments] than they have deserved." Thereupon Paine sets out on a fault-finding study of the books of the Old and New Testaments, picking out inconsistencies, absurdities, and obscenities, after the fashion of a literary critic or Biblical commentator, save that his remarks are always censorious. His observations, however, are but an elaboration of his position already stated in Part I. Not to the Bible would one go for a conception of God, Paine states in Part I, but to his handiworks in creation. There one will behold the character of God, for he is the First Cause.

Paine, it is seen, believed in the idea of God. So, too, did Voltaire and all the deists. They insisted on deriving their idea of God from science and philosophy, however, and not from revelation. Meslier, D'Holbach, La Mattrie, and the atheists denied even the existence of God. According to D'Holbach, who wrote a summary of the position of Meslier, a God cannot be good or just who punishes for faults that he could have remedied. How can a good God permit the existence of a hell? Did God have to make an imperfect world? Could he not have made it perfect and all his creatures happy? If he were good, would he not have done so? "A God filled with implacable fury," says D'Holbach, "is He a God in whom we can find a shadow of charity or goodness?" He continues:

According to theological ideas God resembles a tyrant who, having deprived the majority of his slaves of their eyesight, would confine them in a cell where, in order to amuse himself, he could observe *incognito* their conduct through a trap-door, in order to have occasion cruelly to punish all those who in walking should hurt each other; but who would reward splendidly the small number of those to whom the sight was spared, for having the skill to avoid an encounter with their comrades. Such are the ideas which the dogma of gratuitous predestination gives of Divinity!

Although men repeat to us that their God is infinitely good, it is evident that in the bottom of their hearts they can believe nothing of it. How can we love anything we do not know? How can we love a being of whom all that is told conspires to render him supremely hateful?

He denies that God has the right to punish man, whom he did not create sinless.

He denies the fatherhood of God, the providence of God, and scoffs at the God of the deist as well as that of the theist. He even criticizes the position of skeptics, who "lack the motives necessary to form a judgment." All gods, all ideas of God, come from a barbaric origin, are relics of superstition and ignorance, and hence outmoded. The atheist D'Holbach criticized every aspect of religious belief—God, revelation, miracles, the future life, faith, the soul, even morality whenever and wherever based upon religion. All ideas of morality associated with religion, said D'Holbach, are priestly concoctions for enslaving mankind. "In every religion the priests alone have the right to decide upon what pleases or displeases their God; we may rest assured that they will decide upon what pleases or displeases themselves." Not only morality, but all aspects of religion, according to D'Holbach, are parts of a great scheme of priests to defraud mankind. "The dogmas, ceremonies, the morality and the virtues which all religions of the world prescribe, are visibly calculated only to extend the power or to increase the emoluments of the founders and of the ministers of these religions. . . ." D'Holbach was constantly looking under the bed, so to speak, to see if some lurking priest was not hidden there. Nor was D'Holbach alone; he was joined by virtually all of the eighteenth-century rationalists.

If attack on the miraculous was the prime characteristic of eighteenth-century rationalism, hatred of priestcraft was the second. With hatred of priests went hatred of the church or of organized religion. The eighteenth-century rationalists, in general, looked upon Christianity in the same objective fashion that the eighteenth-century churchmen looked upon the pagan religions of antiquity or of distant lands in their own day. As the churchman regarded the pagan hierarchies as self-centered, grasping for power, and avaricious for wealth, keeping the people in ignorance and profiting from their superstitious reverence, so the deist and skeptic and atheist regarded the churchman as taking advantage of his flock. They looked upon the Christian clergy as vampires sucking the blood of the people. Voltaire, indeed, in his article on "Vampires" in his *Philosophical Dictionary* likens the vampires of European superstition to the clergy, or rather to the monks. In his delightful tale *Candide* he states that Paraguay was a happy state until the Jesuits came into control. In the same book he traces a case of syphilis back to one of the popes. Indeed, it was customary for all the rationalists of the eighteenth century to regard the clergy as Tartuffes, lecherous at heart.

Interestingly enough, these priests were regarded as being always united against the rest of the world for the interests of the sacred order and as using crafty schemes to accomplish their ends; on the other hand, they were regarded as continually at war among themselves over matters of personal ambition and points of belief. Gibbon's *History of the Decline and Fall of the Roman Empire* is filled with stories of the bickering, animosity, and jealousy of the different groups and leaders of the Christians. By their incessant quarreling and strife, chiefly over matters of doctrine, they caused splits in the Roman empire that paved the way for the barbarian invasions. In a very real way, as Gibbon saw it, the quarrels of the clergy over doctrinal points paved the way for Rome's downfall. He closed his great work with the statement: "In the preceding volumes of this History, I have recorded the triumph of barbarism and religion." The idea had come to him when a young man visiting Rome in 1764. One evening he sat on a hill overlooking the site of the ancient forum. In the gathering darkness he heard the tinkling of a bell summoning the monks to vespers in a near-by chapel and saw the monks going to this service. In a flash he caught the idea of the Christian Church triumphant over the Roman world, of interest in the next world eclipsing that in this. With this theme Gibbon wrote his great history.

Gibbon, however, was a gentleman; when writing of a priest like Athanasius whose qualities he admired, he gave due credit. Voltaire, on the other hand, referred to the church as "The Infamous Thing" and could see no good in it. Neither could Paine. Diderot advised Catherine the Great in his *Plan of a University*, drawn up at her request, to watch with a wary eye the preaching of the priests in her land, adding that if he were a ruler it would drive him to despair to have ten thousand or more clergymen rising week by week in pulpits to proclaim their views on every subject. These men, he said, should be carefully watched and controlled.

Certain of the rationalists professed to admire the Quakers, largely because they did not have an organized priesthood. Voltaire in his *Letters on the English* praised them; Paine in his *Age of Reason* admired them for being as he thought, erroneously, most like the deists; Benjamin Franklin is said to have owed not a little of his popularity in France to the fact that many mistakenly thought him a Quaker.

On the shoulders of the church the rationalists placed part of the blame for the severe persecutions frequent in Christian history. Every sect when small and weak pleads for toleration, said Gibbon; but as soon as it is strong, it adopts the policy of persecution. He drew a pathetic picture of paganism being in turn persecuted and stamped out by the Christians. He tended to depreciate the Christian sufferings at pagan hands. The entire number of the Christians put to death throughout the Roman Empire up to the year 313, when Christianity became a recognized religion of the empire, was less than two thousand. Far more numerous have been the victims of Christian persecution at the hands of their fellow Christians. "In the Netherlands alone, more than one hundred thousand of the subjects of Charles the Fifth are said to have suffered by the hand of the executioner; and this extraordinary number is attested by Grotius, a man of genius and learning, who preserved his moderation amidst the fury of contending sects. . . ." When we recall that religious persecution was still a terrible fact in some European countries in the eighteenth century, we can readily appreciate the rationalists' bitterness toward the church on the score.

The rationalists were more severe in their censure of the Catholic Church than of the Protestant churches, partly because the hierarchy of the former was better organized and more powerful, partly because it encouraged belief in relics, saints, and current miracles. Its part in enslaving men in ignorance and superstition was accordingly regarded as greater. Likewise, the rationalists made some slight distinction in treating other religions. The Jews they hated, as being the source of all that was narrow and intolerant in Christianity. One looks in vain for much sympathy toward the Jews in eighteenth-century writers. Bolingbroke, Voltaire, and Gibbon, in particular, described them as narrow, selfish, unsocial, intolerant, and fanatical. Gibbon deplored the mistreatment of them by the Spaniards and the Crusaders during the Middle Ages, but his account of them in Chapter Fifteen of his history, showing them as predecessors of the Christians, makes of them forbidding creatures. On the other hand, Gibbon, Voltaire, and Condorcet esteemed more highly the Mohammedans. Gibbon's chapter on Mohammed and the rise of his religion is one of his best. He saw in the Mohammedans true unitarians, whose God is spirit. He was less critical of their part in overthrowing the Roman empire than he was of the Christians. They were merely one of the groups of barbarians inundating the empire. Condorcet called the Mohammedan religion "the most simple in its dogmas, the least absurd in its practices, and the most tolerant in its principles." Not only Gibbon but other eighteenth-century rationalists as well made a hero of Julian the Apostate, whom they regarded as a man of culture and honor, a just ruler, and a devout pagan, whose only fault was his persecution of Christianity, the religion of his youth. In general, however, the rationalists did not condone·

persecution, from whomsoever it came. They were without exception advocates of toleration.

Eighteenth-century rationalism had no little influence upon policies of the so-called Enlightened Despots of the period 1740-1780 and also upon the legislation and events of the French Revolution of the 1790's. The humanitarian legislation of this period was due partly to the rationalists, even as was the Religion of the Supreme Being of 1793-1794 and the Theophilanthropy of 1796-1801. Thomas Paine complained that he was unable to obtain a Bible for its investigation at the time of writing Part I of his *Age of Reason* in 1794; yet, almost at the same moment, the National Convention, which had discarded Christianity, granted freedom to Negro slaves in the colonies. The influence of rationalism in arousing the social conscience and in promoting legislation of a humanitarian character has been great and has increased with the passing of the years.

The average textbook in history leaves the impression that rationalism of the eighteenth century virtually died out with the French Revolution. This was far from the case. Rationalism continued throughout the nineteenth century despite the strong tides of conservative sentiment in religion during the Romantic Movement; in fact, it gained additional force through the controversies over geological and biological science, and through the developments of the Higher Criticism in biblical study due in part to the Tübingen scholars, Strauss and Bauer. The Roman Catholic Church was quick to detect the scholars in its ranks such as Ernest Renan, Alfred Loisy, and George Tyrrell, who showed a proclivity to this critical study, and to expel them. It has succeeded in a considerable degree in keeping its windows closed to the fresh air of modern thought. With Protestantism it has been otherwise. The Liberal or Modernist Movement has made steady gains and has taken a strong if not a dominant position in such leading sects as the Episcopalians, the Congregationalists, the Presbyterians, and the Methodists. Virtually all of the faculties of theology in the large Protestant universities in Europe and America and virtually all of the leading Protestant theological seminaries have in some degree felt the influence of the methods of higher critical study. This is not to say that the majority of the clergy in any of these denominations are rationalistic or even in favor of the Higher Criticism. Within other denominations, such as the Baptist, the Dutch Reformed, and the Disciples of Christ are many men of Modernist leanings, but in much smaller proportion than in the group first named. Among the Unitarians and Universalists, of course, almost all the clergy are of the Modernist type.

One gauge of the growth of rationalistic spirit in Protestantism is its reaction to Gibbon's *Decline and Fall* since 1776. Even in Gibbon's own day the work was welcomed by the Scotch clergy and by some of the clergy in England, but it was viciously attacked by more conservative Anglicans. After Gibbon's death in 1794, however, attacks greatly diminished, and after 1830 or 1840 they virtually ceased. It is now a century since Protestants have been disturbed in the slightest by his Five Causes for the spread of Christianity, though the book is still on the Catholic Index of Prohibited Books (having been placed there last in 1917). Some years ago the pastor of a large Presbyterian Church in the South praised Gibbon in his pulpit and explained the rapid growth of Christianity in the Roman world on the basis of his Five Causes. We hear little of rationalists today. Perhaps the explanation is that on the one hand the rationalists have lost their fire, and on the other that the churchmen have in part been rationalized.

The Influence of Eighteenth Century Ideas on the French Revolution*

HENRI PEYRE

➤➤➤➤➤➤➤➤➤ *Published in 1949* ◀◀◀◀◀◀◀◀◀◀

Time and time again writers dealing with the eighteenth century have become involved in the debate over the influence of the *philosophes* upon the outbreak of the French Revolution. Anti-Revolutionary writers have often been inclined to ascribe a tremendous influence to the *philosophes,* picturing them as troublemakers who exaggerated enormously the abuses existing under the *ancien régime.* As a result many pro-Revolutionary writers have found themselves in an awkward position. Much as they admire the *philosophes* and much as they consider them as heroes, they have sought to make it clear that the Revolution was not the result of the agitation of a handful of writers. Instead of pointing up the activities of the *philosophes,* they have concentrated on material conditions and grievances under the *ancien régime.* In the following article, Henri Peyre, of Yale University, one of the leading present-day authorities on the history of French literature, attempts once more to deal with the complicated question of the relationship between the Revolution and the writings of the *philosophes.* Pro-Revolutionary in his outlook, he refuses, however, to follow the lead of so many other pro-Revolutionary writers who have belittled the role of the *philosophes.*

N o question is likely to divide students of the past more sharply than that of the action of philosophical ideas and literary works upon political and social events. Our age has been powerfully impressed by the economic interpretation of history proposed by Marxists; but it has also witnessed the important rôle played by men of letters and men

Reprinted by special permission from *Journal of the History of Ideas,* X (1949), 63-87.

* This article was translated into English by Arthur L. Kurth, now of the University of Florida.

of thought in the Spanish Civil War and in the Resistance movement of World War II. The conscience of many writers is more obsessed today than it has ever been by the temptation—some call it the duty—of "engaged literature." The affinities of many of the leading authors in France and other countries link them with the men of the eighteenth century. Sartre, Camus, Giono, Breton are not unworthy descendants or reincarnations of Voltaire, Diderot, Rousseau.

It may thus be useful to attempt a restatement of an old, and ever present, problem, without any presumptuous claim to renovate its data or its solutions, but with an honest attempt to observe a few conditions which are obvious but all too seldom met. A summation of such an immense and thorny question should be clear, while respecting the complex nature of reality. It should be provocative, in the sense that it should suggest that much remains to be said on these matters by young scholars determined to launch upon the study of ideas in relation to the Revolution. Above all, it should be impartial if that is humanly possible, concerning questions on which it is difficult not to take sides, and it should attempt to retain in these questions the life with which they are instinct, without on the other hand sacrificing objectivity or solidity.

I

The problem of the effect of the Philosophy of Enlightenment on the French Revolution is one of the most important problems that confront the pure historian as well as the historian of thought and

BEAUMARCHAIS: Dramatist and secret agent of Louis XVI in the period of the American War of Independence. His *Barber of Seville* (1775) and *Marriage of Figaro* (1784) embodied important social criticisms of the *ancien régime*. The lines that went the rounds of late-eighteenth-century France were those that Figaro spoke in complaining about the Count Almaviva: "Because you are a great Lord, you consider yourself a great genius! . . . Nobility, fortune, rank, offices: all those make you so proud of yourself. What have you done to deserve all that good fortune! You took the trouble to be born, and nothing more."

BOSSUET: French bishop, controversialist, and historian of the age of Louis XIV. An upholder of the traditional Catholic faith and of the divine-right theory of monarchy, he came to serve as a symbol of the reactionary to the *philosophes* of the eighteenth century.

AUGUSTIN COCHIN: Early twentieth-century French historian and devout

of literature. It is without doubt the most complex of the thousand aspects involved in the study of the Revolution, that is to say the origins of the modern world. Together with investigation of the origins of Christianity and the end of the ancient world, this study concerns one of the two most important upheavals that the philosophically-minded historian can conceive: Taine and Renan, as well as Michelet and Tocqueville, the four most important French historians of the past century, had quite rightly realized its magnitude. This problem is inevitable for every teacher of literature who lectures on Voltaire and Rousseau to his students, for every historian of the years 1789-1799 in France, and likewise for every historian of these same years and of the beginning of the nineteenth century in Germany, England, the United States and Latin America. It presents itself to every voter who reflects even a little about the things in his country's past that he would like to maintain and those that he desires to reform.

But because it presents itself so insistently to everyone, this problem has often been met with solutions that are crude or at the very least lacking in necessary overtones; because it closely parallels our present-day preoccupations, it has aroused the partisan spirit; because it concerns not only facts but ideas it has favored excessively dogmatic generalizations on the one hand and on the other, the voluntary blind timidity of chroniclers who have chosen to see in the events of the Revolution nothing but a series of improvisations and haphazard movements.

There is for one thing a long and devious current of ideas which

---

Roman Catholic who was hostile to the French Revolution and presented it as the work of a small, well-organized minority.

ABBÉ MABLY: Authority on international law and writer on social reform who was widely read and quoted in his own time but has been largely ignored in more recent times. One of the most radical of the *philosophes* of the eighteenth century, he viewed economic equality as inseparable from political and legal equality and considered private property the root cause of the troubles of society.

HIPPOLYTE TAINE: Nineteenth-century historian whose *Origins of Contemporary France* was an important statement of the anti-Revolutionary position in French historiography. Taine wrote in the period of disillusionment and humiliation that followed French defeat in the Franco-German War. He was also deeply disturbed by the radicalism connected with the uprising of the Paris Commune (1871).

first springing forth as a swift and turgid torrent in the sixteenth century, becoming a more or less tenuous water-course in the great period of the reign of Louis XIV, and finally like a river encircling the most obdurate islets of resistance within its multiple arms, seems to have engulfed the eighteenth century in the years 1750-1765. More and more clearly, those who set forth and develop these ideas take it upon themselves to influence the existing facts, to change man by education, to free him from out-moded superstitions, to increase his political liberty and his well-being. In no way do they dream of a general cataclysm and several of them are not insensitive to the refined amenity of the life that surrounds them or to the exquisite blend of intellectual boldness and voluptuous refinement that characterizes their era.

Suddenly, this pleasant 18th-century security, "Table d'un long festin qu'un échafaud termine"[roughly, "Scene of a long-lasting feast ended by a scaffold"], as Hugo's beautiful image calls it, crumbles. The Revolution breaks out, and within a few years, rushes through peaceful reforms, produces a profusion of constitutions, sweeps aside the old regime, devours men, and causes heads to fall. This great movement is certainly confused, turbulent and irrational like everything that men accomplish by collective action. However, lawyers, officers, priests, and journalists play a part in it that is often important. These men had grown up in an intellectual climate that had been established by Montesquieu, Voltaire, Rousseau, Raynal and Mably. May we accurately reach a conclusion of "Post hoc, ergo propter hoc"? [after this, therefore because of it]

It would not have been so difficult to answer such a question if partisan quarrels had not needlessly clouded the issue. Frenchmen are incapable of viewing their nation's past dispassionately or accepting it as a whole. For a hundred and fifty years they have not ceased to be of different minds on their Revolution which is doubtless a proof that it is still a live question among them, while in other countries the revolution of 1688 or the revolution of 1776 is calmly invested with the veneration accorded to a buried past. It is a curious fact that the great majority of their political writers from Joseph de Maistre, Louis de Bonald, and Auguste Comte himself, to Le Play, Tocqueville, Taine, at times Renan, Barrès, Bourget, Maurras and many others, has pronounced itself hostile to the "great principles of '89" or at least to that which was drawn from these principles. Three fundamental assertions are the basis of most of the anti-revolutionary arguments. A) The

Revolution was harmful and anti-French; it could only be attributed to foreign influences that perverted the French genius of moderation, restrained devotion, and obedience to the hereditary monarch. It was caused by foreign influences that contaminated eighteenth century thought: Locke, the English deists, the Protestants in general, the Swiss Rousseau, etc. . . . B) These corrupting ideas were introduced among the French people who had been sound and upright until then, by clubs called "Sociétés de Pensée" and by secret groups of conspiring intellectuals, the Freemasons for example and the "Philosophes" themselves, who formed an authentic subversive faction. (Augustin Cochin, *Les Sociétés de Pensée*, Plon, 1921.) C) The Revolutionary spirit is the logical outcome of the classical spirit strengthened by the scientific spirit. This spirit delights in abstraction, generalizes profusely, and considers man as a creature apart from his environment, isolated from his past; it lacks the subtle empiricism which characterizes the English reformists; it is ignorant of everything touching reality. Accordingly it sets out to make laws for universal man, without regard for France's age-old traditions or the local conditions of these provinces. This contention advanced with talent and a semblance of thorough documentation by Taine has beguiled a great number of excellent minds because of its specious clarity.[1]

These contentions have not stood the test of serious scrutiny by literary historians trained in more rigid methods since the dawn of the twentieth century. The penetration with which Gustave Lanson has laid bare many of our prejudices concerning the eighteenth century forms one of his best-established claims upon our gratitude. Numerous investigators, Frenchmen and Americans especially, have since followed upon the path that he had pointed out. Lanson's ideas in their turn have become accepted opinion and doubtless it will be necessary to modify and complete them in the future by adopting new points of

[1] It is well-known that the documentation used by Taine has been checked by Aulard, with disastrous results for the philosopher, who is revealed as a mediocre analyst of documentary evidence and a hasty statistician (*Taine historien de la Révolution française,* Colin, 1907). Aug. Cochin in the work mentioned above has tried with little success to defend Taine against Aulard. Paul Lacombe, in *Taine historien et sociologue* (Giard, 1909), has shown that the sociologist in Taine often causes Taine the historian to advance ready-made or stock theses. A. Mathiez in the *Revue d'Histoire moderne et contemporaine* (VIII [1906-1907], 257-284) and H. Sée in *Science et Philosophie de l'Histoire* (Alcan, 1928), 383-398, have also exposed Taine's weaknesses as a historian.

view. It is none the less true that it is thanks to him and to Daniel Mornet after him that we can state today that the three assertions summed up earlier are contradicted by the facts. The French revolution is truly of French origin. If certain foreigners, in particular Locke, whose name may be found at almost all the century's crossroads of ideas, did exert a real influence in France, this influence was assimilated and naturalized there.[2] It had moreover implanted itself in a group of ideas going back to Bayle, Saint-Evremond, Le Vayer, Naudé and Montaigne, which were quite as indigenous and "French" as the absolutism of Bossuet. The philosophical Clubs and similar groups that made themselves felt in France around 1750 and played an active part after 1789 are not all revolutionary—far from it! Furthermore, the part that they played in preparing the Revolution is nowhere clearly ascertained. The rôle of a gigantic conspiracy attributed by some to Freemasonry is a myth.

Finally and above all, nothing justifies the assertion made with assurance by Taine that the writers of the eighteenth century were men of reason alone with no experience of the realities of life. In their time there was some use of empty rhetoric, as there is in every time; the Revolutionaries for their part will cherish a type of eloquence reminiscent of the ancients, and be occasionally intoxicated with words; they will also have an ambition to proclaim universal truths and formulate principles for all men. It is not certain that this ambition is not one of the finest qualities of the French Revolution. But it would be a mistake to forget that the eighteenth century is a great century in science, as much or more so in experimental science as in deductive and abstract disciplines. The works of M. Mornet have proved that eighteenth-century thinkers were on the contrary suspicious of scholastic generalizations and of systems in general: they made observations and

[2] Tocqueville's work, *L'Ancien Régime et la Révolution* (M. Lévy, 1856), supports a thesis which is in some respects similar to Taine's on the spirit of abstraction of the Philosophes and the influence of their views as theorizing and dogmatic men of letters on their century; but Tocqueville's statements show more subtlety than those of Taine, even if their style is less colorful and sometimes stiffer in its dignified oratorical seriousness. The bulk of Tocqueville's work, which rests on sound documentary research, tends to prove that almost everything attributed to the Revolution (often in order to condemn it) already existed in old France. He puts especially vigorous emphasis on the ownership of land, which came more and more into peasant hands well before '89, and on the general prosperity of the country, which along with discontent increased under Louis XVI.

conducted experiments. They introduced into education the taste for very detailed empiricism and for actual practice in the arts and trades. They praised techniques and described them with care. They traveled like Montesquieu in order to see at close hand constitutions and the way people lived by them. They cultivated the soil, in the case of the physiocrats; lived on their lands, as did Helvetius; or administered provinces, like Turgot. The most thoroughgoing Revolutionaries had not, like Marx or Lenin, spent years in reading-rooms; they were petty lawyers in contact with the people, like Robespierre at Arras, veterinaries like Marat; in short, provincial men who knew the lives of the peasant, the artisan and the humble country priest of France. Taine's abstraction existed chiefly in his mind, and perhaps in that of Descartes and in a few works of Rousseau. But the Revolution was hardly Cartesian and never put into practice as a complete doctrine the ideas of the *Contrat Social*, which are moreover as contradictory as they are logical.

II

So let us differ with those who claim a priori that the Revolution sprang from the teachings of the "Philosophes," only in order to justify their condemnation of both the Revolution and the teaching. But in opposition to this group, the admirers of the "Philosophes" and even more the admirers of Rousseau, who was not exactly one of the "Philosophes," have taken up the cudgels in an attempt to deny the responsibility or even the guilt of the eighteenth-century political writers in the upheaval that ensued. Particularly notable among these efforts is Edme Champion's abstruse but well-informed book: *Rousseau et la Révolution française* (Colin, 1909). Bringing the concept of retroactive responsibility into these matters is a questionable method. "My God!" Karl Marx is said to have exclaimed on one of the rare occasions when he seems to have called upon Heaven, "preserve me from the Marxists!" Rousseau has accused himself of enough sins without our taxing his memory with the errors of his followers. Without inquiring whether the Revolution was good or bad, which would be entirely too naïve in this day, may we not be able to show how and in what way it absorbed, reflected or brought to fruition the ideas of thinkers who had prepared it without wishing for it?

Professional historians generally tend to limit the part played by ideas in world events: the best of them devote, apparently for the sake of form, one or two chapters to the literature, painting and music of the periods studied by their manuals. But the history of civilization and culture is still very clumsily related to general history. Historians prefer to emphasize the purely historical causes of the Revolution: financial disorder, ministerial blunders, or the hostility of parlements that had been alienated by encroachments upon their prerogatives, etc. Perhaps in doing so they are choosing the easiest way. Their history does grasp the events, the things that change, that is, the things that would be presented in today's newspapers as facts or news: a tax-measure, a famine, the dismissal of a minister, a change in the price of bread, or a treaty. But it often fails to apprehend the slow subterranean movements which minds inclined to be too matter-of-fact find intangible, until they one day make their appearance as acts that make news or usher in a historical era. Now there are cases in which they never appear as acts; and orthodox history gives scant consideration to abortive movements or history's side-roads into which the past has ventured briefly only to turn back.

The history of ideas has the advantage of being able to give leisurely consideration to elements of history that changed only slowly and did not necessarily express themselves in events which demand attention by virtue of their suddenness. It would gladly declare that ideas rule the world. This would doubtless be an over-optimistic creed, if one did not add immediately that these ideas often turn into those truths wrapped in the gilt paper of falsehood that our contemporaries call in France "mystiques," or that they crystallize into a few fetish-words which imprison or falsify them. The history of the idea of progress has been sketched, although insufficiently in our opinion, by J. Delvaille and the English writer J. M. Bury. History itself would owe much to the man who would attempt to write the story of the idea of evolution, or the idea of revolution, the idea of comfort, or the idea of efficiency and the myth of success in the United States, among many others. On occasion he would have to go beyond the texts or interpret them, but this should not be forbidden provided that it is done with intellectual honesty. One must also remember the fact that the history of ideas is not simply the exposition of theoretical views expressed in philosophical writings, but at the same time the history of the deformations undergone by these ideas when other men adopt them, and also the history of the half-conscious beliefs into which ideas first clearly conceived by the few promptly transform themselves. In his lectures published in Buenos Aires in 1940 under the title *Ideas y creencias* the Spanish philosopher Ortega y Gasset has rightly claimed for these half-formulated "beliefs" a position in historical works on a par with that of ideas.

The difficulties presented by such a history of ideas when they become beliefs, articles of faith, or emotional drives and impel men to action are enormous: they should, by this very fact, challenge research-men. Up to now, sociology has failed to make over the study of literature to any considerable degree because histories of the prevailing taste and the environment in which a writer lived and of the social and economic conditions in which he was placed while conceiving his work have little bearing on the creation and even the content of the original work. But a knowledge of the public that greeted a literary work or of the work's subsequent career might on the contrary prove extremely fruitful. Such knowledge requires painstaking inquiry into the work's success, based on a great number of facts; it also demands a qualitative interpretation of history and statistics and the occasional intervention of that much-feared "queen of the world" called imagination. For the most read book is not the one that exerts the greatest influence. A hundred thousand passive or half-attentive readers who bought and even leafed through the *Encyclopédie,* for example, count for less than five hundred passionate admirers of the *Contrat Social* if among the latter may be counted Robespierre, Saint-Just or Babeuf. A school-master or a lecturer heard with interest may pass on Marx or Nietzsche to generations of barely literate people who will never guess the source of a thought that has modified their whole lives. It is not even necessary to have understood a book or even to have read it through in order to be profoundly influenced by it. An isolated phrase quoted in some article or a page reproduced at some time in an anthology, may have done more to spread some of the opinions of Montesquieu, Proudhon, or Gobineau than thirty re-editions of their writings bought by private libraries and commented upon by ten provincial academies.

In 1933 Daniel Mornet published on the subject sketched here his work entitled *Les Origines intellectuelles de la Révolution française* (Colin), which is a study of the spread of ideas justly termed a model of intellectual probity and discretion. Henceforth no one can consider this historical and philosophical problem without owing much to this solid book. The author has avoided the error of so many other writers who make the Revolution inexplicable by drawing a rough contrast between 1789 and 1670 or even 1715. He has followed the slow progress of the spread of new ideas from 1715 to 1747, then from 1748 to 1770, the date when the philosophic spirit had won the day. He has made very searching inquiries into the degree of penetration of the reformist spirit among the more or less learned societies and academies, in the letters of private individuals, in provincial libraries and even in educational curricula. His conclusions are new in many respects because of the exact information they offer and because they show those who are misled by the perspective of a later day into the error of limiting the group of "Philosophes" to five or six names, that writers half-unknown to us (Toussaint, Delisle de Sales, Morellet, Mably) were among those most widely read in the eighteenth century. With fitting reserve they tend to show that the thought of the century, by itself, would never have caused the Revolution if there had not been misery among the people as well; and that misery which was not a new thing at the time would not have brought about the Revolution if it had not had the support of opinion that had long been discontented and desirous of reform. It is clear that the Revolution had various causes including historical causes, meaning economic, political and financial causes as well as intellectual ones. However it would seem that Mornet has limited the rôle of the latter causes to an excessive degree and further work still needs to be done after his admirable effort.

The most obvious justification for further research lies in the fact that his investigation leaves off at 1787 because of the very purpose of his work. Now if a revolution was ready to break out at the time of the preparation of the "Cahiers de doléances" [lists of grievances] for the States-General it was not the Revolution that actually developed. Neither the days of June 20th and August 10th 1792, nor the death of Louis XVI nor the Terror, nor the constructive work of the Convention was contained in germ in the convocation of the States-General. In fact we know very little about the influence of Montesquieu, Voltaire and Rousseau himself on the different phases of the Revolution or the way in which they influenced certain actors in the great drama.

The special quality of the French Revolution, compared with other revolutionary movements in France or other countries, obviously lies in the titanic proportions of this upheaval but also in an ardent passion for thought, for embodying ideas in deeds, and for proposing universal laws. This accounts for the unparalleled world-wide influence of the work of destruction and construction which was accomplished between 1789 and 1795. An abstract passion for justice and liberty, the latter being sometimes conceived in strange fashion, inspired the men who made the Revolution and those who prepared it. The original tone that characterizes the Revolution and the verve that enlivens it, which are fundamental things although they elude the grasp of facts and figures, are due in part to the movement of thought and sensibility which goes from Montesquieu to Rousseau and from Bayle to the abbé Raynal.

III

If there is really one almost undisputed conclusion on the origins of the Revolution reached by historical studies coming from radically opposite factions, it is that pure historical materialism does not explain the Revolution. Certainly riots due to hunger were numerous in the eighteenth century and Mornet draws up the list of them; there was discontent and agitation among the masses. But such had also been the case under Louis XIV, such was the case under Louis-Philippe and deep discontent existed in France in 1920 and 1927 and 1934 without ending in revolution. No great event in history has been due to causes chiefly economic in nature and certainly not the French Revolution. France was not happy in 1788, but she was happier than the other countries of Europe and enjoyed veritable economic prosperity. Her population had increased from 19 to 27 millions since the beginning of the century and was the most numerous in Europe. French roads and bridges were a source of admiration to foreigners. Her industries such as ship-fitting at Bordeaux, the silk-industry at Lyons and the textile-industry at Rouen, Sedan and Amiens were active while Dietrich's blast-furnaces and the Creusot were beginning to develop modern techniques in metallurgy. The peasants were little by little coming to be owners of the land. Foreign trade reached the sum of 1,153 million francs in 1787, a figure not to be attained again until 1825. The traffic in colonial spices and San Domingo sugar was a source of wealth. Banks were being founded and France owned half the specie existing in Europe. So misery in France was no more than relative. But truly wretched peoples such as the Egyptian fellah, the pariah of India or even the Balkan or Polish peasant or Bolivian miners for example rarely bring about revolutions. In order to revolt against one's lot, one must be aware of his wretched condition, which presupposes a certain intellectual and cultural level; one must have a clear conception of certain reforms that one would like to adopt; in short, one must be convinced (and it was on this point that the books of the eighteenth century produced their effect) that things are not going well, that they might be better and that they will be better if the measures proposed by the reformist thinkers are put into practice.

Eighteenth-century philosophy taught the Frenchman to find his condition wretched, or in any case, unjust and illogical and made him disinclined to the patient resignation to his troubles that had long characterized his ancestors. It had never called for a revolution nor desired a change of regime; it had never been republican and Camille Desmouslins was not wrong in stating: "In all France there were not ten of us who were republicans before 1789." Furthermore he himself was not one of those ten. But only an over-simplified conception of influence would indulge in the notion that political upheaval completely embodies in reality the theoretical design drawn up by some thinker. Even the Russian revolution imbued as it was with Marxian dialectic did not make a coherent application of Marxism or quickly found it inapplicable when tried. The reforms of limited scope advocated by *L'Esprit des Lois, L'Homme aux quarante écus, L'Encyclopédie* and the more moderate writings of Rousseau struck none the less deeply at the foundations of the ancien régime, for they accustomed the Frenchman of the Third Estate to declaring privileges unjust, to finding the crying differences between the provinces illogical and finding famines outrageous. The propaganda of the "Philosophes" perhaps more than any other factor accounted for the fulfillment of the preliminary condition of the French revolution, namely, discontent with the existing state of things.

In short, without enlarging upon what is already rather well known we may say that eighteenth-century writers prepared the way for the Revolution, without wishing for it, because:

a) They weakened the traditional religion, winning over to their side a great number of clerics, and taught disrespect for an institution which had been the ally of the monarchy for hundreds of years. At the same time they had increased the impatience of the non-privileged groups by uprooting from many minds the faith in a future life which had formerly made bearable the sojourn in this vale of tears that constituted life for many people of low estate. They wished to enjoy real advantages here on earth and without delay. The concept of well-being and then that of comfort slowly penetrated among them.

b) They taught a secular code of ethics, divorced from religious belief and independent of dogma, and made the ideal of conduct consist of observation of this system of ethics, which was presented as varying in accordance with climate and environment. Furthermore they gave first importance in this ethical code to the love of humanity, altruism and service due society or our fellowmen. The ideas of humanity, already present in the teaching of Christ, in Seneca and Montaigne but often dormant, suddenly exerted fresh influence over people's minds.

c) They developed the critical spirit and the spirit of analysis and taught many men not to believe, or to suspend judgment rather than accept routine traditions. In D'Argenson, Chamfort, Morelly, Diderot, Voltaire of course, D'Holbach, Condillac and many others, and even in Laclos and Sade, we will find the effort to think courageously without regard for convention or tradition, that will henceforth characterize the French intellectual attitude. From this time on, inequality with respect to taxation, the tithe paid to the Church, and banishment or persecution for subversive opinions will shock profoundly the sense of logic and critical spirit of the readers of the "Philosophes."

d) Lastly, these very thinkers who have often been depicted as builders of Utopias are the creators of history or the historical sense, or almost so. Montesquieu studiously examined the origins of law and constitutions and saw men "conditioned" by soil and climate in contrast with the absolute rationalists who were foreign jurists and not Frenchmen. Boulainvilliers and many others of lesser fame studied France's past. Voltaire's masterpiece is probably his work on general history. The result of this curiosity about history was two-fold: it encouraged faith in progress and convinced numbers of Frenchmen that it was their task to fulfill humanity's law, to endeavor to increase the sum of liberty, relative equality, "enlightenment" and happiness in the world; it also proved to many men of the law who examined old documents and the titles of nobility and property, that the privileges of nobility were based on a flimsy foundation. The respect that these bourgeois or sons of the people might have felt for the aristocrats was accordingly diminished, at the very moment when the bourgeois saw the nobles not only accept with admiration but take under their protection destructive writings produced by the pens of commoners: sons of tailors (Marmontel), vine-growers (Restif), cutlers (Diderot) and watchmakers (Rousseau). And the history of the origins of royal sovereignty itself seemed to them scarcely more edifying than that of the feudal privileges.

As for the means of dissemination of those ideas or new beliefs that the philosophes were spreading between the years 1715 and 1770 or 1789, it will suffice to enumerate them rapidly, for numerous studies have examined them: they were the salons, although very few of the future revolutionaries frequented society gatherings; the clubs, that more and more called for tolerance, preached deism, demanded the abolition of slavery (*société des Amis des Noirs*) and dreamed of imitating the American Revolution (*Club Américain*); books or tracts which made their appearance as works of small format, easily carried or hidden, lively and sharp in style and prone to surprise and arouse the reader; periodicals; the theatre especially after the coming of the "drame bourgeois" and the "comédie larmoyante" ["sentimental comedy"], and then with Beaumarchais; and the education given in the secondary schools. Mornet's book sums up the essential material on the subject that can be found in documents. The other means of spreading new ideas, such as conversation, which is doubtless the most effective means man has always used to borrow and pass on new views, elude documentary research.

It is among the actors in the great revolutionary drama that investigations of broader scope might show us which of the ideas of the eighteenth century exerted influence and how and why they did so. Sieyès, among others, has been the subject of an exhaustive intellectual biography which has established with precision what the young abbé coming to Paris from Fréjus to devise constitutions owed to Descartes, Locke, and Voltaire in particular (for the negative side of his ideas), to Rousseau (for his impassioned logic) and to Mably. (Paul Bastid, *Sieyès et sa pensée*, Hachette, 1939). Another recent book, by Gérard Walter, is a study of Babeuf (Payot, 1937). It would be instructive to know how the minds of many of the revolutionaries were developed and by what books and meditations they were influenced; such men range from Mirabeau and Danton to Marat, from Rabaut de Saint-Etienne to Hérault de Séchelles and from Desmoulins or Brissot to generals of the Convention who may have read Raynal and Rousseau with passionate interest, as Bonaparte did later. Only when many monographs have been written devoting at least as much if not more attention to the history of ideas and the psychology of the protagonists in the Revolution than to the facts of their lives of action, will we be able to make sure generalizations about the influence of Montesquieu or Rousseau on the France of '89 or '93.

IV

Montesquieu and Rousseau are certainly the two great names worthy of consideration in some detail. The presiding judge of the High Court of Bordeaux obviously did not want the Revolution; had he lived to see it, he would not have approved of its reorganization of the judiciary, nor its audacity in reform, nor the Declaration of the Rights of Man, nor even the interpretation of certain principles he himself had enunciated. Still he is one of the spiritual fathers of the first two revolutionary assemblies. Like so many other men who have made history, he influenced the fateful years of 1789-92 by what he did say almost involuntarily, by the thoughts other men read in his sentences and by the tone even more than by the content of his writings. His great work breathes a veritable hatred of despotism founded on fear; it shows no moral respect for monarchy, and so helped to alienate the most reasonable minds from it. The great principle of the separation of powers presumes the right to seize from the king the united powers that he believed he held as a whole by divine right. Finally, Montesquieu, however elevated his position as a citizen or as a magistrate may have been, uttered words which will assume a mystic authority in later times on the subject of the people's inherent good qualities and its ability to select its leaders: "The common people are admirable in choosing those to whom they must delegate some part of their authority," (II,ii) or "When the common people once have sound principles, they adhere to them longer than those we are wont to call respectable people. Rarely does corruption have its beginning among the people." (V,ii)

Finally, in his admirable XIth book, Montesquieu had defined liberty in terms that were to remain etched in people's memories: this liberty required stable laws, which alone could establish and protect it. These laws were also to correct economic inequality. Certainly its historical examples adduced in great profusion, highly technical juridical considerations, certain generalizations that had been too cleverly made symmetrical and its lack of order made this voluminous treatise hard to read. But Montesquieu's influence was not one of those that can be gauged by the number of readers: it expressed itself in action thanks to a few thoughtful minds who found in it a sufficiently coherent overall plan capable of replacing the old order which obviously was crumbling. Montesquieu's influence inspired a more important group of revolutionaries who were familiar with only a few chapters of his work, but these chapters were filled with the love of freedom and the great feeling for humanity that condemned slavery and the iniquitous exploitation of some men by others.

Montesquieu's influence on the French Revolution began to decline at the time when Rousseau's was coming to the fore. Many studies have been devoted to the subject of Rousseau and the French Revolution; and the subject deserves still further study, for perhaps no more notable case of the effect of thought on life exists in the whole history of ideas and of dynamic ideas in particular. But this broad subject has too often been narrowed down by the most well-meaning historians. So many dogmatic and partisan statements had portrayed Rousseau as the great malefactor who was guilty of the excesses committed by the Terrorists and as the father of collectivism that, as a reaction, the best-disposed scholars set about proving by facts and texts that the author of the *Contrat Social* was guiltless of so many misdeeds. As a result they have belittled his influence. But there is some narrowness and naïveté in these scholarly arguments.

According to some, everything that Rousseau wrote already existed before his coming in the works of a number of writers and thinkers both at home and abroad and Jean-Jacques brought forth very little that was new. That is quite possible, and scholars have been able to make fruitful inquiries into the sources of the *Discours sur l'Inégalité* and the *Contrat*. But the fact remains that whatever Rousseau borrowed from others he made his own; he rethought it and above all felt it with a new intensity and set it off to advantage by his own passion and his own talent. What he owes to Plato or Locke suddenly "shook" the men of 1792 only because Rousseau had charged it with a new electric current.

Furthermore Rousseau is rife with contradictions and the most ingenious men of learning (Lanson, Höffding, Schinz and E. H. Wright) have not yet succeeded in convincing us of the unity of his thought. For Corsica and Poland he proposes finely adapted and moderate constitutions that do not seem to have sprung from the same brain as the *Contrat Social*. He writes a very conservative article on *l'Economie politique* for the fifth volume of the *Encyclopédie* while in his second *Discours* he had propounded anarchical theses burning with revolutionary ardor. "To expect one to be always consistent is beyond human possibility, I fear!" he himself had admitted in the second preface of the *Nouvelle Héloïse*. We will not go so far as to pay homage to Rousseau for his contradictions and may choose to reserve our unalloyed admiration for other systems of thought more dispassionate and logical than his. But an author's influence does not have much to do with the rigor and coherence of his philosophical system. In fact, it would not be hard to show that the thinkers who have contributed the most toward changing the face of the world exerted influence because of their contradictions, since very different periods and highly diverse individuals drew from them various messages of equal validity. Let us add with no ironic intention that because of this the ingenuity of the learned will never tire of seeking the impossible golden key to these disconcerting enigmas and that the hunger for systems, among those lacking the necessary imagination to construct new ones, will always exert itself to bring about a happy synthesis of the successive assertions of a Plato, a Montaigne, a Locke, Rousseau, Comte or Nietzsche.[3]

After all, as the historians tell us quite correctly, the *Contrat Social* is only a part of Rousseau's political thought and not the most important part in the eyes of his contemporaries; the author himself attributed only a rather limited importance to this logical Utopian book. Rousseau never seriously contemplated a revolution in France; he did not think that a republic was viable, or perhaps even desirable for France. One might even make the assertion supported by texts that Jean-Jacques, that *bête noire* of the anti-revolutionaries from Burke to Maurras, Lasserre and Seillière, was a timid conservative.[4] It is quite true (M.

[3] "Inconsistencies are the characteristic quality of men who have thought much, created abundantly and destroyed on a broad scale. They have necessarily said many things and among those things there are a great many that are at variance or even directly contrary to one another." This is the comment on Rousseau made in an article pertinent to the present subject by the solid founder of the School of Political Science: Emile Boutmy, in "La Déclaration des Droits de l'Homme et du citoyen et M. Jellineck," (*Annales des Sciences politiques,* 1902, pp. 415-443).

[4] Rousseau has depicted himself in the third of his *Dialogues* as "the man who is more averse to revolution than any one else in the world, . . . who has always insisted upon the maintenance of the existing institutions, contending that their destruction would only take away the palliative while leaving their faults and substitute brigandage for corruption." It is true that here he is making an effort to present himself in the most favorable light! In his *Jugement sur la Polysynodie de l'abbé de Saint-Pierre* (Vaughan, *The Political Writings of Rousseau* [Cambridge, 1915], I, 416), he gave the following warning in 1756: "Think of the danger of once displacing the enormous masses that make up the French monarchy! Who will be able to check the shock once it is given or foresee the effects it may produce?" In the eighth of his *Lettres de la Montaigne,* he again exclaims: "Eh! How could I approve of any one's disturbing the peace of the State for any interest whatsoever . . . ?"

Mornet has proved this once again) that the influence of the *Contrat Social* was very weak between the years 1762 and 1789; the book caused so little disturbance that Rousseau was not even molested; and it is probable that Rousseau would have been frightened by certain inferences that were later drawn from his ideas. What he wrote in 1765 in no way justifies an assertion on our part that he would still have written the same thing in 1793 and so it is quite as conceivable that Rousseau might have violently changed his point of view and espoused the cause of the revolutionaries, had he lived long enough to receive their acclaim. And above all, without having consciously wanted the Revolution, Rousseau did a great deal, if not to cause it, at least to give it direction when it had broken out. The success of Rousseau's works and the reception accorded them in his life-time have been investigated in sufficient detail. From now on groups of research men might well give their attention to the enormous influence Rousseau exerted on the men of the Convention and on those of the Empire or the Restoration or on the Romantics. Granted that Rousseau was neither a republican nor a revolutionary, he was in revolt and that is no less important. A. Aulard who was not inclined to over-estimate the influence of the intellectuals on the French Revolution neverthe-less accurately described the paradoxical result of any fairly broad study of this subject: "All these men in revolt want to keep the mon-archy and all of them blindly deal it mortal blows. The French, mon-archists to a man, take on republicanism without their knowledge."[5]

Not one of the men of the Revolution adopted Rousseau's phil-osophical system outright in order to put it into practice; that is only too plain. Not one of them understood Rousseau's thought in its subtleties, its contradictions and its alterations as the scholar of the present-day can understand it with the aid of much posthumous documentation: this is scarcely less obvious. Whatever chagrin it may cause minds devoted to strict methods, the unparalleled effect produced on the imagination of posterity by Montaigne, Rousseau or Nietzsche can be credited to quotations drawn from their contexts and probably perverted from their original sense. This influence is not so much an influence of ideas as it is an influence of *idées-forces*, to use Fouillée's expression, and exerts its power more by setting men's sensibilities aflame than by convincing their minds.

[5] A. Aulard, "L'Idée républicaine et démocratique avant 1789," in the *Revolution française*, July-December 1898, tome 35, 5-45.

"Man is born free, and everywhere he is in chains." This peremptory formula from the first chapter of the *Contrat Social,* in conjunction with a few others which declared the sovereignty of the people inalienable and affirmed the right to revolt in the event of the usurpation of powers by the government, contributed immeasurably toward crystallizing in the general mind from 1789 on the resolve to make the king subject to the only true rights which were inherent in the people. On October 5th 1789 Robespierre and Barrère contended that the sovereign could not oppose the constituent power which was superior to him. The passion for equality which wildly inspires the Revolutionaries and the modern world after them owes no less to Rousseau's fundamental idea that law should rectify natural inequality (which he was not foolish enough to overlook) by means of civic equality. The XIth chapter of the 2nd book of the *Contrat Social* stated in striking terms: "For the very reason that the force of things always tends to destroy equality, the force of legislation must always tend to maintain it." The 3rd book of the same work castigated the vices to which kings are prone, for if they are not narrow or evil on attaining the throne—"the throne will make them so." That does not make Rousseau a partisan of republicanism or a democrat; but had it not been for such aphorisms, Saint-Just never would have proclaimed in his fine *Discours concernant le jugement de Louis XVI* of November 13th 1792: "Royalty is an eternal crime against which every man has the right to rise up and take arms . . . One can not reign in innocence."

The *Discours sur l'Inégalité* contained pages of impassioned rhetoric that were even more effective. The English writer C. E. Vaughan, who is a scrupulous commentator on the political writings of Rousseau, did not hesitate to state, after years of reflection on this subject: "Wherever, during the last century and a half, man has revolted against injustice and oppression, there we may be sure that the leaven of the second *Discours* has been working." Doubtless Rousseau had never dreamed of the application of his declamations against property: but he had set forth the idea that inheritances ought to be whittled down by fiscal measures and that those who owned no lands ought to receive some, without necessarily advocating collectivism. He had also uttered against wealth words whose echoes will ring down the centuries: "It is the estate of the wealthy that steals from mine the bread of my children. . . . A bond-holder whom the State pays for doing nothing is scarcely different in my eyes from a highwayman who lives at the expense of the passers-by . . . , every idle citizen is a rogue."

The precautions with which Jean-Jacques had surrounded some of his bold affirmations quickly disappeared in the heat of action. The chapter called "Du Peuple," in the *Contrat Social* (ii, 8), was most cautious: but its author had nevertheless hinted in it that sometimes, in the life of peoples, "the State, set aflame by civil wars, is so to speak reborn from its ashes, and regains the vigor of youth in leaving the arms of death." People retained phrases from the *Emile* too,—the prophetic phrases in which the educator had proclaimed to the people of his time that they were approaching the era of revolutions when men would be able to destroy what men had built. These few phrases, gaining added violence in tone from the fact that they were detached from contexts that often contradicted them, seemed charged with new meaning when the great upheaval had broken out. Such was also the case of the mystic system of happiness taught by the Genevan "philosophe's" entire work. Man is born good; he is made to be happy; he may become so if he reforms himself and if his governments are reformed. We know how the echo of these doctrines will resound in the noble formulas of Saint-Just, who was perhaps the revolutionary most deeply steeped in Rousseau's thought.[6]

The aspect of Rousseau that Albert Schinz called "the Roman Rousseau" exerted no less influence on that other myth which prevailed or raged among the men of the Revolution (and among the women, too, as in the case of Madame Rolland), the myth of the ancients and their passion for liberty and virtue. "The world has been empty since the day of the Romans," cried Saint-Just; and he stated

[6] On March 3rd 1794 (13 Ventôse An II), "The Archangel of the Terror," as Michelet calls Saint-Just, declared before the Convention: "Let Europe learn that you no longer want either a single unhappy victim of oppression or an oppressor in French territory; let this example bear fruit upon the earth; let it spread abroad the love of virtue and of happiness! Happiness is a new idea in Europe." In his *Fragments sur les institutions républicaines,* published after his death, the young disciple of Rousseau and the Romans wrote: "The day that I am convinced that it is impossible to instill in the French people ways that are mild, energetic and responsive but merciless against tyranny and injustice, I will stab myself." It is regrettable that there is in existence only an inadequate Swiss dissertation by S. B. Kritschewsky, *Rousseau and Saint-Just* (Bern, 1859) on the fine subject that the influence of Rousseau and other eighteenth century thinkers on Saint-Just's noble thought would make.

to the Convention on February 24th 1793: "The Republic is not a
Senate, it is virtue." The whole of Saint-Just's remarkable youthful
work entitled: *Esprit de la Révolution et de la Constitution de la
France* is imbued with Rousseauist themes and ends on this cry of
regret: "France has only now conferred a statue upon J.-J. Rousseau.
Ah! Why is that great man dead?"

Robespierre, whom Michelet maliciously called a "weak and
pale bastard of Rousseau" because of his cult of the Supreme Being,
was indebted to Rousseau to no lesser degree than Saint-Just although
he does not show the mark of the born writer that stamps the formulas
of the terrorist guillotined at the age of twenty-seven. It was by assidu-
ous reading of Rousseau that he formed his style: and his style served
him as a powerful weapon. It seems that the young student from
Arras met Rousseau in 1778, the year of his death, and never forgot it.
"I saw thee in thy last days, and this memory is a source of proud
joy for me," he declares later in his *Mémoires*, placed under the aegis
of Rousseau, and promised to "remain constantly faithful to the
inspiration that I have drawn from thy writings." Dozens of sentences
which reiterate formulas from the *Contrat Social* might be extracted
from his speeches. It was Rousseau who had helped to turn Robespierre away from Catholicism, and of course he was the man from
whom Robespierre borrowed his cult of the Supreme Being; his
Observations sur le projet d'Instruction publique presented to the
Convention in 1793 are based on the Rousseauist faith: "If nature
created man good, it is back to nature that we must bring him." His
speech made at the Jacobin Club on January 2nd 1792 against the war
at that time desired by the Girondins rendered homage to Rousseau
in impassioned terms: "No one has given us a more exact idea of the
common people than Rousseau because no one loved them more."[7]
The secret of the enormous influence exerted by Rousseau lay less in
the substance of his thought than in the burning tone of a man who
had lived his ideas and had suffered (or thought he had) because he
had sprung from the people and had known poverty. "According to
the principles of your committee," declared Robespierre to the Constituent Assembly on August 11th 1791, "we ought to blush at having

[7] Here again this large subject deserves a lengthier and more recent monograph than the thesis of Richard Schass: *J. J. Rousseaus Einfluss auf Robespierre,*
(Leipzig, 1905).

erected a statue to J.-J. Rousseau, because he did not pay the property-tax." The history of ideas and their influence on persons and things is full of elements that defy all possibility of quantitative or statistical measurement. How can one estimate all that the men of the Revolution owed Rousseau in the way of fervor, mystic hope, logic that was impassioned and even fierce on occasion and—what is not less important, even for history, as Danton, Saint-Just and Robespierre were aware— the imperious and incisive style that made their formulas resound in twenty countries and across one hundred and fifty years? "One does not make revolutions by halves" or "the French people are voting for liberty for the world"—these aphorisms or decrees of Saint-Just, like certain phrases of Mirabeau, or a multitude of orators of lesser stature,[8] and of Bonaparte himself, would not have been uttered, and would not have had the resonance that has kept them alive, if these men had not been imbued with the spirit and the style of the Citizen of Geneva.

The history of the cult of Rousseau during the French Revolution is easier to trace than that of his deep influence on the revolutionaries. The former has been studied in part, and the manifestations of this idolatry of Rousseau are often amusing. The setting-up of the bust of Jean-Jacques in the Constituent Assembly on June 23, 1790, the consecration of a street of Paris named after him in the same year, the

[8] Among the speakers heard with interest at the time, one might mention D'Eymar, who had the honors of the Pantheon voted to Rousseau; Rabaut de Saint-Etienne, who often quoted Rousseau as one of the precursors of the revolution; the abbé Fauchet, who expounded the *Contrat* before a numerous audience, in 1790, at the "Universal confederation of the Friends of Truth." Mirabeau had long since (letter to Sophie of December 8th 1778) extolled "the sublime creative genius" of Rousseau, and had had homage paid to his widow on May 12th 1790. Marat had, so it is said, annotated the *Contrat* in 1788, and his sister Albertine testified how much he admired it. Let us hope that some historian with a knowledge of psychology will some day treat the great subject of "Napoleon the First and Rousseau." Even the remarks of the Emperor in old age show that he was attracted by Rousseau: the *Nouvelle Héloïse* was one of the first books he read on Sainte-Hélène. At the height of his glory, in 1806, he thought of organizing an official tribute to Rousseau, according to Stanislas Girardin. This same Girardin, in a curious passage in his *Mémoires* (Michaud, 1834, vol. i, 190) reports this reflection (did he understand it correctly?) of the First Consul at Ermonville: "The future will tell whether it would not have been better for the peace of the earth if Rousseau and I had not existed."

repeated editions of the *Contrat Social* (4 editions in 1790, 3 in 1791, etc.), the constitutional articles put under his aegis, the decree ordering that Rousseau's ashes be brought to the Pantheon in 1794 and the pious emotion of the crowd, and lastly, the invocation to "his generous soul" by the Incorruptible One in his speech of May 7th 1794 on the religion of the Revolution and the pompous application of his declamations on the Supreme Being; all these things have been mentioned more than once and recently, too.[9] But the way in which Rousseau's influence profoundly modified the men and women of the revolutionary and imperial era, and then the romantics great and small, and the continuators of the Revolution, in and out of France, in the nineteenth and twentieth centuries: these are the questions that intellectual history seems to have been reluctant to investigate.

Its timidity is regrettable and our knowledge of the past suffers twice over because of it: first, because history that devotes itself too exclusively to what we call material facts such as a military victory, the fall of a ministry or the opening-up of a railroad-track, seriously falsifies our perspective of what took place. The development of the Napoleonic legend, the quietly working influence of Rousseau or Voltaire, the growth of anti-clericalism and the elaboration of socialist myths are phenomena which are partly literary or sentimental in nature, but are second to no other order of phenomena in importance and in the effects they had on the course of human affairs. Our knowledge of the past suffers additionally because historians, by turning aside from the history of ideas and sentiments with their vigorous influence on the lives of men, abandon these research subjects to men less trained than themselves in exact methods of study; the latter are disposed to write with the sole intent of finding in the past arguments to support their political views or their partisan claims.

[9] See Gordon McNeil: "The Cult of Rousseau in the French Revolution," *Journal of the History of Ideas*, April 1945, 196-212. Monglond's work *Le Préromantisme français* (Grenoble, Arthaud, 1930) contains, especially in the second volume, chapters i and vi, the most thought-provoking evidence on the effect produced by Rousseau on sensitive souls of the revolutionary era. Monglond quotes (ii, 157) the curious sentence in which Bernardin de Saint-Pierre, in his *Etudes de la Nature*, had proclaimed some years before '89: "It seems to me that some favorable revolution is in store for us. If it comes, it will be letters that we will have to thank for it. . . . Oh men of letters! . . . . You alone recall the rights of man and of Divinity."

Meanwhile youth is tempted to reject history as it is officially presented, as an endless series of wars, diplomatic ruses, crimes, examples of intense selfishness and the impotent efforts of men to bring more reason into the world. It refuses to lend credence to those who advise it that man has remained a religious and ideological animal even more than an "economic" creature. Youth's awakening, when it is suddenly placed face to face with the terrible power of ideas, myths and fanaticisms in the world, is sometimes a rude shock, as we have seen recently.

The Frenchmen in particular who have thought fit in the past few years to deny their eighteenth-century thinkers as traitors to the classic and monarchical tradition of France have only to open their eyes in order to ascertain that no French tradition is more alive than that of the Century of Enlightenment. Pascal and Descartes are doubtless greater; Montaigne has more charm and Saint Thomas more logical power: but it is Voltaire and Rousseau, and sometimes Montesquieu and Condorcet, that one finds almost always behind the living influence of France on the masses and the ideologies of South America, of the United States itself, of central and eastern Europe and that one will find tomorrow in Africa and Asia. The world of today expects from post-war France, and France herself expects from her political thinkers who had lost the habit of expressing themselves in universal terms during the last fifty years, a renewal and a modernization of her liberal ideas of the eighteenth century, boldly adapted to the social and economic problems of today, but still inspired by the same faith in man and his possibilities.

Students from other countries remind the French of this fact, lest they forget it too readily. Their studies on the influence of Voltaire and Rousseau on the French Revolution and the revolutions that ensued elsewhere in the world are becoming more numerous and sometimes more objective than the French ones. A Slavic scholar Milan Markovitch in a large and exhaustive book on *Rousseau et Tolstoi* (Champion, 1928) set forth in detail the Rousseauism of the Russian novelist, who in his adolescence carried the portrait of Jean-Jacques around his neck like a scapular and wrote the following message to the newly-founded Rousseau Club on March 7th 1905: "Rousseau has been my teacher since the age of fifteen. Rousseau and the Gospel have been the two great influences for good in my life." The German thinker Ernst Cassirer devoted a little book written in

1945 to commemoration of the admiration for Rousseau expressed by Goethe and Fichte as well as Kant who declared: "Rousseau set me right. . . . I learned to respect human nature."[10] Thoreau and D. H. Lawrence are indebted to the Genevan for a good half of their thinking. George Eliot, on meeting the philosopher Emerson in Coventry in 1848, found herself being asked by him what her favorite book was; Rousseau's *Confessions,* she answered; at which the American transcendentalist cried: "It is mine too." Shortly afterwards, on February 9th 1849, she wrote Sara Hennel these extremely lucid sentences on the mechanism of intellectual influence:

> I wish you thoroughly to understand that the writers who have most profoundly influenced me are not in the least oracles to me. . . . For instance, it would signify nothing to me if a very wise person were to stun me with proofs that Rousseau's views of life, religion, and government were miserably erroneous,—that he was guilty of some of the worst *bassesses* [acts of meanness] that have degraded civilized man. I might admit all this: and it would be not the less true that Rousseau's genius has sent that electric thrill through my intellectual and moral frame which has awakened me to new perceptions; . . . and this not by teaching me any new belief. . . . The fire of his genius has so fused together old thoughts and prejudices, that I have been ready to make new combinations.[11]

[10] Ernst Cassirer, *Rousseau, Kant and Goethe* (Princeton University Press, 1945).—Fichte openly proclaimed that he owed the revelation of his philosophical system to "the years when the French nation was fighting passionately for the triumph of political liberty. . . . To the French nation I owe my having been raised to those heights [of his *Doctrine of Science*]. . . . To her in some measure my system belongs." The influence of the French Revolution was equally strong on the philosopher who is often presented as the theorist of Prussian absolutism, Hegel. Two years before his death, in 1829, he wrote: "It was a glorious sunrise. All thinking beings then celebrated that dawn [of the French Revolution]. A sublime emotion then reigned, the enthusiasm for the spirit made the world quiver, as if, then only, a true reconciliation of the divine and the world had been achieved." In the *Phenomenology of the Mind,* a supreme function is also given to the French Revolution—it made a living synthesis between the two conflicting worlds of conscience: through that Revolution, "the two worlds are reconciled and heaven descends upon the earth." (See a posthumous article on "Hegel and Diderot's *Nephew of Rameau*," by the French philosopher Henri Mougin, in *Europe,* August 1926, 1-12.)

[11] For this reference and the one preceding, we are indebted to Professor Gordon Haight, who is thoroughly familiar with all that touches on George Eliot.

In the face of such proofs of a fruitful and life-giving though possibly dangerous influence, an important English historian who was moreover an admirer of Burke and usually more moderate in his statements, but was conscious of the importance of ideas in the events of this world, Lord Acton, was impelled to exclaim: "Rousseau produced more effect with his pen than Aristotle, or Cicero, or St. Augustine, or St. Thomas Aquinas, or any other man who ever lived."[12]

[12] This quotation from Lord Acton is given by Herbert Paul as uttered in his presence. (Lord Acton, *Letters to Mary Gladstone* [New York, Macmillan, 1904], 10.)

XIII

The French Revolution and Napoleon

-»»-»»-»»-»»-»»-»»-»»-»»-»»-«««-«««-«««-«««-«««-«««-«««-«««-«««-

The Place of the American Revolution in the
Causal Pattern of the French Revolution

LOUIS GOTTSCHALK

French Revolution

ALBERT MATHIEZ

Songs—Colorful Propaganda of the French
Revolution

CORNWELL B. ROGERS

Napoleon's Military Bulletins

JOSEPH J. MATHEWS

The Europe of Napoleon: A Synopsis

GOLO MANN

-»»-»»-»»-»»-»»-»»-»»-»»-»»-«««-«««-«««-«««-«««-«««-«««-«««-«««-

The Place of the American Revolution in the Causal Pattern of the French Revolution

LOUIS GOTTSCHALK

⋙⋙⋙⋙⋙⋙⋙⋙⋙ *Published in 1948* ⋘⋘⋘⋘⋘⋘⋘⋘⋘⋘

Virtually every historian who has ever written about the causes of the French Revolution has dealt not only with political, economic, social, and intellectual conditions under the *ancien régime* but with the repercussions of the American Revolutionary experience on developments in France. In the past the American influence was often given only minor importance. It is significant, however, that in the years since World War II many a French historian who fears Soviet Russia and favors cooperation with the United States has read his present concerns into the past and ascribed far more significance than before to the American Revolutionary example. Although easy enough to understand, this is an approach to the past that no fair-minded historian can condone. It is reassuring, therefore, to come upon an analysis of the sort that Louis Gottschalk has written on the relations between the American and the French Revolutions. Professor of history at the University of Chicago, Gottschalk is one of the leading American authorities on eighteenth-century France and the author of a multi-volume biography of Lafayette which when it is completed will stand for years to come as the definitive work on the French leader. In showing the connection between the American and the French Revolutions, Gottschalk keeps his eyes fixed steadily on the eighteenth century, not on the twentieth.

On July 4, 1948 the people of the United States will celebrate the 172nd anniversary of the Declaration of Independence. In other words, it is now almost *twice* four score and seven years ago that "our fathers brought forth on this continent a new nation conceived in liberty and dedicated to the proposition that all men are created equal." And we have just finished—in fact, it may be said that we are still engaged in—a great struggle "testing whether that nation or any nation so conceived and so dedicated can long endure."

The principle of liberty and the proposition that all men are created equal were inherited by the people of the United States from a long tradition. That tradition had Biblical origins; its genealogy can easily be traced by the brilliant pattern it weaves through the history of British and European political philosophy and constitutional practice. Its collateral American lines reached maturity in the constitutions of the separate states (some of which came even before the Declaration of Independence), the Declaration of Independence itself, and in the first ten amendments of the federal constitution.

It is sometimes believed that it was because of the principles for which the Americans fought and which they had incorporated in their widely admired Declaration of Independence that the government of France joined with the young American nation to fight against the tyranny symbolized by the British army and its Hessian mercenaries. That belief, however, contains sentimental overtones that do not ring true. That the ideals of "life, liberty and the pursuit of happiness" had a significant influence in determining French foreign policy before 1778, if it is true at all, is true only in small part. How little truth there is in it can be shown by citing the outstanding contemporary French writers on political theory, the very people whose purpose it should have been to promote the ideals of liberty among the French.

Take, for example, Beaumarchais. He was one of the writers in the period before the French Revolution largely responsible for the spread of the idea of liberty in France. He was greatly interested in

Reprinted by special permission of the American Friends of Lafayette. This essay appeared originally in the series, "Publications of The American Friends of Lafayette," No. 2, 1948. The documentation which originally appeared with this essay has been omitted.

American independence, and was influential in forming the American policy of the French minister of foreign affairs, the Comte de Vergennes. Yet from the letters that Beaumarchais wrote to the minister before 1778, it is clear that he did not intend the ideal of liberty to have the foremost part in that policy. He made the more practical plea that the independence of the American colonies from England would redress the world's commercial balance and would be to the political advantage of the French empire.

And Turgot, also a minister of the king and justly reputed to be one of the outstanding economic reformers of his day, was still less a champion of American freedom. When the minister of foreign affairs sent around a memorandum asking for opinions as to whether the French government should take part in the War of American Independence, Turgot replied: "It seems to me that the most desirable outcome from the viewpoint of the two crowns [the French and the Spanish] would be that England overcome the resistance of her colonies." He went on to say that a long-drawn-out war between the British and the American insurgents would be to the advantage of France. A similar point of view was presented by the Abbé de Mably, generally considered one of the most radical political theorists of the day, in an essay entitled *Notre Gloire ou Nos Rêves*. In short, hard-headed considerations regarding the welfare of France were more typical of the attitude of French writers *before* the Declaration of Independence than the sentimental championing of American liberties.

It is sometimes said that many French soldiers came to America before 1778 to fight on behalf of the ideal of liberty. That is supposed to be particularly true of the Marquis de Lafayette. But it can be shown—I have spent many hours and written many pages in the effort to show—that as a matter of fact Lafayette's interest in political

---

BRISSOT: Minor *philosophe*, worshipper of things American, and French Revolutionary leader of the Girondins, who were often called Brissotins. With the establishment of the Republic in 1792, he and his followers came increasingly to be viewed as reactionaries by reason of their static attitude toward the Revolution, their opposition to the domination of the city of Paris, and their hostility to undue government intervention in economic life. Brissot was guillotined in 1793.

POTATO WAR: The War of the Bavarian Succession (1778-1779) growing out

ideals, if it existed at all before 1776, was not very keen. Its vigorous growth came only *after* he had enlisted in the American service, and was not a cause of his doing so. It was less spiritual motives—such as escape from frustration, desire for glory, and hatred of the British— that led to his heroic behavior. What was true of Lafayette was *a fortiori* true of other European soldiers who volunteered their services to the American army, and was still more true of those soldiers who went as part of the French army, following the formal Franco- American alliance, to fight under Rochambeau on the side of Wash- ington. The attitude of the French people before or shortly after the Declaration of Independence [that] was known to them is well summed up by Morellet, another of that group of writers of the eighteenth cen- tury Enlightenment called "the *philosophes*." In a letter to the British minister Shelburne dated January 5, 1777—i. e., shortly after news of the Declaration of Independence had reached France—Morellet de- clared that many partisans of America in Paris were less friendly to American liberty than hostile to Great Britain.

Offsetting this prevalent attitude, however, was that of other Frenchmen who thought of America as fighting the cause of man- kind. After Benjamin Franklin got to France, he reported a general feeling that America was fighting for the liberty of all in fighting for her own. Franklin, however, is not the best of witnesses in this regard. Naturally he encountered the most pro-American elements, and the less friendly persons he met were not likely to express themselves freely in his presence. And yet Franklin's testimony enables us to note that the news of the Declaration of Independence, which had arrived in France just about a month ahead of him, marked a sig- nificant change in French public opinion. While before the end of 1776 the prevailing attitude toward the American rebellion was Anglo- phobe, by the beginning of 1777 it had become Americanophile.

of the death of the Duke of Bavaria without a legitimate heir and out of Prussian objections to Austrian claims to the Duchy. Brief and uneventful, it was given the label "Potato War" because both sides exhausted their sup- plies and the two hungry armies had to dig up frozen potatoes to avoid starvation.

SECOND HUNDRED YEARS' WAR: Widely used label for the series of struggles between England and France that started in 1689 with the War of the League of Augsburg and ended in 1815 with Waterloo.

For a time after 1776—that is to say, between 1776 and the signing of the treaty of alliance of 1778—the official policy and the opinion of a large part of the population was for the most part Anglophobe and not libertarian. Between 1776 and 1778, the pro-American party in France published a periodical entitled *Les Affaires de l'Angleterre et de l'Amérique*. This periodical appeared to be published in the Belgian city of Antwerp. At any rate, that city was indicated on the title page as its place of origin. It probably was printed and published in Paris, but in order to avoid the censorship authorities, who apparently still were unfriendly to American ideals, it was made to appear to come from a foreign country. This newspaper has often been cited as showing the popularity of republican principles in France before 1778, but recent investigation shows that it endeavored to soften the impact of republican principles against a cushion of anti-English arguments rather than to propound republican principles directly and positively. There was at the same time in Paris also a pro-English, anti-American propaganda intended to counteract that of the friends of America. This English propaganda, organized under the guidance of Isaac De Pinto, played upon the widespread antipathy in France to rebellion and reproached the Americans as insurgents.

The Alliance of 1778 changed the picture thoroughly, making official France outwardly, and the greater part of the French people sincerely, friendly to America as well as hostile to England. That alliance was largely, however, the result rather of the fear that the American colonies might become reconciled to the mother country, thereby re-establishing English supremacy upon the seas and overseas, than of France's interest in the ideals set forth in the Declaration of Independence. The English historian W. E. H. Lecky has well summed up the French attitude of that day. The French, he said, were not moved by American liberty, but they were greatly concerned with American independence. After 1778, however, the spirit of liberty grew in France and cemented the friendliness of the people of France toward the people of the United States.

As a general rule, American history textbooks give the impression that what went on in the thirteen transatlantic British colonies from 1778 to 1783 was the major phase of the War of the American Revolution. Nevertheless, to most contemporaries outside of America, that was only a small part of a much bigger war—one that may indeed be called a "world war," if by that phrase is meant a struggle fought all over the world. Only a portion of the total forces involved were engaged in what is now the eastern part of the United States and Canada. Others fought in the West Indies, South America, Africa and Asia, and on the high seas. The total number of land forces under arms in the United States seldom, if ever, reached more than 40,000 on either side. In only one instance did Washington command more than 16,000 men, and that was at Yorktown, where nearly half of them were French. A bigger army in France had constituted one of the most serious threats of invasion that England had ever had to face before 1940, and in Spain another army nearly as large had besieged Gibraltar and invaded Minorca. The fleets that fought in the East and the West Indies sometimes numbered more men than were engaged in the most decisive land battles of the American phase of the conflict.

Eventually nearly every country of Europe was involved directly or indirectly in the war, which was only another in a century-long series that France had been fighting against England for world hegemony. Since the Treaty of 1763, the French had made a vigorous effort to fan the ill-feeling between the American colonies and their mother country into a flame that could be quenched only with blood. After rebellion started, it would probably have resulted in reconciliation between the colonies and England if the French had been willing that it should end in a peaceful manner. Not only did they form an alliance with the United States, they also brought in the Spanish and the Dutch. Before peace was made, a formidable coalition of world powers was lined up against England instead of merely thirteen under-populated colonies.

France also put a great deal of effort and money into the thirteen colonies themselves. True, the forces sent there were small compared to those sent elsewhere. Likewise, the fleets that sailed there went usually on side-trips from their campaigns in the West Indies. But the visit of one of those fleets proved to be the means by which Cornwallis was cut off from aid or retreat, and the half-army that Rochambeau placed under Washington at Yorktown (after agreeing to wait no longer for the other half to come) was the deciding factor in winning that decisive encounter.

Though France, Spain, Holland, and the United States formed quite a strong coalition, they were not the only countries involved in the war. Practically every other big European state was included in a league of "armed neutrality," organized to fight England "short of war" (to use a phrase not then current). They resisted her on the high seas, seeking to refute the contention that she ruled the waves and that the oceans were not free. Thus, Russia, Prussia, the Holy Roman Empire, the Scandinavian countries, Portugal and the Two Sicilies became indirectly involved in the War of American Independence. The separate German states also became interested in its outcome, since Austria and Prussia were carrying on a little war of their own—the so-called "Potato War" (1778-79)—which remained localized and bloodless because England and France, allies of Prussia and Austria respectively, were busily engaged in fighting each other in America and elsewhere. Thus another important aspect of European history during the eighteenth century—the struggle for leadership in the Holy Roman Empire—was for a while affected by what went on in America.

Nor did the war end when the American phase of it was decided. Yorktown was fought in 1781, but peace was not made until 1783. Several things that occurred in the meantime had a greater influence than the victory at Yorktown on what that peace would be. For example, France was decisively defeated in the West Indies waters, and it became obvious that the siege of Gibraltar would not succeed. These failures rather than Yorktown determined the outcome for the Spanish, the Dutch, and the French. They determined also that Britannia would continue to rule the waves, even though she lost her thirteen Continental colonies.

Thus it happened that, from the military and diplomatic point of view, the Revolutionary War was much more than a war for American independence. Although time was to show that the establishment of a sovereign American federation was perhaps the most important result of that war, to contemporaries the future of the United States appeared to be only one among many issues that had induced the big powers to become involved in the struggle. It is even conceivable that if the Battles of Lexington and Concord had not made the American rebellion the immediate occasion of that struggle, England and France might have engaged about the same time anyway in another round of their hundred-year contest for control of the seas and of the colonies beyond the seas. In that event, it is also conceivable, the strategy on both sides might have been much the same as it actually was, except perhaps for the campaigns on the North American continent.

In other words, the War of the American Revolution was a conflict in which France played the major part on the allied side and the American states a minor one. To Frenchmen the capture of small islands like Grenada and Dominica and naval defeats like the Battle of the Saints in the West Indies were no less important and roused no less enthusiasm or distress than Yorktown. When victory finally was won, Frenchmen rejoiced not so much because the United States was independent as because England had been humbled, her empire torn asunder, and her control of trade and the seas jeopardized.

In 1783, the "Second Hundred Years' War" looked as if it were over and had ended in a decision favorable to France. The conflict was not over, however. The very effort France had made to win the latest bout left her too much exhausted to reap the expected rewards. Exhaustion soon combined with other complications to lead to domestic collapse. Eventually the struggle was renewed, with revolutionary ideologies as one of the weapons in this fight, and came to a close only with the decisive defeat of Napoleon Bonaparte and France.

In preparing that collapse of France with its subsequent revolutionary ideology, the American Revolution played a part that has not always been properly understood, though generally recognized. A few years ago I tried to show that unrest alone is insufficient to create a revolution. In addition, I maintained, there must exist a sense of solidarity among the restless; and they must also have leadership and some program of reform. Even with all these, however, my argument continued, revolutions have been known to fail if they met with effective conservative resistance; and hence it follows that revolutions succeed not so much because the revolutionaries are strong as because the vested interests are weak—or, to use Hegelian terms, not so much because antithesis is irresistible as because thesis has collapsed.

The French Revolution, for example, could hardly have come about without the American Revolution. Unrest, the factor for which one naturally looks first in analyzing the causes of a revolution, would perhaps have been no less pronounced in France if the American Revolution had not occurred. It was caused by many age-old social, economic, political, religious, intellectual, and other provocations, with which the fate of America had very little association. But one important source of dissatisfaction was definitely connected with the American Revolutionary War. While popular uneasiness had been rife for decades, it did not come to a head until the French treasury was threatened with bankruptcy. That danger was in large part due to French sacrifices in the American Revolution. The French had given and loaned great amounts of money to America. They had also made loans to other allies. They had sent huge armies and fleets to every quarter of the globe. The war is generally estimated to have cost France 2,000,000,000 livres. The program of economy and reform that France's comptroller-general, Turgot, had embarked upon before the war had had to be abandoned. Not only were Turgot's sympathizers disillusioned, but also, when the war was over, France's accumulated debt had reached about 4,000,000,000 livres. Meanwhile the cost of living had gone up distressingly.

It is difficult to translate the significance of a 4,000,000,000 livre debt for France of the 1780's into terms that would be intelligible to a twentieth-century American audience. In the first place, our attitude toward national indebtedness has changed, and many, if not most, of us no longer think that having an unfavorable trade balance or being a debtor rather than a creditor nation is necessarily disastrous if the national economy is otherwise sound. In France of the 1780's, however, Adam Smith and his ideas of free trade as the true basis of the wealth of nations were not yet well known, and if the Physiocrats were more renowned, their emphasis was rather upon the virtues of a healthy domestic agriculture than upon those of vigorous international trade and exchange. Hence all but a few in France felt that a large national debt would ruin the country's credit; and that feeling did more to make their fears come true than the logic of the actual situation.

In addition, correctly to appreciate the differences between our reactions and theirs to such a situation, we must make allowances for the differences in population, national income, natural resources, and the comparative price index. France in that day had about one-sixth or one-seventh of the population of the United States of today, and her national income probably was proportionately less, because the chief enterprise was still a relatively primitive form of agriculture. Modestly estimated, a four-billion-livre debt weighed about as heavily on France in the 1780's as a debt of around twenty-five billion dollars would have weighed on the United States of the pre-war period of the 1930's. Even in the present day of astronomical national debts, that is a staggering sum if allowance be made for the inflationary trends since the 1930's. The debt and the rising cost of living could not alone have brought on the French Revolution, but they were major contributing factors in the accumulating unrest. Both were in large measure directly attributable to French participation in the American Revolutionary War.

What is more important, general awareness that dissatisfaction was widespread throughout France, with a resultant solidarity among the dissatisfied, became much more marked after the 1770's. That too was attributable in large measure to French participation in the American Revolutionary War. To be sure, France was an absolute monarchy; the press was censored, and writers were sent to prison for the expression of heterodox opinions. The French had nevertheless been the allies of a confederation that believed in republican institutions. Several of those confederated states had constitutions containing bills of rights guaranteeing civil and political liberty. It became desirable for absolutist France to tolerate—in fact to build up—among its people a sympathy with the republican institutions of America, its ally.

It was now the patriotic duty not only of French writers to promote the interest of French people in the American nation but also of the censors not to interfere unnecessarily with their doing so. For example, in 1778 a collection was published of the constitutions of the states and the Declaration of Independence, which was dedicated to Benjamin Franklin and was referred to as "the code of liberty." In 1783 a much more impressive work reinforced the pro-American impact. It contained, besides the constitutions of the thirteen states, other significant American documents, although it was called *Les Constitutions des Treize Etats de l'Amérique*. It was of special significance that this work was published by the king's official printer. That meant, as was later pointed out when a French Revolutionary assembly issued the famous Declaration of the Rights of Man and of the Citizen, that a declaration of rights actually had been promulgated in France by royal consent several years earlier.

Another reason for the rapid spread of American ideals of liberty in France before the French Revolution was the personal popularity of Benjamin Franklin. He was petted by the ladies and feted by the aristocracy; he was lionized by the court and eulogized by poets, scientists and journalists; and he was envied by Arthur Lee and John Adams. The effect, direct or indirect, of Franklin's personal charm, his wide correspondence, and the writings about him was that the people of France often thought of all Americans as being made more or less in his image. The thought was probably far from true, but it did Americans no harm that their allies tended to think so.

Another channel for the favorable impact of American ideals upon French popular psychology was the impression made upon the soldiers who went from France to fight in the War of American Independence. Lafayette went back to France a worshipper of Washington and, for the most part, an uncritical admirer of American institutions. The Abbé Robin, who had been a chaplain with Rochambeau's army, wrote a book about his experience that spoke of the Americans as if they were a nation of new Arcadians. Chastellux, who already had a great reputation as a *philosophe* and was third in command to Rochambeau, wrote a volume on his journeys through America that induced its readers to believe that American institutions were ideal and the American people admirable. And a number of young men who, like Lafayette, were to become leaders in the forthcoming revolution in France—men like Alexandre de Lameth, Mathieu Dumas, the Comte de Ségur, the Vicomte de Noailles, and that Saint-Simon who became the founder of the famous school of socialist utopians in the nineteenth century—all stated in later years that they had imbibed their first ideas of liberty from their contact with Americans during the Revolutionary War. These people wrote, spoke, and made orations about the American people, American institutions, and American principles. They fondly nurtured idealizations of which they would brook no criticism. They flocked to the defense of the Americans whenever American virtues were questioned by others, like Deux Ponts, Moré, Biron, and Armand, who had hardly less right to speak of the American people than they. And the people of France, it proved, preferred to believe those who eulogized rather than those who disparaged America. The occasional book that criticized the United States won very little audience, whereas books like those of Chastellux and Robin received an enthusiastic welcome; and Lafayette became the most popular Frenchman of the day in France as well as America.

Another factor that led to the spread of American ideals in France was the active propaganda of French agents, both diplomatic and un-official, in America. Crèvecoeur's famous *Letters from an American Farmer* spread broadcast a roseate picture of the United States in vastly different English and French editions. Foremost among the official propagandists was the Chevalier de La Luzerne, the French minister in Philadelphia. La Luzerne subsidized Americans, including Thomas Paine, to write things about America for circulation in France. Paine, according to La Luzerne, proved too lazy to write a reply to a critique of America by an illustrious *philosophe*, the Abbé Raynal, and La Luzerne satisfied himself by carefully going over the French transla-tion of Carver's *Voyages through the Interior Parts of North America* and helping the translation to win approval in France.

So the king's government, on the one hand, promoted interest in American institutions, while, on the other, it opposed freedom in order to uphold absolute monarchy. This predicament arose largely because there was a war going on and France wanted to win it. Money had to be advanced and armies raised if it was to be won, and those things could not easily be done without popular support. The predicament was solved by weakening the royal censorship to the point where, in the famous "flood of pamphlets" of 1788, it practically collapsed.

Thus the 1770's marked a new era in the propagation of the ideas that formed the intellectual foundations of the French Revolution. The change was noticeable in two ways. In the first place, ideas of reform became common property, and no longer belonged exclusively to the literate classes. In the second place, they became concrete rather than abstract. The outstanding students of French public opinion during this period, like Daniel Mornet, find that before the 1770's the *philosophes* had appealed only to a limited audience, consisting almost exclusively of those who could afford to buy the very expensive books produced by the high publication costs of that day, and that they had dealt with mankind in broad general terms. But after the 1770's, as the appeal of the *philosophes* became more popular and was spread more widely than before—through conversations, law courts, sermons, masonic lodges, and club meetings, as well as books, it became more specific. The demand was now not alone for the general reform of mankind in accordance with "the laws of Nature and of Nature's God" but also for practical and immediate changes in French government and institutions. Even the authors of utopias tended to turn from picturing purely imaginary states to describing what an ideal France might someday be; and although none of them spelled *nature's* backward, one of them did spell *Paris* backward to make the name of his ideal city.

Madame d'Houdetot, a friend of Franklin, wrote to him that America had now provided the *philosophes* with "an example and a hope." In other words, America had become a case of Philosophy teaching by Example. In much the same way that speculative socialists of more recent times, unable to make a great impression upon the popular mind if they talked merely of what might be, found that, when they had an actual example in Russia, they could more easily bring about political pressure and effect political action, so the *philosophes,* the political theorists of the eighteenth century, once they could point to a living illustration of the Rights of Man in America, rallied behind them the type of person that could not grasp principles but could visualize the force of political reform in action. Old writers now began to write about American institutions rather than the abstract Rights of Man and the welfare of mankind in general. Condorcet, Raynal, Chastellux, Turgot and Mably were only a few of the figures among the recognized *philosophes* who turned their attention to America, writing critiques of the American constitutions and innovations. A set of new writers who would probably have developed into another generation of *philosophes* if their energies had not been diverted by the French Revolution also became leaders in the new American vogue. Men like Mirabeau and Brissot, not to mention Condorcet and Lafayette again, wrote about the new America, holding it up as an example of what a good state ought to be. France, they thought, could hardly become a republic; it was too big to be anything but a monarchy. Yet otherwise it might follow the American model profitably.

The attention these writers received was heightened by the controversies in which they engaged with Americans like Adams, Jefferson, Livingston, Mazzei and Barlow, and by translations of more sober historical and anthropological writings of American students like Filson, Carver and Ramsay. French journals carried articles on America—sometimes by Americans. Abbé Raynal's popular *History of the Two Indies* in the original edition of 1775 gave only twenty pages to the United States but in that of 1780 almost one hundred and fifty. Thus war, diplomacy and propaganda united to produce a general awareness of the existence of a restless spirit in France.

France had, however, long been restless. Nearly every decade since Louis XIV's death had witnessed a revolutionary crisis. But the repeated crises that had flared up to the danger point had in the end died down without producing catastrophe. One reason for the ineffectiveness of these outbursts was that they had had no enterprising leadership. The American Revolution now helped to supply that deficiency. An actual, though far from exhaustive, count has been made of Frenchmen who took a leading part in both the American and the French Revolution. There were thirty-eight of them, including Lafayette, the Lameth brothers, the Rochambeaus (father and son), Duportail, Estaing, Dumas, Ségur, Jourdan, Gouvion, Noailles, Custine, Beauharnais, Montmorency-Laval—to mention only those who were conspicuously friendly to the French Revolution in its initial stages. Of these, as we have noted, several admitted that they owed much of their interest in revolutionary ideas to America. How far the American Revolution was a factor in training men, like Brissot, Condorcet, Dupont, Marat and Robespierre, who were not soldiers, for their roles in the French Revolution can be only a matter of conjecture. It would be rash to believe that such men, but for the American development, would not have become revolutionary leaders. Yet they followed American affairs and watched the republican experiment with keen interest, as their writings and speeches make abundantly clear.

Thus the American Revolution helped to provide leaders for the French Revolution and made it possible for unrest to result in more effective demands for reform. It did more than that, however. It also furnished a model, a program, and a political philosophy for those leaders. As we have already seen, the French philosophers no longer had to talk about abstractions like natural law, natural institutions and natural morality derived from a hypothetical Common Sense or Reason. They no longer had to seek in the wilds of America or Asia for the theoretical Child of Nature. In live Americans like Benjamin Franklin they now found an impressive exemplar of a people who had actually achieved a life and a society that a philosopher might embrace. Across the Atlantic, as anyone who was not willfully blind could see, vigorous states prospered with governments based upon the Rights of Man.

To be sure, the *philosophes* deceived themselves somewhat. Franklin fell a little short of being a paragon, and the United States of being Arcadia. Yet it was more convincing to cite concrete cases than to point to sublimated primitives or to hypothetical societies. The American Arcadia, if not examined too critically, fully justified the speculations of the philosopher. Why could not Arcadia be located also in France?

With such queries political propaganda in France took on a more specific, pragmatic and effective form. The illiterate on the café terrace of the smallest village could grasp what the new generation of *philosophes* was saying as readily as the learned in the salons of the capital. Lafayette was not alone in noting that liberal ideas spread rapidly throughout France after the American Revolution. Talleyrand remarked that subsequent to the victory over England America became "the sole topic of conversation" among the aristocracy; and the English agriculturalist Arthur Young observed in his travels in France in 1787 "a strong leaven of liberty, increasing every hour since the American revolution."

No man's testimony in this regard can be more convincing than Thomas Jefferson's. As American minister to France, he was sympathetic with the reform party, particularly with Lafayette, who had no secrets from him, and he knew more about the American Revolution than any other man in France. When the French Revolution was unmistakably on its way, he wrote the well-known English liberal Dr. Richard Price his interpretation of how it had come about: "Though celebrated writers of this and other countries had already sketched good principles on the subject of government, yet the American war seems first to have awakened the thinking part of this nation in general from the sleep of despotism in which they were sunk. The officers too who had been to America were mostly young men, less shackled by habit and prejudice, and more ready to assent to the dictates of common sense and common right. They came back impressed with these. The press, notwithstanding its shackles, began to disseminate them; conversation, too, assumed new freedom; politics became the theme of all societies, male and female, and a very extensive and zealous party was formed, which may be called the Patriotic party, who, sensible of the abusive government under which they lived, longed for occasions of reforming it."

Yet, if my theory of the causes of revolution is right, provocations, crystallized public opinion, popular leaders, and a program of reform, even when they occur together, do not make a revolution unless the conservative forces are too weak to resist change effectively. Here, too, the American contribution was significant. The royal debt, by weakening the French treasury, made revision of the fiscal system inescapable. Furthermore, although there was still very little republicanism in France after the American Revolution, many more among the influential circles than before favored thoroughgoing reform of the monarchy. Important, too, in creating weakness of the conservative forces was the fact that aristocratic officers who had returned from the war in America could no longer be counted upon to obey if ordered to shoot down opponents of the government. An "American faction" also grew up in the parlements, and a "liberal aristocracy" at court, with Lafayette foremost among them. The same conditions that provided leaders for the revolutionaries created disaffection among the conservatives at the very time when the conservatives should have presented a united front if the Old Régime were to be preserved.

It goes without saying that the conditions which together made reformers willing to risk revolution and conservatives unable to resist it—a combination which makes revolution inevitable—naturally did not come exclusively from the American shore. The American Revolution had less effect on the French peasants, who formed about three-fourths of France's population, or on the city workers, or on the lower clergy than on the upper classes, except as its influence seeped down from the aristocracy and the middle class or as it was reflected in general agitation, fiscal difficulties and the rising cost of living. But upon the aristocracy and the middle class that influence was great. And the French Revolution at the outset was a movement of the aristocracy and the middle class.

On the eve of the French upheaval, Baron Friedrich Melchior de Grimm, though himself a friend of the *philosophes,* intimated that Frenchmen might well regret America if they stopped to think. "Her liberty has cost France nearly two billions," he wrote. ". . . That costly glory will serve only to hasten a revolution the outbreak of which all the nations of Southern Europe would seem well advised at least to put off, if the force of circumstances should make it inevitable." Louis XVI himself recognized that the American Revolution was the source of his troubles. The French Revolution had just begun when Sultan Tippoo of Mysore asked for French aid in driving the English out of India. Louis XVI, hesitating to comply, commented dryly: "This occasion greatly resembles the American affair, of which I never think without regret. On that occasion they took advantage somewhat of my youth, and today we are paying the penalty for it. The lesson is too vivid to be forgotten."

It is now about half a century since Lord Acton gave his deservedly famous lectures on the French Revolution at Cambridge University. I can find no better words to end my argument than those he used to begin his lecture on "The Influence of America":

> "The several structures of political thought that arose in France, and clashed in the process of revolution, were not directly responsible for the outbreak. The doctrines hung like a cloud upon the heights, and at critical moments in the reign of Lewis XV men felt that a catastrophe was impending. It befell when there was less provocation, under his successor; and the spark that changed thought into action was supplied by the Declaration of American Independence. It was the system of an international extra-territorial universal Whig, far transcending the English model by its simplicity and rigour. It surpassed in force all the speculation of Paris and Geneva, for it had undergone the test of experiment and its triumph was the most memorable thing that had been seen by men."

French Revolution

ALBERT MATHIEZ

Published in 1931

French scholars agree about most of the facts concerning their Revolution, but they disagree violently about the interpretation of those facts, and it is likely that battles of the books will rage as long as writers turn to the Revolution. The literature on the subject is, of course, enormous, and some of the finest minds of the last century and a half have contributed to it, among them such literary figures as Mme. de Staël, Lamartine, Michelet, and Taine; such political figures as Thiers, Louis Blanc, and Tocqueville; and such gifted scholars as Aulard, Cochin, and Labrousse. Among writers of the last generation the towering figure was Albert Mathiez (1874-1932). Author of many controversial books and articles on the subject, Mathiez almost always had a thesis to defend; nor did he ever conceal his sympathy for the Revolution, the First French Republic, and the Robespierrite regime. In the present article he analyzes some of the main currents in French Revolutionary history and presents some of the novel interpretations which he did much to popularize in the last few decades. Not easy to read, the essay deserves to be studied with care. No better brief discussion of the Revolution exists.

There are many approaches to the cataclysm which overturned the institutions of France and degenerated rapidly into a bitter warfare of twenty-three years between the young democracy and its monarchical neighbors.

There is the purely French approach, such as that of de Tocqueville or Taine. For the former the revolution in unifying France was but the achievement of the work of centralization begun by the absolute monarchy; the Committee of Public Safety was the legitimate heir of

Reprinted from the *Encyclopaedia of the Social Sciences,* Vol. VI. Copyright 1931 by The Macmillan Company and used with their permission.

Francis I, of Richelieu and of Colbert. For Taine, concerned more with ideas than events, the revolution was the product of the classic spirit— of that lucidity of analysis and abstraction which characterized the golden age of French literature but which subsequently became crystallized and emptied of all real content.

For present day historians, more disposed to emphasize the European angle and more conversant with the doctrines of historical materialism, the French Revolution is merely the outstanding episode of a much vaster tragedy, whose protagonist is the bourgeoisie. Such is the thesis of Jean Jaurès. While skilfully using the authority of the Feuillant, Barnave, as a cloak for his own conception of the close and inevitable parallelism between the economic and the political movements, Jaurès succeeded in orienting the French Revolution in terms of contemporary Europe, in explaining clearly why the crisis broke out in France rather than in England or Germany or Italy.

The English bourgeoisie, which for a century had been in possession of political power, was enjoying the fruits of the industrial revolution, then in its first flush. It was not bothered by the crown and had nothing to gain from attacking the feudal orders either lay or ecclesiastical since both had been dispossessed. There were no class discriminations in the levying of taxes, no restrictions on circulation within the country, no abusive regulations. Individual liberty went hand in hand with religious toleration. The freehold tenant, accorded the franchise, was essentially conservative in temperament. Satisfied interests make poor revolutionaries. Alarmed by Burke as to the possible consequences of the French Revolution, English landed proprietors arrayed themselves behind Pitt to meet the threat by war.

FEUILLANTS: The members of the club which met in a Cistercian convent. Believers in limited constitutional monarchy, they feared further revolutionary changes and therefore thought in 1791 that the king, despite his attempt to flee from France, should be forgiven provided that he would abide by the revolutionary settlement. They formed a right-wing group in the Legislative Assembly that met in October 1791.

JEAN JAURÈS: Leading Socialist in early-twentieth-century France and author of a multi-volume history of the French Revolution that was written from a socialist point of view. He considered it the purpose of the Revolution to bring the bourgeoisie to power. At the same time, he argued that the Revolution prepared the way for the coming to power of the proletariat.

In Germany and Italy the minute parceling out of land and the particularism of the small princes were sufficient to prevent a concerted movement of any vitality. The faint beginnings of industrialism in Germany were confined to three or four localities, and the German bourgeoisie had as yet no conception of its strength, no ambition to power. It was content to vegetate in the shadow of the royal or princely houses.

The outbreak of the revolution in France rather than elsewhere may be attributed not only to the fact that the French bourgeoisie had become increasingly powerful because commerce had quadrupled since 1714, that monarchical centralization facilitated a concerted movement, that the writings of the *philosophes,* especially of the physiocrats, had kindled discontent and formulated in advance a program of reforms, but primarily to the fact that the resistance of the nobility, which had become increasingly powerful throughout the entire century, had produced a situation where the prerequisite of progress was force. In an age characterized by enlightened despotism France alone clung to the outworn tradition of autocracy.

The feudal reaction, which began as far back as Louis xiv, continued throughout the eighteenth century. The *parlements,* whose members had come to constitute the dynamic force within the nobility, took the lead. Now that they had become nobles themselves and owners of fiefs they perverted the *arrêts de justice,* which had formerly been instruments for protecting the rights of the king or the public interest, to the service of the feudal lords, sanctioning their encroachments on the common property. In the second half of the century especially, there was a multiplication of hunting preserves and *triages* with a correspond-

LEVÉE EN MASSE: Wholesale conscription system introduced in France in August 1793. The decree which put it into effect stated: "Young men will go to the front; married men will forge arms, and carry food; women will make tents and clothing, and work in hospitals; children will turn old linen into bandages; old men will be carried into the squares to rouse the courage of the combatants, and to teach hatred of kings and republican unity."

THERMIDORIAN REACTION: The period following the execution of Robespierre in Thermidor (July) 1794, which saw the undoing of many of the social, economic, and political reforms that the Robespierrites had favored.

ingly increased number of peasants deprived of their traditional rights. In the place of the older monarchical maxim, "Fief and jurisdiction have nothing in common," the new feudal jurists—Boutaric, Fréminville, Renauldon—substituted a maxim purely feudal, inspired by Montesquieu: "Fief and jurisdiction are one."

The feudal reawakening manifested itself not only in changes in jurisprudence but also in the increasingly arrogant claims of the provincial estates, whose encroachments on the royal power proceeded with remarkably few pauses. In the province of Brittany, for instance, the administration of the tax passed almost entirely from the hands of the intendant to those of the estates. The offensive of the nobles eventuated in the reconstitution, which ordinarily accompanied augmentation of feudal dues, of the officials known as *chartriers,* or guardians of title deeds.

But above all else the opposition of the *parlements* to every share of reform completely enfeebled the monarchy and drove it to bankruptcy. The magistrates not only set the bad example of resisting the orders of the king but in their remonstrances formulated a program of representative monarchy which was later to be turned to profitable use by the insurgent bourgeoisie.

While the nobles of the robe were thus undermining confidence in the very foundations of absolute monarchy the economists and especially the physiocrats were waging against the time honored economic institutions an increasingly ardent and fruitful campaign. Organs of agrarian and industrial capitalism with a veneration for private property, they advocated the suppression of all regulations and corporations and the establishment of absolute commercial liberty. The ancient artisan class, which had been the symbol of the union between the petty bourgeoisie and the king, tottered under the assaults of ministers won over to the new doctrines. But the large manufacturers, who for a century had been fighting the corporations and who were practically exempt from public burdens, were still unsatisfied with the partial reforms made in their behalf. Now that they were meeting with the nobles in the councils of administration of the new joint stock companies they felt themselves their equals since they enjoyed the same rights. Their ambition was kindled and they were no longer to be content with half measures. It is an eloquent commentary that the first revolutionary assembly in 1789 was held in the chateau of the great metallurgist Périer at Vizille in Dauphiné and that noble, bourgeois and priest plotted together to change the social order.

The campaign of the physiocrats combined with the anti-administrative assaults of the *parlements* had seriously impaired the royal prerogatives in the economic sphere. Hitherto the king as the personification of the public interest had been able to issue decrees whenever an economic crisis seemed to necessitate recourse to such measures, limiting the exercise of property rights—even to the extent of imposing a tax on prices. The rights of the individual were subordinated to the rights of society. But now the situation was reversed. The right of property appears as prior and superior to the state—to the king. The duty of the state consists solely in protecting liberty and property; it has no other justification. In the past, law had been no more than the expression of the personal will of the king. The physiocrats succeeded in transforming it into an eternal impersonal truth of the natural order, which independent of the monarch limits his sovereignty. The ideal government is that which is reduced to its simplest expression and which leaves the maximum of control to the great social forces. Physiocratic utilitarianism was the antithesis of the old Christian morality—a point of contact with the *philosophes,* who in addition welcomed from the physiocratic program all those elements conducive to the rise of capitalism.

The revolution existed in the realm of ideas from the middle of the century. It was carried over into the realm of actuality not only by the intransigency of the *parlements* and the partial application of the program of the physiocrats but also by the incoherence of the king's political policy.

The feudal reawakening seconded by the *arrêts de justice* subjected the peasants more grievously to the seigniorial yoke. The nobility attempted to reestablish itself in rural society in the midst of its former serfs. The aristocracy which the revolution had to fight was not a detached, passive class, but on the contrary a class which was awake to the economic life going on around it and swayed by new and mounting ambitions. The succession of edicts between 1761 and 1785 dealing with enclosures, with the old pasturage lands, with the dividing up of the commons, with the clearing of land, made it obvious to the peasants that the king was deliberately abandoning them in favor of their natural enemies.

The intermittent freedom of grain exportation caused an increase in the price of bread at the very time when royal taxation was increasing. In the single *bailliage* [bailiwick] of Reims royal taxation tripled or quadrupled during the period from 1704 to 1788. From 1765 to 1789 prices doubled, while salaries averaged only a 10 to 20 percent increase. The growing overpopulation produced a huge proletariat both rural and urban, which furnished the revolution with the man power for its mobs.

Hitherto the monarchy had rested upon the traditional docility of the French artisanry, on the fidelity of the army, on the loyalty of the intendants, on the gospel of resignation preached by the clergy. One after another these supports crumbled. The artisans, especially after Turgot's taxation of them, considered themselves sacrificed to the manufacturers. The army became permeated with the spirit of reform, which was still heightened, especially among the young nobles, by the American Revolution. The intendants, no longer men of the people as under Louis xiv but instead recruited from the nobility, to whose interests they catered, displayed less and less zeal. The lower clergy instead of counseling submission began to advance claims.

Brienne's very attempt to counteract the feudal claims of the *parlements* and of the provincial estates by the creation of provincial assemblies—hybrid bodies, more consultative than representative—precipitated the crisis which was generally expected. This crisis continued for at least a dozen years. It described an ascending curve toward democracy until the fall of Robespierre, 9 Thermidor, year 11. Thereupon it descended again to the bourgeois oligarchy of the Directory, to eventuate finally in the Napoleonic dictatorship, which endured despite its suppression of public liberties by reason of its consolidation of the material and legal accomplishments of the revolution. It is a question really not of a single revolution but of a series of different revolutions bound together by an inner logic.

In the first of these revolutions, which extended from the convocation of the Notables by Calonne in 1787 to the assembling of the Estates General in 1789, only the privileged classes were involved. It was begun by the nobility of the robe, who were joined immediately by the nobles of the sword and the higher clergy. In order to safeguard their fiscal immunities against the threat of the new schemes of taxation these privileged orders struck a blow at the royal government, thereby setting a bad example to the lower classes. The significance of this prelude to the revolution is too often ignored. It is extremely important to note that the monarchy was threatened by its own agents. The revolt was not yet the work of a political party or the outgrowth of a conspiracy. Political parties did not exist. There was no plot, no secret organization planning a sudden overthrow of secular institutions and the substitution of others. On the contrary, it was in the name of the past through invocation of time honored customs—of the rules of feudal law—that the *parlements* unleashed resistance and revolt.

The role of conspiracy which is sometimes attributed to Freemasonry is pure legend. The lodges in the period before 1789 bore no resemblance except in their ritual to continental Freemasons' lodges of the present day. They were composed of *grands seigneurs,* of officers, of priests, of rich bourgeois. Salons rather than clubs, they were frequented by the flower of the army, by men of the world, by champions of the status quo. Their members celebrated the Feast of St. John the Baptist by a solemn mass. Their activities were never, as is evidenced by the reports of the intendants, a source of disquietude to those in authority. Louis xvi and his brothers, Marie Antoinette herself, participated in the ceremonies at the Loge des Trois Frères in the Versailles district. More than three fourths of the French Freemasons, especially those in the military lodges, became émigrés. The smallness of the minority which aligned itself on the side of the revolution eliminates the possibility that the movement of 1789 was the result of a Masonic conspiracy.

The insurgent forces at the outset were the constituted bodies of the states—the *parlements* and the Notables. The revolution was cast within the existing mold. These judges, these Notables, were the representatives of a class which was no longer satisfied with its privileges and which desired through the attainment of dominant political power to rejuvenate them.

But this first revolution, superficial and ephemeral, soon brought in its train a second, more profound and utterly different. Behind the judges, behind the nobles, behind the priests, was the bourgeoisie, which toward the end of 1788 pushed its way to the front. It became aroused for a variety of reasons. Royal absolutism constituted as grievous a burden to the bourgeoisie as to the privileged classes, while the imminent bankruptcy of the government threatened to engulf bourgeois property. Finally, the bourgeoisie felt itself capable of assuming in its turn the direction of the state in order to free itself from those legal encumbrances which held it down as a vassal and prisoner of the unproductive and privileged classes. It was suspicious of a revolution by the noble and feudal class and in order to forestall such a contingency it went into action under the banner of unwritten natural law, which it opposed to feudal law.

From the outset the bourgeoisie possessed the double advantage of wealth and intellect. Since most of the writers were in its ranks, control of public opinion was guaranteed. In addition it controlled the army, for the soldiers, to whom the higher ranks were closed, perceived in the revolution the path to opportunity. This bourgeois revolt, which followed on the heels of the revolt of the nobility, was not apparently the result of long premeditation or the outgrowth of a conspiracy. It was for that reason all the more vigorous. It was the expression of reflections stored up from the reading of authors who for fifty years had been criticizing existing institutions, and it was infected with the contagious enthusiasm of the American precedent.

The influence of abstract thinkers on great social crises has sometimes been denied. "The most eloquent dissertations on revolution," writes Georges Sorel, metaphysician of revolutionary syndicalism, "have no practical issue, and the course of history is not altered by literature." If this statement implies simply that literature alone is incapable of bringing about a social movement it is on firm ground; but if it pretends that literature is an utterly negligible factor it lays itself open to serious question. The great majority of men are unaware of injustice until it is pointed out to them. The denunciation of abuses is an essential preliminary to a demand for reform; a clearly formulated ideal, the prerequisite of a loyal following. It is extremely doubtful whether without the writings of the *philosophes* the bourgeoisie would have risen in 1789 with the same unanimity, the same resoluteness; whether without the writings of Karl Marx the Russian Revolution would have been the same. Robespierre without Rousseau remains an enigma; so does Lenin without Marx.

The revolt of the judges and the Notables, being essentially a revolt of officially constituted bodies, did not have to build up a special organization. The bourgeoisie faced an entirely different problem. Almost from the outset the nucleus of the organization consisted in meetings sponsored by the "Américains" at the homes of Lafayette and the councilor Adrien Duport. It was from these centers that the Société des Trente despatched orders to the barristers and lawyers who carried them into effect in their respective local provinces. In Burgundy the detection of the movement of the corporations and the supervision of elections were in the hands of the lawyers. In Brittany the law students

of Rennes under the leadership of Moreau, the future general, took
up arms against the nobles and in the course of the fighting were
supported by reenforcements sent from youthful bourgeois in adjoin-
ing towns.

Proof that the entire movement was the execution of a carefully
coordinated and matured plan may be found in the universal application of the same tactics and in the formulation—even in the *cahiers de
doléances* drawn up on the eve of the election—of the same general
claims. From the east to the west, from the north to the south, the
revolutionary bourgeoisie extended one hand to the peasants, the other
to the curés and the lower clergy, with a view to binding together,
as in a *fascis*, all the potential forces of renovation. So permeated were
they with a jealous class spirit that in accordance with the counsels
of the abbé Sieyès they elected the deputies who should represent them
in the Estates General almost exclusively from the third estate.

At Versailles the leaders became aware almost immediately of the
necessity of a compact organization in order to present a solid front to
the court and to the privileged classes. On the eve of the opening they
assembled at the Club Breton, which became the cradle of the Club
des Jacobins. Victory depended, it was felt, on their remaining in close
contact with the masses and on their ability to match force with force.
Accordingly they entered into endless correspondence with their constituents both to stimulate their zeal and to keep them posted concerning
the difficulties encountered at Versailles. Several of these correspon-
dences have been published, and constitute—especially those of the
lawyer Bouchette, of the curé Barbotin and of Duquesnoy from Lorraine—documents of great interest. When the king called out the
troops following the tennis court oath, the correspondents encouraged
the bourgeois of Paris to form the national guard, which was to become the military force of the revolution. After the fall of the Bastille
permanent committees, i.e. revolutionary and dictatorial municipalities,
which spread as if by magic through France, hastened to distribute
arms to their partisans. From that time on the *ancien régime* was defeated, inasmuch as the bourgeoisie had taken possession of both the
municipal administration and the public forces. By the side of the
permanent committees and the national guards were shortly created the
clubs which formed a federation under the direction of the Jacobins.
The club was the organ of surveillance. It was wide awake to the
dangers that threatened the revolution. At the time of the convention

there were no fewer than four or five thousand clubs at work. In all this activity the French were merely following the example of the permanent committees, the militia and the clubs which had been such significant factors in the prosecution of the American Revolution. Revolutions are contagious.

Vaulting into power on the fourteenth of July the bourgeoisie proceeded to intrench itself. It restored the king to the helm by a constitution which guaranteed his political power. It lowered the clergy and the nobility to its own level by writing large into the constitution equality before the law. Deviating from the real spirit of the Declaration of Rights it refused the franchise to the unpropertied classes, who were rated as passive citizens. To save the property owners threatened with bankruptcy it confiscated church property and offered it for sale by the ingenious system of assignats. An immense transfer of property resulted.

The work of reconstruction proceeded parallel to the work of destruction. Above the débris of the privileged classes and the suppressed orders the Assembly erected a logical and harmonious structure. Its foundation was the Declaration of the Rights of Man and the Citizen—the document which was to instal individualism as the dominant feature of the modern world. This eloquent apostrophe to personal initiative, to the force of individualism, was heard from afar and provided for the revolution itself a magic spring of energy endlessly renewed. The dawn of romanticism was already coloring the horizon.

But the Assembly would not have been victorious if it had not in accordance with Sieyès' theory on the constituent power constituted itself a veritable dictatorship. The fundamental distinction between constitutional laws, exempted from royal sanction, and ordinary laws, which were alone subject to veto, provided a means of nullifying the evils of the royal will and of raising the new order.

The committees governed and at the same time administered by methods which the Convention was to do no more than take over and expand. They corresponded directly with the new authorities, gave them instructions which were tantamount to orders and treated the ministers as their agents.

The *Comité des rapports* and the *Comité des recherches,* which were in charge of political policing, kept themselves informed regarding the various municipalities, conducted investigations, issued orders for arrests and brought those apprehended before the Châtelet, which at the outset of the revolution served as the seat of the High Court. The renowned *Comité de sureté générale* of the Convention was to do no more. The *Comité diplomatique,* formed after the king had been shorn of his prerogative of declaring war and making peace, received communications from ambassadors and was the dominant force in the direction of foreign policy. After December 19, 1789, the *Comité des finances* had its own special treasury called the *Caisse de l'Extraordinaire,* which was distinct from the royal treasury and filled with special contributions such as the *contribution patriotique.* Its chief responsibility, however, was the administration of the assignats and of the receipts accruing from the sale of national property. The *Comité de l'aliénation des biens nationaux,* charged as its name indicates with the sale of church property, divided France into twenty territorial districts and at the head of each of these placed one of its members. The active correspondence published by Raymond Delaby between Camus, head of one of these districts, and the department of Côte-d'Or indicates in a striking manner that contrary to a widely held opinion the locally elected authorities enjoyed no initiative in the intepretation or application of the laws. Camus insisted on being consulted in reference to all decisions made by the administration of the department which concerned national property. No anonymous notice of auctions could be published without his consent and his visa, and he concerned himself with the most minute details. The *Comité des droits féodaux* did not confine its activities to drawing up laws on the redeeming of the feudal dues of the nobles, but carried on an active correspondence with the local authorities, guiding them and making decisions on the practical difficulties submitted by them. Nor did the *Comité ecclésiastique* limit itself to elaborating the civil constitution of the clergy, which harmonized the older ecclesiastical organization with the new organization by departments. In addition it supervised at close range its actual application and made final decisions on all contentious points in the legislation affecting religion. The aristocrats could with some justification accuse it of having usurped the status of a conciliar body. One of its notable accomplishments was the inventories which it took of confiscated ecclesiastical furnishings in order to exempt from sale rare and precious objects. The *Comité militaire* from the outset worked in close touch with the Ministry of War and kept a sharp eye on the administration of the army in all its ramifications.

As a result of this elaborate system of committees the great principle of the separation of powers, which the Constituent borrowed from Montesquieu and wrote into the constitution of 1791 as the corner stone of essential liberties, was never applied or observed as long as the great assembly continued to function. Moreover, its members did not believe that they were going back on their own doctrines in vigorously usurping the dictatorship and in applying it on a large scale. Sieyès had taught them that they were the constituent power. Consequently the constitution would function only after their exit, when the powers which they had constituted would begin to be applied. Their dictatorship was justified by the obligation of clearing the way for these new powers. They were forced to remove all obstacles beforehand.

If Louis xvi had resigned himself to the position of constitutional monarch, the bourgeoisie would have kept him at the helm. All it asked of him was not to take the side of the privileged classes. But Louis xvi began to conspire. He was disgruntled at the curtailment of his power. He sought the aid of foreign kings. Within France he precipitated religious war. He fled to the frontier and was brought back humiliated. From that time on a new revolution was in process. The first had been that of the aristocracy; the second, of the bourgeoisie; the third was to be, in part at least, of the people both urban and rural.

The first revolution had forced the king to summon the Estates General. The second had suppressed the institutions of the *ancien régime*. The third overturned the throne. The first had been provoked by the resistance of the privileged classes to fiscal reforms. The fundamental cause of the second had been the fear of bankruptcy. The third sprang from foreign war and invasion. It was at once a patriotic and a popular revolution. It resulted in the liberation, at least partial and provisional, of the peasant and the worker.

Since the fall of the Bastille the peasants had been attacking the chateaux and had forced the nobles to surrender and burn the title deeds which authorized the collection of feudal dues. The artisans of the town had on their side burned the customs barriers and forced a reduction in prices. These disorderly popular outbursts had surprised and annoyed the bourgeois membership of the Constituent. Their permanent committees and their national guards were designed as much against the threat of the jacquerie from below as against that of the aristocracy from above. It was with bad grace that they granted concessions to the peasants. The legislation of August 20 and the following days constituted but a very superficial suppression of the feudal regime, abolishing personal servitude but maintaining all the rest. The most immediately felt feudal dues, those in kind or in money, continued to be paid by the tenants, until they redeemed them. At the same time the Constituent deprived the people of the franchise. The new constitution handed over France to an oligarchy of men in possession.

If the bourgeoisie, victorious over the peasants as well as over the nobles, had remained united, the revolution would have been over. The discontented peasants continued to create sporadic disturbances, but in default of concerted action they were incapable of overturning by their own efforts the remnants of the feudal order or of dispossessing the bourgeoisie.

But after the flight of the king the bourgeoisie split into two factions. The Feuillants frightened by the possibility of democracy fired upon the republicans on the Champ de Mars, July 17, 1791. After the massacre they found themselves in the position of being forced to consolidate the royal power and, because of class egotism, of restoring to the crown a part of the force which it had lost. The other great faction, the Girondists, took the opposite course; defiant of the king and fearful of the reestablishment of absolutism, they opposed any backsliding. As a method of solving the internal difficulties of the country, of checking the priests and the aristocrats, of reissuing the assignats, of forcing the king to entrust them with power, they plunged the revolution into foreign war, despite the warnings of Robespierre and the Montagnards.

The war was the decisive event which underlay the third revolution, that of August 10, 1792. It brought in its train not only the fall of the monarchy, which trafficked with the enemy and worked for its victory, but also the confiscation of the property of émigrés serving in the Austrian and Prussian armies. And the confiscation of émigré property following the confiscation of church property completed the dispossession of the older ruling class. Moreover, the war resulted in the suppression without indemnification of those feudal dues which the Constituent had allowed to stand. The revolutionary bourgeoisie was forced to offer this bait to the peasants in order to interest them in victory. It was likewise forced in the same spirit and from the same necessity finally to abolish amid the booming of cannon directed against the Tuileries the distinction between active citizen and passive citizen—in short, to grant universal suffrage to the proletariat. It marked the arrival, as yet more theoretical than real, of the fourth estate.

But the Girondists, who flattered themselves that they could manage the people just as earlier they had flattered themselves that they could manage the king, perceived to their amazement and irritation that in the aftermath of August 10 the people were turning from them to follow the Montagnards, who had been the true authors of the overthrow of the king and of the emancipation of the peasants. In their declaration of war the Girondists had promised that it would be short and victory rapid. They had nourished illusions regarding the strength of the Declaration of the Rights of Man as a rallying cry. They had predicted that the people in foreign lands would rise against their tyrants at the call and example of the French people. But the foreign people seemed asleep or subdued, and the war prolonged itself endlessly, waxing in its proportions. The rapid fall of the assignat, issued in increasingly large amounts to keep pace with the enormous aggravation of expenses, produced a colossal rise in the prices of all merchandise. The salaried classes began to murmur. The Girondists, committed to commercial liberty, turned a deaf ear to their complaints and rejected the remedies proposed by the Montagnards— remedies borrowed from the interventionist legislation of the *ancien régime*, such as censuses, regulations, requisitions, control of prices, economic and administrative centralization. A vast agitation began, born of suffering and misery. The Girondists fearing the proletariat held out their hands to the reactionaries. They were ready to give pledges. They incited the provinces against Paris, the citadel of the Montagnards. They attempted vainly to save the king as they had tried earlier to save the throne. They brought Marat to the bar. They called in the generals to help them. They overlooked the insubordination and intrigues of a Dumouriez.

The Montagnard minority in the Assembly drew its strength from the communes of the large cities and from the Jacobin clubs, which were rapidly being purged of rival elements. Since the Montagnards had opposed the war the people could not hold them responsible for the grievous economic crisis which it had precipitated. Their social program kept them in close contact with the populace. The defeats of the spring of 1793, the treachery of Dumouriez, the revolt in the Vendée, allowed them at last to assume power. Their *coup de force*, extending from May 31 to June 2, purged the Convention of their adversaries and was followed up shortly by the organization of a dictatorship—the collective dictatorship of the Committee of Public Safety and the Committee of General Security supported by a Convention which had become provisionally Montagnard in spirit. This event was equivalent to a new revolution—the fourth. The dictatorship of the committees was the dictatorship of the Montagnard party and to a certain extent the dictatorship of the sans-culottes.

This dictatorship, which lasted a little over a year, sprang much less from a preconceived theory than from the immediate necessities of the military situation at home and abroad. The enemy had to be pushed back from the borders, the royalist and Girondist insurrections had to be suppressed. Food had to be supplied to the armies and cities starved by the English blockade. The millions of soldiers that were being shipped off to the frontier had to be clothed. Terror became the order of the day. For the enemies of the regime the guillotine was set up. Elections were suspended. Resistance was beaten down by the medium of *commissaires de la Convention* armed with unlimited power. To the generals went out the order, "Victory or death." In place of liberty authority was enthroned. The Montagnard revolution rested upon principles which had little in common with those of the individualistic revolution. In the name of public safety, as formerly in the name of the king, individual wills were over-ridden and when necessary the rights of property. Necessities of life were communized; provisions and merchandise were requisitioned for the defense of the nation and the revolution. Municipal bakeries and butcher shops were set up. In short, there arose under the pressure of circumstance an embryonic collectivism. The emergency character of the experiment is indicated by the fact that the very ones who were resorting to it considered it as a temporary expedient, all traces of which should be wiped out as rapidly as possible.

The new dictatorship contrasted strikingly with that exercised by the Constituent. The latter had been accepted, even welcomed, while the success of the new was detested or at best condoned. The Constituent was supported by public opinion, which urged it on to more and more severe measures against the enemies of the revolution. Its committees had been obeyed without complaint by the elected authorities, who met its desires. By 1793 a profound change had taken place. The foreign war had its counterpart in civil war. The revolts of the Vendée and of the federalists, the execution of the king, the military defeats, the requisitions, the misery consequent on inflation, official repudiation of Christianity and the closing of the churches, the regime of the suspects and the overworked guillotine, all these terrifying manifestations of the crisis brought discouragement to large sections of French society and pushed them into the opposition, desirous above all of peace even at the price of the reestablishment of the *ancien régime.*

It was no longer possible to justify the new revolution as Sieyès had the old by the single theory of the *pouvoir constituant* [constituent power]. It was too obvious that it was no longer an application of the sovereignty of the people but rather the exact opposite. Accordingly, in rebutting an attack of the Dantonists Robespierre justified the dictatorship by drawing a fundamental distinction between a state at war and a state at peace, between the constitutional regime and the revolutionary regime. His speeches of 5 Nivôse and 17 Pluviôse expounding this thesis contain the theory of the revolutionary government, which was already an adumbration of the dictatorship of the proletariat. The constitutional regime according to Robespierre is capable of functioning only in time of peace. In time of war it must give way; otherwise it would destroy liberty. "The aim of constitutional government is to preserve the Republic; that of revolutionary government, to establish it. Revolution is the war carried on by liberty against its enemies; constitutionalism, the regime of liberty victorious and at peace." Revolution being essentially civil war, "revolutionary government entails an extraordinary activity for the very reason that it is at war . . . and forced to endlessly deploy new and rapid resources to meet new and pressing dangers." Whereas the theory of constituent power had grounded dictatorship upon the unanimous will of the people, the theory of revolutionary government grounded it upon the political and patriotic necessity growing out of the war. Robespierre admitted the dangers of such a regime. What would become of the state if the dictators should selfishly capitalize their power? There was only one protection, as far as he could see—the moral virtue of the dictators.

The revolutionary groups in France had believed that as soon as they acquired political power they could immediately settle the social question. They perceived quickly enough that they were mistaken. Their work was thwarted by the wealthy classes, who coalescing against the revolutionary legislation impaired its effectiveness. They did not entertain the idea, however, of recasting their principles. They had no inclination to introduce limitation of property as the normal and abiding foundation of the social order. Private property still seemed to them sacrosanct. They wished only to correct its momentary abuses and they were reduced to this expedient of a revolutionary dictatorship, which they conceived as being provisional. They imagined that it would be sufficient merely to strike terror into the aristocrats, to imprison them, to banish them, and that then the social question— which they continued to regard as a political rather than an ethical question—would be solved. Their attitude is readily understood if it is borne in mind that a good number of them were property owners —well to do bourgeois, lawyers and professional men. The terrorist dictatorship was popular in its aims, but it was carried out by bourgeois.

Only a small minority composed of those who had been taught by experience understood that the maintenance of the sans-culottes in power could not be perpetuated except by means of a progressive and lasting limitation of individual property. Robespierre, Saint-Just and Couthon proposed in the laws of Ventôse to turn over the property of the suspects to the poor. But their colleagues turned a deaf ear to the proposition. The Committee of Public Safety had already refused to nationalize the food supply. Carnot had opposed the taking over of manufactures, even of those which had been founded by the representatives on mission. The Committee of General Security, in concert with certain members of the Committee of Public Safety, blocked the laws of Ventôse and their authors were driven from power, 9 Thermidor.

The great majority of the members of the Convention were individualists bitterly opposed to anything that savored of communism. The true communists, those who were convinced that the reign of the fourth estate is possible only on condition of the suppression of individual property, were isolated figures without influence and in the main not looking beyond a communism of provisions and, by implication, of land. When Babeuf attempted in the post-Thermidor period to bring them together into one large party, it was too late. The dictatorship had collapsed and Babeuf was powerless to reestablish it. He paid with his life for his experiment—a belated experiment and at the same time premature; belated because it was advanced at a time when the Montagnard party had already fallen from power and was already decimated by the Thermidorian proscription; premature because public opinion had not been prepared for communistic ideas.

The revolution of July, 1789, which had brought the bourgeoisie into power, was the child of eighteenth century philosophy, a philosophy liberal and individualistic to its roots. The revolution of June, 1793, which swept the Montagnards into power, was the work of circumstance and necessity. It was not the product of a campaign of education, of a systematic view of government and society or of a penetrating analysis of economic evolution. It could scarcely have been otherwise at a time when machinery was in its infancy and its fatal offspring, industrial concentration, not yet manifest. The most daring of the revolutionary thinkers, Babeuf himself, hardly conceived of communism other than in an agrarian context. The majority of the communists of the time distinguished clearly between industrial property, which they wished to respect as being the product of labor, and landed property, which alone their program affected.

This fact clarifies not only the basic difference between the Jacobin dictatorship and more recent dictatorships but also the fundamental reasons for its frustration. Although the Bolshevist dictatorship is similar to the Jacobin in that it sought justification in the circumstances of war, it at least rested in contradistinction to the latter on the coherent doctrine of Marxism, which it proposed to put into practise. The Bolshevists had no qualms about destroying either individual property or even the structure of the state which they had usurped. The Jacobins, on the contrary, tampered only timidly and partially with the system set up by the Constituent. They merely superimposed their economic dictatorship on the older individualistic legislation without destroying it. Their requisitions and their taxes did not abolish private property. They merely restricted the use of it. Their communism, which was never more than provisional and relative, was only an expedient. They themselves made apologies for being forced to resort to it.

In the political realm similar differences are apparent. The Russian communists, loyal to the ideology of Marx, have been anxious from the first to transfer power to the proletariat. The government which they have set up is consistently a government by a class. The Montagnard Jacobins, on the contrary, although they were obliged to lean upon the sans-culottes and to govern in their behalf and in their interests, never really grasped the idea of class. They hounded the royalists, the Feuillants, the Girondists, not as members of a hostile class but as political adversaries and as accomplices of the enemy. This is readily explicable. The Montagnard leaders who sat in the committees and in the Convention were not members of the proletariat but merely its friends and allies. They still clung to eighteenth century philosophy—a philosophy which is the negation of class, which ignores social groups in favor of the individual.

That is why the Montagnards, in contrast to the Bolshevists with their basic doctrine of class antagonism, remained fundamentally individualistic and never developed a thoroughgoing, organic dictatorship. Lenin and his associates realized that the establishment and perpetuation of the proletariat dictatorship were handicapped by the separation and division of the powers of the state. The Council of the Commissaries of the People legislates and at the same time executes. In France under the Terror it was different. Unity was never entirely realized in the revolutionary government. The Convention, to be sure, was purged. Theoretically it combined the legislative and the executive. But actually the Committee of Public Safety was responsible for the prosecution of the war, for the handling of diplomatic relations and for general administration, while the Committee of General Security directed political policing and the suppression of conspiracy. Thus there was a division of the executive and the legislative power: the Convention on one side, the committees on the other. There was a dualism even in the executive power, which was divided between two separate committees. The revolutionary machine of the Montagnards was infinitely more complicated and its manipulation correspondingly more delicate than the revolutionary machine of Soviet Russia.

With the fall of Robespierre individualism reasserted its rights to the full. The system of requisitions and taxes passed with the Terror. The bourgeoisie after a momentary curtailment of its power sprang up again fully triumphant. The Girondists, freed from prison, resumed their seats in the Convention. The last Montagnards were exterminated in abortive risings. Their agents, who had had the courage to organize and to operate the revolutionary government, were branded with the name of terrorists and disarmed en masse. There is no record of those who fell, massacred during the white terrors. The proletariat sank again into silence and subjection. If it later welcomed the dictatorship of Bonaparte it was because he gave them work and bread. The revolution by and large had done no more than replace one class with another, an aristocracy of birth with an aristocracy of wealth, but it had flung out to the world the idea of social justice.

The French Revolution succeeded, it would seem, only to the extent that it had been prepared for. The work of the bourgeoisie, it redounded to the profit of the bourgeoisie. This class, possessed of wealth and intellectual superiority, was destined to triumph over a nobility which, despite the significant attempt at rehabilitation undertaken during the last days of the monarchy by the higher ranks, was essentially impoverished and already half dispossessed. It was destined to triumph over the people, because the people, still untrained, was dependent upon it for its leaders. The bourgeoisie alone was endowed with a sufficiently developed class spirit to seize and maintain power.

It is a most striking fact that during this period the artisan classes of France entered the struggle only in a political sense, even when the struggle was directed toward social demands. Corporations were suppressed. Syndicates did not yet exist. The guilds were weakened by division. Strikes were forbidden. It was in the clubs and the popular societies, in the communes and in the sections, that the sans-culottes, thrown in with the advance party of the bourgeoisie, were forced to fight for their interests. They were bent on getting complete control of public power. To get control of the state they did not hesitate to resort to the mobs which were being organized in the political societies and which were achieving results only because the armed force, the national guard, was on their side, as were frequently the communal authorities as well. July 14, for instance, was mapped out by the assembly of electors which had appointed the deputies from Paris to the Estates General, and this assembly of electors sat in the Hôtel de Ville next to the legal municipality. August 10 similarly was the work of the sections and of a part of the commune. The same is true for May 31.

After Thermidor the bourgeoisie once more came into its own. It purged the national guard and soon afterwards disarmed it; the mobs, which no longer had the support of the communal authorities, suffered a succession of failures. The clubs were closed, robbing the famished and disarmed mobs of a place of meeting and of a *point d'appui.* They drifted helplessly. The situation would have been different if the proletariat of this period instead of borrowing its political organization from the bourgeoisie had succeeded in working out a class organization. But as it was, when the sans-culottes lost political power they lost everything.

The triumph of the bourgeoisie was perhaps too complete. Hounded mercilessly by the *lois d'exception,* the last democrats disappeared or took refuge in surly abstraction. The Thermidorians remained isolated, surrounded by a hostile nation.

The great majority of Frenchmen, surfeited with politics, their spirits broken by the sufferings of war, pined only for peace. They no longer bothered to perform their duties as electors when the suffrage was restored to them. Only the professional was interested in politics. The average Frenchman no longer mentioned public affairs except with irony and disgust. Dictatorship, which under diverse forms had been continuous since 1789 and which was perpetuated by the coups d'état of the Directory, forced the individual to withdraw into himself. Idealism was dead among the royalists as well as among the republicans. Generous enthusiasm gave way to egoism. The time was ripe for Bonaparte with his reassurances and consolidation of interests. In default of political liberty he brought to the French the assurance of civil liberties. In his code he preserved equality, their most cherished possession. He maintained the greater number of the institutions of the revolution, fusing them at times with adaptations made from those of the *ancien régime*. So forceful was his work that the door was forever closed to an integral restoration of the past.

The influence of the French Revolution on France and on Europe was so important that it is no exaggeration to say that it marks the beginning of a new era in the history of the world. France found herself greatly strengthened by the destruction of the *ancien régime*. No other state was so homogeneous. The suppression of orders, of bodies, of privileges, the unification of legislation, the standardization of institutions, the decisive advancement of the national language, had already generated a tremendous *élan*. It was only in France that for a long period of time the all powerful state ruled over citizens endowed with equality.

The individualistic program of the physiocrats was in a large measure realized. The right of property, recognized as absolute, allowed the French full enjoyment of economic and civil liberties. The road was wide open to the rise of capitalism, and it was not simply a coincidence that the great capitalists were in the majority of cases ardent revolutionaries.

In principle the revolution proclaimed itself peaceful. It solemnly renounced all conquest—a spontaneous gesture which won many sympathizers abroad—but the violent clash of the revolutionary program with the monarchical rendered the maintenance of peace impossible. War changed the aspect of the problem. The kings of neighboring countries were forced to resort more and more to French methods as a war measure. In 1794 the king of Spain inaugurated a confiscation of the church treasury. The following year he appropriated the revenues of vacant ecclesiastical benefices and at the same time began the issue of paper money. The Austrian emperor was reduced to the same necessity. Confronted with a shortage of troops, he resorted in the third year of the war to the device of the *levée en masse*. Pitt kept in power only by loans. Fortunately the crowned heads of Europe did not dare prescribe universal military service, which saved France, because as Mallet du Pan has pointed out they were almost as afraid of their subjects as they were of the enemy.

Victory intoxicated the French. Under the pretext of bringing liberty to their neighbors they brought conquest in the form of a rejuvenation of the old theory of natural frontiers. They became a perilous threat to the liberty of Europe. Napoleonic militarism brought into being nations which had hitherto had no national consciousness. Thus the nationalistic struggles so numerous in the nineteenth century were the direct offspring of the French Revolution. In the past, wars had been purely dynastic; the people had played but a passive role. The wars of the future in direct contrast were to put into the field larger and larger armies recruited according to the French system of military service extended progressively to the entire nation. In 1793 France had equipped 1,200,000 men. It was the first time since antiquity that an equal number of effectives had been assembled together. Never had there been recruited an army equally nationalistic in spirit, which went out not only to defend its national independence but to impose on others its political and religious credo.

With the progress of the nineteenth century the struggles between peoples became increasingly bitter. Europe was split up into hostile nationalistic systems. But early in the century conditions were different. The conflict was as yet more social than political. In all nations there were minorities of varying strength, which shared the French ideal and more or less secretly expressed their wishes for its success. In order to prevent these minorities from expanding and contaminating the rest of the subjects, monarchs were forced to grant increasingly important concessions. Thus the efflorescence of nationalism was accompanied by a liberal movement which gradually undermined the walls of France's neighbor states. Moreover, both nationalists and liberals belonged to the same social class—to that enlightened bourgeoisie which had reformed France and subsequently become the model for Europe.

At the outset the revolutionaries in France although tinged with the spirit of Voltaire had nourished little hatred against the church and still less against religion. They dreamed, on the contrary, of securing the collaboration of the clergy in the defense of their political work. Their union with the lower clergy had been very close. But the refusal of the pope to ratify their religious reforms, the schism within the clergy, which was divided into juring and non-juring priests, their ineffective efforts to repair this schism—all of these factors led them gradually to a policy of hostility toward the church. They wound up by secularizing the republic through the separation of church and state. The Concordat of Bonaparte, designed primarily to reassure the classes which had acquired national property during the revolution, was powerless to reestablish the former close alliance between throne and altar. The civil state remained in the hands of civil magistrates. Anticlericalism, which before 1789 was nothing more than a point of view, became a program which was to be adopted by the majority of liberals throughout Europe.

Similarly the divine right of kings had received a fatal blow in the proclamation of the principles of 1789. The idea of sovereignty had undergone a change of meaning. From the king it had passed to the people, and the scaffold of January 21 had shorn it of all supernatural prestige. When Charles x at his coronation made for the last time the gesture of touching the scrofulitic he was greeted with laughter.

The American Revolution had been primarily a political revolution. It had respected the privileges of the wealthy classes and had established without exception an electoral system based on the census. It had not even struck at the remnants of the feudal system which here and there were still in evidence. The seignorial rents in the state of New York, for example, were not suppressed until the middle of the nineteenth century.

The French Revolution was profound in a different sense. It thoroughly exterminated without indemnification feudal dues and the *dîme* [tithe]. It nationalized the property of the church and the property of the émigrés. It completely remodeled the commercial industrial regime. It revealed itself almost from the beginning as imbued with a keen sense of equality, which reached its apogee in 1793-94. Under the stress of necessity rather than theory a social democracy made its début and attempted to take its place in the world of men. The attempt was premature and failed. But it did not disappear without leaving traces, at least in the realm of ideas. The de facto collectivism realized by the terrorist regime, the control of prices, the requisitions, the communizing of all the resources of the nation, were cited over and over again by the social reformers during the century after Babeuf.

If the Terror continued to freeze the blood of nineteenth century bourgeois it kept alive the hope of champions of social justice. It acted upon their imaginations like a grandiose myth, a breeder of devotion and sacrifice. The historian Gabriel Monod in his preface to Mathiez' *Contributions à l'histoire religieuse de la Révolution* recounts that at Nantes toward the middle of the last century the woman at whose house he was boarding was singing the praises of her father, who had enthusiastically welcomed the revolution and had fought for it in his youth against the Vendeans. "He sorrowfully witnessed the extermination by the imperial regime of the democratic liberties which had been bought so dearly. At each new revolution—1814, 1830, 1848—he had believed that the ideal republic, dreamed of in 1793, was about to reappear. He died under the Second Empire, more than ninety years old; at the moment of death, raising his eyes ecstatically toward the sky, he murmured, 'O sun of '93, I shall then die without having again seen thy rays!'" He was no exception, this old Breton. The sun of '93 which had illumined his youth had ill succeeded in cloaking itself behind the darkened horizon, for in his heart he had kept bright its undying rays.

Mankind has need, in the course of its trying and discouraging march forward, to have its illusions rekindled by the warm rays of the past. The revolutionaries of 1789 drew sustenance for their struggles from the memory of the republics of antiquity or from the more recent example of the American Revolution. Plutarch was before their minds and his spiritual elevation served to exalt their courage, to increase their faith in the revolution. They imitated the heroes of Greece and Rome and like them gave up their lives for their faith—becoming in their turn heroes. For their descendants they became what Aristides, Brutus and Cato had been to them—martyrs who by their lives and their deaths bear witness to the abiding strength of devotion to justice and selfless love of humanity. The republicans of France have faithfully nourished their memory, and the revolution has served in contemporary history as a spring, ever fresh, of precedent and inspiration.

Songs—Colorful Propaganda of the French Revolution

CORNWELL B. ROGERS

Published in 1947

Anyone who wants to find out what Frenchmen of the revolutionary period were thinking has many sources to which to turn. He can consult such materials as the laws Frenchmen enacted, the speeches they made, the books they wrote, and the newspapers and pamphlets they published; it is, in fact, such data that historians have usually investigated in order to study the ideas of Frenchmen in the revolutionary period. There are, however, other sources, too—less obvious ones but certainly no less revealing than those that have generally been used. Consider, for example, the plays Frenchmen saw, the works of art they produced, and the songs they composed and sang. It is these songs, indeed, that recently came into their own in an unusual doctoral dissertation by Cornwell B. Rogers. Dissertations, of course, have often been criticized for their pettiness, their dullness, and their singular lack of originality; and, when they deal with some aspect of the French Revolution, they are likely to be especially vulnerable, for so much has been written on the subject that it is extremely difficult to find anything new to say. But anyone who has read Rogers' thesis on *The Spirit of Revolution in 1789* (1949) will quickly concede that the usual antidissertation jibes do not apply. The present article, based in part on his dissertation, gives the essence of Rogers' ingenious approach to a dramatic and meaningful subject that has at last received the attention it deserves.

The French Revolutionists believed that they were ushering in a new day for mankind. It would not be strange had such a proud supposition turned out to be entirely a delusion; instead, we see today that it was laden with prophetic insight.

Reprinted by special permission from *Public Opinion Quarterly*, XI (1947), 436-444. The footnotes which originally appeared with this essay have been omitted.

Indeed, the influence of their work has profoundly altered the life of succeeding generations. As Jan Masaryk said after the termination of the Second World War: "We are in the midst of the greatest revolution that ever befell the human race. It started with the French Revolution and we have never finished it."

Students of the great upheaval at the end of the eighteenth century have agreed on one thing at least—that a remarkable store of energy was released; but on the nature, merits, and proper uses of that energy there has been little accord. As a matter of fact, the French Revolutionists themselves, for all their insight, were generally unaware of the complexity of the forces they were unloosing, and were strikingly—almost pathetically—incapable of controlling them. And now, a century and a half later—with the slogan "Liberty, Equality, Fraternity" continuing to mean different things to different men—it is obvious that the French Revolution, although abundantly described in a vast store of scholarly writings, still contains many enigmas.

The Factor of Emotion in Human Affairs

Not a few of the unanswered questions fall into a field of inquiry that is being much explored in our own times—namely, that area of social science which is concerned with mass behavior and, especially, with mass emotions. Current emphasis on so-called "ideologies" indicates our recognition today that there is a factor in human society that cannot be reduced to purely political or economic terms, or explained even in the light of time-honored "reason." Increasing attention is accordingly given to the part which emotion plays in human affairs. To be sure, up to a certain point, it has always been recognized that the reactions of the crowd play an important part in determining the

---

MARIE-JOSEPH CHÉNIER: Author of one of the great hymns of the French Revolution, the *Chant du Départ*. Much more important, he wrote a number of historical plays which dealt with subjects that were of topical interest in the late eighteenth and early nineteenth centuries. His *Charles IX*, presented shortly after the fall of the Bastille, was an attack on tyranny. His *Tiberius* was an attack on Napoleonic despotism. He should not be confused with his brother André, the great French poet of the eighteenth century.

HÉBERTISTS: Ultrarevolutionaries, followers of Hébert, the owner of an

course of events; but only in the era of the common man, and especially in an industrial era, is one made fully aware of the tremendous weight of this factor. If one would investigate this matter, he must have recourse to the most popular media of expression and opinion—to the daily press, the pulps, the cartoons, the movies, and the radio. The analysis of these media is accordingly becoming an increasingly important part of public-opinion study.

A somewhat comparable interest may well be taken in so critical an era in history as that of the French Revolution; for this period, more than any other, marks the transition in Europe from the aristocratic society of the old regime to the democratic society of today. Indeed, many of the most fundamental problems of the present first confronted the peoples of Europe with the outbreak of that movement in 1789. It was then that "mass thought" and "mass action," in the modern sense of those terms, first emerged.

To be sure, by 1789 industrialization as a whole had not advanced far, but by that time one of its most important features, a people's press, was coming into its own. In the France of that day newspapers expanded prodigiously. The Revolutionary presses turned out pamphlets, too, in great profusion. All this was in addition to a continuing flow of books—the most characteristic being, no doubt, little handbooks of all sorts, adapted to spreading widely the Revolutionary message.

These products of the new democratic press are essential for the study of popular opinion during the Revolution. They have been given, as one would expect, careful attention by scholars, with the result that the main trends of opinion expressed in these media have been written into the general histories of the period. It is true, besides, that the role of the theaters in relation to public opinion has been given a fair degree of consideration.

---

important Parisian yellow journal. Vigorously anti-Roman-Catholic, they went about attacking priests and burning churches. The Robespierrites, fearing that the Hébertists were discrediting the Republic, secured the arrest and execution of their leaders in March 1794.

MONITEUR: French newspaper, remarkable for its colorlessness, which was founded in November 1789. Its generally careful accounts of parliamentary proceedings make it the most valuable newspaper source for the study of French Revolutionary history.

Songs—Vehicle of Popular Opinion

One phase of popular expression, however, seems to have been relatively neglected—the songs, political and patriotic, of the times. The Revolution produced an abundance of such songs, or "hymns," as many of the songs were called. This literature conveys not only the main trends of popular opinion in the French Revolution, but also, it seems to me, the essence of the spirit of that movement. It contains, besides, in concentrated form, many of the emotional overtones and subtleties that are apt to be lost in the welter of journalistic writings. Indeed, owing to its emotional intensity and suggestive exaggeration, the song literature is particularly revealing of such individual and group predispositions as are found today to be of psychological importance.

No adequate account of the contents of this literature as a whole, or of its significance in terms of popular-opinion analysis, can be given in brief compass. In this article I shall undertake, however, to touch on three phases of the subject: to suggest the extraordinary popularity of Revolutionary songs; to show how profoundly this vogue impressed the government, and how the government, in turn, used it for purposes of propaganda; and, finally, to indicate one or two of the principal strains of Revolutionary enthusiasm that were effectively broadcast through the songs.

It is strange that this literature, despite its interest and importance, has not been extensively treated by historians, especially in view of the fact that many years ago pioneer bibliographical work was undertaken on an impressive scale. In 1898, the municipality of Paris—to which scholars are indebted for monumental bibliographies in the field of the French Revolution—provided for a work by Constant Pierre on the songs and hymns of the period. Pierre brought to light in his *Catalogue* the existence of some three thousand songs of a political nature which came out between 1789 and 1800. But despite this impressive bibliographical achievement, there has been no adequate recognition of the part which they played.

The Spontaneous Vogue of Songs

To a remarkable extent, as the Revolution progressed, songs were used by community and club leaders as an instrument of enlightenment, and from 1793 they were exploited by the national government as a primary agency of propaganda. But in the beginning the vogue was spontaneous.

The Revolutionists took to singing political songs for pleasure, as they had previously sung folk songs or other popular airs. Paris journals made mention from time to time of their increasing popularity. One of them, the *Chronique de Paris,* noted in May, 1790, that "Songs within the reach of the people and made in the spirit of the Revolution are current in the streets." The editor reproduced verses to which a crowd had listened "with great satisfaction." In a subsequent issue of the same journal, mention was made of patriotic stanzas which had been sung on the Pont-Neuf "to the great pleasure of all those present and of the singers, who made a considerable sale." What the street singers sold were brochures or leaflets, carrying the words, but rarely the music, of the pieces of their repertoire. An abundance of material could be cited to show the remarkable extent to which political songs had caught the popular fancy.

Club meetings, banquets, and reunions of various sorts afforded the patriots—as the Revolutionists customarily called themselves—ample opportunity for singing in unison, a form of expression which they particularly enjoyed. In this connection an interesting custom developed at the theaters. Early in the Revolution actors adopted the practice of singing one or more political songs in the course of a performance. It was usually intended that only the performers should sing, but the audience could not resist taking part. "The desire to sing in concert with the actors is so compelling in France," an English observer was reported to have said, "that in the case of a familiar song, he had sometimes seen the music leader of a theatre play almost the same role as the precentor in the churches, who serves only to intone the psalm and whose voice is then absorbed by that of the entire audience." Thus, political songs came to be sung in almost all the theaters and at the opera as well. This practice, at the height of the Revolution, transformed these places of entertainment into centers of great political excitement.

For some time the favorite song of the French Revolutionists was *Ça ira.* The vogue of *Ça ira*—consisting of catchy lyrics to an irresistible dance tune—commenced on the occasion of the first anniversary of the fall of the Bastille. The celebration of that event on July 14, 1790, was doubtless the greatest demonstration of mass enthusiasm that had occurred in modern times. At the gathering at the Champs de Mars,

Paris, it is estimated that three hundred thousand persons attended. This was the master meeting in a nation-wide celebration of freedom and brotherly love. How utterly gay was the spirit of Frenchmen at that time! So, too, was *Ça ira*—at least in its early versions. Later, as the Revolution became grim, the lyrics of *Ça ira* in turn became sanguinary. But the metamorphosis took time. Even by 1791, France, as a whole, was overflowing with good feeling, though by then the aristocrats were admittedly dangerous enemies. The King, too, was gradually losing popularity; and in the following year his leadership, at first dear to the Revolutionists, was discredited.

But this brings us already to 1792—a year which plunged France into cataclysmic changes and which launched Europe on a conflict that was to last, with slight interruption, over twenty years. The outbreak occurred on April 20, when the constitutional monarchy of the Revolution declared war on reactionary Austria. Prussia was allied to the Hapsburg power, and before long the armies of both powers were invading France. In the face of this advance, the French Assembly on July 11 made its stirring declaration that *la patrie* was in danger.

Of the patriots who responded, the most notable were those from Marseilles who arrived in Paris on July 30 singing the great song of Rouget de Lisle that was later to become the national anthem of France. These new arrivals played an important part in the insurrection of August 10—an event by which Louis XVI, already suspected of treason, was virtually overthrown. When in September, 1792, the National Convention came into power, its first act was to proclaim France a Republic.

Song and Cannon

With the arousal of the French masses to resist the professional armies of Europe, the great role of propaganda in modern warfare emerged. Here, to be sure, we are concerned with but a single part of that propaganda—and yet perhaps with its most colorful and revealing phase.

The success of the *Marseillaise*, as it resounded through the streets of Paris, was instantaneous. Such was its popularity that astute observers began to foresee that some deliberate use might be made of it and of other patriotic songs to spread the spirit of the Revolution. "I propose," wrote a contemporary, "to add our songs to our cannon; the former will be for the peasants' cottages, the latter for the chateaux. . . . Songs will have a more prompt effect than writings, will be their precursors, and will scatter sparks of light in advance. The *Marseillaise* enlightens, inspires and cheers all at the same time; it alone sufficed to subjugate the entire youth of Brabant. I conclude to the effect that four singers be attached to each of our armies." The Convention did not follow exactly the terms of this proposal; but the notion behind it, that the song could be exploited to quicken the spirit of the fighting forces of France and to stimulate among foreign peoples a universal uprising, exerted a potent influence on the minds of Revolutionary leaders.

The amazing successes of the armies of the French Republic, which by 1793 were battling the royalist forces of Sardinia, England, Holland, and Spain, as well as those of Austria and Prussia, and which a year later were driving them all back, naturally added fuel to the flames of patriotic self-confidence.

By 1793 the National Convention, fully aware of the important effect of songs on morale, began to use them to reach and arouse the masses. Since the French people at the end of the eighteenth century were still largely illiterate, much of the propaganda of that day had to be oral; and apparently lyrics remembered for enjoyment's sake proved to be at least as stimulating as the reasoned arguments of political discourse.

It may be said in passing that the members of the Convention had ample opportunity to gain firsthand knowledge of the "delightful frenzy" of popular singing. They entertained at their sessions numerous delegations representing both sexes, all ages, and most classes of French society, and they frequently permitted these visitors to sing in their presence. Just as the theaters were transformed into centers of political excitement, so on occasions did the Revolutionary parliament become an arena of theatrical effects. The sessions of July 4 and 5, 1793, may serve as an example. On the former day, groups of "*jeunes citoyennes*" ["young women citizens"] twice regaled the National Convention with song: five girls rendered "an invocation to the love of *la patrie* and the hymn of the men of Marseilles"; presently, another group of girls sang "patriotic hymns" to the legislators. They had come with deputations from the forty-eight sections of Paris to pay honor to the Constitution. On the following day several delegations together sang a Hymn to Liberty and other patriotic lyrics, "accompanied by drums and musical instruments." One of the deputations included some of the best operatic talent of the capital. No doubt, a striking effect was attained when the opera star Chenard, after singing the *Marseil-*

laise, turned to the benches of the dominant Jacobin party and added a new stanza to the "true defenders of the people."

The legislators occasionally enjoyed an advance audition. For example, on November 8, 1793, the band of the National Guard played for the Convention a new Hymn to Liberty two days before it was heard at the remarkable "Festival of Reason" in Notre Dame Cathedral. The words of the hymn were by Marie-Joseph Chénier; the music, by Gossec. Both Chénier and Gossec, together with an important delegation of musicians and officials, attended the hearing before the Convention. The account in the *Moniteur* tells of repeated applause by deputies and spectators. Also present on this occasion was a group of pupils of the band, introduced as "among the poorest citizens of each section." They, too, were given a chance to play in the presence of the legislators. One purpose of the visit of the musicians was to request that a national institute of music be created. Acting as spokesman, Chénier called the attention of the Convention to the influence which music had exerted "on the patriots at Paris, in the departments, on the frontiers." Chénier's proposal was approved in principle, and the National Institute of Music, renamed in 1795 the Conservatory, was brought into being.

When on January 15, 1794, a deputation of boys, "pupils of *la patrie,*" went before the Convention on behalf of the *Section des Piques,* and one of them sang a patriotic song, Laloi, a member of some prominence, demanded that the lyrics be inserted in the *Bulletin.* Danton protested that this publication was not intended "to circulate verse in the Republic, but good laws written in good prose." His objection prompted another member, Dubouchet, to give the following interesting testimony: "Nothing is more appropriate than patriotic hymns and songs to electrify the souls of Republicans. When on mission in the departments [i.e., administrative divisions of France] I was witness to the prodigious effect which they produce. We used always to end the meetings of official bodies and of the popular societies in singing hymns, and the enthusiasm of the members and spectators followed as an inevitable consequence." Danton, without denying the efficacy of the songs, nevertheless insisted that the Convention could not pass judgment on the sense and words of a song that had not been well heard. He urged that the matter be referred to the Committee of Public Instruction.

This proposal was accepted, but the custom of interrupting the sessions of the Convention with song continued. On March 16, twenty

CORNWELL B. ROGERS

days before his death, Danton rose to protest again. A delegation from the Section of Mont-Blanc had congratulated the Convention on the firmness with which it had struck down the Hébertist "traitors." The spokesman of the delegation then undertook to sing a song of his own composition. Danton stopped him. He denounced the practice of permitting the work of government to be thus delayed, and concluded as follows: "I do justice to the civic devotion of the petitioners, but I demand that from now on one hear at the tribunal only reason in prose." A motion to this effect was passed. From then on there were auditions, but only of a more dignified sort, as when the Convention had certain festivals celebrated in the midst of its deliberations. On such occasions hymns were played or sung by members of the National Institute or of its successor, the Conservatory.

Music for Morale

In the meantime the government had been using its authority to heighten the morale of the people by means of songs and ritual. In the autumn of 1793 the Committee of Public Safety issued a decree requiring that the *Marseillaise* be played at all theatrical performances in the Republic—"regularly on all the *decadi* [the tenth day, or day of rest, under the new Revolutionary calendar] and at any time the public may demand it."

The introduction by the Convention of a non-Christian calendar—which dated a new era from the establishment of the Republic in 1792—afforded opportunities for much Revolutionary ceremonial. This calendar substituted for Sundays the *decadi* to which reference has been made. These newly decreed days of rest were celebrated by festivals, at which the singing of patriotic songs and hymns played an important part.

Such celebrations were presently incorporated in the new religion—the "Worship of the Supreme Being"—inaugurated by the Convention in May, 1794, at the behest of Robespierre. It was hoped that the Revolutionary religion would take the place of Christianity. The essence of the new democratic faith—which in the course of the Revolution was embodied in four different cults—was the equality and liberty of man, revealed by Nature, fostered by the State (*la patrie*), kept alive through brotherly love (*fraternité*), and consecrated by patriotic devotion and sacrifice—if need be, by death.

Much of this spirit was expressed somewhat informally in numerous

Revolutionary handbooks devoted in whole or in part to political songs. The most typical of these were called *almanachs chantants*, or *chansonniers*. In the preface of one of these an editor remarks: "The French, more than any other people, know how to intersperse the garlands of glory with the flowers of enjoyment. Every phase of their beneficent revolution is marked by Hymns. This sort of chronology electrifies Republican souls, and depicts the happy public spirit."

A more strenuous note was sounded in the preface of the *Nouveau chansonnier patriote*, dated, in terms of the new Calendar, "Year II." The following passages are of particular interest:

"Popular songs are with the French what morality is with other peoples: there are no events or remarkable deeds which have not been put into verses. It is therefore to give to posterity a new proof of that delightful frenzy which fills the heads of all Frenchmen, that we have gathered together in an anthology the best productions of this kind.

"A eulogy of the martyrs of our revolution appears at the beginning of this collection: this eulogy . . . was read in all the sections of Paris and was everywhere greeted with transports of patriotism. . . .

"Peoples of all nations . . . unite with the French. Blush to wear your chains any longer, and, in imitating us, hasten to become worthy of liberty."

This was world revolution.

State Aid for Song and Hymn Production

The legislators, confronted by a vast task of indoctrination, repeatedly voted subsidies to further the spread of patriotic songs and hymns. Important financial aid was given a music publishing association, called the *Magasin*. This Association, which was an outgrowth of the newly created National Institute, hoped to bring out, in the form of a monthly serial, scores for the decadal and national festivals, and in January, 1794, proposed that the government subsidize the undertaking. The memoir of the Association supplied various patriotic reasons why the Convention should occupy itself with the matter. The Committee of Public Safety examined the proposal, and pronounced it "important in revolutionary connections"; it would, according to their analysis, improve public spirit, arouse courage, and offer a means of strengthening the moral effect of civic festivals. The Committee accordingly decreed that the Association should provide the government, each month, 550 copies of the proposed serial, which was to be published in quarto. In return, the Association was to receive from the government a sum of 33,000 livres. The enterprise developed tardily, but essentially as planned. The new publication, *Musique à l'usage des fêtes nationales*, consisted of twelve issues, and contained scores by Catel, Cherubini, Gossec, Lesueur, Méhul, and others, some of the scores being known today only through this series. The first number having appeared on April 9, 1794, a deputation of artists, headed by Gossec, went before a meeting of the Jacobins the following day, to proclaim the new publication and to present the Society with one of the first copies.

This activity of professional musicians was evidently not sufficient. On May 7, the Convention called on all with talents "worthy of serving the cause of humanity," to contribute civic hymns and songs to the successful establishment of decadal and national festivals. Ten days later, the Committee of Public Safety repeated the invitation, calling on all composers and others interested in music to provide for the festivals, "plays, martial music, and whatever else their art might offer as being best suited to recall to republicans the most cherished sentiments and memories of the Revolution." These promptings no doubt account in part for the record number of songs—some one hundred and twenty are extant—which were written to celebrate the Festival of the Supreme Being, June 8, 1794.

The *Magasin*, encouraged by its initial success in obtaining a subsidy, soon projected a second enterprise. The new plan called for the issuance of "a collection of songs and *romances civiques* in the form of a journal," to be underwritten by the government. The Committee of Public Safety, viewing the proposal with favor, decreed on July 9, 1794, that "the Association of Artists, Musicians, and Composers shall distribute to the various armies of the Republic, on land and sea, 12,000 copies of patriotic songs and hymns such as are suitable for propagating the republican spirit and the love of public virtues." The decree bears the signatures of an important company of Jacobins: Carnot, Barère, Billaud-Varenne, Collot d'Herbois, C. A. Prieur, and Saint-Just. For the support of this journal for one year, the government paid in installments a total of over 60,000 livres.

Along with these serial issues, the Convention financed the publication and distribution of hymns for particular occasions. Obviously,

such music was of a relatively formal character. At the same time, songs
of the most popular sort were appearing in great profusion. Pierre,
whose *Catalogue* has already been mentioned, reports for 1793 nearly
six hundred Revolutionary songs still extant. For 1794, the peak
year, he reports the existence of just over seven hundred. Pierre depended primarily on the libraries of Paris, and there is no way of
knowing what additional material may yet be found in the provinces,
or even outside France. Furthermore, there are indications that many
songs of the Revolution have been lost in the course of time. For these
reasons one must be reserved in estimating popular trends; but, in
any case, it is clear from existing evidences that the exploitation of
songs as official propaganda reached the height of its importance under
the Jacobin supremacy in 1793-94.

The first half of the latter year was the period of Robespierre's
greatest influence. As head of the all-important Committee of Public
Safety, he not only determined party policies but also was the outstanding leader in matters of Revolutionary culture and morale. On July
24, three days before his sudden fall, the Committee of Public Safety
was giving attention to the need for more speed in the circulation of
patriotic songs, shipments of which had been ordered sent "to the
departments and to the armies of the Republic."

The Convention continued in existence for a year and three months
after the overthrow of Robespierre. During this period, July 27, 1794,
to October 26, 1795, decisions in regard to music were relegated, for
the most part, to the Committee of Public Instruction. This Committee
paid one Perrin twelve hundred livres to enable him to furnish to the
forty-eight sections of Paris 12,000 copies of his hymn in honor of
Jean Jacques Rousseau. On another occasion, the Committee—at the
instance of the National Institute—provided for 1,000 copies of engraved music to be sent to each of the fourteen armies of the Republic.
There is no need to multiply examples. They all point to the same
fact: the Convention regarded music as highly effective propaganda,
and was willing to pay well for it.

The Convention hoped to propagate Revolutionary ideas even in
foreign countries through the influence of songs. Perhaps it was encouraged in this expectation by the report of contemporaries that in
some areas the *Marseillaise* had caught the imagination of foreign
populations and had helped to convert them. In any case, the Committee of Public Safety exempted engraved music from the ordinary

customs regulations, in order to facilitate its distribution abroad. It is known that boxes of patriotic music were shipped to Zurich, and it may be that similar shipments were made elsewhere across the borders. The fact that evidence on the subject is scanty suggests that the business of exporting music did not become very considerable. It stands, however, as one of many interesting instances of the conviction of the Revolutionists that their program would be favorably viewed by all other nations, or, as people said in those days, by the "entire universe."

When, in the fall of 1795, the National Convention gave way to the new government of the Directory, the initial wave of Revolutionary enthusiasm was spent—and the great day of the Revolutionary song was passing.

But while their popularity lasted, the songs of the French Revolution recorded evidences of the utmost importance—those which disclose a state of mind or lay bare the human heart. This vast literature provides, in short, a rich store of materials for the study of popular opinion. It contains the spirit—and, no doubt, some of the unexplored meaning—of the emergence of the revolutionary world of today.

Napoleon's Military Bulletins

JOSEPH J. MATHEWS

Published in 1950

Historians have generally been suspicious of the military bulletin—the rough equivalent of today's communiqué—as a historical source. The reason for this wariness is obvious. The bulletin has often been shockingly inaccurate in the information it conveys; it has grossly magnified successes and toned down defeats. For all that, it can be an enormously valuable source. Though it may do little to further the search for historical truth, it does reveal what those in positions of command wished their own people as well as their enemies to believe the truth to be. In the case of Napoleon, for example, as Joseph J. Mathews, of Emory University, indicates in the present essay, the military bulletin was an important instrument of propaganda and of psychological warfare; and if Napoleon was able to exploit it as effectively as he did, the reason was that for so long he had one theme above all on which to concentrate: success.

The military bulletins of Napoleon Bonaparte have been regarded by most serious students of the Napoleonic era as extremely limited, or even useless, sources of information. Bias and factual inaccuracy make these documents treacherous material for students of Napoleon's military campaigns, a fact which is almost universally recognized. Although they have been correctly labeled as instruments of Napoleonic propaganda, the bulletins have not been studied from this viewpoint with sufficient care. An examination of their contents, of the methods of distributing them, and of their reception is revealing

Reprinted by special permission from *Journal of Modern History*, XXII (1950), 137-144. Publisher, University of Chicago Press. The footnotes which originally appeared with this essay have been omitted.

in the light that it sheds on Napoleon's attempts to master the art of psychological warfare.

Napoleon is often called the "inventor" or "father" of the military bulletin; but this, like most historical "firsts," is a question of definition. The term "bulletin," as applied to official accounts containing war news, was fairly widely but loosely used prior to Napoleon's popularization of the term. In the latter half of the eighteenth century it was the accepted practice for a commanding general to send accounts of his battles to his home government, which would then issue them to the public, usually in an official gazette. Long before the time of Napoleon the British inaugurated the practice of publishing "extraordinary" numbers of the *London Gazette* on the receipt of war news of special interest. In France the Revolutionary period was an unprecedented one in all manner of propagandistic activity. Fate could scarcely have chosen formative years for young Bonaparte which would have presented him with better opportunities for observing such activities and for drawing lessons from them. The factual validity of much of the military news issued by the Republic is as open to question as anything in the Napoleonic bulletins, and some of the Republican generals were as boastful and inaccurate in their reports as Napoleon ever was. For all his exaggeration, Napoleon never equaled the account of a battle sent in by General Pierre de Ruel Beurnonville. "After three hours of tremendous fighting," stated Beurnonville, "the enemy lost 10,000 men; the loss of the French was confined to the little finger of a drummer." But, if Napoleon learned his lessons from earlier practices, he possessed the genius to apply them with unparalleled vigor.

From the beginning of his military career Napoleon gave evidence of that "psychologico-dramatic sense" which distinguishes him from other great military leaders such as Wellington, Frederick the Great, and Moltke. At Toulon he attempted to electrify his soldiers by calling them *les hommes sans peur* [men without fear]. Even if, as seems probable, Napoleon actually composed his famous address to the army of Italy many years later at St. Helena, there were other stirring messages for his soldiers, and his dispatches to the Directory were glorified, exaggerated, and exciting accounts of his victories. Dissatisfied with existing means of disseminating news, the young Republican general established two newspapers of his own in Italy and later launched one in Egypt. It was in the period prior to the coup d'état of Brumaire that Napoleon's ingenuity for self-advertisement was put to its severest test. He had no control of the French press, and his dispatches, like those of any other general, were channeled through the suspicious and intrigue-ridden Directory, which exercised the usual prerogatives of the home government in editing the general's accounts before submitting them to the public. No one would deny the significance of Napoleon's military victories in making possible the overthrow of the Directory; but his skill in presenting these victories in the most favorable manner, and particularly in creating the impression of his personal responsibility for them, was as essential for success as the victories themselves.

Technically, the bulletin system was not inaugurated until late in 1805, when Napoleon forsook his projected invasion of England and led the Grand Army into Austria. Beginning on October 7, 1805 and continuing through the famed twenty-ninth and last bulletin of the Russian campaign of 1812, official news of the activities of the Grand Army was given in numbered bulletins which appeared irregularly but frequently when the army was on campaign: 37 bulletins were issued from Germany in 1805, 87 during the war against the Prussians and Russians in 1806-7, and so on. On a more limited scale, dispatches from the French forces in Italy and in Spain were issued as bulletins. The numbered bulletin system came to an end after 1812, and all dispatches were subsequently issued in the name of the empress-regent, but the change was one in name only, since the emperor relaxed none of his vigilance in controlling the news. The official accounts continued to be referred to as "bulletins" by the newspapers, and many contemporary and later sources refer to any of Napoleon's military dispatches as his "bulletins."

A Napoleonic bulletin can probably best be described as a newsletter from the emperor when he was with the army. Even though the chief purpose of the bulletins was to convey the news of the army—

GEORGE CRUIKSHANK: One of the most gifted political artists of all times. His hatred of Napoleon found expression in caricatures which bore such titles as "Quadrupeds, or Little Boney's Last Kick," "Little Boney Gone to Pot," and "Snuffing out Boney."

JOSEPH FOUCHÉ: French politician and bureaucrat who has come to serve, along with Talleyrand, as the symbol of the turncoat. A Jacobin, he played an important part in the overthrow of Robespierre. Napoleon's minister of police, he did much to organize and direct the internal security program

often they were the sole source of news directly from the army—they went far beyond modern military communiqués. They not only contain battle accounts but a wide scope of information and comment, ranging from ill-mannered attacks on enemy sovereigns to descriptions of distant villages and terrain; from analyses of diplomatic situations, defenses of French policy, and soliloquies on the horrors of war and the benefits of peace, to "human-interest" stories of the heroic deeds of individual soldiers. There were no artificial limitations as to what might or might not go into a bulletin. Often proclamations, orders of the day, treaties, and other diplomatic documents were attached as supplements to the bulletins.

Aside from their factual undependability, the characteristic of the bulletins which has drawn greatest comment is Napoleon's unabashed egocentrism, evidenced in all manner of disgusting self-glorification and shameless appropriation of credit rightly due others and in the blaming of subordinates for his own errors. In the Marengo bulletin, François-Christophe Kellerman, one of the real heroes, was virtually ignored, and the other hero, Louis Desaix, received fame of a sort when the bulletin manufactured for him a dying speech in which he expressed his regret at having but one life to give for the First Consul. The picture of Napoleon rousing disheartened troops with a stirring speech, or even by his mere appearance among them, is a relatively frequent one in the bulletins. The Austerlitz bulletin reads like a fairy tale in its portrayal of the omnipotent emperor as he directed every move of the battle, both those of his own troops and those of the enemy. Perhaps the most quoted single remark in any of the bulletins is the last sentence of the twenty-ninth bulletin of the Russian campaign: in the midst of one of the most disastrous defeats in history, when thousands of men were meeting horrible deaths from cold, hun-

of the Napoleonic Empire. With the collapse of the Empire imminent, he went over to the side of Louis XVIII.

FRIEDRICH VON GENTZ: German publicist and politician. At first a supporter of the French Revolution, he soon became an opponent of Jacobinism and Napoleonic expansionism. He translated Burke's *Reflections on the French Revolution*; and, after 1802, when he gained official recognition in high Austrian political circles, he emerged as a leading figure in the struggle against Napoleon.

ger, disease, and the Cossacks, the bulletin states that "the health of
His Majesty was never better."

Whatever all this may prove of the personal character of Napoleon,
it has too often been subjected to superficial interpretation. It all fits
into the structure of imperial ideology, the very keystone of which was
the legend of Napoleon's military infallibility, and that legend was
created no less by the pen than by the sword. If one reads the bulletins
as a whole, one can scarcely escape the impression of a careful, orderly,
systematic, and purposeful story rather than one of mere egotistical
boasting or callous disregard on the part of the emperor for the contributions and lives of his soldiers. In 1808 an English magazine recognized the crux of the matter in discussing a book which made much
of Napoleon's boastfulness. "Be it remembered," commented the English writer, "that if the French general had cultivated the delicacy and
candour, for want of which he is here reproached, he would never have
reached the elevation which he now occupies."

If individual bulletins are studied in their relation to the circumstances of the moment, they add to the emperor's stature as a propagandist, if not to his stature as a man. At Marengo in 1800 Napoleon's
political position was too recently established and the acceptance of the
concept of a general whose mere presence on the battlefield was worth
an army was as yet too doubtful to permit the admission of errors or
the just allocation of credit. More significant than the question of accuracy in the account of Marengo is the fact that this battle, for all
Napoleon's errors, became one of his most famous personal victories.
The tendency to emphasize Napoleon's personal role in battles is
more noticeable in the early years of the expansion of the empire than
later. In 1814 the Parisian press undertook on its own to reassure its
readers of victory by emphasizing the ingeniousness of the emperor
as a counterbalance to the inferior numbers of the French troops. But
on this occasion French strength was inferior, and Napoleon's fury at
the stupidity of the journalists knew no bounds. Napoleon used his
bulletins as a means of rewarding officers and units with praise, no
less than other commanding generals have done; and, as might be
expected, he gave or withheld praise as it suited his purposes. The
bulletins are full of bouquets for men and units, and Napoleon's marshals vied with one another no less than generals of other armies have
for this type of recognition. The interpretation of the line, "the health
of His Majesty was never better," as mere callous insensitivity to the

loss of life is entirely misleading. In the ideology of the Napoleonic system the matter of the emperor's health was one of real consequence. The bulletins usually referred to the emperor's health as a matter of course. As the final line of the account of a serious defeat, the sentence was, or at least was intended to be, the most reassuring news that could be offered.

Napoleon's mastery of the techniques of wartime propaganda went far beyond the clever presentation of his own military prowess. It is, of course, impossible to separate Napoleon's handling of war news from the activities of his vast propaganda machine, which extended to the church, to the press and literature as a whole, to the educational system, and to the theater. The manner and timing of the distribution of military news, as well as the emasculation, contradiction, or suppression of counternews, were made possible by the existence of these general controls. It is obvious, too, that the centralization of political authority and military leadership in the hands of one man gave him an unusual tactical advantage. But, even if one simply assumes the existence of an effective propaganda machine and the various advantages indicated, the skill of the emperor is evident in a special sense in his meticulous supervision of every phase of the composition and distribution of war news.

Napoleon himself wrote, or at least edited, virtually all the bulletins of the Grand Army, and there is very little evidence of polishing or other alterations in the accounts by anyone else. They represent, then, the views which Napoleon wanted to have accepted. The bulletins were usually rushed by courier to Paris, where they were first published in the *Moniteur*, the official government organ. There exist a few copies of single bulletins which were published separately by the government printer, but the almost invariable rule was to distribute individual bulletins in the form of reprints from the *Moniteur*. Napoleon appears to have viewed this as the only really safe method of handling the official accounts. On numerous occasions he gave strict instructions to officials regarding the precise time and manner of publication. The following instructions of 1806 to Talleyrand, who at the time was in Germany, may be taken as typical: "I am sending you some bulletins. You must not have them printed as I do not wish for them to have arrived so quickly. You will send them to M. Cambacérès for him to put them in the *Moniteur* and you will send copies to Prince Eugene. You will have a copy made for the

King of Holland, but you will tell him that I do not wish to have them printed; our enemies would receive them five or six days too soon." Napoleon's care during the campaigns of 1806-7 to prevent the bulletins from arriving too quickly in Germany led him to send General Henri Clarke in Berlin regular directions concerning the information which should be published both officially and unofficially. Prince Eugene in Italy was roundly upbraided for publishing the destination of some outgoing ships and was told: "My son, it is essential that one print very little . . . in general, the less one has printed the better." Nor was Napoleon unaware of the possibility of misleading his opponents through the publication of false information. Sir Robert Wilson, British commissioner with the Russian army in 1812, tells of a letter which the Russians captured in which Napoleon instructed Hugues-Bernard Maret to demand that Austria, Prussia, and the other French allies double in their official-gazette statements the number of troops they were actually supplying for the campaign. The emperor's concern with news which went to his enemies, however, was incidental; his major interest was always in giving proper direction to news in France and in the territories which he controlled.

The proper timing of the publication of news for the best possible effect was a point to which Napoleon gave careful attention. Normally he tried to have his version of a particular battle arrive first, especially if it were impossible to shut out other accounts. Precautions were taken throughout Germany to have the Eylau bulletin distributed before the Russian account should arrive. Possibly the time of a bulletin's publication was never more important to Napoleon than that of the final bulletin of the Russian campaign. The emperor was extremely anxious to have the bulletin appear in Paris just long enough before his own return to permit excitement over his defeat to die down but not long enough to encourage anti-imperial intrigue.

Newspapers were by no means the only media for spreading the tidings of battle to the French public. On occasions Napoleon instructed Joseph Fouché, minister of police, to broadcast specified news in the salons before permitting it to appear in the papers. The traditional practice of firing guns at the Invalides, followed by the announcing or posting of news, was continued. Managers of theaters were instructed to read victorious bulletins to their audiences, although on one occasion a greater commotion was created by a lady in the audience who swooned on hearing a relative's name given in the casualty list than by the news of victory. Of all the channels for distributing war news in France, the church appears to have given the emperor greatest concern. In 1805 he wrote to Fouché as follows: "I see difficulties in permitting the bulletins to be read in the churches; I do not consider this advisable for it gives more importance to the priests than they deserve. It gives them the right to comment and should the news be bad, they will not fail to remark on it." Somewhat later Napoleon attempted to get around this problem by instructing Fouché to have the prefects post bulletins on the doors of the churches. The prohibition of priestly participation in the distribution of war news did not, however, mean the prohibition of religious manifestations of joy over the emperor's victories. Napoleon kept a strict eye on the singing of "Te Deums" for his victories even to the point of cautioning Empress Marie Louise not to have "Te Deums" chanted too often, since it is "because they are so rare that they are imposing." It is worth noting that, while Napoleon was anxious to have the Lord's representatives on earth join in the celebration, he was unwilling to share credit with the Almighty for his victories. The writer has not found in Napoleon's bulletins the phrase, "with God's help," which, in the nineteenth century at least, was the almost invariable preamble to a victorious communiqué.

The distribution of French war news outside France varied with time and circumstances. It is well known that the extension of Napoleon's political control over Europe was paralleled by control, direct or indirect, over existing means of disseminating information, and the evidence indicates that he took no less interest in what was published in newly acquired territory than in old. He was interested, too, in supplying the right news to neutral states and particularly to countries which were wavering in their attitude toward the Napoleonic empire. The smaller German states and the Turkish empire furnish two examples of the policies followed in the two-year period prior to the treaties of Tilsit. Fauvelet de Bourrienne, at the time a French agent in Germany, states that he was ordered to distribute two thousand copies of the Eylau bulletin in the Hanse towns, an obvious attempt to reach the general public of these towns. Napoleon's correspondence of the period contains numerous instructions for sending news as speedily as possible to Constantinople, but in the latter case it was merely an attempt to get the word to high government officials. Apparently, Napoleon made no attempt to distribute his military-news wares to England, but here the factor in the equation was demand rather than supply: British newspapers gave full and free distribution to Napoleon's bulletins throughout the Napoleonic wars, including the period of nonintercourse regulations between England and France. William Jerdan, editor of the *Sun* (London), states that in 1813 a smuggled French newspaper containing bulletins or accounts of Bonaparte's German campaign would sell to a London paper for ten, twenty, or even one hundred guineas. The activities and difficulties of the *Times* in obtaining continental news during the period are relatively well known.

The problem of evaluating the effectiveness of Napoleon's propaganda efforts is, for obvious reasons, a difficult one. A fairly weighty body of evidence can be produced to show that the bait was not always swallowed, at least not all of it. Even in France the iron curtain was not entirely effective, and bad news especially found ways of getting in. Paris papers continued throughout the Napoleonic period to quote from enemy journals, especially the English, although this news was selected and usually an attempt was made to discredit it. Enemy dispatches were often quoted by Napoleon in his bulletins and ridiculed, of course. The Russian official account of the battle of Austerlitz was given in its entirety in the *Moniteur* in parallel columns with comments by an anonymous French officer: the anonymous officer is accepted by the editors of the official correspondence of Napoleon as the emperor himself. There can be no question but that many intelligent Frenchmen discounted official war news with something approaching accuracy; perhaps virtually all Frenchmen discredited it to a greater or lesser degree. Nor would mere passive acceptance in itself be an adequate measure of effectiveness. The monotony of endless victories began in time to pall on the French, and questions of cost became more important than assurances of victory—a weighty point in explaining the increasing opposition to conscription for the army. It is a significant fact that newspaper circulation declined steadily in France with Napoleon's increasing control over the press. If we may accept the implications in the published correspondence of Joseph Fiévée, a Napoleonic agent who for years had had the assignment of informing the emperor of the state of French public opinion, Napoleon was aware of the tendency in France to discredit his bulletins and to greet them with apathy. When finally it became necessary to admit the failure of the Russian campaign in 1812, Napoleon expressed his conviction that it would have been better to have prepared the French public for the reception of such news than to have been forced to issue it without warning. In the period of the Hundred Days he accepted, albeit reluctantly, a relatively free press for France.

On the other side of the ledger it must be recognized that the ultimate victory of the allies was accomplished against odds, at least in the matter of military news. If the larger question of the total propaganda effort is raised, it may be that the greater spontaneity in allied writings and the apparent spontaneity of much officially inspired literature were better calculated than Napoleon's propaganda to produce favorable response. Certainly, the significance of the magnificent literature of national awakening in Germany, and to a lesser extent in Spain and Italy, can scarcely be overemphasized; but these outpourings were designed essentially for internal consumption and were unsuitable for export to other allies. The English, for their part, maintained the longest and most serious attack of all against Napoleon, but their attacks also tended to be a diet on which the English fed themselves. No more than a fractional part of the excellent caricatures of George Cruikshank or of the ingenious and varied efforts of the British press to keep alive the spirit of opposition to Napoleon found their way to the continent. The British government did, of course, subsidize such continental writers as Friedrich von Gentz; render limited financial aid to anti-Napoleonic newspapers, such as Jean Peltier's *L'Ambigu*; and distribute military dispatches, newspapers, and pamphlets through its agents on the continent. Even so, the British government looked on its agents primarily as collectors rather than as distributors of intelligence. One agent, disgusted with his country's failure to supply him with news for distribution, compared England to Eternity, "whither everything goes but from whence nothing returns."

In their attempts to combat Napoleon's weapon of military news the British were handicapped on several important counts. Not only was the control of most of the European press in the hands of Napoleon for the greater part of a decade and a half, but the British had relatively little in the way of victorious news to export. The victories were Napoleon's, and the British were reduced to the tiresome and unpalatable task of endlessly minimizing the extent of the emperor's victories. When there was good news, the Trafalgar victory, for example, the British made unusual efforts to spread it. Sir George Jackson tells how he rushed with the greatest possible speed in specially arranged transportation to carry to Berlin packets of the *London Gazette* which gave the news of Nelson's great victory. When successes came to the British in the Peninsula campaign, it was difficult for them to make the most of the Duke of Wellington's unimaginative dispatches; for, whatever may be said of the Iron Duke's military qualities, he was scarcely the man to compete with Napoleon in the writing of exciting battle descriptions. John Quincy Adams, at the time United States minister in London, is said to have declared on reading Wellington's Waterloo dispatch that it obviously was written by a defeated general and that the duke's forces had surely been annihilated.

If Napoleon's primacy in the field of war news went largely unchallenged, it cannot be said to have gone unrecognized. Journalists and pamphleteers in all countries unfriendly to France kept up regular denunciations of his methods. The anti-Napoleonic French newspapers, which were published in London, constantly attacked the veracity of the French bulletins. Gentz, one of the ablest propagandists of the time, devoted most of a lengthy introduction of one of his books to denouncing the new French method of warfare. Among the statesmen of the period, none recognized more clearly the force and importance of Napoleon's techniques of word warfare than did Clemens von Metternich. Writing from Berlin in 1805, he warned the Austrian government:

> We cannot . . . help seeing that public opinion ends by taking more or less the shape our enemies wish to give it. The dignity of silence observed by the right side does not impress the people . . . it is only necessary to be in a foreign country [Prussia], especially a place where Bonaparte has chosen to spread all that the odious pamphleteers emit daily against us, to be convinced of the truth of what I say. The daily Bulletins which are published for the French Army, and which inundate Germany and the whole of Europe, are a new invention which deserve the most serious attention. Designed less to report military facts than to mislead the public as to the spirit of our government and people, Bonaparte's cabinet thus brings itself into daily contact with all classes of society. It has cast off official style and adopted the most familiar language.

Three years later Metternich declared: "The French have the game to themselves."

In summary, the evidence seems overwhelming that Napoleon

seized existing tools of propaganda and utilized them so extensively as to make the control of military news in wartime a distinct and significant arm of his warfare. By the very nature of the problem, the question of the extent to which these activities were effective defies precise measurement. Evidence that the views which Napoleon wished to have accepted were not accepted in their entirety is, in a sense, beside the point. Propaganda of this type is scarcely intended for complete acceptance. The bulletins were merely one aspect of a larger propaganda program, and their effectiveness cannot be isolated from the whole. The student of the problem, moreover, is confronted with difficulty in distinguishing between cause and effect. Successful propaganda is dependent in large measure upon successful military action. In one sense, then, the efficacy of Napoleon's war news derived from his victories in battle. Even so, this does not answer the question of the extent to which those victories were made possible by that skilful exploitation of events commonly called "propaganda."

The Europe of Napoleon: A Synopsis

GOLO MANN

➤➤➤➤➤➤➤➤➤➤➤➤➤➤*Published in 1942* ◄◄◄◄◄◄◄◄◄◄◄◄◄◄

Hardly had the Battle of Waterloo been fought and hardly had Napoleon reached St. Helena than the great debate over the collapse of the Bonapartist hegemony got under way. Spanish patriots insisted that it was their Peninsular War that played the decisive role in bringing about the fall of the French Empire. Russian patriots insisted that it was the disastrous Moscow Campaign of 1812. German patriots insisted that it was the Battle of Leipzig. And Britons insisted that it was their navy that mattered primarily. That spokesmen of different nationalities have stressed the contribution of their own nationality is in itself highly revealing. For what perhaps mainly explained the string of Napoleonic successes was the squabbling within the ranks of the anti-French forces. Though coalition after coalition was formed to oppose Napoleon, these coalitions existed for the most part in name only. As Golo Mann, author of an admirable biography of Friedrich von Gentz, makes clear in the present essay, the fall of the Napoleonic Empire was long delayed because of disunity within the ranks of the so-called allies.

W here human fate is concerned there is hardly a question that does not admit of different or contradictory answers. An abyss separates our age from that of Napoleon and in this sense nothing useful may be learned from the latter. Yet there is a mechanism of power politics, even a mechanism of the human soul, that remains constant throughout the ages and in this sense the past elucidates the present. Vice versa, the present elucidates the past. Contemporary statesmen may very seldom have sufficient time to view the present in the light of past experience. Historians have time to view the past

Reprinted by special permission from *The American Scholar,* XI (1942), 133-148.

in the light of recent experience. That is why an episode like the Napoleonic crisis is studied anew by every generation, and always with different results.

In retrospect the conflicts that checkered the fourteen years of Napoleon's European adventure can be considered as one single war, interrupted by lulls and armistices, resumed by the Allies time and again in unsuccessful offensives. But if we look at the individual events of the period from the perspective of those who lived through it we are able to distinguish four separate phases. The first, covering the years 1801 to 1805, may be called the appeasement period; the second, 1805 to 1807, the period of continental resistance; the third, 1807 to 1812, the period of continental peace, collaboration, or, as the expression ran, of the New Federative System; the fourth, 1812 to 1814, the revolutionary period.

Albert Sorel, in the introduction to his *L'Europe et la Révolution Française*, gives a shrewd analysis of the character of the great wars against the French Revolution:

> The French Revolution, from its beginning, and as a direct conse-
> quence of its basic principles, undermined the foundation and ruined
> the whole structure of ancient Europe. . . . The strangest factor in this
> picture is neither the character of the new doctrine nor the ardor with
> which it was propagated; it is the indifference of the other European
> governments. They had not noticed the first signs of the storm and
> when it finally broke they witnessed it with egoistic tranquillity; it
> was only after the inundation had flooded their own countries that
> they began to understand what a serious thing was going on. They had
> not recognized the danger nor were they able to cope with it. Incoherent
> efforts, contradictory maneuvers, plans that were wrecked again and
> again—this was all they had to offer in opposition.

The great historian's judgment seems to contradict popular tradition, according to which the war began with an arbitrary aggression by Europe's kings against the cause of liberty. But it does not contradict the opinions of witnesses of the time—not, that is, if we take the word of those who were really competent and ignore the poets and doctrinaires. In 1805 Frederick Gentz thus characterized the attitude of the European Powers:

> To escape the common danger in every imaginable way, once par-
> ticipation could not be refused; to restrict it to the poorest, most in-
> effective measures; and as soon as an exit was offered to quit the scene

on any condition—this comprised the substance of all political wisdom. We have seen the egoistical Allies converted, in the very midst of the common disaster, into real foes by the hope of grasping an elusive prey before the flames should reach their own house.

Similar accusations, exhortations to a radical change in tactics, can be found as early as 1793 in the writings of moderate French royalists. The war against the French Revolution was launched too late in the day to save the *ancien régime* either in France or in the rest of Europe; once undertaken, the defense of the old order proved as inadequate as it was belated.

There were manifold reasons for this failure. Some of them hold good for the whole period, 1789 to 1814, and others for its early years only.

During the first phase there was complete blindness as to what the Revolution meant or could mean. It was understood neither in its national nor in its international implications. To European intellectuals it was a moral spectacle, beautiful or dreadful in its absolute meaning but without immediate consequences in terms of their own destiny. To European diplomats it was an event much more disagreeable for the King of France than for his royal brothers, because a revolution spelled the political and military decadence of the country in which it took place. Their mistake in judgment led de Tocqueville to remark:

> It is a common error of the people who are called wise and practical in ordinary times to judge by fixed standards those men whose very object it is to change or to destroy those standards. But when passion usurps the guidance of affairs, the beliefs of men of experience are

JACQUES MALLET DU PAN: Royalist editor of the *Mercure de France* and advocate of constitutional monarchy on the English model. His *Memoirs and Correspondence* are a valuable source for the study of the reactions of a thoughtful royalist to the Great French Revolution.

ALBERT SOREL: Official of the French Foreign Office, bureaucrat, and historian of foreign affairs. His multi-volume *Europe and the French Revolution* (1885-1904) offers an example of diplomatic history at its best.

STEIN: German publicist and statesman. In the period after Jena, when Prussian power had collapsed, he insisted that the key to recovery was to

less worthy of consideration than the schemes that engage the imagination of dreamers.

That early period was also marked by a vague expectation of tremendous, unavoidable historical changes in the near future; by a contempt, shared by members of the ruling caste even, for everything associated with foreign policy; by a secret hope that the period of great wars was over; by a philosophical pacifism, in vogue throughout Europe but especially strong in Northern Germany.

Still other influences operated to make defense of the *ancien régime* ineffectual. There was sympathy for the Revolution, which had been quickly identified with the great transformation the intellectual élite had hoped for; and this sympathy tended to give vigor to the formal principle of non-intervention, which declared the sovereignty of a state inviolate, with domestic and foreign affairs regarded as strictly separated fields.

But the factor that did most to paralyze the anti-French forces—and this during the entire period—was the character of the training their leaders had had. These men had been educated in the tradition of other issues and conflicts: for example, the inveterate continental hatred of England's commercial policy, a fear of Russia's recently developed power and ambitions, the hostility between Prussia and Austria. Each government cherished its own private aims, greeds and apprehensions, in the face of which sentiment on behalf of a common cause grew very slowly, even under the impact of monstrous experiences.

The ignorance that delayed the resort to arms was matched by the conduct of the war waged upon revolutionary France. A penetrating observer, Mallet Du Pan, could say in 1794:

---

be found in imitation of the French. Considered too radical because of the political, social, economic, and military reforms that he advocated, he was dropped from office by the King of Prussia after little more than a year. Officially he was dismissed on Napoleon's orders.

ALEXIS DE TOCQUEVILLE: Nineteenth-century statesman, writer, and acute political observer. Best known in the United States for his classic volumes on *Democracy in America,* he was equally thoughtful and penetrating in his comments on the France of 1848, of the *ancien régime,* and of the Great Revolution.

> They [the Allies] do not want, nor are they able, to understand that
> this is a *revolutionary* war which must be waged in a revolutionary way
> with weapons adapted to the genius and the means of their enemy.

In the preceding year the same publicist had written:

> The greatest number of those who have passed 50 or 60 years of
> age cannot but view the revolution from the perspective of antiquated
> habits. . . . With their eyes fixed upon the fortifications of a frontier
> town they tie their destiny with a confident simplicity to a spot on the
> map: the gulf widens and these observers see the last fortress still
> standing in defense of the remains of civil society totter to its base.

When, however, the enemies of the Revolution finally awoke to a
realization of the superiority of the military forces it had mobilized
they did not redouble their own efforts. The realization led, instead,
to the first of the peace treaties with the Republic.

The treaty was signed, in 1795, between France and Prussia. Many
different motives led to its conclusion: reasons of power politics, of
economy, the particular kind of philosophical thought then current.
In addition, however, we find the Prussian ministers presenting to
their king an argument that may be summed up as follows: We are
told that to escape the Revolution we must wage war against the
revolutionary Power. The contrary is true. A war against the Revolution would be the surest way to attract it to our own country. For,
inasmuch as it has now been proven that the Revolution furnishes
France with hitherto unimagined economic, military and moral
resources, it is clear that we cannot fight France without the sans-
culottization of our own army and government. A war would offer
the French all desired pretexts and occasions for employing their
propaganda machine against us and for undermining the morale of
our population; whereas we might hope, if we arrived at a diplomatic
understanding with them, not only to escape the dangerous impact
of revolutionary France but even to exert a moderating influence on
its system of government.

For ten years Prussia shaped her course to this policy. Her statesmen, conscious of a glorious but somewhat obsolete military tradition,
secretly haunted by doubt as to the real might of their nation, never
for a moment forgot the fate of the French aristocracy. Their hesita-
tions, their lack of self-assurance sprang from fear of a like destiny.
Furthermore they had been taught by popular philosophers that war,

as a barbaric form of human coexistence, must be avoided at any price; that theirs was an age of reason; and that inner reform constituted the best foreign policy. But the social reforms paralyzed Prussia's foreign policy and were themselves crippled by fear of war.

The final dissolution of the first anti-French coalition, however, was inspired by few if any philosophical considerations. In their dealings with the French the Prussian ambassadors had adopted, though not without irony, the idealistic language of the former—world peace, justice, reason, no conquests. But when, two years later, General Bonaparte met with the representatives of Austria he talked in the familiar terms of power politics to which the Austrian plenipotentiaries were accustomed. Out of the conferences came a treaty in the old style—revolutionary only in the sense that it pushed the *"système copartageant,"* the principle of concluding peace at the expense of the weakest neutrals, further than the most rapacious king of Prussia would have dreamt possible.

The first coalition disappeared in a peace that was merely an armistice. After eighteen months, spent in peaceful conquests by the French and in futile pleas and the publication of confused tracts by the conservative Powers, the world war began anew, automatically and with no formal declaration. Russia now joined England, Austria, Naples, Portugal, Turkey. And again a tremendous agglomeration of states was overwhelmed "by a handful of bandits," to quote the Austrian leader, Thugut, "who have already too often taught the amazed world the priceless advantages deriving from a single planning agency and a ruthless determination in thought and action." The republican government of France prosecuted the first phase of the war; the dictator, or First Consul, Bonaparte, concluded the peace—supposed to be a lasting one. For at least three years the continental Powers not only hoped for peace but earnestly tried to appease the new French ruler.

This peace policy was dictated by several considerations. The Allies had come to realize the military superiority of the French. They had had bitter experience with the French Army; and this direct knowledge had been supplemented by numerous theoretical studies—books on revolutionary warfare, strategy, propaganda, which have a modern counterpart. On the other hand they clung to the belief, or the fallacious hope, that Bonaparte was somebody with whom one could deal. There was nothing of genuine sympathy for him or for his system in this belief; on the contrary, there was hardly a government in Europe that would not have preferred a downright restoration of the old dynasty. Bonaparte, however, was there, he was very strong, he had a reputation for being a prudent politician, at least he seemed preferable to a new outburst of Jacobinism. Characteristically, when a new, strong, opportunistic government, a government not tied to a particular class or party and therefore free to dally with all and to change its course to suit the exigencies of each occasion, a government having only one aim—to maintain itself in power—appears on the international scene, the most disparate parties believe themselves entitled to claim it as their own. Europe's leftist intellectuals adored Bonaparte; conservative rulers hoped to attract him into their own camp. The instructions handed to a new Austrian ambassador to Berlin, Count Metternich, read in part:

> The crucial question is, therefore, whether Bonaparte is really the insatiable world conqueror England and her friends would like to make us believe, or whether this shrewd statesman could not be persuaded to adopt a more moderate policy. The domestic pressure exerted upon him, added to the incredible lack of resistance he has met from the princes of Europe, has until now determined his violent operations. Would it not be in the interest of the First Consul to make an end to this fatal course? In that case he should be assured that we are ready to take into account the particular situation of his government, and that we should be far from asking any striking concession or steps which could do harm to his personal position.

It goes without saying that in this peace effort the arguments habitually advanced by isolationists played their part. In 1804 Gentz, then an adviser to the Austrian foreign minister, Cobenzl, attributed an amazing piece of wisdom to his chief:

> Let us close our eyes and ears to everything going on in the outside world! Away with all this talk about foreign influence and balance of power and resistance to a force which is now too firmly established and against which there are no measures left to be taken. And why should they be? Let Europe help herself as she can; what are our obligations toward Europe? Let us stay at home, let us mind our own business, and nobody will disturb our peace.

Gentz adds:

> Such an excess of weakness and blindness indeed passes all imagination! These are things posterity will refuse to believe; and even we,

who are condemned to witness this spectacle of shame and misery, sometimes ask ourselves whether it is really true or whether all this is not a dream.

When an individual is on bad terms with the majority of his neighbors the source of the trouble must be within himself. By his character and deeds he provokes reactions which drive him to, or give him the pretext for, other actions that make things worse and worse; a vicious circle takes shape. If we arbitrarily select a certain point on this circle we can easily demonstrate the guilt of the other parties, the neighbors, but not if we consider the circle as a whole. The same holds true for relations between states. The treaties of 1801-02 had confirmed France in possession of territories or zones of influence to which neither England nor the remaining continental Powers could in the long run resign themselves. The natural consequence was a reciprocal and universal distrust which in turn led to allegedly defensive precautions on the part of Napoleon—the taking of new steps in those regions given him by the peace treaties.

A new outbreak of hostilities between England and France was inevitable. Unable to attack England on the high seas, Napoleon was forced to strengthen his positions against England's potential allies on the Continent. In doing so he provoked the coalition he had set out to prevent. During the period 1802 to 1805 (one year of universal and three years of continental peace) he refused to evacuate Holland and Naples; annexed Piedmont; invaded Switzerland and arbitrated her internal dissensions; invaded a German state in order to seize a French émigré living there; occupied another German state formally belonging to the King of Great Britain; and founded a North Italian kingdom for himself. These acts he justified on the ground that they represented the common interest of Europe—defense against British arrogance; that they occurred in countries of no concern to Russia, Austria and Prussia; or that they were purely defensive. Historians have said they were dictated by fear (a thesis developed in Ferrero's recent books, *The Gamble* and *The Reconstruction of Europe*). But instead of fear the appeasement policy adopted by the great nations of the Continent provoked its opposites, contempt and presumption, in Napoleon. If those Powers were in any way responsible for the war of 1805, the most fateful of the Napoleonic wars, they may be blamed for the weakness and ineptitude with which they had allowed Napoleon to do things against which there was ultimately no other recourse but war. "Napoleon," the Prussian diplomat Lucchesini remarked in 1805, "is exploiting Europe's desire for peace and rest." The annexation of the Ligurian (Genoese) Republic finally filled the cup to overflowing. Fournier, in his *Gentz and Cobenzl*, quotes the Austrian foreign minister, Cobenzl, as writing to his sovereign:

> Recent events in Italy demonstrate only too clearly that Emperor Napoleon is indeed governed by an insatiable lust for world domination. . . . No longer can we hide from ourselves the mortal danger with which the Austrian Monarchy is now threatened.

But the third coalition (England, Austria, Russia) ended like its predecessors—not after years, but after a few months.

Prussia, still believing in perpetual peace, remained neutral and waited until her natural allies were beaten; eight months later she precipitated herself into a desperate struggle against France. In naive and pathetic language the Prussian war manifesto of 1806 reviewed the whole story of the abortive appeasement policy. It enumerated the crimes committed by France and dwelt upon Prussia's unlimited patience.

> The policy of France has been for fifteen years the scourge of humanity. . . . It is painful to declare that there has been no change even under the new ruler. . . . It would be superfluous to enumerate everything that Napoleon owes to Prussia. . . . The peculiar contest has taken this course: On the one side moderation, forgiveness, probity, faithful adherence to the given pledge; on the other side abuse of force, a cynical assumption, based on past good luck, that success will attend any and every enterprise, and the habit of relying exclusively upon opportunism. . . . A conflict between a policy desiring all it can possibly get and a probity trusting in obligations and in particular in promises will be at all times an unequal contest. The moment had come when the King, out of his own experience, had had to realize the nature of the contest. It had been the most painful moment in his reign. . . . The Emperor Napoleon had informed His Majesty it had pleased him to dissolve the German Reich and to establish a Confederation of the Rhine; he had suggested to the King that he set up a similar confederation in the north. This had been Napoleon's usual device—crowned by longstanding success—namely, to offer a kind of bait, at the moment of the birth of a new project, to those courts which might place obstacles in the path of that project.

And yet the King of Prussia finally began the war and the Emperor of the French implored him for humanity's sake not to resort to this most murderous of human follies. The Napoleonic wars were never started by Napoleon.

Obviously only the appeasers could call a halt to the appeasement policy. By his exploitation of every preceding peace treaty, by the very character of his regime, Napoleon was aggressive in peace time. He had no interest in declarations of war and most sincerely did not want war. Gentz commented in 1806:

> Those who began the general destruction [the French] had without much genius found out that there was nothing more desirable for them than to go on with their work, irresistibly proceeding under the veil of a faithless sham peace. This was war of the most disastrous kind, because it raged on the one side without resistance from the other. If the French could push forward in this manner they could reach a point at which a single decisive blow would smash the last frail palisades still separating them from world domination. This system, the most assured and the most comfortable, they preferred to a declared and real war whose outcome always remained in doubt. . . . For this reason they did not want war; for the same reason others were forced to want it.

Once these conservative statesmen had decided to resort to war they flattered themselves upon having wrested the initiative from Napoleon. Would he not withdraw, seeing himself suddenly confronted with a serious resistance to which he was unaccustomed? Or if he accepted war would the odds not be on the side of those who had begun it? But Napoleon was only too ready. He may not have wanted war, formally or consciously; but he wanted it in the way we are bound to want to exercise a skill in which we feel superior to our competitors and upon which our whole economy of life is built. The bare fact of his immense military superiority was tantamount to a perpetual aggression. Undeniably, however, he had implored his enemies to keep the peace; he had warned them; and after his victorious campaign he was again right and his enemies wrong. He annexed new provinces and things were worse than ever.

Organized resistance on the Continent ended in 1807 with the Treaty of Tilsit. By the terms of this pact, drawn up between Napoleon and the Tsar, Prussia was partitioned, a "new order" was set up in Germany, Napoleon's brothers were recognized as Kings of Holland, Westphalia, Naples and presently of Spain. But from the moment the New Federative System was definitely established it began to crumble—in reality it was never established at all. It was a magnificent form given to a mass of contradictions, a gilded improvisation, crude, accidental and irrational. A few months after the signing of the Treaty of Tilsit the Spanish rebellion broke out. In 1809 the Spaniards were joined by the Austrians. And yet, although for a time Napoleon was victorious in his campaign against the Spanish and Austrians, nevertheless it was in these campaigns that the seeds of revolutionary (and, from 1812 to 1814, decisive) changes in the attitudes and techniques of Napoleon's enemies—his pseudo-allies—began to germinate. Finally, just when Austria seemed firmly bound to the New Federative System, Russia embarked on an independent course. Collaboration with Napoleon was a hybrid product, the collaborators embracing protected states (like Switzerland, the Confederation of the Rhine, the Grand Duchy of Warsaw), vassal states (for example the Italian States, Holland until her annexation, Spain) governed by members of the Bonaparte family, and those formally independent states allied with Napoleon. After her defeat in 1806 Prussia became to all intents and purposes a protected state, as did Austria after 1809. The Tsar alone remained an ally in his own right—and therefore a potential enemy, for in Napoleon's system there was no place for independent allies. When the pact dividing the Continent between France and Russia was concluded, shrewd observers foresaw the inevitable outcome. Gentz commented in a letter written in 1807:

> It goes without saying that this *societas leonina*, this unnatural, abject duumvirate will end like former attempts of this kind. Octavian shares the world with Antony only to dominate it alone after a battle of Actium—which is perhaps not so far off. The Emperor of Russia will be punished! But *we* meanwhile! . . . This barbaric fight over the question whether the world shall belong to one or to two tyrants—this is the last act in the 18-year-old tragedy played for the sake of *universal freedom!*

The administration of the subjugated countries was prevailingly French where French-speaking rulers were imposed by Napoleon; prevailingly indigenous where the old dynasties were preserved. While they were completely bound to Napoleon's foreign, military and commercial policy, his vassals were free to deal with their own subjects as they pleased; they adopted French forms of administration because they seemed efficient and timely. Nor were the German and Italian populations at first very unhappy under these new forms. Napoleon was eager not to antagonize national sentiment if without great cost he could avoid doing so. German intellectuals were still more eager not to hurt Napoleon; many brains were overstrained and much printer's ink was wasted in an effort to prove the new order natural, unavoidable and beneficial and its founder godlike. But there was one—and it proved decisive—factor that gradually poisoned the New Federative System and roused the German and Italian peoples to enmity toward the Emperor: the economic misery caused by the continental blockade. The war against England had led Napoleon to found the New Federative System; the war against England forced him to institute the continental blockade; the continental blockade ruined the New Federative System.

Collaboration and imitation, born of defeat and subjection, in one sense prepared the ground for deliverance. Statesmen had understood, ever since the military disasters of the early nineties, that the French Revolution had mobilized forces theretofore unimagined. These forces were not invincible but they could not even be matched by the old methods of warfare employed by absolutist states. Appeasement represented an attempt to avoid the efforts and convulsions attendant on an adaptation to the new element in Europe. Once appeasement had proved futile, there remained nothing but complete capitulation or an attempt to fight the enemy with his own weapons. The reforms that Stein introduced in Prussia were instigated by this realization. Consciously he and his government undertook the sans-culottization from which Prussian statesmen had refrained ten years earlier. Surrender to an international necessity must not in this case be equated with a renunciation of national tradition and individuality; Stein was not a Bonapartist merely because he began to organize that democratic mass-army which was needed to beat the democratic mass-army of the French.

The gradual adoption of revolutionary methods by Napoleon's adversaries made the change in Napoleon's own position the more striking. France ceased to be a revolutionary Power. This transformation is attributable not so much to the temperament of the dictator as to the laws inherent in all imperialism and wars of conquest. The Jacobins had been unable to tolerate really independent republics as neighbors; Napoleon could not tolerate strong governments, popular armies or flourishing industries outside the borders of France. Consequently he began to connive with the reactionary caste in the occupied countries and the Revolution turned against him.

Since there was no historical analogy to enlighten them, those living in the midst of the turmoil were utterly mystified by the puzzle they were watching. They could not see that Napoleon was impelled to continued aggression and expansion by his powerlessness on the high seas. They could not see that the New Federative System, allegedly a product of the Emperor's planning and an organic necessity, was merely incidental to the inevitable clash between England and a France dominating the European Continent. They did not know the future, they wanted so to proceed that in the end they would have made the right choice, whatever shape the future might assume. Even Stein, a born leader of men, in his darkest moments feared that the Napoleonic Empire might last for several hundred years; those gifted with less imagination took it almost for granted. Almost—but not quite. And the fact that in the darkness they had discerned, though only dimly, another course became the armor whereby they saved their honor. Secretly they had always prayed for an English victory.

Actually, almost every continental Power had been, during this twenty-year crisis, more or less, time and again, at war with England: Spain in 1804, Prussia in 1806, Germany ever since the creation of the Confederation of the Rhine, Russia in 1808. If their declarations of war lacked deadly earnestness and could do England no serious harm, they were certainly no contribution to the "common cause." But had there been a common cause there would have been no Napoleonic Empire; once there was recognition of such a common cause, taking precedence over all other considerations, the Napoleonic Empire went to pieces within a few months. Before 1813, however, only the intellectual *avantgarde* understood that England, while fighting England's war, was also fighting for the liberty of the nations of Europe.

The very existence of the British Empire depended upon the survival of free nations on the Continent, whereas the existence of the Napoleonic Empire was incompatible with their independence. This basic contradiction was obscured, however, by superficial factors. Although Napoleon overthrew so many old dynasties and suppressed so many ancient states, he nevertheless seemed ambitious to become a member of the family of kings, to enter their order. It was an ambition that presupposed the conservation of their order and as such could not fail to be a source of constantly renewed endeavors at appeasement. Moreover England, in her treatment of the rights of neutrals, was hardly less ruthless than the Emperor. The bombardment of peaceful Copenhagen, the rape of the Danish fleet or the Dutch Colonies had at first glance not much to do with the fight for man's freedom. Because of such acts, Napoleon's propagandists were free to point out how greatly it was to the interest of Europe to unite against England's tyranny on the seas. France was Europe; to hope for an English victory was not merely anti-French—it was "anti-European." The coalitions against France were interpreted as forged by the British solely to serve Britain's self-seeking interest—everybody knew, for example, what strange help Austria or Russia had obtained from England once they had taken up arms in a cause in which England alone was interested. Russia looped the loop in 1807 partly because she felt she had been cheated and deserted by the English. Her disappointment was expressed in the words, perhaps legendary, with which Tsar Alexander greeted Napoleon when the two met for the first time: "I hate the English as much as you do." "In that case peace is established," Napoleon answered.

Fortunately the British statesmen knew how to overcome their contempt and to manage the continental Powers whose aid they were sooner or later bound to need. The dubious position in which the enforced partners to Napoleon's system found themselves led them to equivocal and dishonest practices. Although he shrank from a complete severance of his relations with Britain, the Tsar took advantage of the New Federative System to conquer Finland and Bessarabia. Similarly Metternich, the Austrian, whispered promising words in the ears of his British ex-allies on the very day of the wedding between Napoleon and an Austrian princess. Napoleon's reluctant partners excused whatever they did by pointing to the frightful pressure under which they undeniably existed. They also made a virtue of necessity and drew all possible profit from their collaboration with the enemy, plundering small neutrals, even plundering one another. What they were "really" intending and planning they did not know. Time had to decide for them.

When Tsar Alexander in the summer of 1812 exhorted the Germans to revolt against Napoleon, an Austrian diplomat had commented:

It really takes a rare degree of insolence to invite one's neighbor to a common fight after having deserted, cheated, sold out and plundered this very neighbor for so many years; or to tell us that a war which the Tsar himself presents as purely defensive and which he begins with a retreat beyond the Dnieper has the liberation of Germany as its principal aim!

But the urgencies of the moment carried more weight than the sins of the past or any moralistic reflection. Russia, at war with Napoleon, fell into a *de facto* alliance with England, to be signed later on in due form. When, five months afterward, Napoleon's expeditionary force was broken and Russia decided to pursue her victory beyond her own frontiers, North Germany fell into a *de facto* alliance with Russia, and Austria could not long avoid being drawn down the stream. During this crisis the English diplomats were extremely energetic, the Austrian extremely astute. Those most intimately acquainted with their activities, however, felt there was something automatic about the formation of the great alliance. For the first time since the outbreak of the Revolution, France was faced with an alliance of all the European Powers and with such a mobilization of social forces as she herself had mustered in 1793. Napoleon could not hold out for even three months against assault from this combination of Powers.

At that critical moment the statesmen of Europe once again played with the idea of appeasement—but now an appeasement calculated to bring a halt not to Napoleon's rising but to his declining course, an attempt to save what remained of his position. For three months the leaders of Europe had recognized and treated the Napoleonic problem as the one paramount political issue; they now remembered other conflicts. There was danger of a Russian hegemony, of a nationalistic movement in Germany, of a social revolution in France.

The task, however, of sloughing off the burdens of the Napoleonic Empire while preserving its social assets proved too difficult for even the accomplished diplomats of the day. At this juncture the dissensions, inherent in any coalition, that had made Napoleon's adventure possible, merely prolonged his agony. Words and treaties could control the mechanism of his downfall as little as words and treaties could have ordered the mechanism of his conquests. Indeed it was the same mechanism, now running in reverse. If Napoleon could be forced

to disgorge Germany and Italy he could be compelled to relinquish
all other territory, the fruits of his own campaigns and those of
revolutionary France alike.

To subdue England, Napoleon had been driven to form his New
Federative System. To rid themselves of the New Federative System,
the European Powers had finally been driven to form the great alliance
of 1813. Neither the Napoleonic nor the anti-Napoleonic unity of
Europe survived the occasion to which they owed their existence.
Despite treaties, sermonizings, Christian compacts, after seven years
nothing remained of the great coalition. States, social classes, intellectual movements, bound together for a single moment by an unbearable common suffering, reaffirmed their individuality.